YORKSHIRE ARCHAEOLOGY 3

DALTON PARLOURS

Iron Age Settlement and Roman Villa

edited by

Stuart Wrathmell and Andrew Nicholson

© West Yorkshire Archaeology Service 1990

ISBN   1-870-453-10-7
ISSN   0959-3500

Published by: West Yorkshire Archaeology Service, on behalf of West Yorkshire
                   Archives and Archaeology Joint Committee
Typeset by: West Yorkshire Archaeology Service, output by Autograph, Bradford
Printed by: Witley Press, Hunstanton, Norfolk

This publication has been made possible by a substantial grant from English Heritage
(Historic Buildings and Monuments Commission for England).

Contents

List of Plates

List of Figures

List of Tables

Preface

The excavation of Dalton Parlours was carried out by the Archaeology Unit of the former West Yorkshire Metropolitan County Council. It was organised by the then County Archaeologist, Philip Mayes, in response to increasing plough damage to the remains; this damage was brought to the Unit's attention by Mrs Margery Woodhead of Wetherby, who investigated the site after ploughing in the winter of 1975-76, and who recorded surface finds.

The work was supervised by A.B. Sumpter assisted by A.S. Tindall; excavation of the well was conducted by R.E. Yarwood. The labour force consisted of Unit staff, temporary staff employed through the Job Creation programme of the Manpower Services Commission, and volunteers; among the latter, special thanks must go to Mrs M. Woodhead, Mrs P. Cross and Mrs D. Welbourn. S. Nelson and A.C. Swann were in charge of the drawn record; J. Marriott dealt with finds administration and S. Wager with the photographic record. Permission to excavate was generously granted by the trustees of The Lady Elizabeth Hastings' Estate Charity (owners) and Mrs P.I. Langrick of Compton Grange Farm (tenant). Funding was provided by the Department of the Environment, by the Manpower Services Commission and by the Metropolitan County Council.

The responsibility for the production of the site archive and the publication of the excavation report was inherited by the West Yorkshire Archaeology Service. The programme of post-excavation analysis was largely funded by English Heritage (then the DoE), with additional resources provided by the West Yorkshire Archives and Archaeology Joint Committee. The post-excavation project was first directed by A.B. Sumpter (1979-85) and subsequently for brief periods by A. Wilmott and S.A. Moorhouse. The organisation of the site archive in 1987-88 was carried out by A.P. Nicholson, an unenviable task considering the serious deficiencies in the primary recording system. S. Wrathmell, during 1988-89, directed the major part of the post-excavation

work and the production of this publication. Artefact conservation, also funded by English Heritage, was carried out by M. Brooks, J. Greenwood and S. Omar of the Conservation Department, Doncaster Museum on behalf of the Museum and Art Gallery Service for Yorkshire and Humberside.

Authorship of the various sections of this published report is indicated at the head of each chapter. The location map, site plans, and sections are by C. Philo and M. Thacker. Artefact drawings are by J. Callister (most wooden objects), J. Heron and K. Keith (pottery), A.P. Nicholson (querns), A.C. Swann (leather, iron, glass, lead and jet objects and architectural stonework), M. Thacker (worked bone) and P. White (bronze and silver objects). C. Philo, in addition to drawing further artefacts (brooches, Iron Age pottery, wallplaster, tile and miscellaneous stone objects), also numbered and pasted up the figures for printing. P. Gwilliam prepared the plates; M. Schofield undertook the initial typing of the report, and L. Turner carried out the sub-editing and typesetting. The index was prepared by R. Turner, who also helped to check the report at page-proof stage. The Archaeology Service wishes to express its thanks to those named above and to all the other people who have contributed to the excavation, post-excavation and publication of Dalton Parlours.

This published report includes full details of what have been identified (mainly by the specialists concerned) as significant artefacts and assemblages. The omission of other details from this publication is indicated at appropriate points by reference to the Archive Report. One copy of this full report is housed with the rest of the site archive by Leeds City Museums. Another copy has been retained by the Archaeology Service, and is available for inspection at the Service's address printed on the inside cover.

John D. Hedges
County Archaeologist

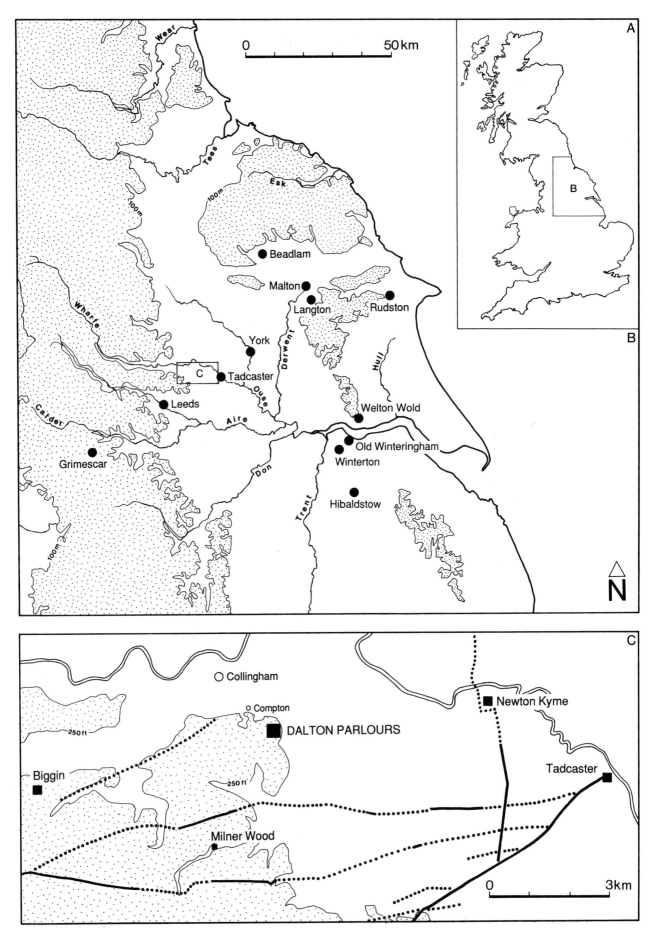

Fig. 1. Location map showing places mentioned in the report (B) and Roman roads and sites in the vicinity of Dalton Parlours (C) (after Faull and Moorhouse 1981, map 9). Black squares on (C) indicate Roman sites; dotted lines are possible Roman roads.

Part One
The Site and its Structures

1 Introduction

by Andrew Nicholson

The site and its setting

The Iron Age and Roman settlement known as Dalton Parlours lay in the parish of Collingham, West Yorkshire, about 2½ miles (4km) south of Wetherby (SE 4025 4454; Fig. 1). It was situated at a height of 84m (275ft) OD on a moderately level elevation, overlooking the Vale of York. The farmland around the settlement occupies the fertile Magnesian Limestone which extends along the eastern boundary of the modern county and is largely under crop. During the past two decades these crops have revealed to aerial survey the extensive remains of prehistoric and Roman fields, trackways and farmsteads; the place of Dalton Parlours within this landscape is discussed later (Chapter 35). A major Roman road (Margary 1957; 72b)

linking the fort at Ilkley to Tadcaster ran only about 1.5km south of the site; eastwards, the fort and *vicus* at Newton Kyme were less than 5km away, on a north-south Roman road (Margary 1957; 280). The widespread evidence of early agricultural activity, and the proximity of important Roman roads and settlements readily provide a context for the Iron Age farmsteads and, in the 3rd and 4th centuries, the fully romanised villa at Dalton Parlours (Pl. I).

The site was located close to the eastern boundary of Compton, now a minor settlement in Collingham but recorded in the Domesday book as a vill (Faull and Moorhouse 1981, 350). The boundary is unquestionably an ancient one: it was not only the medieval township boundary between Compton and Bramham, but also the division between Skyrack and Barkston wapentakes (Faull and Moorhouse 1981, map 17). Dalton Lane, which follows this boundary, is the post-enclosure remnant of a droveway which connected Wothersome Warren, to the south, with Collingham and Clifford Moors (Jefferys

Pl. I. Aerial view of the site and its setting, facing north-west. (Photo: WYAS)

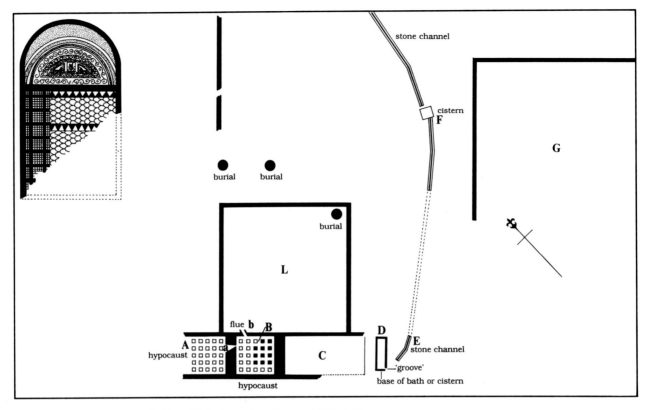

Fig. 2. Villa structures recorded in 1854 (redrawn from Procter 1855, pl. 7).

1775). In the early 18th century the fields containing the villa were called Drover Fields; the name Dalton, which is not known to be a medieval name (Smith 1961, 175), was then applied to the field south of Great Drover Field ('A Map of the Lordship of Compton', 1735, Leeds City Archives LF/117/22). By 1777 the villa site had been planted with trees, and the plantation was named 'Parlours' ('A Survey of the Manors of Collingham and Compton', 1777, Leeds City Archives LF/M14), presumably because tree holes had revealed the stone walls of rooms. The 1848 Ordnance Survey map indicates a rectilinear enclosure and calls it 'Dalton Parlours. Site of Ancient Hall' (OS 1st edition 6", Sheet 189).

The site had for a number of years yielded Roman coins, oyster shell, building materials and reportedly 'a silver ring ... set with an intaglio engraved on a pale blue onyx, having for a device a winged victory standing upon a globe' (Procter 1855, 278). However, the first record of discoveries at the site appeared in the *Leeds Intelligencer* of 11 March 1854. A farm labourer, while routinely digging a field for building stone, uncovered 'between fifty and sixty stone pillars of very rude workmanship, not quite three feet long each, standing upright, singly, about three feet apart'. At some distance from this place were discovered 'a quantity of brick pillars ... about one foot high and four feet apart, standing on a floor ...'

These were presumably the discoveries which prompted a group of local gentlemen to examine the site further during the spring of 1854. An account of the excavations, which were supervised by F. Carroll, was published by William Procter, Honorary Secretary to the Yorkshire Antiquarian Club (Procter 1855). Although the

work was severely hindered by growing crops, it was established that the site was that of a Roman villa.

Three buildings were partly revealed (Fig. 2). An apsidal room with a mosaic portraying Medusa was found at the side of the field amongst trees; the mosaic was subsequently lifted and preserved (Pl. XXIX, p. 147). To the south-east the excavators exposed the remains of a hypocaust range consisting of two chambers with an adjoining room. Further east they located the foundations of a building furnished with an oven. In addition, a series of cisterns and conduits was discovered running northwards from the hypocaust remains.

Since the mid-19th century the combination of a light well-drained soil, a hilltop position and modern agricultural operations has steadily reduced the soil cover to as little as 0.35m over the limestone bedrock. In the 1950s and 1960s the continued ploughing up of Roman artefacts and building debris caused the site to be kept under observation by local amateur archaeologists, and by the Royal Commission on Historical Monuments. Mr H.G. Ramm predicted from surface indications the locations of the buildings recorded in 1854 (drawing in RCHM(E) files).

In 1976 the Archaeology Unit of the former West Yorkshire Metropolitan County Council was notified that the plough was disturbing heavy stonework; on inspection this was seen to include monolithic millstone grit *pilae* from a hypocaust. It was quickly established by manual trial trenching that in places only the lowest wall foundations remained, and that these would be seriously threatened by a further season of ploughing. Since no other Roman villa in West Yorkshire had been examined,

2

and as Dalton Parlours was the only known example not overbuilt, it became an urgent priority for large-scale rescue excavation. Permission for this was immediately granted by the then landowner, the trustees of the Lady Elizabeth Hastings' Estate Charity, and by Mrs P.I. Langrick, the tenant farmer.

The Archaeology Unit commenced excavations in October 1976, with the aim of totally exposing the villa complex in a single operation (Pl. II). The enclosure marked on the 1848 Ordnance Survey map had been eroded by ploughing and was visible to the north, west, and south only as a very slight lynchet in the ploughsoil. With this vague guide, slit trenches were dug which located stone building remains and ditches over a wide area in two adjacent fields. The ditches were further delineated by staff from the Department of Archaeological Sciences, Bradford University, using a proton magnetometer.

The hedgerow which crossed the site from east to west was removed and the villa enclosure was mechanically stripped of ploughsoil, following boundary ditches as they were exposed; these were found to be more sinuous than the 1848 map suggested. The machines employed, all tracked vehicles, were a Priestman Mustang hydraulic excavator, working in tandem firstly with a Komatsu hydraulic shovel fitted with a four-in-one bucket, and subsequently with a Caterpillar 951C of similar specifications. A total area of 1.43ha (3.5 acres) was stripped to a mean depth of 0.30-0.40m. In places this exposed the top of the bedrock; elsewhere 0.15-0.20m of soil cover remained, with up to 0.60m under the plough

headlands along the hedgeline. The limestone surface was heavily cryoturbated, to over 1m in depth on the east of the site, though bedded limestone outcropped occasionally. The building foundations and other features were then cleared manually using draw hoes, since shovels proved inadequate to clean the fragmented surface of the limestone.

It was found that no stratification remained except in a few isolated patches. Archaeological features were not generally visible until at or just above bedrock level, whilst in places proper definition required the removal of up to 0.15m of shattered bedrock. The hollow features were largely filled with medium brown earth with few colour changes, and sections were frequently uninformative. Intermittent permafrost cracking had occurred on a north-east to south-west alignment producing irregular linear gullies with a distinctive filling of firm ginger-brown earth. There was some disturbance from tree roots, notably near the former hedgerow, and also from rodent activity.

It was observed during machining that the stone buildings of the villa overlay earlier archaeological features, and it became apparent that these represented a substantial Iron Age settlement. Few such habitation sites have been investigated in the county, and it was decided to extend the duration of the work in order to make a detailed study of the pre-Roman occupation.

The excavation lasted almost continuously until June 1979. Six weeks were lost in the winter of 1978-79 when the site was under snow and ice, and work was hindered at other times by the extremes of weather in this elevated

Pl. II. Aerial view of the site, facing south.(Photo: R.E. Yarwood)

and exposed location. The labour force comprised County Council staff, DoE-paid personnel, Job Creation Programme workers, and unpaid volunteers. Numbers varied between 2 and 22; this large site was continually undermanned.

The importance of the remains prompted the County Council to purchase the site in 1978, in order to restrict further plough damage. In 1988 ownership was vested in Leeds City Council. The Lady Elizabeth Hastings' Estate Charity generously donated the artefacts recovered during the first two years of the excavations to Leeds City Museums, where they are kept together with those presented by the County Council after its acquisition of the land, and those given by individuals. The material from the 1854 excavations is in the Yorkshire Museum at York, whilst other finds are in private hands. The excavation archive is held by Leeds City Museum; copies of the Archive Report are with the Museum and the Archaeology Service.

The excavation recording system

The excavated area was staked out in 10m squares based on the Ordnance Survey grid, and each 20m square was allotted a number from 20 to 69 (Fig. 3). In addition, major types of structure were assigned individual numbers and letters as follows:

| Iron Age enclosures | I-IX |
| Roman structures | A-Z |

Each square and each putative Roman building was allotted a block of context numbers. These are the basis of the finds recording system, and were assigned as shown below; some designations were altered or abandoned during the course of excavation:

Area	Context
All unstratified and unprovenanced material	001
Major ditches	002-099
Structure A	100-199
Structure B	200-299
Structure C (part of B)	300-399
Structure D (not a structure)	400-499
Structure E	500-599
Structure F	600-699
Structure G (not a structure)	700-799
Structure H (part of A)	800-899
Structure I (part of J)	900-999
Structure J	1000-1099
Structure K (wall 1101)	1100-1199
Structure L (part of M)	1200-1299
Structure M	1300-1399
Structure N (part of M)	1400-1499
Structure O	1500-1599
Structure P	1600-1699
Structure Q	1700-1799
Structure R	1800-1899
Structure S	1900-1999
Square 20	2000-2099
Square 21	2100-2199
Square 22	2200-2299
Square 23	2300-2399
Square 24	2400-2499
Square 25	2500-2599
Square 26	2600-2699
Square 27	2700-2799
Square 28	2800-2899
Square 29	2900-2999
Square 30	3000-3099
Square 31	3100-3199
Square 32	3200-3299
Square 33	3300-3399
Square 34	3400-3499
Square 35	3500-3599
Square 36	3600-3699
Square 37	3700-3799
Square 38	3800-3899
Square 39	3900-3999
Square 40	4000-4099
Square 41	4100-4199
Square 42	4200-4299
Square 43	4300-4399
Square 44	4400-4499
Square 45	4500-4599
Square 46	4600-4699
Square 47	4700-4799
Square 48	4800-4899
Square 49	4900-4999
Square 50	5000-5099
Square 51	5100-5199
Square 52	5200-5299
Square 53	5300-5399
Square 54	5400-5499
Square 55	5500-5599
Square 56	5600-5699
Square 57	5700-5799
Square 58	5800-5899
Square 59	5900-5999
Square 60	6000-6099
Square 61	6100-6199
Square 62	6200-6299
Square 63	6300-6399
Square 64	6400-6499
Square 65	6500-6599
Square 66	6600-6699
Square 67	6700-6799
Square 68	6800-6899
Square 69	6900-6999

Extra blocks of context numbers were added for squares with more than 100 features:

| Square 25 | 7000-7099 |
| Square 27 | 7100-7199 |

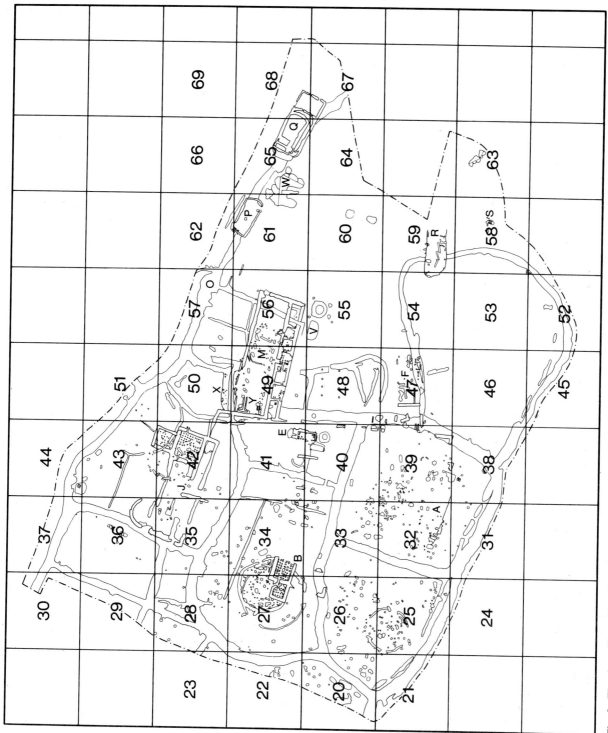

Fig. 3. The site grid used for allocating context numbers.

5

Additional structures were designated:

Structure T (part of M)	8000-8099
Structure U (part of M)	8100-8199
Structure V	8200-8299
Structure W	8300-8399
Structure X	8400-8499
Structure Y	8500-8599

Layers within a feature were recorded by letter suffixes to a group context number, from the uppermost layer down, e.g. 7301A, 7301B. Sections through a feature were recorded by numerical suffixes, e.g. 002/1, 002/2. Thus layers in sections became e.g. 002/1A, 002/1B. Uncertainty between two contexts was indicated by a linking dash, e.g. 210-211, 003/5A-003/5B.

This cumbersome numbering system has been retained in the present report, so that the reader who wishes to consult the archive will find it easy to do so. The report begins with the structural evidence from each of the Iron Age enclosures (I-IX), dealing with pre-Roman and undated earth-cut features. These are followed by the Roman structures (A-Y) designated during excavation, and then by other Roman-period buildings recognised since. Reports on the artefacts recovered from the site in general are followed (in a separate section) by descriptions and discussions of the large assemblage of material from the excavated well. The text indicates where data on the artefacts have been omitted from this publication, but appear in the Archive Report. Discussions of the settlement as a whole, and its development through time are followed by several appendices, one of them listing all the published 'smallfinds' by context.

2   The Iron Age Structures

by A.B. Sumpter

Introduction

The most conspicuous features of the settlement were the enclosure ditches, some of them as much as 3m wide, and originally perhaps 2m deep. They were part of a more extensive ditch system which has been recorded in aerial survey, and which is discussed in Chapter 35.

The ditches were not all dug at one time; they seem, for the most part, to have been accretions to one or two foci (Enclosures II and, probably, VI). The priority of the ditches was most apparent in the profiles and alignments at junctions; the filling layers were less helpful because of recutting. There is no means of dating absolutely either the initial ditches or the accretions, other than by the general artefactual evidence for the settlement as a whole. Nor is it certain when the ditches fell into disuse; most were obviously not much more than shallow depressions by the time the Roman buildings came to be erected, but there are

also signs that some peripheral stretches were recut in that period.

The following descriptions of the pre-Roman structural features are grouped according to the enclosures in which they lay. This is not to imply that they were all secondary to their enclosing ditches; some were demonstrably earlier. For the most part, however, relationships are either uncertain or sufficiently complex to require separate discussion in Chapter 36. Unless stated otherwise, the features were cut into the Magnesian Limestone bedrock and their fillings were of uniform medium brown earth with small fragments of limestone in differing proportions.

The enclosures were numbered after the initial clearance, before detailed excavation began; these original numbers have been retained here, to facilitate reference to the Archive Report. The numerical order has been retained except for Enclosures I and II: the latter, being the primary enclosure, is described before its addition, Enclosure I. The account of each enclosure and the structures within it is preceded by a small key plan to enable the reader to see at a glance the location of the particular element within the complex as a whole.

Enclosure II (Figs 4-8)

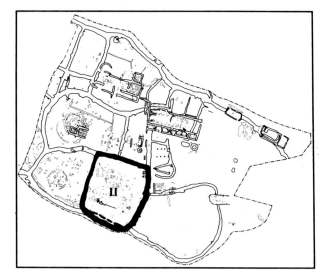

Fig. 4. Location of Enclosure II.

The boundaries

Ditches 018-022 formed the sub-rectangular Enclosure II, which contained about 1090m². The ditches were generally 1.90-3.30m wide and 0.80-1.60m in depth (from the bedrock surface), with fairly uniform, steep-sided profiles (Fig. 6, S.191; Pl. III). The west ditch, however, changed from flat bottomed and 0.80m deep, to almost V-shaped and 1.25m deep between two sections 4m apart (020/1 and 020/2). This could indicate a secondary cutting of the original causeway.

The plan suggests that Enclosure II pre-dated the enclosures linked to it, and this was confirmed by the bedrock profiles where the ditch angles were excavated (Fig. 6, S.191). The sections were in some places at

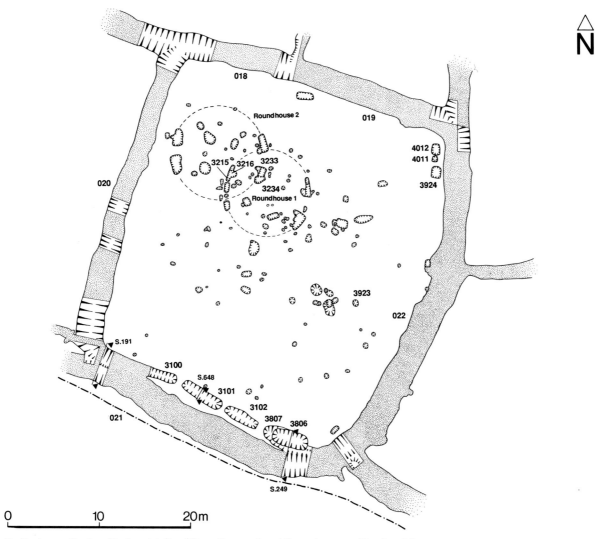

Fig. 5. Enclosure II: plan. Further details of Roundhouses 1 and 2 are shown on Figs 7 and 8.

variance; they showed the fill of this ditch cutting through those of adjoining ditches. This probably represented recutting after the partial or total filling of the adjoining ditches. The lower fill of the north ditch and the adjacent part of the west ditch contained large amounts of limestone rubble with voids; the tip lines suggested that the rubble had been derived from within Enclosure II.

At the south-west angle two recuts of the south ditch were seen to cut the fill of the west ditch, they both continued along the south side of Enclosure I (Fig. 6, S.191). A deposit of uniform, medium brown earth with limestone fragments (021B) was overlain by a darker grey-brown layer (021A), 0.40-0.60m thick and with much Roman material and building debris. This indicated a second recutting in the Roman period (Fig. 6, S.249), probably open for a considerable time since the top surface of the lower fill 021B was relatively compact.

The north and east ditches had been partly overbuilt by a villa precinct wall, the east ditch also by Structure F, and the west ditch by Structure A.

The interior

Running along the north side of the south enclosing ditch (021) were four lengths of a shallower, interrupted ditch (3100, 3101-2 and 3807). They were probably earlier than the enclosure, otherwise the westernmost stretch (3100) might have been expected to appear in section (Fig. 6, S.191). The easterly stretch (3807) was certainly earlier than the recut of 021 (Fig. 6, S.249). All of them had symmetrical V-shaped profiles (Fig. 6, S.648). The general line of the interrupted ditch was continued both east and west by trenches which lay just inside the southern ditch of Enclosures I and II. There is, however, no reason to suppose that they had all been cut together to form a simple boundary: the adjoining trenches had markedly asymmetrical profiles, more in keeping with palisade trenches, and they survived in longer stretches.

The northern half of Enclosure II contained a number of post-pits which have been interpreted as the remains of two roundhouses (Roundhouses 1 and 2). The first (Fig. 7) had an entrance on its east side, 1.90m wide, flanked by a pair of elongated multiple post-pits (3907 and 3915). The two elongated pits were 1.90-2.10 by 0.40-0.60 by 0.38-0.50m, though effectively widened by neighbouring post-pits, and the filling incorporated redeposited limestone.

The other remains attributed to this structure, forming its west side, comprised an arc of three post-pits. By

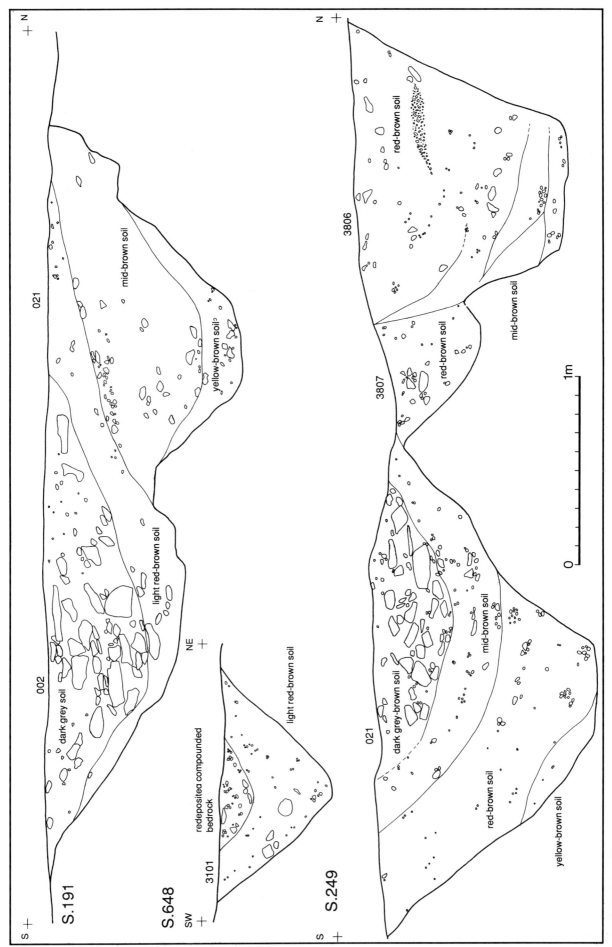

S.191

N

021

mid-brown soil

yellow-brown soil?

light red-brown soil

002

dark grey soil

S

S.648

NE

light red-brown soil

redeposited compounded bedrock

3101

SW

S.249

N

3806

red-brown soil

mid-brown soil

3807

red-brown soil

mid-brown soil

021

dark grey-brown soil

mid-brown soil

red-brown soil

yellow-brown soil

S

1m

0

Fig. 6. Enclosure II: sections.

8

Pl. III. Ditch 020 between Enclosures I and II, facing south. (Photo: S. Wager)

analogy with other roundhouses at this site, the arc may have been expected to form a second entrance, diametrically opposed to the first. Only the northernmost pit (3215), 1.80 by 0.45 by 0.33m, seemed, however, to have the characteristic elongation and multiple post-settings. The two adjacent pits (3228 and 3229) were 0.90-1.20 by 0.50 by 0.28-0.37m and separated by 0.80m, but the gap was occupied by a smaller and seemingly contemporary post (3285). All three peripheral pits had clean redeposited limestone within the earth filling. Pit 3215 was cut by a large post-hole (3216) which, with adjacent post-hole 3203, was probably part of the later Roundhouse 2 to the west.

Around the northern periphery were seven irregularly spaced smaller post-holes (3323-4, 3331, 3967 and 4013-15) between 0.25-0.35m in diameter and 0.08-0.25m deep, which may have marked a wall-line belonging to this building. A few post-holes on the southern periphery (3270, 3273 and 3948-9) may also have been associated.

Scattered post-holes inside the roundhouse did not conform to any obvious pattern; though three large post-pits (3231, 3234 and 3931) and a smaller post-hole (3940) may signify the kind of four-post internal structure more evident in some of the other roundhouses (e.g. Roundhouse 2, below).

Roundhouse 2 (Fig. 8) lay to the west of, and partly overlapped Roundhouse 1. It had opposed entrances; the post-pits which framed them had presumably survived because they had been cut deeper than the trenches or post-holes of the linking walls. The west entrance was

defined by two elongated post-pits (3218 and 3222) spaced 1m apart, measuring 1.80-2.10 by 0.80 by 0.40-0.70m and each containing several post-settings. To the east, an opposite pair (3233 and 4008) with a gap of 1.40m had dimensions of 1.90m by 0.60-0.80m by 0.37m. Redeposited limestone was present in the filling of all four entrance post-pits.

Four large post-holes (3216 3225-6 and 3326), 0.70-1.10m in diameter and 0.24-0.52m deep, were arranged in the manner of a four-post structure, measuring about 3 by 3m. The structure was, however, positioned symmetrically within the roundhouse; it is therefore interpreted as a roof support system, rather than as a distinct building. Diagonally outside each corner of the square was a smaller post-hole (3203, 3291, 3325 and 3329-30). These, too, have been assigned to Roundhouse 2 on the basis of their symmetrical placing.

Roundhouse 2 was shown to be later than Roundhouse 1 by a single stratigraphic relationship: a major internal post-hole (3216) in Roundhouse 2 cut one of the peripheral post-pits (3215) of Roundhouse 1. In addition, at the east entrance of Roundhouse 2, the southern flanking pit (3233) cut through pit 3234; the latter has, therefore, been assigned to Roundhouse 1.

Within Enclosure II were seven pits interpreted as storage pits, which lay around the perimeter of Roundhouse 1. The largest was at the south-east angle: pit 3806, measuring *c.* 3.90 by 1.60 by 1.20m. It cut one length of the interrupted ditch 3807 (Fig. 6, S.249). Of the others, three pits partly underlay the Roman villa precinct wall (3924 and 4011-12).

9

N

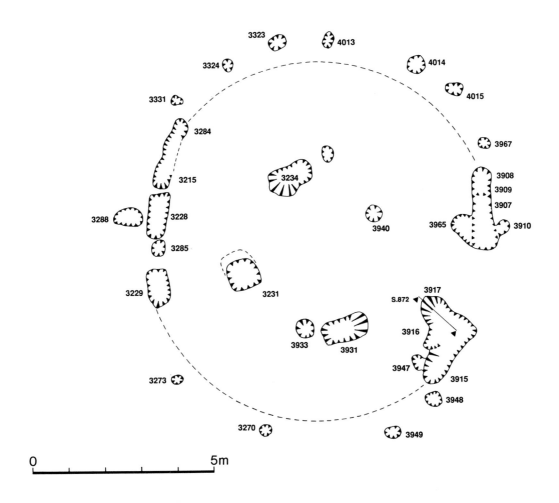

0   5m

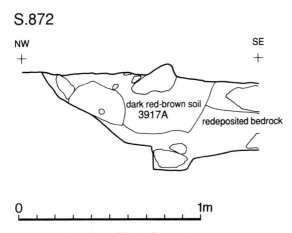

S.872

NW

SE

dark red-brown soil
3917A

redeposited bedrock

0   1m

Fig. 7. Plan and section of Roundhouse 1.

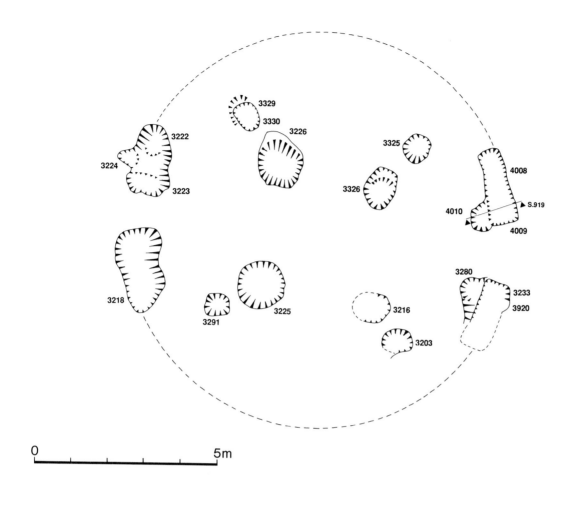

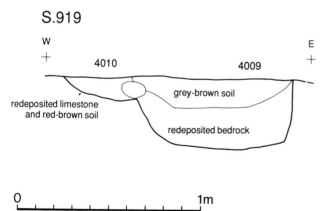

S.919

W   E
+   +
        4010   4009

                                    grey-brown soil

redeposited limestone
and red-brown soil
                        redeposited bedrock

0   1m

Fig. 8. Plan and section of Roundhouse 2.

11

Pl. IV. Roundhouse 3 in Enclosure I, facing south, with palisade trench and enclosure ditch beyond; all features unexcavated. (Photo: S. Wager)

Towards the east side of Enclosure II a sunken hearth (3923) had been dug into the bedrock. It was roughly circular in plan with almost vertical sides and a flat base, 0.70m in diameter and 0.27m deep. The sides had been burnt, and the filling was blackish earth with sub-rounded gritstone erratics but no artefacts. The upper fill (3914) consisted of heavily burnt sandstone flags.

Enclosure I (Figs 9-13)

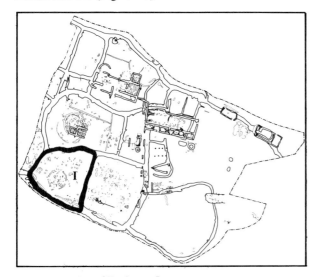

Fig. 9. Location of Enclosure I.

The boundaries
Initially, the area to the west of Enclosure II was delimited on the south side by three lengths of shallow trench. The west end stretch (2100) was very depleted by plough damage, in places only 0.15m deep. It would originally have formed a continuous feature with the better preserved central stretch (2101). The latter had an asymmetrical profile, steep sided on the south (Fig. 11,

S.187). It may have been a palisade trench; the filling stones visible in the published section were probably the remains of post-packing.

A gap of 5.50m separated trench 2101 from the third eastern stretch of trench 2550. This gap, unlike the much smaller one further west, was clearly a deliberate break, perhaps an entrance. It was positioned in front of the southern gap in the wall-trench of Roundhouse 3 (Pl. IV).

Trench 2550 had a similar profile to trench 2101 and can be assigned to the same structure (Fig. 11, S.415). It depended at its east end upon the corner of Enclosure II, and was therefore additional to that enclosure. We should note that the shallow, interrupted ditch which resumed the alignment of trench 2550, along the southern side of Enclosure II, was entirely different from it in profile. It may have been a contemporary feature; it was not a continuation.

There was no indication that trench 2100 had continued north or west of its junction with Ditch 003. It is possible that the course of the boundary had been followed more precisely (and therefore destroyed) by Ditches 003 and 006. Alternatively, the enclosure may originally have been defined by a palisade trench on one side, and ditches on the others. Whatever the arrangement, the southern trenches were at some stage replaced by Ditch 002.

The fully ditched enclosure, bounded by 002, 003, 006 and 020, occupied an area of 860m^2. The ditches were 1.90-2.70m across and 0.56-1.10m deep, with sides of varying steepness (Fig. 11, S.187 and S.201). At both relevant junctions the ditches were seen to be additional to those of Enclosure II. On the south side, the cutting of Ditch 002 had caused a realignment of Ditch 021 at the south-west corner of Enclosure II. A southward bulge at the mid-point of the northern Ditch 006 implied that Roundhouse 5, to the north, was already in existence.

Pl. V. Roundhouse 3 in Enclosure I, facing south; after excavation. (Photo: S. Wager)

Ditch 007, however, was cut later than Ditch 003, as was Ditch 005.

A 2.50m length of Ditch 020, the west side of Enclosure II, had been backfilled after partial silting. It was filled with earth and consolidated by a 0.40m capping of limestone which had, early in the excavation, completely masked the underlying section of ditch. It is probable that the causeway was established to provide permanent access between Enclosures II and I, and therefore post-dated the creation of the latter area.

The south and west ditches had been recut during the Roman period, in the same manner as the south ditch of Enclosure II. The north ditch was overlain by Roman Structure B.

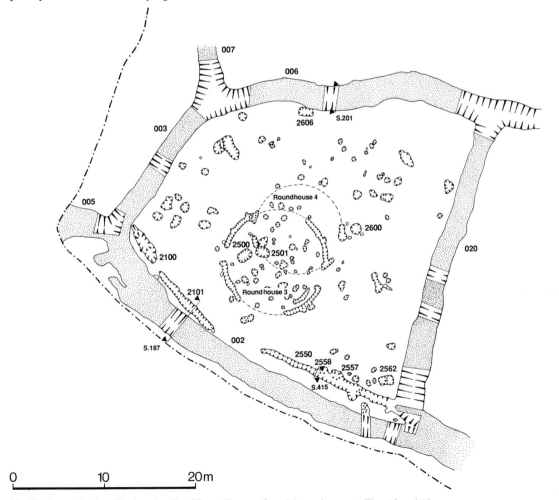

Fig. 10. Enclosure I: plan. Further details of Roundhouses 3 and 4 are shown on Figs 12 and 13.

13

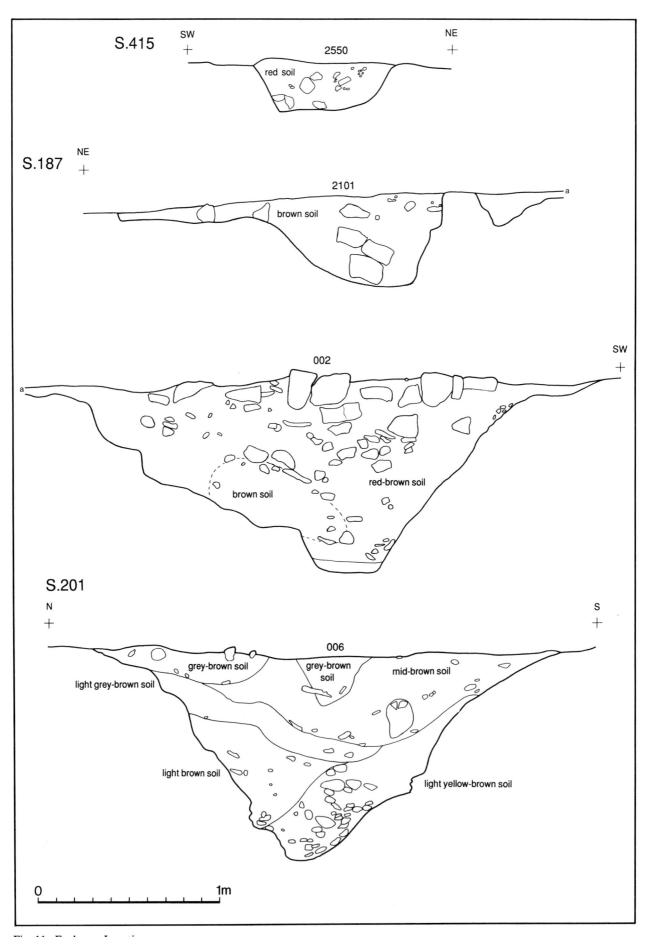

S.415

SW

NE

2550

red soil

S.187

NE

2101

a

brown soil

002

a

SW

brown soil

red-brown soil

S.201

N

S

006

grey-brown soil

grey-brown soil

mid-brown soil

light grey-brown soil

light brown soil

light yellow-brown soil

0   1m

Fig. 11. Enclosure I: sections.

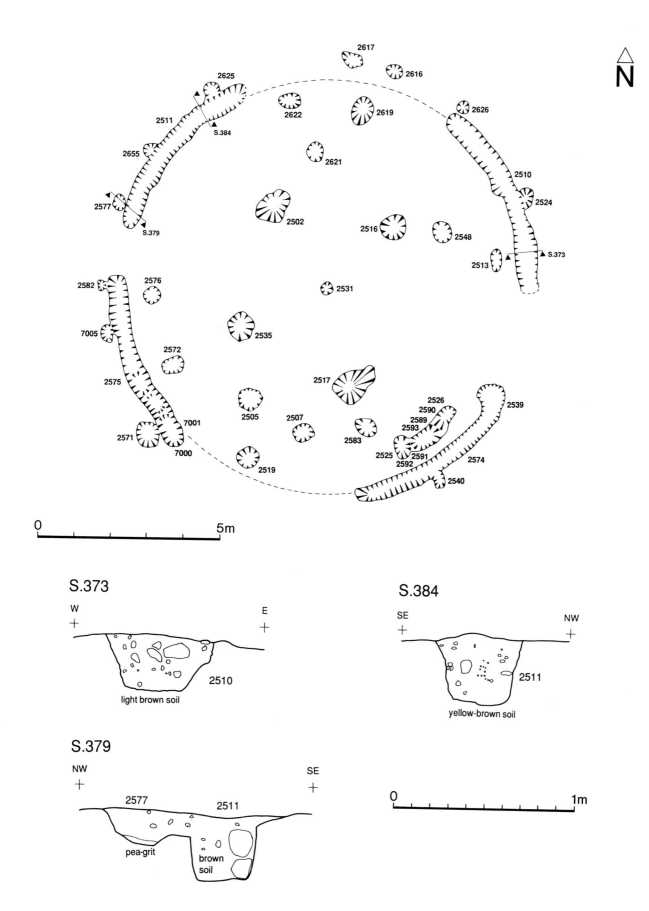

N

S.373

W
+

E
+

2510

light brown soil

S.384

SE
+

NW
+

2511

yellow-brown soil

S.379

NW
+

SE
+

2577   2511

pea-grit

brown
soil

0   5m

0   1m

Fig. 12. Plan and sections of Roundhouse 3.

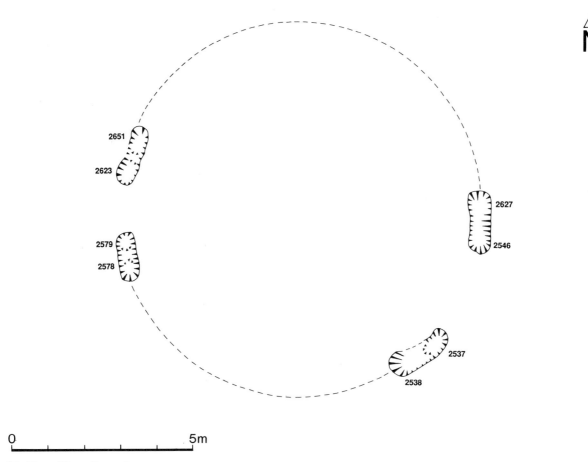

Fig. 13. Plan of Roundhouse 4.

Two radiocarbon dates were obtained from animal bone in the lower filling of the enclosure ditch. In the north-east angle a sample from section 006/2 gave a date in the range 743-212 BC (HAR 6727; see Table 55). In the opposite south-west angle, bone from section 003/2 was dated to the range 346-1 BC (HAR 6716; see Table 55).

The interior

Roundhouse 3 (Fig. 12; Pl. V) was represented by four independent segments of wall-trench (2510, 2511, 2574 and 2575) on a circle 11.50m in (external) diameter. At the centre was a small post-hole (2531), 0.25m in diameter and 0.10m deep. The trenches did not peter out but terminated abruptly, leaving four unequal gaps which measured: north, c. 5.20m; east, c. 2.50m; south, 4.80m; west, 1.25m. The southern gap faced the gap between boundary trenches 2550 and 2101, suggesting possible contemporaneity.

The segments were almost vertical sided and fairly flat based, 0.45-0.55m wide and 0.22-0.41m in depth. Each segment was about 5.20m long though the ends of three were lost in other features; two of them in post-pits of Roundhouse 4 which was thought to be later (see below). The external edge of the south-west quadrant was also affected by later disturbance.

Evidence for post positions in the trenches was scanty and only two (7000 and 7001) were confirmed, both in the south-west segment. Occasional possible but inconclusive traces of post-pipes were seen in sections cutting through the filling, amongst which small gritstone erratics were perhaps for packing. However, close to and mainly outside the ring-trench were several post-holes which could have been replacements or reinforcements for posts in the trench. These were: north-east quadrant, 2524 and 2626; south-east, 2539 and 2540; south-west, 2571, 2582 and 7005; north-west, 2577, 2625 and 2655. Most had diameters of 0.25-0.50m and depths of 0.05-0.25m. Some post-holes within this area could have marked one or more inner rings of supports; a further four large post-pits (2502, 2516-17 and 2535) were centred upon the circular structure in the same fashion as in Roundhouses 1 and 2 (Enclosure II).

Two pairs of elongated pits, in the centre of the enclosure, were interpreted as post positions for the opposed entrances of Roundhouse 4 (Fig. 13). No linking wall-trenches or lines of post-holes could be observed, but such features may have been sufficiently shallow to be removed entirely by ploughing. On the west, the elongated post-pits (2623 and 2651; 2578 and 2579) measured 1.30-1.60 by 0.50 by 0.23-0.30m, and were 1.20m apart. On the east side, the opposed pair (2546 and 2627; 2537 and 2538) had dimensions of 1.60-1.80 by 0.60 by 0.20-0.29m, with a gap of 2.20m. In all four the filling was homogeneous, but each appeared to have held two principal posts. Where pits 2651 and 2538 met segments of the ring-trench for Roundhouse 3, no distinction between the fills was observed. All that can be said is that Roundhouses 3 and 4, if correctly interpreted, could not

16

have been contemporary. Many post-holes of varying sizes which lay in the area could not be satisfactorily assigned to either roundhouse.

Four storage pits were identified in Enclosure I, of which two lay on the perimeter. On the north side, pit 2606 measured 1.70 by 0.90 by 0.25m. In the south-east angle pit 2562 was 1.70 by 1.00 by 0.45m. The two remaining possible storage pits were less regularly cut than most of those found; they were 1m apart and may have been contemporary. Pit 2501 crossed the wall-line of Roundhouse 4; it measured 1.40 by 1.00 by 0.40m. Pit 2500 lay a short distance to the west and measured 1.60 by 1.10 by 0.50m. It was within the area of Roundhouse 3, but there was no means of relating it to that structure.

There were also two sunken hearths in Enclosure I. Both were roughly circular, flat-bottomed pits about 1m in diameter with near-vertical sides, dug 0.25-0.30m into the bedrock; their sides and bases showed signs of burning. Hearth 2600 lay to the north-east of the roundhouses, while hearth 2558 was cut into trench 2550 on the south side of the enclosure. They contained black ashy material; both produced numerous sherds of coarse Iron Age pottery. Adjacent and to the east of hearth 2558 was an irregular pit (2557), of similar size but with sloping sides, filled with much burnt material. It, too, cut trench 2550.

Enclosure III (Figs 14-15)

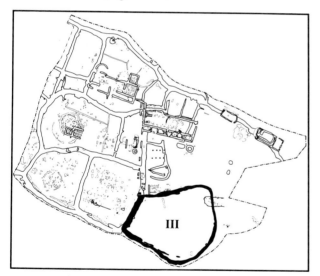

Fig. 14. Location of Enclosure III.

The boundaries

The earliest boundary in this part of the site was a trench similar to, and continuing the alignment of trench 2550 in Enclosure I. As can be seen from the published sections (Fig. 15, S.255 and S.985) the profiles were again asymmetrical, the steep side being to the south. The gaps between the three stretches of trench (3812, 4500 and 4600; 5201 could be a fourth) may have been the result of erosion, as the central and eastern lengths survived to a depth of only c. 0.25m. As in Enclosure I, the trench is interpreted as the foundation for a palisade. Its east and north sides have been lost – if they ever existed.

The palisade was replaced by a ditch which encompassed an area of 1610m^2. The ditches were about 1-2m wide and 0.60-0.90m deep, with fairly steep-sided profiles (Fig. 15, S.267). Several sections showed signs of recutting at least once, and most consistent was a shallower recut ditch (023-025) which diverged at the south-west angle by 0.70m inside the line of the original Ditch 040. The recut was c. 1-2m broad and 0.50-0.60m deep, and recognisable more by the profile than by marked differences in the filling.

The north ditch was partly overlain by Roman Structure F and the east ditch by Structure R (pp. 59 and 67 respectively).

The interior

This was the largest enclosure to be completely exposed, but no evidence was found for roofed structures. Towards the north-west angle a short slot or gully (625) ran almost at right-angles to, and within 1.50m of the north ditch. It was steep sided, measured 6.00 by 0.70 by 0.40m, and produced no finds. The slot may have retained a timber barrier or fence but there were no associated features.

Of several inhumations on the site, Enclosure III provided the only demonstrably Iron Age burial. It occupied a shallow grave (602) in the north-west corner of the enclosure, oriented north-north-east to south-south-west on the Ordnance Survey grid, with head to the south-west. It was the crouched skeleton of an adult female, lying face upwards with the knees drawn to the chest, and unaccompanied by grave goods (Chapter 23, No. 2). Radiocarbon analysis of a bone sample gave a date in the range 355-94 BC (HAR 6715; see Table 55).

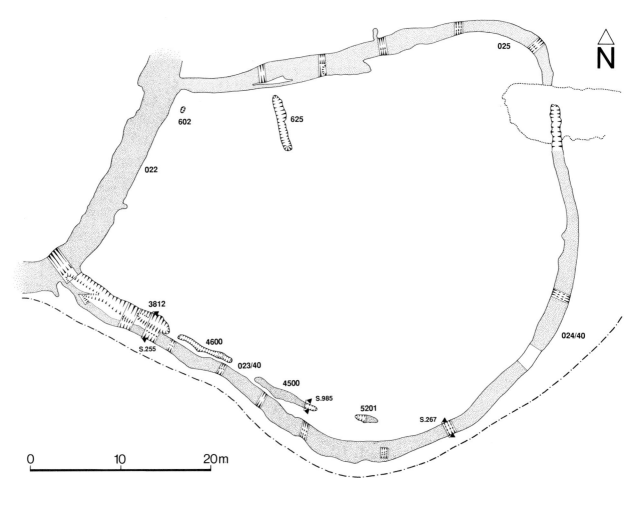

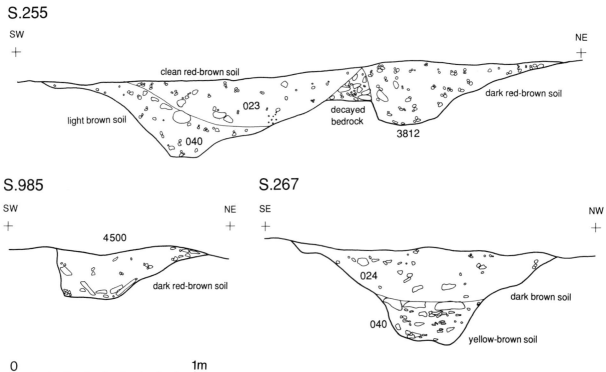

Fig. 15. Enclosure III: plan and sections.

Enclosure IV (Figs 16-21)

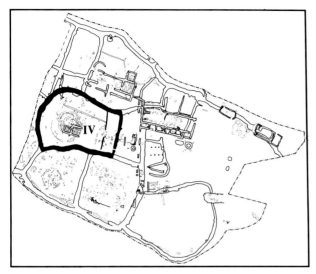

Fig. 16. Location of Enclosure IV.

The boundaries

The east side of this enclosure seemed originally to have been defined by a fence or palisade. The two gullies which marked this boundary were 3307/3308 and 3467/4101. They had fairly steep-sided profiles, and were about 0.70m wide and 0.25-0.45m deep (Fig. 18, S.736 and S.825). A gap about 3.80m wide between the two stretches

may have marked an entrance. The southern gully began about 0.80m from the northern ditch of Enclosure I, upon which it clearly depended. The north end of the northern stretch turned into Ditch 016: it may indicate that Enclosure IV was originally fenced on one side but ditched elsewhere.

The ditches numbered 007, 015 and 016 were unquestionably part of a single cutting which seems to have respected (or to have been designed to accommodate) Roundhouse 5. Their profiles and dimensions were similar to those of the other enclosure ditches (Fig. 18, S.227). Ditch 007 post-dated the Enclosure I ditch (Fig. 18, S.205). On the east, the fence line was at some stage replaced by Ditch 017 about 7m further east. Ditch 017 was shallower than the earlier ditches (Fig. 18, S.233). It must have been at this time, or later, that Roundhouse 7 was erected.

The interior

Enclosure IV provided evidence of three roundhouses. The earliest of these was Roundhouse 5 (Fig. 19). It seemed, in fact, to have pre-dated the ditches of this enclosure, since it pre-dated the northern ditch of the earlier Enclosure I: the central part of Ditch 006 can be seen on the plan to have been diverted southwards, to avoid the southern arc of the structure. Roundhouse 5 was represented by a ring-gully in three segments (2656, 2700,

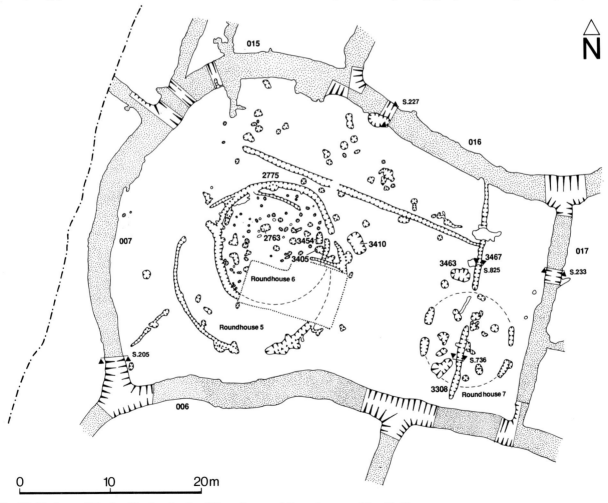

Fig. 17. Enclosure IV: plan. Further details of Roundhouses 5-7 are shown on Figs 19-21.

19

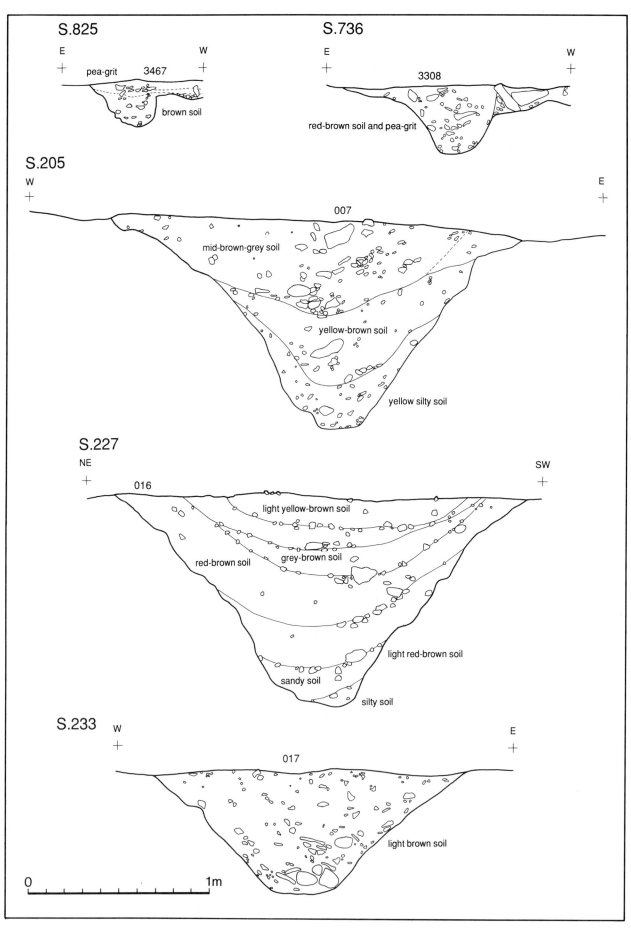

S.825

E   W

pea-grit   3467

brown soil

S.736

E   W

3308

red-brown soil and pea-grit

S.205

W   E

007

mid-brown-grey soil

yellow-brown soil

yellow silty soil

S.227

NE   SW

016

light yellow-brown soil

grey-brown soil

red-brown soil

light red-brown soil

sandy soil

silty soil

S.233 W   E

017

light brown soil

0   1m

Fig. 18. Enclosure IV: sections.

20

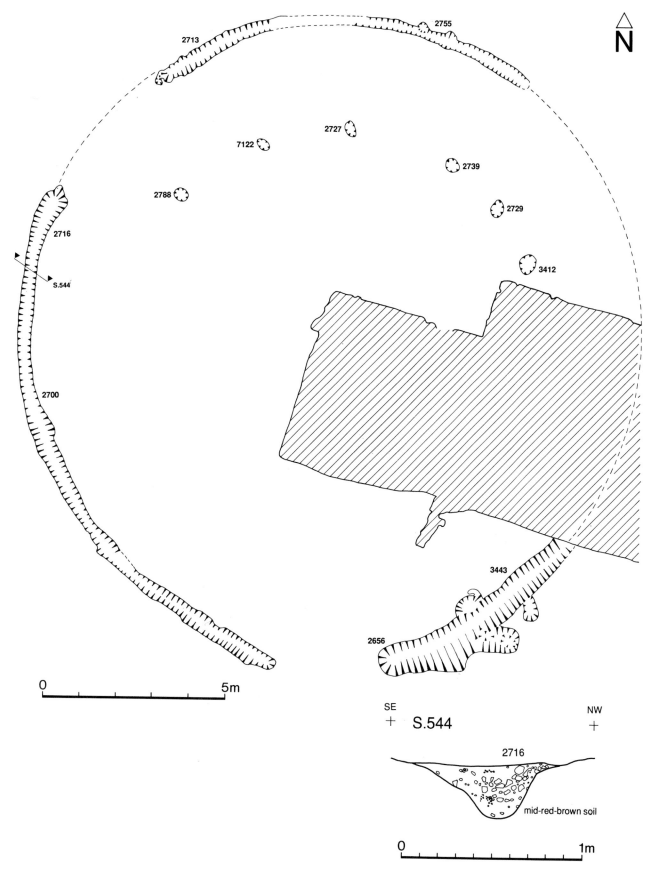

2713

2755

2727

7122

2739

2788

2729

2716

3412

S.544

2700

3443

2656

0   5m

N

SE

+   S.544

NW

+

2716

mid-red-brown soil

0   1m

Fig. 19. Plan and section of Roundhouse 5.

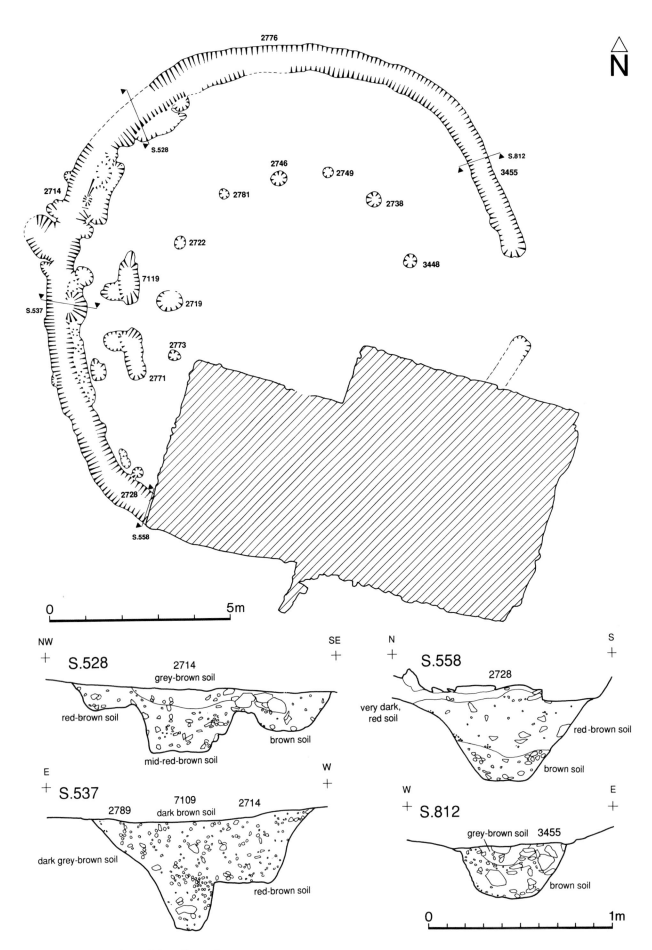

Fig. 20. Plan and sections of Roundhouse 6.

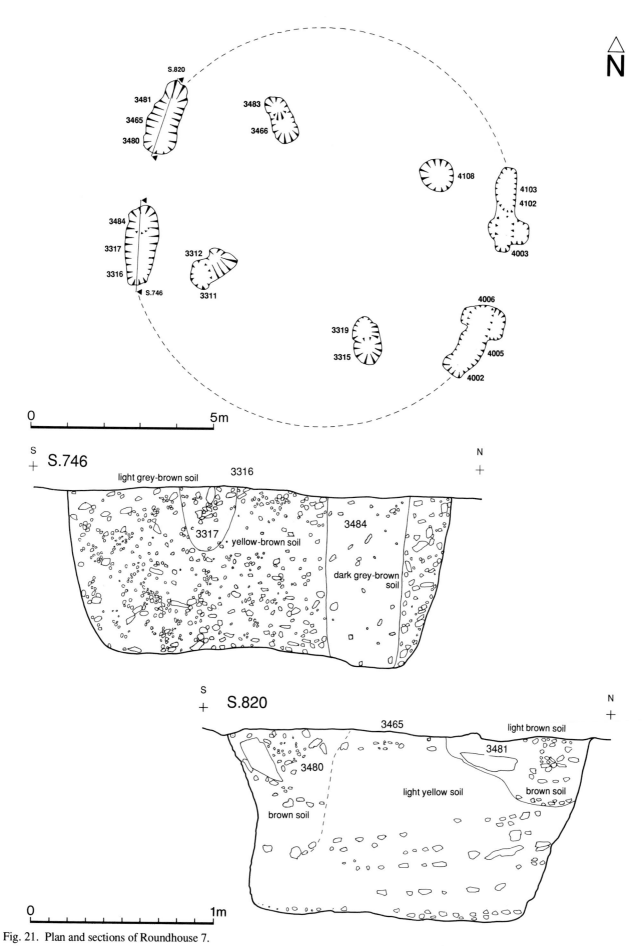

N

S.746

S
+

N
+

light grey-brown soil
3316

3317 • yellow-brown soil

3484

dark grey-brown soil

S.820

S
+

N
+

3465
light brown soil

3480

3481

light yellow soil

brown soil

brown soil

0   5m

0   1m

Fig. 21. Plan and sections of Roundhouse 7.

2713, 2716, 2755 and 3443) of a near-circle with a mean internal diameter of 17m and an enclosed area of *c.* 220m^2. The southern and north-western gaps in the ring may have marked entrances. The ring-gully had a U-shaped profile and was more pronounced to the south-east where it was 0.80m wide and 0.37m deep; on the north side it diminished to 0.30m across and as little as 0.10m in depth.

About one-fifth of the interior including the centre point had been destroyed by Roman Structure B, which cut through the eastern segment. A concentration of post-holes within Roundhouse 5 was largely in the area of overlap with the later Roundhouse 6 (see below), but 2727, 2729, 2739, 2788, 3412 and 7122 may have been internal post-holes associated with Roundhouse 5.

Roundhouse 6 (Fig. 20) was located nearer the centre of the enclosure. Indeed, it was approximately concentric with Ditches 007, 015 and 016. Either the roundhouses pre-dated the ditches, or the various elements were created simultaneously.

The building was defined by a ring-gully (2714, 2728, 2776 and 3455), about 0.60-0.90m in width and 0.29-0.40m deep. A gap, interpreted as an entrance, faced east; there was no sign of enlargement for entrance posts. Where the ring-gullies for Roundhouses 6 and 5 coincided, sections were cut; these failed to reveal a stratigraphic relationship. From a section (3455/2) through the north-east section of the ring-gully for Roundhouse 6, a sample of animal bone gave a radiocarbon date in the range 480-235 BC (HAR 6725; see Table 55).

Numerous post-holes and post-pits were located within the area of Roundhouse 6. Some of them may have represented internal supports: a roughly concentric circle was formed by pits 2719, 2722, 2738, 2746, 2749, 2773, 2781 and 3448. Others may have belonged to different structures: two elongated pits (2771 and 7119), each containing several post-settings, could indicate the entrance of another roundhouse. Since they appear to have been concentric with Roundhouse 6, however, they may signify a different phase of this building, one with a smaller floor area.

Roundhouse 7 (Fig. 21) was an opposed-entrance structure, similar to Roundhouse 2. It was located in the south-east corner of the enclosure. Two elongated post-pits formed the west entrance (3465 and 3480-81; 3316-17 and 3484). They were 1.40m apart and measured 2.00 by 0.85 by 0.95m. Both pits had been backfilled largely with clean redeposited limestone, and at the inner ends (3480 and 3484) each contained a post-pipe 0.40m in diameter. In the middle of the south pit (3317) there was a shallower pipe 0.30m in diameter.

On the east side the other two opposed pits (4003 and 4103; 4002 and 4006) were 1.50m apart; their dimensions were 2.10-2.30 by 0.55-0.65 by 0.55m. The fill was medium brown earth with a high concentration of redeposited limestone and gritstone lumps probably marking post-packing. The inner end of the south pit (4006) contained a post-pipe 0.46m in diameter. In the middle of both pits there were post-pipes (4005 and 4102) *c.* 0.30m in diameter.

Within the floor area of this roundhouse were four large post-holes which formed a square. Its sides were 4.80m from centre to centre. These post-holes (3311, 3315, 3483 and 4108) were 0.60-0.80m in diameter and 0.55m deep. Except for 4108 each was joined by an irregular shallower pit (3312, 3319 and 3466) on the side nearest the centre. The roundhouse could not have co-existed with the fence gully 3308. There was, however, no means of determining which came first. The suggested boundary development would imply that the fence pre-dated the structure.

Three storage pits were identified in Enclosure IV. Pit 2763, near the centre of the area occupied by Roundhouse 6, was 1.22 by 0.75 by 0.53m. To the east of Roundhouses 5 and 6 was pit 3410 which measured 1.20 by 0.48 by 0.50m. Pit 3463, just north of Roundhouse 7, was 2.03 by 1.17 by 0.45m. After use it had been levelled with a layer of gritstone erratics.

A sunken hearth (2775) was located in Enclosure IV. It was oval in plan, and measured 0.97 by 0.79 by 0.25m. It contained black ashy earth, and cut the filled-in ring-gully 2776 on the north side of Roundhouse 6. The hearth yielded one small sherd of coarse Iron Age pottery, and four indeterminable Roman sherds from the uppermost fill. There were numerous other post-holes and pits in Enclosure IV, particularly to the north of Roundhouse 6, which could not be resolved into discrete structures. Near the centre two large pits (3405 and 3454) contained animal burials (Chapter 24, pp. 176-7).

Enclosure V (Figs 22-3)

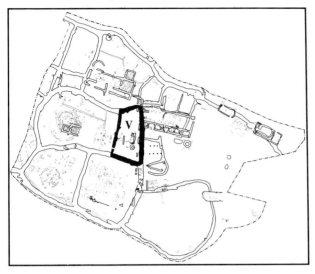

Fig. 22. Location of Enclosure V.

The boundaries
This enclosure was formed by Ditches 017, 019, 026 and 027 in the angle between Enclosures II and IV. Its position in the sequence of boundaries was demonstrated at the intersections with both these enclosures. At the south-east corner, the 026/022 ditch was secondary to the 022/019

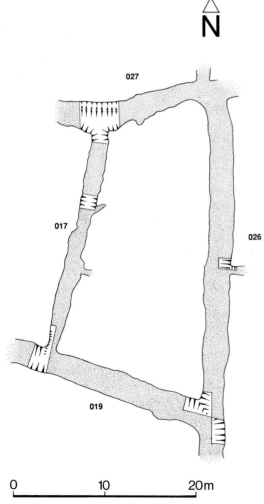

Fig. 23. Enclosure V: plan.

line. At the north-west corner, Ditch 027 cut through the filling of Ditch 017 to meet Ditch 016. Indeed, it is possible that Enclosure V was not a separate area, but a further eastward extension of Enclosure IV. Its ditches were about 2.20m wide and 0.80m deep.

The interior
The ground level in this area had been lowered by at least 0.50m since antiquity, judging by the limited survival of the hypocaust of Structure E which occupied the centre of the enclosure. Erosion by plough probably accounts for the absence of demonstrably Iron Age features.

Enclosure VI (Figs 24-5)

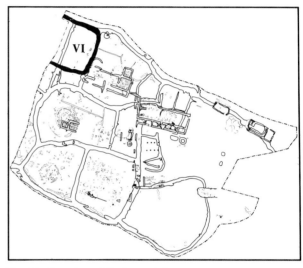

Fig. 24. Location of Enclosure VI.

The boundaries
Only part of this enclosure fell within the excavation area; it was bounded on the north by Ditch 011/036, on the east by Ditch 012 (Fig. 25, S.214), and on the south by Ditch 010/013. When the surfaces of the filled-in ditches were exposed, the alignments of the inner edges, in particular, indicated that Enclosure VI was originally an isolated, sub-rectangular structure, like Enclosure II; it had later been incorporated into larger and more complex units.

The initial indications were confirmed by the excavated sections, which showed that the ditch linking the south-east corner of the enclosure to Enclosure IV was a recutting and extension of Ditch 012, probably to define the adjacent area eastwards as Enclosure VII. Similarly Ditch 014 was a recutting (on a slightly more northerly line) and extension of Ditch 011. This recutting may have continued west as far as Ditch 009, which crossed Enclosure VI and continued southwards to meet Enclosure IV. Both 009 and 014 may be attributable to the Roman villa period.

The interior
Centrally positioned on the east side of Enclosure VI was a pair of elongated and lobed post-pits (3606 and 3617), each c. 2.00 by 0.90 by 0.30-0.50m and lying 2m apart; they were parallel to the east ditch. Within both pits were

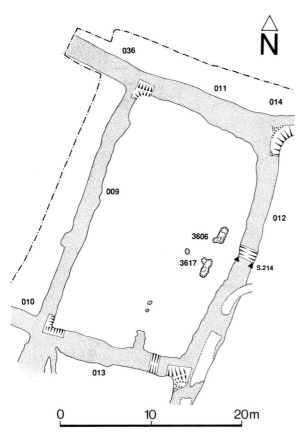

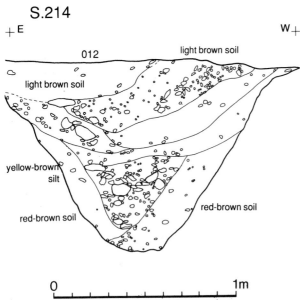

S.214

+E   W+

012

light brown soil

light brown soil

yellow-brown silt

red-brown soil

red-brown soil

0   1m

Fig. 25. Enclosure VI: plan and section.

settings for two large posts, with smaller subsidiary posts and signs of replacement. The fill contained some clean redeposited limestone. The structure resembled the entrances of some of the roundhouses but the pits were in a straight line rather than angled; no related features were detected. The only other man-made features in this enclosure were a few scattered post-holes.

Enclosure VII (Figs 26-8)

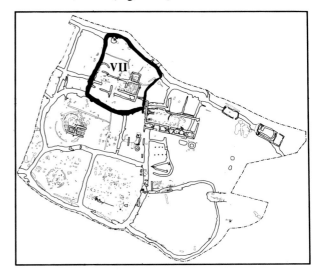

Fig. 26. Location of Enclosure VII.

The boundaries

This enclosure, like some others, produced evidence of smaller gullies which presumably held fence posts. Features 4201, 4303 and 5001 were two stretches of a curvilinear gully which underlay the north-east room of Structure J (Fig. 27, S.967), and which could not have co-existed with Roundhouse 8. They ran from the northern half of Ditch 029 to a point about 5.50m south of Ditch 014; on the west there was a 2.20m wide gap between them. Near the northern end an apparently associated gully (4302) ran westwards as far as Ditch 012 (Fig. 27, S.965). It is possible that these gullies pre-dated the definition of Enclosure VII: that they were part of an earlier enclosure formed when this area was an external space on the east of Enclosure VI.

Enclosure VII was formed by recutting the east ditch (012) of Enclosure VI and joining it to the north ditch (016) of Enclosure IV; by extending the north ditch of Enclosure VI eastwards (014; Fig. 27, S.219), and by cutting an east ditch (029) roughly in line with the east ditch (026) of Enclosure V. The north ditch was *c*. 2m wide and up to 0.95m deep. The east side had been drastically lowered by 19th-century excavations, and the east ditch was reduced to 0.60-1.20m in width and 0.43m in depth.

The north ditch had been recut, perhaps as late as Roman times, in the same manner as the north ditch of Enclosure VI. The west ditch had been overbuilt by Roman Structure J, and the south-east angle by the linking wall between Structures J and F.

The interior

Close to the centre of Enclosure VII was Roundhouse 8 (Fig. 28), an opposed-entrance structure. The western entrance comprised two elongated post-pits each with several post-settings; they were joined by an irregular gully on the interior. The pits (4212 and 4213) were about 2.20 by 0.50 by (max.) 0.53m, and lay 1.20m apart. They contained much redeposited limestone. The gully (4211),

26

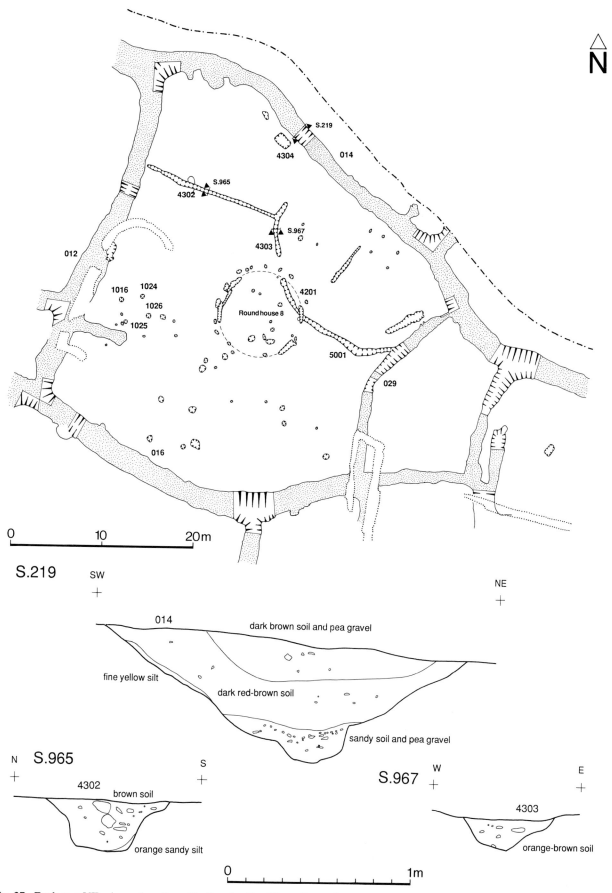

Fig. 27. Enclosure VII: plan and sections. Further details of Roundhouse 8 are shown on Fig. 28.

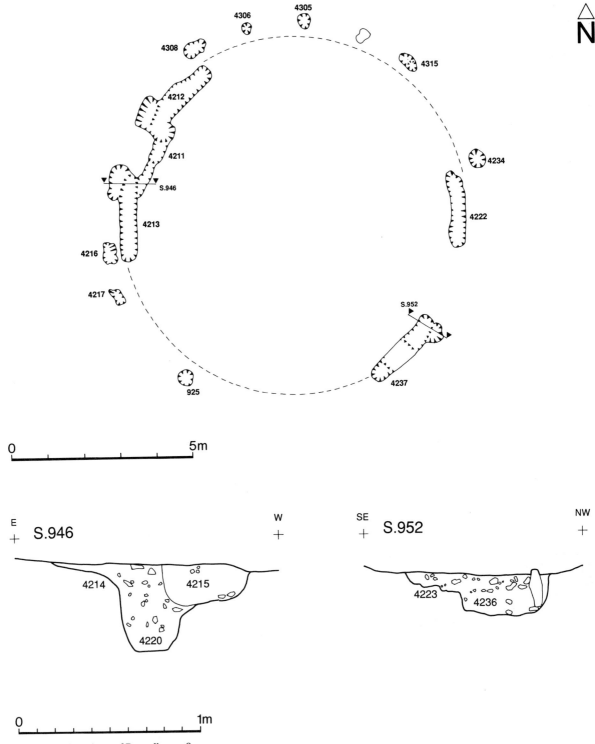

S.946

S.952

E
+ S.946
W
+

SE
+ S.952
NW
+

4214   4215

4220

4223   4236

0   5m

0   1m

Fig. 28. Plan and sections of Roundhouse 8.

interpreted as the slot for a threshold timber, was 0.20m wide and 0.10m deep. On the east side, the opposing pits (4222 and 4237) were 2.00-2.20 by 0.40-0.50 by (max.) 0.43m; each contained at least two major post-settings, spaced 2m apart.

A circle centred upon the entrances would pass through a number of post-holes: 4234, 4305-6, 4308 and 4315 to the north; and 925 and 4216-17 to the south. These

may therefore have been post positions for the wall timbers of the building. They were intermittent and shallow; others could have been lost entirely through erosion.

From among the general scatter of post-holes, one possible four-post structure could be defined. It comprised post-holes 1016 and 1024-26 which formed a square of mean side 2.40m across the post-hole centres. The post-holes were 0.43-0.60m in diameter and 0.30-0.38m deep, all with heavy gritstone packing. No artefacts were found in their fills.

One pit (4304) in the area of Enclosure VII was probably associated with Iron Age occupation. It lay close to the north ditch, and had probably been used for storage. It was sub-rectangular and measured 1.75 by 1.05 by 0.20m. There were no finds from it. There were a few other isolated and undatable pits, gullies and post-holes, some of which probably belonged to the overlying Roman Structure J.

Enclosure VIII (Figs 29-30)

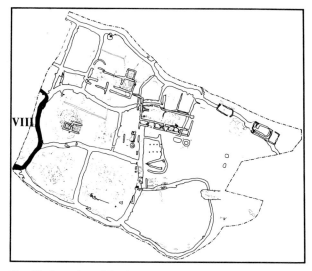

Fig. 29. Location of Enclosure VIII.

The boundaries
Enclosure VIII was one of the settlement enclosures extending westwards from the excavated area (Chapter 35, Fig. 155); only a narrow strip was exposed along the edge of excavation. It was bounded by two east-west

Pl. VI. Storage pits in Enclosure VIII, facing south-west; before excavation. (Photo: S. Wager)

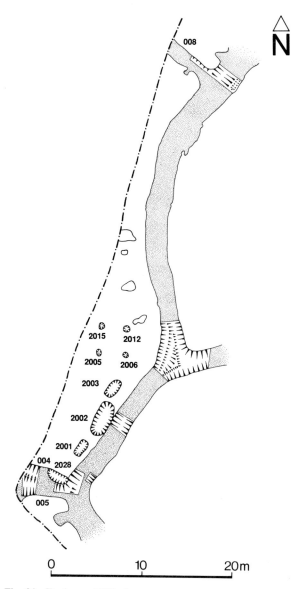

Fig. 30. Enclosure VIII: plan.

ditches, the profiles at the intersections showed these to have been added to the west side of Enclosures I and IV. Ditch 008 was the less substantial where seen, 1m across and not more than 0.30m in depth; Ditch 005 was 2m wide and 0.60m deep.

The interior
A four-post structure was identified in the southern half of the enclosure. It was 3m square, measuring between the post-hole centres. The four post-holes (2005-6, 2012 and 2015) were 0.50-0.74m in diameter and 0.18-0.28m deep; they did not contain packing stones.

Four regularly cut pits lay in a group in the south-east angle (Pl. VI). Three of them (2001, 2003 and 2028) measured about 2.00 by 1.00 by 0.40-0.60m; the fourth pit (2002) was much larger (3.85 by 1.87 by 1.08m). They may have been used for storage.

West of these pits were several poorly defined hollows or shallow pits, and other irregular features lay to the north. A shallow irregular gully (004), about 0.65m wide and 0.20m deep, lay just inside the south ditch. It ran for 2m to the edge of the excavation.

Enclosure IX (Figs 31-2)

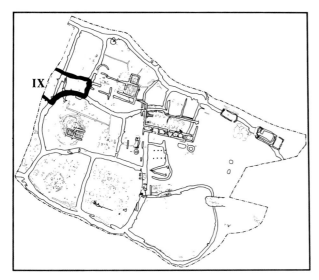

Fig. 31. Location of Enclosure IX.

The boundaries

Enclosure IX was like Enclosure VIII to the south, only marginally within the excavation area. The exposed part contained fewer structures than Enclosure VIII, from which it was separated by Ditch 008. It occupied the space between pre-existing Enclosures IV and VI. It may originally have been part of the open area later converted to Enclosure VII. Enclosure IX was traversed by the north-south ditch (009) probably of Roman origin, which also crossed Enclosure VI to the north.

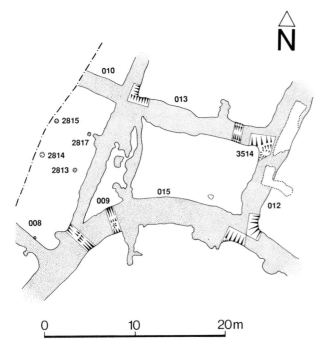

Fig. 32. Enclosure IX: plan.

The interior

A four-post structure was represented by substantial post-holes (2813-15 and 2817) arranged in a near-geometrical square of mean side 3.90m across the post-hole centres. The holes were 0.35-0.64m in diameter and 0.13-0.33m deep, with gritstone packing in each.

A storage pit (3514) which could not have been contemporary with the usage of Enclosure IX or Enclosure VII was cut into the bedrock within the western half of Ditch 012. It was roughly elliptical, with maximum surviving dimensions 1.40 by 1.10 by 0.80m. Its fill could not be differentiated from that of the ditch, and it was revealed only in the base of the ditch; it therefore probably pre-dated the ditch. Apart from a small isolated post-hole on the edge of the south ditch, no other archaeological features were found inside Enclosure IX.

Enclosures east of V and VII (Figs 33-5)

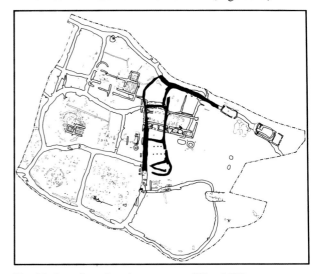

Fig. 33. Location of enclosures east of V and VII.

The boundaries

A series of small ditched areas along the east side of Enclosures V and VII mark the final additions to the Iron Age settlement: gullies 035, 5600, 5601 and 5605 further east are assigned to the Roman period (see p. 47).

The earliest gully in this area was 4800, which clearly pre-dated Ditches 026 and 042. It was a shallow cut surviving no more than 0.30m deep; further south Ditch 5515, with a similar depth, may have been an associated boundary feature.

At some period after the creation of Enclosure V a *c.* 10m wide strip of land further east was annexed to it, either as a subsidiary enclosure or (if Ditch 026 was then backfilled) as a continuation of the existing area. It was formed on the north side by the extension eastwards of Ditch 027. Though most of this stretch of ditch had been removed in the construction of Structure X (Fig. 46, S.63), its east end clearly curved south, beneath the walling of Structure M (Fig. 35, S.287), to become the east side Ditch 042. The latter was at some stage recut as Ditch 043 (Fig. 35, S.287 and S.319), perhaps when this enclosure or extension was itself extended northwards by the cutting of

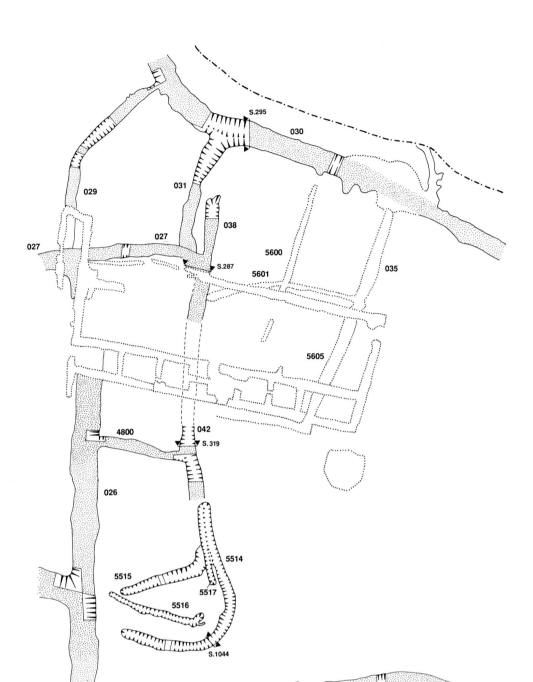

S.295
030
031
029
038
027
027
S.287
5600
035
5601
5605
4800
042
S.319
026
5514
5515
5517
5516
S.1044
025

0   10   20m

Fig. 34. Enclosures east of V and VII: plan.

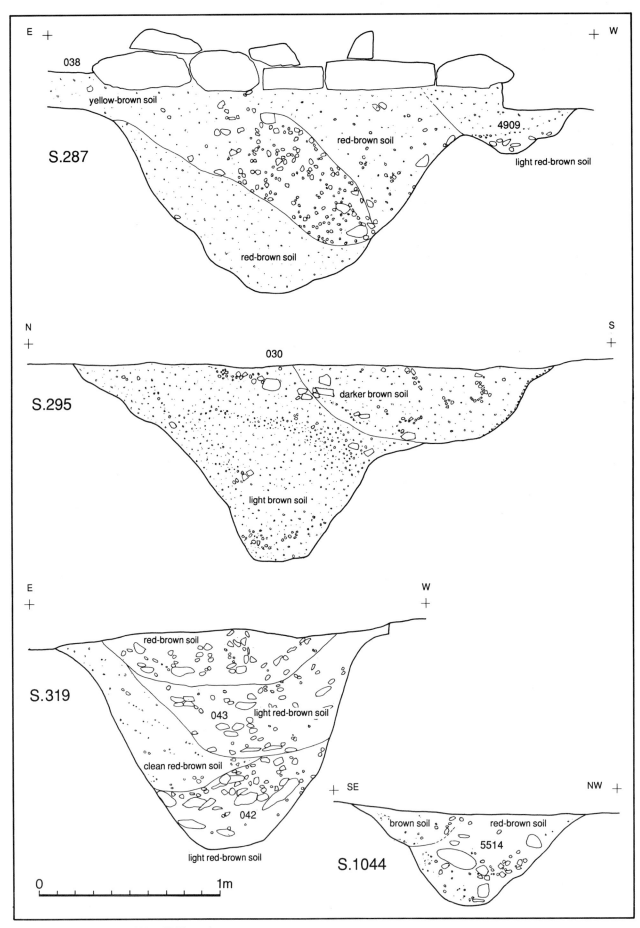

E +
038
yellow-brown soil
S.287
red-brown soil
4909
light red-brown soil
red-brown soil
+ W

N +
030
S.295
darker brown soil
light brown soil
S +

E +
red-brown soil
S.319
043 light red-brown soil
clean red-brown soil
042
light red-brown soil
W +

SE +
brown soil
red-brown soil
5514
S.1044
NW +

0 _____ 1m

Fig. 35. Enclosures east of V and VII: sections.

Ditch 038. Southwards the line of Ditch 042 was continued by 5514, a rather shallower ditch which showed evidence of even shallower recutting (Fig. 35, S.1044). Gullies 5516 and 5517 were possibly a later version of the same boundary.

The area north of the extended Ditch 027 was enclosed at a later stage. It is not clear whether Ditch 038 preceded or replaced 031 as the east side of the new area; the latter evidently replicated the alignment of Ditch 029, the earlier east side of Enclosure VII. The relationship of Ditches 030 and 031 was not established, but, again, alignments suggest that 030 was originally an 8m extension of Ditch 014, to link with 031. It was later extended (or developed, piecemeal) eastwards as a spinal land division boundary, partly recut in the Roman period (Fig. 35, S.295).

The interior

No internal features could be attributed to the Iron Age. The series of post-holes forming Structure Z (p. 73), south of 4800, has been attributed to the Roman period: one of the holes was cut into the backfilled Ditch 043.

3   The Roman Structures

by Adrian Tindall

Structure J (Figs 36-7)

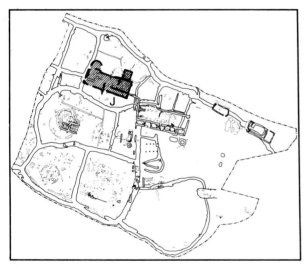

Fig. 36. Location of Structure J.

Structure J was, in the 4th century, the principal residential building of the villa. It was aligned approximately east-west, and consisted of a central suite of three rooms with a corridor along the south side, and two wings – one apsidal and one square – projecting to the north. The apsidal west wing had been investigated as a discrete structure in the excavations of 1854, and it was from here that the 'Medusa' mosaic pavement, now housed in the Yorkshire Museum at York, was recovered.

By the 1970s the building was in an extremely poor state of preservation due to the effects of, successively,

tree planting, stone robbing and ploughing. The 1855 report, referring to what has now been identified as the east wing, states that:

> No excavation of any value could be carried on, at present, here, for the whole ground is strewn over with stones and the remains of a hypocaust, which had been destroyed by the farmer in obtaining stones for building. (Procter 1855, 277)

The report also records that the south portion of the apse 'was so incomplete that the precise character and form of its termination could not with accuracy be decided.' (Procter 1855, 274).

The degree of plough damage could be gauged by the fact that no distinction existed between the level of the hypocaust basement and that of the surrounding bedrock. Despite its fragmentary condition, however, the evidence of robber trenches and of the stretches of surviving walling allowed the ground plan to be determined. The approximate external dimensions of the building were as follows: 30m long, 16.50m wide at the west wing, 17m wide at the east wing, and 10.50m wide at the centre. The building comprised six rooms (Rooms 1-6 on Fig. 37), which will be described in turn.

Room 1

Room 1 was a corridor, running the entire length of the south side of the building. It measured internally 27.80 by c. 2.40m. On its northern side it was bounded by walls 907 and 911 and by robber trench 1004. Wall 907 (average width 0.90m) was the best preserved of these, consisting of a single course of dressed gritstone blocks, mortared and with a rubble core; parts had been robbed. Wall 911 (average width 0.90m, maximum surviving height 0.70m) continued the line of wall 907 to the west, but was composed of a single course of limestone nodules, mortared in places. After a break of some 10.50m, this wall-line was continued at the western end of the building by robber trench 1004, 1.30m wide and 0.10m deep at maximum. It may be noted that, in cases where intermittent stretches of walling survived, the width of the robber trench often exceeded that of the remaining wall by as much as a third. Except where otherwise stated, the material filling the robber trenches consisted of a black soil matrix containing building debris – dressed stone, sandstone roof flags, roof tile, box-flue tiles, *tesserae*, mortar and painted plaster.

The east wall of Room 1 (919) was fairly well preserved, having been robbed only at its northern end. The surviving stretches consisted of two, or in some places three courses of dressed, mortared gritstone with a rubble core, the lowest course being slightly offset. The average width was again 0.90m, and the maximum surviving height 0.26m.

The southern limit of the room was marked by wall 906 and robber trenches 1006 and 1008. Wall 906 survived at its eastern end as two courses of dressed, mortared gritstone (average width 0.85m, maximum surviving height 0.18m) with a rubble core. The remainder of its length was robbed. Robber trenches 1006 and 1008 continued its line to the west, and these varied in width from 0.80-0.95m, with a maximum surviving depth of 0.17m. Trench 1006 contained 3rd and 4th-century pottery. Two breaks occurred in this south wall: one (2.70m wide) near the western end and another (1.70m wide) exactly in the centre. The latter was flanked by a pair of clay-packed post-holes (913 and 1022); and also at this point a cross-wall (1009), consisting of a single course of gritstone and limestone blocks, bisected Room 1 and extended southwards from the building for a distance of at least 2.50m. The pair of post-holes and wall 1009 may represent successive features associated with the entrance. The western side (1003) of Room 1 was marked only by a scatter of rubble in the top of enclosure ditch 012.

Room 1 contained a layer of black soil of maximum depth 0.35m. This occurred throughout the building (numbered variously as 900, 901, 903-5, 1000 and 1001), and clearly represented backfilled material from 19th-century stone robbing and from the excavations of the 1850s. Finds from this general level include two sherds of Iron Age pottery and late 2nd to late 4th-century pottery (including quantities of plain and decorated samian ware); but there were also post-medieval sherds. In addition, the layer contained building debris such as dressed stone, roof tile, sandstone roof flags, box-flue tiles, *tesserae*, *opus signinum* flooring, mortar and painted plaster. No surfacing survived below, and the bedrock was heavily cratered by tree roots.

Room 2

The westernmost of the central suite of rooms measured 6.20 by 7.60m internally (approximate dimensions derived from present excavations and 1854 measurements). It was bounded to the north by feature 1027, described in the 1855 report as 'the foundations of a wall (which may have been for the foundation of pillars) 1 foot 10 inches broad.' (Procter 1855, 274).

No structural evidence was located on the assumed line of the east wall (in line with the east side of apsed Room 5), but the southern and western limits of Room 2 were represented respectively by robber trenches 1004 and 1003. Room 2 had originally contained the fragmentary tessellated pavement described in the report of 1855 (Procter 1855, 274). The entire area was found to be covered with the general layer of 19th-century backfill material, here numbered 1000 and 1001. No occupation levels survived.

An irregular spread of hard-packed mortar and building debris (1010) lay on the eastern side of the room. Immediately below it, and extending into the area of Room 3, was an oven or furnace (1017, 1023). It consisted of a stoke-hole cut into the bedrock, aligned with the long axis of the building and about 3.50m in length, and a chamber, *c.* 0.70m square, at the western end (Fig. 37, S.60 and S.61). Gritstone facing blocks survived along the north side of the stoke-hole, and depressions in the bedrock around its perimeter suggested that the entire

structure had originally been faced in this way. The maximum surviving depth was 0.35m, and both chamber and stoke-hole were filled with ash and burnt material containing building debris, *tesserae* and other artefacts. Areas of the surrounding bedrock showed signs of burning. This structure might have been identified as the *praefurnium* for a hypocaust in Room 2, were it not for the fact that Procter (1855, 276) states that there was no hypocaust below the pavement.

To the south of the oven was a shallow depression (1007) containing an infant burial (Chapter 23, No. 9), and to the north an irregular hollow (1020) filled with brown soil containing *tesserae* and fragments of tile.

Room 3

The central room of the building, rectangular in shape, measured 12.70 by 5.50m internally. To the north it was bounded by robber trench 917, 1011. This had a sinuous outline, varying from 0.80-1.20m in width and up to 0.15m in depth, and was filled with stone-free brown soil. At its western end, a single course of unmortared limestone fragments survived in places. The east wall (918) was also robbed except at its southern end, where one course of dressed gritstone blocks was partially preserved to a maximum height of 0.07m. The southern limit of the room was partially defined by wall 911.

One area of flooring had survived: it occupied the south-east corner of the room and comprised an even surface of powdered mortar and painted plaster (902), 0.10m in depth and covering *c.* 3.00 by 1.50m. Three other features were found in this area: an oval pit (926) containing *tesserae* and painted plaster; a small circular pit (912) containing painted plaster and a fragment of window glass in a burnt soil matrix; and a further post-hole (930). These were overlain by the general backfill level, here numbered 905.

Room 4

The eastern room of the central suite was *c.* 6.85m square internally, and had originally contained a hypocaust. Its northern limit was marked by robber trench 929, 1.20m wide and 0.17m deep, filled with stone-free brown soil. At the eastern end of the trench, a stub of walling (0.96m wide, maximum surviving height 0.15m) was preserved: it comprised two courses of mortared, dressed gritstone with a rubble core.

The east wall of Room 4 was a northward continuation of wall 919 (Room 1), of identical build but slightly narrower (0.80m). Towards its northern end wall 919 was pierced by a 0.35m wide stoke-hole (915) which was faced with fire-reddened dressed gritstone blocks. The same material was used to flank the stoke-hole outside the line of wall 919, to a distance of 0.60m. The south and west walls of Room 4 (907 and 918) have been described above (Rooms 1 and 3).

The only surviving archaeological levels in this room consisted of a band of burnt debris (914) alongside the east wall, lenses of burnt material (923 and 931) in the south-east corner of the room and in the base of stoke-hole

915, and grey ash and mortar filling the sockets in which the robbed hypocaust *pilae* had once stood. These sockets were 50-100mm in depth, and oval or rounded in plan. They were cut into the bedrock floor of the hypocaust basement (which was at the same level as the surrounding bedrock) and were disposed in rows of ten (on average) in each direction. Their distribution was, however, irregular. Above these features was, again, the 19th-century backfilling material (903).

Room 5

Room 5 was the apsidal western wing of the building, measuring internally 6.20 by 3.25m (the latter based on the 1854 measurements). The apse wall (1005) was partially robbed and ploughed out, but survived on the western side where it overlay enclosure ditch 012. It consisted of a single course of dressed gritstone blocks, mortared and with a rubble core, 0.92m wide and up to 0.20m high. The facing stones were noteworthy for both the smoothness and regularity of their dressing, and for their large size (up to 0.58m long). The southern limit of Room 5 was bounded by trench 1027. The Medusa mosaic pavement was removed from Room 5 in 1855, and the report records (of this and the mosaic in Room 2) that: 'No hypocaust could be found below this pavement ...' (Procter 1855, 276). Consequently, apart from the usual layer of backfilled material, no levels survived in Room 5. An irregular sub-rectangular pit filled with brown soil (1002) outside wall 1005 produced tile fragments, mortar and *tesserae*.

Room 6

The square eastern wing of the building measured internally 4.40 by 4.08m. Like Room 4, it originally housed a hypocaust. The north and east walls (921 and 920) consisted of two, and in places three courses of dressed gritstone blocks, mortared and with a rubble core. Both walls had an average width of 0.65m and the basal course of wall 921 was offset externally. The maximum surviving height was 0.27m. The room was bounded to the south by robber trench 929, and to the west by robber trench 922, which was *c*. 1m wide and filled with a stone-free brown soil to a maximum depth of 0.26m. A stub of walling (0.66m wide, and up to 0.25m high) remained at the northern end of trench 922, and this consisted of two courses of dressed gritstone, mortared and with a rubble core. The robbing backfill 903 extended over Room 6, and below this nothing remained of the hypocaust except for the shallow sockets of the robbed *pilae*, again filled with grey ash and mortar. The *pilae* seem to have been arranged in rows of six or seven in each direction, but their positions were not very regular.

Dating evidence

The dating evidence for the Medusa pavement (see Chapter 17) indicates that the floor in Room 5 (and probably the apse as a whole) should be assigned to the second quarter of the 4th century. The apse may have been contemporary with, or additional to the main structure: the

evidence was too slight to give a firm indication either way. Room 2 contained a mid-4th-century pavement which, being slightly later in date that the Medusa pavement, was presumably inserted in an existing room; it is just possible that the room had originally been hypocausted, heated from furnace 1017, 1023, and that it acquired a solid floor only when the mosaic was installed. There is no means of knowing how long the residence continued in use.

Structure A (Figs 38-9)

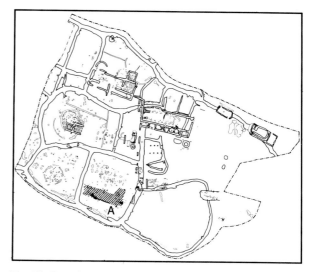

Fig. 38. Location of Structure A.

This structure lay at the southern end of the villa complex. It contained two ovens or kilns, and clearly showed at least two building phases: Phase I represented by post-holes, and Phase II by stone footings (Pl. VII).

Phase I

Phase I was a rectangular building consisting of six pairs of outer posts and probably at least five pairs of smaller internal ones; these appeared to subdivide the building into 'nave' and narrow 'aisles'. Whether it should be regarded as a true aisled building is a difficult question: in a post-Roman structure of this kind one would expect the arcade posts, carrying the nave roof, to be marked by post-holes larger that those which signified the wallposts. The building was aligned approximately east-west and measured externally 11.30 by 6.70m. The internal width of the 'nave' was 3.20m and that of the 'aisles' about 1m or less.

The northern side of the building was formed by six post-holes (3248, 3250, 3252, 3258, 3261 and 3263) spaced 2.00-2.25m apart. These were broad and flat bottomed, varying in diameter from 0.52-0.60m, and with a maximum depth of 0.28m. In each case, the upper 0.15-0.20m was filled with fine brown soil, without packing stones, and the remainder with clean redeposited magnesian limestone. No finds were recovered.

The post-holes of the south side (3212 and 3237-3241) were spaced 1.50-2.25m apart and were circular in plan

Pl. VII. Structure A, facing east. (Photo: S. Wager)

with a U-shaped profile. Their diameters ranged from 0.52-0.74m, and their maximum surviving depth was 0.38m. The filling differed from that of the northern row: the upper 0.15-0.20m was puddled red clay, and the remainder clean redeposited limestone with packing material of gritstone and limestone blocks. No post-pipes were visible and no finds recovered. Post-hole 3237 was out of line with those further east; it may in fact have belonged to a different structure.

The internal post-holes were less clearly defined, but at least eight were identified. The four northern ones (3247, 3249, 3254 and 3259) were spaced 1.80-2.40m apart and were circular in plan with a U-shaped profile. Their diameters, which were consistently smaller than the outer posts, ranged from 0.28-0.48m, and they survived to a maximum depth of 0.26m. They were filled with stone-free brown soil and produced no finds. The four southern post-holes (3214, 3236, 3244 and 3292) had diameters from 0.41-0.46m, and the maximum surviving depth was 0.30m. They were again filled with fine brown soil (in the case of 3214, with gritstone packing material), and produced no finds. Post-hole 3236 was cut on its western side by pit 3211, and oven 103 occupied the presumed position of the post between 3236 and 3214. No evidence was found for internal posts at the eastern end of the building, and no occupation levels survived.

Phase II

Phase II was represented principally by a stone footing (104) which replaced the southern wall of Phase I. The surviving stretches displayed a single course of unmortared, dressed gritstone and limestone blocks. The width varied from 0.52-0.60m, and the maximum surviving height was 0.22m. One of the better preserved stretches sealed a post-hole (3212) of the Phase I building (Fig. 39, S.2). In other places the stonework was too badly robbed to allow the relationship with the post-holes to be determined. In general, however, the alignment of the stone foundation followed the Phase I wall line so precisely as to indicate that it marked the reconditioning of an enduring building, rather than the complete replacement of one structure by another. The roof structure probably remained intact, the earthfast posts being underpinned. The post in 3241 may even have survived as an earthfast member.

There was no sign of a stone wall on the north side: it may have been destroyed entirely, or the Phase I wall may have continued in use. Traces of a west wall (108) survived in the form of several blocks of dressed gritstone and limestone which had subsided into the top of enclosure ditch 020.

Towards the east, the building was considerably extended: the south wall (104) ran 6.50m beyond the observed east end of the Phase I structure. No east end wall was discovered, but its course may have been indicated by the eastern edge of flooring, context 107, which survived as a thin surface of powdered mortar. It extended about 4.05m north-south and 3.10m east-west, and had a maximum surviving thickness of 0.12m, but was severely damaged by ploughing.

Pl. VIII. Structure A, oven flue 103, facing south. (Photo: S. Wager)

Several features within the western half of the building seem to have been associated with the Phase II structure. A rectangular stone-lined furnace or oven (103) was set against the inside face of the south wall (Fig. 39, S.1; Pl. VIII). The oven was 1.26 by 0.54m internally, and it was bounded to the east, south and west by mortared, roughly dressed gritstone walling, varying from 0.38-0.60m in width, and surviving to a maximum height of 0.30m. A gritstone hypocaust *pila* had been incorporated in the west wall. To the north was a roughly paved area of dressed gritstone flags. The base of the oven was cut into bedrock to a maximum depth of 0.32m and the bedrock sides were heavily burnt. The fill consisted of a homogeneous blackened soil containing dressed masonry, iron nails and late 4th-century pottery. The position of the oven was such that it would have butted against wall 104.

Directly to the west of oven 103 was a second oven or furnace (105), of similar shape but without enclosing walls. It consisted merely of an elongated pit, *c.* 1.60 by 0.58m, cut into the bedrock to a depth of 0.26m and again with burning around its edges. The west wall of 103 lay exactly along the edge of 105 and the two may therefore have been contemporary.

Immediately to the west of oven 105 was a large sub-rectangular pit (3211). It measured 1.84 by 1.04m and was cut into the bedrock to a maximum depth of 0.65m. It had been neatly dug and had smooth, near-vertical sides. The filling showed two clearly defined layers. The upper layer, 0.25-0.30m thick, was a dark grey soil containing a large quantity of building debris, domestic refuse and pottery mainly of 3rd to 4th-century date, including a near-complete Dales ware cooking jar (Chapter 15, No. 7). The remaining 0.35-0.40m was filled with clean compacted limestone, containing considerable quantities of small white *tesserae* and an openwork bronze box lid or plaque (Chapter 5, No. 33). On its eastern side, pit 3211

cut one of the southern internal post-holes (3236) of the Phase I building.

Unphased features

A number of other features in the area produced Roman material, and may be associated with one of the phases of Structure A. Feature 3209 was a small hole cut into the bedrock to the west of pit 3211. It was circular, with a diameter of 0.40m, and its profile was slightly angular with a maximum depth of 0.19m. A small near-complete jar with a gritty fabric (not illustrated) stood upright within the hole, snugly fitting its sides. The hole was capped by a sandstone slab whose upper surface was flush with the surrounding bedrock. Feature 3210 was a small, irregular oval hollow near the north-western corner of the building. It was filled with fine brown soil. Small post-holes 3207 and 3208, at the eastern end of the Phase I building, were also filled with fine brown soil and both contained pieces of *tegula* used as packing material. In the eastern portion of the Phase II building a possible post-hole (3901), filled with grey soil and with gritstone packing, produced fragments of painted plaster; while south of Structure A, two possible post-holes (3800 and 3803) were filled with a grey soil matrix containing sherds of late 2nd to late 3rd-century pottery. At the eastern end of the building were two hearths: 3914, just to the north of wall 106/109, consisted of burnt sandstone flags bedded in black soil overlying feature 3923; while 3802, south of surface 107, was a single fire-cracked gritstone flag. No finds were associated with either of these features.

The east end of the building may have been abutted by walling 106/109, which formed the fragmentary south-east corner of a room, building or enclosure. It displayed two constructional phases. Wall 106 consisted of a single course of dressed gritstone and limestone blocks with an unmortared rubble core. It was *c.* 0.52m wide and stood to a maximum height of 0.30m, and it formed a right-angled return from north-south to east-west. Walling 109 represented a thickening of the east-west stretch of wall 106 along its northern side, and was of identical dimensions and build except that its rubble core was mortared.

To the north-east of 107 was a *c.* 4 by 6m rubble spread (802) in a black soil matrix up to 0.15m thick. Finds from this area include sherds of 3rd or 4th-century pottery. Within it were two stretches of curving wall foundation (803) which seems to have been part of a roughly circular building about 2m in diameter.

The southern portion of the building was overlain by a brown soil level (numbered variously as 100, 102, 800 and 801), reaching a maximum depth of 0.22m south of wall 104. It contained late 2nd to late 4th-century pottery, as well as an Iron Age rim sherd and a single post-medieval body sherd. Other finds include building debris such as roof tile, iron nails, painted plaster, glass fragments and *tesserae*.

Structure B (Figs 40-41)

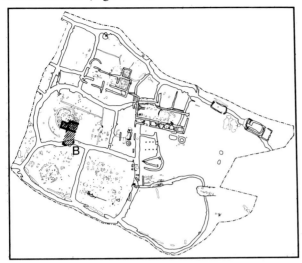

Fig. 40. Location of Structure B.

Structure B was a rectangular building, aligned approximately north-south, with an annexe on the western side. It overlay several Iron Age features, including two roundhouses and enclosure ditch 006. The structure was 15.80 by 11.30m, and it comprised three rooms.

Room 1

The southernmost room, measuring 8.80 by 5.00m internally, had no hypocaust and had consequently been severely damaged by ploughing. Except on its northern side, where it adjoined the hypocaust basement of Room 2, only two short lengths of walling survived (225 and 304), largely through having subsided into the fill of the underlying enclosure ditch 006. These remaining fragments represented the two lowest foundation courses, consisting of a mortared rubble core faced internally and externally with roughly dressed gritstone and limestone blocks, the lower course slightly offset from that above. Their width varied, being on average 0.90m. Apart from a lens of burnt soil over the top of enclosure ditch 006, no occupation levels survived in Room 1, and modern ploughmarks were visible on the limestone bedrock.

Room 2

Room 2 (Pl. IX), to the north, measured 4.30 by 5.20m internally, and contained a hypocaust basement surviving to an average depth of 0.36m below the surrounding bedrock. No wall remained on the eastern side; but the walls revetting the friable limestone on the north, south and west sides (227, 229 and 230) survived to a maximum depth of 0.64m, or six courses of masonry (Fig. 41, S.4). At least one, and in many places two of these six courses survived above the level of the bedrock outside the building. As in Room 1, the walls consisted of a limestone rubble core faced (on the interior below basement level, and on both faces above it) with roughly dressed gritstone and limestone, and in places sandstone blocks, mortared throughout. The walls were bonded to those of Room 1 and were butted by those of Room 3. The mode of construction varied, apparently at random, between regular coursing, edge-setting and crude herringbone. Wall thickness varied, the north and west walls (227 and 230) being on average 1.10m thick, the south wall (229) 0.75m.

The west wall was interrupted just north of its centre by a 0.44m wide flue (234), linking Room 2 with the hypocaust basement of Room 3. The flue, faced with mortared blocks of dressed gritstone, was heavily burnt, and it was flanked at its eastern end by a pair of box-flue tiles mortared into the angles of wall 230.

The *pilae* in Room 2 were of two types: mortared stacks of undressed limestone (and less frequently gritstone) blocks, and neatly dressed gritstone monoliths. Both types were bedded in shallow sockets in the natural limestone floor of the basement, and both showed signs of plough damage to their tops.

The *pilae* were arranged in rows of eight, but their distribution was rather irregular: some rows consisted of seven or nine. Some *pilae* around the perimeter of the room butted against the surrounding wall, while others were free standing. Two of the monolithic gritstone *pilae* (Chapter 19, Nos 3-4) were reused column shafts.

Room 3

Room 3, to the west, was smaller (3.10 by 3.60m internally) and also contained a hypocaust basement, surviving to an average depth of 0.33m below the surrounding bedrock. The walls were again mortared with a rubble core, but were faced internally almost exclusively with dressed limestone, and stood to a maximum height of four courses. The basal course of the south and west walls (232 and 233) was offset from those above by as much as 0.14m. The overall width of the walls varied between 0.65-0.75m. Walls 231 and 232 butted against Room 2; the finely dressed stone and uniformity of building style in Room 3 was in marked contrast to that in Room 2.

The north wall (231), unlike the others, was also dressed externally, and the level of the surrounding bedrock had been considerably reduced to form a stoke pit. A diagonal flue (235) was 0.40m wide, and it was faced with five courses of dressed gritstone and tile. Heavy burning was visible on both faces and on the pit base, which was cut into the bedrock slightly below the level of the side walls. The flue was aligned so as to feed both the basement of Room 3 and the connecting flue into Room 2.

The *pilae* in Room 3 were almost entirely of monolithic gritstone type, neatly dressed, and founded in shallow sockets in the bedrock. They were arranged in rows of four or five, but several were irregularly positioned as if to provide supplementary support. Many bore signs of plough damage on their tops, and in some cases *pilae* had been completely removed from their sockets by the plough.

The basements of Rooms 2 and 3, as well as flue 234, were filled with a layer of brown soil (numbered variously as 204-7 and 210-19, corresponding to arbitrary horizontal divisions) from 0.33-0.50m deep. It contained large quantities of building debris, with extensive indications of

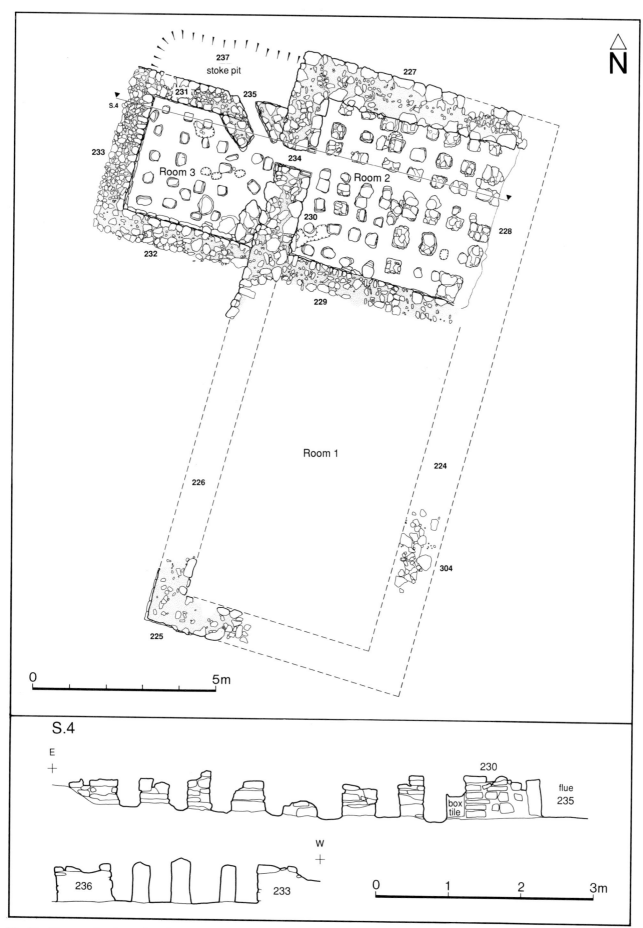

N

237
stoke pit

231 235

233

Room 3

234

Room 2

230

232

228

229

Room 1

224

226

304

225

0   5m

S.4

E

230

flue
235

box
tile

W

236   233

0   1   2   3m

Fig. 41. Structure B: plan and sections.

Pl. IX. Structure B, facing east. (Photo: S. Wager)

burning and a great density of painted plaster. Portions of the decorated plaster were able to be reconstructed (see Chapter 18).

Pottery from Room 2 and flue 234 (contexts 210-19) is mainly of Crambeck and Huntcliff wares, with some sherds of colour-coated, Oxfordshire and Rhenish wares. Room 3 (contexts 204-7) again includes colour-coated, Crambeck and Huntcliff wares. A coin in unworn condition dating to AD 322 was also found in this level (Chapter 4, No. 31).

Flue 235, in the north wall of Room 3, was filled with a homogeneous layer of black ash, containing late 3rd to 4th-century pottery (again mainly Crambeck and Huntcliff wares) and several *tesserae*. Above this was a mixture of reddened soil and burnt mortar (208). The stoking area (237) outside the mouth of the flue was covered by a thin lens of black ash and burnt mortar (202), containing sherds of colour-coated and Crambeck wares.

The basement filling layers were capped by a layer (201 and 220) about 0.12m deep. This, too, consisted of building debris in a matrix of brown soil. Pottery again includes 3rd to 4th-century colour-coated, Crambeck and Huntcliff wares, together with a single post-medieval sherd.

Above was a further layer of brown soil (200 and 221-2) of maximum thickness 0.10m, which contained large quantities of iron nails, window glass, roof and flue tiles, painted plaster, *tesserae*, *opus signinum* and mortar. Some of this debris showed signs of burning. Pottery is again predominantly of 3rd to 4th-century date.

The occupation material filling these hypocausts was probably derived from a single source, perhaps in a single levelling operation: this is indicated by the number of joining sherds from different layers. One greyware vessel, for example, has sherds from 200, 201, 204-6, 208 and 210; an Oxfordshire product has sherds from 200 and 215, and a colour-coated flagon is represented by sherds from 201 and 205. Deliberate levelling suggests that occupation of the villa continued after this building had been demolished: otherwise the filling of the basement would presumably have occurred by gradual silting and decay. Demolition may have taken place before the middle of the 4th century.

Structure E (Figs 42-4)

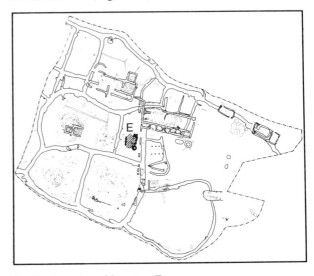

Fig. 42. Location of Structure E.

Structure E was a heated building about 30m east of Structure B. It was parallel to, and just west of enclosure wall 1101, and overlay the fill of a ditch running east from enclosure ditch 017. The building had suffered serious plough damage and several areas may also have been robbed.

The structure was rectangular and on the same general alignment as the other stone buildings. It had an external length of 6.36m and a maximum surviving width of 2.80m. The absence of the west wall prevents the exact width of the hypocaust being ascertained, but the distribution of *pilae* suggested that it may not originally have been much wider than its surviving extent.

The north wall consisted of a narrow primary phase (505) with a secondary thickening (506) along its northern side (Pl. X). Wall 505 survived as two courses of mortared gritstone and limestone blocks (predominantly the former), dressed on both its north and south faces. It was 0.48-0.52m wide and stood to a maximum height of 0.26m. Its western end had been destroyed. At the centre of the surviving portion was a flue (511), 0.84m wide at the northern end and 1.04m wide at the south. The sides of the flue were faced with heavily burnt gritstone blocks and the base was neatly paved with rectangular bricks of uniform size (280-90 by 120-40mm), and several were

Pl. X. Structure E, facing south. (Photo: S. Wager)

scored with loop signature marks on their upper surface (Chapter 22, p. 170). They were laid across the flue so as to span exactly the width of wall 505. Structure 506 ran along the northern side of wall 505, effectively thickening it. The fabrics differed in construction, 506 consisting of a single facing course of large gritstone blocks along its northern side, with a broad core of mortared gritstone rubble to the south. The wall was 0.98-1.04m wide and had a maximum surviving height of 0.26m. Like wall 505, its western end had been destroyed. At its centre was a flue (512), which formed a continuation of 511: it was 0.46m wide to the north, narrowing to 0.22m to the south. The sides of the flue were faced with heavily burnt large gritstone blocks, and its base, which was not paved, was cut slightly into the bedrock. A shallow depression in the bedrock (513) at the northern end of 512 formed the stoke-pit.

The east and south walls of Structure E (507 and 508) were faced internally with a single surviving course of dressed gritstone blocks, fronting a mortared gritstone and limestone rubble core. The exterior was not faced. Wall 507 was 0.80-0.82m wide and stood to a maximum height of 0.18m, while wall 508 was narrower (0.57m) but of similar height. Wall 508 was destroyed at its western end.

The hypocaust basement was 4.50m long internally and survived to a width of 1.94m (Fig. 43, S.11 and S.14). The level of the *opus signinum* basement floor (514) was only 0.18-0.20m below that of the surrounding bedrock, an indication of the extent of plough damage in this area. The *pilae* bases were formed by large tiles, 220-350mm square, each mortared to the floor of the basement and

supporting a mortared stack of smaller tiles (180-230mm square) above. Traces of thirteen *pilae* survived, attaining a maximum height of 0.29m (i.e. four tiles). Although unevenly spaced, the *pilae* appear to have been disposed in rows of eight by (at least) four.

The building was overlain by a general level of brown soil (500 and 503), containing building debris (including *tesserae* and roof tile) and late 2nd to late 4th-century pottery. The maximum depth of this level was 0.20m, and it directly overlay the *opus signinum* floor of the hypocaust basement. An area of brown soil (515), relatively free of building debris, overlay the fill of a ditch to the west of Structure E. Flues 511 and 512 were filled with black ash (501 and 504) to a depth of 0.32m.

Pl. XI. Well 2 (4017), facing south. (Photo: S. Wager)

41

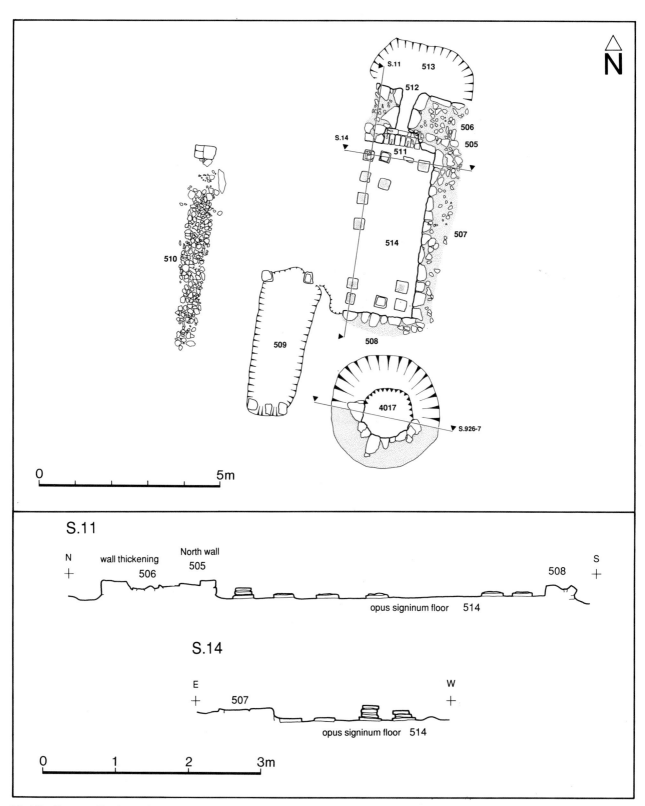

Fig. 43. Structure E: plan and sections.

S.926-7

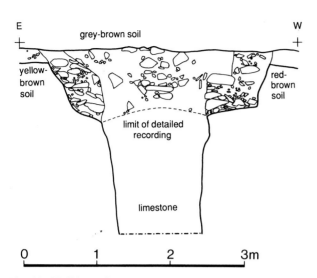

Fig. 44. Well 2: section.

Three other features to the south and west of Structure E may have been associated with it. The first was Well 2 (4017; Pl. XI), located just beyond its south-east corner. Only the upper filling layers were excavated (Fig. 44, S.926-7); the rest remain intact for future investigation. The top of the well was in the form of a wide 'basin', about 3m diameter and 0.70m deep. This led to the shaft proper, which had a diameter of only 1.20m. The purpose of the basin was evident in the nature of the bedrock: the top 1.50m of limestone were softer and more fragmented than the very solid rock beneath. The basin would have allowed the upper part of the shaft to be lined with stone; some of the revetting blocks had survived.

Secondly, a large rectangular pit (509), west of the well, measured 3.80 by 1.64m at the north end, 1.18m at the south, and was up to 0.17m deep. Flat, squared gritstone blocks were situated at each of the four corners, with an additional block in the centre of the southern end. The sides of the pit were steep, and the base was on approximately the same level as the hypocaust base. The east side may well have been overcut, either during robbing or in excavation. The pit seemed to have been associated with the hypocaust building in view of its position, alignment and depth. It was filled with brown soil containing building debris but no other finds.

Finally, west of Structure E, and aligned with it, was a 5.50m long stretch of wall foundation (510) consisting of a single course of small, undressed limestone blocks. The wall was 0.70m wide and stood to a maximum height of 0.14m; at its northern end were three large squared gritstone blocks.

It is impossible to say whether Structure E was the remnant of a small, discrete building or whether it was once part of a much larger complex. If the hypocaust and the rectangular pit were indeed associated features, then the latter might indicate a cistern or a plunge bath, water being derived from the adjacent well.

Structure X (Figs 45-6)

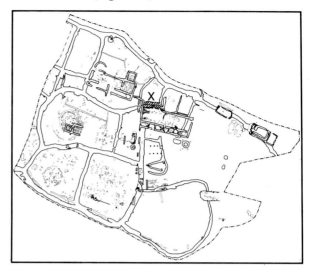

Fig. 45. Location of Structure X.

Structure X adjoined the north side of Structure M, towards the west. It was aligned east-west, occupying the course of Ditch 027, and had external dimensions of c. 14.00 by 4.30m. Its relationship with Structure M is considered in detail below (p. 58): Structure X was probably in existence when Structure M, Phase I, was being built, but went out of use before its final phase.

Structure X consisted of a roughly sub-rectangular hollow terraced into the sloping bedrock, and into the fill of Ditch 027, to a maximum depth of c. 0.55m at its western end (Pl. XII). The level of the bedrock fell away towards the eastern end of the structure, and consequently the flat basement floor of the building was at this end flush with the bedrock surface. The southern edge of the building, and possibly also the northern, had been revetted with gritstone walling (Fig. 46, S.1002).

The walls were bedded directly on the limestone floor of the basement, acting as a revetment to its friable sides. The north wall (5022) was represented only by three roughly dressed gritstone blocks near the western end of the building. The south wall (1219) was much better preserved, consisting of a single row of large unmortared gritstone blocks, dressed on the interior face; parts of a second course survived in places. Wall 1219 varied in width from 0.20-0.60m, and stood to a maximum height of 0.45m above the basement floor. There were no surviving traces of a west wall.

In the base of Structure X, overlying the upper levels of Ditch 027, were several areas of rough gritstone paving (5023) in a matrix of burnt soil. Areas of the surrounding bedrock floor also showed signs of burning. Set into this flooring were the bottom stones of four beehive querns, three of which were bedded into the top of Ditch 027. The fourth quernstone (Chapter 10, No. 13; Fig. 46, S.1001) was bedded in a socket cut into the bedrock alongside the south wall of Structure X, and sealed by lens 4905 (Pl. XIII). The socket (4910) was neatly cut to fit exactly the contours of the underside of the quern, and measured some 0.55m in diameter and 0.53m in depth.

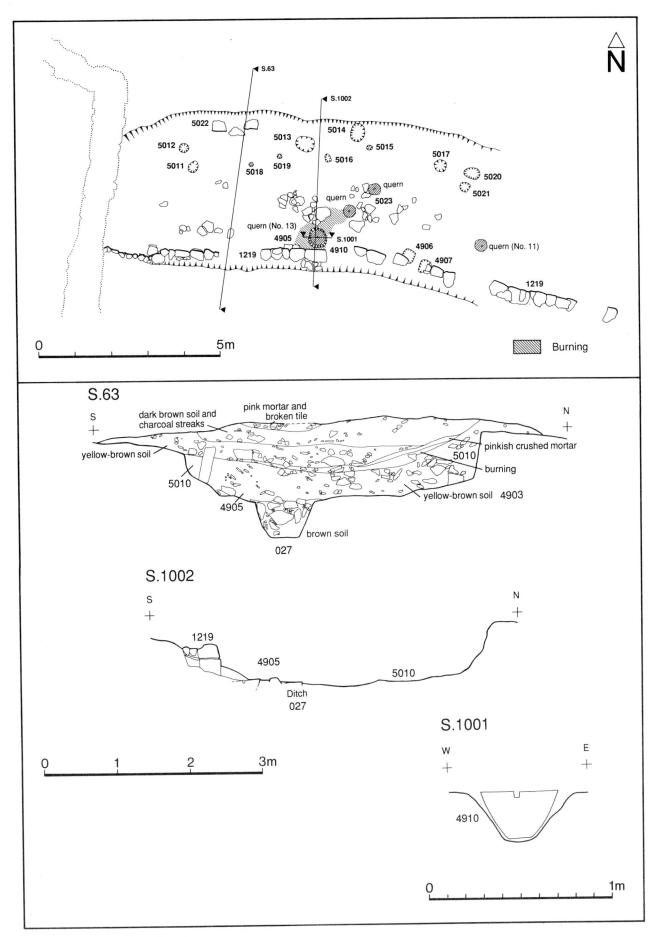

Fig. 46. Structure X: plan and sections.

Pl. XII. Structure X, facing east. (Photo: S. Wager)

A number of post- and stake-holes (or in some cases, perhaps, further quernstone sockets) were found around the edges of the basement floor, cut into bedrock and sealed by the filling layers. Two of them (4906 and 4907) were partially overlain by the south revetment wall of Structure X. The ten holes (4906-7, 5011-14, 5016-17 and 5020-21) were of variable shape and size, ranging from 0.25-0.50m in diameter. Their U-shaped or flat-based profiles varied in depth from 0.07-0.27m. The fill was

Pl. XIII. Structure X, quern No. 13 next to its socket in the floor. (Photo: S. Wager)

uniformly homogeneous brown soil with small limestone inclusions; four of them (4906-7 and 5013-14) contained gritstone packing material but no visible post-pipes. The only find was a fragment of a yellow glass bracelet (Chapter 9, No. 30) from post-hole 5020.

As a sunken-floored building with stone-revetted sides, Structure X is reminiscent of Structures P, Q and R. Some at least of the Structure X post-holes were presumably roof supports; those in the south need not have been earlier than the revetment, since they could have contained posts set against the stones. The evidence of burning and discovery of quernstones again invites comparison with Structures P and Q. In this case, the setting of the four lower stones in the floor show beyond reasonable doubt that beehive querns were used in this building.

The interior of the building was filled with three distinct deposits of which the uppermost was associated with Phase II of Structure M (Fig. 46, S.63). The lower two layers (4905 and 4903) were associated with, respectively, the occupation and abandonment of Structure X. The first of these, in the base of Structure X alongside its south wall, was a small lens of black burnt soil (4905), of maximum depth 0.12m, which produced no finds. Layer 4903 was a yellow-brown soil with limestone inclusions, filling the entire basement to a depth of *c.* 0.50m around the edges and *c.* 0.30m in the centre. It contained 2nd to 4th-century pottery (including quantities of colour-coated ware).

Structure Y (Figs 47-8)

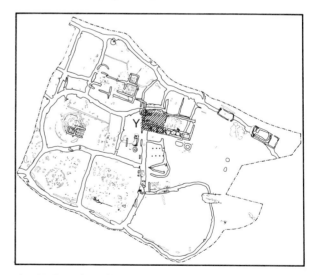

Fig. 47. Location of Structure Y.

This structure lay beneath the west end of the aisled Structure M. It was represented by a rectangular sunken floor measuring about 15m by at least 10m. It may have extended southwards into an area later occupied by the hypocausts of Structure M: any evidence would have been removed by the cutting for the hypocaust basements (Fig. 48, S.65). Structure Y was positioned directly south of Structure X, separated from it by a ridge of bedrock about 2m wide. It unquestionably pre-dated the aisled building,

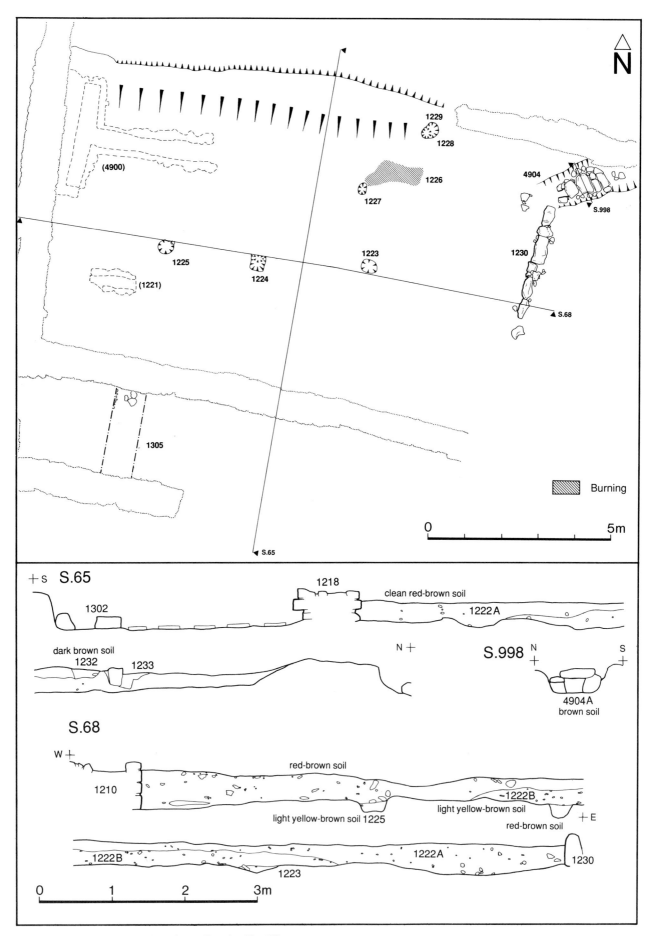

N

(4900)

1229
1228

1226
1227

4904

S.998

1230

S.68

1225
1224
1223

(1221)

1305

Burning

0   5m

S.65

+s S.65

1218   clean red-brown soil

1302   1222A

dark brown soil
1232   1233   N +

S.998 N   S
        +   +

4904A
brown soil

S.68

w +
                    red-brown soil

1210   ~1222B
                light yellow-brown soil
        light yellow-brown soil 1225   red-brown soil
                                    + E

~1222B   1222A   1230
        1223

0   1   2   3m

Fig. 48. Structure Y: plan and sections. (See also Fig. 50)

46

since the holes for the aisle posts had been cut through the filling of the sunken floor. Because of the superimposition of Structure M it was, however, possible to excavate only parts of Structure Y. Two opposed quadrants revealed the rock-cut floor and several associated features.

The basement area was cut into the bedrock to a maximum depth at the western end of *c*. 0.50m. No revetment was found to the north or west, but the eastern edge was revetted by a single row of limestone blocks (1230) of irregular shape and size (Fig. 48, S.68). These were roughly dressed on the interior and were unmortared. Wall 1230 varied in width from *c*. 0.20-0.40m, and stood to a maximum height above the basement floor of 0.45m.

At the north-eastern corner of the basement a rock-cut drain (4904) ran north-eastwards. It was 0.60-0.90m wide, with a maximum depth of 0.35m, and was for some distance lined and capped with large, unmortared, dressed gritstone slabs (Fig. 48, S.998). The interior was filled with stone-free brown soil. Drain 4904 passed beneath wall 1463, which was associated with the first phase of Structure M, and continued eastwards as gully 5601 (Fig. 50); this in turn seems to have been linked to gully 035/5605. The full sequence of gullies is discussed below (p. 50).

Six post-holes could be attributed to Structure Y. Three of these (1223-5) may have been positioned along the central axis of the building; they were oval or squarish in plan with diameters of 0.38-0.46m; they were flat based and about 0.15-0.20m deep. Their fill was a yellow-brown soil with limestone inclusions, and they contained no packing material or finds. The remaining three post-holes (1227-9), none of which produced finds, were situated in the north-eastern quadrant of the building, again cut into the bedrock of the basement floor. They were circular or slightly oval in plan, with diameters of 0.24-0.40m, and depths of 0.11-0.19m. Their fill consisted of redeposited limestone, while two of the holes (1227 and 1228) contained fragments of gritstone and limestone packing material. Two other features, an oven (1221) and a T-shaped kiln (4900), were possibly associated with Structure Y; but they were more probably related to Structure M, and are discussed below (p. 58).

In the north-eastern corner of the building, directly overlying the bedrock of the basement floor, was a thin lens of burnt soil (1226), up to *c*. 50mm deep. Above this, the interior of Structure Y was filled with a homogeneous brown soil level (1220, 1222 and possibly 1305) containing limestone fragments. This had a maximum depth of *c*. 0.50m around the edges of the building and an average depth of *c*. 0.30m at the centre. It contained pottery of the 2nd to 3rd or 4th centuries, as well as several Iron Age sherds.

The positioning, alignment and depth of Structure Y strongly indicate that it was contemporary, for at least part of its life, with Structure X. Though its full extent was not uncovered, the proportions of the building seem to have differed from those of Structures P, Q, R and X. Structure Y may, in fact, have been more closely comparable with the so-called 'threshing floor' (P) at the villa of Langton,

North Yorkshire (Corder and Kirk 1932, 48-9, figs 52 and 58).

Structure M (Figs 49-53)

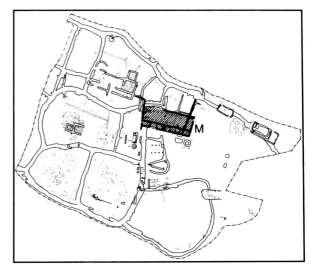

Fig. 49. Location of Structure M.

Structure M was the largest building on the site, and lay south-east of the main residential block, Structure J. Rectangular in plan, it was aligned approximately east-west and directly overlay Structure Y. In its later phases, at least, Structure M also post-dated Structure X.

Structure M was better preserved than most other buildings on the site because a hedgeline along the northern side had protected it from recent ploughing. A suite of hypocausts along the southern side had also, by virtue of its depth, escaped serious plough damage. These rooms had, however, suffered extensive wall robbing, and had been cleared in the excavations of 1854. It is certain that the hypocausts and associated rooms described in the report of those excavations (Procter 1855, 271-4) represent the eastern portion of Structure M (see below). The structure as a whole had three building phases (Fig. 53), as well as a number of minor modifications.

Phase I

Phase I was a rectangular aisled building, aligned approximately east-west and measuring externally about 27.00 by 9.50m. The building contained at least eleven pairs of aisle post-holes, each pair of posts having at some stage been replaced (Pl. XIV); it is clear therefore that Phase I must be considered as two sub-phases, representing the initial construction and the rebuilding.

The north wall (1463; underlying 1402) consisted of one, and in places two courses of river-worn gritstone cobbles set in red and yellow puddled clay. The wall stood to a maximum height of 0.18m and its width varied from 0.80-1.00m. The former hedgeline, although ensuring its survival, had caused much disturbance to the wall. West of the surviving stretch, wall 1463 had run along the bedrock ledge between Structures X and Y, but it had been robbed out. The extreme west end, along with the west wall (1207) did, however, survive.

Pl. XIV. Structure M, facing east. (Photo: S. Wager)

The east wall (1423) was very poorly preserved and in places absent; it lay within the floor area of the Phase II building. At best it survived as a metre-wide scatter of water-worn gritstone cobbles directly overlying bedrock. It seems probable that wall 1423 was that located in 1854 and described as the west wall of 'Room L' (Procter 1855, 273). The south wall of the Phase I building presumably underlay the Phase II south wall (1218) which was not removed.

At its north-western corner, the Phase I building was connected to Structure J by walls 1203 and 1205 (Fig. 52). Wall 1205 continued the line of wall 1207 for a distance of *c.* 5m northwards, before turning west for a further 4.50m (wall 1203), to connect with the south-east corner of Structure J, Room 4. Walls 1203 and 1205 each consisted of a single course of (predominantly) gritstone facing blocks, with a mortared rubble core. The width of the walls varied from 0.55-0.70m and they stood to a maximum height of *c.* 0.15m, having suffered severe plough damage. They were overlain by walls 1202 and 1204, which performed a similar function in connecting the Phase II building to Structure J.

The aisle post-holes of Phase I were cut into bedrock in the eastern half of the building, and, in the western half, into the soft brown fill (1222) of Structure Y. The similarity between the filling material of the post-holes and fill 1222 made the exact position and extent of the aisle posts in this area uncertain; several post-holes may have been removed by the insertion of features associated with the Phase II structure, and others may have been

missed in the course of excavation, obscured by underlying features. On the basis of their spacing (*c.* 1.50m apart) in the bedrock areas, it seems likely that there were originally eleven pairs of aisle posts, most at some stage replaced. Two sets of holes could be identified. One comprised nine holes on the northern side (1417, 1432, 1435, 1458, 1460, 1462, 1466-7 and 4902) and nine or ten on the south (1419, 1431, 1438, 1444-6, ?1452, 1454, 1456 and 1481). The other group of post-holes included seven of the northern row (1405, 1424, 1436-7, 1457, 1459 and 1461) and nine or ten of the southern row (1409, 1415, 1420, 1428-9, 1440, 1449, 1453, ?1455 and 1482). The post-hole fills were all very similar, and in most cases it was impossible to determine which came first. Of pair 1405 and 4902 on the north side, however, the former showed at a higher level than the latter; and on the south side post-hole 1455 appeared to have cut 1454. It is possible, therefore, that the first of the sets described above was the earlier.

In general, the aisle post-holes were circular or slightly oval in plan, 0.50-0.80m in diameter, and with broad U-shaped profiles 0.20-0.40m deep. Those in the northern rows tended to be slightly larger in diameter, and those cut into fill 1222 slightly deeper than those cut into bedrock; but no distinction of shape and size existed between the holes of Phase Ia and those of Phase Ib. Nearly all the post-holes were filled with homogeneous brown soil containing gritstone and some limestone packing material. Exceptions were post-holes 1453 and 1454, both of which were filled with black ash. The relationship of these and

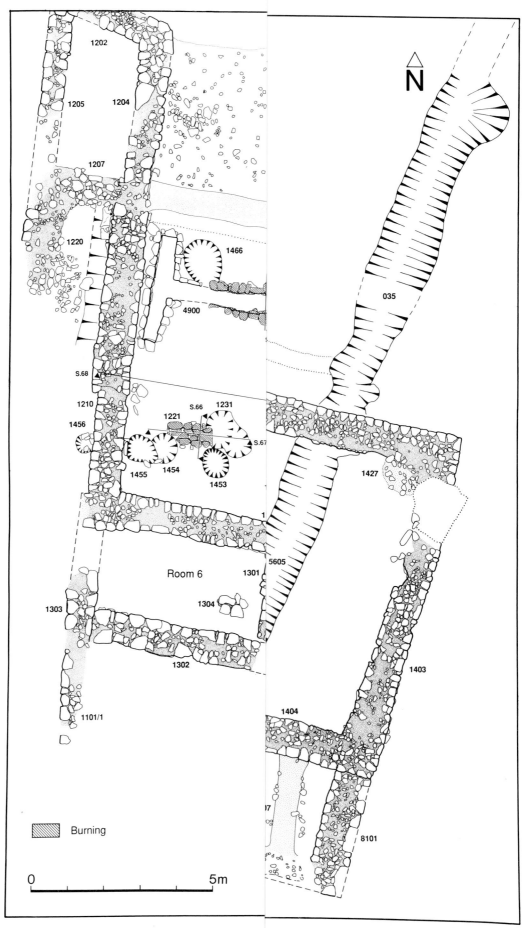

Fig. 50. Structure M: plan.

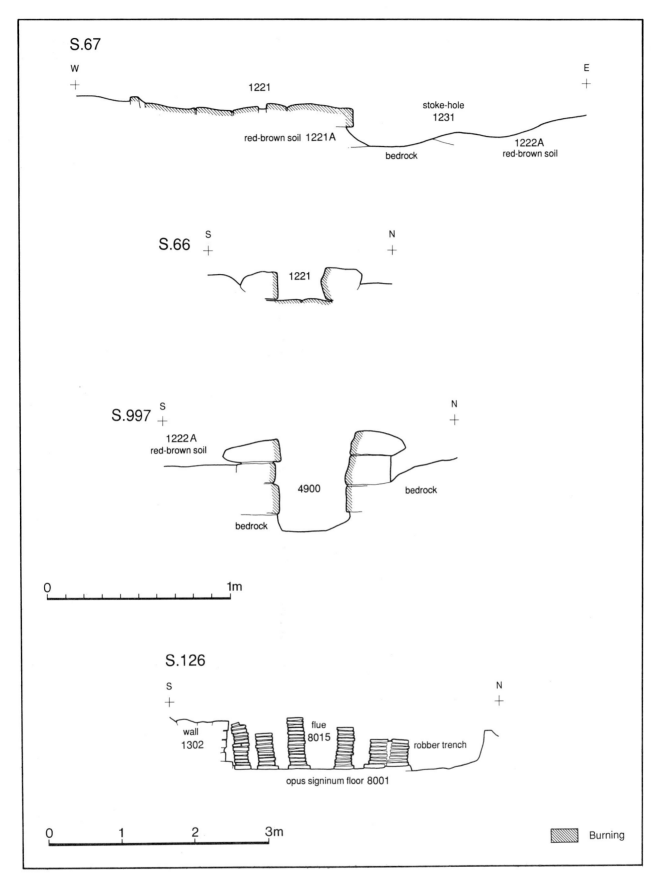

S.67

W
+

1221

red-brown soil 1221A

bedrock

stoke-hole
1231

E
+

1222A
red-brown soil

S.66

S
+

1221

N
+

S.997

S
+

1222A
red-brown soil

4900

bedrock

N
+

bedrock

0   1m

S.126

S
+

wall
1302

flue
8015

robber trench

N
+

opus signinum floor 8001

0   1   2   3m

Burning

Fig. 51. Structure M: sections.

49

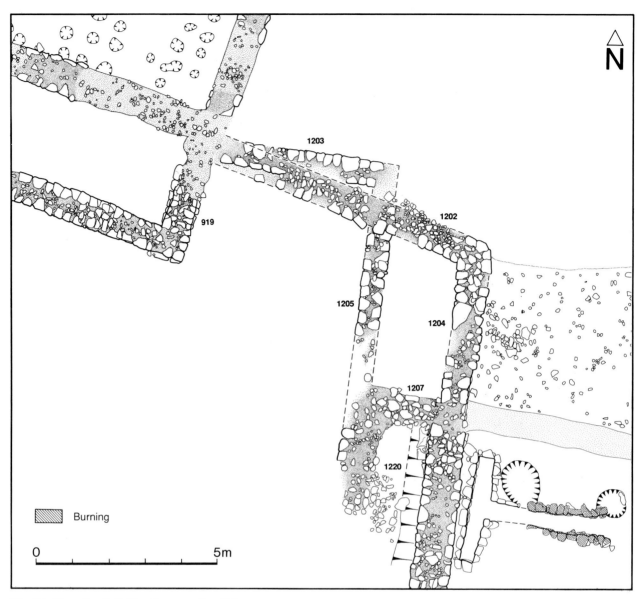

Fig. 52. Plan of walls linking Structures J and M.

the other west end post-holes to kiln 4900 and oven 1221 is considered below.

A number of post-holes (1232-3, 1406-8, 1410-14, 1418, 1430, 1433-4, 1439, 1441-3, 1447-8, 1451, 1464-5, 1476-80 and 1483-4) may have been associated with internal divisions of the building, but could equally well belong to earlier structures on this site. These features were concentrated towards the eastern end of the building, although it is possible that others may have existed at the western end, but remained undetected within brown fill 1222. Most of the post-holes were circular or slightly oval in plan, 0.30-0.48m in diameter, with U-shaped profiles 0.10-0.21m deep. They were filled with brown soil and contained gritstone and some limestone packing material. Post-holes 1433 and 1480 were, however, considerably larger, being 0.55-0.65m in diameter and c. 0.33m deep, and may represent further replacement of aisle posts.

The Phase I building was precisely aligned with the earlier Structure Y; it was, therefore, probably an immediate replacement for that structure. Drain

4904/5601, which had run north-eastwards from Structure Y, was blocked by the Phase I north wall of Structure M. It is possible, however, that the new building was provided with a new drainage system, incorporating gullies 5065 and 035. Gully 5605 was certainly earlier than Phase II of Structure M; its association with Phase I may be inferred from its position and alignments.

Phase II

The second phase of Structure M principally involved the rebuilding of both ends, giving internal dimensions of about 30.50 by 7.50m (Fig. 53).

The north wall (1402) was a reconstruction of the Phase I wall (1463), but for much of its length it had been robbed out, and was represented by a robber trench (1208) filled with dark grey soil. It was, however, better preserved towards the east, especially beyond the east end of the Phase I structure (Pl. XV). Two foundation courses of well-constructed walling survived, faced internally and externally with dressed gritstone blocks. The wall was

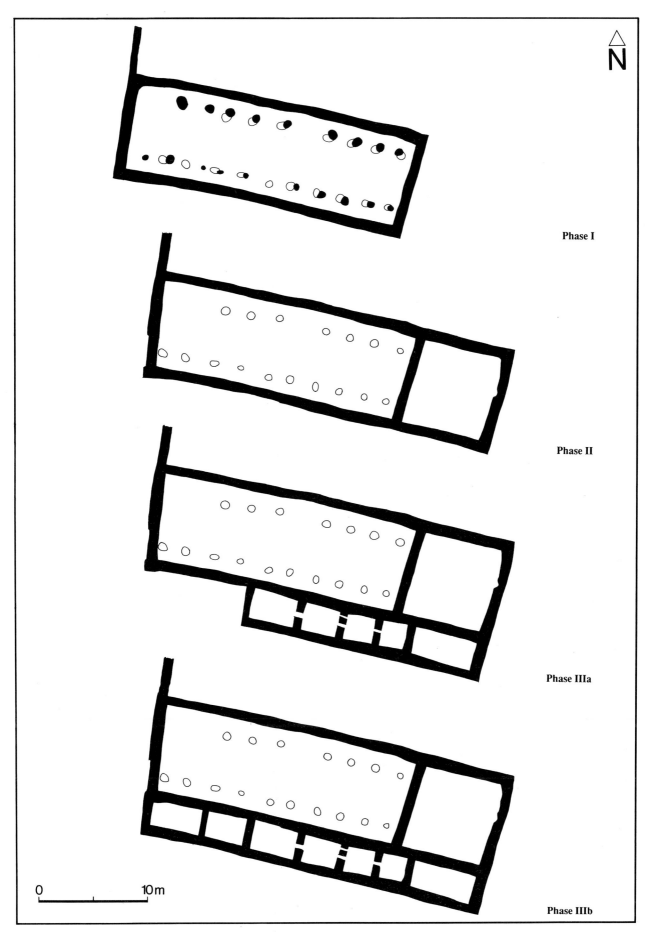

N

Phase I

Phase II

Phase IIIa

0   10m

Phase IIIb

Fig. 53. Phase plans of Structure M.

Pl. XV. Structure M, facing west. (Photo: S. Wager)

0.90-1.00m in width, and stood to a maximum height above bedrock of *c.* 0.35m. Where it cut the line of an earlier gully, 5605, the foundations had been carried down to the gully base by a further two courses of roughly dressed limestone blocks, giving here a maximum height of *c.* 0.70m.

The east wall (1403) was of identical build and dimensions to north wall 1402, and the two were bonded. At its northern end wall 1403 had been penetrated by concrete foundations of an electricity pylon.

Wall 1403 also bonded with the south wall (1218/1404), which was presumably a rebuild of the south wall of the Phase I structure. Wall 1218/1404 was neatly faced with dressed gritstone blocks along both sides; its width varied from 0.70-1.00m, and it had slightly offset foundations. The maximum surviving height above the bedrock on the north side was 0.25m (two courses). On the south side, where it bounded the hypocaust suite (see below), its maximum height above the basements was 0.55m (four courses). Again, where it cut gully 5605 it was underpinned by two further courses of roughly dressed gritstone and limestone blocks, giving it a maximum height of *c.* 0.70m.

It is clear that walls 1402, 1403 and 1218/1404 corresponded respectively to the north, east and south walls of room 'L' of the 1854 excavations (Fig. 2). The west wall located at that time was almost certainly wall 1423 – i.e. the east wall of the Phase I structure. The 'room' thus formed would have measured *c.* 8.50 by 8.20m. This corresponds exactly to the dimensions given for room 'L' in the report of 1855: 'from north to south 28 feet, from east to west 27 feet' (Procter 1855, 273). Additional evidence for this identification was provided by the location of flue 8018 in the south wall, where it is clearly identifiable with flue 'b' shown on the 1855 plan, and by the fact that the report describes the south wall as having at its base 'a species of ledge, formed by the upper course of masonry, being narrower than the lower' (Procter 1855, 273), clearly a reference to the offset foundations of wall 1218/1404.

The west wall (1210) of the Phase II building was bonded to wall 1218, and two distinct sections could be discerned. The southern section, *c.* 3.40m long, was faced on both sides with dressed gritstone and limestone blocks, with a mortared rubble core. It was 0.80-0.90m wide, and stood to a maximum height of 0.25m (two courses). Post-hole 1456, associated with the Phase I building, was overlain by this stretch of walling. The northern section, *c.* 5m long, was of similar construction but with a broader core, forming a wall 1.00-1.05m wide. Incorporated into the rubble core were several large fragments of *opus signinum* flooring including two sections of quarter-round fillet. Where it overlay the junction of enclosure ditches 026 and 027, wall 1210 was underpinned with two further courses of very large, roughly dressed gritstone and limestone blocks, giving an overall height of *c.* 0.45m (Pl. XVI).

At the west end of the building there were two internal structures: a 'T'-shaped kiln (4900) and a rectangular oven flue (1221). Kiln 4900 was faced internally with

52

Pl. XVI. Offset foundation carrying wall 1210 through Ditch 027. (Photo: S. Wager)

neatly dressed gritstone blocks fronting a mortared rubble fabric (Fig. 51, S.997). Signs of severe burning were visible throughout. The base was unlined; the excavation records indicate that it had been cut into the underlying fill (1222) of Structure Y. The flue was 3.50m long and 0.40-0.50m wide internally – fanning out slightly towards its eastern end – and its wall stood to a maximum height of 0.50m (three courses of masonry). The transverse flue was 2.76m long and 0.38-0.44m wide internally, and again stood to a height of 0.50m. The west wall of kiln 4900 lay close to wall 1210, and its other walls were recorded as cutting two Phase I aisle post-holes (1466 and 1467). The base of the flues was filled with black ash (4900B).

South of kiln 4900 was oven or kiln 1221, of which only the flue and stoke-pit survived. The flue walls consisted of a single course (0.15m high) of gritstone blocks, dressed on the interior face only (Fig. 51, S.66 and S.67). The same material was used to line the base. The north wall incorporated the inverted upper stone of a beehive quern (Chapter 10, No. 22) which was, like the rest of the masonry, extremely heavily burnt. The surviving portion of the flue was 1.24m long and 0.24-0.30m wide internally. The stoke-pit at the eastern end (1231) was marked by a depression in the top of level 1222 (the filling of Structure Y) measuring c. 1.00 by 0.60m, and with a maximum depth of 0.37m. Both the flue and stoke-pit of kiln 1221 were filled with black ash, although the area around the stoke-pit was also characterised by a number of thin lenses of grey, red and yellow ash, and burnt clay, each covering less than 1m^2 in area and none more than c. 20mm thick.

Above the filling layer (1222) of Structure Y (Fig. 48, S.65), the western third of Structure M was covered extensively by a layer of black ash (1216) presumably associated with kilns 4900 and 1221. A layer of pale orange-coloured soil (1215) lay above this; its maximum thickness was 0.12m. It contained dressed masonry, roof tile and mortar, but produced no other finds. Although

layer 1215 survived only in the north-western corner of the building, it was identical in character to two other deposits in the area: layer 1217, which survived in places along the southern side of the building, against wall 1218; and layer 4900A, which was the material filling the upper part of kiln 4900. It is almost certain that these deposits represent a single activity.

Above 1215, and again surviving only in the north-western corner of the building, was a thin surface of friable white mortar (1211), up to c. 60mm thick. It extended over an area of approximately 4m^2 and directly overlay the fabric and fill of kiln 4900. The northward and westward limits of the layer coincided exactly with the edges of robber trench 1208 and wall 1210, but ploughing had obliterated its eastward and southward extent – indeed, it was only by virtue of its position on the edge of the ploughing headland that it had survived at all. It presumably represented a relatively late phase of flooring, perhaps associated with refurbishment in Phase III. Above it, and covering the whole building interior, was a general brown soil layer (numbered variously as 1200, 1201, 1400, 1401 and 1422) of maximum depth 0.35m. The layer contained large quantities of building debris, including dressed masonry, iron nails, glass fragments, roof and box-flue tiles, *tesserae*, *opus signinum* flooring, painted plaster and mortar. Pottery is largely of 3rd to 4th-century date.

In the eastern two-thirds of the building, the general brown soil layer (here numbered 1400, 1401 and 1422) directly overlay bedrock, although three features in this area (1425-7) may be noted. Near the east end, two shallow pits (1425 and 1426), c. 1m square, were cut into the bedrock to a depth of c. 0.10m. They were filled with dark grey soil and building debris but produced no other finds. The nature of their filling suggests that they represented trial pits associated with the excavations of 1854. A pit (1427) of similar size, though somewhat deeper (c. 0.30m), was cut into bedrock at the north-east corner of Structure M. It was filled with material identical to that in pits 1425 and 1426. On the assumption that the eastern end of the building corresponds to room 'L' of the 1855 report (see above), pit 1427 was located precisely where 'in the north east corner about one foot from the surface the skeleton of a child was discovered.' (Procter 1855, 274). Also referring to room 'L', the 1855 report states that: 'As a quantity of large red stone and coloured *tesserae* were dug out of this room, it had in all probability possessed a tessellated floor.' (Procter 1855, 273). It may be noted that the brown soil layer in this area produced a mortared block of five *tesserae* (SF 807) – in contrast to other areas of the site where they tended to occur singly and less numerously.

From the north-western corner of Structure M, wall 1204 ran northwards for a distance of 4.50m; it then turned westwards (wall 1202) for a further 7.50m to join the south-eastern corner of Structure J (Fig. 52). Walls 1202 and 1204 therefore fulfilled the same function as had walls 1203 and 1205 in Phase I. Walls 1202 and 1204 were of the same build as elsewhere in the Phase II structure, being 0.75-0.85m wide and surviving to a maximum height above bedrock of *c.* 0.20m (two courses).

Approximately 9m further east another wall (1214) ran north-eastwards from Structure M. It was composed of large, cleanly dressed gritstone and limestone blocks, without a core, and was 0.48-0.50m wide. This wall directly overlay the subsided fill (4903) of Structure X (see p. 45), and here its foundations were accordingly dug deeper. It separated two distinct filling layers which had been deposited in the hollow of the abandoned Structure X after the erection of wall 1214.

Of these, layer 1212 was a homogeneous band of brown soil abutting the eastern face of wall 1214. It had a maximum depth of *c.* 0.80m over the edge of Structure X, tapering to *c.* 0.15m at its edges, and contained large quantities of building debris. One basal sherd of a colour-coated beaker joins a sherd from layer 1213, which lay to the west of wall 1214 and abutted its western face.

Layer 1213 was a heterogeneous level composed of a series of rubble deposits, containing much burnt debris, interspersed with lenses of brown soil. Its overall depth was *c.* 0.82m at the eastern end, tapering to *c.* 0.20m towards the edges and western end of the underlying Structure X. Three broad subdivisions (numbered 1213A, 1213B and 1213C) could be discerned within layer 1213. These were tipping layers, and seem to have been derived from a single event: one pottery vessel (Chapter 15, No. 32) provides sherds from all three bands. The tipping evidently took place from west to east, perhaps incorporating debris from the occupation of Structure J. Pottery, which was abundant, ranges from the 2nd to 4th centuries.

Phase III

Attached to wall 1218/1404, and stretching the entire length of Structure M, was a range of small rectangular rooms consisting of two unheated rooms (6 and 7) at either end of a hypocaust suite (1-5). The walls which separated these rooms, and the east end wall of the range all abutted the south side of the main building; this is why they have been assigned to a third phase (Fig. 53). On the other hand, there is no evidence to indicate whether they were erected long after the construction of Phase II, or whether they were merely a later stage of the same building campaign. Nor is it certain that all the rooms were constructed at the same time.

The east wall of the range (8101) abutted the south wall of the main building (1403). The two were, however, very similar in construction, with mortared rubble cores faced with gritstone and limestone blocks. Their widths were uniform, at just over 1m.

The south wall (1302) was heavily robbed at its eastern end, the backfill consisting of a dark grey soil (8102). It survived better at its centre and western end, and in both areas consisted of a mortared rubble core faced on both sides with neatly dressed gritstone and limestone blocks, above a slightly offset foundation course. It may be noted however, that, whereas at its centre wall 1302 was some

0.65m wide and largely composed of gritstone, at its western end it was broader (0.75-0.85m) and showed a predominance of limestone. Where it bounded the hypocaust suite, wall 1302 stood to a maximum height of five courses (0.66m) above the basement floor level. In this area, too, the fabric of the wall was very heavily burnt throughout. A foundation trench (8026) for this wall was located along its southern side. It was 0.90-0.95m wide and post-dated gully 5605 immediately to the south.

The west wall (1303) was robbed at its northern end but survived elsewhere as a single course (maximum height 0.15m) of dressed gritstone and limestone blocks fronting a mortared rubble core, with an overall width of 0.78-0.90m. Three observations concerning wall 1303 should be noted. First, although forming a southward continuation of wall 1210, wall 1303 displayed a slightly more south-easterly orientation. Secondly, the junction of walls 1210 and 1218 was faced externally – showing that wall 1303 had not been bonded to it. Thirdly, the western end of wall 1302 butted against wall 1303 and was not bonded to it.

The space formed by walls 1218, 8101, 1302 and 1303 was subdivided by a series of cross-walls into Rooms 1-7.

Room 6

The westernmost room (Room 6) was unheated. It was bounded to the east by wall 1301, which was 0.45-0.55m wide and consisted of three courses of dressed gritstone and limestone blocks fronting a mortared rubble core. The southern end of wall 1301 was robbed, but its northern end butted against wall 1218. The rectangular room thus formed measured internally some 4.50 by 2.20m.

The lowest layer in this room was a homogeneous layer of brown soil with limestone inclusions (1305), of maximum depth 0.32m. It contained only small quantities of building debris and may have represented part of the general level (1220/1222) filling Structure Y (see p. 47). In the south-eastern quarter of Room 6, directly overlying layer 1305, were traces of a mortared foundation of roughly dressed limestone blocks (1304), which covered an area of some 1.48 by 0.84m. Above 1305 was a layer of dark grey soil (1300), *c.* 0.13m deep, containing large quantities of building debris.

Room 1

Room 1, east of Room 6, had originally contained a hypocaust. It measured internally some 3.35 by 2.20m, and the basement survived to a depth of 0.55-0.60m below the level of the surrounding bedrock. The room was bounded to the north, south and west by walls 1218, 1302 and 1301 respectively. Wall 1302 had been extensively robbed. It had clearly abutted the south wall of Room 2, which is also numbered 1302 in the excavation record, and which bonded with the east wall of Room 1. This latter wall (8005) consisted of four courses (maximum height *c.* 0.60m) of dressed gritstone and limestone blocks fronting a mortared rubble core, with an overall width of 0.60-0.66m. Its northern end abutted wall 1218, while its southern end had been broken through in order to form a flue (8014) 0.30m wide. The southern side of the flue was marked by a single course of dressed limestone blocks (8027), 0.33m wide and 1.16m long, which incorporated a laid *tegula* at its west end.

The remains of five basal *pila* tiles were mortared onto the natural limestone floor of the hypocaust basement. They were 230-80mm square and 45-50mm thick, and in two cases a second tile course, smaller in size (180mm square and *c*. 40mm thick), also survived. The distribution of the *pilae* was irregular, but they appeared to be disposed, at least nominally, in rows of six by five.

The basement was filled to a depth of 0.40-0.45m with a layer (8008) characterised by an abundance of building debris in the form of dressed masonry, iron nails, roof, *pila* and flue tiles, painted plaster, *tesserae*, *opus signinum* and mortar. Pottery is mainly of 3rd to 4th-century date. Two lenses were discernible within this general level: layer 8006, in the north-western corner of the room, was distinguishable as a concentration of friable *opus signinum* and painted plaster (of maximum depth 0.31m); while layer 8007 consisted of an area of heavy masonry around the centre of the room. Layer 8008 was overlain by dark grey soil (8000).

Room 2

Room 2 is interpreted as the *praefurnium* of the hypocaust suite, with flues leading to the adjacent hypocausts of Rooms 1 and 3. It measured internally 4.10 by 2.40m, and the basement survived to a depth of 0.60-0.70m below the level of the surrounding bedrock. The room was bounded to the north, south and west by walls 1218, 1302 and 8005 respectively. Its flue opening into Room 1 was, as indicated above, a secondary feature, built to serve the added hypocaust. The eastward extent of Room 2 was marked by wall 8002 and subsequent modifications. Wall 8002 was constructed of dressed gritstone and limestone blocks (predominantly the former) fronting a mortared rubble core, and standing to a maximum height of 0.75m, or four courses of masonry. Just north of its centre it was cut by a flue (8015), 0.45m wide, connecting with the hypocaust of Room 3. Both sides of flue 8015 were faced with mortared tiles, laid horizontally and standing to a maximum fourteen courses high. The tiles were rectangular in shape and uniform in size, measuring 350-400mm long, 180-200mm wide and 45-50mm thick, and were severely fractured by heat. The western end of these tile courses was flush with the west face of wall 8002, but at the eastern end they extended beyond wall 8002 for a distance of some 0.30m, thus effectively lengthening the flue to 1.06m.

At some subsequent stage, flue 8015 was extended further westwards, for a distance of some 0.95m, by the addition of cheek-walls 8029 and 8024 to the north and south respectively. These were poorly constructed walls consisting of large, mortared gritstone and limestone blocks, roughly dressed on the exterior only, and fronting a cavity filled with loosely packed rubble. They abutted the side walls of Room 2 and stood to a maximum height of 0.60m (five courses of masonry), with heavily burnt

exterior faces. Flue 8015 was further lengthened on its northern side by the addition of wall 8025. This abutted walls 1218 and 8029 to the north and east respectively, and consisted of five courses of dressed gritstone and limestone blocks. The overall width of 8025 was 0.40m.

The limestone bedrock floor of this room was itself heavily burnt. Above it were alternating bands of black ash (8023C, 8023E and 8023G) and sand/mortar (8023D and 8023F) none more than 10mm thick. A 30mm thick layer of pink plaster (8023B) overlay these, beneath another layer of ash (8023A) containing 3rd to 4th-century pottery. Above was a 0.45m layer of building debris (8009). The material filling flue 8015 (8022) was very different in character from that in Room 2, having much in common with the deposits in Room 3. It is therefore described below.

Room 3

Room 3 was the best preserved room of the hypocaust suite, although even here much of its eastern half had been destroyed (Pl. XVII). The room measured internally 3.10 by 2.40m, and the basement survived to a depth of 0.65-0.75m below the level of the surrounding bedrock. The room was bounded to the north, south and west by walls 1218, 1302 and 8002 respectively; it communicated with Room 2 via flue 8015. The eastward limit was marked by the fragmentary remains of cross-wall 8011, which abutted wall 1218 to the north and survived at its northern end as a 0.64m wide course of mortared, dressed gritstone blocks. The southern end of wall 8011 had been destroyed, and it was clear that this wall represented the approximate western extent of the excavations of 1854. The 1855 report describes the excavation of a pair of hypocausts ('A' and 'B': see Fig. 2) which evidently correspond to Rooms 4 and 5 of the present excavations. In describing the more westerly of these ('A'), the report records:

> This room, when first opened, was much longer than it appears at present; for a portion of it at the west end, has been heedlessly destroyed … by visitors, so that … the original dimensions could not be accurately ascertained. (Procter 1855, 271)

The report goes on to state that:

> Beyond this ruined portion were the remains of a praefurnium or furnace, likewise imperfect, but when discovered appearing to be of similar construction to the one found at the York baths, and containing a large quantity of wood ashes. (Procter 1855, 271-2)

This is either a reference to the *praefurnium* located in the present excavations (i.e. Room 2), or else a misinterpretation of the hypocaust of Room 3.

Wall 8011 was cut just north of its centre by a flue (8016) connecting the hypocausts of Rooms 3 and 4. The flue was 0.30-0.40m wide, but its exact dimensions were uncertain due to the fragmentary nature of wall 8011. Flue

Pl. XVII. Structure M, Room 3, facing north-west. (Photo: S. Wager)

8016 was clearly positioned to align with the flue connecting Rooms 2 and 3 (8015), but there were traces of a possible additional flue (8028), 0.20m wide, through wall 8011 at its northern end.

With the exception of those in the south-eastern corner, the *pilae* in Room 3 were very well preserved (Fig. 51, S.126). They consisted of large basal tiles (220-80mm square, and 30-50mm thick) mortared to the *opus signinum* basement floor, supporting stacks of smaller tiles (160-240mm square, and 30-50mm thick). The tiles were squared or with rounded corners, and were severely fractured by fire. The best preserved of the *pilae* stood to a height of 0.74m, or seventeen tile courses. The *pilae* formed rows of seven by six, and were fairly regularly distributed except at the western end of the room, either side of flue 8015, where they were more closely spaced and where the westernmost row abutted wall 8002.

The basement floor of Room 3 was a compact skin of *opus signinum* extending westwards to form the base of flue 8015 (terminating at the western face of wall 8002), and eastwards through flue 8016 into neighbouring Room 4. The floor was covered with a thin layer of black ash (8020, 8021 and 8022B), of maximum thickness 0.10m; this layer also filled the bases of flues 8015 to the west (as 8022B) and 8016 to the east (as 8021).

Above the ash, the deposits in the western half of Room 3 were undisturbed. The upper 0.55-0.60m consisted of a pink-coloured level of very heavily burnt building debris (8001 and 8022A), comprising crushed

tile, *opus signinum*, sandstone flags and painted plaster, and containing a few sherds of Crambeck and Huntcliff wares. This level extended westwards to fill the upper part of flue 8015 (as layer 8022A) as far as the west face of wall 8002.

In the eastern half of the room, however, the basement was filled to its entire depth with a uniform deposit of dark grey soil and building debris. This deposit (variously numbered as 8003, 8010 and 8104) extended uninterrupted over Rooms 4 and 5 to the east, and contained large quantities of building debris and artefacts. It was evident from its general nature, and the presence within it of such modern finds as a steel pin (SF 1120) and a clay pipe fragment (SF 1174), that the layers 8003/8010/8104 represented backfilled material from comparatively recent activity in the area, and this can almost certainly be identified with the excavations of 1854. It may be noted that the 1855 report, describing hypocausts 'A' and 'B', records that:

> the pillars in the two chambers seem to have supported a floor of thick concrete, composed of mortar and powdered bricks, laid on flat tiles passing across the top of the pillars, thus forming the floor of an ornamented chamber above them, as large masses of painted stucco, coloured in different ways, were found in this place. (Procter 1855, 272)

Room 4

It is clear that Room 4 corresponds to 'hypocaust A' of the 1854 excavations. It measured internally about 2.62 by 2.30m, and its basement survived to a depth of 0.55-0.60m below the level of the surrounding bedrock. The 1855 report gives comparable dimensions of 8 feet 6 inches by 8 feet 2 inches (Procter 1855, 271; or 2.59 by 2.49m), either internally or externally. Room 4 was bounded to north, south and west by walls 1218, 1302 and 8011, and it communicated with Room 3 via flue 8016. The eastward limit of Room 4 was marked by cross-wall 8012, which had been almost totally destroyed, being represented only by a 0.60m wide break in the *opus signinum* floor. There were also two mortared, dressed gritstone blocks near the centre of wall 8012. Just to the north of these blocks, and aligned with flues 8015 and 8016 to the west, was flue 8017. This was marked by a 0.30m wide tongue of *opus signinum* flooring, running eastwards across the line of wall 8012. The 1855 report states that the wall separating hypocausts 'A' and 'B' (i.e. wall 8012 of the present excavations) stood to a height of 2 feet 4 inches (0.71m), and was:

> a well built wall of sandstone … communicating with the second hypocaust (B) by a small opening (a) like a flue, which was stopped up on one side with Roman concrete. (Procter 1855, 272)

Flue (a) is identifiable with flue 8017, although no evidence of its blocking was found in the present excavations.

None of the *pilae* remained, these apparently having been removed in 1854 and deposited in the collections of the Yorkshire Philosophical Society. The only surviving traces consisted of eleven mortar patches on the basement floor surface, their distribution suggesting that the *pilae* had originally been disposed in five rows of five. The 1855 report describes hypocaust 'A' as having:

> contained five rows of pillars, each row consisting of five pillars, built of the ordinary flat Roman tiles 8, 9 and 10 inches square, with layers of concrete, made of mortar and powdered brick, between them. These pillars, especially towards the lower part, showed the action of fire, and in the spaces between them bones of various animals and the skulls of one or two sheep were discovered. The floor is a cement composed of brick and lime. (Procter 1855, 271)

The dimensions quoted for the *pila* tiles (*c*. 200-250mm) conform with those of the surviving examples in Rooms 3 and 5. The entire depth of Room 4 was occupied by the general backfilling layer 8003/8010/8104 associated with the excavations of 1854.

Room 5

Room 5 was the easternmost of the heated rooms, and corresponded to hypocaust 'B' of the 1854 excavations.

Internally it measured 2.30m square and its basement survived to a depth of 0.65-0.70m below the level of the surrounding bedrock. The dimensions given for hypocaust 'B' in the 1855 report are 8 feet 4 inches by 7 feet 10 inches (Procter 1855, 272; or 2.54 by 2.38m). The room was bounded to the north, south and west by walls 1218, 1302 and 8012 respectively, although these were almost entirely robbed in this area. Communication with Room 4 was via flue 8017. The east wall (8013) was also poorly preserved, and formed the eastward limit of the suite of heated rooms. The wall revetted the limestone bedrock in the neighbouring, unheated, Room 7. The west face of wall 8013 was largely robbed, but traces of an east face of dressed gritstone and limestone blocks, with a mortared rubble core, survived. The wall was 0.65-0.75m wide, and it stood to a maximum height of *c*. 0.55m (four courses of masonry) above the basement floor level.

The north wall (1218) was interrupted just west of its centre by flue 8018, a 0.30m wide feature lined on both sides with mortared tile courses – a design closely resembling that of flue 8015. The tiles were rectangular in shape, measuring 300-400mm long, 180-200mm wide and 40-50mm thick; they stood to a maximum of four courses high, and showed no indication of burning.

At its northern end, flue 8018 communicated with a small rectangular chamber (8019). This was cut into the bedrock to a depth of 0.70m and measured internally 0.84 by 0.62m. The chamber sides were faced with large, dressed limestone blocks backed by mortared rubble; it was lined throughout with a thin skin of *opus signinum*. Like flue 8018, the chamber showed no traces of burning.

Flue 8018 corresponds to flue 'b' of the 1854 excavations, which, according to the report:

> has been for the escape of the smoke from the hypocaust; only a few feet from it existed, so that neither its course nor destination could be traced. (Procter 1855, 273)

This may indicate that flue 8018 was only partially excavated; and it would explain a further discrepancy: the report refers to room 'L', to the north, as being 'on the same level' as hypocausts 'A' and 'B'. However, as noted earlier, room 'L' corresponded to the east room of the Phase II structure of the present excavations, which had no hypocaust. It must be concluded that the excavators of 1854 misinterpreted the partially exposed *opus signinum* base of chamber 8019 as representing one corner of a hypocaust basement in room 'L'.

The *opus signinum* basement floor, continuing from Room 4, extended over the entire area of Room 5 and terminated at the southern end of flue 8018. Above it, the only filling layer in Room 5 was the general level (8003/8010/8104) associated with the excavations of 1854. This layer also filled flue 8018 and chamber 8019 (here numbered as 8105 and 8106 respectively).

None of the Room 5 *pilae* remained, but the position of some of them was marked by five mortar patches on the floor surface and two basal *pila* tiles *in situ*. The latter were identical in size to those in Rooms 1 and 3, being

230-60mm square and 40-50mm thick. The *pilae* again seem to have been disposed in five rows of five, conforming to the distribution recorded for room 'B' of the 1854 excavations:

> [it} contained five rows of pillars, each row consisting of five pillars, eleven of the whole being of sandstone ... the remainder of brick. (Procter 1855, 272)

The reference to 'sandstone' *pilae* – which occupied the central and eastern portion of room 'B' – almost certainly indicates the monolithic gritstone *pila* type encountered elsewhere on the site.

Room 7

Room 7, at the eastern end of the range, was unheated and corresponded to room 'C' of the 1854 excavations. It measured internally 5.70 by 2.45m, and this compared closely with the dimensions given for room 'C'. The room was bounded by walls 1218 and 8101 to the north and east respectively, and by the largely robbed remains of walls 1302 and 8013 to the south and west.

The only internal features were two gullies (8103 and 8107) cut into the bedrock base. Gully 8103 ran north-westwards across the western half of the room. It was irregular in plan, some 3.40m long and 0.40-0.60m wide, and had an irregular U-shaped profile, 0.15-0.35m deep. It was filled with dark grey soil with gritstone and limestone inclusions, and contained building debris and a fragment of a clay pipe stem (SF 1319). A similar feature (8107) was located at the eastern end of Room 7, but was not excavated. It was 0.80-0.90m wide and spanned the entire width of Room 7 parallel to, and just west of, wall 8101. Like gully 8103, gully 8107 was filled with grey soil, although with a concentration of limestone rubble in the top. Similar grey soil (8100) overlay the whole room.

Referring to room 'C' of the 1854 excavations, Procter states that this was an area 'through which trenches in several directions were dug'; gullies 8103 and 8107 clearly represented the remains of such trial trenches. He also records that considerable quantities of 'large *tesserae* of chalk and tile measuring an inch square' were recovered, and surmises that these 'doubtless had formed the floor of a chamber in this situation' (Procter 1855, 272).

Finally it may be noted that the plan in the 1855 report depicts room 'C' as extending eastwards beyond the east wall of room 'L'. The present excavations have shown this to be erroneous, since the east wall of Room 7 (8101), and that of the main Phase II building to the north (1403), shared a common alignment.

Discussion

Structure M was the best preserved of the major buildings on the site. It therefore presents the most complicated structural sequence. Three phases have been identified, but their relationships to each other were not entirely clear. The form of the earliest phase was clearly an aisled building. Its west end precisely overlay Structure Y, suggesting that it was a direct and immediate replacement. Such precision would have allowed Structure X to continue in use for some time; the quite different character of its filling layers from those of Structure Y certainly indicates that the two were levelled in separate operations.

Phase I of Structure M survived long enough to require the replacement of aisle posts, and the replacement post-holes (Ib) may in fact be related to (or may have survived) the expansion of the structure in Phase II. Though the Phase I east wall (1423) was much depleted when excavated, it evidently remained a substantial enough foundation to be recorded in the 1854 excavations; it is likely, therefore, to have continued as a partition wall when the building was extended eastwards in Phase II.

The new eastern room produced no evidence of aisled construction; its square shape may have been designed to permit an alternative roof structure. A two-part plan such as this, with a main aisled room and a smaller partitioned unit at one end, is also recorded for building IV (phase one) at Hibaldstow, Humberside (Smith 1987, 190-91, figs 12-13). The addition of the hypocaust suite, marking Phase III, seems to have been a two-stage expansion of facilities: initially Rooms 2, 3, 4, 5 and 7 to which were added, later, Rooms 1 and 6.

A final problem is the relationship of kiln 4900 and oven 1221 to these phases. Both features are recorded as cutting the fill of Structure Y; therefore they did not, presumably, belong to that structure. That said, there are grounds for denying their association with any phase of Structure M.

The site records show that, at the time of excavation, kiln 4900 was thought to cut post-holes 1466 and 1467 of Phase Ia, yet on plan post-hole 1467 in particular could be interpreted as cutting and disrupting the stone flue lining. Similarly, post-hole 1454 on the south side could have cut short flue 1221. If so, both features would have to be assigned either to Structure Y or to an intermediate phase preceding the erection of the aisled building. Such an interpretation might be seen to gain support from the fact that two aisle post-holes on the south side (1453 and 1454) were filled with black ash: the posts seem therefore to have been removed at times when ash had already been deposited and was available to fill the voids. On the other hand, the absence of any record of Phase Ib post-holes at the north-west corner of the building, on the line of the axial flue of kiln 4900, supports the initial interpretation, that the kiln post-dated the aisle post-holes.

Whatever the correct place (or places) of these features in the structural sequence, they may have caused only minor disruption to one end of an existing building, with perhaps a few aisle posts being removed to make way for them. There is no reason to suppose they mark the replacement of one complete structural phase by another.

Structure F (Figs 54-5)

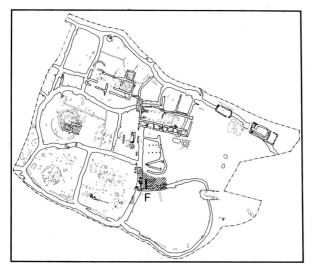

Fig. 55. Location of Structure F.

Pl. XVIII. Structure F, oven flue 639, facing west. (Photo: S. Wager)

Structure F was a rectilinear building at the south-east corner of the villa settlement. Except at its western end, where it overlay enclosure ditch 022, it was severely damaged by ploughing, and its eastern extent remains largely conjectural.

The structure was aligned east-west, with external dimensions of *c.* 26.00 by 7.50m, and seemed to have been divided into two parts by wall 610. The western part was the more clearly defined due to its position over the top of Ditch 022. The north wall (609) survived for a length of 1.80m and consisted of a single course of large, roughly dressed limestone facing blocks, with a mortared rubble core. The wall varied in width from 0.66-0.78m, and stood to a maximum height of 0.25m; it showed signs of burning along its southern face.

The east wall (610) was of similar construction, although rather better made and incorporating some gritstone. It was 0.64-0.70m wide and survived to a maximum height of 0.22m. A short stretch of the south wall (608) survived in the top of Ditches 022 and 025, and consisted of one course of (predominantly) gritstone facing blocks, with a mortared rubble core. It stood to a maximum height of 0.24m and was 0.76-0.80m wide.

Although the west wall was absent, a rectangular stone-lined flue or oven (639) survived in the presumed south-western corner (Pl. XVIII). It was aligned east-west, with internal dimensions of 1.08 by 0.20m, and was cut into the bedrock to a maximum surviving depth of 0.24m. It was lined on its north, south and west sides with one, and in places two courses of heavily burnt, dressed gritstone, fronting a mortared rubble core. The base was paved with sandstone flags, again heavily burnt (Fig. 54, S.15). At the mouth of the flue was a lens of fire-reddened soil (606), while flue 639 itself was filled with a dark brown sandy silt with limestone and charcoal inclusions (607). A spread of burnt black ash (604) in the top of Ditch 022 also seemed, from its position and alignment, to have been related to the use of this oven or kiln.

In the centre of the area defined by these walls were traces of further foundations (637) which may have partitioned off a small room, measuring 2.40 by 3.30m. The wall was in a very fragmentary state, consisting of a single course of roughly dressed gritstone and limestone blocks with an unmortared rubble core. It varied in width from 0.56-0.80m, and stood to a maximum height of 0.12m. The wall overlay layer 604, a black ash deposit which has been associated with flue 639. Therefore wall 637, if part of this building, was a modification rather than an original element.

Also overlying ash 604 was a spread of sandstone flags and roof tiles (638) in a brown soil matrix around wall 637. There was no evidence to demonstrate whether it should be regarded as a discrete feature or merely as a constituent of the overlying general layer 603. This was a level of building rubble in a brown soil matrix, which reached a maximum depth of *c.* 0.20m and covered the entire building. Cut into it, towards the east end of the building, was an infant burial (Chapter 23, No. 12). Layer 603 was itself overlain by brown soil (600).

The building east of wall 610 was, apart from certain internal features, less clearly defined. Its conjectured internal dimensions were 19.00 by 7.50m. The north and east walls were entirely destroyed except for two possible lengths of a gritstone and limestone foundation course (620 and 622). The south wall was also destroyed, although it may have run just outside slot 621. The west wall (610) has been described above.

The most obvious internal features were several linear slots (612-13, 619, 634 and 636) cut into the bedrock, each containing black ashy material and displaying signs of burning along their sides and base. All but one had U-shaped cross-sections. They seemed, on the basis of their alignment and extent, to have been features associated with this building. In the western part of the room, slot 613 was aligned north-south. It was 3.08m in length and 0.62m wide to the south, narrowing to 0.52m to the north, and had a maximum depth of 0.16m at the southern end. Slot 636 was at right-angles to 613, and adjoined the centre of its western side (Fig. 54, S.32). It was 2.66m long and varied from 0.44-0.52m wide. The western end of the slot was slightly bulbous in plan, having a diameter of 0.62m. Its maximum depth (at the eastern end) was 0.30m, and it contained fragments of a box-flue tile, and a *pila* tile. Slot 634 was parallel to, and east of 613. It was 1.80m long and bulbous in plan, being 0.34m wide to the north and 0.78m to the south. Its maximum depth was 0.18m at the southern end.

Slot 612 was further to the south and aligned east-west. It was 4.20 by 0.21m, and up to 0.17m deep at the western end. Its sides were more exactly parallel, and its base flatter than those of the other slots. It produced no finds, but was partly overlain by a large, dressed limestone slab which may have been associated with paved area 614. Slot 619 was aligned east-west, just to the north of paved area 618. It was 3.56m long, while its width varied from 0.40-0.74m, and its depth from 0.14m to the east to 0.25m at the western end. The central section was partially overlain by several gritstone slabs which may have been associated with paved area 618.

In the presumed south-eastern corner of the building was a slot (621) of a different type, running westwards from paved area 618 for a distance of some 5.80m. Its sides were parallel and its terminals rounded; it was flat based, and had a maximum depth of 0.66m (Fig. 54, S.23). The fill consisted of building debris (including dressed stonework and tile fragments) in a grey soil matrix; only the western end was fully excavated.

Above these gullies, and within the general rubble level (603) were two areas of crude gritstone and limestone paving (614 and 618). The latter was the larger (*c.* 6 by 4m), and was situated at the southern edge of the structure, alongside and partly overlying the presumed course of the south wall. It consisted predominantly of large, roughly dressed gritstone slabs bedded in the top of Ditch 025. Paving 614, further to the west, was mixed gritstone and limestone laid directly onto the bedrock and extending for about a square metre.

Several other features in the area may have been associated with Structure F. There were a number of post-holes within and around the building, of which one (615) was filled with burnt material and produced several sherds of 3rd to 4th-century pottery. A lens of burnt material (629) in the top of Ditch 022 may also have been associated with the building.

A few fragments of other, possibly associated masonry structures lay to the north-west of Structure F. Some 2.20m north of wall 609, and apparently parallel to it, were several blocks of roughly dressed limestone (630). These may have represented the remains of an east-west wall, but this could not be established with certainty. A further 2.30m to the north were more conclusive traces of a wall (632), again aligned east-west and surviving for a length of *c.* 2.80m. It consisted of a single course of large, roughly dressed limestone facing blocks, without any traces of mortaring or core. It was *c.* 0.94m wide and stood to a maximum height of 0.15m. Midway between walls 630 and 632 was an area of gritstone cobbles in a grey soil matrix (631).

The remains of Structure F were so fragmentary that a detailed interpretation is impossible. The presence of a flue or oven (639) similar in shape and size to 103 in Structure A, and of burnt slots like those in Structure R, suggests that it was another ancillary building (or range of buildings) devoted to agricultural use.

Structure P (Figs 56-7)

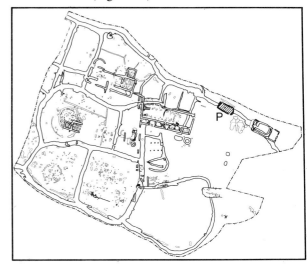

Fig. 56. Location of Structure P.

Structure P was situated on the north-east edge of the settlement, and was one of two buildings inserted into enclosure ditch 030-034. It was aligned approximately east-west and had a bowed eastern end (Pl. XIX). A slightly irregular building, it varied in width from 4.40m at the west to 5.10m at the east, and was 10.50m long. It contained a sunken floor cut into the bedrock to a

Pl. XIX. Structure P, facing west. (Photo: S. Wager)

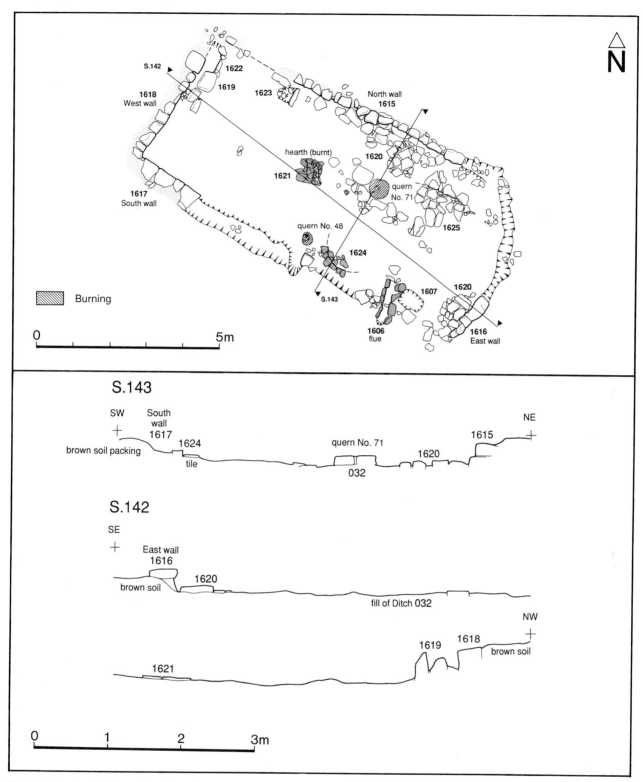

Fig. 57. Structure P: plan and sections.

maximum depth of *c*. 0.50m at the western end. A fall in the level of the bedrock towards its eastern end allowed the floor there to be cut to a lesser depth (*c*. 0.30m) to form a level surface (Fig. 57, S.142 and S.143). The friable limestone sides of the sunken floor were partly revetted by gritstone walls 1615-18, but these did not extend down to the floor; they rested instead on a broad shelf cut into the sides, 0.30-0.40m above the floor.

Where they survived the walls consisted of single lines of unmortared gritstone blocks, dressed on the interior face only. The north wall (1615) was 0.26-0.38m wide and had a maximum height of *c*. 0.20m. The eastern and western ends had been destroyed by ploughing. Only the southern portion of the curving east wall (1616) survived. The wall may have been dressed on the exterior as well as the interior face, and was *c*. 0.30-0.40m wide and up to *c*.

Pl. XX. Structure P, flue 1606, facing north. (Photo: S. Wager)

0.20m high. The south wall (1617) was almost entirely destroyed except at its western end. It was 0.32-0.48m wide and had a maximum height of *c.* 0.20m. The west wall (1618) was reasonably well preserved, being 0.30-0.48m wide and up to *c.* 0.15m high.

Several stone features occupied the interior of the building. Near the centre was an open hearth (1621) consisting of four fire-cracked gritstone flags. These formed a 0.65m square, set obliquely to the alignment of the building but on its main axis. To the north-west, against the north wall, was a stone-lined ?post-setting (1623), and beyond this, in the north-west corner of the building, was a ?pit (1622) associated with several large squared blocks of stone (1619). Neither 1622 nor 1623 was fully excavated, and their function is not apparent from the existing records.

The eastern part of the building contained two patches of gritstone flagging (both numbered 1620) against the north and east walls; these may have been the remnants of more general paving on the south side. Kiln or oven flue 1606 apparently vented through the south wall (Pl. XX). It measured internally 1.20 by 0.18m, and was lined on both sides by fire-reddened, edge-set gritstone blocks. At the surviving north end of the flue was a possible baffle, formed by a slab and a hypocaust *pila*. Close to the east side was a hole in the floor (1607) containing an upright pottery vessel: the lower part of a Dales ware jar which had clearly been set in the floor as a container. West of the flue, but not apparently served by it, was part of what was probably a circular oven base; it was marked by curved edging stones and paving (1624). The stones were reddened by heat. Another edging (1625), near the north-east corner of the building, was not so well defined, but seems to have been unburnt. It may have marked the edge of a threshing floor: a kerb at Catsgore, Somerset,

delimiting a paved area next to a drying kiln, has been so interpreted (Morris 1979, 27).

The floor of the building was overlain by several lenses of red-brown soil with limestone inclusions up to 0.30m deep (1609-10 and 1612-14); these were mainly distributed around the edges of the basement. Above and beyond these, a layer of blackish ash and soil (variously numbered as 1604, 1608 and 1611) covered much of the western part of the building to a maximum depth of *c.* 0.20m. It contained fragments of roof and box-flue tile, iron nails and 3rd to 4th-century pottery. Layer 1604 ran out towards the eastern end of the building, where there was a heterogeneous layer of ash and clayey soil (1603) of maximum depth *c.* 0.20m. This contained fragments of sandstone roof tiles, *pila* tile, *tesserae*, and querns (Chapter 10, Nos 48 and 71).

Layers 1603 and 1604 were overlain by a more compacted brown soil (1601 and 1602) up to *c.* 0.15m deep. This contained building rubble, roof tile fragments, iron nails, further quern fragments (Chapter 10, Nos 27, 46 and 62), and 3rd to 4th-century pottery. It also contained a piece of stamped lead (Chapter 7, No. 1). Above this deposit was the brown ploughsoil (1600).

The building was clearly an ancillary structure. In the absence of industrial waste, its hearths, ovens and kilns were probably used in the processing of agricultural produce. This suggestion is supported by the presence of numerous quernstone fragments on and above the floor; one flat stone (Chapter 10, No. 71) and a beehive quern top stone (unnumbered) were found complete. There is a marked concentration of quern fragments in this and similar buildings (see Fig. 46), including Structure Q which was at one phase almost identical to Structure P. The Dales ware jar set in hole 1607 is a clear indication of use in the 3rd to 4th centuries.

Structure P, together with its neighbouring, similar but better preserved Structure Q (see below), was constructed in the fill of a major Iron Age ditch (032-034); it is very probable that the ditch line was chosen because it was still, in late Roman times, marked by a depression: this would have facilitated sunken-floor construction. By analogy with Structure Q, Structure P may have had an entrance in the east wall. Except at this end the walls were marked by blocks of stone which were faced internally; there was no external face. This could mean that there were, effectively, no walls at all: that a low roof was formed by rafters sitting on the ledges. It seems, however, most unlikely that a building which apparently contained an open hearth had such a low roof. The walls may well have been destroyed entirely, leaving only the lowest course of foundation blocks set on the ledge.

The roof may, instead, have been supported independently by post-and-truss construction, dividing the building into two bays. Slight discontinuities and shifts in alignment at the centres of both long walls may have marked a truss position; the east curving wall was probably beneath a hipped end.

Structure Q (Figs 58-61)

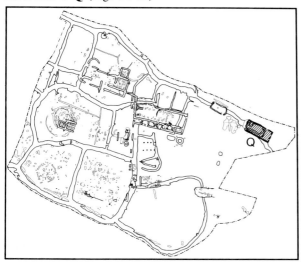

Fig. 58. Location of Structure Q.

Like Structure P, Structure Q was a sunken-floored building set into the fill of Ditch 030-034. Three distinct phases were represented (Fig. 61), one being almost identical in shape and size to Structure P. The phases, described separately, were most evident in the successive east end walls 1711, 1706 and 1710 (Pl. XXI).

Phase I

The earliest east wall was foundation 1711, a curving wall with a threshold stone (1712) at its centre. Site records show conclusively that the north and south ends of this wall ran beneath the side walls (1707 and 1705) of the larger, rectilinear structure. The latter presumably overlay the foundations of the Phase I side walls; they were not dismantled. On the north side, however, facing stones 1719 may have represented the remains of the Phase I north wall. At the south-west corner, the curved facing 1720 may also have belonged to this phase; if so, the west end wall must also have been curved. Thus defined, the building would have measured about 10m internally on its long axis, and about 6m in width. The threshold stone 1712 remained *in situ*. It was about 1.60m long and had a raised rib along the external edge. Several small holes had been cut in its upper surface; these may have taken door fittings, but are more likely to indicate the reuse of a stone which had once served a different purpose.

At the east end, a general layer of burnt soil can be associated with this phase: it was confined to the west side of wall 1711 and is unlikely to belong to the Phase II building which continued further east. Other patches of burnt earth against the south side of the building may also have belonged to this phase. In part, notably along this south side, the floor of the building had been terraced into the natural to provide a level surface. In places it was cut down by as much as 0.70m.

Phase II

The east wall of the Phase I building was reduced to its foundations, which were then incorporated into the paving of a larger Phase II structure. This had a straight east end wall (1706) composed of dressed gritstone and limestone blocks. Like its predecessor, it contained a centrally

Pl. XXI. Structure Q, facing north-west. (Photo: S. Wager)

63

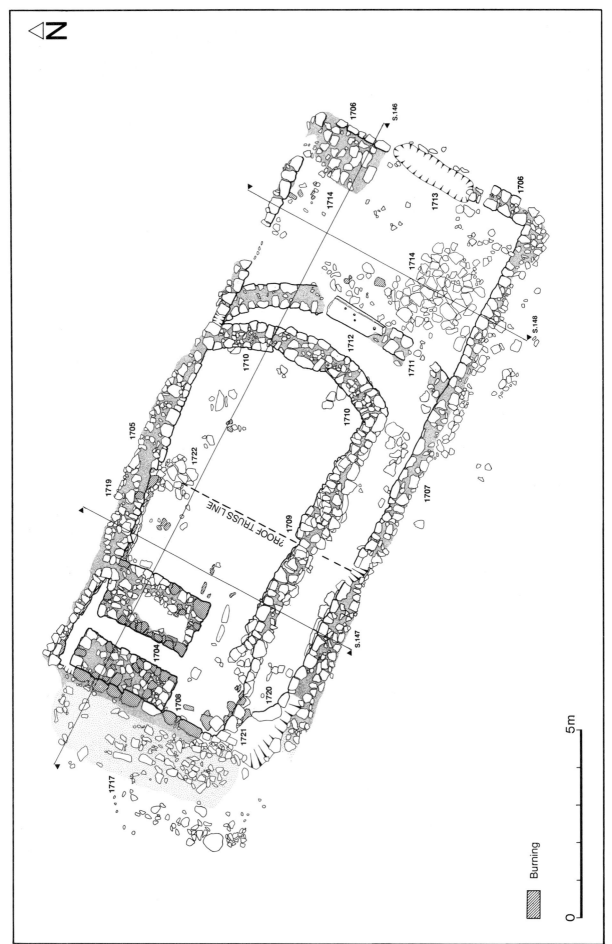

Fig. 59. Structure Q: plan.

Burning

0   5m

placed doorway. In this case, however, the threshold stone did not survive: only the trench (1713) which had contained it remained, together with a stone-lined post-hole or setting at the south end which may have held a square-section doorpost. The side walls 1705 and 1707 varied in width. Some of these variations were probably due to the incorporation of Phase I walling. The records are not sufficiently detailed to document the changes comprehensively, but two phases of walling were clear in section S.147 where it crossed 1707 (Fig. 60). Many of the inner facing stones of both walls showed signs of burning: these may have been Phase I remains.

The west end of the Phase II building is rather more problematical. The end of wall 1705 had been obscured by the insertion of a T-shaped kiln (1704). Wall 1707 petered out: it may have been robbed out in the 19th-century excavations, which seem to have located the kiln (see below). The known west wall (1708) seems to have been of one build with the kiln, and therefore of a later phase. On the west side of 1708 there was, however, a rectangular area of dark brown soil, mortar and rubble (1717). The north and south ends of this context lined up precisely with the interior faces of the Phase II side walls. Context 1717 was not excavated; in retrospect it seems very probable that this was a continuation of the Phase II structure, representing the rubble and soil filling the sunken-floor area. The deposition of 1717 would mark a shortening of the building and the construction of the kiln in Phase III. It would give the Phase II structure an internal length of about 18m, the internal width being about 6m.

Towards the centre of the north wall (1705), against the inner face, was a heap of collapsed masonry (1722). This lay at the junction of two distinct stretches of walling: to the west the inner face was battered, to the east it was not. A rebuilding, perhaps in Phase III, is signified. Masonry 1722 may also have marked the position of a post, the decay or removal of which caused the collapse; it is in line with a gap in the inner face of the south wall (1707). A further gap in the face of the Phase III wall (1709) could indicate that a truss in this position served both the Phase II and III structures.

The east end of the Phase II floor was partly paved (1714; Fig. 60, S.148), the southern patch incorporating the foundation of wall 1711. The dark brown soil around the stones was very distinct from the red-brown layers west of wall 1711; it contained fragments of roof tile.

Phase III

The third structural phase was marked by a decrease in the size of the building and a return to a curving east wall. This wall (1710) survived to a height of three courses, and abutted wall 1705. Once again, this phase had a central entrance, marked not by a single threshold stone, but by a stretch of rough blocks which abutted the coursed walling of 1710 at each end. Close to the south end was a pivot stone, probably *in situ*.

The north side reused the wall of the earlier phases; the western part may have been rebuilt at this time, its inner

Pl. XXII. Structure Q, facing south-east. (Photo: S. Wager)

face battered to prevent collapse. The wall survived to a height of 0.80m above the basement; five courses of stonework remained. The west end of the south wall (1709) deteriorated to a line of inner facing stones which had begun to curve northwards. Wall 1709 was very rough, composed of loosely stacked, unmortared blocks of gritstone and limestone and an unmortared rubble core. Stones on both faces showed signs of burning, and the wall survived to a maximum height of four courses. A gap in the centre of the inner face, in line with the suggested Phase II truss position or partition may indicate the location of a post.

At some stage the west end of the building was reconstructed to allow the insertion of a T-shaped kiln (Pl. XXII). The new west wall (1708) had an inner face of large, neatly dressed and heavily burnt blocks. On the outside it butted soil layer 1717, interpreted above as the backfilled west end of the Phase II structure. The facing stones (1721) appeared to mark the realignment of south wall 1709 to accommodate the stoke-hole of the kiln. The kiln (1704) was a well-built structure, formed by a pair of massive rectangular platforms. That on the west butted against 1708; the eastern platform had been bonded into wall 1705 at its north-east corner. The structure generally survived to a height of five courses. The heavily burnt axial flue was 2.80m long and 0.56m wide; the transverse flue was 2.52m long and tapered from west to east. On the north side, beyond the western arm of the transverse flue, was an earlier facing behind the flue lining; its phasing is unknown as the masonry was not dismantled.

The floor of the Phase III building was cut even further down than that of the Phase I structure: it had a maximum depth in the centre of 0.90m below the level of the

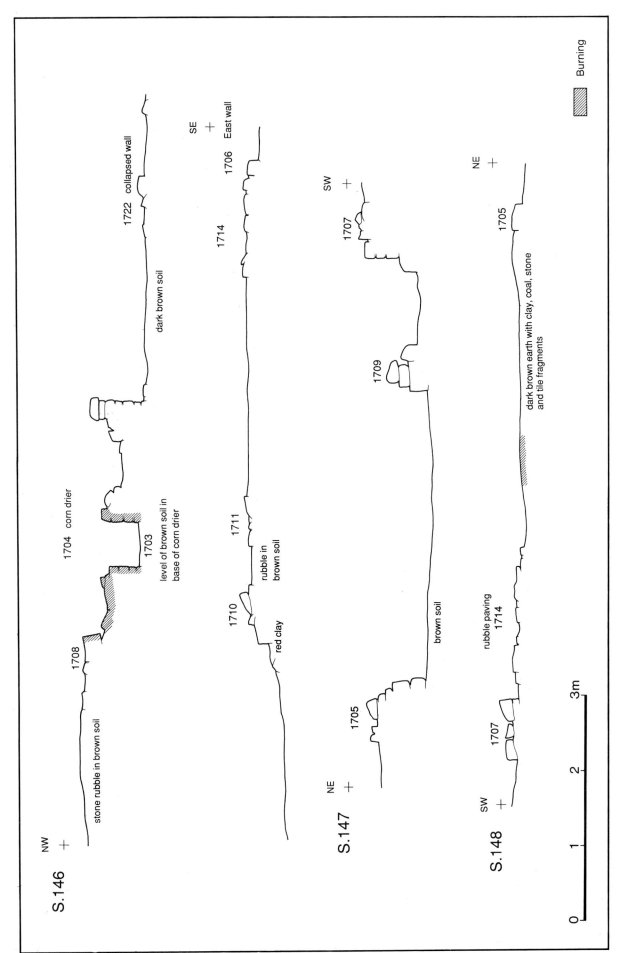

S.146

NW +

stone rubble in brown soil

1708

1704 corn drier

1703

level of brown soil in
base of corn drier

1710

1711

rubble in
brown soil

red clay

1722 collapsed wall

dark brown soil

SE +

East wall

1714

1706

S.147

NE +

1705

SW +

1707

1709

brown soil

S.148

SW +

1707

rubble paving
1714

NE +

1705

dark brown earth with clay, coal, stone
and tile fragments

Burning

0   1   2   3m

Fig. 60. Structure Q: sections.

66

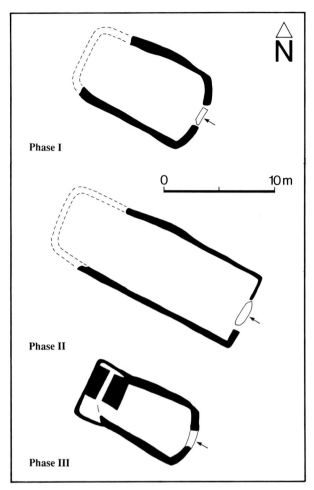

Fig. 61. Phase plans of Structure Q.

surrounding bedrock (Fig. 60, S.146 and S.147). A large part of the floor area was covered by a thin spread of heat-reddened clay (1702).

Structure Q should probably be identified with building G recorded by Procter:

> a large square of foundations (G) formed of the best worked stone that was met with, measuring 10 by 18 yards, was excavated: the west wall of which is marked strongly with fire and displays some remains of a fire-place. The floor had been covered with that coarse kind of pavement called *Ruderatio*, formed by embedding refuse pieces of tiles and stones in a structure of mortar. (Procter 1855, 273)

There was no sign of an *opus signinum* floor in the recent excavations.

The various sunken-floor areas and the kiln flues were filled with homogeneous layers of brown soil (1701, 1703 and 1715). These contained such building debris as dressed stonework, iron nails, roof and flue tiles, *tesserae* and fragments of painted plaster, with several quern fragments and 3rd to 4th-century pottery. Above was a brown ploughsoil layer (1700), of maximum depth *c.* 0.15m. At the mouth of the kiln, some 0.74m below the level of the surrounding bedrock, were found two fragments of clay pipe stem (SF 1555), confirming that

this part of the structure had been disturbed either for stone robbing or during the course of the 1854 excavations.

Structure Q was clearly an ancillary building rather than a dwelling. Its situation, orientation, shape and (in Phase III) size invite the comparison with Structure P. The only internal structure was the T-shaped kiln of (modified) Phase III, but all phases showed signs of burning. In Phase II, at least, there seems to have been a tiled roof, rather than a combustible covering. Fragments of several querns were discovered (Chapter 10, Nos 28, 47, 56 and 64), another point of comparison with Structure P.

The constructional details of the two buildings were also similar. The north wall of Structure Q (used in all phases) changed markedly in construction at context 1722. Walls 1707 and 1709 showed distinct changes in width and alignment directly opposite 1722. There may have been posts and a principal roof truss in this position, dividing Phases I and III into two bays and perhaps marking one of two or three bay divisions in the larger Phase II structure. The clear reuse of the north wall in all three phases and of the first south wall in Phase II, combined with the longitudinal symmetry of Phases I and (unmodified) III, indicate that Structure Q was a single building modified substantially at various times, and not three separate buildings on the same site. Such modifications would have been easier to achieve if the roof had been supported by vertical posts, rather than by the extant stone walls.

Structure R (Figs 62-3)

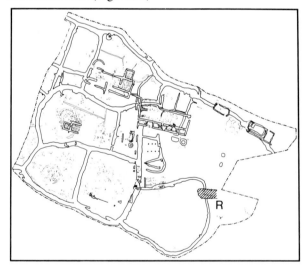

Fig. 62. Location of Structure R.

Structure R lay in the south-eastern corner of the villa complex and overlay enclosure ditch 024-025. The building consisted of a shallow depression, roughly oval in plan, cut into the bedrock to a maximum depth of 0.25m, and aligned east-west. Its overall dimensions were *c.* 11.50 by 7.25m. A number of post-holes were disposed around the perimeter, and the interior contained traces of crude gritstone paving overlying several rock-cut slots, each of which displayed signs of severe burning (Pl. XXIII). Plough damage was evident on many of the

Pl. XXIII. Structure R, facing west; during excavation. (Photo: S. Wager)

paving slabs, as well as on the surrounding bedrock. Moreover, the cratered condition of the bedrock over the entire area made the exact identification of rock-cut features difficult; this was especially true of many of the possible post-holes.

Around the perimeter of the building were ten holes (1804-8, 1816-17, 1819, 1824 and 1830). Of these, only 1804-5, 1816 and 1819 had undoubtedly contained posts. The holes displayed little uniformity of shape or size, having irregular oval or circular plans, varying in diameter from 0.24-0.65m, and having U-shaped or flat-based profiles from 0.08m-0.39m deep. All were filled with homogeneous brown soil; 1804 contained heavy gritstone and limestone packing. Post-holes 1804, 1817 and 1819 each produced sherds of 4th-century pottery, that from 1817 cross-matching with sherds from levels 1812 and 1815 (Chapter 15, No. 57).

In addition to the perimeter post-holes, four others were located within the building (1818, 1822, 1829 and 1831). These displayed a similar variety of shape and size to those of the perimeter, and were again filled with homogeneous brown soil.

At the northern end of Structure R there was a large sub-rectangular pit (1821), measuring 1.40 by 0.81m. It had a maximum depth of 0.56m, and had a homogeneous brown fill with small gritstone and sandstone inclusions. The pit contained fragments of tile and several sherds of 2nd to early 3rd-century pottery. Along the eastern side of the building, aligned north-south, was shallow slot 1823. This was 1.40m long, varied in width from 0.37-0.50m, and had a maximum depth at the north of 0.11m. It again contained brown soil.

The remaining internal features of the building consisted of a series of slots cut into the bedrock and overlain in places by paved area 1814 (Fig. 63, S.150). All were filled with black ashy material and had undergone severe burning on their sides and base; all had a regular U-shaped cross-section. Slots 1809, 1810 and 1820 were aligned approximately east-west along the central axis of the building. The westernmost of these (1820) was 2.08m long and varied in width from 0.32-0.50m. The maximum depth of slot 1820 was 0.53m at the eastern end, where it appeared to take a slight northward turn; it contained several fragments of roof tile. Slot 1810, overlying Ditch 024-025 in the centre of the building, was 2.66m long and slightly bulbous in plan, being 0.29m wide at the western end and widening to 0.54m to the east. Its maximum depth, at the eastern end, was 0.21m, and it again produced fragments of roof tile. The easternmost of the three (1809) was of comparable length (2.70m), varied in width from 0.40-0.44m, and had a maximum depth of 0.40m at the western end. It contained several fragments of roof tile.

Further slots were situated at the south-east corner of the building. Slot 1826 ran northwards to join 1809. It was 1.06m long and tapered from 0.34m wide at the north to 0.16m at the south. The maximum depth at the northern end was 0.26m. Slot 1827 ran parallel to, and east of 1826. It was 1.78m long and slightly bulbous in plan, being 0.36m wide to the south and 0.58m to the north. The maximum depth was 0.25m at the southern end. Slot 1827 produced a single *tessera*. Finally, a possible east-west slot (1828) connected 1826 and 1827. It was *c*. 1m long and 0.40m wide, with a maximum depth to the west of 0.13m.

Above and between these slots several areas of the floor (mainly towards the eastern end) were crudely paved with large roughly dressed gritstone and limestone slabs (1814). Some of these showed traces of burning around the edges. Two of the gritstone slabs (Chapter 20, No. 27) had deep grooves on their undersides; they were parts of a reused threshold stone from a cart entrance. Crambeck and Huntcliff sherds were recovered from the thin layer of

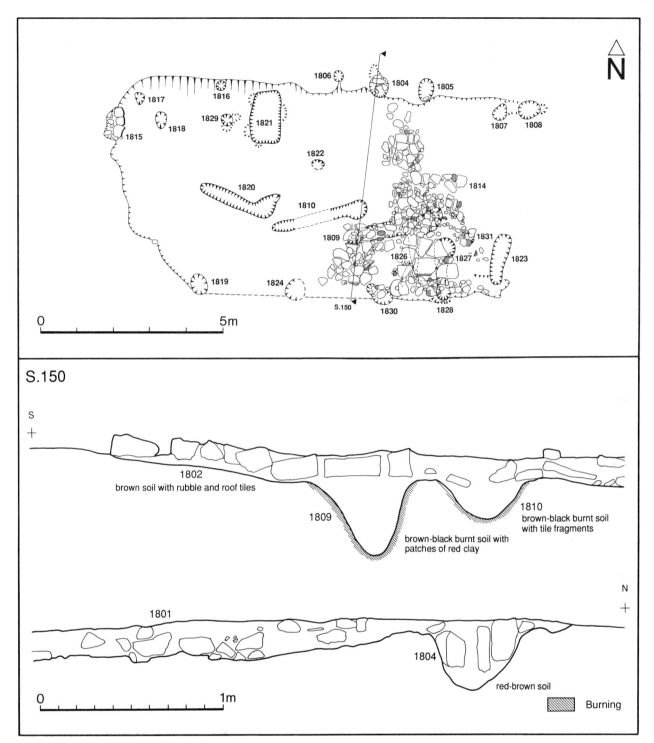

Fig. 63. Structure R: plan and sections.

brown soil (1825) in which the paving was bedded. The slabs overlay several of the slots.

The unpaved areas of the building were again filled with a homogeneous brown soil layer (1815) containing building rubble, a column fragment (Chapter 19, No. 6) and a quernstone (Chapter 10, uncatalogued). A further general level of brown soil, numbered as 1801-3 and 1811-13 (representing arbitrary horizontal divisions) reached a maximum depth of *c.* 0.15m. This layer contained building rubble (dressed stone, mortar, roof and flue tile, and *tesserae*), and was overlain by a general

brown ploughsoil level (1800), which was up to 0.10m deep.

Structure R seems to have been post-built, and the south-east corner timbers may have been set in trenches. The three slots 1809, 1810 and 1820, with their burnt sides, bases and ashy fills were perhaps flues for ovens or kilns; as the easternmost of the three underlay paving 1814, the slots may have been successive rather than contemporary features. The occurrence of roofing tiles in the slot fills suggests a non-combustible covering. The structure, which was partially terraced into the sloping bedrock, was probably used for crop-processing; similar in general function to the other sunken-floored buildings.

Minor structures (Figs 64-7)

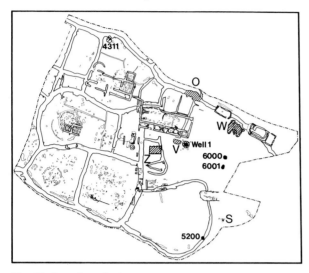

Fig. 64. Location of minor structures.

In addition to the major buildings described above, a number of minor structures and features can be assigned to the villa phase of occupation.

Structure O (Figs 64 and 67)
This was an oval depression, measuring about 8 by 5m and up to 0.25m deep. It had been cut into Ditch 030-034. Like Structures P and Q, which were also cut into this ditch, it was first visible as a spread of rubble; unlike them, it failed to emerge as a coherent building, having been almost completely levelled by the plough.

At the base of the hollow, a slot (1502) had been cut partly into bedrock and partly into the fill of Ditch 030-034. It was *c.* 1.50 by 0.40m, and was *c.* 0.25m deep. Its sides were heavily burnt and its black ashy fill contained Crambeck ware sherds. It was reminiscent of the slots in Structure R. The hollow was filled above this level with a medium brown soil (1501), which produced building debris and 3rd to 4th-century pottery. The ploughsoil (1500) overlying this contained much more building debris.

Structure V (8201) (Figs 64-5)
On the west side of Well 1 was another 'sunken-floored' structure. It was sub-rectangular, measuring 4.30 by 2.30m, and was flat bottomed (Fig. 65, S.183). There were three main filling layers. The lowest (C) was a dark grey soil with building rubble and pieces of tile. Above this, layer B was recorded as a pale brown soil containing pottery, tile and painted plaster. Both layers C and B had been tipped into the eastern end of the structure; above and to the west, layer A was similar to layer C. These characteristics suggested that the filling of Structure V was a single operation, rather than a gradual silting and accumulation.

There was nothing to indicate the function of this structure (there were no oven flues, for example); nor was any walling recorded along the edges. The filling contained no less that nine barbarous coins (Chapter 4, Nos 72, 74, 78-9, 81 and 84-7) of the 3rd and 4th centuries.

Structure S (Figs 64-5)
A small group of features was found to the east of Enclosure III. It comprised several post-holes (1903-6), an oval pit (1902) and a stone-lined oven flue (1907) set in another pit (1901; Fig. 65, S.175). The dressed, burnt stone of the oven was clearly Roman in date, as was the tile packing of post-hole 1906. Otherwise, there was nothing to suggest a date, or to indicate which, if any, of these features were associated with one another.

Structure 4311 (Figs 64 and 66)
A sub-square pit (4311) had been cut into the southern edge of Ditch 014. It measured 3 by 3m, and was about 0.23m deep (Fig. 66, S.978). The north-east corner contained a square stone-lined feature (4317) formed by vertical gritstone slabs founded at a lower level (Fig. 66, S.979; Pl. XXIV). Its fill was a mixture of coal and slag. Similar material surrounded the stones, filling the hollow in which they were set. Two adjacent post- or stake-holes were filled with coal; structural remains (4319) in the south-east corner of the hollow consisted of a series of larger stones set in brown soil. To the east of these, a second oval hollow (4312) contained lumps of slag (Fig. 66, S.981).

The presence of slag, coal and hammer scale indicates that these structures were associated with smithying. It has been suggested that the stone setting was the packing for an anvil base; if so, it is interesting that the base was a squared timber.

Pl. XXIV. Structure 4311, facing south; after excavation. (Photo: S. Wager)

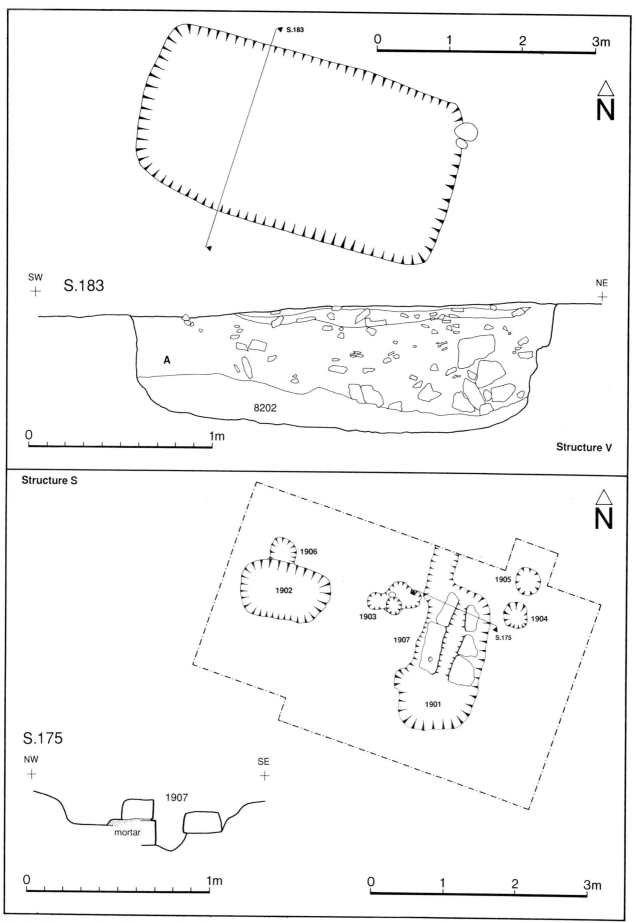

S.183

SW

NE

A

8202

Structure V

Structure S

S.175

NW

SE

1907

mortar

1906

1902

1903

1905

1904

1907

S.175

1901

Fig. 65. Structures V and S: plans and sections.

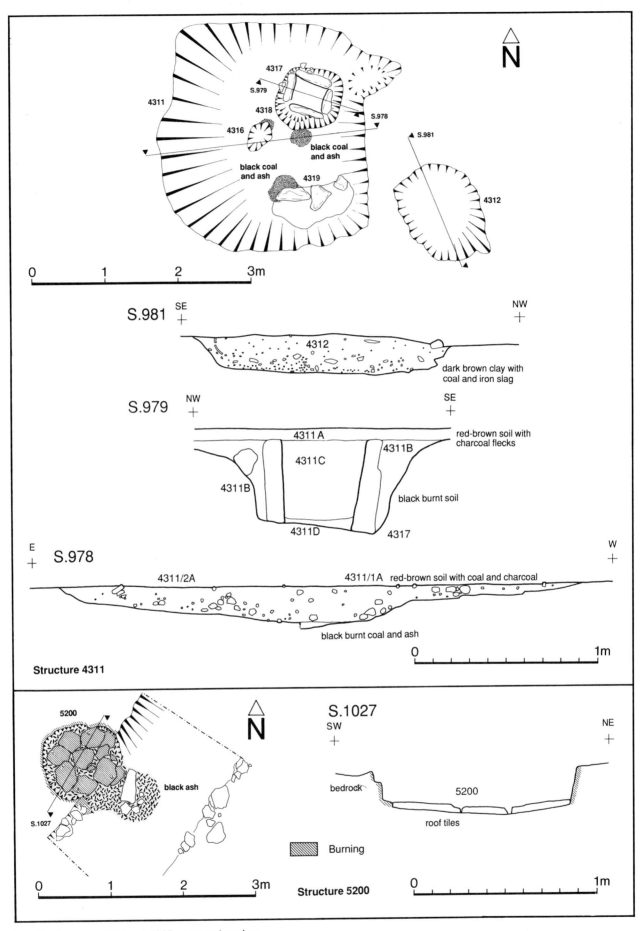

Fig. 66. Structures 4311 and 5200: plans and sections.

Structure Z (4801-8) (Figs 64 and 67)

South of the aisled building (Structure M) were eight uniform post-holes which clearly represented a single structure. It measured 6.40 by 4.30m, and consisted of three bays. It may have been an open-sided agricultural building, though ploughing could easily have obliterated less deeply cut wall-trenches. The structure is undated, but post-hole 4808 was cut into the filling of Ditch 042. It was probably a villa outbuilding.

Structure 5200 (Figs 64 and 66)

A circular oven base was found on the south-east periphery of Enclosure III. It was positioned so that the stoke-hole occupied the line of Ditch 024, presumably taking advantage of a depression in the surface of the ditch fill. The oven itself was cut into the bedrock side of the ditch, and was paved with sandstone roofing tiles (Fig. 66, S.1027; Pl. XXV).

Pl. XXV. Oven 5200 (south-east corner of Enclosure III) with base of roofing slabs. (Photo: S. Wager)

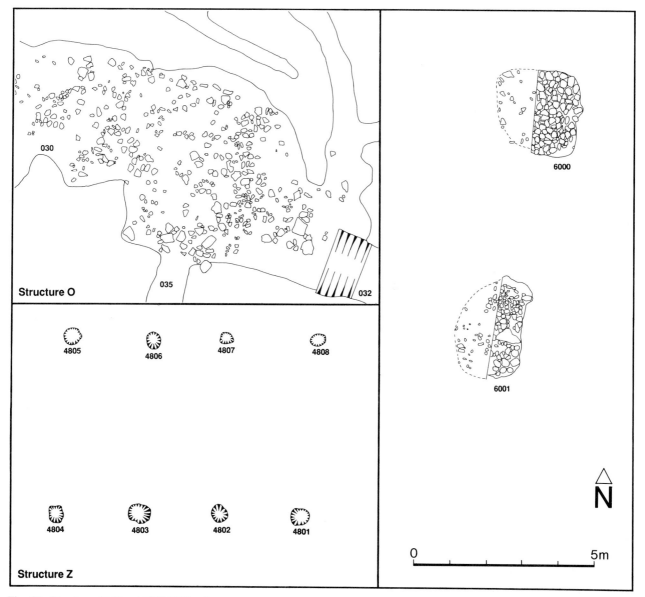

Fig. 67. Structures O, Z and 6000/6001: plans.

Structures 6000/6001 (Figs 64 and 67)

Outside the enclosed areas, to the north-east of Enclosure III, were a pair of irregular oval-shaped pits, about 3.30m apart. They were clearly associated features: both had fills of gritstone cobbles set in a reddish-yellow clay matrix. Neither was fully excavated; their date and function are unknown.

Structure W (Fig. 64)

A group of pits and gullies, located between Structures P and Q, should probably be assigned to the villa period. Its surface indication – an area of dark earth and rubble – was similar to that of the neighbouring structures. The relationships of several intercutting features are unclear, and their function is unknown; but the presence of burnt soil in a pit (6509) and a gully (8301) may signify another oven and flue.

Well 1 (5500) (Fig. 64)

The well at the south-east corner of Structure M, and its contents, are described in Part Four of this report (pp. 195-272).

Part Two
The Artefacts (mainly excluding Well 1)

(In the catalogues which follow, illustrated items are marked by an asterisk after the catalogue number.)

4 The Coins

by E.J.E. Pirie, with some identifications

by H.B. Mattingly

Introduction

The following list, with its commentary, is based only on those coins recovered during excavations by the West Yorkshire Archaeology Unit. It is perhaps necessary to put on record the fact that surface finds of coins have been made over a period of many years, principally by people living in the Wetherby area.

Summary of Coin List

Severan (pre-200)		3
Severan (post-200)		2
Radiate (early)		9
Radiate (Gallic)		9
Radiate (British)		1
Radiate (barbarous)		12
Diocletian		1
Constantinian (pre-324)		3
Constantinian (324-46/8)		19
Constantinian (barbarous)		1
Constantinian (346/8-50)		2
Constantinian (barbarous)		22
Magnentius		2
Valentinianic		1
	Total	**87**

Length of the Roman occupation

Perhaps surprisingly on a site which has produced evidence of early Iron Age activity, there is a complete dearth of numismatic material from the 1st and 2nd centuries AD. The earliest pieces, Severan, from the end of the 2nd century (of which there are only five, including the only true silver on site) need not have been new when they were lost, though their date matches that for the earliest pottery.

The first sign of the coins reflecting intensive activity (rather than initial settlement) on the site comes with the radiate *antoniniani*, when the total for Gallienus and Claudius is equalled by that for issues from the Gallic empire, and each group is smaller than that of the barbarous 'Tetrican' radiates which linger on until about AD 284 or until Carausius started issuing coins in Britain, AD 287-93.

The coins are sparse again at the turn of the century, and remain so until the years following AD 330: the coinage of 330-346/8 is represented by twenty specimens. Unusually, this peak is in effect a plateau since there is no noticeable decline in coin loss during the next few years: the later Constantinian *Fel Temp Reparatio* issues are represented by two regular specimens and no less than 22 imitations which, taken with two coins of Magnentius, must reflect continued vigorous occupation until perhaps as late as AD 367. By that time the smallest counterfeits must have ceased when coins of Valentinian were in full circulation (Boon 1974a). After that there is no gradual tailing off, only a rather abrupt and, in relation to other sites, early end, since there is only one specimen (and that, rather indeterminate) to represent the Valentinianic coinage.

It would seem from the coin record that the Roman site was occupied effectively for little more than a century: from the time of Gallienus, *c.* AD 260, to just after the late Constantinian period, *c.* AD 370.

Some comparative sites

A rather limited survey has been attempted in order to bring the site's coins into focus alongside a few other such records. The fort at Malton, North Yorkshire (Corder 1930), of course, has a much longer history, having been established earlier, and retaining some form of activity until as late as AD 395. Yet, for the overlapping phases, although it has some expected differences (because of the type of site), it has some unexpected factors. A comparatively small number (21) of Severan issues is about four times that which has been found at Dalton Parlours; percentages are about the same: 4.92% of Malton's total (5.76% of the comparative phases) and 5.74% at the villa. The 3rd-century radiates and the Constantinian issues of the following century are, however, not in the same proportion: 157 radiates (of which 44 are barbarous) bear no such comparison with the 31 from the villa, especially when twelve of the latter group are barbarous. In percentage terms, the Malton figure is 36.85% of the fort's coinage, 43.13% of the coins representing the life-span of the domestic site. The villa's figure is 35.63% of its total coin loss; considered separately, the barbarous radiates form 13.79% of the site's numismatic evidence.

Unlike Dalton Parlours, the fort at Malton has no mention of Diocletian in its record. The first phase of Constantinian occupation is reflected by 130 coins at the

75

fort, 23 at the villa; this is, comparatively, 30.5% of the total (35.7% of the overlap) for Malton and 26.43% for Dalton Parlours. The second phase (*Fel Temp Reparatio*) yields 52 specimens (of which seven are barbarous) from the fort and 24 (of which 22 are barbarous) from the villa. Percentages can be quoted as 12.2%/14.28% for the former, 27.58% for the latter; again, the villa shows a remarkably high result for its barbarous coins of the period, since these groups are alike in each having two coins of Magnentius, although more might have been expected at Malton. Valentinianic issues at the fort are more numerous: 3.7% of the total, 4.3% of the overlapping phases.

Comparison with the villas at Langton, North Yorkshire (Corder and Kirk 1932) and at Winterton, Humberside (Stead 1976) shows first what one might expect: that coin losses at domestic sites are far fewer than at military bases. Both Langton and Winterton were active longer than Dalton Parlours, starting earlier and finishing later. Site totals (of specimens recovered during excavation) are 105 for the former, 101 for the latter; figures for the periods covered by Dalton Parlours are 69 and 89 respectively; that for Winterton is remarkably similar to the total at the West Yorkshire villa. Yet the rate of coin loss, period by period, differs throughout in most particulars. Severan activity at both Langton and Winterton seems slight: a single coin has been recovered from Langton (1.44% of 69); three from Winterton (3.3% of 89). Late 2nd-century occupation is represented by twelve radiates (17.39%) at the first site, 27 (30.33%) at the second; in these groups, Langton has four barbarous specimens, Winterton five. First-phase Constantinian occupation seems reasonably vigorous at each place: 29 coins (42.02%) at Langton, 32 (35.9%) at Winterton. However, both sites dwindle at the beginning of the second half of the 4th century, showing only five coins each (7.24% and 5.6% respectively). They both then reach another peak with the Valentinianic coinage: 22 specimens (31.88%) from Langton, 20 (22.47%) at Winterton.

In relation to the coinage patterns determined by Alison Ravetz (1964) as a reflection of inflation in the 4th century, Malton conforms to pattern A, since it peaks in the coinage of AD 330-346/8 (Ravetz, group III). Perhaps oddly for a site nearby, Langton is of pattern C, peaking in the same group III, Constantinian issues, as well as in the Valentinianic (group V) and Theodosian (group VII) coinage. Although it is near Brough and Old Winteringham, both in Humberside (recognised as pattern A sites), Curnow (1976) identifies Winterton as marginally that of pattern B, since it peaks in groups III and V.

As far as one can judge, Dalton Parlours conforms to no such pattern, not only because the Roman occupation terminates earlier than it does at the other sites, but because it is apparently alone in having such a high number of *Fel Temp Reparatio* coins (Ravetz, group IV) in relation to those of the other periods. Even if one were to allocate the smallest of the counterfeits to the

Valentinianic group V (allowing for their having been produced as late as AD 367), the picture would not alter appreciably.

Individual coins

Only two coins need to marked out for comment: the first, for what it is; the second, for its relationship to the site. First is the coin purporting to be a *denarius* of Julia Maesa (No. 5, Pl. XXVI). Both hoards and site finds of the period are known to include specimens of contemporary hybridisation and forgery. The first category involves the muling of two regular dies in unauthorised combinations. The second category is usually that of straight copying of official dies in styles that are in various degrees less than perfect, to produce what is in effect a duplicate of an official coin. The *denarius* of Maesa is neither a hybrid nor a normal forgery. Apart from the fact that the piece is made up of a base-metal core dipped in silver, and the style, particularly of the obverse legend, leaves much to be desired, the choice of reverse type must place it in a category of its own; the figure of Pax, with the legend PAX AVGVSTI, is not known for *denarii* of the period and must have been concocted for the occasion rather than copied from a genuine coin in the Severan range.

The *follis* of Diocletian (No. 29) is the second coin. Neither Langton nor Winterton, with their small site totals, includes a specimen from this reign. Ravetz remarks on the circumstance that such records are of too few coins for them to produce examples of the missing issues in their normal proportions. Yet the much larger record from Malton also shows the absence of coins of Diocletian. It is a great pity that, when such an item has been found at Dalton Parlours, it cannot be related to any of the structures.

Coin catalogue

The items are recorded by period of issue. The mint is Rome, unless otherwise stated. Numbers 70-87 were identified by Professor H.B. Mattingly. It has been thought best to keep the two sets of identifications separate. This leads, however, to a slight maladjustment in the longer section; quite apart from the single coin of Carausius going before the slightly earlier barbarous radiates, the single coin from the period AD 364-78 has been placed before rather than after the register of barbarous pieces, the majority of which may properly belong to AD 350-60 (although the smallest may be as late as AD 367). The following abbreviations are used:

BMC: *Coins of the Roman Empire in the British Museum:* Vol. V by Mattingly, 1950; Vol. VI by Carson, 1962
LRBC: *Late Roman Bronze Coinage I and II by Carson, Hill and Kent, 1965*
RIC: *Roman Imperial Coinage:* Vols I-V edited by Mattingly and Sydenham, 1923-49; Vols VI-VII edited by Sutherland and. Carson, 1966-73; (Vol. V by Webb, 1962; Vol. VI by Sutherland, 1967; Vol. VII by Bruun, 1966)

Pl. XXVI. Plated *denarius* of Julia Maesa, *c.* AD 225-50 (No. 5). (Photo: P. Gwilliam) Scale 2:1

Pl. XXVII. *Follis* of Constantinus Caesar; minted at Trier, AD 322 (No. 31). (Photo: P. Gwilliam) Scale 2:1

1 Septimius Severus: sole reign; *denarius*; AD 196.
Rev.: Minerva with spear and shield. Legends worn by oxidisation: IMP VII or VIII; cf. *BMC* 134 and 139. *212 (Structure B); SF 319*

2 Caracalla, as Caesar; *denarius*; AD 196-8.
Obv.: M AVR ANTON CAES PONTIF; Rev.: [IMPERIIF] ELICITAS, Felicitas with child and caduceus; *BMC* (Septimius) 199-200. *5500M (Well 1: 14.5-15.5m); SF 1751*

3 Septimius Severus: joint reign (with Caracalla); *denarius* (?base AR); AD 198-200.
Rev.: Emperor on horseback, right. Legends worn or off flan; ?*Profectio* type; cf. *BMC* 134. *4900B (Structure M); SF 1250*

4 Severus Alexander; *denarius*; AD 230.
Rev.: V [IRTVS] AVG, Virtus seated left, on cuirass, with spear and branch. Wear, particularly on rev., caused by heavy oxidisation; *BMC* 653-7. *5500M (Well 1: 15.5-16.2m); SF 1878*

5 Julia Maesa, sister-in-law of Septimius Severus; *denarius*; *c.* AD 225-50.
Obv.: IVLIA MAESA AVG, bust facing right; Rev.: PAX AVGVSTI, Pax standing, with branch and sceptre. Type unrecorded for the period; 'plated' forgery. *Ditch 014/1A; SF 1956;*
Plate XXVI

6 Gallienus: joint reign (with Valerian I); *antoninianus*; AD 253-60.
Rev.: Felicitas, with caduceus and cornucopiae; *RIC* 134-5. *5500H (Well 1: 1.6m); SF 1257*

7 Gallienus: sole reign; *antoninianus*; AD 260-68.
Rev.: AETERN [ITAS AVG], Sol holding globe; *RIC* 160. *Ditch 002/9A; SF 1951*

8 Gallienus: sole reign; *antoninianus*; AD 260-68.
Rev.: A[POLLONI] CONS AVG, animal to right; identity uncertain – ?poorly struck Pegasus; mint-mark: N; cf. *RIC* 166-7. *603 (Structure F); SF 1674*

9 Gallienus: sole reign; *antoninianus*; AD 260-68.
Reverse mis-struck and uncertain; *RIC* ?. *222 (Structure B); SF 459*

10 Gallienus: sole reign; *antoninianus*, very worn; AD 260-68.
Possibly Pax on reverse; *RIC* ?. *001; SF 83*

11 ?Gallienus; *antoninianus*, (fragment); AD 260-68.
Obv.: ?[AL]...; Rev.: ?Fides with standard; cf. *RIC* 192a (sole reign). *001; SF 452*

12 Claudius II (head in style of Milan mint): posthumous; *antoninianus*; struck after AD 270.
Obv.: legend off flan; Rev.: CON [SECRATIO], lighted altar; *RIC* 261. *200 (Structure B); SF 101*

13 Claudius II: posthumous; *antoninianus*; struck after AD 270.
Obv.: DIVO CLA [VDIO]; Rev.: CONS [ECRATIO], eagle; mint-mark uncertain; *RIC* 265-6. *1602 (Structure P); SF 1467*

14 *Antoninianus* fragment, unidentifiable. *001; SF 658*

Gallic Empire
(The coins of the Tetrici may be from a southern mint.)
15 Victorinus; *antoninianus*; AD 268-70.
Rev.: Salus feeding serpent in her arms. ?Cologne mint (detail of obverse legend is uncertain); cf. *RIC* 122. *1602 (Structure P); SF 1469*

16 Tetricus I; *antoninianus*; AD 270-73.
Rev.: H[ILARITA]SAVGG, Hilaritas with palm and cornucopiae; cf. *RIC* 79-81. *600 (Structure F); SF 436*

17 Tetricus I; *antoninianus*; AD 270-73.
Rev.: Laetitia; detail uncertain; cf. *RIC* 86-8. *600 (Structure F); SF 437*

18 Tetricus I; *antoninianus*; AD 270-73.
Rev.: Pax with olive branch and sceptre; *RIC* 100. *1200 (Structure M); SF 762*

19 Tetricus I; *antoninianus*; AD 270-73.
Rev.: Pax with olive branch and sceptre; *RIC* 100. *603 (Structure F); SF 513*

20 Tetricus II; *antoninianus*; AD 270-73.
Rev.: [PIETAS AVG...], sacrificial implements; cf. *RIC* 254-9. *001; SF 661*

21 Tetricus II; *antoninianus*, worn and chipped; AD 270-73.
Rev. is all but illegible, but most probably shows the Pietas figure. *1701 (Structure Q); SF 1493*

22 Tetricus II; *antoninianus*; AD 270-73.
Rev.: COME[S AVG], Minerva with laurel branch and shield. Variety not in *RIC* but cf. 224-6 (the style seems too good for attribution as barbarous). *001 (surface find); SF 211*

23 Tetricus II; *antoninianus*; AD 270-73, or barbarous and later.
Rev.: ?Pax; cf. *RIC* 247. *001; SF 664*

British Empire
24 Carausius; *antoninianus*; AD 287-93.
Rev.: Pax; mint-mark uncertain (because of poor striking) – possibly MC for mint of Camulodunum (Colchester); style, particularly of obverse, quite distinctive; cf. *RIC* VII, pl. XVIII, nos 2-3. *3491; SF 668*

Barbarous radiates (uncertain 'mints')
(see also 70-77)
25 'Tetricus'; *c.* AD 273 and later.
Obv.: CTVETRIC[....; Rev.: I[.....]V[., Spes (cartoon figure). *1200 (Structure M); SF 773*

26 Cartoon head; *c.* AD 273 and later.
Obv.: ...]FIICΛI[; Rev.: indeterminate female figure, headless (head is off the sub-rectangular flan) – traces of 'lick-and-a-promise' legend. *Surface find, near Compton Grove Farm; SF 1954*

27 Cartoon head (to left) dominated by radiate crown; *c.* AD 273 and later.
Rev.: tiny female figure within wreath, off-centre of oval flan. No legends. *3413; SF 456*

28 Very worn oval flan with ghost of radiate head, but no reverse detail; *c.* AD 273 and later. *001 (surface find); SF 2*

77

Later bronze or billon issues: a) Pre-AD 324

29 Diocletian; *follis* (fractional); *c.* AD 297-8.
Rev.: VOT XX, in wreath; *RIC* VI, Rome 79, *officina* H. *001; SF 80*

30 Crispus Caesar; *follis*; AD 318.
Rev.: SOLI INVICTO COMITI, Sol holding globe; *RIC* VII, London 143, *officina* P. *001 (surface find); SF 4*

31 Constantinus Caesar; *follis*; AD 322.
Rev.: BEATA TRANQVILITAS, altar inscribed VO/TIS/XX; *RIC* VII, Trier 352, *officina* P. The coin's condition is as new. *204 (Structure B); SF 233; **Plate XXVII***

32 Constantine I; *follis*; AD 323-4.
Rev.: SARMATIA DEVICTA, Victory and captive; *RIC* VII, Trier 435, *officina* P. *1300 (Structure M); SF 404*

Later bronze or billon issues: b) Post-AD 324

(see also 78-79)

i AD 324-30
No specimens.

ii AD 330-35

33 *Constantinopolis.*
Rev.: Victory on prow; Trier, *LRBC* 59, *officina* P. *300 (Structure B); SF 98*

34 Constantinus Caesar; *Gloria Exercitus.*
Rev.: soldiers with two standards; Trier, *LRBC* 63, *officina* P. *1800 (Structure R); SF 385*

35 *Constantinopolis.*
Rev.: Victory on prow; Lyons, *LRBC* 185, *officina* P. *1001 (Structure J); SF 733*

36 Constans Caesar; *Gloria Exercitus.*
Rev.: soldiers with two standards; Arles, *LRBC* 381, *officina* S. *001; SF 9*

37 *Urbs Roma.*
Rev.: Wolf and Twins. Extremely worn, and mint detail uncertain; *LRBC* ?. *001; SF 659*

iiia AD 335-7
No certain specimens.

iiib AD 337-41

38 Constantius II; *Gloria Exercitus.*
Rev.: soldiers with one standard; Trier, *LRBC* 126, *officina* P. *1300 (Structure M); SF 421*

39 Constans; *Gloria Exercitus.*
Rev.: soldiers with one standard; Trier, *LRBC* 131, *officina* P. *200 (Structure B); SF 79*

40 *Gloria Exercitus* (one standard).
Uncertain issuer and mint. *001; SF 662*

41 *Gloria Exercitus* (one standard).
Uncertain issuer and mint. *200 (Structure B); SF 82*

42 *Gloria Exercitus* (one standard).
Uncertain issuer and mint. *001; SF 292*

43 *Gloria Exercitus* (one standard).
Uncertain issuer and mint. *001; SF 464*

44 *?Gloria Exercitus* (one standard).
Uncertain issuer and mint. *001; SF 663*

45 *Virtus* (VIRTVS AVGGNN).
Uncertain issuer and mint. *1809 (Structure R); SF 1340*

iv AD 341-346/8

46 Constantius II; *Victoriae.*
Rev.: two Victories; Trier, *LRBC* 141, *officina* P. *3493; SF 674*

47 Constans; *Victoriae.*
Rev.: two Victories; Trier, *LRBC* 149, *officina* S. The coin's condition is as new. *5500L (Well 1: 14-14.5m); SF 1441*

48 Constans; *Victoriae.*
Rev.: two Victories; Arles, *LRBC* 456, *officina* S. *1300 (Structure M); SF 400*

49 Constans; *Victoriae.*
Rev.: two Victories; mint detail uncertain. *8000 (Structure M); SF 784*

50 *Victoria.*
Rev.: Victory, advancing left; issuer and mint uncertain. *1300 (Structure M); SF 401*

51 Unidentifiable: fabric of the period, but worn to illegibility. *216 (Structure B); SF 294*

v Post-AD 346/8

52 Constans; *Fel Temp Reparatio* (AD 346/8-50).
Rev.: Emperor and Victory in galley; Trier, *LRBC* II 41, *officina* uncertain. *8104 (Structure M); SF 1128*

53 Constantius II; *Fel Temp Reparatio* (AD 346/8-50).
Rev.: Virtus spearing fallen (sitting) horseman; Trier, *LRBC* II 47, *officina* P. *8001 (Structure M); SF 1695*

54 Magnentius; *Victoriae* (AD 351-3).
Rev.: two Victories, with shield inscribed VOT/V/MVLT/X (no column); Trier, *LRBC* II 60, *officina* P. *001; SF 24*

55 Magnentius; *Salus* (AD 351-3).
Rev.: Chi-Rho monogram, flanked by Alpha and Omega (no wreath); mint detail off flan; *LRBC* II? *903 (Structure J); SF 335*

56 *Securitas Reipublicae* (AD 364-78).
Rev.: Victory, to left, with wreath and palm; issuer uncertain (Valens, Gratian, Valentinian I or II); Arles, *LRBC* II? *8104 (Structure M); SF 1126*

Barbarous copies of *Fel Temp Reparatio* (uncertain 'mints')

(see also 79-87)

a) Medium flan

57 Obv.: large bust; no recognisable legend; Rev.: Emperor on horseback, left; single captive facing him. ?Contemporary imitation. *001; SF 3*

58 Obv.: small bust; legend indecipherable; Rev.: falling horseman type. ?Contemporary imitation. *8102 (Structure M); SF 1185*

59 Obv.: small bust and attempt at legend; border of pellets; Rev.: falling horseman type, in cartoon style, with recognisable]REPARA[TIO of legend; linear border but no exergue. The flan is slightly oval. ?Contemporary imitation. *8010 (Structure M); SF 1264*

60 Obv.: large bust, and attempt at normal legend; Rev.: falling horseman type. The style is cramped and heavy on a fairly thick flan. *001; SF 1301*

61 Obv.: large bust, and some attempt at legend, of which only the end appears; Rev.: falling horseman type, with parts of nonsense legend, within border (?of blurred pellets). *1803 (Structure R); SF 465*

62 Obv.: crude bust and trace of legend behind head; Rev.: outline of falling horseman type, with exaggerated exergual space and nonsense mint signature: CPIC. *8104 (Structure M); SF 1199*

63 Obv.: cartoon bust and attempt at legend; Rev.: falling horseman type and attempt at legend. *001; SF 660*

64 Obv.: cartoon bust; Rev.: falling horseman type and attempt at legend, in chunky, cartoon style. *8104 (Structure M); SF 1115*

65 Obv.: cartoon bust and attempt at legend; Rev.: falling horseman type in cartoon style, within border of pellets (blurred); struck off-centre. *8010 (Structure M); SF 1263*

66 Obv.: cartoon bust and attempt at legend; Rev.: falling horseman type in cartoon style, with attempt at legend. The flan is oval, and detail, particularly on the obverse, is worn. *3420/3; SF 709*

b) Small flan

67 Obv.: small head with miniature legend:]CONT[... ; Rev.: sketch of falling horseman type with legend in miniature. *8102 (Structure M); SF 1187*

68 Obv.: cartoon head, no legend; Rev.: part only of falling horseman type – fallen horseman, in close-up. *8201/4A (Structure V); SF 1260*

69 Obv.: cartoon head and end of legend; Rev.: part of falling horseman type and legend. The dies seem to have been too big for the flan. *1400 (Structure M); SF 785*

Further barbarous coins (small flan)

70 Claudius II.
?Rev.: *Virtus Augg*, ?left. Barbarous radiate minim (12mm). *1813 (Structure R); SF 540*

71 Tetricus II (*c*. AD 284).
Rev.: *Pietas Augg* (decorative). Barbarous radiate minim (8mm). *303 (Structure B); SF 593*

72 Tetricus II.
?Rev.: uncertain female figure. Barbarous radiate minim (9mm). *8201/4A (Structure V); SF 1261*

73 'Tetrican' (*c*. AD 284).
Rev.: *Fides Exercitus*. Barbarous radiate minim (7mm). *Ditch 021/2A; SF 1971*

74 Uncertain obverse; Rev.: ?*Providentia Augg*. Barbarous radiate minim (10mm). *8201/6B (Structure V); SF 1248*

75 Uncertain obverse; Rev.: ?female figure. Barbarous radiate minim (9mm). *8104 (Structure M); SF 1107*

76 Thickish barbarous radiate minim (11mm). Detail very unclear – especially of reverse type. *8104 (Structure M); SF 1200*

77 'Billon' barbarous radiate minim (11mm); *c*. AD 284. Uncertain reverse. *8104 (Structure M); SF 1108*

78 Obv.: ?diademed head; Rev.: *Gloria Exercitus* (2 soldiers)? AE 4 (9mm). *8200 (Structure V); SF 922*

79 Obv.: 'Constantius' head; Rev.: *Gloria Exercitus* or *Fel Temp Reparatio* (falling horseman)? AE 4 (10mm). *8200 (Structure V); SF 1088*

80 Obv.: good 'Constantius' head; Rev.: *Fel Temp Reparatio* (falling horseman). AE 4 (10mm). *8000 (Structure M); SF 806*

81 Obv.: neat little 'Constantius' bust; Rev.: neat *Fel Temp Reparatio* (falling horseman). AE 4 (7mm). *8200 (Structure V); SF 929*

82 Obv.: Constantius II type head; Rev.: *Fel Temp Reparatio* (falling horseman)? AE 4 (10mm). *8000 (Structure M); SF 805*

83 House of Constantine.
Rev.: *Fel Temp Reparatio* (falling horseman). AE 4 (9mm). *1300 (Structure M); SF 394*

84 Obv.: head almost gone; Rev.: *Fel Temp Reparatio* (falling horseman). AE 4 (9mm). *8200 (Structure V); SF 920*

85 Obv.: part of diademed head; Rev.: *Fel Temp Reparatio* (falling horseman)? AE 4 (9mm). *8200 (Structure V); SF 921*

86 Obv.: ?diademed head; Rev.: *Fel Temp Reparatio* (falling horseman)? AE 4 (8mm). *8200 (Structure V); SF 928*

87 Obv.: uncertain head; Rev.: *Fel Temp Reparatio* (falling horseman)? AE 4 (8mm). *8200 (Structure V); SF 1085*

5 Silver and Copper-Alloy Objects (other than brooches) (Figs 68-73)

by H.E.M. Cool

Introduction

During the excavations 6 silver (Nos 1-6) and 53 copper-alloy (Nos 7-59) objects of certain or probable Roman date were recovered, in addition to about 90 fragments of rings, rods, sheet, etc. which are not closely datable. Less than a third of this material was found in stratified contexts which, being mainly ditch fills or destruction deposits, are of relatively little use in helping

to date objects more precisely. In this assemblage the types of objects which can be relatively closely dated are late Roman. The only object which is typologically likely to have been connected with the Iron Age occupation on the site is the spiral finger-ring (No. 7). With so much undatable material, however, the possibility that some fragments of rod or sheet may have been in use at that time cannot be ruled out; fragments of an annular and a penannular ring (Nos 64 and 67), for example, fall into this category as they were found in contexts probably dating to the Iron Age.

In its overall composition the assemblage is comparable with those that have been recovered from villa sites such as Rudston (Stead 1980, 99-103) and Winterton (Stead 1976, 202-15), both in Humberside, in that personal ornaments, toilet implements, fittings for furniture, etc. are well represented. Most of the objects found are common, widespread forms but there are certain noteworthy features about the assemblage. One is the relatively high proportion of silver to copper-alloy personal ornaments (4:9, Nos 1-4 and 7-15), and another is the unique copper-alloy candlestick (No. 30, Pl. XXVIII). Five objects of military equipment may also be identified (Nos 25-9) possibly suggesting some form of military presence in the 3rd century.

The personal ornaments

Number 7 is a spiral finger (or toe) ring. This type has a long history stretching from the Bronze Age into the Anglo-Saxon period. They were the commonest type of finger-ring in use during the Iron Age but are relatively uncommon on Roman sites (Cool 1983, 224-5, finger-ring group II). They have, however, been found in 4th-century graves at Lankhills, Winchester, Hampshire (Clarke 1979, 318, fig. 80, no. 250) and Poundbury, Dorchester, Dorset (unpublished). The context No. 7 was found in is not helpful for determining its date. In such circumstances it could be associated either with the Iron Age or the late Roman activity on the site, but is perhaps more likely to belong to the former.

Silver finger-ring No. 2 is also a type with antecedents in the Iron Age. It is an expanding wire ring whose ends have been twisted into a rosette to form a bezel. Although copper-alloy rings of this form are not infrequent finds (Cool 1983, 221-4, finger-ring sub-group IC), they have rarely been found in dated contexts. One with a double rosette was found in one dated to *c*. AD 49-55 at Balkerne Lane, Colchester, Essex (Crummy 1983, 47, fig. 50, no. 1756) and an example from Rudston with a single rosette was found in a ditch fill that post-dated the end of the 2nd century (Stead 1980, 17, 99, fig. 63, no. 28). Number 2 was found in a context from Structure Y (the levelling layer for Structure M) that may be of early 4th-century date and it is quite likely that this form of finger-ring continued in use into the 4th century.

Rings with constricted shoulders like the silver example No. 1 were a relatively common form in use during the 2nd and 3rd centuries (Cool 1983, 249-53, finger-ring sub-group XIIIA). Number 1 may be more closely dated to the 3rd century because of the type of moulded glass intaglio it contains (see separate report in catalogue by Dr Henig).

Number 8, from a level in Well 1 dated to the mid to late 4th century, belongs to a range of light trinket finger-rings in use during the 3rd and 4th centuries (Cool 1983, 273-5, finger-ring group XXII). It is not common for these to have separately soldered on bezels like No. 8 but other examples with this feature are known at Caerwent, Gwent and Stockton, Wiltshire (Cool 1983, 1127, no. 10; 1132, no. 41).

Bracelets are the most numerous type of personal ornament represented in this assemblage. There is one example of a cable twist bracelet (No. 9) which was the commonest type of copper-alloy bracelet in use in Roman Britain from the later 1st to the 4th century (Cool 1983, bracelet group I). Simple examples like No. 9 cannot be more closely dated within this period. There are also two examples (Nos 10 and 11) of the type of light bangle which was very common during the 4th century (Cool 1983, 152-81). These were decorated with a variety of different patterns and both the ones seen at Dalton Parlours (No. 10 ring and dot: Cool 1983, bracelet sub-group XXVB; No. 11 simple zig-zag: Cool 1983, bracelet sub-group XXIIA) are common ones, especially the simple zig-zag of No. 11. Number 13 may also originally have been from a bracelet of this general variety. It has been bent into a small ring with the two ends held together by a small strip soldered onto the interior. It is decorated with an incised zig-zag, a pattern that is one of the relatively rare ones used on these bracelets. Though it is not uncommon to find broken lengths of light bangles bent into smaller rings presumably for reuse as finger-rings, as may have happened to No. 12, the degree of care taken with No. 13 is unusual.

The short length of torc-twisted rod (No. 12) probably also came from a bracelet which, from the expansion at one end, probably had a hook-and-eye terminal like one found at Lankhills, Winchester, in a grave dated to c. AD 350-70 (Clarke 1979, 304, fig. 85, no. 442). Torc-twisted bracelets (Cool 1983, 135-8, bracelet group IV) were primarily in use during the late 3rd and 4th centuries.

Number 3 consists of a D-sectioned kinked bar broken at one end and tapering to a point at the other. The upper surface is cross-hatched. This may tentatively be identified as the tail of a spiral snake bracelet. Most frequently these have straight tails as on the golden pair in the treasure from Boscoreale buried by the eruption of Vesuvius in AD 79 (Baratte 1986, 49), but ones with tails kinked in a manner very similar to No. 3 are also known (Marshall 1911, 325, nos 2780-81). In both cases the scales of the snake are frequently indicated by cross-hatched lines. Spiral snake bracelets (Cool 1983, 151, bracelet group XII) are not common finds from Roman Britain and those that have been found all differ markedly in precise details and could have been in use at different times. Number 3 may perhaps have come from a

3rd-century example as it was found in an early 4th-century pit fill.

The only hairpin that can definitely be identified is No. 4 which has a cubic head decorated with diamond and triangle facets. Faceted-head pins were one of the two commonest 4th-century pin types and came into use during the late 3rd century (Cool 1983, 81, hairpin group XVII). It is possible that No. 15 was also a hairpin. The basic head type consisting of curved mouldings between sets of narrow ribs is one which occurs on a large and varied group of hair pins in use from the 1st to 3rd centuries (Cool 1983, 51-4, hairpin group III). The perforated expansion below the head, however, is most unusual and No. 15 may have been some form of needle instead, though again it is unusual to have needles with such ornate heads.

It is interesting to note that four of the personal ornaments, finger-rings Nos 1, 8 and ?14, and bracelet No. 10, were found in the silts towards the bottom of the well. These are precisely the type of ornaments that are most at risk from casual loss while drawing water and it is presumably this type of loss that is represented here rather than that of someone's trinket box.

Toilet implements

The two pairs of plain sheet tweezers (Nos 16 and 17) are examples of a very common and widespread type which appear to have been in use throughout the Roman period. We may note, for example, ones from Cirencester, Gloucestershire, in a sealing layer where virtually all of the samian pottery was of Neronian or early Flavian date (Viner 1982a, 93, fig. 26, no. 25); in a demolition deposit relating to occupation of c. AD 200-275/300 at Lion Walk, Colchester (Crummy 1983, 59, fig. 63, no. 1882); and in a late 4th-century context at Canterbury, Kent (Jenkins 1952, 128, fig. 6, no. 4). It is not possible, therefore, to date tweezers of this sort closely within the Roman period, although No. 16 is likely to be of 4th-century date from its position in the well.

Another toilet implement is probably represented by No. 18 which was found unstratified. It is cast with a cable pattern down one side. Both ends are broken but it could originally have been a small scoop from a chatelaine. It is not closely paralleled and cannot be closely dated.

Spoons and vessels

The presence of metal vessels is attested by the rim fragments of Nos 22 and 23 which are probably from bowls rather than jugs though they are too small for the types represented to be identified. Number 24 has been tentatively identified as coming from a skillet. The handle is, however, only 1mm thick and this would be very thin for such a vessel although a skillet handle from Doncaster appears to be only 2mm thick (Lloyd-Morgan 1986, 85, fig. 19, no. 3).

A slight downward expansion at the broken end of No. 19 suggests it may have come from a spoon but the type cannot be identified. Numbers 20 and 21 may also be parts of spoon handles but could as easily be from the shanks of pins, needles or medical implements. It is unfortunate that No. 20 is so undiagnostic as it is one of the few fragments to come from a securely stratified early context (the ditch below the aisled Structure M).

Military equipment

The belt plate and buckle loop (No. 25) found in the deliberate infill of Well 1 is a most interesting object. The loop is a reused penannular brooch, lacking its pin, which has diagonally grooved terminals. It is not possible to see whether it is an example of a type A4 brooch with a rib between the terminals and the hoop (Fowler 1960, 152; see for example Allason-Jones 1983, 112, fig. 71, no. 52) or whether it was one of type A2 without the rib (Fowler 1960, 152; see for example Allason-Jones and Miket 1984, 110, nos 113-14) as the belt plate is made of a rectangle of repoussé decorated sheet folded to enclose them. It is probable that the 'buckle' did not have a tongue as there is no point of articulation for it between the terminals.

Penannular brooches of types A2 and A4 were a common form and cannot be closely dated within the Roman period. Sheet belt plates with repoussé decoration similar to that of No. 25, by contrast, appear to be relatively rare. Two with more conventional oval buckles have been found in mid-4th-century contexts. One came from the Alchester Road suburb at Towcester, Northamptonshire (Brown and Woodfield 1983, 106, fig. 38, no. 7), and the other with a damaged belt plate was found in a grave dated to AD 350-370/90 on horizontal stratigraphy at Lankhills cemetery, Winchester (Clarke 1979, 273, fig. 34, no. 126). Other examples from Ospringe, Kent (Whiting *et al.* 1931, pl. LVII, fig. 3), Richborough, Kent (Wilson 1968, 94, no. 107, pl. XXXV), Woodyates, Dorset (Pitt-Rivers 1892, 139, fig. 2, pl. CLXXXIV) and Colchester, Essex (Hull 1958, 118, fig. 47, no. 8) are undated. The evidence thus suggests that these repoussé belt plates were in use during the early to mid-4th century.

The openwork mount No. 26, by contrast, belongs to a common range of harness fittings with curvilinear openwork patterns, such as the heart-shaped pendants studied by Oldenstein (1977, 127-30, 246-7, nos 217-27, Taf. 31). This style was in use during the later 2nd and 3rd centuries. In Britain we may note, for example, part of a mount pierced for attachment like No. 26 found in a layer dated to the Hadrianic/Antonine period at the amphitheatre, Caerleon, Gwent (Wheeler and Wheeler 1928, 169, fig. 1, no. 6, pl. XXXIII), and a heart-shaped pendant from Vindolanda, Northumbria, found with mid-3rd-century material (Allason-Jones *et al.* 1985, 119, fig. 40, no. 16).

Hexagonal harness mounts such as No. 27 are primarily a 3rd-century form though they came into use during the late 2nd century (Oldenstein 1977, 139, 248, nos 267-72, Taf. 34). In Britain they are normally found on military sites, see for example ones from Brancaster, Norfolk (Green and Gregory 1985, 209, fig. 89, no. 38) and South Shields, Tyne and Wear (Allason-Jones and Miket 1984, 237, no. 3, 870-71), though they are sometimes found on sites which appear to lack such a presence such as Colchester, Essex (Allason-Jones and Miket 1984, 237, note to no. 3, 870).

Number 28 is a tie loop used to help fasten the plates of a *lorica segmentata* together (Brewer 1986, 175, fig. 57, nos 29-31; 184, fig. 61, no. 148). Its shank shows the characteristic burring to one side caused when it was fastened into the iron plate. Several of these have been found in later 2nd and 3rd-century contexts at Caerleon (Brewer 1986, 175) and, as is to be expected, they are common on military sites; see for example those noted in connection with the ones from South Shields (Allason-Jones and Miket 1984, 206-7, fig. 206, nos 689-93).

Number 29 may be tentatively identified as a *lorica squamata* scale. One long side is broken so a pair of perforations may be missing. It measures 37 by 24mm which would be large for such a scale, but it is clear that they were made in a variety of sizes with different patterns of lacing. In a group of 30 from a late 3rd-century context at the legionary baths at Caerleon, each scale measures 16 by 11mm and has pairs of vertically arranged perforations in the centre of the top and both sides (Brewer 1986, 186, fig. 62, no. 155), while ones from a Flavian context in the amphitheatre of the same fort are larger (24 by 14mm) and have all three pairs of perforations placed in the upper part of the scale, the ones on the upper edge horizontally and those on the sides vertically (Wheeler and Wheeler 1928, 166, no. 29, fig. 14). Ones found in a well in the *principia* at Newstead, Scotland (Curle 1911, 138, fig. 12, pl. XXIV) also have all the perforations at the top of the scale, a large central perforation with a pair of vertical perforations on each long side. Others from Malton, North Yorkshire (Mitchelson 1966, 253, fig. 19, no. 24) have a pair of vertical perforations placed in the centre of each of the four sides. It is at present unknown to what extent these differences have a chronological significance, but given this variation, it seems reasonable to include No. 29 as a possible piece of military equipment despite its large size.

As will now be clear three of the objects included in this section, Nos 26-8, are definitely pieces of military equipment and one, No. 29, may also be. The status of the belt plate No. 25 is more equivocal. In the early Roman period belt fittings were almost exclusively the preserve of the military, but by the 4th century they may also have been used by some civilian officials. It will be observed in this case that several of the sites which have produced similar repoussé belt plates are not ones with an obvious military presence. The date of No. 25 also seems to be later than that of the other military pieces. Whether the number and variety of objects indicates an official military presence at Dalton Parlours, or casual losses by soldiers on their way to another destination is open to question. Whatever the nature of the event that led to the presence of Nos 26-8 and possibly also to that of No. 29, it is likely to have taken place in the 3rd century and to have been concentrated in the area of the aisled Structure M, where three of the pieces (Nos 26, 28 and 29) were found.

Furniture, fixture and fittings

The outstanding copper-alloy object from the excavations is undoubtedly the candlestick, No. 30 (Pl. XXVIII). It consists of a flower-like drip pan, a tripod stand and a shallow cylindrical base supported by three feet in the shape of stylised dolphins and is made up from many different elements. Most of these are cast but some are made of sheet. The base now contains a heavily corroded mass that must be the remains of some material like lead which would have given stability to the piece. An iron rod runs through the centre of the vertical axis. This seems to have been an integral part of the original design as its upper end forms the pricket and it also serves to keep the different elements tightly joined together. The candlestick has been constructed in a most complex manner, but the workmanship is not always very competent. An additional piece had to be wedged between the tripod and base at one point, for example, so that the latter would be level. At some point the dolphin feet have been damaged and repairs using iron have been made.

The candlestick was found in a hollow that appeared to be natural in origin, perhaps the result of tree disturbance, and its context thus gives no indication of its date. Apart from being found on a site occupied in the 3rd and 4th centuries, a Roman date is strongly suggested for this piece because of the dolphin feet. These clearly belong to the long established Roman tradition of using zoomorphic cast feet on both furniture and smaller items such as chests and lamp stands (Henig 1970, 182). A small cast foot, variously interpreted as representing a goat, antelope or panther, was found in the bed of the Walbrook at Tokenhouse Yard, London (Henig 1970, 185, no. 6, pl. XXVIII). It has projections at the back of the head very similar to those on the dolphin feet of the candlestick which support the base. The Tokenhouse Yard foot is very likely to be of 1st or 2nd-century date as finds from the bed of the Walbrook generally pre-date the mid-2nd century.

A group of small copper-alloy candlesticks on display in the Mittelrheinische Landesmuseum in Mainz, Germany also have tripod zoomorphic feet. They are much smaller and less complex than No. 30, consisting of a small cup-shaped drip pan and three tall feet. Not all need have been candlesticks, but one certainly was as the pricket is still clearly visible.

Roman candlesticks made of copper alloy are extremely rare. In Britain the only others known to me are ones found at Caerleon, Gwent and Branston, Lincolnshire. The one from Caerleon was found in a deposit dating to the 2nd century at the Prysg Field barracks (Nash-Williams 1932, 85, fig. 34, no. 43). It consists of a cylinder supported by three plain feet and is very similar to the much commoner iron candlestick form (Viner 1982b, C04, fig. 40, nos 122-3). The one from

Branston (Moore 1974) is a much larger and more elaborate piece consisting of a lily-shaped drip pan, a cylindrical body with expanded base and, originally, three feet with panther heads at the top and five-toed bases. The original context is unknown as it was found in a potato harvesting machine, but unworn coins of Constantine II (AD 337-41 and 335-7) were found lodged by the pricket. Neither of these is similar to the Dalton Parlours candlestick although the one from Branston does share the use of zoomorphic feet with it.

It has been suggested (Moore 1974, 212) that the Branston candlestick was intended for use in conjunction with some form of stand, perhaps like the one from Flixborough, Humberside (Henig 1970, 185, no. 5, pl. XXVI). The Dalton Parlours candlestick undoubtedly must have stood on some form of base or stand as the small pegs at the bottom of the dolphins were clearly intended to fit into sockets. The type of the stand might have been a low one similar to the Flixborough example or perhaps a taller one like the candelabra found, for example, at Pompeii (Ward-Perkins and Claridge 1979, no. 141a), although these normally supported oil lamps. The presence of such candelabras has been suggested in Britain by finds from London (Wheeler 1930, 59) and possibly Shakenoak, Oxfordshire (Henig 1970, 187, no. 13).

It is impossible to date objects as rare and unparalleled as the Dalton Parlours candlestick by analogy to other objects. A late Roman date would seem to be implied by the general period of occupation on the site, but the possibility that it may already have been old when it arrived at Dalton Parlours cannot be ruled out. A long life for the object is certainly implied by the iron repairs that were made to the foot.

The Dalton Parlours candlestick is a most important addition to our knowledge of the lighting furniture available in Roman Britain, standing alongside such finds as the Branston candlestick and the copper-alloy hanging lamp from London (Lowther 1936, 205, pl. XXXV) as an example of the, perhaps unappreciated, range that was in use.

Another unusual find is the cast openwork plate No. 33. This has a perforation in each corner and the metal surrounding the perforations on the upper face has been left rough. This is in marked contrast to the rest of the surfaces which show careful finishing. The irregularities around the corner perforations must have been left because they would have been hidden by the heads of studs or nails used to fix No. 33 in position. Although it is clear that it must have been attached to something, its purpose is obscure. It could have been used as a decorative mount for furniture or a casket. It is, however, more substantial than such decorative mounts normally are: see, for example, the fittings from a casket found at Butt Road, Colchester, Essex, in a grave dated to the period after AD 320 (Crummy 1983, 85, figs. 90-91, nos 2171-98). A possible, more likely use is as a grill. It was found in a pit that also contained complete 4th-century pottery vessels and the bolts Nos 37-9.

It is tempting to see objects like Nos 30 and 33 as being indicative of a high status site because of their rarity. This may, however, be misleading: their apparent rarity may simply be the result of numerous similar objects being remelted for scrap during antiquity. Artefacts like Nos 30 and 33 with large amounts of metal in them must always have been more at risk of such a fate at the end of their useful lives than those with small amounts such as brooches and personal ornaments. The larger objects are also far less likely to enter the archaeological record through casual loss by their users. On both counts, therefore, larger objects are far less likely to survive than smaller ones, making it difficult for a true picture of their level of use to emerge.

Two lever lock keys were also found. Number 31 has a copper-alloy handle and an iron key. Such keys more commonly have handles with three lobes (Crummy 1983, 126, fig. 142, no. 4161) than the simple ring handle used here. Number 32 is also slightly unusual in that the upper end of the stem is smoothly finished and the handle, if the key had one, would have been made from a separate piece. Small lever lock keys for caskets similar to No. 32 are not uncommon finds on late Romano-British sites (see for example Wheeler 1930, 74, pl. XXXI, nos 1-6).

The other finds in this section call for little special comment as they are the common range of terminals, mounts, studs, etc., that are not closely datable but which are found on most Roman sites in large numbers. Noteworthy is the presence of seven sheet clips (Nos 51-7). These are a typical example of the type of copper-alloy find which is frequent but which has only recently started to be included in the published records of the site (see, for example, Gadebridge Park, Hertfordshire: Neal and Butcher 1974, 135, nos 104-6; Whitton, South Glamorgan: Webster 1981, 187, nos 99-100; Cirencester, Gloucestershire: Viner 1982b, C02, fig. 56, no. 78).

Catalogue

Silver (Fig. 68)
Personal ornaments
1* Finger-ring. Oval box bezel with chipped edges; constricted junction with D-sectioned shoulder tapering towards hoop. Back of hoop and other shoulder missing. Moulded glass intaglio, now loose, of dark yellow/brown glass appearing black with blue/green glass down one edge. Schematised figure holding ?spear and ?shield. Box bezel dimensions 14 x 12mm; depth 5mm; intaglio dimensions 8 x 6.5 x 1.5mm. *5500 (Well 1, sieving); SF 1829*

Report on the intaglio by M. Henig
The ring contains an intaglio of black glass depicting a male figure holding a ?spear and ?shield. The type was produced in Britain in a variety of coloured glasses. Most examples are from south of a line running from the Wash to the Bristol Channel (cf. Henig 1978, 255, nos 543 and 552) and this seems to be a northern outlier (Henig 1978, 132, fig. 2 for distribution), although a bronze stamp, perhaps used for producing intaglios of this sort, has been found near Brough-on-Humber (Henig 1984a).

2* Finger-ring. Rectangular-sectioned, widest to finger strip, tapering to circular-sectioned wire at either end. Ends of wire spiral around each other to form a central rosette, each free end is wrapped around hoop on opposite side 6½ times. Now broken into two pieces and bent out of shape. Circumference of ring *c.* 80mm; original diam. *c.* 25mm; hoop section 2.5 x 1mm. *1222/1 (Structure Y); SF 1853*

3* Terminal of spiral or penannular snake bracelet? Kinked D-sectioned tail tapering to point; upper convex surface decorated with cross-hatched grooves. L. 40mm; section (max.) 4 x 2mm. *8201 (Structure V); SF 1249*

4* Hairpin. Cube head with diamond and triangle faceting; circular-sectioned shank with slightly faceted point. L. 48mm; head section 4mm; shank section 1.5mm. *001; SF 234*

Miscellaneous
5 Disc. Part of white metal disc with very uneven surfaces. One extant edge folded back on itself. Dimensions 26 x 25mm; th. 1mm. *5500L (Well 1); SF 1433*

6 Disc. ?Silver gilt. Part of slightly convexo-concave disc; concentric polishing marks on underside. Dimensions 12 x 8mm; th. >0.5mm. *001; SF 624*

Copper alloy
Personal ornaments (Figs 68-9)
7* Finger-ring. Oval-sectioned wire with pointed ends bent into spiral ring of 1½ turns. Diam. 17 x 15mm; section 1.5 x 1mm. *2802; SF 544*

8* Finger-ring. Circular-sectioned wire with bevelled flattened ends bent into a closed penannular ring; flat bezel plate soldered over ends of wire. Edges of plate cut to resemble two small discs either side of a large one, each 'disc' has central punched ring and dot. One end of hoop now free and ring bent out of shape. Circumference *c.* 56mm; original diam. *c.* 20mm; hoop section 1mm. *5500L (Well 1); SF 1430*

9* Cable twist bracelet. Three circular-sectioned wire strands loosely twisted together with right-hand twist; one end broken with four fragments now detached; other end has one strand finishing before terminal and two other twisted strands forming an elongated loop with one strand twisting around hoop 1½ times to fasten it. Broken end of bracelet passes through loop. Diam. of hoop 50 x 43mm; hoop section 1.5mm. *001; SF 560*

10* Ring and dot bracelet. Rectangular-sectioned hoop with rounded edges, widest to wrist; hook-and-eye terminal with rounded eye terminal. Eye perforation surrounded by four grooves arranged in a diamond and has a pair of edge nicks separating it from hoop; central row of punched ring and dots around hoop. Now bent out of shape. Circumference 186mm; original diam. *c.* 60mm; hoop section 5 x 1mm. *5500L (Well 1); SF 1500*

11* Zig-zag bracelet. Rectangular-sectioned, narrowest to wrist hoop; both ends broken. Upper surface decorated with edge nicks forming a simple zig-zag pattern. Straightened. L. 27mm; section 3 x 1.5mm. *1604 (Structure P); SF 1523*

12* ?Torc-twisted bracelet. Rectangular-sectioned torc-twisted hoop; both ends broken, one expanding toward terminal. L. 46mm; section 2 x 1.5mm. *903 (Structure J); SF 766*

13* ?Bracelet. Rectangular-sectioned, widest to wrist hoop; one end broken, other thinning to straight-ended terminal. One groove parallel to each edge producing three ribs. Now bent into small ring with overlapping ends. Diam. 23 x 18mm; hoop section 5 x 1mm. *001; SF 441*

14* Bracelet or ring. Brass-coloured alloy. Rectangular-sectioned, widest to wrist hoop with straight ends bent into a penannular ring; small fragment of sheet soldered below one end, probably also originally soldered below other end to join both together to form a closed ring. Upper surface decorated with diagonal grooves in a zig-zag pattern, a punched circle in each triangle formed by zig-zag. Diam. 22.5 x 21mm; section 4 x 1mm. *5500M (Well 1); SF 1676*

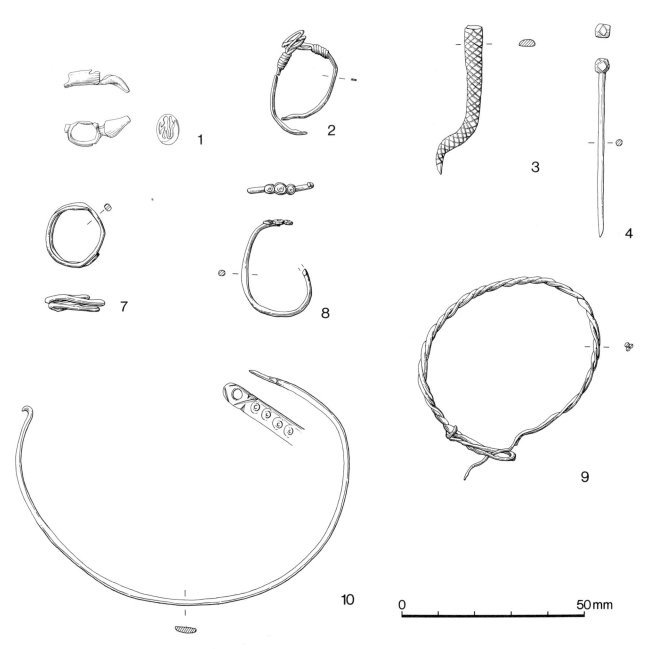

Fig. 68. Silver (Nos 1-4) and copper-alloy objects (Nos 7-10). Scale 1:1

15* Pin. Circular-sectioned. Squashed spherical finial with diagonal notches around sides; two ovoid mouldings separated from each other, finial and shank by groups of two or three narrow ribs. Rectangular-sectioned, diamond-shaped perforated expansion at top of circular-sectioned shank which tapers to point over lower part. L. 118mm; head section 3.5mm; shank section 2.5mm. *1213/3 (Structure M); SF 1370*

Toilet implements (Fig. 69)

16* Tweezers. Rectangular-sectioned strip bent in half to form tweezers with loop at top and straight-ended, inwardly curved jaws. L. 45mm; section 4 x 1mm. *5500L (Well 1); SF 1516*

17* Tweezers. Description as No. 16. L. 48mm; section 4 x 1mm. *901 (Structure J); SF 334*

18* Scoop. Circular-sectioned shank with cast concave, diagonal channels down front to produce effect of right-hand cable or torc-twist; both ends thin to rectangular section and are broken, one end probably part of a scoop. L. 53mm; shank section 2mm. *001; SF 390*

?Spoons (Fig. 69)

19* ?Spoon handle. Circular-sectioned handle tapering to point at end, other end broken across a slight downward expansion. L. 81mm; section 3mm. *1220 (Structure Y); SF 1116*

20 Spoon handle or pin/needle shank. Oval-sectioned shank; one end broken, other tapering to blunt point. L. 35mm; section 2.5 x 2mm. *Ditch 031/2A; SF 801*

21 Spoon handle or pin/needle shank. Description as No. 20. L. 32mm; section 2mm. *001; SF 376*

Vessels (Fig. 69)

22* Vessel. Two rim and one crumpled body fragments. Rim has internal angular bead. Polishing marks on interior of rim. Present ht of rim fragments 9 x 6mm; rim th. 5mm. *3222; SF 1733*

23* Vessel. One rim fragment with internal angular bead. Small patch of metal riveted on immediately below rim edge, shank of rivet visible on interior but not on exterior. Present ht *c.* 10mm; rim th. 4.5mm. *001; SF 629*

24* ?Skillet handle. Part of flat handle and rim of vessel; rim and handle edges thickened. Rough hammering marks parallel to edges on underside of handle. Now crumpled and bent out of shape with one

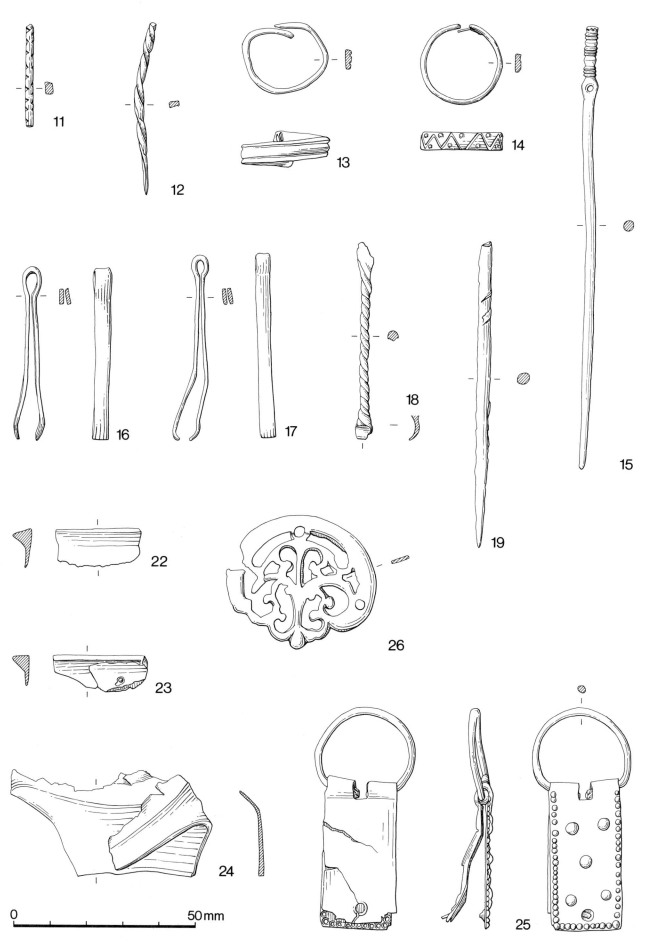

Fig. 69. Copper-alloy objects (Nos 11-19 and 22-6). Scale 1:1

small fragment detached. Handle section 33 x 1mm. *1000 (Structure J); SF 356*

Military equipment (Figs 69-70)

25* Belt plate. Rectangular-sectioned rectangular strip with central rectangular perforation. Half of strip decorated with five repoussé bosses arranged in quincunx with a border of smaller bosses down one short end and along the two sides. Strip bent in half enclosing the terminals of the penannular brooch which acts as a 'buckle loop'. Central perforation through both thicknesses of strip at end opposite loop, perforation in upper decorated part retaining shank of rivet. Penannular brooch has circular-sectioned hoop with blunt-ended spherical terminals decorated with diagonal grooves. Plate dimensions 39 x 20mm; brooch diam. *c.* 28mm; brooch hoop section 2mm. *5500J (Well 1); SF 1331*

26* Openwork mount. Rectangular-sectioned, approximately oval plate with curved outer edges. Openwork decoration with bevelled edges to cut-outs in some places; decoration is symmetrical about short axis and consists of curving scroll patterns either side of a central spine. Outer frame broken on one side with small fragment missing. Small circular perforation centrally at upper end of central spine, a similar perforation in outer frame at side and a third perforation approximately opposite the second may have been in missing fragment. Polishing marks on back. Original dimensions *c.* 41 x 35mm; th. 1mm. *5605/2A; SF 1452*

27* Hexagonal harness mount. Elongated hexagonal mount with central oval hollow boss, narrow indentation down centre of boss. Two short sub-circular sectioned shanks with disc terminals on underside, these cast in one with rest of mount. Upper face, underside of flange and terminals polished, underside of boss rough and shank sides show irregular finishing marks. Dimensions 31 x 20mm; diam. of terminals 7mm. *001; SF 622*

28* Tie loop. Cast spade-shaped block with central perforation; rectangular-sectioned shank slightly burred to one side at end. Polishing marks. Dimensions 21 x 16mm; shank section 7 x 3mm. *1422 (Structure M); SF 1873*

29* ?*Lorica squamata* scale. Elongated D-shaped sheet with one upper corner and majority of one long edge missing. Two circular perforations on extant long side and four circular perforations arranged in a square slightly off-centre on straight narrow side. Some polishing marks on front. Dimensions 37 x 24mm; th. 0.5mm. *5605; SF 1844*

Furniture fixtures and fittings (Figs 70-72)

30* Candlestick. Composite made from ten copper-alloy pieces and one of iron. Description from top to bottom as follows:

(i) Cast copper-alloy cylindrical drip pan. Upper part concave-sided and crown/flower-shaped terminating with alternate short rounded and long pointed projections each with a small knob finial. Short elements having a crescentic cut-out. The two extant long elements are curved out and down, outer parts appear to have been made separately and joined by hammering as junctions are visible at a level equivalent to the upper edge of the short units. The third long element is also broken at this point. Lower part of drip pan concave sided and split in places.

(ii) Shallow cylindrical copper-alloy pan inserted into bottom of (i) and forming its base.

(iii) Cast copper-alloy tripod consisting of a disc with three long legs attached to underside of (ii). Legs have a pointed oval section with their outer faces and outer edge of disc diagonally channelled.

(iv) Flat cast copper-alloy plate in shape of concave-sided equilateral triangle with hemispherical knob finials with facet marks from hammering at points. Legs of (iii) joined to (iv) just inside finials and channelling on legs continues onto edge of (iv).

(v) Thin flat copper-alloy disc with three squared projections between (iv) and (vi) with a small wedge-shaped piece of copper alloy inserted between bottom of (iv) and top of (v) under one of legs probably to even the level.

(vi) Narrow copper-alloy collar split in places below (v).

(vii), (viii) and (ix) Three cast dolphin feet with heads attached to (vi) at point opposite to junctions of (iii) and (iv) One retains a projection from the head which fitted below (vi); this dolphin also has a cylindrical peg which projects between tail and ventral fin. On another this has been replaced by an iron peg and on the third dolphin part of the peg remains but the back part and the tail are broken off and missing.

(x) A faceted iron spindle passes through the centre of all the other parts and may have been expanded at its base as the underside of the collar (vi) is filled with iron corrosion products. Upper part of this spindle now broken just above base of pan (ii) but may originally have formed the pricket for a candle. Present ht *c.* 165mm; ht to (v) 54mm; diam. of base 40mm; max. diam. of drip pan 29mm. *2601; SF 104*

31* Lever lock key. Copper-alloy handle, iron key. Approximately shallow D-sectioned ring terminal with ridged flattening across top; hollow cylindrical handle with rib around lower end. Iron key

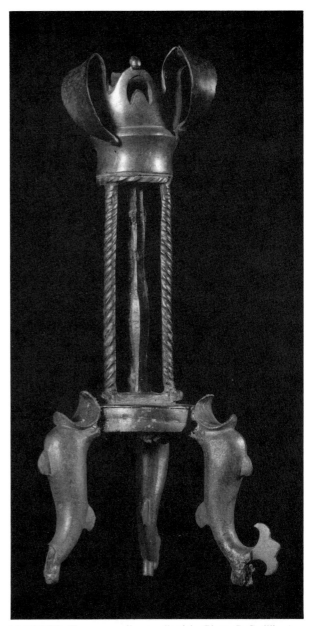

Pl. XXVIII. The copper-alloy candlestick. (Photo: P. Gwilliam)

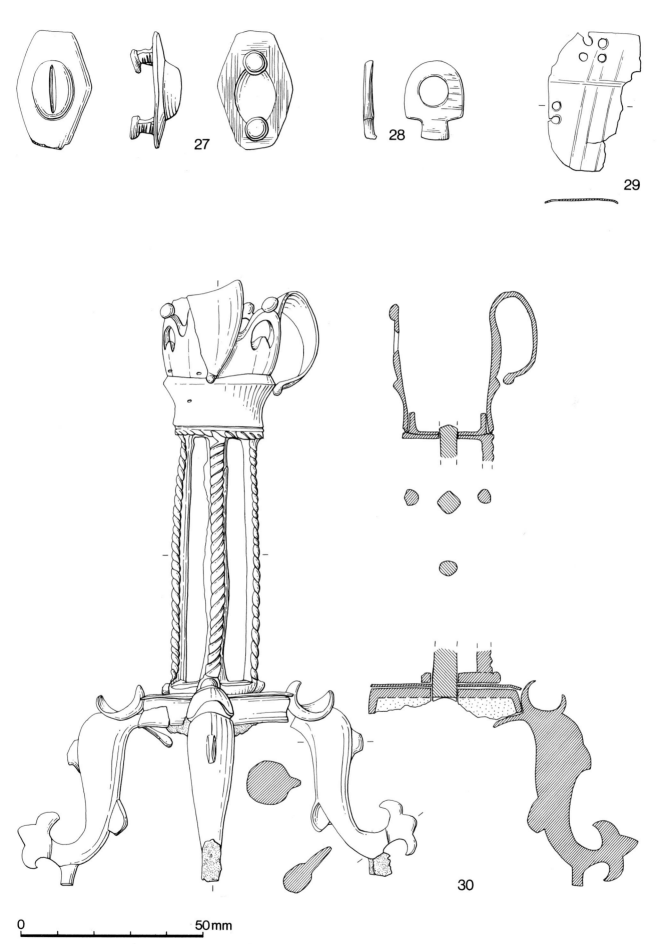

Fig. 70. Copper-alloy objects (Nos 27-30). Scale 1:1

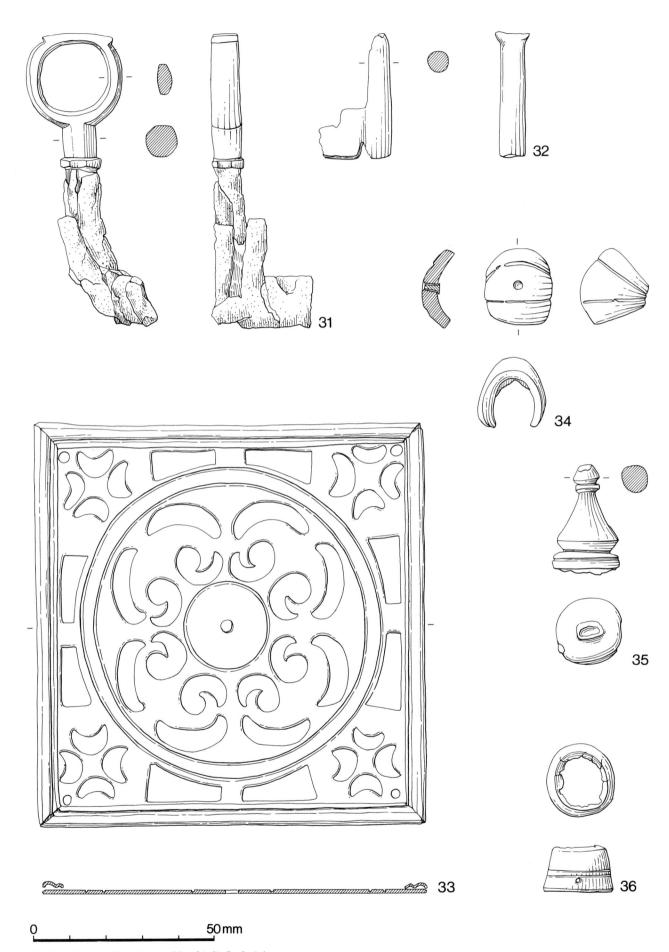

Fig. 71. Copper-alloy objects (Nos 31-6). Scale 1:1

0   50mm

with piped stem set into handle. Key much corroded and bent out of shape. Total l. 75mm; l. of copper-alloy handle 24mm. *1213 (Structure M); SF 1832*

32* Lever lock key. Piped stem; square ward with one notch on lower edge by stem and one centrally on upper edge, outer corner of ward beyond this notch broken off and missing. Upper part of stem solid and tapering with small crescentic terminals projection on either side. Upper face of stem smooth. L. 32mm; diam. of stem 5mm. *001; SF 210*

33* Openwork mount. Square plate with symmetrical openwork design, cut-out elements have neat vertical edges. Cut-outs produce a pattern of four pelta shapes surrounding a central roundel inside a circular frame; area between circular frame and outer frame formed by edge of plate is filled by a framed cross in each corner and a small bar centrally. On upper face of mount there is a circular groove around edge of central roundel and two similar concentric grooves on circular frame. Outer edge of mount has four lengths of sheet each with two beaten up ribs soldered onto edges to form a raised frame around the openwork pattern, ends of frame lengths neatly mitred. A small circular perforation in each corner inside raised frame and one similar perforation centrally, all five cut through from back of plate leaving small flanges of metal around their edges on the upper surface. Dimensions 106.5 x 105mm; th. of plate 1mm. *3211 (Structure A); SF 1717*

34* Mount. Cast saddle-shaped mount with small central perforation at apex retaining fragment of rivet shank; deep groove parallel to each edge forming a 'V' pattern on both sides. L. *c.* 20mm; max. section 20 x 4mm. *1611 (Structure P); SF 1563*

35* Terminal. Cast carinated pear-shaped terminal with hemispherical knob and cordon finial above and ribbed disc below. Underside of disc rough and has central square-sectioned stump of shank. Ridge, possibly part of casting flash, down one side of main pear-shaped element. L. 28mm; max. diam. 18mm. *001; SF 382*

36* Ferrule. Thimble-shaped sheet cap with top mostly missing. Two small perforations opposite each other punched through into interior and two fine shallow grooves around sides. Diam. of base 18mm; present depth 12mm; th. 0.5mm. *8104 (Structure M); SF 1184*

37* Bolt. Conical head slightly flattened at top; square-sectioned shank tapering to blunt point and slightly curved over lower part. L. 100mm; head diam. 18mm; shank section 6mm. *3211 (Structure A); SF 1721*

38* ?Shank of bolt. Square-sectioned shank tapering to blunt end; other end broken. L. 41mm; shank section 4mm. *3211 (Structure A); SF 1712*

39* ?Shank of bolt. Square-sectioned shank tapering to chipped chisel shaped end; lower part bent to one side and irregular gauge marks on one angle at bend. L. 57mm; shank section 6.5mm. *3211 (Structure A); SF 1722*

40* ?Terret. Approximately one-third of circular-sectioned ring, upper part becomes square-sectioned and slightly angled down from apex on either side of a knob finial. Original inner diam. *c.* 25-30mm; section 5.5mm. *1815 (Structure R); SF 1216*

41* Angle strip. Rectangular-sectioned strip bent into 'L' shape; both ends broken. Outer face has two channels parallel to edges producing three ribs. Total l. *c.* 28mm; section 4 x 1mm. *300 (Structure B); SF 1913*

42* Boss. Circular head with repoussé decoration of central boss and surrounding ridge; two pointed strips on opposite sides of circumference bent under back, one broken. Diam. 12mm; th. 0.5mm. *104 (Structure A); SF 1719*

43* Stud. Flat circular head with chipped edges now bent out of shape; short blunt-ended shank with remains of corroded circular washer still attached. Upper face of stud decorated with a ring of punched ring and dots and an incised star of six rays each with a small triangular terminal. Underside of head has two concentric shallow ribs inside edge. Trace of ?gilding on upper face. Head diam. *c.* 20mm. *Ditch 039/1; SF 1399*

44* Stud. Shallow hemispherical domed head with chipped edge and central perforation. Rivet with flat head and rectangular-sectioned

tapering shank with broken tip acts as shank of stud. Stud head diam. 21mm; l. of rivet 14mm. *3463; SF 570*

45* Stud. Hemispherical domed head with chipped edges; square-sectioned blunt-ended shank. Head diam. 10mm; l. 7mm. *100 (Structure A); SF 1890*

46 Stud. Head description as No. 45; shank broken. Head diam. 6mm. *8202 (Structure V); SF 1294*

47 Stud. Fragment of domed head and broken shank. Present dimensions 19 x 12mm. *1700 (Structure Q); SF 447*

48 Stud. Rectangular-sectioned tapering shank with broken point and eight fragments of head. L. of shank 9mm. *5600/4; SF 840*

49* Tack. Flat oval head; bent circular-sectioned shank tapering to point. Head diam. 3 x 2mm; l. 8mm. *001; SF 1240*

50 Tack. Small flat head; broken and bent shank. Head diam. 3.5mm. *903 (Structure J); SF 761*

51* Clip. Diamond-shaped piece of sheet, ends folded in towards centre and then back out; the whole flattened. Dimensions 19 x 16mm; th. of sheet 0.5mm. *Field walking; SF 33*

52* Clip. Description as No. 51. Dimensions 23 x 14mm; th. of sheet 0.5mm. *200 (Structure B); SF 375*

53 Clip. Description as No. 51, in four fragments. Present dimensions 17 x 13mm; th. of sheet 0.5mm. *200 (Structure B); SF 377*

54* Clip. Description as No. 51. Dimensions 18 x 14mm; th. of sheet 0.5mm. *4017B (Well 2); SF 1883*

55* Clip. Description as No. 51. Dimensions 15 x 14mm; th. of sheet 0.5mm. *3218A; SF 1737*

56* Clip. Description as No. 51; pointed outer ends project beyond outer fold. Dimensions 17 x 13mm; th. of sheet 0.5mm. *Ditch 020/4; SF 1786*

57* Clip. Description as No. 56. Pointed ends bent out at 90° and not 180°. Dimensions 20 x 10mm; th. of sheet 0.5mm. *900 (Structure J); SF 368*

58* Washer. Square sheet washer with central perforation. Also two crumpled fragments of sheet. Dimensions 14 x 14mm; th. 1mm. *001; SF 1813*

59* ?Washer. Sub-diamond-shaped fragment of sheet with chipped edges and central circular perforation punched through. Dimensions 19 x 15mm; th. 0.5mm. *207 (Structure B); SF 307*

Miscellaneous (Figs 72-3)

60* Hollow boss. Hollow pear-shaped boss with short end broken and small solid hemispherical finial centrally on wide end. Convex surface well-finished, concave surface rough. Dimensions 29 x 18mm; th. 2mm. *001; SF 304*

61* Cylinder. Hollow cylinder slightly curved to one side at one end, other end has shallow rib below the beaten-out and slightly outsplayed edge. L. 47mm; diam. 6mm. *001; SF 1586*

62* Casting. Heavy oval casting with rough and uneven underside; upper face has sides sloping up to central ridge running down long axis with broken oval-sectioned projections at either end. Upper surfaces undulating and uneven. Dimensions 41 x 28mm; th. to ridge 16mm. *001; SF 10*

63* Curved fitting. Curved rectangular-sectioned bar expanding evenly to ovoid terminal with parts of rectangular-sectioned scrolls with bevelled edges on either side. Groove down centre of bar; upper surface silvered/tinned over outer part. Present l. 51mm; section of bar (min.) 5 x 1mm. *1003 (Structure J; SF 736*

64* Annular ring. Circular-sectioned. Diam. 25 x 24mm; section 5mm. *2775; SF 651*

65 Annular ring. Oval-sectioned with casting flash on interior and exterior filed in places. Diam. 28mm; section 3.5 x 2mm. *001; SF 917*

66* Penannular ring. Circular-sectioned wire bent into penannular ring. Diam. 14 x 12mm; section 2.5mm. *001; SF 236*

67 Penannular ring. Description as No. 66. Diam. 12 x 9mm; section 1.5-1mm. *2558; SF 521*

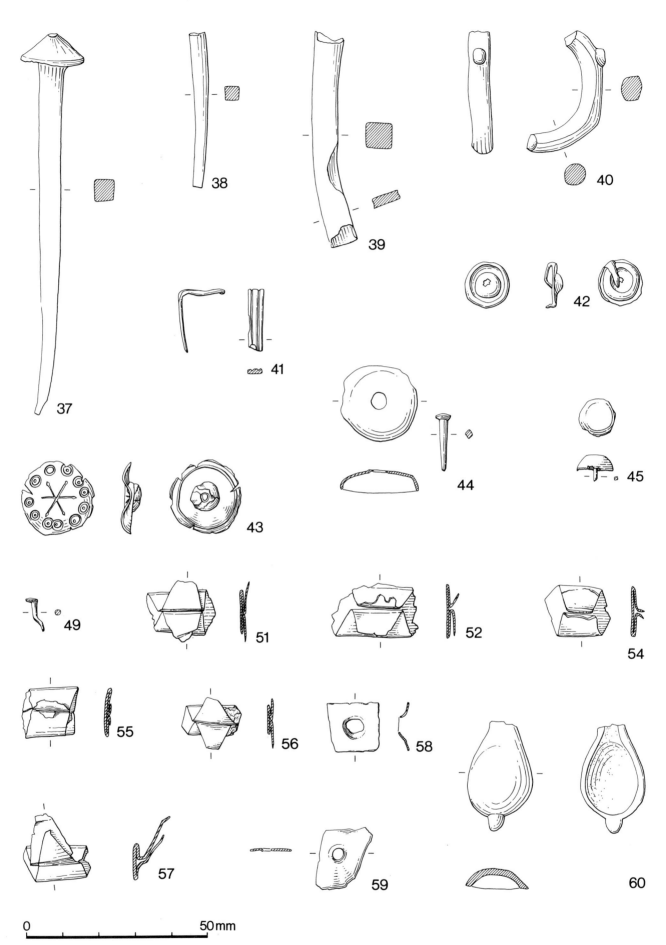

Fig. 72. Copper-alloy objects (Nos 37-45, 49, 51-2 and 54-60). Scale 1:1

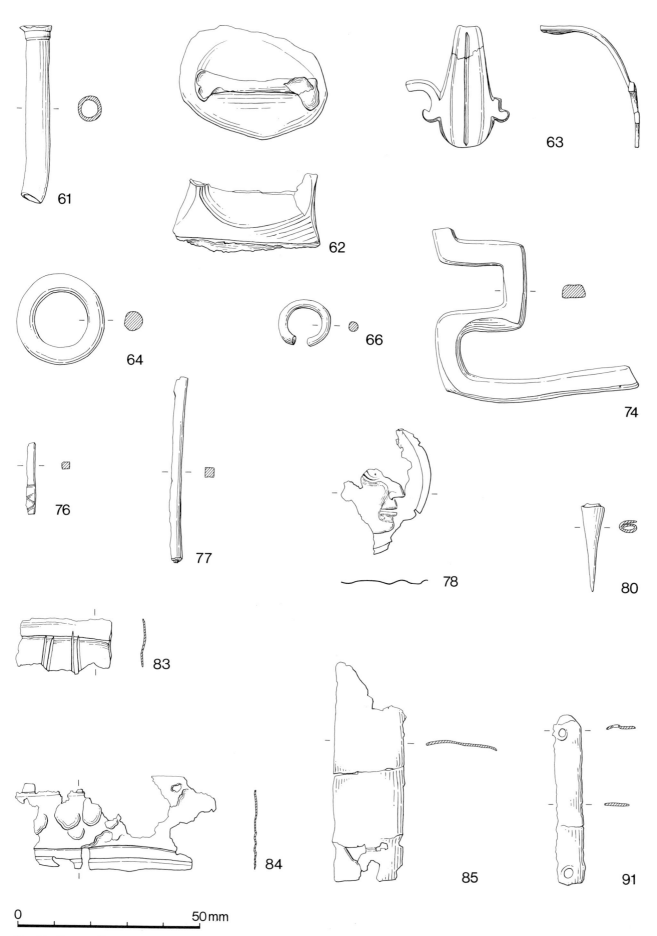

Fig. 73. Copper-alloy objects (Nos 61-4, 66, 74, 76-8, 80, 83-5 and 91). Scale 1:1

68 Ring. Part of oval-sectioned hoop, bent out of shape. Diam. *c.* 45mm; section *c.* 4 x 3mm. *1701 (Structure Q); SF 1547*

69 Rod. Square-sectioned bent rod; one end broken, other retains an angular butt joint. L. *c.* 20mm; section 1.5mm. *903 (Structure J); SF 767*

70 Rod. Circular-sectioned, slightly faceted curved rod; both ends broken. L. 18mm; section 4.5mm. *4903/2 (Structure X); SF 1282*

71 Rod. Circular-sectioned curved rod; both ends broken. L. 25mm; section 6mm. *001; SF 1817*

72 Rod. Circular-sectioned curved rod; one end broken, other a slightly expanded terminal. L. 28mm; section 6mm. *001; SF 453*

73 Rod. Oval-sectioned rod; both ends broken. L. 4mm; section 6.5 x 5mm. *001; SF 842*

74* Bar. Rectangular-sectioned bar; both ends broken, one end bent into angular 'S' shape. Overall dimensions 52 x 47mm; section 6 x 4mm. *001; SF 76*

75 Rod. Rectangular-sectioned rod with broken ends bent into a curved 'L' shape. L. 19mm; section 2 x 1mm. *1212 (Structure M); SF 1117*

76* Rod. Square-sectioned with broken ends; hammering marks on sides. L. 19mm; section 2mm. *2010; SF 463*

77* Rod. Description as No. 76; rectangular-sectioned. L. 49mm; section 3 x 2.5mm. *001; SF 379*

78* Repoussé disc. Five fragments of thin sheet disc; most edges broken and one side found bent back on itself. Repoussé decoration, perhaps the lower part of a face in profile. Underside coated with white metal. Dimensions (largest fragment) 25 x 20mm; th. 0.5mm. *8201/2 (Structure V); SF 1229*

79 Disc. Edge of thin sheet disc. Dimensions 18 x 10mm; th. 1mm. *3454; SF 585*

80* Cone. Triangular piece of sheet bent into a flattened cone. L. *c.* 22mm; diam. (max.) 5 x 2mm. *200 (Structure B); SF 191*

81 Sheet. Bent fragment with one long edge rolled outward, outer edges broken. Dimensions 27 x 10m; th. 1mm. *001; SF 212*

82 Sheet tube or binding. Fragment of sheet bent into open tube. L. 13mm; w. 3mm. *8200 (Structure V); SF 1100*

83* Decorated sheet. Rectangular fragment with one straight chipped edge, all other edges broken. Two pairs of grooves running towards straight edge at 90° and dying out at slight ridge parallel with it. Dimensions 26 x 15mm; th. 1mm. *001; SF 306*

84* Decorated perforated sheet. Part of very thin strip with two short ends and parts of long sides broken. Repoussé decoration with parts of two narrow ribs parallel to each sides and other decoration, now obscure, centrally. Fragment retains one circular perforation close to one edge. Dimensions 57 x 25mm; th. >0.5mm. *5605; SF 1884*

85* Perforated sheet. Rectangular strip with one short end broken; two broken perforations at other short end. Traces of silvering. L. 57mm; th. 20 x 0.5mm. *8300; SF 1912*

86 Perforated sheet. Twelve fragments of crumpled sheet retaining parts of perforations and two flat-headed rivets. Th. of sheet 1mm; rivet head diam. 6mm. *4903/3 (Structure X); SF 1397*

87 Perforated sheet. Two fragments of perforated sheet joined together by shank of rivet. Th. 0.5mm. *001; SF 1119*

88 Perforated sheet. Curved fragment with broken edges broken across perforation. Dimensions 27 x 10mm; th. 0.5mm. *Ditch 002/4; SF 538*

89 Perforated Sheet. Fragment with one straight edge and other edges broken, broken across square perforation. Dimensions 16 x 9mm; th. 0.5mm. *1216/2 (Structure M); SF 1233*

90 Perforated sheet. Crumpled fragment with two perforations. Th. 1mm. *001; SF 535*

91* Perforated strip. Rectangular strip with chipped edges; circular perforation at either short end. L. 45mm; section 7 x 0.5mm. *001; SF 625*

92 Perforated strip. Rectangular-sectioned strip, both short ends broken across perforation. L. 19mm; section 6 x 0.5mm. *Ditch 006/1; SF 552*

93 Perforated strip. Rectangular-sectioned strip, three edges broken, two small perforations. Dimensions 10 x 5mm; th. 0.5mm. *001; SF 1138*

94 Fragment of sheet broken along hollow rib. Dimensions 14 x 10mm; th. 0.5mm. *001; SF 107a*

95 Two fragments of sheet. Larger has a straight finished edge parallel to a curved straight edge and other edges broken; all edges broken on second fragment. Dimensions 19 x 15mm and 15 x 12mm; th. 0.5mm. *001; SF 166a*

96-113 Twenty fragments of sheet with broken edges: listed in Archive Report.

114-119 Seven fragments of rectangular-sectioned strip: listed in Archive Report.

120-132 Twenty-one unidentifiable corroded lumps and fragments: listed in Archive Report.

133 Iron loop bent in half with loop of copper-alloy wire bent through ends. *001; SF 265c*

6 The Brooches (Fig. 74)
by D.F. Mackreth

All are made from a copper alloy unless otherwise stated.

1* Trumpet brooch. Pin is hinged, its axis bar housed in a half-round projection across the back of the trumpet head. Above this rises a loop and collar, the ends of the loop being lodged in the ends of the hole for the pin's axis bar. The collar is a simple, plain strip bent round the waist. The trumpet head is narrow in its lower part and flares out to fill an elongated oval. On the top is a nib now lodged in the collar; it may have been intended to fix that, but more probably to prevent the loop and collar from falling over the front of the brooch. At the top of the head is a ridge sweeping down to form a small scroll sitting on a step which runs over the head in front of the ridge. The result is that the narrow part of the trumpet seems to end in a circle between the scrolls. The knop consists of a grooved central disc with petalling on each side, ending above and below in single grooved mouldings. Two of the grooves have traces of a white metal appliqué strip. The lower bow is chamfered down each side. The foot-knob, topped by a small cross-moulding, is an inverted cone with petals formed by grooves, from its dished base rises a small conical boss. Traces of a white metal coating on the central face of both the trumpet and the lower bow. Also traces of a white metal coating round the upper perimeter of the trumpet head. *900 (Structure J); SF 291*

Hinged-pin trumpet brooches are only a small proportion of the whole class. Almost all come from England south of the Pennines, especially in the south and the south-west. However, those with relief moulding come from the north of Roman Britain and beyond: County Durham (Hattatt 1985, 109, fig. 44, no. 434); Settle, North Yorkshire (British Museum, 96.5.1.9); Traprain Law, the Borders, and a parallel for the present example (Curle 1915, 168, fig. 23, no. 2). This is hardly an impressive total and none is dated, but the distributional differences between this particular group of hinged, plain or relief-moulded and sprung-pin relief-moulded is very marked, the last occurring mainly in the West Midlands, the Welsh Marches and in Wales itself. Such discrimination is not often found. The dating of white metal appliqué trim, probably beaded on the head and lower bow here, is in the 2nd century and the bulk of

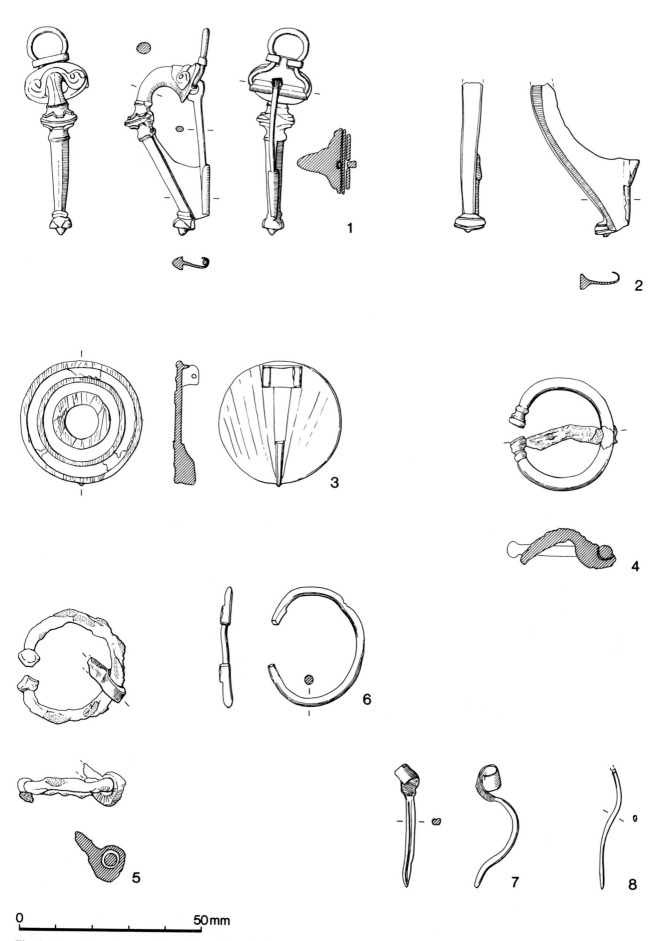

Fig. 74. Brooches of copper alloy and iron (Nos 1-8). Scale 1:1

0   50mm

trumpet brooches passed out of use between AD 150 and 175, very few continuing to the end of the century; those from later contexts should be regarded as having been residual in their contexts.

2* Unclassified brooch. Upper bow with the pin-fixing arrangement is missing. The surviving part has flat front face with a groove down each side and a suggestion of a second one on the right. Lower bow tapers towards a foot-knob made up of a boldly projecting moulding with two grooves across the front face. Small nib on the underside. Top edge of the catch-plate sweeps up the back of the bow as a deep, but thin, flange ending in a rounded top. *001; SF 102*

The type to which this brooch belongs is not explicit. The length of the surviving bow is, however, too long to suit a trumpet brooch. The prominent foot-knob might point to a member of the headstud type (e.g. Collingwood 1931, 82, fig. 7), but the thin section of the casting is uncharacteristic. Similarly, it is difficult to find a Colchester derivative which would suit the style of the piece. The result is that no firm date can be proposed. The behaviour of the catch-plate and the nature of the foot suggest that the brooch does not date to before *c.* AD 75. It is unlikely to have been made after *c.* AD 150 and it should not have survived in use beyond *c.* AD 175.

3* Plate brooch. The sprung-pin was housed between two pierced lugs joined across the top by a slight flange. Plate is circular and flat. Three concentric recessed zones on the front face. Central circular one is empty, middle one has discoloured enamel, and outer one contains remains of a pale turquoise colour. Whole of the front of the brooch was roughly filed in antiquity. *001; SF 43*

The pattern is not uncommon and is related to a group of either oval or round enamelled brooches which were the precursors of the popular gilded series of the earlier 3rd century. The group has a sprung-pin mounted on a single pierced lug and it is not yet certain whether the system used on the present piece represents either a separate workshop tradition, or is a chronological stage in an overall development. Dating evidence for those with double lugs for the spring is scant: from *c.* AD 120 (Potter 1979, fig. 84, no. 15); and the 3rd century (Down 1978, 287, fig. 10, nos 28 and 55). Neither provides a satisfactory clue of the true date. If there was a progression through the decorative sequence, then those with the single lug should be later because of the proven development from the enamelled brooches into the gilded ones which have stamps on the outer recesses and a paste gem or intaglio in the centre. The date of these can be placed in the first half of the 3rd century, although some may have carried on in use. On typological grounds only, the present brooch should be 2nd century, probably not carrying on in use until the end.

4* Penannular brooch. Of iron; circular in section. Each terminal has a flat circular end with two mouldings, then a waist and a smaller single moulding separated from the rest of the ring by a groove. Profile has a bow. *Ditch 030/2; SF 1904*

5* Penannular brooch. Of iron, complete; circular section. Each terminal is in the form of a round nail-head. Pin has a bow. *102 (Structure A); SF 443*

Multiple mouldings used as in No. 4 are not common and do not easily fit into any classification system. Dated pieces are rare, but two from Newstead in the Borders which are only broadly comparable, should date from the late 1st century through to, perhaps, the earliest 3rd century (Curle 1911, pl. lxxxviii, nos 3 and 17). Another from Wall, Staffordshire (Ball and Ball 1985, 14, fig. 10) has punched decoration running along the ring from each terminal and this should be more characteristic of the Principate than of the late empire. The most likely period for its popularity should be the later 1st and 2nd centuries. The simpler form of No. 5 is less easily paralleled and iron specimens are rare. One from Poole's Cavern, Buxton, Derbyshire (Bramwell *et al.* 1983, 59, fig. 4, no. 8) was found with a collection whose bias is towards the 2nd century (Bramwell *et al.* 1983, 49), but which was not in itself dated. However, a blanket acceptance that this is a proper reflection of the *floruit* would be unwise as a specimen from Maiden Castle, Dorset was dated *c.* AD 25-75 (Wheeler 1943, 264, fig. 86, no. 3).

6* Penannular brooch. Circular section, broken into two. Each terminal is cast in with the ring and has a square step up from that. Top surface is flat and has a groove across each end and a small concave chamfer on each side between. Well preserved apart from the modern break, and shows signs of having been carefully finished. The pin is missing. *1702 (Structure Q); SF 1556*

The design of the terminal as such, with the grooves and the chamfers, can be found in the Principate, but only when the terminal is folded back along the top of the ring. Fowler's system does not allow either the bent or the cast-in decorative form as here to be allocated securely to any of her types (Fowler 1960, 150-53, fig. 1). This may be of little moment as it is the type of terminal which is of importance. Here, there has been no attempt to imitate the older form by incising a groove down each side. This is either by omission or by typological development. It should be noted that there is nothing on the present brooch which could by any stretch of the imagination be described as being zoomorphic or proto-zoomorphic. The writer has recorded no other cast terminal of this pattern. In fact, dating of cast versions of originally turned-back terminals is very hard to come by; this matches the general problem which afflicts the dating of zoomorphic brooches which may be of either type. All that is possible is a suggestion that, as cast terminals of this basic form are not 1st or 2nd century, and as they are hard to assign to the 3rd century, then the date is probably in the 4th century, but not necessarily beyond.

7* Penannular brooch. Pin only; complete with high bow in its profile. *001; SF 251*

8* Fragments of brooch. Piece of wire, broken at one end and pointed at the other; profile suggests it may have come from a sprung-pin brooch. Section for half the length and running to the break is square, this is more the mark of a Nauheim derivative than of any other type. If so, the date is likely to be found before the last ten or twenty years of the 1st century. *1813 (Structure R); SF 534*

7 Lead Objects (Fig. 75)

by Quita Mould

Discussion

The excavations at Dalton Parlours produced eighteen objects of lead and just over 2kg of lead scrap and waste. The types of object and various categories of scrap and waste are given in Table 1.

Among the objects, three circular plugs (Nos 12-14) and three cramps (Nos 7-9) occurred within levels L and M of Well 1. One of the plugs (No. 12) and a cramp (No. 7) were both found attached to pottery, indicating that they had been used for repair. The pots were evidently repaired to prolong their useful life before being eventually discarded. A flat-headed nail (No. 3) was found at the north-west corner of Structure M between walls 1208 and 1218. It lay within destruction debris and mixed ploughsoil. A fragment of stem (No. 17) and a small ?pierced disc (No. 18) occurred along with pieces of tile in the burnt upper fill (1213) of Structure M.

A truncated ellipsoidal-shaped weight (No. 2), possibly a *sescuncia* (1½ *unciae*), was found unstratified, as were a plug fragment (No. 10), two centrally-pierced caulkings (Nos 5 and 6), a small lead shot (No. 4) and three fragments of round-sectioned stem (Nos 15 and 16). Fragments of stem are likely to be scrap lead broken from larger objects, but they have been included amongst the lead objects in Table 1 as they are of distinct, recognisable form.

Table 1. Lead objects and waste.

Artefact	Quantity
caulking	2
cramp	3
nail	1
plug	5
sheet, stamped	1
shot	1
stem	4
weight	1

Scrap and waste	Weight in grammes
sheet	161.0
sheet, offcut	682.8
scrap fragment	756.0
molten waste	485.3
Total	**2085.1**

The majority of the lead recovered is scrap and waste deriving from lead fittings (plumbing, flashings, etc.) associated with the Roman buildings. Most occurred unstratified as surface finds or in topsoil. A stamped sheet (No. 1) was found in demolition debris (1601) in Structure P, associated with pottery of 3rd to 4th-century date. It has been randomly struck at least five times, apparently to try out a rectangular stamp. The stamp reads A (VLVS) FL (AVIVS) VITALIS. Flavius Vitalis is a commonly occurring name, the 'A', however, is rarely found (I am grateful to Dr M.W.C. Hassall for this information). It is likely to represent the name of the owner and/or worker of the lead. The stamp was probably used to distinguish the salvaged scrap lead, recast for ease of transportation, of one worker from that of others.

The scrap consists of fragments of broken sheet, sheet offcuts and trimmings with blade-cut edges and a small quantity of unrecognisable fragments. Nearly 8% of the scrap and waste comprises fragments of broken sheet, probably resulting from the decay or demolition of buildings with sheet lead fittings. The sheet offcuts and trimmings, produced when cutting the sheet to shape, represent scrap fragments discarded during the installation and repair of lead fittings; these account for 32% of all the scrap and waste recovered from Dalton Parlours. Molten waste, that is solidified droplets, dribbles, runnels and pools of spilt molten metal, make up 25% of the scrap and waste. Due to the low melting point of lead, such molten waste may be the result of accidental fire and cannot be interpreted as waste from deliberate melting and casting without the support of other evidence. The presence of the molten waste does indicate destruction debris, but whether deliberate demolition or accidental fire is unknown.

The amount of lead is relatively small. One might have expected a larger quantity in the vicinity of Structure B, which is interpreted below (p. 281) as the bath house. That this was not the case, suggests that the lead fittings were deliberately salvaged for use elsewhere when the building was abandoned.

Catalogue

The catalogue is arranged according to type of artefact in smallfind number order; the descriptions have been kept to a minimum. I am most grateful to Dr M.W.C. Hassall of the Institute of Archaeology, London for commenting on the stamp, and to P.T. Wilthew formerly of the Ancients Monuments Laboratory, HBMC for his helpful comments and XRF analysis of selected items. Measurements have been included for the objects and complete offcuts only.

1*   Stamped sheet. Thick sheet of sub-circular/trefoil shape with cut edges and rough lower surface. Smooth upper surface has been randomly stamped at least five times, the stamp reading A FL VITALIS. The lead is pierced by a rectangular nail hole. L. 112mm; w. 111mm; max. th. 14mm; wt 838g. *1601 (Structure P); SF 383*

Fig. 75. Lead objects (Nos 1-3, 5-9, 12-14 and 17-18). Scale 1:2

2* Weight. Truncated ellipsoidal weight with plano-convex section. Flat upper surface has two holes from the seating of the suspension loop. Diam. 30mm; ht 8mm; wt 43.5g. *001; SF 631*

3* Nail. Nail with square-sectioned shank and flat, round head, now folded. Shank l. 38mm; head l. 18mm; wt 15.5g. *1201 (Structure M); SF 780*

4 Shot. Diam. 3mm; wt 1.9g. (XRF analysis PTW 19/11/86.) *001; SF 530*

Caulkings

5* Sub-biconical caulking centrally pierced by a hole and formed from thick sheet wrapped around and moulded in the hand. L. 54mm; max. w. 27mm; wt 149.7g. *001; SF 623*

6* Circular caulking of plano-convex section with central hole. Flat face is smooth, the other rough. Diam. 22mm; th. 8mm; hole diam. 6mm; wt 19.5g. *001; SF 630*

Cramps

7* Pottery cramp comprising an irregular strip with an irregular-headed shank at each end. The cramp remains attached to a sherd of pottery by one shank. L. 42mm; max. w. 35mm; shank l. 6mm; wt 48.6g. *5500L (Well 1: 14-14.5m); SF 1428*

8* Pottery cramp comprising two irregularly shaped strips joined at each end by a shank. L. 64mm; max. w. 14mm; shank l. 8mm; wt 20.2g. *5500L (Well 1: 14-14.5m); SF 1444*

9* Pottery cramp, as No. 8, distorted. L. 36mm; max. w. 12mm; shank l. 8mm; wt 14.1g. *5500L (Well 1: 14-14.5m); SF 1515*

Plugs

10 Plug fragment with waisted section, smooth upper and irregular lower surface. L. 32mm; th. 9mm; recess ht 4mm; wt 42.7g. *001; SF 338*

11 Roughly circular plug with deeply waisted section. Diam. 29mm; th. 7mm; recess ht 3mm; wt 33g. *001; SF 846a*

12* Large circular plug with flat, circular, upper face and irregular lower face with a series of scored grooves present. Deeply waisted section with pottery fragments remaining. Diam. 49mm; max. l. 61mm; max. th. 10mm; recess ht 5mm; wt 178.8g. *5500L (Well 1: 14.2m); SF 1409*

13* Circular plug with slightly waisted section, smooth upper and lower surfaces with an irregular runnel present on the underside. Diam. 40mm; max. l. 50mm; recess ht 5mm; wt 43g. *5500M (Well 1: 14.3m); SF 1454*

14* Circular plug of deeply waisted section with smooth upper face and smaller, irregular lower face with pitted surface. Diam. 33mm; recess ht 12mm; wt 45.7g. *5500M (Well 1: 14.8m); SF 1490*

Stems

15 Two lengths of round-sectioned stem, the thicker with tool marks visible. Diam. 6mm; l. 36mm: diam. 4mm; l. 25mm; combined wt 11.6g. *001; SF 352a*

16 Round-sectioned stem with an oblique and an irregular end. Diam. 8mm; l. 60mm; wt 33g. *001; SF 849a*

17* Round-sectioned stem with a cut and a broken end. Diam. 7mm; l. 75mm; wt 40.8g. *1213/2 (Structure M); SF 1302*

18*? Pierced disc. Flat disc, pierced toward one end, with smooth but pitted upper and rough lower surface. Similar to a solidified droplet of spilt metal but the edges appear to have been deliberately shaped. Diam. 21mm; th. *c.* 2mm; wt 8.4g. *1213/3 (Structure M); SF 1337*

19 a-g. Sheet fragments; all edges broken: listed in Archive Report.

20 a-p. Sheet offcuts; blade-cut edges: listed in Archive Report.

21 a-f. Sheet offcuts; nailed: listed in Archive Report.

22 a-o. Scrap fragments: listed in Archive Report.

23 a-o. Molten waste; solidified droplets, dribbles and pools of spilt molten metal: listed in Archive Report.

8   Ironwork (from contexts other than Well 1) (Figs 76-7) by Ian R. Scott

The largest and most important group of iron objects was recovered from Well 1; it is described and discussed along with other finds from the well in Chapter 27. The remaining ironwork, from various contexts, is catalogued below.

Tools

1* Smith's chisel, or punch, with battered head. There are examples of similar smith's chisels, or punches, from Frocester Court Roman villa, Gloucestershire (Scott 1980, 31, fig. 13, no. 2), and from Verulamium, Hertfordshire (Manning 1972, 164, fig 60, no. 5); see also Manning 1985, 8-11 (especially nos A23 and A26). L. 88mm. *4903/2 (Structure X); SF 1612*

2* Smith's chisel, or punch. Head may be battered. Similar to No. 1. L. 80mm. *1600 (Structure P); SF 439*

3* Axe head. This axe does not quite fit into any of the types recently defined by Manning (1985, 14-16, fig. 3); nor am I aware of any exact parallel to this axe from a Roman context. Its date must be in some doubt, especially as it was unstratified. L. 166mm. *001; SF 395*

4* Drill bit head. The stem and blade are lost. See Manning 1985, 25-7 (especially nos B58-9). L. 54mm. *1422 (Structure M); SF 915*

Knives

Knives have been discussed in some detail by Manning and a scheme of classification proposed (1985, 108-23); any comment here, beyond the identification of the forms, would be superfluous.

5* Knife blade of triangular cross-section, with tang. Manning type 11 or 13. L. 106mm. *001; SF 1957*

6* Knife blade of triangular cross-section, with tang of rectangular cross-section. Manning type 11. L. 124mm. *001; SF 582*

7* Knife blade of triangular cross-section, with tang. Probably Manning type 11. L. 138mm. *1216/2 (Structure M); SF 1234*

Fittings and miscellaneous items

8* Linch pin, with spatulate head and rolled over loop. See examples from Verulamium (Manning 1972, 174, fig. 64, nos 33-5). L. 155mm. *001; SF 450*

9* Loop hinge, with nails *in situ*. There are good examples from the Roman fort at Heilbronn-Böckingen in Germany (Schönberger 1967, 142, Abb. 9, nos 1-8 and 10-13). L. 130mm. *1213/3 (Structure M); SF 1371*

10* L-shaped staple for drop hinge. One arm is of circular cross-section, the other of square cross-section. The square-sectioned arm was driven into the door post, while the round-sectioned arm acted as a pivot for the hinge attached to the door (cf. Manning 1985, fig. 31, no. 1a-b). L. 65mm. *Ditch 011/1A; SF 720*

11* L-shaped staple for drop hinge. L. 80mm. *221 (Structure B); SF 298*

12* Chain link, oval. L. 50mm. *1213 (Structure M); SF 1837*

13* Elongated link, bent in the middle, with ?split spike loops attached to each end. May be part of a snaffle bit, but seems more likely to be some form of structural fitting. L. *c.* 80mm. *1213/1 (Structure M); SF 1176*

14* Clamp, or cleat. Could be a cleat from a boot, or, more probably, a clamp for timber. See the examples from Rushall Down, Wiltshire (Manning 1985, 131, especially nos R54-5). L. 45mm. *Ditch 021/2A; SF 719*

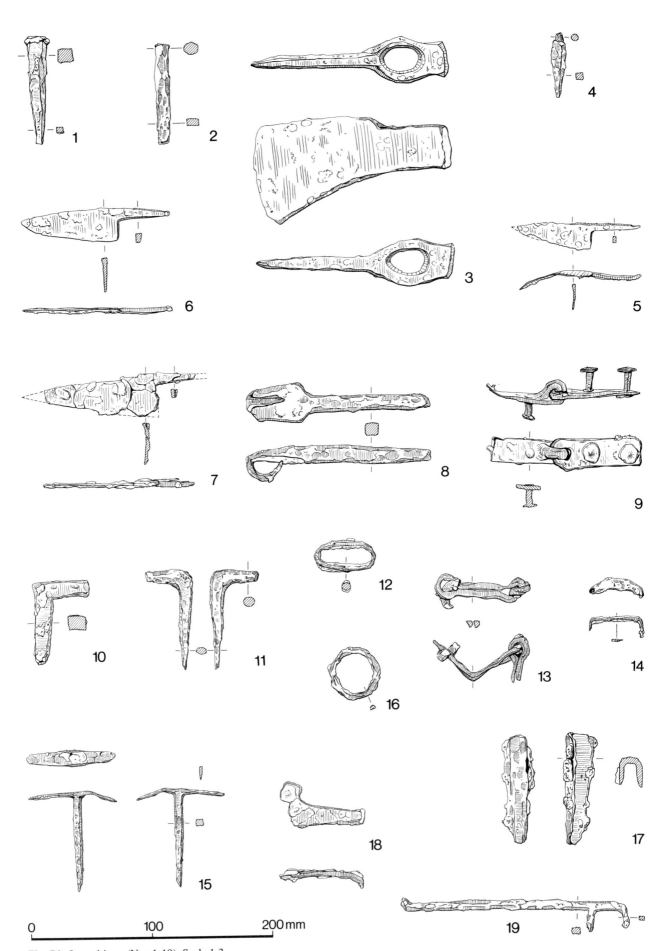

Fig. 76. Iron objects (Nos 1-19). Scale 1:3

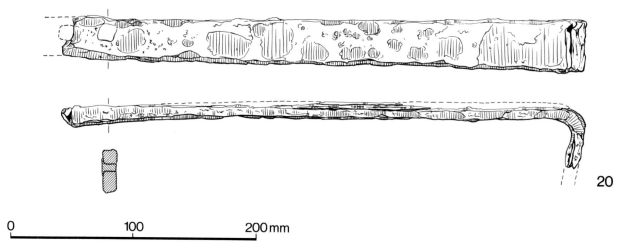

20

Fig. 77. Iron object (No. 20). Scale 1:3

15* T-staple. L.80mm. *001; SF 1690*

16* Ring of ?circular cross-section. Diam. 42mm. *3463; SF 572*

17* U-shaped channel, or spout. Function uncertain. L. 88mm. *3902; SF 1697*

18* Object of uncertain function. L. 72mm. *1400 (Structure M); SF 116a*

19* Bar with two teeth at one end. L. 190mm. *1213/2 (Structure M); SF 1300*

20* Bar of rectangular cross-section, slightly tapered. Wider end bent at a right angle. One certain rivet hole, and one possible rivet hole at the other end. L. *c.* 440mm. *501 (Structure E); SF 414*

9 The Glass (Figs 78-9)

by Jennifer Price

Discussion

The excavations have produced 271 pieces of Roman glass, of which 138 come from vessels and 103 from window panes; there are also two completely melted small lumps and 28 objects and fragments of objects. Among the vessel glass fragments, one (0.72%) is polychrome, fourteen (10.14%) are greenish colourless, 38 (27.54%) are bluish-green and 85 (61.60%) are colourless.

Very few vessels are represented by more than one fragment, and most of the pieces are quite tiny. The range of vessel forms is considerable, and indicates that glass was widely used throughout the occupation of the villa; nonetheless, the surviving assemblage of vessel glass is very small for a site of the size and status of Dalton Parlours. This may be explained either by an efficient system of collection and recycling of broken vessel glass during the life of the villa, or by events such as scavenging and ploughing which post-date the Roman occupation of the site. It is noteworthy that the excavations at another Yorkshire villa published in recent years, at Rudston (Stead 1980), also yielded only a small quantity of glass.

Where the forms are identifiable, the vessel glass has been divided into two broad categories: tablewares, which

are mostly bowls, cups and jugs, and containers. The 2nd to 3rd-century tablewares were made in polychrome, colourless or bluish-green glass, while the late Roman tablewares were either colourless or greenish colourless. None of these vessels was particularly rare or luxurious, though most of the 2nd to 3rd-century tableware was of good quality, and the presence of a piece of 'snake-thread' glass (No. 1) is interesting. The containers, which account for 71% (27 fragments) of the bluish-green glass, are all bottles of 1st or 2nd-century types, and where the bodies have survived they appear to be either square or rectangular.

The glass bangles (Nos 28-33), and some of the beads (Nos 34-5) were the earliest glass forms in use at the site. These objects were manufactured in the late 1st century or early years of the 2nd century, and were almost certainly associated with the pre-villa occupation. By contrast, most of the vessel glass ranges in date from the later 2nd to the late 4th century, though a little material (such as Nos 3 and 9) was produced in the late 1st or first half of the 2nd century, and some of the square bottles (Nos 14-17) may well have been manufactured before the late 2nd century, although similar containers probably continued to be made until the end of the 2nd century.

Two types of window glass were found on the site. There are 94 pieces from the cast matt-glossy panes produced in the 1st, 2nd and early 3rd century (Harden 1974), of which 47 (50%) are bluish-green, 24 (25.53%) greenish colourless and 23 (24.47%) colourless. In addition, there are nine pieces (three of each colour also found in the matt-glossy fragments) from the blown double glossy panes which were produced in the later 3rd and 4th centuries.

The fragment of 'snake-thread' glass (No. 1) is too small for the form to be identified, though the straight wall suggests that it may come from a cylindrical or conical vessel. A wide range of colourless vessels decorated with unmarvered, scored, serpentine trails, which were either self-coloured or opaque white, yellow or blue, occur in later 2nd and early 3rd-century contexts in the north-west provinces, especially in the lower Rhineland, and it is probable that many of them were produced in Cologne (cf. Fremersdorf 1959).

Fragments of 'snake-thread' vessels have been found quite frequently in Britain (see Price 1981, 154-5 for a list of the pieces noted up to 1978; several more are now known), but they do not occur in large numbers, and they have not been recorded in burials. Finds from sites in northern Britain include several pieces from York (Harden 1962, fig. 88; excavations in Blossom Street, unpublished); Aldborough, North Yorkshire, South Shields, Tyne and Wear, Carrawburgh, Northumbria and Covesea, Morayshire (Charlesworth 1959, 54, fig. 10, pl. III, no. 4); and Catterick, North Yorkshire, Piercebridge, Co. Durham, Old Penrith and Carlisle, both in Cumbria (all unpublished). There is little doubt that the finds in Britain were imported from the Rhineland.

Number 2 comes from the body of a hemispherical bowl decorated with 'rice-grain' facets, and an abraded line which may have been intended to mark out the areas of cutting. Colourless hemispherical bowls, decorated with a wide variety of facet- and linear-cutting, were produced in the later 2nd and 3rd centuries, and some appear to have continued into the 4th century. They are quite common in the western provinces (Isings 1957, form 96), and fragments have frequently been found in Britain, as at Verulamium (Charlesworth 1972, 208-10, fig. 78, nos 48-53), London (Wheeler 1930, 121-2, fig. 42, nos 1-3) and York (Harden 1962, 137, fig. 88, HG 162, 205, no. 1, 210, 211). Many of the patterns are much more complex than the lines of vertical cutting on this piece, but fragments with comparable cutting are known from *Insula XXI*, Verulamium (Charlesworth 1984, 154, fig. 62, nos 37-8), Shakenoak, Oxfordshire (Harden 1968, 76, fig. 26, no. 5), Woodcuts, Wiltshire (Pitt-Rivers 1887, 126, pl. 44, no. 7) and Kenchester, Hereford and Worcester.

Fragments of four colourless vessels (Nos 3-6) decorated with horizontal bands of wheel-cutting and abrasion were found. Two colourless curved rim fragments with narrow wheel-cut lines (No. 3) come from a drinking cup, though too little survives for the precise body form to be identified. Cups with similar rims occur in 2nd-century contexts on many sites in Britain, and there is little doubt that their production began at the end of the 1st century and continued until soon after the middle of the 2nd century. A wide variety of body and base forms are known; several examples were found in an Antonine pit at Felmongers, Harlow, Essex (Price 1987, 188-92, fig. 2, nos 8-17), and additional forms are known at Verulamium (Charlesworth 1972, 206-8, fig. 77, nos 43-6) and Park Street, Towcester, Northamptonshire (Price 1980a, 64, fig. 14, nos 4-5). A large number of fragments from cups of this kind have been found during excavations in the *vicus* at Castleford, and other local finds include pieces from York.

Number 4 also has wheel-cut and abraded decoration at and below the nearly vertical rim. It probably belongs to the same period as No. 3, or a little later, though alternatively it might come from an early or mid-4th-

century vessel. Although it is not possible to identify the vessel form with certainty, the fragment appears to come from a hemispherical or shallower cup or small bowl. Number 5 is a body fragment from a cylindrical or conical cup, and No. 6 may also come from a cylindrical cup, though the diameter of the body suggests that it is more likely to be from a 2nd or early 3rd-century cylindrical jug or bottle. Several fragmentary examples have been noted in Britain, and a complete specimen was found at Hauxton, Cambridgeshire (Harden 1958, 12-15, fig. 6, pl. 3b).

Fragments from three vessels with ribs and pinched projections (Nos 7-9) were noted. Two were colourless; the upper body and neck fragment, No. 7, may come from a late 2nd or 3rd-century flask or jug, perhaps rather similar to the bluish-green jug, with vertical ribbing on the upper body pinched into 'spectacle trails' in the middle of the body, which was found in Colchester, Essex (Harden *et al.* 1968, 84, no. 111). The small curved body fragment with two spikes of a vertical pinched projection (No. 8) also comes from a late 2nd or 3rd-century vessel, probably a drinking cup. Fragments with similar projections, and sometimes also with indents, have been recorded from several Romano-British sites, as at Chichester, West Sussex (Down 1979, 163, fig. 56, no. 5) and Colchester (unpublished), but only one complete example is known, from the 3rd-century cemetery at Brougham, Cumbria (Cool and Price forthcoming).

The bluish-green neck fragment with vertical ribs (No. 9) very probably comes from a jug with folded rim, long neck, angular handle with central rib, and either a conical or a globular body. These jugs are widely distributed within the north-west provinces, and were produced in this region during the later 1st and early 2nd centuries (Isings 1957, forms 52 and 55). They are very commonly found on sites of this date in Britain, and some examples have also been found in contexts dating from the third quarter of the 2nd century, as at Park Street, Towcester (Price 1980a, 66, figs 15-16, nos 7-10), and Felmongers, Harlow (Price 1987, 193-5, fig. 3, no. 20), which may indicate that some production continued until at least the middle of the 2nd century. The uneven distribution of the vertical ribs on the lower part of the neck is a recurring feature of these jugs.

Numbers 10, 11 and perhaps 13 come from colourless cylindrical cups with fire-rounded and thickened rims and tubular pushed-in base-rings with an inner trailed ring. These cups are found throughout the north-west provinces in late 2nd and early 3rd-century contexts (Isings 1957, form 85), and they are the commonest drinking cups on Romano-British sites, occurring in great numbers on most sites occupied during this period. Sites such as Verulamium (Herts.), Caerwent (Gwent), Piercebridge (Co. Durham), Corbridge (Northumbria) and Carlisle (Cumbria) have produced many fragments, and finds in Yorkshire include pieces from York, one of which shows a figured scene in scratched decoration (Harden 1962, 137, fig. 88, HG 202, no. 6; Charlesworth 1976, 17, fig.

13, nos 49-51; Charlesworth 1978, 55-7, fig. 30, nos 169, 172 and 279), Well (Gilyard-Beer 1951, 59, fig. 19, nos 1-2), Malton, Catterick and elsewhere.

The convex-sided drinking cup represented by No. 12 is not such a common form, though it was in use at the same time as or a little later than the cylindrical cups. Very few examples have been noted in Britain; an example with a thick concave base was found in the main drain at East Grimstead villa, Wiltshire (Sumner 1924, 43, pl. 8, no. 3), others come from burials at Brougham (Cool and Price forthcoming), and fragments of similar bases are known from Bishophill, York (Charlesworth 1978, 57, fig. 30, no. 177) and the Minster site, York.

The bottle fragments (Nos 14-17) have already been mentioned above. Bluish-green bottles were manufactured in very large quantities as containers for liquid or semi-liquid substances from the Neronian or early Flavian period onwards. The commonest forms are square or cylindrical (Isings 1957, forms 50-51), though rectangular and hexagonal examples were also produced. The square bottle was the most long-lived, as it continued in common use until around the end of the 2nd century, while the other forms disappear early in the 2nd century. Square bottle fragments are also known in later contexts, but this is not very surprising as the bottles were of robust construction, and many examples are likely to have survived in use for a long time after production ceased.

The basal designs (Nos 15-17) consist of one or more raised concentric circles, in one case with a central pellet. These are the commonest designs on square bottle bases. They are very frequently found in Roman Britain (see Charlesworth 1959, fig. 9, for some of the basal designs recorded in northern Britain) and they occur throughout the Roman world, so there is very little chance of identifying the centres of production.

The fragments from 4th-century drinking vessels were made in bubbly colourless or greenish colourless glass. With the exception of No. 27, all of them are decorated with horizontal bands of abraded lines. Number 27 probably also comes from a vessel with horizontal bands of abraded lines, but the surviving fragment is decorated only with a horizontal trail pulled down into loops.

Two forms of drinking cups are represented: hemispherical cups or small bowls (Nos 20 and 25-7) and conical beakers (Nos 18-19 and 23-4); both are commonly found in the middle and lower Rhineland and northern Gaul in 4th-century contexts (Isings 1957, forms 96 and 106). They also occur frequently in Britain, in burials, as at Glaston, Leicestershire (Webster 1950) and Lankhills, Winchester, Hampshire (Harden 1979, 211-4, fig. 27, classes I-II), and on very many settlements, as at the Frocester Court and Barnsley Park villas in Gloucestershire (Price 1980b, 41-2, fig. 16, nos 8-11; Price 1983, 176-7, fig. 59, nos 11-17), and the Alchester Road suburb, Towcester, Northamptonshire (Price and Cool 1983, 116-17, fig. 46, nos 11-25 and fig. 47, nos 30-34).

Numbers 21-2 come from 4th-century colourless jugs, flasks or bottles. Rims similar to No. 21 occur on a wide range of late Roman colourless and bluish-green vessels

(see Isings 1957, forms 102, 120-21 and 126-7), though the dimensions of this piece, which is part of a wide funnel mouth with a thick folded trail below the rim outside, suggest that it is probably from a large bottle. A bluish-green two-handled bottle came from grave 398 at Lankhills, Winchester (Harden 1979, 219, fig. 27, class VIII), a similar colourless bottle came from the Butt Road cemetery in Colchester, Essex (unpublished), and a fragment was found at Shakenoak, Oxfordshire (Harden 1968, 76, fig. 26, no. 6). Other identifiable pieces in Britain include some colourless cylindrical flasks from York (Harden 1962, 140, fig. 89, H 13, fig. 90, HG 146, nos 3-4), but most fragments are only small parts of the rim and mouth and the vessel forms cannot be identified.

There are two categories of glass objects: bangles and beads. Fragments of six bangles were found. Five of these (two type 2, three type 3A) conform to the tripartite classification proposed by Kilbride-Jones (1938), and subsequently extended by Stevenson (1956; 1976), and one (No. 33) falls outside this classification. Four of the Dalton Parlours bangles (Nos 28-30 and 33) have been examined in a recent study of the glass bangles found on sites in eastern Yorkshire (Price 1988, nos 6-7, 59 and 94), so they will not be considered in detail here. It is, however, most unlikely that these objects were in current use during the villa occupation phase of the site, as they appear to have gone out of production very early in the 2nd century. The sites of several other late villas in Yorkshire have also produced bangles, as at Rudston (Charlesworth 1980; Price 1988, nos 28, 35-6, 39, 47 and 63-6), Harpham (Price 1988, no. 26), Wharram Grange (Price 1986, section 26.12; Price 1988, no. 17), and Wharram Le Street (Price 1986, section 12.18; Price 1988, nos 31 and 75), and it is probable that these finds also relate to the pre-villa phases of activity. The undecorated bluish-green fragment (No. 33) comes from an unusual Romano-British bangle, which is much more robust than the other pieces found, and has a larger internal diameter. The broken ends of the fragment have been carefully shaped and polished smooth, perhaps for mounting in a metal setting or some other secondary purpose.

Numbers 34-5 are probably the earliest beads at Dalton Parlours. Number 34 is part of a Guido class 9A bead (Guido 1978, 77, fig. 26, pl. II, no. 14), a large bluish-green annular bead with meandering trails of brown and opaque white cord. The earliest examples appear to be ones from Hembury, Devon and Meare, Gloucestershire which may date from about the 1st century BC, and several others occur on sites of the 1st century AD. Number 35, a dark blue annular bead with an opaque white spiral trail, is comparable with Guido's group 5A beads (Guido 1978, 63, fig. 21, no. 1). This is a long-lived type with Iron Age origins which also occurs on many Romano-British sites.

Parallels for No. 36 have not been easy to find, and it is possible that this is not an ancient bead, but the rest of the beads (Nos 37-43) are normal Roman types (see Guido 1978, 92-100, fig. 37). Numbers 37-8 are small blue globular/cylindrical beads (Guido 1978, 94-5, fig. 37, no.

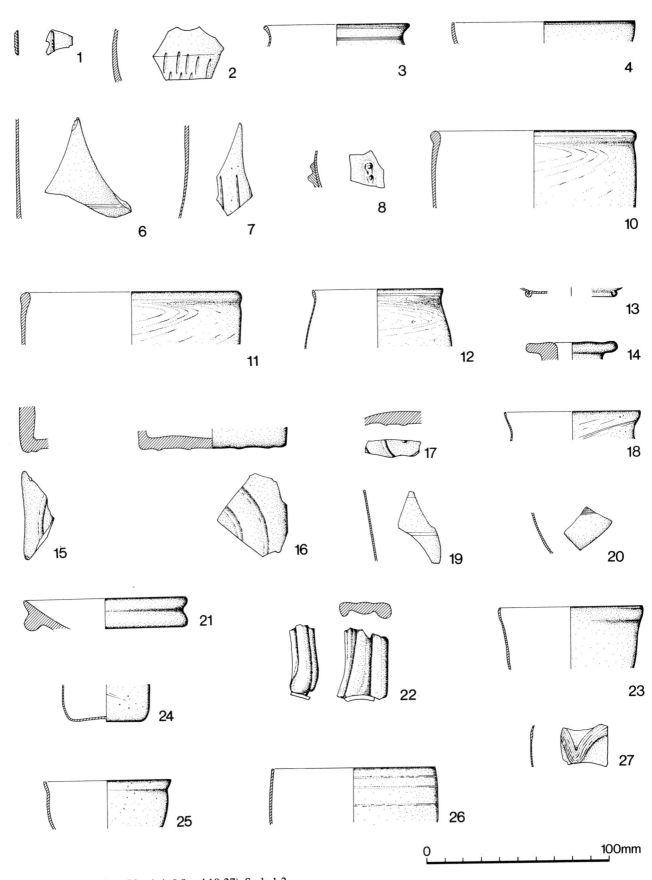

Fig. 78. Vessel glass (Nos 1-4, 6-8 and 10-27). Scale 1:2

5) which have been noted throughout the Roman period but became more common after the 2nd century. Numbers 39-40 are small biconical beads (Guido 1978, 97, fig. 37, nos 12-13) which are usually found in late Roman contexts, and Nos 41-2 are narrow tubular beads. Number 41 is very distorted, and the colour is unusual but a few have been noted in Roman contexts in Britain (see Guido 1978, 96), while No. 42 is made in bluish-green glass. Fifteen very small beads were found with a fragment of cord (No. 43); these are a type which has sometimes been recorded in early Roman contexts but only became very common in Britain in the late Roman period (Guido 1978, 96-7, fig. 37, no. 8).

Catalogue

Blown vessels: 2nd to 3rd centuries AD (Fig. 78)
Polychrome
1* Small body fragment. Colourless; opaque yellow trail. Straight side, perhaps from thin-walled cylindrical or conical vessel. One prominent unmarvered trail with short scored lines. Dimensions 13.5 x 14mm; th. 0.5mm. *001; SF 686*

Monochrome
Cut decoration
2* Body fragment, hemispherical bowl. Colourless. Surfaces covered with iridescent and enamel-like weathering deposits. Convex lower body. Two rows of vertical 'rice-grain' facet-cuts. Dimensions 30 x 37.5mm; th. 1.5-4mm. *Ditch 002/2A: SF 415*

3* Two rim fragments, cup. Colourless. Small curved rim, edge cracked-off and ground smooth, upper body expanding out. Two fine wheel-cut horizontal lines on rim, band of abraded lines on upper body. Present ht 11mm; rim diam. 80mm; th. 1-1.5mm. *Ditch 014/1A; SFs 722 and 1955*

4* Rim fragment, ?hemispherical cup. Colourless. Dull, surfaces covered with enamel-like weathering deposits. Vertical rim, edge cracked-off and ground smooth, slightly convex side. Horizontal wheel-cut line below rim. Present ht 11mm; rim diam. 100mm; th. 1.5mm. *1213/2 (Structure M); SF 1291*

5 Body fragment, ?cylindrical cup. Colourless. Dull, flaking iridescence. Straight side. Six closely set horizontal abraded lines. Present ht 28mm; body diam. *c.* 80mm; th. 0.6mm. *1213/3 (Structure M); SF 1376a*

6* Two body fragments, not joining, ?cylindrical jug or bottle. Colourless. Dull, flaking iridescent weathering deposit. Straight side. Three closely set horizontal abraded lines. Present ht 54mm; body diam. *c.* 100mm; th. 1.5-2.5mm. *1213/3 (Structure M); SFs 1346 and 1376b*

Pinched decoration
7* Body fragment, flask or jug. Colourless. No visible weathering. Cylindrical neck with slight constriction, expanding out to upper body. Three vertical ribs, terminals extending to lower neck. Present ht *c.* 47mm; neck diam. *c.* 42mm; th. 1-2.5mm. *5500M (Well 1; 14-15.5m): SF 1679*

7a Body fragment. Colourless. One rib. Dimensions 8 x 16mm; th. 1mm. *1213/2 (Structure M); SF 1291a*

8* Body fragment, ?cup. Greenish colourless. Dull, weathering spirals. Convex side. Vertical pinched projection, two surviving points. Dimensions 21 x 19mm; th. 0.5-1.5mm. *101 (Structure A); SF 70*

9 Neck fragment, ?jug. Bluish-green. Dull. Cylindrical neck. Six vertical ribs in low relief (ribs on one part of neck only). Present ht 13.5mm; neck diam. *c.* 26mm; th. 3.5-4mm. *3480; SF 854*

Undecorated
10* Rim fragment, cylindrical cup. Colourless. Dull, weathering spirals. Vertical rim, edge fire-rounded and thickened, straight side. Present ht 41mm; rim diam. 110mm; th. 2-3mm. *1200 (Structure M); SF 771*

11* Two rim fragments, not joining, cylindrical cup, as No. 10. Present ht 30mm; rim diam. 120mm; th. 2-3mm. *1200 (Structure M); SF 771a*

12* Rim fragment, cup. Colourless. Dull, pitted surfaces. Slightly everted rim, edge fire-rounded and thickened, upper body slightly convex. Present ht 31mm; rim diam. 70mm; th. 0.5-1mm. *001; SF 353*

13* Base fragment, ?cylindrical cup. Colourless. No visible weathering. Tubular pushed-in base ring. Present ht 4mm; base diam. *c.* 50mm; th. 1mm. *001; SF 222*

Square bottles
14* Rim fragment, bottle. Bluish-green. Dull, pitted surface. Horizontal folded rim, edge bent out, up, in and flattened. Present ht 9mm; rim diam. *c.* 50mm; th. *c.* 4mm. *1300 (Structure M); SF 391*

15* Body and base fragment, square bottle. Bluish-green. Dull, lightly pitted outer surface. Straight side with small hollow in centre near base, concave base, one raised concentric circle. Present ht 22mm; th. 4.5-7.5mm. *1300 (Structure M); SF 406*

16* Base fragment, square bottle. Bluish-green. Dull, weathering swirls. Straight side, concave base, two raised concentric circles. Present ht 10mm; th. 5-7.5mm. *1300 (Structure M); SF 425*

17* Base fragment, ?square bottle. Bluish-green. Concave base, two raised concentric circles, central pellet. Present ht 7.2mm; th. 4-6.5mm. *6400; SF 1339*

4th-century vessels (Fig. 78)
Colourless
18* Rim fragment, conical cup. Colourless. Dull, weathering streaks. Small bubbles visible. Curved rim, edge cracked-off, straight-sided upper body, tapering in. Thin horizontal band of abraded lines below rim. Present ht 15mm; rim diam. 76mm; th. 0.7mm. *5500M (Well 1; 14.5-15.5m); SF 1739*

19* Body fragment, conical cup. Colourless. Dull. Bubbly. Straight side tapering inwards. Fine abraded horizontal line below rim (missing), two closely set abraded lines on body. Dimensions 38.5 x 22.5mm; th. 0.8mm. *001; SF 44*

20* Body fragment, ?bowl. Colourless. Small bubbles. Wide convex curved side. Horizontal band of abraded lines. Dimensions 23 x 16mm; th. 1mm. *001; SF 398*

20a Body fragment. Dimensions 19 x 24.5mm; th. 1.2-2mm. *1815 (Structure R); SF 1215*

20b Two body fragments. Dimensions 19.5 x 22.5mm; th. 0.5mm. *1305 (Structure M); SF 1315*

21* Rim fragment, jug or bottle. Colourless. Dull, iridescent weathering. Small bubbles. Wide everted rim, edge fire-rounded, funnel mouth with folded solid ridge below rim. Present ht 16mm; rim diam. 90mm; th. 4-6mm. *001; SF 856*

22* Fifteen fragments, several joining, handle and body, ?jug. Colourless. Dull, enamel-like weathering; devitrification fractures. Convex body, lower handle attachment, three rounded ridges. Present ht *c.* 40mm; handle w. 28mm; th. 2.5mm. *Ditch 014/1A; SFs 721 and 724*

22a Very small handle fragment, as No. 22. Dimensions 17 x 7.5mm. *001; SF 504*

Greenish colourless
23* Two joined rim fragments, conical cup. Greenish colourless. Flaking iridescent and enamel-like weathering. Bubbly. Curved rim, edge cracked-off and not ground, straight-sided upper body tapering in. Two faint bands of abraded lines on body. Present ht 33mm; rim diam. *c.* 80mm; th. 1-1.25mm. *8020 (Structure M); SF 1810*

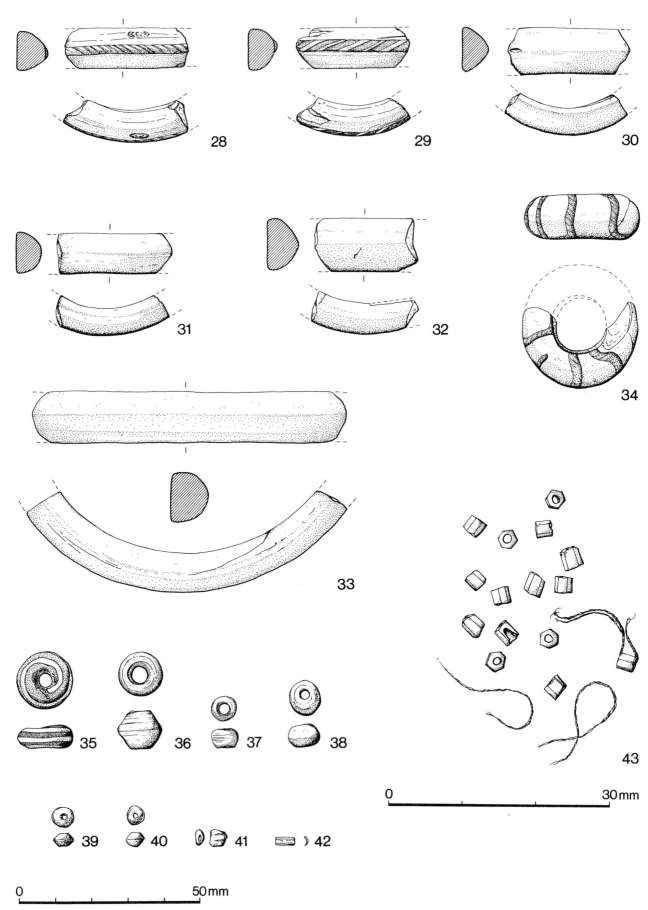

Fig. 79. Glass objects (Nos 28-43). Scale 1:1, except No. 43 which is scale 2:1

24* Body and base fragment, conical cup. Greenish colourless. Flaking iridescent weathering. Straight side tapering in, small concave base. Present ht 20mm; base diam. 38mm; th. 1-1.5mm. *8004 (Structure M); SF 1237*

24a Five joining fragments, body, conical cup. Yellow-greenish colourless. Abraded lines. Dimensions 36 x 34mm; th. 1-1.5mm. *8010 (Structure M); SF 1286*

24b Small body fragment, conical cup. Yellow-greenish colourless. Abraded lines. Dimensions 20 x 21mm; th. 1mm. *8010 (Structure M); SF 1286a*

24c Small body fragment, conical cup. Greenish colourless. Abraded lines. Dimensions 21 x 14.8mm; th. 1mm. *1400 (Structure M); SF 1160*

24d Small body fragment, conical cup. Greenish colourless. Abraded lines. Dimensions 18 x 23mm; th. 1mm. *1300 (Structure M); SF 397*

24e Small body fragment, conical cup. Greenish colourless. Abraded lines. Dimensions 26.5 x 17.5mm; th. 1mm. *1300 (Structure M); SF 399*

24f Small body fragment, conical cup. Greenish colourless. Abraded lines. Dimensions 29.5 x 14.5mm; th. 1mm. *8010 (Structure M); SF 1295a*

25* Rim fragment, hemispherical cup. Pale yellow-green. Dull. very bubbly. Small curved rim, edge cracked-off, convex curved side. Present ht 25mm; rim diam. 70mm; th. 1.5-2mm. *5500L (Well 1; 14.0-14.5m); SF 1455*

26* Rim fragment, hemispherical cup. Yellow-greenish colourless. Dull, flaking enamel-like weathering deposits. Small bubbles. Slightly inturned rim, edge cracked off and not ground, convex side. Three bands of abraded lines on body. Present ht 30mm; rim diam. 90mm; th. 1mm. *8009 (Structure M); SF 1278*

27* Two body fragments, hemispherical cup. Pale yellow-greenish colourless. Dull, weathering swirls. Small bubbles. Convex side. Unmarvered horizontal trail pulled into loops (two surviving). Dimensions 29.5 x 22.5mm and 16.5 x 26.5mm; th. 1mm. *8010 (Structure M); SF 1295b*

Objects (Fig. 79)

Bangles

28* Fragment, D-sectioned bangle. Bluish-green; dark blue and opaque white cord and 'eye'. Dull. Bubbly. Central unmarvered anticlockwise cord, (Z-twist); spiral 'eye'. Ht 11mm; w. 8.5mm; internal diam. *c.* 50mm; present l. 34mm. *1800 (Structure R); SF 455*

29* Fragment, D-sectioned bangle. Bluish-green; dark brown and opaque white cord; dark blue and opaque white 'eye'. Dull. Bubbly. Central unmarvered clockwise cord, (S-twist); spiral 'eye' very broken. Ht 11mm; w. 8mm; internal diam. *c.* 50mm; present l. 31mm. *4200 (Structure J); SF 372*

30* Fragment, triangular-sectioned bangle; type 3A. Opaque white. Shiny outside, dull inside. Ht 12.5mm; w. 7mm; internal diam. *c.* 44mm; present l. 33mm. *5020 (Structure X); SF 1907*

31* Fragment, triangular-sectioned bangle; type 3A. Opaque white. Dull, pitted surfaces. Ht 10mm; w. 7mm; internal diam. 50mm; present l. 31mm. *918 (Structure J); SF 790*

32* Fragment, triangular-sectioned bangle; type 3A. Opaque white. Dull, pitted surfaces. Ht 14mm; w. 8mm; internal diam. *c.* 65mm; present l. 28mm. *902 (Structure J); SF 800*

33* Fragment, massive D-sectioned bangle. Bluish-green. Flaking iridescent weathering, lightly pitted surfaces. Approximately ⅓ of bangle surviving. Broken ends reworked by flaking and polishing. Ht 13mm; w. 9.5-11mm; internal diam. 90mm. *Ditch 020/4; SF 547*

Beads

34* Fragment, large annular bead, plano-convex section. Bluish-green; brown and opaque white cord. Flaking iridescent weathering. Marvered cord in meandering trails across convex surface. Ht 11.5mm; diam. 31.5mm; diam. of perforation 14mm. *5500M (Well 1); SF 1589*

35* Annular bead, flat top and bottom surfaces. Dark blue and opaque white. Marvered spiral trail wound round bead from top to bottom. Ht 6mm; diam. 15mm; diam. of perforation 4mm. *101 (Structure A); SF 56*

36* Biconical bead. Greenish-blue (peacock blue). No weathering. May be post-Roman. Ht 11mm; diam. 12mm; diam. of perforation 5mm. *900 (Structure J); SF 365*

37* Small globular/cylindrical bead. Dark blue. Dull. Ht 5.2mm; diam. 7mm; diam. of perforation 3mm. *101 (Structure A); SF 74*

38* Small globular/cylindrical bead. Greyish-blue. Ht 5.5mm; diam. 9mm; diam. of perforation 3mm. *101 (Structure A); SF 57*

39* Small biconical bead. Dark blue. Ht 3.8mm; diam. 5.5mm; diam. of perforation 1.5mm. *001; SF 789*

40* Small biconical bead. Dark blue. Ht 3.5mm; diam. 5.2mm; diam. of perforation 1.5mm. *303 (Structure B); SF 596*

41* Narrow tubular bead. Dark glass, appearing black. Distorted, surfaces very uneven. L. 4.8mm; w. 2.6mm. *001; SF 696*

42* Fragment, narrow tubular bead. Bluish-green. L. 6.1mm; w. 2.6mm. *1616 (Structure P); SF 1607*

43* Fifteen very small hexagonal beads on fragment of cord. Dark blue. Average l. 2.5mm; average w. 2.3mm. *Ditch 004; SF 2025*

10 Quernstones (Figs 80-88)

by D.G. Buckley and H. Major

Introduction

The excavations at Dalton Parlours produced pieces from a substantial number of quernstones. They came from a variety of contexts located within the area of both the Iron Age settlement and the 2nd to 4th-century Roman villa complex. The collection is one of the largest from a Yorkshire site of these periods recovered under excavation conditions in recent years. As such it is of regional importance and merits detailed study.

The Archive Report contains a catalogue giving full details of each stone. They are listed firstly by form and secondly by smallfind number. The form types comprise saddle querns, beehive lower and upper stones, lava querns, Romano-British flat querns and millstones. With the exception of the lava querns, all appear to be gritstones deriving from sources within the Carboniferous sequence, principally Millstone Grit, of northern England.

The following discussion draws upon the details within the catalogue. It aims to establish the principal features of the Dalton Parlours querns and to place them within a wider context.

Saddle querns

Two stone fragments, Nos 1 and 2, retain traces of smooth, concave surfaces such as are likely to derive from use as saddle querns. Only one is from a dated context.

Saddle querns have been recovered from many sites in England and the evidence for parts of Yorkshire and for the north generally has been reviewed (Hayes 1974, 23-5: Challis and Harding 1975, 22-3). They were in use from the Neolithic period and are often found on 1st millennium BC sites. During the middle to late Iron Age they were

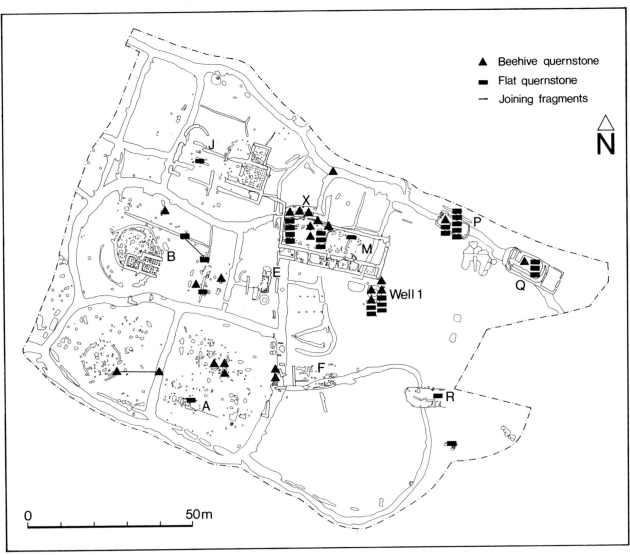

Fig. 80. The site distribution of quernstones.

gradually superseded by rotary querns, although at some sites, such as Gussage All Saints, Dorset (Wainwright 1979), saddle and rotary querns were found in direct association in pits. They also occur on Roman sites in a variety of contexts (Hayes 1974, 25). Although one of the Dalton Parlours stones is from a Roman context, it may be residual and have derived from earlier settlement in the area.

Beehive querns (Figs 81-7)

Pieces from 37 beehive rotary querns were recovered, comprising parts of 16 lower stones and 21 upper stones. Three of the lower stones were not available for examination. Two were unfortunately removed from the excavation before they could be fully recorded and a third, No. 13, disappeared after being photographed and drawn (section only). However, all of these stones were found set into the floor of Structure X and appear on the plan of that building (Fig. 46). Details of a further upper stone, No. 74, found near Dalton Parlours are also included in the catalogue.

The large assemblage of beehive querns from Dalton Parlours can be added to the substantial number already recorded from Yorkshire (Hayes 1974; Challis and Harding 1975, fig. 98; Hayes et al. 1980). These are generally acknowledged to be a native form of rotary quern. They have a wide date range (see below) and considerable variation exists in their form, which raises difficulties when considering the finds from a particular site. Any study is further complicated by a general lack of comparative information in published reports regarding the precise context, stone type and overall form of excavated querns. A systematic survey of all Yorkshire beehive querns is currently being undertaken by the Yorkshire Archaeological Society (Spratt 1987) and comments which follow regarding the Dalton Parlours querns should therefore be seen as provisional.

The principal features of the Dalton Parlours beehive querns are summarised for lower stones in Table 2 and upper stones in Table 3 and can be related to a number of published classifications. Curwen (1937; 1941) divided beehive querns into Wessex/Sussex southern types, Hunsbury Midland types and Roman legionary types from northern England and Scotland. The latter were so called

Table 2. Querns: beehive lower stones.

SF no.	Fig.	Cat. no.	Approx. % survival	Stone size (mm) diam.	height	Spindle size (mm) diam.	depth	Context no.	Description
12	–	3	25	320	>160	–	–	001	Topsoil
474	81	4	80	310	144	24	50	001	Topsoil
564	81	5	100	312	190	20	30	3505	Post-pit (unassigned)
569	81	6	100	345	333	25	c. 65	3312	Post-pit (Roundhouse 7)
638	–	7	25	c. 380	>200	28	14	4103	Post-pit (Roundhouse 7)
775	81	8	100	370	128	24	32	001	Topsoil
1269	82	9	100	344	176	20	49	5500H	Well 1
1703	82	10	unfinished	370	320	–	–	627	Pit (Iron Age)
1820	82	11	80	326	158	22	44	5010	Str. X
1827	82	12	40	388	124	27	23	001	Topsoil
1928	–	13	100	420	245	25	40	4910	Str. X
1963	83	14	100	348	160	26	20	001	Topsoil
1975	83	15	100	c. 340	250	20	36	001	Topsoil
2026	–	16	–	–	–	–	–	001	Topsoil

Table 3. Querns: beehive upper stones.

SF no.	Fig.	Cat. no.	Approx. % survival	Stone size (mm) diam.	height	Form of top	Handle	Context no.	Description
128	83	17	100	300	224	rounded	1	001	Topsoil
⌈141	83	18	100	280	174	rounded	1	001	Topsoil
⎨510								2539	Post-pit (Roundhouse 3)
⌊518								020/1	Ditch
153	84	19	80	290	188	rounded	1	001	Topsoil
310	–	20	fragment	–	>180	–	–	001	Topsoil
776	84	21	40	c. 312	142	flat	1	1200	Str. M
1175	84	22	40	360	154	flat	–	1221	Str. M
1205	–	23	fragment	–	–	rounded	1	5500E	Well 1
1219	84	24	50	322	212	rounded	2	5008	Pit (Iron Age)
1292	84	25	80	322	144	rounded	2	5500J	Well 1
1314	85	26	60	290	170	rounded	–	5500J	Well 1
1477	85	27	fragment	c. 300	>130	flat	1	1602	Str. P
1536	85	28	40	c. 280	168	rounded	1	1701	Str. Q
1702	85	29	100	312	180	raised	2	627	Pit (Iron Age)
1727	85	30	100	306	c. 220	rounded	1	3917	Post-pit (Roundhouse 1)
1728	86	31	25	c. 280	250	raised	–	3916	Post-pit (Roundhouse 1)
1821	86	32	40	344	150	flat	1	1463C	Str. M
1824	86	33	100	330	?	rounded	2	3917	Post-pit (Roundhouse 1)
1841	86	34	35	290	138	rounded	1	1213	Str. M
1845	86	35	70	312	208	rounded	1	001	Topsoil
1847	87	36	20	c. 320	122	rounded	–	4903	Str. X
1962	87	37	50	256	249	rounded	2	001	Topsoil

because of their recovery from numerous Roman military sites on the Northern Frontier and were distinguished from the Hunsbury type by being lower and more bun-shaped in form. Philips (1950) subdivided the Hunsbury type into a Hunsbury type characterised by a handle hole piercing through to the hopper, a Yorkshire type in which the handle did not pierce the hopper, and an East Anglian type, usually of puddingstone, which often lacked a handle hole. These terms were considered inappropriate by Caulfield (1977) since the Hunsbury type is found in Yorkshire and the Yorkshire sub-type is not confined to that county. He favoured the descriptive terms 'pierced' and 'unpierced', a distinction which relates directly to the functioning of the quern since on the pierced querns the inner end of the handle would be attached to the spindle of the lower stone, an arrangement not possible with the unpierced type.

The Dalton Parlours beehive querns are consistent in respect of two features – the handle hole and the form of the grinding surface. Of the sixteen upper stones with handle holes, all are cut into the side of the stone and are of Philips' Yorkshire and Caulfield's unpierced type. In all cases the grinding surfaces are almost flat or only slightly convex on lower stones, with correspondingly concave upper stones. However, there is evidence to suggest, notably No. 8, that the stones may have been used with the grinding surface set at an angle, a functional property noted for the beehive lower stones at Thorpe Thewles, Cleveland (Heslop 1987, 89). In other respects the stones can be very variable.

Diameters range from 310-420mm in lower stones and 256-360mm in upper stones, and height from 124-333mm in lower stones and 122-250mm in upper stones. Grinding surfaces are generally smooth although lower stone No. 9 has worn traces of an originally pecked surface. Occasionally mismatched stones have been used together resulting in a slight ridge round the outer edge of the grinding surface as on upper stone No. 24 and lower stone No. 9. There is considerable variation in the degree of dressing of the outer surface. Upper stones tend to be better finished with smooth surfaces, occasionally pecked, but sometimes left rather rough. Lower stones are generally rougher, ranging from a flattened, well-finished, pecked base on No. 12 through to those with only a roughly worked base such as No. 5, or in the case of No. 4, left in a natural state. Lower stone No. 15 was made from a natural boulder, resulting in an assymetric stone which is almost vertical on one side and sloping on the other.

Apart from the size and state of finish, the main feature of lower stones is the spindle hole. This survives on eleven stones and is usually round, ranging in diameter from 20-28mm and set from 14-65mm into the stone. Number 9 is different in that it is square at the top, becoming cylindrical towards the bottom. There are also lower stones with features of particular interest. Number 9 has a hole cut low down on the side suggestive of a handle slot. It seems likely that this was intended for an upper stone but was converted into a lower, possibly because the stone

broke badly when the top was being worked. Number 10 has no spindle hole and appears to be an unfinished rough-out for a truncated conical lower stone. The base is flat and the sides fairly well dressed but the top is unfinished, possibly due to accidental breakage of the stone on one side. The top was being dressed from the edge towards the middle at the time when work stopped.

The upper stones have differences in profile, hoppers, feed-pipes and handle holes. Three broad forms of profile can be identified comprising rounded, flat and collared. In the rounded form the sides curve over into the hopper without any flattening of the top of the stone as with Nos 25-6; the flat form has a broad area of surface between the side and the hopper as with No. 32; and the collared form has a constricted top to the stone resulting in a raised hopper with a narrow flat surface round it, as with Nos 29-30. Hoppers vary in form from V-shaped to U-shaped and lead to feed-pipes of variable diameter. The majority are straight, occasionally widening slightly towards the grinding surface, but in two instances (Nos 18 and 31) there is a marked kink or change of direction. The base of the feed-pipe of No. 17 widens to form a double hole to take the spindle, which is also a feature of No. 74, a stone found near the site. Numbers 19 and 33 have a depression on the grinding surface round the bottom of the feed-pipe, probably to assist the movement of the grain outwards. The feed-pipe to No. 24 is assymetrically positioned and that to No. 27 askew. Handle slots are generally placed well down on the side of the stone and in one instance, No. 34, the hole appears to have broken through to the grinding surface as a result of the wearing down of the stone. Five stones have two handle slots which are diametrically opposed, with the exception of No. 24, where they are at an angle of 120°.

It is considered likely that the wide variation of form within the beehive querns from Dalton Parlours reflects different places of manufacture and date. Querns of rounded profile are the most numerous form present. These have similarities with the 'Roman legionary' form of quern identified by Curwen (1937, 147, figs 28-32) and which predominates between Yorkshire and Scotland. The flat-topped forms have closer affinities with querns found south of Yorkshire, of Curwen's (1941, 17) unpierced Hunsbury type. Similarly, the two querns with collared hoppers are comparable with Hunsbury querns of the pierced form (Curwen 1941, 17, figs 11-12). The most likely explanation is that during its long period of occupation Dalton Parlours obtained querns from a variety of sources. The differences in detail may reflect particular quarries where they were produced or the workshops at which they were finished. However, lower stone No. 10 was apparently abandoned in the process of being finished which raises the question of the extent to which stone from immediately local sources was used, or whether the trading of rough-outs direct from quarry to site occurred. Many differences of form could then reflect individual craftsmen, possibly peripatetic, producing querns after the fashion of the workshop or area in which they learnt their trade. Clarification of this question awaits

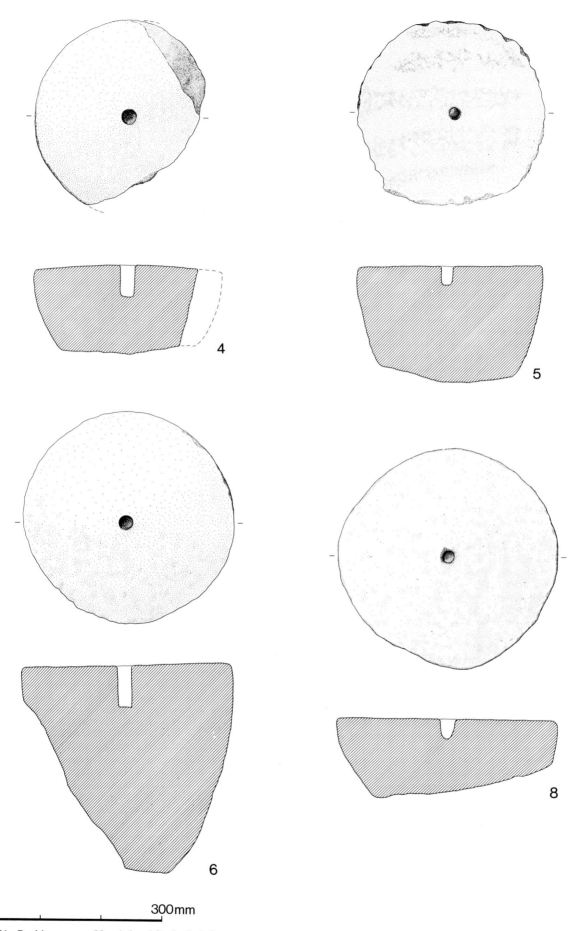

0   300mm

Fig. 81. Beehive querns (Nos 4-6 and 8). Scale 1:6

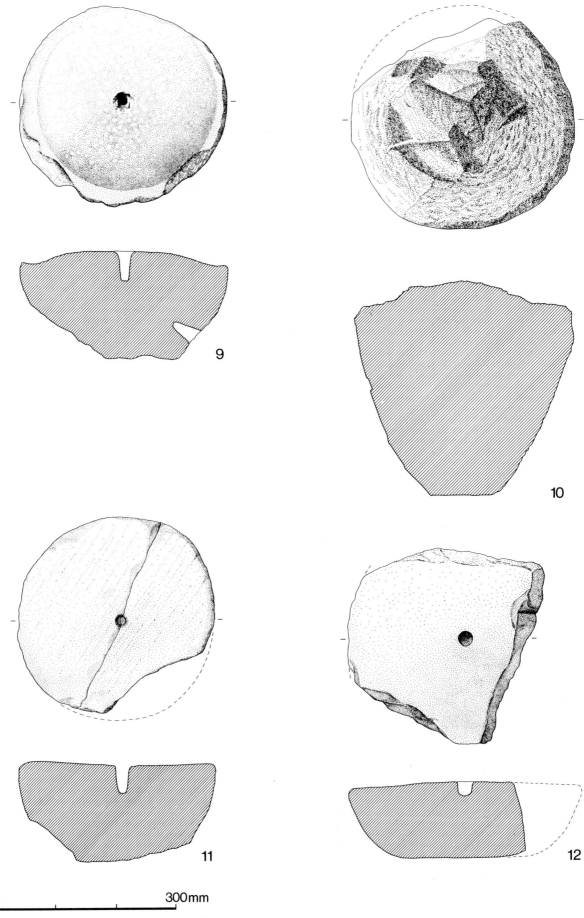

Fig. 82. Beehive querns (Nos 9-12). Scale 1:6

0   300mm

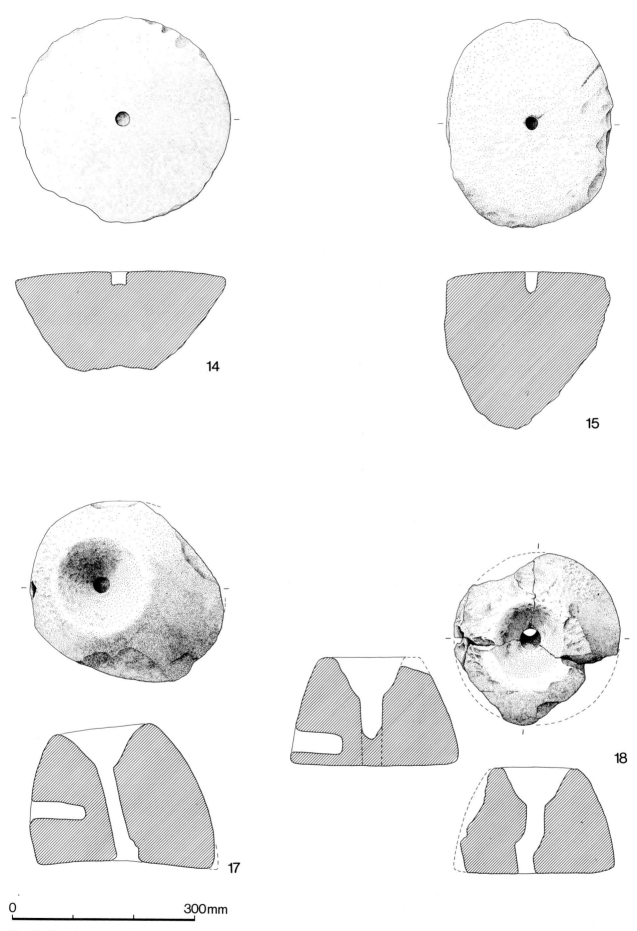

Fig. 83. Beehive querns (Nos 14-15 and 17-18). Scale 1:6

0   300mm

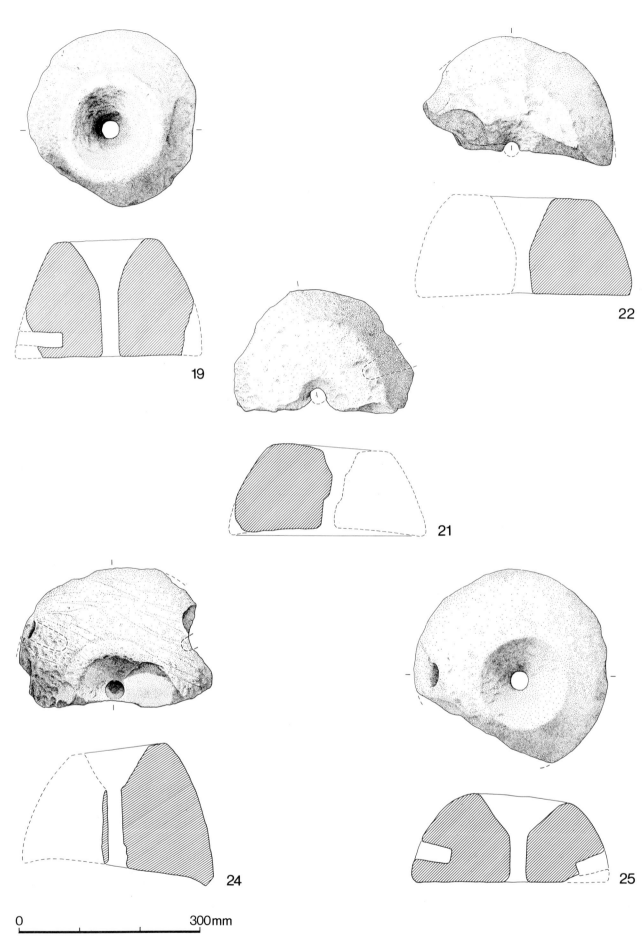

19

22

21

24

25

0   300mm

Fig. 84. Beehive querns (Nos 19, 21-2 and 24-5). Scale 1:6

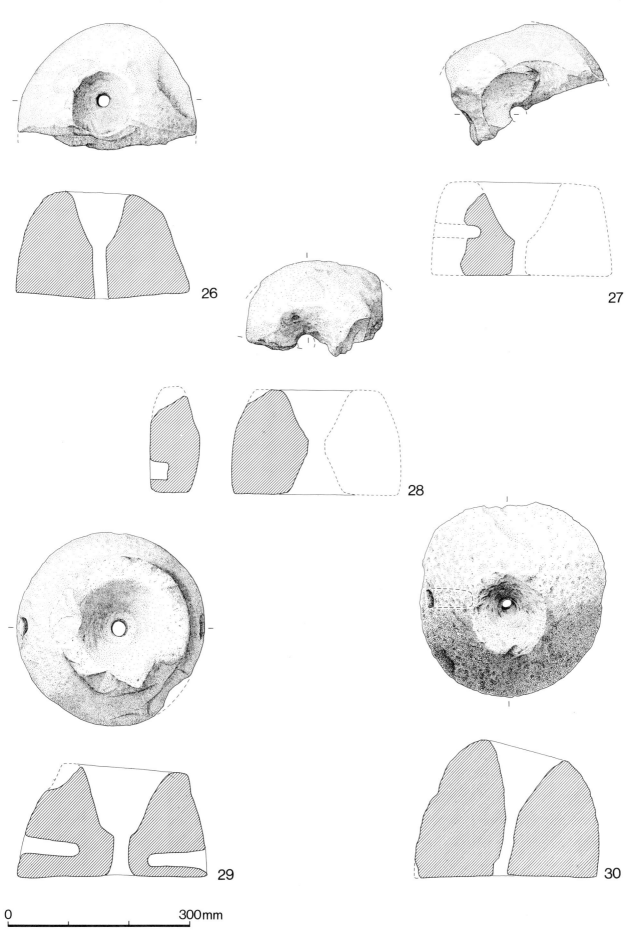

0   300mm

Fig. 85. Beehive querns (Nos 26-30). Scale 1:6

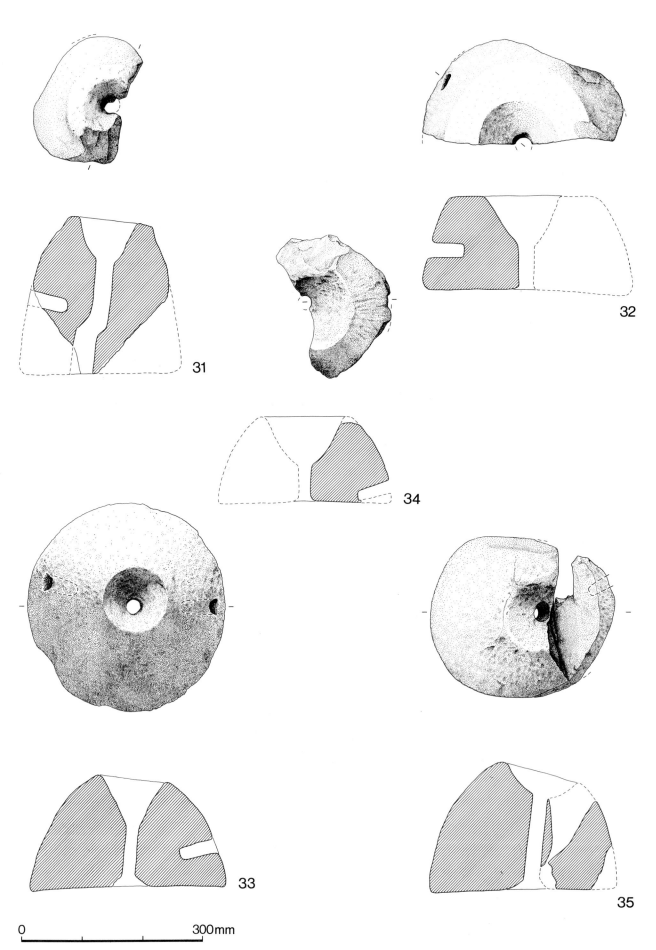

31

32

34

33

35

0   300mm

Fig. 86. Beehive querns (Nos 31-5). Scale 1:6

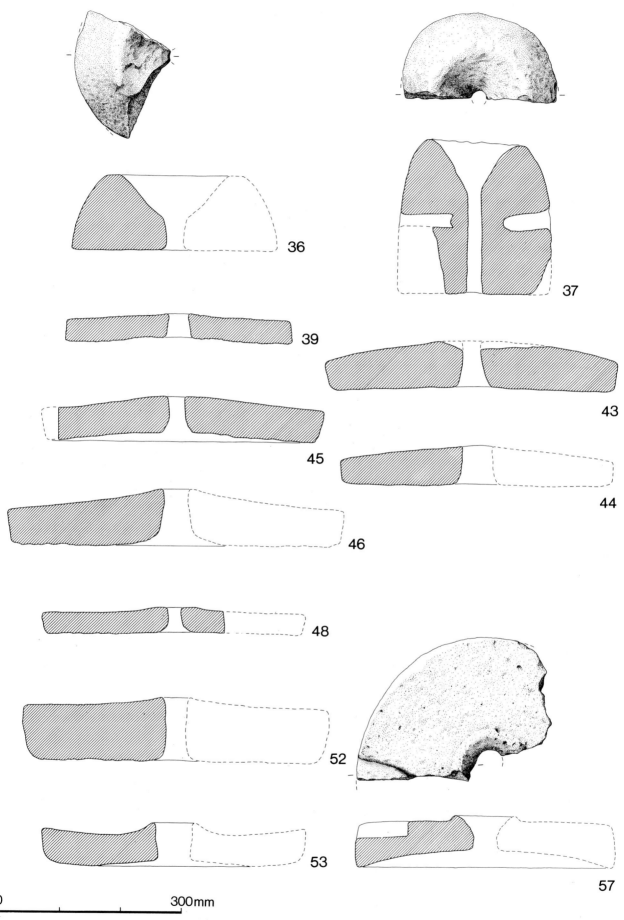

Fig. 87. Beehive querns (Nos 36-7); lava quern (No. 39); Romano-British flat querns (Nos 43-6, 48, 52-3 and 57). Scale 1:6

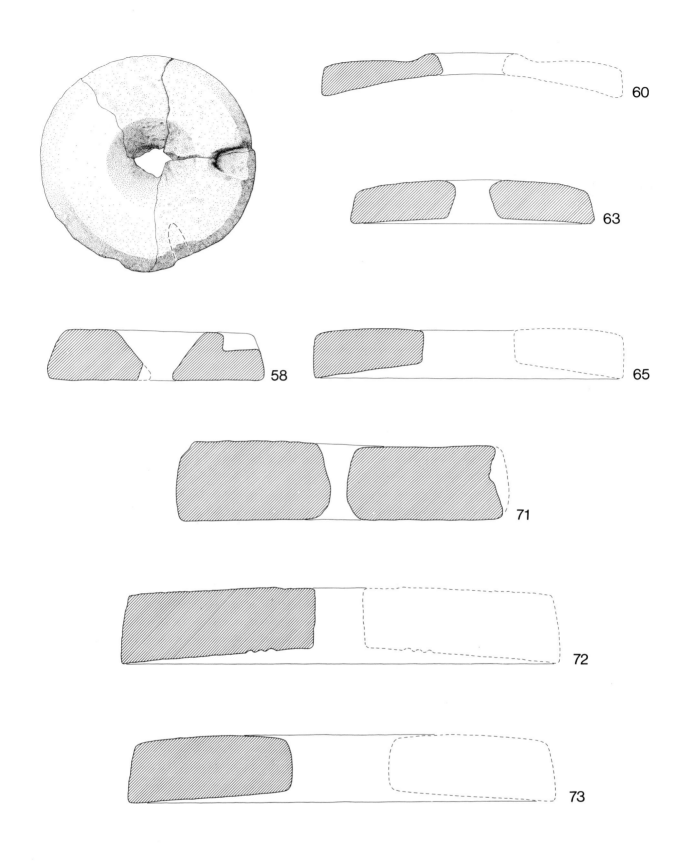

0   300mm

Fig. 88. Romano-British flat querns (Nos 58, 60, 63, 65 and 71-3). Scale 1:6

the results of much detailed work on the distribution and forms of large numbers of beehive querns throughout northern England, and the location of more quarries and production centres, few of which are yet known.

Dalton Parlours does have a number of querns from broadly dated Iron Age or Roman contexts and these are of particular value for future research into the evolution of beehive querns. Generally, the dating of beehive querns is difficult. Welfare (1985, 154) has indicated that production in the north of England may have begun by the 2nd century BC, and this date has been accepted as reasonable for Yorkshire by Spratt (1982, 188) based upon pottery associations. In the south of England, beehive querns appear to have been rapidly superseded by flat forms following the Roman conquest. However, in the north of England, although flat forms appeared with the Roman army before the end of the 1st century AD (Buckley and Major forthcoming), beehive querns continue to be one of the most widespread finds on Romano-British sites in Yorkshire, Durham and Northumberland of 2nd to 4th-century date (Caulfield 1977, 107).

Iron Age contexts producing beehive querns include Roundhouse 3 (No. 18), Roundhouse 1 (Nos 30, 31 and 33) and Roundhouse 7 (Nos 6-7). These all derive from post-pits within the buildings, where they were used for post-packing, and include upper stones of rounded (Nos 30 and 33) and collared form (No. 31). An isolated post-pit (5008) cut by an Iron Age boundary ditch contained an upper stone of rounded form (No. 24). A further post-pit (627) located beneath Structure F and apparently cut by an Iron Age boundary ditch, also contained an unfinished lower stone (No. 10) and an upper stone of collared form (No. 29). These are the earliest rotary querns from the site, and since with the exception of No. 10 all were used before breakage and reused as post-packing, it is probable that the stones were produced during an earlier phase than that in which they were found. It is therefore quite possible that, as at Thorpe Thewles (Heslop 1987, 119), rotary querns may have been used for grain processing at Dalton Parlours from the earliest stages of the occupation.

Roman contexts producing beehive querns include Structures M, Q, X and Well 1. A number of these are from the topsoil over the buildings or came from 19th-century backfill and therefore may not be directly associated with the structure. Others appear to be part of the Roman backfill and cannot with certainty be related to the structure in which they were found. However, Structure X is of particular interest in that it contained four *in situ* lower stones: Nos 11 and 13 (see Fig. 46, S.1001; Pl. XIII), and two which were stolen from the site. There can be little doubt that milling was a primary activity carried out within Structure X and that beehive querns were in use during the later Roman period at Dalton Parlours (see below). The four beehive uppers with flat tops (Nos 21-2, 27 and 32) all derive from Roman contexts and may represent a later form.

Lava querns (Fig. 87)

Fragments of lava quern were recovered from only two contexts at Dalton Parlours. Number 38 comprised no more than four, possibly burnt, fragments from the topsoil, but No. 39 comprised 54 conjoining fragments from a complete lower stone, found overlying kiln or furnace debris in Structure M.

These conform to the standard characteristics of lava querns imported into Britain in large quantities during the Roman period, the majority from the Mayen area of Germany (Hörter et al. 1952; Crawford and Röder 1955). They comprised a new form of quernstone to the beehive querns, incorporating improvements to the stone which were dependent upon the use of the rynd and the spindle and are reflected in the fully perforating spindle hole of No. 39. This made it possible to adjust the stones and for the grain to be reduced by a shearing and grinding process rather than the crushing and tearing of the heavy beehive quern, thereby enabling greater gradation in the milled grain.

Lava querns are difficult to date. They were a standard item of legionary equipment, fragments of which have been found on many military sites in Britain (McIlwain 1980, 132) and appeared in Yorkshire with the invading army in the later 1st century. It has been argued that the lava quern trade declined by the 3rd century (Peacock 1980, 50). Number 39, however, comes from a later Roman context, and its completeness suggests that it may have remained in use until shortly before deposition. In southern Britain, particularly East Anglia, lava querns appear to have become a regular part of civil trade (Buckley and Major 1983), but their distribution in the north suggests that they remained essentially military. Dalton Parlours, in common with other Yorkshire rural sites, produced virtually no lava querns, and can be contrasted with the military site at Castleford where they were numerous in both fort and *vicus* contexts (Buckley and Major forthcoming: see this report for further discussion of the dating of lava querns).

Romano-British flat querns (Figs 87-8)

Pieces from 36 flat rotary querns were recovered comprising parts of eighteen lower stones, fourteen upper stones and four indeterminate. Two stones, from Structures P and R, disappeared following preliminary recording and were not available for detailed examination.

Production of flat millstone grit querns began soon after the Roman conquest of the north in the late 1st century AD, almost certainly influenced by the appearance of the flat lava quern. The type continued in use throughout the Roman period. They have been recovered from many Yorkshire sites but there has been no survey comparable to that undertaken for the beehive querns. Nor has there been detailed examination of the stones, although a study is currently being made of the

Table 4. Querns: flat lower stones.

SF no.	Fig.	Cat. no.	Approx. % survival	Stone size (mm) Diam.	Thickness at edge	Max. height	Spindle hole diam.	Context no.	Description
760	–	40	30	420	40	–	–	1023	Str. J
838	–	41	30	*c.* 420	66	–	40	5500E	Well 1
1177	–	42	15	*c.* 460	50	64	40	1216/1	Str. M
1178	87	43	100	490	48	74	56	1216/1	Str. M
1280	87	44	25	*c.* 460	40	60	64	5500J	Well 1
1390	87	45	50	466	54	70	26	5500K	Well 1
1475	87	46	40	*c.* 560	50	60	38	1602	Str. P
1537	–	47	20	590	84	–	–	1701	Str. Q
1545	87	48	25	430	34	40	26	1603	Str. P
1628	88	71	100	555	130	–	48	1603	Str. P
1822	–	49	20	612	58	–	–	100	Str. A
1823	–	50	15	510	50	–	–	1615	Str. P
1825	–	51	fragment	490	78	–	–	1606	Str. P
1828	87	52	30	510	90	?	40	001	Topsoil
1846	87	53	15	436	54	?	60	1213	Str. M
1863	–	54	fragment	>548	–	68	*c.* 44	1432-33	Str. M
1932/ 1941	–	55	20	380	60	–	–	5500J	Well 1
1969	–	56	fragment	–	60	–	–	1701	Str. Q

Table 5. Querns: flat upper stones.

SF no.	Fig.	Cat. no.	Approx. % survival	Stone size (mm) Diam.	Thickness at edge	Hopper diam.	Context no.	Description
410	87	57	40	434	65	*c.* 100	001	Topsoil
568	88	58	100	360	80	150	3312	Post-pit (?Roundhouse 7)
575/ 590	88	72	50	730	110	80	3436/ 3461	Post-pit (unassigned)
786	–	59	20	432	58	*c.* 100	1400	Str. M
1178a	88	60	20	496	48	90	1216/1	Str. M
1188	–	61	15	428	70	–	1222	Str. Y
1217	–	–	100	*c.* 480	60	35x40	1815	Str. R
1474	–	62	fragment	>500	45	–	1602	Str. P
1478	–	–	50	526	50	?	1602	Str. P.
1631	88	63	80	400	55	80x58	5500M	Well 1
1688	88	73	15	715	100	–	001	Topsoil
1826	–	64	10	*c.* 410	82	–	1701	Str. Q
1842	88	65	fragment	512	72	150	1900	Oven
1866	–	66	fragment	470	48	–	1221	Str. M

South Yorkshire Wharncliffe quarries (Liz Wright pers. comm.). The large assemblage from Dalton Parlours is a significant addition to the recorded sites and of importance to any future study. The principal features of the lower stones are summarised in Table 4 and upper stones in Table 5. They equate with the class of Romano-British domestic quern which was identified by Curwen (1937). This class had two main groups: an earlier form characterised by flat-topped stones with a radiating groove for the handle on the top of the stone (Curwen 1937, figs 15-18), and a later form which had projecting hoppers, was thinner, of greater diameter and much better finished (Curwen 1937, figs 19-20). Curwen's classification of flat querns was largely based on southern examples and although certain characteristics of the Dalton Parlours flat querns can be related to one or other of these classes, there are overall variations which distinguish them as distinctly northern forms. Most of the upper stones are flat topped with a V-shaped hopper and are similar to Curwen's earlier group. However, No. 60 and the missing stone from Structure P have slightly projecting rims round the hopper which, though not pronounced, are comparable to Curwen's later group. A further variation not considered by Curwen is represented by No. 61 which has a flat rim only 34mm wide round a large hopper occupying most of the top of the stone. Unfortunately only a small amount of the stone survives, but this does include a small part of the edge of the feed-pipe. This appears to be set off-centre, suggesting that the stone was of a type which had a central rib. This rib usually has a handle slot set into it, and probably served to strengthen the stone at its weakest point. Querns of this type were recorded from Doncaster by Buckland and Magilton (1986, 100-102) and they, citing several parallels, claim this to be a widespread form on Roman military sites in northern Britain. A number of stones of this form have recently been reported from the military site of Castleford (Buckley and Major forthcoming).

There is considerable variation in the size and thickness of the stones (Tables 4 and 5). Upper stones range from 360-730mm in diameter and 45-110mm in thickness at the edge of the stone. Lower stones range from 380-612mm in diameter and 34-130mm in thickness at the edge of the stone. This is a considerable range, and it is likely that at least three of the larger stones, Nos 72-3, and lower stone No. 71 derive from geared mills. Since there is no stream at Dalton Parlours these would need to be turned by either animal or man power. Four stones retain handle slots: Nos 57-8, 64 and the missing stone from Structure R. In the case of No. 58 there is a handle slot on the top, but also a 20mm deep groove in the grinding surface which may represent an original handle hole in the side of the stone. Number 63, although substantially complete, has no handle slot, but a suggestion of wear round the edge of the stone may have been caused by an iron band round the stone from which a vertical handle would have projected.

There is considerable variation in the overall finish of the stones. The upper stones are generally better finished than the lower stones, which are usually left rough on the underside. Most dressed faces have a smooth finish, though traces of pecking are present on the top surface of Nos 57 and 62, there is crude vertical tooling on the side of No. 50, and No. 51 may also originally have had vertical pecked lines. Upper stone No. 63 appears to have been worked from a water-worn boulder.

Grinding surfaces are slightly convex on lower stones, with corresponding slightly concave surfaces on upper stones. They are mostly smooth, with the exception of No. 49 which has harp dressing, a feature of many Roman lava querns. Several of the grinding surfaces have a slightly raised rim round the outer edge resulting from use with a mismatched stone. Feed-pipes are round or oval, but that of No. 64 is irregular in shape, suggesting that it might originally have had a slot for keying the rynd. This stone also has a groove from the hopper which appears to be an original feature and may have assisted the outward flow of the grain. Lower stones Nos 42, 44, 46 and 48 have a raised lip round the spindle hole, and lower stone No. 54 also has concentric striations on the grinding surface.

It is difficult to assign close dates to particular forms of flat rotary querns. Very few have been recovered from well-dated contexts, making it impossible to develop Curwen's original classification. Study is also hampered by the fact that individual stones could have remained in use for many decades with periodic re-dressing and modification. Stones were also readily reusable for a variety of purposes before being finally discarded. Challis and Harding (1975, 25) suggested that flat rotary types became dominant in the 3rd century AD, and the Dalton Parlours assemblage is in accord with this in that all of the flat stones, with the possible exception of No. 58, derive from contexts associated with later Roman buildings (Structures A, J, M, P, Q, R and Y) and Well 1. However, almost every variation of form represented is paralleled in late 1st to early 2nd-century AD contexts at Castleford (Buckley and Major forthcoming). While some of the Dalton Parlours querns may have been in use at an earlier period, most were without doubt brought to the site and used during the main occupation of the villa during the 3rd to 4th centuries. This would suggest that once production was established, only minor innovations occurred in the form of flat querns between the late 1st and 4th centuries.

Discussion

Further progress in understanding the production and morphology of these stones is most likely to result from the location of more quarries and petrological study, as demonstrated by Peacock (1987) for the Greensand querns of southern England. Such work may also help to resolve questions about the dual production of beehive and flat millstone grit querns. In southern England beehive querns were rapidly superseded by flat querns early in the Roman period, using local stone types or imported lava. Later in the Roman period, large numbers of flat millstone grit querns and millstones were traded to the south. This process appears to have begun during the 2nd century, as evidenced by an unfinished millstone grit millstone found in the Blackfriars boat (Marsden 1966), and during the 3rd and 4th centuries millstone grit querns were a major import into London, replacing the former almost exclusive supply of lava querns and millstones from Gaul and Germany (Milne 1985, 122). However, in the north of England, where these flat stones were being produced, the change was less evident. Although flat querns appear on many sites throughout the Roman period they are complemented by beehive querns. This is the case at Dalton Parlours where both forms are present in 3rd to 4th-century contexts, and there is little doubt that they were in use at the same time. Structure X had four beehive lower stones set for use into the floor and together with Structure M, which contained a kiln and had fragments of flat quern in its makeup, appears to form part of a bakery complex. Similarly, the accumulated debris used to backfill Well 1 contained both beehive and flat querns apparently all disposed of at the same time. The number of beehive querns from late contexts at Dalton Parlours and many other sites suggests that production continued on some scale, but that nationally the production of flat stones was much more extensive.

What is not clear is how production of the two forms was organised. The extensive quarry at Wharncliffe, South Yorkshire has produced numerous rough-outs for both beehive and flat querns and this has been seen as a chronological development (Challis and Harding 1975, 23). The working of stone for beehive querns on an industrial scale had almost certainly begun by the late Iron Age, and by the later Roman period it is probable that the large scale trade in millstone grit flat querns was supported by large quarries. Did a small number of quarries come to take over most of the quern production, making a variety of forms to suit regional requirements, or did numerous small quarries continue to exist as well, maintained by local craftsmen? The range of querns from Dalton Parlours, many only crudely finished, would support the latter theory.

The number of querns from Dalton Parlours serves to emphasise the importance of grain cultivation throughout both periods of occupation. Spratt (1982, 185) has used the many beehive querns recorded to cast doubt on any nomadic-pastoralist view of Iron Age Yorkshire, and the site can be added to the list of mixed farming settlements of that date from the county. In the later Roman period, grain production clearly played a major role in the agricultural activities of the villa. The concentrations of querns in Structures X, M, P and Q, with associated hearths and ovens, indicate that all of these buildings were probably used for activities associated with the processing of grain. The range of forms used – beehive, flat and millstones – suggests that a variety of grain crops were being grown. Continued use of the beehive quern is unlikely to be simply anachronistic, but rather indicates milling to produce coarse forms of meal. A finer product was obtained by using adjustable flat querns, and it is possible that the replacement of Structure X during the 4th century, with its four in situ beehive querns, by the more

substantial Structure M reflects both intensification of grain processing and increased use of more efficient flat querns. The presence of a number of larger millstones may also be an indication of this process.

Acknowledgements

Thanks are given to Don Spratt and Liz Wright for reading and commenting on this report.

11 Miscellaneous Stone and Ceramic Artefacts (excluding structural stonework) (Figs 89-92) by J.C. Clarke

Ceramic objects (Fig. 89)

Spindlewhorls
1* Grey ware; spindlewhorl, made from a base sherd. Diam. 38mm; th. 7mm; hole diam. 6mm. *001; SF 381*

2 Grey ware; spindlewhorl, fragment made from a base sherd. Diam. 28.5mm; th. 7mm; hole diam. 5mm. *Ditch 002/9A; SF 1952*

3 Grey ware; spindlewhorl, made from a base sherd; broken. Diam. 34mm; th. 7mm; hole diam. 7mm. *Ditch 036/1; SF 703*

4 Grey ware; spindlewhorl, made from a body sherd; broken. Diam. 38.5mm; th. 8.5mm; hole diam. 7mm. *1213/3 (Structure M); SF 1326*

5 Grey ware; spindlewhorl, made from a base sherd; abraded. Diam. 35mm; th. 6.5mm; hole diam. 7mm. *5500 (Well 1); SF 1734*

6* Black Burnished ware 2; spindlewhorl, made from a body sherd, the edge chipped in places. Diam. 38mm; th. 5mm; hole diam. 5mm. *8023G (Structure M); SF 1711*

Counters made from vessels
7* Grey ware; counter, made from a body sherd, roughly chipped into shape. Diam. *c.* 32mm; th. 8mm. *001; SF 1905*

8* Grey ware; counter, made from a body sherd, roughly chipped into shape and with a small central hole. Another hole has been started on the inner surface nearer the edge. Diam. *c.* 38mm; th. 5mm; hole diam. 3mm. *200 (Structure B); SF 449*

9 Grey ware; counter, made from the base of a vessel. Diam. 71mm; th. 16mm. *5500M (Well 1); SF 1801*

10 Orange oxidised ware; counter, made from a body sherd with smoothed edges, but almost heart-shaped. Approx. diam. 56 x 52mm; th. 8mm. *8301/2; SF 1920*

Counters made of tile
11* Counter with roughly chipped edges; made from a box tile with combing on its upper surface. Diam. *c.* 52mm; th. 18mm. *001; SF 1804a*

12 Counter with smoothed edges, but approx. oval in shape. L. 68mm; w. 58mm; th. 23mm. *001; SF 1804b*

13 Counter with roughly chipped edges, almost square in shape. L. 70mm; w. 67mm; th. 26mm. *001; SF 1804c*

14* Counter with quite well-chipped edges; probably made from a box tile as it has a slight angle. Diam. *c.* 60mm; th. 20mm. *001; SF 1804d*

15 Counter with roughly chipped edges. Diam. *c.* 45mm; th. 20mm. *Ditch 002/3; SF 507*

16 Counter with quite well-chipped edges; probably made from an *imbrex* as it has a slight curve. Diam. *c.* 44mm; th. 18mm. *Ditch 005/2; SF 1797*

17 Counter with smoothed edges. Diam. *c.* 49mm; th. 23mm. *1213/1 (Structure M); SF 1129*

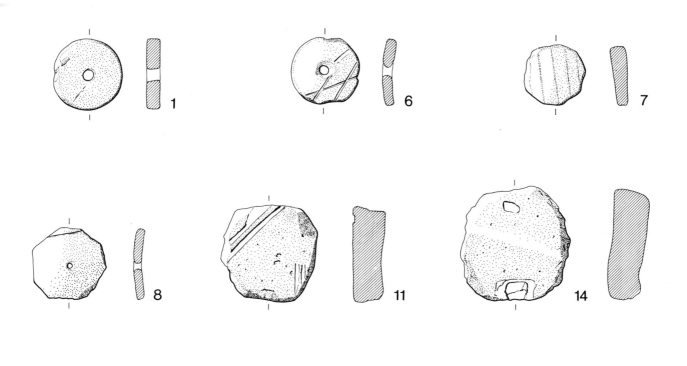

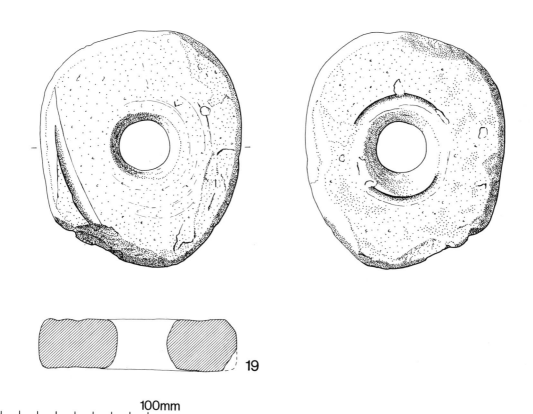

Fig. 89. Miscellaneous ceramic objects (Nos 1, 6-8, 11, 14 and 19). Scale 1:2

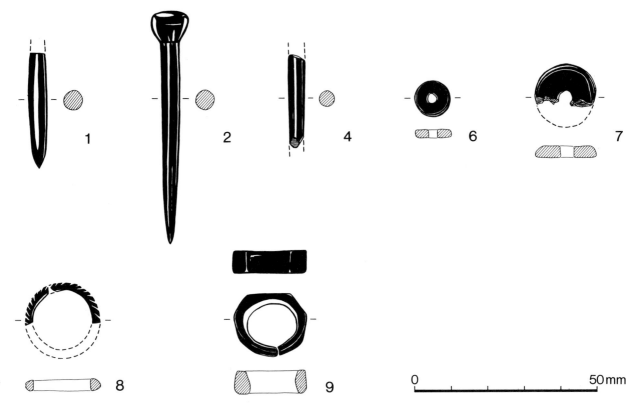

Fig. 90. Objects of jet (Nos 1-2, 4 and 6-9). Scale 1:1

18 Counter with smoothed edges, but oval in shape and varying in thickness. L. 60mm; w. 54mm; max. th. 28mm. *5500M (Well 1); SF 2006*

Loomweight
19* Approx. oval loomweight formed from a *tegula* with a perforation made during manufacture; part of a signature mark on its upper surface. L. 125mm; w. 110mm; th. 28mm; hole diam. 28mm. *5500M (Well 1); SF 1967*

Discussion
The pottery spindlewhorls show a greater uniformity of size than those of stone (see below), five of the six having diameters between 34-38.5mm, and all having thicknesses and hole diameters within close limits.

Size is much more variable among the pot and tile counters, but they are generally smaller than those of stone. Number 8 is the only example of the pierced counter type which also displays an unfinished attempt close to the completed perforation (cf. Crummy 1983, 95, fig. 99, no. 2463). The tile counters seem to have been produced from *tegulae*, *imbrices* and box tiles. The loomweight, made from a *tegula* with part of a signature mark remaining, has well-smoothed edges despite its somewhat irregular shape.

Objects of jet (Fig. 90)
Hairpins
1* Fragment of swollen-waisted shaft, broken a little above the swelling. Not lathe-turned. L. 30mm; max. diam. 6mm. *001; SF 396*

2* Complete pin with a flattened, fairly irregular head; knife marks at the point, but the rest well polished. Not lathe-turned. L. 60mm; max. diam. of head 10.5mm; max. diam. of shaft 5mm. *Ditch 011; SF 360*

3   Fragment of tapering shaft, broken at both ends near to point. Not lathe-turned; soft jet. L. 12mm; max. diam. 3.5mm. *1200 (Structure M); SF 774*

4* Fragment of tapering shaft, broken at the tip and crudely repointed with the new surface unpolished. Not lathe-turned. L. 24.5mm; max. diam. 4.5mm. *8200 (Structure V); SF 919*

5   Fragment of tapering shaft, broken at both ends. Not lathe-turned. L. 25mm; max. diam. 3.5mm. *8201/1 (Structure V); SF 1221*

Beads
6* Oblate disc bead. Diam. 9.5mm; th. 3mm. *1500 (Structure O); SF 430*

7* Fragment of disc bead with bevelled edge, broken across its diameter and tapering towards the break. Soft jet. Diam. 17mm; th. at edge 3mm; th. at centre 2mm. *2550/9; SF 526*

Finger-rings
8* Fragments of a D-shaped section ring with incised cable decoration on the outer surface. Soft jet. Int. diam. *c.* 16mm; th. 2mm; ht 3.5mm. *303 (Structure B); SF 834*

9* Complete ring, slightly distorted to oval shape, with the hoop split opposite the bezel; this is flat and rectangular (length twice its width), with almost square, flat shoulders at unequal angles on either side; these in turn become flat, shield-shaped areas merging into the rest of the slightly narrower beaded hoop. The internal surface is not smoothed and polished; soft jet. Int. diam. oval 13 x 11mm; ht at bezel 7mm; th. at bezel 2mm; th. of hoop 2.5mm. *1302 (Structure M); SF 1900*

Discussion

The small number of artefacts made from jet can be accounted for by the fact that it occurs in the British Isles only in the Whitby area of North Yorkshire, making it a rare and expensive commodity in Roman Britain. Direct evidence is lacking that it was exported in the raw state (Crummy 1983, 20), although evidence for pin manufacture was found at York during excavations on the site of the new railway station in 1873 (*RCHM* 1962, 141-4, pls 68-70).

The only complete hairpin (No. 2) is of type 1 (Crummy 1983, 27, fig. 24, nos 446-8; Allason-Jones and Miket 1984, 133, no. 6) and can be dated by analogy to bone pins of types 3 (Crummy 1979) and B1 (Greep, forthcoming), the former giving a date of *c*. AD 200-400+, the latter *c*. AD 150/200-400. The shaft fragment (No. 1) appears to have been repointed asymmetrically, but the new point polished (unlike No. 4). This would have resulted in a rather dumpy pin, ineffective as a hairpin (cf. Crummy 1983, 27, fig. 24, no. 447). Late pin shafts such as these were either lathe-turned or hand-carved (Crummy 1983, 27), all five examples being produced in the latter manner. Numbers 1 and 2 have irregular cross-sections and Nos 3-5 have slight knife-cut facets.

The beads (Nos 6-7) fall within the disc bead category adapted by Crummy from Beck (1928): length less than one third of the diameter. Given the nature of the 'soft' jet it is possible that bead No. 7 is part of a thicker one that has split, but continued in use, as the 'back' surface is less polished than the others. There is no reason for the date of these beads to be outside the general range for the site, given that the Colchester examples are mainly from a 4th-century cemetery.

Jet finger-ring decorative motifs are often similar to those of armlets (Crummy 1983, 45) and examples of cable decoration similar to the smaller ring (No. 8) occur in Colchester, Essex (Crummy 1983, 36, nos 1556 and 1558) and Cirencester, Gloucestershire (Viner 1986, 116; McWhirr 1986, 245) in 3rd to 4th-century contexts. The complete ring (No. 9) is rather crude: the angles of the shoulders are unequal and the inner surface is unfinished. It may have been intended that an incised design or inscription was to be cut in the flat bezel (cf. Crummy 1983, 49, no. 1787, an inscribed copper-alloy ring). Again, a 3rd to 4th-century date can be assigned to these two rings.

The term 'soft jet' has been borrowed from Allason-Jones and Miket (1984) and applied to Nos 3 and 7-9. The material falls between shale and true jet, having some organic inclusions and a slight tendency to laminate (Dr G. Hornung, pers. comm.).

Stone objects (Figs 91-2)

Whetstones

1   Sandstone; tapering, triangular-sectioned stone; fairly rough on all surfaces. L. 78mm; max. w. 29mm; max. th. 19mm. *001; SF 1*

2   Siltstone; rectangular-sectioned stone; smooth on three sides, one end faceted. L. 112mm; max. w. 30mm; th. 20mm. *001; SF 41*

3   Micaceous sandstone; approx. triangular-shaped stone, split from a larger one. L. 63mm; max. w. 32mm; max. th. 14mm. *001; SF 42*

4   Sandstone; rectangular-sectioned stone, pointed at one end, broken at the other; fairly smooth on all surfaces. L. 108mm; max. w. 40mm; max. th. 37mm. *001; SF 224*

5*   Micaceous sandstone; approx. circular-sectioned stone, rounded at one end, broken at the other. L. 69mm; diam. *c.* 38mm. *001; SF 1787*

6*   Fine micaceous sandstone; oval-sectioned stone, rounded at one end, broken at the other. L. 112mm; w. 43mm; max. th. 27mm. *Ditch 005/2; SF 574*

7*   Micaceous sandstone; rectangular-sectioned, flat fragment; the longer narrow surface the smoothest. L. 86mm; max. w. 47mm; th. 20mm. *2747; SF 1784*

8   Fine-grained volcanic ?ash; fragment of flattish stone, one side broken; broad surfaces all well used and polished. L. 86mm; max. w. 33mm; max. th. 29mm. *3211 (Structure A); SF 1752*

9   Fine-grained micaceous sandstone; triangular fragment, broken and split from a larger stone; sides and top fairly smooth, but possibly not a whetstone. L. 82mm; max. w. 83mm; max. th. 22mm. *5500M (Well 1); SF 1807*

10* Fine-grained micaceous sandstone/siltstone; oval-sectioned stone, broken at both ends. L. 76mm; w. 18mm; th. 9mm. *5500M (Well 1); SF 2005*

11* Micaceous sandstone; oval-sectioned stone, broken at one end and tapering slightly to the flat, unbroken end; all surfaces smooth. L. 58mm; max. w. 29mm; max. th. 25mm. *8010 (Structure M); SF 1284*

12* Micaceous sandstone; D-sectioned stone, broken at one end, pointed at the other; flat surface smoother than the other. L. 77mm; max. w. 25mm; max. th. 17mm. *8023D (Structure M); SF 1692*

Spindlewhorls

13* Fine-grained sandstone; complete, cylindrical spindlewhorl. Diam. 50mm; th. 14mm; hole diam. 8mm. *001; SF 266*

14   Micaceous sandstone; complete, cylindrical spindlewhorl. Diam. 39mm; th. 8mm; hole diam. 4mm. *001; SF 388*

15* Gypsum; complete spindlewhorl, double-chamfered. Diam. 29mm; th. 8.5mm; hole diam. 5mm. *1213/3 (Structure M); SF 1325*

16* Carboniferous limestone; fragment of approx. oval-sectioned spindlewhorl with a slight groove around the edge. Diam. *c.* 60mm; th. 12mm. *3454; SF 643*

Counters

17   Micaceous sandstone; counter with roughly chipped, slightly sloping edges. Diam. *c.* 62mm; th. 14.5mm. *001; SF 328*

18   Micaceous sandstone; counter with its edges varying from straight to well rounded; uneven in thickness. Diam. *c.* 87mm; max. th. 23mm. *001; SF 1802*

19   Micaceous sandstone; counter with quite well-chipped edges. Diam. *c.* 71mm; th. 15mm. *001; SF 1803*

20   Micaceous sandstone; five counters of varying degrees of circularity, one being almost square. Diams *c.* 90mm, *c.* 80mm, *c.* 65mm, *c.* 64mm and *c.* 60mm. *001; SF 1805*

21   Micaceous sandstone; counter with its edges roughly chipped. Diam. *c.* 64mm; th. 17mm. *Ditch 005/2; SF 1798*

22   Micaceous sandstone; counter with its edges roughly chipped, but with a high degree of circularity. Diam. 49mm; th. 18mm. *101 (Structure A); SF 1789*

23   Micaceous sandstone/siltstone; counter with smoothed edge. Diam. 29mm; th. 6mm. *218 (Structure B); SF 295*

24   Micaceous sandstone; counter with roughly chipped edges. Diam. *c.* 118mm; th. 17mm. *802 (Structure A); SF 2003*

25   Micaceous sandstone; counter with roughly chipped edges. Diam. *c.* 71mm; th. 12mm. *1001 (Structure J); SF 695*

26   Micaceous sandstone; counter with fairly smooth edges, but oval in shape. L. 61mm; w. 57mm; th. 10mm. *1213 (Structure M); SF 1831*

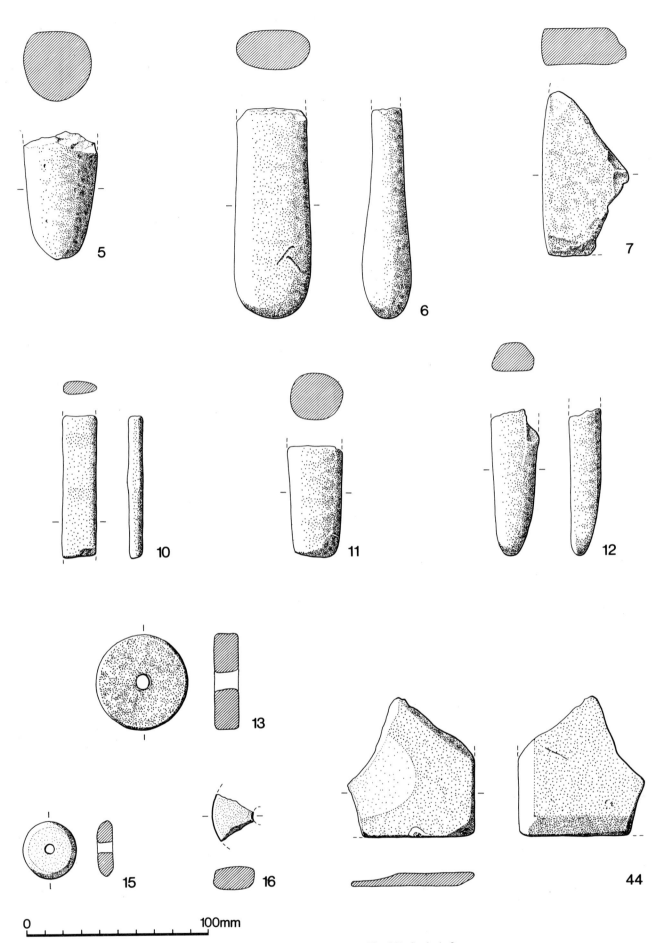

Fig. 91. Stone objects (Nos 5-7, 10-13, 15-16 and 44; No. 42 is shown on Fig. 92). Scale 1: 2

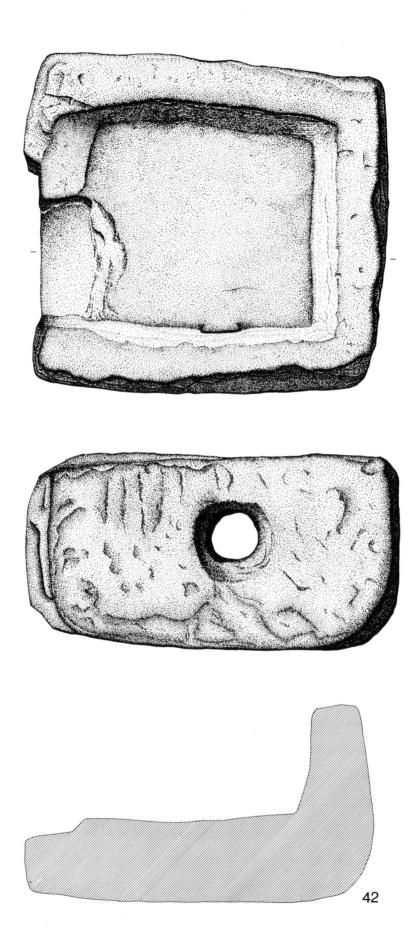

Fig. 92. Stone object (No. 42). Scale 1: 6

27   Micaceous sandstone; counter with fairly smooth edges. Diam. 43mm; th. 9mm. *1213/1 (Structure M); SF 1130*

28   Micaceous sandstone; counter with roughly chipped edges. Diam. *c.* 80mm; th. 22mm. *1213/3 (Structure M); SF 1347*

29   Micaceous sandstone; counter with roughly chipped edges. Diam. *c.* 62mm; th. 12mm. *1213/3 (Structure M); SF 1344*

30   Micaceous sandstone; counter with roughly chipped edges. Diam. *c.* 65mm; th. 15mm. *1801 (Structure R); SF 1799*

31   Micaceous sandstone; counter with roughly chipped edges, two sides almost straight. Diam. *c.* 66mm; th. 11mm. *1801 (Structure R); SF 1800*

32   Micaceous sandstone; counter with fairly smooth edges. Diam. 54mm; th. 11mm. *2518; SF 499*

33   Micaceous sandstone; three counters, two with roughly chipped edges, one smoothed but virtually pentagonal. Diams *c.* 59mm, *c.* 56mm and *c.* 53mm. *5500 (Well 1); SF 1749*

34   Sandstone; large ?counter with fairly smooth edges; broken. Diam. *c.* 115mm; max. th. 40mm. *8201/5 (Structure V); SF 1983*

35   Micaceous sandstone; counter with roughly chipped edges. Diam. *c.* 63mm; th. 13mm. *8300; SF 1898*

36   Micaceous sandstone; counter with roughly chipped edges, two almost straight. Diam. *c.* 60mm; th. 12mm. *8301/1; SF 1923*

37   Micaceous sandstone; counter with roughly chipped edges. Diam. *c.* 64mm; th. 26mm. *8301/1; SF 1924*

38   Micaceous sandstone; counter with roughly chipped edges. Diam. *c.* 62mm; th. 18mm. *8301/1; SF 1925*

Troughs and cisterns

39   Millstone grit; rectangular trough, broken at one end. The internal sides slope inwards and the rim is rounded. A shallow, V-shaped overflow channel has been cut into the rim a little off-centre along the complete side. Ext. l. 270mm; ext. w. 560mm; ht 220mm; int. w. (top) 395mm, (bottom) 330mm; depth 145mm. *5500J (Well 1); SF 1334*

40   Sandstone; fragment of side of trough or cistern, well finished internally. Max. ext. l. 220mm; max. ext. w. 180mm. *5500K (Well 1); SF 1358*

41   Sandstone; rectangular trough or cistern fragment with sharpening score marks across its rounded rim. Max. ext. l. 290mm; max. ext. w. 380mm; ht 310mm; depth 190mm; int. w. 180mm. *5500K (Well 1); SF 1373*

42*   Millstone grit; rectangular, open-ended cistern with a circular hole at the bottom of one long side. The opening at the end is off-set to one side and has a sloping channel stepped down from the flat bottom. The rim of the short side next to the channel is missing and the area around the channel is set back slightly. The rim is flat topped. Ext. l. 600mm; ext. w. 540mm; int. l. 380mm; int. w. 380mm. *5500K (Well 1); SF 1374*

Other finds

43   Micaceous sandstone; fragment with two straight edges and one curved. L. 215mm; w. 95mm; th. 20mm. *1701 (Structure Q); SF 1985*

44*   Slate; mixing palette fragment with bevelled edges on the lower surface and a hollow worn in the upper. L. 69mm; w. 74mm; th. 7mm. *1806 (Structure R); SF 1806*

45   Micaceous sandstone; probably circular fragment. Diam. 230mm; th. 20mm. *1809A (Structure R); SF 1987*

46   Fibrous gypsum; hexagonal-sectioned fragment, flat and polished at both ends. L. 46mm; w. 27mm; th. 15mm. *4903/2 (Structure X); SF 1283*

47   Millstone grit; ?beehive quernstone with dressed sides, but unfinished grinding surface, with a circular flat-bottomed hollow in the top; part of the rim broken; possibly used as a mortar. Max. diam. 285mm; max. ht 180mm; diam. of hollow 155mm; depth 60mm. *5500J (Well 1); SF 1297*

48   Sandstone; large, approx. cylindrical stone with a flat base and a large off-centre hollow in its top; the rim is partly flat, partly rounded. Max. ht 370mm; max. diam. 460mm; diam. of hollow 300mm; max. depth 170mm. *5500K (Well 1); SF 1360*

Discussion

All the whetstones recovered are of local sandstone, with the exception of No. 8 which is probably from the Lake District. It is perhaps surprising that so few whetstones (twelve) have been found on a villa site of long occupation where many agricultural and other implements would have needed sharpening.

Of the four spindlewhorls, two are of local stone (Nos 13 and 14), and two probably from North Yorkshire (Nos 15 and 16). The largest single group of artefacts is the total of 28 counters, all of local sandstone. The range of diameters is wider than that recovered from Castleford (Clarke forthcoming): 29-118mm, twelve falling within the 60-69mm range. It is presumed that counters made of various materials were for use in board games, the varying sizes indicating differing values (Crummy 1983, 94). The large size of the Dalton Parlours examples would indicate that the 'boards' could have been marked out on the ground.

Of the four troughs or cisterns recovered (all from the well), No. 42 is worthy of comment. It would seem to have been a junction box, with water entering it from a pipe via the hole in the side, and flowing out along the channel which, presumably, opened into a stone drainage channel. A number of such channels were discovered during the 19th-century excavation (Procter 1855, 272-3).

The two sandstone fragments (Nos 43 and 45) from among the miscellaneous stone objects are much too large to be classed as counters. The degree of reddening of No. 43 may support the theory that discs were used as 'mats' for hot cooking pots (Addyman and Priestley 1977, 139). The slate mixing palette fragment (No. 44), probably from North Yorkshire or the Lake District, shows a considerable degree of wear on its upper surface. It is of almost exactly similar dimensions to an example found in York during excavations in 1868 (*RCHM* 1962, 174, pl. 65, no. 146).

Acknowledgements

The writer wishes to acknowledge the help of Dr G. Hornung of the Department of Earth Sciences, Leeds University, who provided the identification of the stone types.

12 Objects of Worked Bone (Fig. 93)

by S.J. Greep (Report first submitted in 1981)

Hairpins

1*   Type A1 pin with simple flat head and long tapering stem (Greep forthcoming). L. 122.6mm, complete. *216 (Structure B); SF 289*

2*   Pin similar to No. 1. L. 109.5mm, complete. *Ditch 016/1; SF 566*

3*   Pin with conical head surmounting an oval moulding and collar, and with tapering stem. L. 106.8mm, complete. *607 (Structure F); SF 1706*

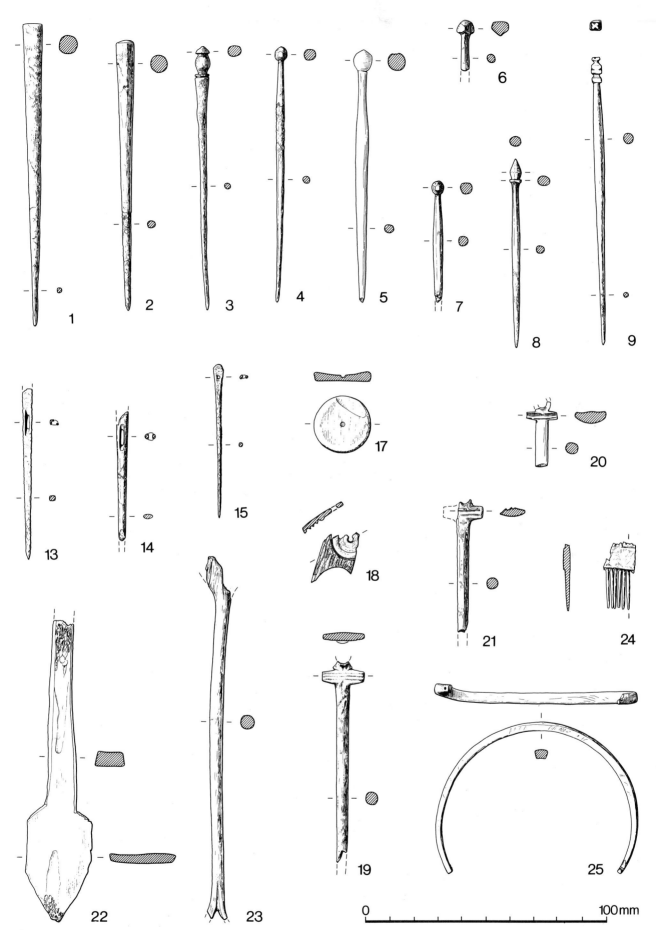

Fig. 93. Objects of worked bone (Nos 1-9, 13-15 and 17-25). Scale 2:3

127

4* Type B1 pin with spherical head and swelling stem (Greep forthcoming). Jewry Wall type B (Kenyon 1948, fig. 90, nos 7-8), Colchester type 3 (Crummy 1979, fig. 1, nos 3-4), and Shakenoak type B (Brodribb *et al.* 1971, 124). L. 103.6mm, complete. *Ditch 021/1; SF 543*

5* Pin similar to No. 4. L. 103.6mm, complete. *5500 (Well 1); SF 1691*

6* Pin similar to No. 4. L. 20.5mm, broken. *Ditch 004/2; SF 559*

7* Pin similar to No. 4. L. 49.1mm, broken. *1213/3 (Structure M); SF 1330*

8* Pin with a cone or 'flame-shaped' head above a single collar with a swelling stem. Jewry Wall type Dii (Kenyon 1948, fig. 90, no. 11), Colchester type 5 (Crummy 1979, fig. 1). L. 73.6mm, complete. *Ditch 002/1B; SF 588*

9* Pin with squarish head, cut on each corner between two collars, both decorated with a number of short incised lines; swelling stem. L. 117.1mm, complete. *1612 (Structure P); SF 1602*

10- Three pin stems of type A, tapering form. *1001 (Structure J), 1003*
12 *(Structure J) and 8201/2 (Structure V); SFs 694, 759 and 1227*

Pins 1-3 are of types datable to *c.* AD 40-200/250 and should belong to the early phases of the villa settlement; the rest are common late Roman forms, of *c.* AD 150/200-400+.

Needles
13* Type 3.2 needle with flat, pared head, and rectangular eye (Greep forthcoming). Jewry Wall type E (Kenyon 1948, fig. 91, no. 7), and bronze form type C (Kenyon 1948, fig. 89, no. 19). L. 69.3mm, broken. *Ditch 011/1; SF 710*

14* Needle similar to No. 13. L. 52.1mm, broken. *5605; SF 1882*

15* Small needle with simple club-shaped head, and small oval perforation. L. 61.5mm, complete. *802 (Structure A); SF 1655*

16 Needle similar to No. 13. Broken across the eye. L. 73.1mm, broken. *1001 (Structure J): SF 738*

Counters
17* Gaming piece, type 2 (cf. Greep 1986, 202), with a countersunk obverse surface. These forms date to *c.* AD 150/200-400. Diam. 23mm; th. 3.8mm. *1600 (Structure P); SF 1458*

18* Small fragment of waste material from the manufacture of type 3 gaming pieces; upper surface has series of thin concentric circles (Greep 1986, 202); as finished each counter would have been 15mm diam. and 2.3mm th.; a small example of its type. Of cancellous bone, probably rib or scapula. *1300 (Structure M); SF 428*

Such waste has not been recorded elsewhere in Britain, although similar fragments occur on the continent at Trier (unpublished, Rheinisches Landes Museum Trier, Acc. no. 16050), Speyer (unpublished, Historisches Museum Der Pflaz, Speyer Inv. no. 29.9.1912) and Cologne (unpublished, Römisch-Germanisch Museum, Köln Acc. no. 23.601).

?Spoons
For a discussion of perforated spoons (Nos 19-21 and 23) see Greep forthcoming.

19* Stem with cruciform terminal; probably from a perforated spoon. L. 80.5mm, broken. *100 (Structure A); SF 1888*

20* Stem as No. 19. Possibly made from ivory. L. 26mm, broken. *001; SF 833*

21* Stem as No. 19. L. 54mm, broken. *4310; SF 770*

22* Crude spoon-shaped object. It has been very roughly worked and is possibly a rough-out for a spoon. A number of similar objects were found at Woodyates, Dorset (Pitt-Rivers 1887, pl. 46, especially no. 4). L. 121.5mm, broken. *8301/2; SF 1909*

23* Object broken at both ends but possibly originally a perforated spoon. L. 146.8mm. *3921; SF 1750*

Other objects
24* Small fragment of a comb plate from a double-sided, composite comb; six teeth remain on one side. L. 27.3mm. *900 (Structure J); SF 358*

25* Plain bracelet of rectangular section, with lapped, pierced terminals, one broken. This would have been held together by copper or iron rivets which have corroded or broken away, allowing it to spring apart (cf. Crummy 1983, 37-8, no. 1584). A 4th-century type. Int. diam. *c.* 51mm; th. 5mm. *5500L (Well 1); SF 1442*

26 Fragment of red deer antler consisting of a sawn section of beam and three tines, one of which has been removed by sawing. A waste product. *5500K (Well 1); SF 1964*

27 Sliver of bone with an irregular, rectangular cross-section. Probably a waste product. *1001 (Structure J); SF 713*

28 Red deer antler tine sawn and hollowed at the proximal end, worn and broken at the terminal end. Possibly used as a handle but more likely to be a simple waste product. L. 105mm. *001; SF 216*

29 Proximal end of a *Bos* metatarsal ?turned and cut from the shaft. A waste product. L. 39mm. *Ditch 006/6; SF 2022*

13 Iron Age Pottery (Fig. 94)
by A.B. Sumpter

Introduction

The excavation produced easily the largest assemblage of Iron Age pottery yet known from West Yorkshire, a total of almost 300 sherds. It is estimated that at least 40 vessels are represented, though no precise quantification may be made owing to the fragmentary state of many sherds and the degree of variation seen to occur between joining sherds of individual vessels.

The most noteworthy aspect of the native pottery is its lack of sophistication. The vessels are entirely hand-made in a range of coarse mineral-gritted fabrics, fired to varying degrees of hardness with no apparent control over oxidation/reduction conditions. Some, notably No. 2, were in a state of extreme fragility as excavated and had to be dried at room temperature for several weeks before cleaning could be attempted. Decoration is entirely lacking, and surface finishing is minimal. No full profiles were recovered and so the range of vessel types cannot be adequately assessed, though it appears to be limited apart from variations in size. The forms are generally very basic and often with little attempt at fashioning rims.

The distribution of the pottery shows a widespread scatter across the western half of the excavated area where the density of Iron Age features was greatest. Concentrations of sherds occurred in the ring-gully for Roundhouse 5 and nearby gullies, and in two sunken hearths (2558 and 2600) in Enclosure I. Individual sherds

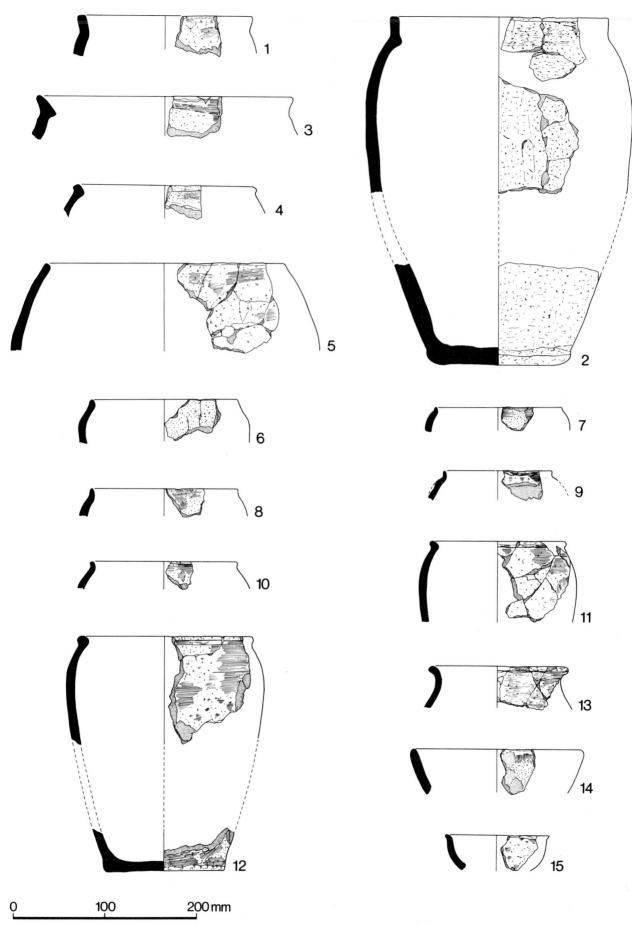

0   100   200 mm

Fig. 94. Iron Age pottery (Nos 1-15). Scale 1:4

came from post-holes and enclosure ditches, with some in Roman contexts and disturbed layers.

As this section examines the pottery pre-dating the establishment of the Roman villa in *c*. AD 200, in addition to the native pottery mention should be made here of three small fragments of Flavian South Gaulish samian ware, forms 37 and 30, from unstratified deposits. Their significance in the context of the Iron Age settlement is further discussed below.

The fifteen vessels figured represent the total justifying illustration, and this restricted number is an indication of the preservation conditions of the native Iron Age pottery.

Description of vessels

1* Shoulderless jar with upright rim. Soft, friable dark grey fabric with pink surfaces; abundant large mixed grit; Fabric C. Heat-cracked. For the form, cf. Thorpe Thewles no. 240 (Swain 1987, 70, fig. 47). One rim sherd, one body fragment. *Ditch 006/1; Ditch 003/4*

2* Large shoulderless jar with upright rim and internal ledge. Soft, extremely brittle dark grey fabric with light brown surfaces; excessively charged with grit including cemented grains of millstone grit; Fabric B. External reddened and grey reduced areas from heat. A total of *c*. 70 sherds and fragments including 4 rims and 7 basal sherds, several joining. *2700; 3402/1; 3403/1; 3406/3; 3411*

3* Large shoulderless jar with triangular-section rim and internal ledge. Soft, very brittle dark grey fabric, internally light brown; heavily charged with grit including cemented grains of millstone grit; Fabric B. Some external sooting. Fabric very similar to No. 2 but with slightly less grit. One rim sherd and one body sherd (not certainly from the same vessel). *001*

4* Jar with stubby rectangular-section rim and internal ledge. Soft, dark grey fabric with light pinkish-brown surfaces; abundant tiny sparkling grit; Fabric D. One rim sherd. *Ditch 020/2*

5* Large jar with uneven plain rim. Soft, dark grey fabric; much of the exterior and some of the interior light brown; scattered grit of wide size range, including cemented grains of millstone grit; Fabric C. External sooting towards the rim. A total of 27 sherds including 9 rims, several joining. *200 (Structure B); 303 (Structure B); 3400; 3402/1; 3403/1; 3406; 3410, 3411*

6* Jar with plain rim. Soft, dark grey fabric with variable pink cortex, externally light pinkish-brown; abundant tiny sparkling grit, also larger soft chalky inclusions; Fabric A. Two joining rim sherds. *Ditch 040/2*

7* Jar with plain rim. Soft, blackish fabric; profuse fine sparkling grit; Fabric B. One rim sherd. *001*

8* Jar with lightly pinched upright rim. Soft, blackish fabric with variable light brown cortex towards the interior; fine sparkling grit; Fabric D. Internal sooting on rim. One rim sherd. *1300 (Structure M)*

9* Jar with unevenly pinched rim. Soft, grey fabric with light brown surfaces; fine sparkling grit; Fabric D. Sooting inside and outside rim. One rim sherd. *Ditch 026/1*

10* Jar with small bead rim. Soft, light brownish-grey fabric; profuse small white calcite grit; Fabric A. One rim sherd. *Ditch 006/6-018/2*

11* Jar with bead rim. Soft, brownish-grey fabric with brown surfaces and pink cortex towards the interior; scattered grit including calcite and occasional cemented grains of millstone grit; Fabric A. External sooting towards the rim. A total of 31 sherds including 5 rims, many joining to upper profile. Also one rim from Ditch 020/2. *2558*

12* Jar with bead rim. Soft, brownish-grey fabric, externally brown with pinkish-brown cortex, internally blackish; abundant unevenly distributed calcite grit of varying size; internal pitting from loss of grit, much external spalling; Fabric A. External sooting towards the rim. A total of 73 sherds including 9 rims, many joining to upper profile, and 6 joining to complete base. The form is a larger version of No. 11. *2600*

13* Bowl with S-shaped profile and bead rim. Soft, greyish-brown fabric with dark grey surfaces; abundant calcite grit of varying size; Fabric E. External sooting. This is the most developed coarse Iron Age vessel form from Dalton Parlours and the only one showing signs of so-called Gallo-Belgic influence, though the finish is altogether inferior apart from vestiges of burnishing: cf. Camulodunum form 221 (Hawkes and Hull 1947, 261, pl. 78), a type which recurs in Corieltauvian territory at Dragonby, North Lincolnshire (May 1970). Six joining rim sherds. *Ditch 002/9A*

14 Dish or bowl with plain rim. Soft, dark grey fabric, externally brownish-grey with intermittent pinkish-brown cortex; abundant small sparkling grit giving sandpaper-like surfaces; Fabric B. This vessel is not Iron Age beyond all doubt, as the fabric resembles hand-made West Yorkshire ware of the 3rd to 4th centuries AD (see Chapter 15). One rim. *001*

15 Dish or bowl with pinched rim. Soft, dark grey fabric, externally light brown; abundant small sparkling grit; Fabric D. One rim sherd. *100 (Structure A)*

Discussion

Despite the fact that this assemblage constitutes the greater part of the Iron Age pottery so far retrieved in West Yorkshire, it comprises relatively few vessels to represent several centuries occupation of a site with such a density of structural remains. The physical weakness of the pottery explains why it had not previously been located in fieldwalking, as much must inevitably have disintegrated in the ploughsoil, but even so there is a strong implication that ceramic vessels were not in abundant use here during the Iron Age. Whether this was because of primitive potting technology, or whether it was a lack of demand for pottery which created no stimulus for ceramic advancement, is an open question.

The limited quantity combines with the lack of stratification on the site to restrict deductions about the chronology either of the pottery itself or the features in which it was found. However, the distribution of sherds from vessel Nos 2 and 5 implies that they were contemporary in use; and vessel Nos 11 and 12, from two sunken hearths (2558 and 2600), are evidently to be associated with the use of the hearths and suggest their contemporaneity.

Whilst the sources of the pottery are discussed below under the petrography, it may be noted here that only one vessel, No. 13, is sufficiently distinct from the rest on macro-examination to suggest itself as an import. Although not a particularly striking example, the type hints at an origin in Corieltauvian territory where Iron Age pottery manufacture was immeasurably more developed (cf. May 1970).

It remains to comment on the three fragments of Flavian samian ware. The possibility of their being heirloom vessels in the villa is greatly reduced by the presence of contemporary bronze brooches and glass ornaments (Chapters 6 and 9). Therefore they would seem to suggest that Iron Age occupation extended into the second half of the 1st century AD.

14 The Petrography of the Iron Age Pottery by P.C. Buckland, R.B. Runnacles and A.B. Sumpter

Introduction

The paucity of pottery from Iron Age sites in the western half of Yorkshire (cf. Keighley 1981, 131) places the relatively large assemblage at Dalton Parlours in a pivotal position in the interpretation of Iron Age ceramics in the region. Consequently the material provided the core of a post-graduate study at the University of Bradford (Runnacles 1985). Subsequent additional thin sections and closer examination of both the pottery and the geological background to the site and finds have led to some modification of the initial conclusions.

The application of petrological techniques to the study of pottery in Britain was placed upon a firm footing by the work of Dr D.P.S. Peacock (e.g. Peacock 1968; 1969; 1977). Attempts to characterise sources have used a wide range of techniques from thin sectioning and heavy mineral analysis to geochemical methods, with varying degrees of success. In much of eastern England, from the Norfolk coast to the Pennine foothills, the problems of localising production centres are compounded by the redistribution and mixing of rock types occasioned by the several Quaternary glaciations (Penny 1974). In the archaeological context, this has meant for example that Loughlin (pers. comm.), in a search for the manufactories of the distinctive Roman Dales ware cooking pots (Loughlin 1977), found few significant differences in the heavy mineral suites of sherds from a number of Yorkshire and Lincolnshire grey ware pottery kiln sites. Accepting this caveat, however, and with an awareness of the immediately local geological context of the Drift-mantled dipslope of the Magnesian Limestone at Dalton Parlours, some progress can be made with the pre-Roman pottery from the site.

The coarsely tempered nature of most of the material means that coherent rock fragments, as well as individual mineral grains, appear in most sherds; and a basic subdivision of the assemblage is easily achieved by examination with a hand lens. Initial scrutiny assigns most of the sherds to one of two groups: those tempered with crushed calcite or limestone (Fabric A), and those with sandstone or other rock fragments (Fabric B). Closer study, however, suggests that this division may be a little over simplified, and the second group has been refined into Fabrics B, C and D. Two vessels lying outside these criteria have been designated as Fabrics E and F.

The calcite/limestone-gritted group (Fabric A)

At least nine vessels, of which four are illustrated, occur in Fabric A. It is easily distinguished from other fabrics in the assemblage by large (up to 5mm) angular rhombs of calcite, occasionally dissolved out to leave characteristically shaped voids. Some vessels (e.g. No. 12) include crushed limestone rather than calcite, often surviving as partly decalcified angular areas of off-white powder; no fragments of fossils have been noted. Despite the visual prominence of the calcite, the temper also includes varying amounts of grog, i.e. crushed fired clay of similar composition to the matrix (e.g. a sherd from Ditch 030/2B), and quartz. The quartz ranges from sub-angular to rounded grains with reddened outer surfaces; a few approach a 'millet seed' form. With the calcite and grog, these give the pottery a distinctive multi-coloured appearance, the inclusions standing out against the base colour, which extends from dark red-brown to grey, with surfaces ranging from black to light reddish-brown, dependent upon firing conditions. Occasional other material occurs in the temper of sherds: vessel No. 11 includes crushed cohesive rock fragments of an arkosic grit.

The frequency of calcite, limestone, quartz and grog shows considerable variation both between and within vessels. The pot of which most survives (No. 12) includes sherds which might appear wholly calcite-gritted, whilst elsewhere on the same vessel smashed fragments of an unfossiliferous, fine-grained limestone are more evident. The surface finish of the vessel is such that the limestone content is often indicated only by voids, the small grains of quartz being the sole inclusions visible at the surface. This vessel also contains scattered small fragments which may derive from a shale or mudstone.

The origins of the calcite/limestone-tempered group

Although the varying nature of the temper in Fabric A led initially to some subdivision (Runnacles 1985), this largely served merely to place sherds of the same vessel together; and re-examination suggested that the variation was no more than might be expected with the work of a single group of potters or even one individual. It is recognised, however, that further research may lead to renewed subdivision.

The rock and mineral assemblage from these sherds, clearly polygenetic, points to origins in the glacial Drift and is not exclusive of an immediately local origin. The arkosic sandstone in vessel No. 11 is likely to derive from the Millstone Grit, outcropping not far to the north-west of the site and very widely dispersed in the Drift of the Vale of York (e.g. Gaunt 1970). The rhombs of calcite do not appear to be the result of crushing crinoid or echinoid fossils but are more likely to come from authigenic calcite in the parent rock. Small blocks of calcite/dolomite crystals have been noted, derived from large vugs in the parent rock, being broken down by frost on the cleared surface of the excavated area; and similar pieces were recovered by sieving from the infilling of Well 1. All come from the lower beds of the Lower Magnesian Limestone on which the site lay. The crushed limestone in sherds also reacts sparingly with 10% hydrochloric acid, suggesting a dolomitic rather than a purely calcitic rock, which again implies a Permian origin in the same parent rock.

The range of quartz temper in the pottery implies a polygenetic origin for this also. The angular grains derive from the Millstone Grit, evident elsewhere in sherds, and the well-rounded ones from Triassic sandstones outcropping to the north-east and east of the site and flooring, often at depth, beneath thick Quaternary deposits in the Vale of York (Gaunt 1981).

This mixture of eastern and western derived elements in the temper might at first appear to exclude manufacture actually on the Dalton Parlours site. Certainly the site itself lacks suitable deposits, although pre-Devensian glaciation involved the transport of Permian limestones to the west of its escarpment (Gaunt 1981); and Triassic sandstones occur on the Permian Limestone dipslope, both as erratics and, disaggregated, as part of the till matrix. But clay and temper sources, almost certainly a single locality, lie within a few hundred metres in most directions from the site.

Mineral calcite does not form a significant proportion of the erratic content of local Drift, from which the temper might more easily have been derived by crushing blocks of crinoidal limestone from the Carboniferous, a major constituent of Devensian tills in the area. The mixture for the pottery does not therefore appear to derive from a till, tempered by the random breaking of erratics from the same source, but by the deliberate adding of calcite and/or crushed limestone to the clay. Whilst there is no need to imply that Fabric A is anything other than of local manufacture, the calcite temper would require collection and it is possible that it reflects a by-product of some other, larger-scale utilisation of the limestone, rather than its recovery purely as temper for pottery, particularly in view of the widespread occurrence of calcite and limestone gritted fabrics in both Iron Age and Roman contexts. In the Roman period, the use of the rock as building stone and in mortar is widespread (Buckland 1988) but such options seem improbable in the pre-Roman Iron Age, where an agricultural function for lime might provide a possible explanation. Pliny (*Natural History*, XVIII, 53) refers to the practice of marling fields in Britain, utilising material (*creta argentaria*) dug from pits up to 100 feet deep (White 1970, 139); and the numerous pits on this site could have provided a convenient source of crushed limestone for marling (cf. Fowler 1983, 170) besides, as a by-product, more than sufficient temper for potting. The problem requires further, more wide-ranging research.

The erratic-tempered group (Fabric B/C/D)

In the initial study of the material Fabrics B, C and D were regarded as distinct (Runnacles 1985). However, they are better considered as a single grouping, based upon Rigby's suggestion (pers. comm.) of a rather heterogeneous group termed erratic-tempered pottery. This might be subdivided in the light of further research, as the nature of the temper perhaps owes more to the laws of probability than to the deliberate selection of particular erratics for temper. The group is primarily characterised by the presence of crushed sandstone as temper, most conspicuously in Fabric B. Fabric C is distinct in the use of igneous rock and iron slag in the temper which could warrant separation, but the iron slag may be incidental; a more extensive programme of sectioning sherds in Yorkshire and northwards is required before conclusions can be based upon it. Fabric D, of six sherds, is quartz gritted, lacking in distinct rock fragments. Although the slightly finer fabric, with the addition of considerable quantities of grog in some sherds, might serve to distinguish the fabric archaeologically, its mineralogy remains insufficiently distinct and would appear merely to indicate the finer disaggregation of the rock used as temper.

A minimum of eighteen erratic-tempered vessels were recovered. They are typified by a heavy temper of quartz, predominantly of medium to coarse, angular to sub-angular grains up to 3mm. Occasional cohesive rock fragments also occur in the temper of most vessels and these are clearly the source of the disaggregated grains, none of which show clear evidence of crushing. The rock fragments are dominated by an arkosic sandstone but fragments of quartzite are also present, the latter derived as detrital grains from the sandstone. Temper size ranges from individual grains of 0.25mm to angular sandstone fragments up to 14mm across. Visually, the individual grains of quartz dominate, although occasional fresh feldspar cleavage flakes may be found, the former often standing out from the softer matrix of the sherds, which range in colour from very dark grey to light grey with a light reddish-brown surface. In thin section, the quartz grains invariably show undulose extinction and many contain acicular and less regular inclusions, both as voids and other minerals. Feldspar is infrequent and the few grains noted in section are either cleavage flakes or anhedral partly rounded grains, and are frequently much altered. The cross-hatched twinning of microcline and lamellar twins, probably of oligoclase, has been noted.

Fabric C is also largely dominated by the use of a similar crushed sandstone temper but, in addition, there are also varying quantities of other materials. These fragments, to a maximum noted size of 6.5mm, are angular, suggesting deliberate crushing, rather than purely the inclusion of detrital grains from a sedimentary source. In thin section, the temper of one sherd (from Ditch 028) is sufficiently coarse to allow the identification of the rock type as a quartz dolerite. The remaining mineral temper is more difficult to typify, being initially noted as 'dunite' and 'dendritic olivine' (Runnacles 1985), in that it consists of olivine, usually with growths of an opaque mineral, probably magnetite, along two cleavage planes lying virtually at right angles. The Vale of York Drift contains no suitable rock types and, despite the problems of dealing with the small fragments in the pottery, it is evident that a man-made origin for the material is likely. Slag from the smelting, rather than the smithing of ironeads to the formation of olivine-magnetite/pyrolusite (MnO) intergrowths, depending upon the efficiency of the process (cf. Bestwick and Cleland 1974), and this material in finely crushed form appears to have been employed in the temper (see Dugmore below).

The origins of the erratic-tempered group

Although perhaps initially appearing a rather heterogeneous group, Fabric B/C/D is principally tempered with a crushed sandstone, sufficiently lightly indurated to disaggregate easily into individual grains. Both in hand specimen and in thin section, it is evident that the temper shows many of the characteristics which Gilligan (1920) describes in his extensive study of the Millstone Grit, and further subdivision as to which particular Namurian sandstone provided the temper is presently impossible. Grain size is very variable amongst the Grits, and fragments of igneous and metamorphic rock are not infrequent but invariably of acidic rather than basic composition (Gilligan 1920). Fabric C must therefore derive its temper from an alternative source. The dolerite fragments in the sherd from Ditch 028 closely match the Whin Sill, with its extensive outcrop in northern England (Emeleus 1974) and frequent occurrence in the Vale of York Drift.

The combination of iron smelting slag with crushed gritstone is more problematic and the appearance of a similarly tempered sherd on the Iron Age site at Ledston, 20km to the south (Runnacles 1985), compounds the problem. Workable ironstones are absent from the Vale but do occur to the west in both Millstone Grit and Coal Measures, the latter outcropping some 10km to the south-west around Leeds, and also in the Jurassic of the Yorkshire Moors and Cleveland Hills over 30km to the north-east. Ironworking has been claimed from an Iron Age site at Meltham, near Huddersfield (Toomey 1976) but there is little surviving evidence elsewhere in West Yorkshire (Yarwood 1981, 43). The easterly sources have produced more evidence of iron smelting, and furnaces have been excavated on Levisham Moor above Pickering, North Yorkshire (Challis and Harding 1975, 16). Although the rock temper in the same sherds would exclude this area, sources further north, along the base of the Cleveland Hills and on the Coal Measures of County Durham, cannot presently be ruled out (Challis and Harding 1975). The problem must presently rest unsolved until more extensive studies of the more frequent erratic-tempered wares of the East Yorkshire Iron Age have been carried out.

It is probable that the selection of temper was not a random process, as such would undoubtedly result in at least an equal representation of acidic and intermediate igneous rocks and, unless a decalcified till from the Older Drift was employed, Carboniferous Limestone would be equally likely to be present. The reasons for the use of crushed dolerite and sandstone, rather than calcite and limestone temper in this fabric remain obscure, but can be paralleled amongst Iron Age pottery from Thorpe Thewles (Swain 1987) and several other sites in Cleveland (Harbord and Spratt 1972). Until more data are available, it is tentatively suggested that a similar origin is probable for the Dalton Parlours material.

Fabric E

Fabric E is represented by one vessel, No. 13, a narrow-necked bowl of a form similar to Camulodunum 221 (Hawkes and Hull 1947, 261, pl. 78). The vessel is itself a unique type on the site. Its temper, of a crushed fossiliferous limestone, includes fragments of a pectiniform bivalve and it is probably of North Lincolnshire origin, the fabric being not too dissimilar to Dales ware.

Fabric F

Fabric F is represented by a single sherd (not illustrated) which in some respects, notably the use of fairly coarsely crushed limestone temper, might perhaps be better regarded as a subgroup of Fabric A. The limestone in Fabric F, however, as distinct from the amorphous fragments in Fabric A, is a crushed oolitic limestone, with individual ooliths up to 1mm in diameter appearing as disaggregated individual grains in the fabric of the vessel. Their concentric layers of calcite are evident where partial solution of the temper has taken place. Although molluscan shell fragments are evident in thin section, the sherd contains no distinctive fossils and a Lower Carboniferous or Jurassic source remains possible. In view of the extent of evidence for erratic-tempered pottery on the site, it is probable that the sherd could be included within this grouping. The presence of small angular quartz grains in the fabric also supports a matrix origin from a till.

Discussion

Despite the present problems of locating an origin for the iron slag used as temper in Fabric C, it is possible that all the Dalton Parlours pottery was manufactured within 10km of the site; yet a number of features would suggest caution in ascribing the material to a domestic rather than a professional source, and the possibility of several sources contributing to the proposed fabric groupings cannot be resolved by petrology. The use of calcite temper in Fabric C, if from pits dug into the Lower Magnesian Limestone on the site, might be taken to imply domestic manufacture; whilst the use of dolerite and iron slag in Fabric C could be argued as denoting the contrary. The crude nature of the products cannot be taken as an indication of domestic production for similarly coarse fabrics achieved wide distribution in the Iron Age of the south-west Midlands (Peacock 1968) and find frequent ethnographic parallels (Peacock 1982).

In a study of Iron Age pottery from three sites along the northern edge of the Yorkshire Moors, Harbord and Spratt (1972) identified fragments of igneous rock temper in several vessels. All sites produced both Cleveland Dyke basaltic andesite and Whin Sill quartz dolerite in their temper. The former has a limited linear outcrop, between 5 and 25m wide, south-eastwards across the Moors from near Eaglescliffe, south of Stockton-on-Tees, to Blea Hill Rigg, south of Whitby. The probability of this rock being utilised as temper and mixed with Whin Sill from a similar erratic source is very slight, and the fact that similarly tempered sherds are now also known from Thorpe Thewles, north-east of Stockton, where on-site manufacture has been claimed (Swain 1987), suggests that a single source should be sought. If temper selection was merely for dark grey or black rock, then numerous erratics of both Carboniferous and Jurassic limestones are also present in the local Drift and would not be immediately distinguishable to the layman.

The implication has to be either that both the Cleveland and Dalton Parlours potters selected igneous rocks for use in temper (and the additional identification of millstone grit in the latter would imply that this is the case), or that at least some of the vessels derive from a common source in Cleveland, at the foot of the north slope of the Yorkshire Moors, where Millstone Grit, Whin Sill and Cleveland Dyke are present as erratics. The problem remains as to whether the potters or their products moved. Peacock's work (e.g. 1968) would imply the latter, but the problems of Drift make the problem much less easily solved in Yorkshire and Cleveland.

The presence of crushed iron slag in vessels from both Dalton Parlours and Ledston provide a further line of evidence which may be linked to the working of ironstones in the Cleveland Hills. Peacock (1982) has pointed out how pottery manufacture is often a means of supplementing subsistence in a marginal environment and his arguments might be extended to iron smelting since much of the Jurassic ironstone outcrop lies in the uplands, among areas of heavily podsolised soils of low productivity. If a single source area is to be sought for Dalton Parlours Fabric B/C/D, and the material from Cleveland, it has to lie towards the base of the Cleveland Hills, at their west end, where the Cleveland Dyke and Drift containing Millstone Grit and Whin Sill are juxtaposed with Jurassic ironstones; this suggests that evidence for Iron Age ironworking should lie around Ayton and Easby. The reality, however, may be more complex and an alternative model could involve ironworkers being itinerant. Their need for clay for both furnace and *tuyères* makes pottery an obvious subsidiary activity. Only a more extended programme of thin sectioning of the Yorkshire erratic-tempered wares, begun by Rigby (pers. comm.), may hold the answer.

The Dalton Parlours Iron Age features failed to provide a chronological sequence for the calcite-gritted and erratic-tempered fabrics, although the overlap in temper might imply continuity in manufacture on the same site. It remains to be seen whether the millstone grit tempered sherds from Roman contexts in West Yorkshire and the Vale (Sumpter 1988, and this volume p. 144) reflect a continuation of an Iron Age potting tradition beyond the conquest.

Acknowledgements
The initial study by R.B. Runnacles was carried out in the University of Bradford and thanks are due to S. Warren, P. Wardle and I. Betts for their assistance. C. Grimley of the University of Sheffield produced additional thin sections. The text has benefited considerably from discussions with C. Cumberpatch, G.D. Gaunt, V. Rigby and I.M. Stead.

Analysis of Mineral Grains
by Andrew J. Dugmore

Optical examination of thin sections of the pottery revealed that in some pots one of the dominant minerals in the temper was an olivine with intergrowths of an opaque mineral. In order to determine their geochemical characteristics, these grains were analysed on a Cambridge Instruments Microscan V electron microprobe. The piece of pot elected for analysis was from context 600.

A standard WDS technique was employed, using an accelerating voltage of 20KV and a probe current of 30nA. Data were reduced by ZAF correction similar to that used by Sweatman and Long (1969).

Microprobe analysis of the opaque minerals indicated that they are intergrowths of magnetite (Fe_3O_4). Results of the microprobe analysis of the olivine surrounding the magnetite are shown in columns DP1 and DP2 on Table 6.

Olivine, $(Mg,Fe)_2SiO_4$, forms a solid solution series between forsterite, Mg_2SiO_4, and fayalite, Fe_2SiO_4; forsterite is virtually unknown in natural contexts (Wahlstrom 1947; McBirney 1984). The analysed minerals are iron-rich end members of the Olivine series

Table 6. Microprobe analysis of Iron Age pottery.

| | Pure and natural olivines (from McBirney 1984) | | | | | | Dalton Parlours analyses | |
	Pure forsterite	Fo 96	Fo 86	Fo 47	Fo 3	Pure fayalite	DP1	DP2
SiO_2	42.71	41.07	39.87	34.04	30.15	29.49	28.39	29.20
TiO_2	–	0.05	0.03	0.43	0.20	–	–	–
Al_2O_3	–	0.56	–	0.91	0.07	–	0.34	0.11
Fe_2O_2	–	0.65	0.86	1.46	0.43	–	(67.00)	(66.90)
FeO	–	3.78	13.20	40.37	65.02	70.51		
MnO	–	0.23	0.22	0.68	1.01	–	1.62	1.85
MgO	57.29	54.06	45.38	20.32	1.05	–	0.70	1.21
CaO	–	–	0.25	0.81	2.18	–	0.25	0.18

and their composition is close to a pure fayalite. Natural occurrences of fayalite are rare, it occurs in rhyolitic and other volcanic rocks, pegmatites and certain iron-rich igneous rocks, but is most common in industrial slags.

The implication is, therefore, that the pots were being made with by-products from the iron-making industry.

15 Roman Pottery (from contexts other than Well 1) (Figs 95-8)

by A.B. Sumpter

Introduction

Comprehensive area excavation produced a total of 14,840 sherds. Of these, 1910 (13%) were in the ploughsoil, and 5940 (40%) formed a large accumulation in Well 1 which is reported separately (Chapter 30). The majority of the remaining 6990 sherds (47%), apart from sizeable deposits in the extreme north and south boundary ditches, came from the villa buildings. The concentrations of pottery in and around these buildings demonstrated that ploughing had caused little horizontal displacement; but each substantial excavated group showed a chronological mix which typically spanned the late Antonine period to the mid-4th century, indicating the effects of vertical displacement. Damage to the pottery has also been severe, with excessive fragmentation and frequent erosion and abrasion.

Although the pottery in use at the villa embraced two centuries and came from several different manufactories, on examination the range of types was found to be limited. Apart from samian and colour-coated wares most are of Yorkshire or North Lincolnshire origin, and several are long-lasting forms already well known in the region. However the assemblage furnishes a catalogue of the commercial connections of the villa during the 3rd and 4th centuries, and sources are dealt with more fully below.

The pottery from Well 1, which in bulk constitutes about half that from the entire site, is in a good state of preservation with a number of restorable vessels. But this is exceptional, and over the remainder of the site the factors outlined above – the lack of sealed deposits, the poor condition of sherds, and the frequency of long-lasting types – combine to limit the detailed information which the material might be expected to provide concerning the structural development of the villa. The pottery cannot be used, for example, to date successive phases in the modification of a particular building; it can offer only a broad date range for the occupation of that part of the site. The unsatisfactory preservation was emphasised when a preliminary extraction of sherds for drawing was seen to be more than usually weighted by the robustness of the types: mortaria, flanged vessels, and heavier wide-mouthed bowls were predominant, whereas jars and smaller bowls were much less evident, and flagons and the ubiquitous colour-coated beakers were too fragmentary for illustration. This physical bias is still partly reflected in the final choice of vessels for illustration, an inevitably economical selection but as representative as circumstances justify. In total 135 vessels have been drawn, of which 65 are from Well 1.

Owing to the relatively large size of the unstratified component a detailed fabric analysis of the coarse wares was not attempted. Consequently no fabric series has been devised; for at the macro-level, the unstandardised nature of much of the material, often showing wide variation within the same vessel, does not facilitate a realistic and usable categorisation.

This constraint applies to much of the grey ware, and also especially to the numerous fragments of coarse, very gritty wares. Among these last, however, one type is more definable: for reasons discussed later the name West Yorkshire ware has been assigned to this class of pottery and appears in the vessel descriptions.

Another term meriting definition is 'sandwich fabric', whose use to describe certain grey ware follows Wacher (1969, 135):

> It was always fully reduced, with a dark grey core, but the dark surfaces were invariably separated from the core by sharply demarcated paler bands, often almost white ... whether all these vessels originate at Throlam must await further enquiry.

By analogy, 'reverse sandwich fabric' has a light grey core and surfaces separated by a dark grey cortex.

For established types conventional nomenclature is adequate. All references to Gillam types are from Gillam (1970). Dales ware refers to Gillam 157 in shell-gritted fabric; and Huntcliff jar to Gillam 163 in calcite-gritted ware, on which a more detailed note has been included under Well 1 (Chapter 30). Black Burnished ware category 1 is abbreviated to BB1. Flanged bowls and dishes are of straight-sided form unless stated otherwise.

Where vessels have been ascribed to particular manufactories, reference has usually been made to the original kiln excavation reports. In the case of South Yorkshire products, quoted parallels ought not to be taken as exclusive to a named kiln since some individual potteries had similar repertoires (Buckland et al. 1980).

Catalogue

The following catalogue is organised by structure or main structural feature. Each structural section is prefaced by a brief analysis of the ceramic evidence from that part of the site; the description of individual vessels is confined to those selected for illustration. A fuller listing of sherds by context is available in the Archive Report. In addition, the date ranges of pottery from significant contexts have been incorporated in the structural descriptions (Chapter 3).

Structure J (Fig. 95)

Structure J had been badly depleted by a combination of systematic stone robbing, the 1854 excavations,

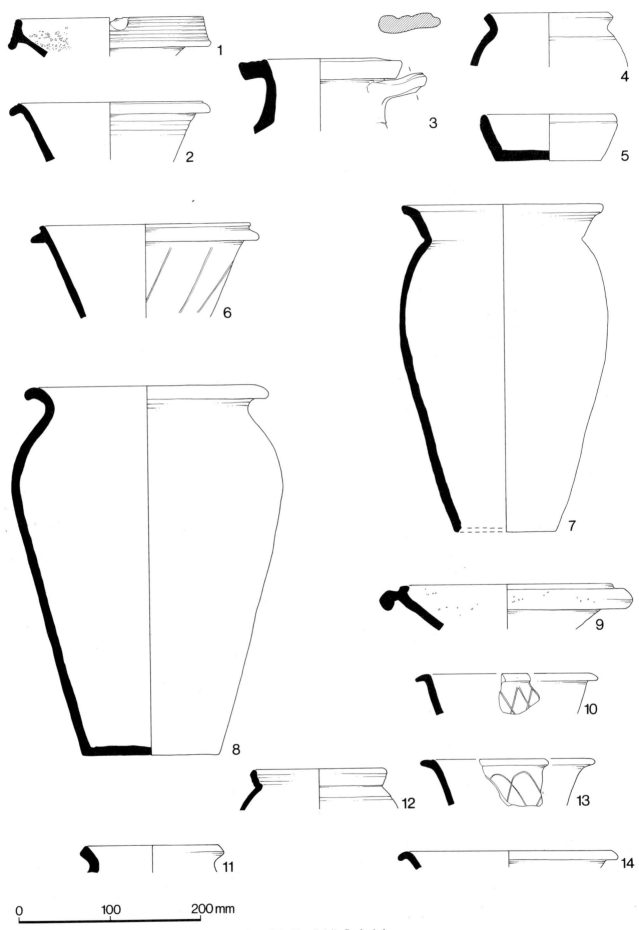

Fig. 95. Roman pottery from Structures J (Nos 1-6) and A (Nos 7-14). Scale 1:4

0   100   200 mm

ploughing, and root activity particularly under the modern hedgeline. Even the basement of the hypocaust in the east wing had been destroyed and in consequence virtually all the pottery came from disturbed contexts. Symptomatic was the retrieval of a recent sherd from the oven chamber (1023), one of the few contexts which at first sight appeared to be relatively intact. While the destruction deposits contained 639 sherds from over 200 vessels, no other context yielded more than 17 sherds.

Context 1023

The ash and debris of the oven stoke-hole in Room 2 included:

1* Mortarium with reeded rim and vestigial spout in hard, off-white fabric showing traces of pale yellow slip; mixed trituration grit; surfaces slightly eroded.

2* Flanged dish with short bead in hard, buff-grey fabric with smoothed surfaces; slight external sooting.

Context 1003

The rubble spread along the western side of Rooms 1 and 2 produced an eroded mortarium fragment, probably Oxfordshire ware and possibly the same vessel as No. 17 in Structure B, context 215. Amongst other vessels was:

3* Large amphora-like jar with reeded rim in uniform pink fabric relatively fine-grained for its size.

Context 900

The black soil layer which represented the backfilling of 19th-century stone-robbing activity contained numerous sherds including:

4* Hand-made, wheel-finished jar with rectangular-section rim in brittle, gritty grey-brown West Yorkshire ware, internally pink; sooted externally and inside the rim.

5* Plain-rimmed dish in pinkish-grey fabric with smoothed black surfaces; reconstructed to 40% complete. Same vessel also in context 903 (19th-century backfill in Room 4).

6* Flanged bowl in coarse, grey-brown fabric with profuse fine mineral grit; surfaces smoothed to a uniform dark grey, with faint hairpin decoration. Kiln marks on the side from two smaller vessels; internally eroded.

Structure A (Fig. 95)

Plough damage which had obliterated the wall foundations of Structure A except to the south and south-east had inevitably destroyed the occupation layers. The bulk of the pottery, 293 mostly fragmentary sherds from a maximum 120 vessels, was amongst the destruction deposits of earth and rubble in and around what remained of the structure; its disturbance was attested by the occurrence of two recent sherds. Other pottery came from internal features cut into the bedrock.

Context 3211

The sub-rectangular pit west of oven 105 contained:

7* Dales ware jar in shell-gritted fabric with prominent fossil inclusions, notably *chlamys valoniensis*; reconstructed to 70% complete. A thoroughly used vessel with internal hard water scaling; externally eroded, and base entirely absent. Gillam 157.

8* Large jar with hand-made body and wheel-thrown rim in calcite-gritted fabric; reconstructed to 95% complete. Gillam 161, dated AD 300-70 on the Northern Frontier.

Contexts 100, 101 and 800

The brown soil overlying the southern part of Structure A produced a range of late 2nd to late 4th-century pottery including:

9* Flanged mortarium in soft, light greyish-brown fabric; small mixed trituration grit scattered on flange; fractured edges rolled. From context 100.

10* Flat-rimmed dish in BB1, coarse, brownish-grey fabric with smoothed darker surfaces and acute-angled lattice decoration. From context 100.

11* Hand-made, wheel-finished jar with rectangular-section rim in brittle, brownish-grey West Yorkshire ware with abundant fine mineral grit; sooted externally and inside the rim. From context 100.

12* Lid-seated jar in hard, sandy, uniform light grey ware. Probably a South Yorkshire product; cf. Cantley kilns 2-6 and 8, no. 86 (Annable 1960, 41, fig. 9). From context 100.

13* Flanged dish or bowl with short bead in sandy, medium grey ware with thin light grey cortex; smoothed darker surfaces with faint hairpin decoration. cf. Gillam 314, dated AD 220-360 on the Northern Frontier. From context 800; same vessel also in context 801.

Context 3800

One of two post-holes on the south side of the structure contained:

14* Dish or bowl with down-turned flat rim in coarse, grey fabric with pink core; smoothed dark grey surfaces.

Structure B (Fig. 96)

Most of the pottery came from the well-preserved hypocaust basement of Rooms 2 and 3 (250 sherds of an estimated 60 vessels); two recent fragments may have entered as a result of robbing sandstone slabs from the remains of the suspended floor. The unheated Room 1 had virtually disappeared. The destruction deposits (contexts 200 and 300) yielded a further 207 sherds from up to 60 vessels; context 300 was also contaminated by recent sherds.

Contexts 204-7 and 210-18

The main filling layers of the hypocaust basements produced:

15* Large heavy jar with semi-circular section rim in sandy, medium grey ware, external surface smoothed darker and partly eroded. From contexts 204, 205 and 206; same vessel (25 sherds in total) also in contexts 200, 201, 208 and 210.

16* Small S-shaped bowl in hard, uniform medium grey fabric, smoothed externally and inside the rim. The general form was produced at both Crambeck and Throlam, but this fabric is not certainly from either. cf. Throlam no. 52 (Sheppard and Corder 1934, 24, fig. 12). From context 204.

17* Mortarium in hard, smooth pink fabric with partial thin grey core and orange-red colour coating, rouletted on the flange; small translucent and white trituration grit; reconstructed to 50% complete. Oxfordshire ware, dated to the 4th century (Swan 1975, fig. 10, no. 60). A total of 21 sherds of this vessel came from contexts 200, 215 and 222; also possibly from Structure J (context 1003).

18* Dish, hand-made and wheel-finished, with internal lip in calcite-gritted ware indistinguishable from Huntcliff jar fabric, sides and base externally smoothed; internal lattice decoration on the base; some external sooting; reconstructed to 55% complete. From context 210; same vessel also in context 200.

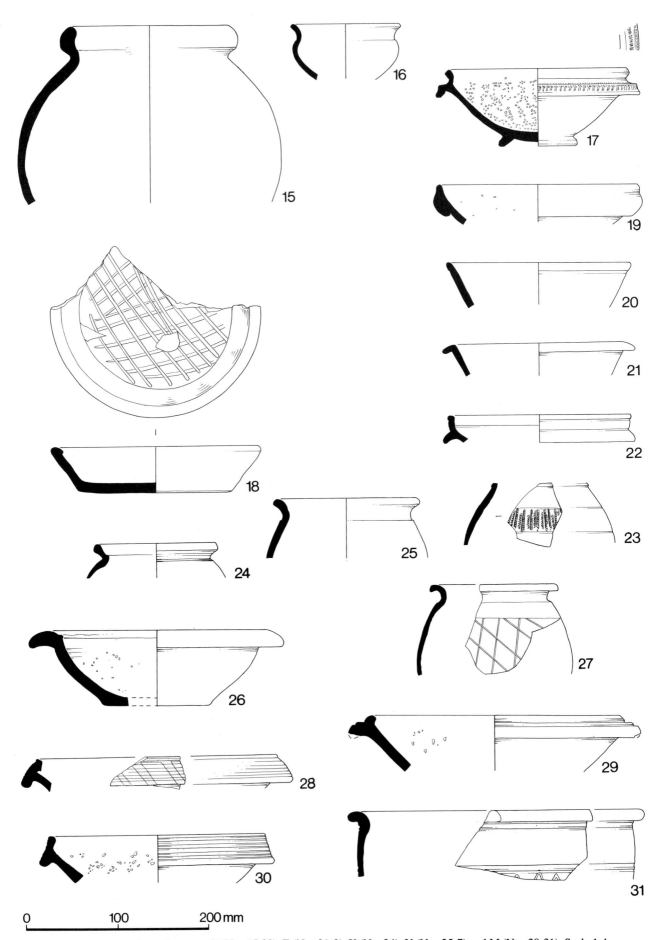

0   100   200 mm

Fig. 96. Roman pottery from Structures B (Nos 15-20), E (Nos 21-3), X (No. 24), Y (Nos 25-7) and M (Nos 28-31). Scale 1:4

Context 200

The upper filling of Rooms 2 and 3 produced:

19* Mortarium with semi-circular section rim in cream fabric with traces of brown slip; sparse white trituration grit visible.

20* Plain-rimmed dish in pink fabric with medium grey core and smoothed dark grey surfaces.

Structure E (Fig. 96)

In Structure E little more survived than the lowest 0.20m of the hypocaust basement; hence the pottery was limited to 33 mainly fragmentary sherds from no more than twenty vessels.

Contexts 500 and 503

The brown soil overlying the hypocaust contained:

21* Bowl or dish with down-turned flat rim in sandy, light grey ware with darker surfaces. Probably from South Yorkshire; cf. Cantley kilns 2-6 and 8, no. 37 (Annable 1960, 37-9, fig. 56).

22* Segmental flanged bowl in off-white fabric, spalled and discoloured by burning after breakage. Crambeck type 5b, without visible decoration (Corder and Birley 1937, 401, fig. 3).

Well 2 (Fig. 96)

Context 4017

The limited excavation of the upper fill produced 70 sherds, including:

23* Stamped Parisian ware sherd of a jar or beaker in fine-grained, light grey fabric externally smoothed to medium grey; Elsdon's fabric 2 (1982, 8-10). Zone of irregularly spaced vertical fern stamps, bearing some resemblance to Corder's stamp 3 from Rudston (Corder 1958, fig. 1).

Structure X (Fig. 96)

The sunken-floored Structure X was partly overlain by Structure M and might have been expected, from its position and depth, to retain occupation debris *in situ*. However no pottery came from internal features; all the sherds retrieved, totalling 70 from up to 30 vessels, were in the lowest filling layers and their deposition therefore post-dated the use of the building. Among these vessels was:

Context 4903/2

24* Lid-seated jar in hard, sandy, medium grey ware; slight sooting around the rim. Probably a South Yorkshire product; cf. Cantley kilns 2-6 and 8, no. 89 (Annable 1960, 41, fig. 9).

Pottery from the upper filling layers, associated with Structure M, is discussed below.

Structure Y (Fig. 96)

Sunken-floored Structure Y was neither completely defined nor fully excavated because of an intention at that time to preserve the overlying stone range, Structure M. Nevertheless a substantial sample of the basement fill was removed, yielding 60 sherds of approximately 30 vessels; but as in Structure X internal features were devoid of pottery, with the exception of two sherds from context 4904: these were two fragments of a jar in medium grey ware with right-angled lattice decoration.

Context 5601/3

The drainage gully which has been associated with this structure (see p. 47), and which pre-dated Structure M, contained:

25* Jar in coarse, brittle, gritty blackish fabric, probably hand-made and wheel-finished; traces of sooting.

Context 5605

A gully which seems to have been initially linked with 5601, but which may have continued in use after the erection of Structure M, Phase I, produced:

26* Mortarium with bead and roll rim in hard, sandy pink fabric with broad medium grey core, cream-slipped; small white and translucent trituration grit, mostly worn away through use.

Context 5605/2A

27* Jar with upright turned-over rim in thin, hard, sandy dark grey fabric, with red core increasing in thickness towards the rim; smoothed inside the rim, and externally above a reserved zone bearing acute-angled lattice decoration approaching a right angle; slight sooting inside and outside the rim. Sherds from same vessel also in gully 5601.

Structure M (Figs 96-7)

Structure M produced more pottery than any other building: over 1500 sherds, despite depletions by the excavators of 1854. However the degree of disturbance was comparable to the other structures, with an absence of floors or securely sealed levels. All contexts with a high pottery content were effectively destruction deposits; of these, context 1213 yielded over 600 sherds.

Context 1213

Layers of rubble and soil had been tipped on to the area of Structure X, above the initial brown soil fill 4903. These dumps of material contained large quantities of pottery, including:

28* Mortarium with lightly reeded rim in smooth cream fabric with traces of yellow slip, and red-brown paint decoration.

29* Mortarium with deeply reeded rim in coarse off-white fabric with external pale yellow slip; sparse black trituration grit; sooting on rim; slightly eroded.

30* Mortarium with lightly reeded rim in coarse cream fabric showing eroded yellow slip; sparse mixed trituration grit.

31* Wide-mouthed bowl in medium grey ware with thin, pale grey cortex, well smoothed externally and inside the rim; wavy line decoration below double girth-groove; eroded internally and on the rim; 30% of rim present. Probably a South Yorkshire product; cf. Cantley kilns 9-25, no. 165 (Cregeen 1958, 385, fig. 5).

32* Jar in BB1, wheel-made, in sandy, dark grey fabric with thin pink external cortex, smoothed to a lustrous black inside the rim, and externally above a reserved zone bearing obtuse-angled lattice. Gillam 145, dated AD 230-300 on the Northern Frontier. Sherds from all three main sectors of this deposit.

33* Dish with triangular-section rim in hard, dense, medium grey ware with thin, light grey cortex, well smoothed overall; sharp linear fractures; reconstructed to 30% complete. Possibly Norton type 2a (Corder 1950, 28, fig. 10).

34* Plain-rimmed dish in sandy, light grey ware with smoothed surfaces; hairpin decoration on the side and scribble beneath the base; sooted on the side and basal edge; internally pitted; 50% of vessel present. Gillam 329, dated AD 190-340 on the Northern Frontier.

35* Hand-made, wheel-finished, lid-seated jar in coarse, gritty grey-brown fabric with dark grey surfaces; sooted externally and inside the rim.

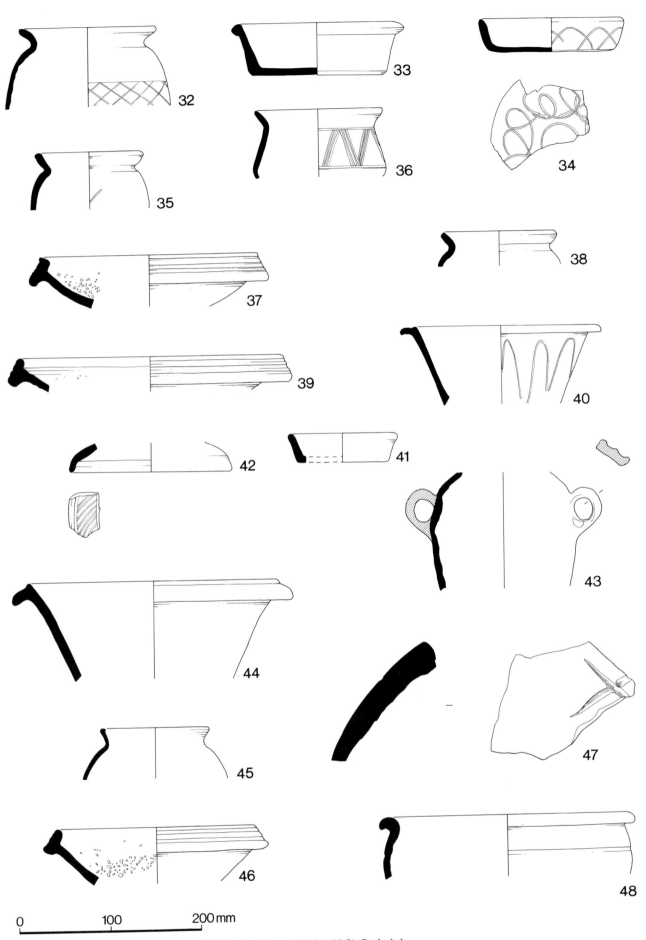

Fig. 97. Roman pottery from Structures M (Nos 32-45) and F (Nos 46-8). Scale 1:4

36* Biconical bowl in hard, medium grey ware with thin pale cortex, smoothed inside and outside the rim. Form as Norton type 10a (Corder 1950, 32, fig. 11). However the groups of sloping lines and sandwich fabric are both Throlam characteristics; and while this form is not among the established repertoire at Throlam (Sheppard and Corder 1934), it has since appeared at the neighbouring kiln site of Hasholme, Humberside, which also used groups of sloping lines, though there the illustrated example is rouletted (Hicks and Watson 1975, 65, fig. 9, no. 22). cf. also Gillam 178, dated AD 290-350 on the Northern Frontier.

Context 1216/2

The black ash associated with the use of kilns 4900 and 1221 contained:

37* Mortarium with reeded rim in dense, smooth, off-white fabric with traces of pale yellow slip; small mixed trituration grit; sooting on rim.

38* Hand-made, wheel-finished jar with slight lid-seating in brownish-grey fabric with internal thin pink cortex, and much fine mineral grit; sooted on the rim.

Contexts 1200, 1201 and 1400

The brown soil layer overlying the main building contained:

39* Mortarium with reeded rim in hard, sandy, brown fabric with medium grey core and eroded grey slip; sparse brown trituration grit visible. From context 1201.

40* Flanged bowl with short bead in hard, sandy, grey-brown ware, smoothed medium grey surfaces and hairpin decoration; Gillam 227, dated AD 210-300 on the Northern Frontier. From context 1200.

41* Shallow plain-rimmed dish, possibly hand-made and wheel-finished, in calcite-gritted ware indistinguishable from Huntcliff jar fabric; base smoothed from wear. From context 1200.

42* Lid in sandy, medium grey ware with pale grey cortex, internally ornamented with lightly incised diagonal lines. From context 1200.

43* Lug handle of a large jar in hard, sandy, dark grey ware with thin brown core, luted on without countersinking. From context 1200.

Context 8023B

In Room 2 of the hypocaust suite the initial destruction layers contained:

44* Flanged bowl in calcite-gritted ware, hand-made and wheel-finished, in medium grey fabric with thin pink cortex and smoothed dark grey surfaces.

Context 1300

The brown soil fill below ploughsoil lying over Structure M yielded:

45* Lid-seated jar, hand-made and wheel-finished, in thin, brittle, gritty medium grey West Yorkshire ware with oxidised patches.

Structure F (Figs 97-8)

Structure F had been largely destroyed by ploughing, and was most evident as a dense concentration of rubble around very fragmentary structural remains. Inevitably the pottery was also heavily disturbed: about 80% of sherds came from the destruction deposits 600 and 700, with 73% from the former – 146 sherds of some 60 vessels. Most internal features contained little or no datable material.

Context 603

46* Mortarium with reeded rim in dense, hard, smooth cream fabric; mixed trituration grit.

47* Body sherd of a globular amphora in coarse, sandy, pinkish-buff fabric; incised with an X before firing; also other sherds of the same vessel.

48* Wide-mouthed bowl in coarse, dark grey ware with medium grey core, smoothed externally and inside the rim. Probably a South Yorkshire product.

Context 600

The destruction deposits included:

49* Stamped Parisian ware sherd in smooth dark grey fabric with thin, light grey cortex; Elsdon's fabric 1 (1982, 8-10). Two stamps: a circle and a comb block. Two fragments apparently from the basal angle are of conventional jar form rather than a pedestal.

50* Flanged mortarium in soft, pinkish-cream fabric with pale grey core.

51* Bowl with flat rim in medium grey ware, smoothed externally and on the rim; reconstructed to 50% complete.

52* Jar in soft, medium grey fabric with darker core and thin light grey cortex; sparse sub-rounded mineral grits, obtruding where the surface has eroded.

Structure P (Fig. 98)

The pottery from the ash and soil dumps which filled this sunken-floored building totalled 360 sherds of an estimated 130 vessels; this was considerably more than from Structures O or Q. Of these sherds, 140 came from the upper deposits 1600, 1601, 1602 and 1615; at a lower level there were small concentrations to either end of the basement.

Context 1608

The black ash and soil covering the western part of the floor produced:

53* Wide-mouthed bowl in hard, sandy, medium grey ware; 30% of rim present. Probably a South Yorkshire product; cf. Cantley kiln 7, no. 163 (Annable 1960, 43, fig. 11).

Context 1603

The ash and clayey loam at the eastern end of the building contained:

54* Small wide-mouthed bowl in uniform, sandy, light grey ware. Probably a South Yorkshire product; cf. Cantley kilns 9-25, no. 140 (Cregeen 1958, 383, fig. 4).

Structure Q (Fig. 98)

Although Structure Q was structurally the best preserved of the sunken-floored buildings, its stratification was not; for at least part of the basement had been excavated to its full depth in 1854. Therefore only two pottery-yielding contexts were recorded and both had been comprehensively disturbed. From context 1701 came 82 sherds of an estimated 24 vessels; context 1700 overlying the whole building produced 54 sherds from some 26 vessels.

Context 1701

The general brown soil filling below ploughsoil included:

55* Wide-mouthed bowl in hard, fine-grained dark grey ware, internally light grey and externally orange-buff; perhaps misfired but also subsequently burnt. Possibly Crambeck type 4 (Corder and Birley 1937, 399-401, fig. 2).

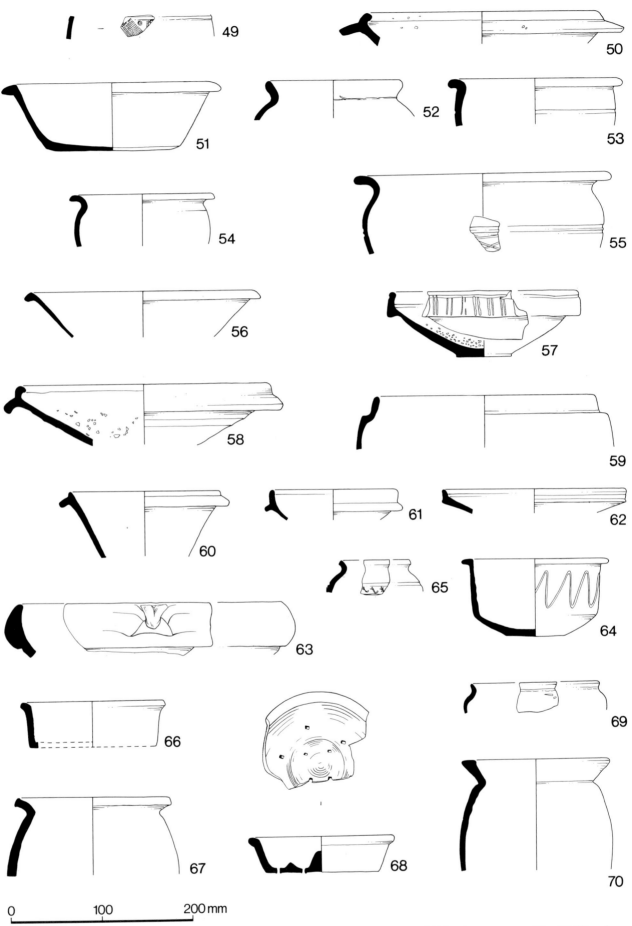

Fig. 98. Roman pottery from Structures F (Nos 49-52), P (Nos 53-4), Q (No. 55), R (Nos 56-7), minor structures (Nos 58-63) and Iron Age ditches and unstratified (Nos 64-70). Scale 1:4

142

Structure R (Fig. 98)

The sunken-floored Structure R was in a poor state of preservation, as was the pottery found in it: 190 mostly small sherds of about 70 vessels, some of them badly eroded. All but 12 sherds came from the main basement filling layers.

Context 1821

A sub-rectangular pit at the north end of the structure contained:

56* Dish or bowl with triangular-section rim in cream fabric; eroded.

Context 1817

The fill of a post-hole in the north-west corner produced:

57* Wallsided mortarium in cream fabric, decorated with red-brown paint; small black trituration grit; rim warped, a second; 25% of vessel present. Crambeck type 7 (Corder and Birley 1937, 401-3, fig. 4). Sherds of same vessel also in contexts 1815 and 1812.

The occurrence of other sherds in the general filling layers suggests this vessel was deposited after the building had gone out of use.

Minor structures (Fig. 98)

Structure O

The remains of sunken-floored Structure O had little substance and there were few definable contexts. More than half the pottery (124 sherds of about 38 vessels) came from context 1500, and most of the remainder (53 sherds of 22 vessels) from context 1501.

Structure S

This isolated group of features east of Enclosure III produced some 40 sherds of colour-coated beakers, Dales ware and Crambeck ware from contexts 1900 and 1902.

Structure V (context 8201)

The fill of this sub-rectangular, sunken-floored structure contained a relatively high concentration of pottery: some 300 sherds from up to 90 vessels. Excavation was in six arbitrary sectors, and three apparent layers were recorded. However the number of sherds of the same vessels which recurred throughout demonstrated that the whole represented one contemporary deposit; the pottery has therefore been reported as a single context.

58* Flanged mortarium in hard, pale pink fabric with thin grey core, and cream slip; large black trituration grit.

59* Bowl or jar with sharply defined shoulder in light grey ware with eroded darker surfaces; in profile like a large castor box. A more rounded version also in grey ware occurred at Langton villa, North Yorkshire, no. 95 (Corder and Kirk 1932, 83, fig. 26).

60* Flanged bowl in light grey ware with smoothed darker surfaces; 55% of the side present, base missing. Crambeck type 1 (Corder and Birley 1937, 398-9, fig. 2).

61* Segmental flanged bowl in pink fabric; eroded. Crambeck type 5 (Corder and Kirk 1932, 401, fig. 3).

Context 6302

One of a group of intercutting pits at the south-east corner of the site produced:

62* Shallow dish in cream fabric. cf. Crambeck no. 55, though in grey at the kilns (Corder 1928, 30, pl. 3).

Contexts 6500 and 8300

The pit complex beyond the south-east corner of Structure P produced about 160 sherds. Among these was a type uncommon on the site:

63* Mortarium in hard, slightly sandy, cream fabric with projecting spout; no trituration grit visible. From context 8300.

Pottery from the Iron Age ditches (Fig. 98)

The enclosure ditches yielded occasional Roman sherds from their topmost filling layers, especially in the vicinity of Roman buildings. This suggests that settlement of the filling had created hollows, where rubbish accumulated.

Much larger quantities of Roman material were recovered from the ditches which are interpreted as having been recut for villa boundaries: 510 sherds from the north ditch 011-014-030, and 670 sherds from the south ditch 002-021. A link was provided by a basal sherd of a mortarium from Ditch 011 which joined with another from Ditch 002. The assemblages were chronologically jumbled over a broad span: Iron Age sherds were present, while the Roman pottery ran from samian ware through 3rd-century vessels to Crambeck forms and Huntcliff jars, reflecting the types already described from the villa buildings. The Roman pottery from the post-Roman levelling deposits adds nothing of significance to the understanding of the villa, and consequently is not detailed here except for pieces of intrinsic interest.

Ditches 031/1 and 031/4

64* Carinated bowl in sandy, medium grey ware; wavy line decoration, sooted on the base; reconstructed to 45% complete.

Ditch 040

65* Small rusticated jar in uniform, sandy, medium grey ware.

Ditch 002/4

66* Hand-made, wheel-finished everted-rim dish in medium grey shell-gritted fabric with pink cortex and smoothed dark grey surfaces.

Ditch 002/8A

67* Hand-made, wheel-finished jar with rectangular rim in brittle, very gritty grey-brown West Yorkshire ware; externally sooted.

Ditch 011

68* Cheese press in uniform, fine-grained medium grey ware, smoothed externally and inside the rim; rectangular drain-holes pierced before firing, probably by a nail. Faint kiln marks from other vessels on the rim. One sherd, representing 45% of the vessel.

Unstratified

69* Small bowl in cream fabric smoothed externally and inside the rim, with eroded orange paint decoration surviving only as a horizontal band in the angle of the neck.

70* Wheel-made jar of Dales ware profile in very gritty grey-brown fabric, externally blackish and internally pink.

The Roman pottery from other Iron Age contexts is unremarkable, though numerous fragments of two ring-necked flagons, uncommon on the site came from features associated with Roundhouse 2.

Discussion

A few sherds of 1st-century Roman pottery, comprising fragments of three South Gaulish samian vessels, pre-date the establishment of the villa. The remaining samian ware, despite its wide distribution across the site, is limited in quantity. It is mainly Central Gaulish and Antonine in date, with a minority of East Gaulish sherds, and predominantly of form 31.

Almost all the other fine ware consists of colour-coated beakers, probably mostly of Nene Valley origin, in what is still widely known as castor ware: cream or off-white fabric slipped in various shades of brown, commonly producing a characteristic mottled effect. There are abundant fragments showing 3rd and 4th-century variations in form and finish, with rouletted, indented and scale-indented beakers, plain and painted barbotine decoration and hunt cups. A few fragments of Rhenish beakers in hard, thin, dark red fabric with lustrous metallic coating are also present.

The coarse pottery in use at the villa emanates largely from the Yorkshire-North Lincolnshire (historic) region, with types characteristic of major established manufactories besides others yet to be firmly provenanced. Owing to conservative potting traditions many have either a broad or an imprecisely known date range, which there is little opportunity to refine here in the absence of sealed stratified groups. The emphasis throughout is on functional vessels; exotic imports are lacking.

The grey wares of South Yorkshire are represented by wide-mouthed bowls and more noticeably lid-seated jars; the latter form, commonly in hard, gritty fabric, was made in greatest quantity at Blaxton, South Yorkshire c. AD 160-250 (Buckland and Dolby 1980, 20-21). However, both types persisted at the Doncaster area kilns from the Antonine period until well into the 4th century (Buckland et al. 1980, 158-9, 161). The small amount of Black Burnished ware is probably from the same area, on grounds of proximity alone, since visually it cannot be distinguished from the products of Dorset and other centres (Buckland et al. 1980, 152). Conceivably also from South Yorkshire are No. 65, the sole example of Rustic ware, which was produced into the late Antonine (Buckland et al. 1980, 158), and the few sherds of Parisian vessels such as Nos 23 and 49, with a roughly contemporary date range (Buckland et al. 1980, 156-7).

Possible alternative sources for the Parisian ware are Market Rasen, Lincolnshire and Roxby in Humberside, where manufacture may have lasted into the 3rd century (Rigby and Stead 1976, 185-7). This origin would be unsurprising since a North Lincolnshire connection is strongly indicated by one of the commonest types found on the site: the Dales ware jar, predominantly the typical hand-made vessel with wheel-finished rim, in reduced fabric sometimes with oxidised cortex, and filled with Rhaetic fossil shell. Dales ware jars had a long life, taken as c. AD 200-350 following a recent intensive study (Loughlin 1977).

In West Yorkshire no civilian kiln sites have yet been attested; the only known Roman pottery production was at the military tilery of Grimescar near Huddersfield, which was in operation c. AD 100-120 (Purdy and Manby 1973). However at Dalton Parlours there appear vessels which, it is suggested, are the products of a previously unrecognised industry located in the geographical western half of Yorkshire, and accordingly designated West Yorkshire ware. The dominant form is a jar with hand-made body of uneven thickness, and a wheel-finished, everted, rectangular-section rim marginally thickened at the lip, sometimes with a slight lid-seating. The fabric is brittle and heavily charged with fine mineral grit, sparkling where cleanly exposed, giving a distinctive sandpapery surface. It is normally reduced but the colour varies even within the same vessel from grey to black, brown or buff occasionally tinged with pink, indicating uncontrolled firing conditions. Examples are Nos 4, 11 and 45.

Although direct comparisons have yet to be made, related forms with similar fabric descriptions have been published from the following sites: Catterick (Gillam 1958, 255, fig. 10, no. 7); Well (Gilyard-Beer 1951, 49, fig. 15, nos 34-7); Aldborough (Myres et al. 1962, 36, fig. 11, nos 24, 31 and 33; also Jones 1972, 54, fig. 9, no. 27); and Ilkley (Hartley 1966, 59, fig. 11, no. 57: two examples). The suggested dates for these vessels, when collated, embrace the 3rd and 4th centuries.

The above sites are all on or towards the western edge of the Vale of York, and significantly Dr P.C. Buckland has confirmed (pers. comm.) that the inclusions in the Dalton Parlours vessels are derived from Millstone Grit, which outcrops on the west side of the county. There are many blackish and brownish-grey sherds with similar inclusions in differing proportions, probably from the same source(s) as the more standardised fabric described, and other forms are likely to be more definable when better preserved material is available. Though further investigation is necessary, the quantity found at Dalton Parlours raises the possibility of local manufacture, perhaps in the area of Wetherby, where the Wharfe cuts the gritstone, and evidence for 2nd to 4th-century occupation exists (Kent and Kitson Clark 1934; Mellor 1934). In this connection it is worth noting the evidence adduced in Lincolnshire for the deliberate siting of potteries to serve nearby villas (Mostyn-Lewis 1966). As a cautionary note, in fabric and to an extent form, West Yorkshire ware can deceptively resemble some middle Saxon pottery, for example the earlier material excavated at the Archbishop's Manor House, Otley, dated c. AD 650-850 (Le Patourel and Wood 1973, 134-6, fig. 10).

Inevitably a high proportion of the coarse pottery is from the prolific East Riding kiln centres, which became increasingly dominant in northern Britain during the later Roman period. A few vessels have been interpreted as possibly, though not certainly, from Norton, North Yorkshire; and grey ware indented jars of Norton type 9 recur, though their fabric suggests a different source. More conspicuous are Throlam types, which in turn are considerably outnumbered by products of Crambeck – even allowing for the many small sherds of forms common to both, which are sometimes hard to distinguish.

The dates given to East Riding kilns in the original excavation reports, principally by Corder, have on the whole endured with little modification; although it is debatable whether this would be entirely so if more closely dated stratified groups had become available for examination. At Norton, Corder's dating was c. AD 220-80, with a frequently overlooked postscript suggesting possible extension into the early 4th century (1950, 35-7; Hayes and Whitley 1950, 41-2). Throlam was assigned to the narrow range of c. AD 250-80 (Sheppard and Corder 1934, 32-5). The 4th-century overall dating of Crambeck pottery, with certain types – mainly in cream or so-called Parchment ware, and often painted – confined to AD 370-95 (Corder and Birley 1937, 408-13), has been generally supported by findings on the Northern Frontier (Gillam 1970).

Queries have been raised by associations in well-stratified groups at Brough-on-Humber, where it was suggested that Norton types spanned c. AD 200-350/70. Also at Brough, Throlam wares were identified in late 2nd-century deposits and it was said that the Throlam kilns 'certainly continued in production during the first half of the 4th century' (Wacher 1969, 134-5). The products of Throlam in particular have sufficient in common with Crambeck to imply a possible overlap; but in Well 1 at Dalton Parlours, deposition of the bulk of the Throlam vessels pre-dated that of Crambeck grey ware (see Chapter 30). It may be that there is a distinction to be drawn between the actual working period of the manufactories and the period within which their wares enjoyed large-scale distribution. It should also be borne in mind that the apparently numerous kilns around Hasholme, adjacent to Throlam, have so far been only partly investigated (Hicks and Watson 1975).

Most frequent of all are Huntcliff jars, whose manufactories presumably in the East Riding have yet to be identified. Traditionally associated with the late 4th-century Yorkshire signal stations (Hull 1933) they are conventionally dated, as Gillam 163, to AD 360-400. These hand-made vessels with wheel-finished rims in calcite-gritted ware are prolific on late Roman sites north of the Humber – remarkably so for such a relatively short date range, but often unaccompanied by other dating evidence. Dr P.C. Buckland has suggested (pers. comm.) that the start date should be revised to c. AD 340 on the evidence of the Cridling Stubbs hoard, which comprised 3300 coins buried in a worn Huntcliff jar in AD 345/6 (Pirie 1971). This has wide implications for the dating of northern sites.

In addition to the wares cited, there is a small number of vessel types each represented by a single example. Worthy of mention are a bowl in York red-painted ware, probably Antonine (not illustrated); a 4th-century Oxfordshire ware mortarium (No. 17), and a small colour-coated segmental flanged bowl of unknown origin (Chapter 30, No. 88).

The pot groups from the villa buildings display a marked uniformity one with another. The vessel descriptions above emphasise the broad chronological and typological coverage of the major excavated groups, and their inadequacy for the relative dating of structures. This lack of differentiation may be further emphasised by examining the recurrence of individual types. For example samian ware was found in all the buildings except Structure O; colour-coated beakers in every building; Dales ware in all but Structure X; West Yorkshire ware in all but Structures E and Y; and Crambeck ware and Huntcliff jars in all except Structures X and Y. The last exclusion is not unexpected for Structures X and Y had been demolished and levelled at an earlier stage to make way for Structure M. Nevertheless the fill of Structure Y yielded two fragments of Roman calcite-gritted fabric, which from identifiable vessels does not demonstrably occur on the site before c. AD 300.

Apart from Well 1, which produced the only function-specific concentration of vessels from the villa, the pottery provides no outstanding revelations for the use of other structural features. The specialised forms present were widely scattered across the site. Amphora sherds were not uncommon, though probably from few vessels in total. Flagons seemed in short supply, and mostly in orange or pink rather than cream fabrics. Mortaria, on the other hand, occurred in every building. A single recognisable cheese press (No. 68) came from the north boundary ditch, and two fragments perhaps from strainers came from Structure O.

Pottery adapted for secondary uses included a Dales ware jar apparently employed as a paint-pot for the interior decor of Structure J, and a fire-shovel improvised from a broken mortarium found in the north boundary ditch. Home-crafted potsherd spindlewhorls and counters are described elsewhere (Chapter 11). Mention may be made of pit 3211 in Structure A, in which two near-complete vessels were found: a Dales ware jar and a 4th-century calcite-gritted jar of Gillam type 161 (Nos 7 and 8). Most of the material from the remaining pits and ditches presumably represents rubbish disposal, though repair was preferred to rejection, especially for water containers.

The pottery is statistically the strongest evidence for the overall dating of the villa occupation within the 3rd and 4th centuries AD. Whether it began before or after the end of the 2nd century depends on the extent to which the samian ware and the small number of Antonine coarse vessels had survived in use. Samian occurred in very small amounts, tending towards proportionality with the total sherd count for each building. The best that can be said from the pottery is that the villa was probably established within a decade or two either side of AD 200.

Intensity of activity by period cannot realistically be gauged, given the wide and overlapping date ranges of wares especially in the 3rd century. For example there is no way of knowing how the acquisition of Dales ware was quantitatively apportioned across a 150 year span; or at what period, if any, East Riding pottery and West

Yorkshire ware were obtained simultaneously. In the absence of the means to assess purchasing policy at the villa relative to the market suppliers at a given time, it can only be assumed from the diversity of sources that certain needs were fulfilled with whatever contemporary products were most readily and economically available.

Intrinsic to the dating problem, and a striking aspect of the Dalton Parlours assemblage, is the abundance and persistence of hand-made pottery with wheel-finished rims, seemingly inferior to the wholly wheel-thrown grey wares. Dales ware and Huntcliff jars have long been recognised, and the designation of West Yorkshire ware merely adds another to the same broad category, whilst being of some regional significance. Perhaps because of its brittle quality this local product did not achieve the widespread success of the other two wares; it may be that future research will clarify the development of its forms to an extent which has not been possible with the Dales ware and Huntcliff jar industries, since their command of the market was in each case based largely on a single outstanding product.

The volume of Crambeck grey ware and Huntcliff jars is such as to imply that the villa attained its *floruit* in the 4th century. There is however a virtual absence of exclusively late 4th-century Crambeck forms with the exception of the type 7 mortarium, for which a slightly earlier beginning is therefore implied. The segmental bowl type 5b and the dish type 10 are sparsely represented, but with no clear example of the extravagantly painted vessels known from late sites in the region (Corder and Birley 1937, 401, fig. 10). This indicates that the villa did not survive as late as the end of the century, and suggests desertion sometime around *c.* AD 370.

The author of the excavation report on the Rudston villa has said:

> That most useful of artefacts, coarse pottery, suffers from a deep-rooted and long-lasting tradition which made little use of the potter's wheel, leaving the archaeologist with masses of undecorated hand-made sherds which allow none of the precision of chronology normally associated with a Romano-British site. (Stead 1980, 35)

This limitation is equally applicable at Dalton Parlours, where closer dating from the pottery would still have presented difficulties even if stratified layers had been preserved across the site. More than anything it impels the need to integrate all available forms of evidence into the process of site interpretation.

16 Wooden Object from Enclosure I, pit 2604 (Fig. 99) by Carole A. Morris

Fragment of double-sided comb comprising a section of the middle bar, 12 coarse teeth and 23-4 fine teeth, cut

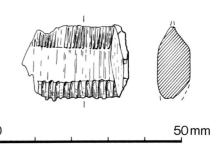

Fig. 99. Wooden object from Enclosure I, pit 2604. Scale 1:1

with fine saws. This type of comb has many parallels, for example from Castleford (Morris forthcoming a), London (Chapman 1980, 678, fig. 73) and Vindolanda, Northumbria (Birley 1977, 123-4, pl. 60). These combs are usually assumed to be domestic items for combing hair, but one boxwood comb from Vindolanda had traces of cow's hair in its teeth, and the Castleford comb was found in an area associated with leatherworking. Combs such as these could well have been used at some stage in the tanning process. L. 30mm; w. 21mm; th. 10mm. (*Buxus sempervirens*, boxwood). *2604A; SF 467*

17 The Mosaic Remains (Pl. XXIX)
by Neil Cookson

Introduction

The only significant mosaic remains from Dalton Parlours were unearthed during the 19th-century excavations of the site, reported by Procter. The pavement was then transported to the Yorkshire Museum, York (Procter 1855, 270), where it has remained, in various states of rearrangement. At present it hangs on the wall of the central stairway, carefully restored to reproduce the design as originally drafted by its excavators (Procter 1855, pl. 7; Speight 1902). Considering the degree of care necessary to lift and transport the mosaic to York, it is surprising that no other records or drawings have survived. Yet this appears to have been the case, notwithstanding the collection of other finds from the same excavation also deposited with the museum (Elizabeth Hartley pers. comm.).

The much more extensive and detailed excavations in the 1970s revealed many more *tesserae*, though no more complete mosaics. Plough damage was severe and, in common with a large proportion of the remainder of the site, few Roman floor levels were preserved, either in Structure J, the building containing the Medusa mosaic, or in Structure M, the location of further remains of *tesserae* (Procter 1855, 271-2). Nevertheless, a reasonably complete settlement plan has been obtained, and in general we are able to accept the chronology of the site with a good deal more confidence than before.

Tesserae were found throughout the site in large quantities. Reconstruction in antiquity, eventual

Pl. XXIX. The Medusa mosaic, as currently reconstructed. (Photo: courtesy of John Rose Associates)

destruction, and continuous damage by robbing and plough since this time will have all contributed to their dispersal. In some instances they appear to have been dumped as debris (in Well 1, and in Structure A), but generally, where evidence for individual mosaics can be inferred, they comprise broad scatters of stones ranging from 15-25mm cubed. Structure J gave examples of smaller *tesserae* (7.5mm, usually cubic), but without exception these were unbonded and uniformly distributed across the floor. Only three structures can be considered with any certainty to provide further evidence for the existence of mosaic: B, M and J; the remainder are doubtful.

Structure B

Convincingly interpreted as a bath house with hypocaust (p. 281), this produced a hundred or more *tesserae* of various sizes, ranging from 10-20mm. These are predominantly of red, creamy-white, and deep yellow. It seems likely that they comprised the floor covering of the corner of the ?*tepidarium* (210); for although unbonded they show traces of mortar. There can be little doubt that this was a polychrome floor, probably with a simple geometric design. This structure also produced fragments of a painted plaster ceiling (see Chapter 18).

Structure M

This block provided the second highest concentration of *tesserae* on the site. Unfortunately, most of these were from fill 1422, possibly the backfill of the 19th-century excavations. The present excavations have, however, confirmed the presence of tessellation in the hypocaust rooms of Structure M, and have provided a patch of five *tesserae* still bonded together. The latter are small

(7.5mm, mainly cubic), of dark red and creamy-white. Interestingly, they follow a curving alignment – red within the white – and so attest in Structure M another polychrome mosaic. The *tesserae* size suggests a finer work than that of Structure B. Heavy wear on the surface confirms them to be floor rather than wall mosaic.

Structure J

Structure J produced the Medusa mosaic (Pl. XXIX), the most significant mosaic remains from the site. The pavement was uncovered during the original excavations, when the apsidal room of this building was one of the few discrete structures revealed. The room is now seen to be the western wing of a larger structure (Fig. 37), with a corridor and at least three other rooms (some of which also appear to have been tessellated).

Many hundreds of *tesserae* were recovered from Structure J. These are generally of 15-20mm or 7.5-10mm cubed, and include the colours red, buff, creamy-white, yellow and grey. Most were backfill material, although some do appear to have been missed by the original excavators. One notable find includes a fragment of eight *tesserae*, in which a band of three white *tesserae* encloses two bands of yellow. These are approximately 7.5-10mm cubed. Unfortunately, the context does not allow the find to be closely associated with the geometric pavement to the south of the Medusa panel. The uneven setting and coarse mortar in this fragment might indicate a repair.

This geometric pattern, reproduced by Procter (1855, pl. 7), is composed of a series of spaced lines running the entire length of the southern section of Room 5. It occupies approximately the western third of the floor, with the remainder divided laterally into rectangular panels, each decorated by an all-over scale pattern. The whole is separated from the Medusa panel by a ?wall (see below)

147

and a mosaic border of filled triangles ('blue and white pyramids' in Procter's report).

The Medusa panel itself almost fills the apse. The only space not covered by polychrome decoration contains a broad border of monochrome, which is relieved by two lighter bands as it approaches the first polychrome element, a continuous scroll featuring stylised ivy-leaves.

The scroll, like the rest of the mosaic, is set against a background of cream-coloured *tesserae*. The lines here are of blue-black, two *tesserae* wide for the main band, and only one *tessera* wide for the curving stems. The scroll has single, scale-like fillers in the angles of the volutes and stylised crests at each of three tendrils. The leaves point alternately towards and away from the centre of the pavement. They are shaded either red or light brown, usually in the sequence one red followed by one brown – although this was a sequence which, apparently, could accommodate a gadrooned bowl or could be broken, to Medusa's right, where three light brown leaves separate two of red.

The next element comprises a band of three-strand guilloche worked in cream, buff, red, and blue-black on a blue-black background. This is loosely drawn, betokening some shortcomings in ability, and occasionally – for example, above the light brown ivy-leaves, and at the return of the band in the only surviving angle of the design – signs of confused workmanship.

Following the guilloche is a cream-coloured band four *tesserae* wide which, in turn, encloses a simple cable pattern. The latter is again loosely drawn – this time in cream, buff, grey, red, and blue-black – but avoids the mistakes of the guilloche. It is this decoration which describes the three parts of the central field, where its alternating shading of strands (red, buff and grey) is particularly effective.

In the central field, the panels to Medusa's right and left are emphasised by a thin line of buff *tesserae*. These enclose distinctive urn-lotus motifs, delineated in blue-black, both comprising a small triangular pedestal, splayed 'handles', and calyces highlighted at their tips by red against buff brown. They are angled away from Medusa, a feature which, when coupled with the line of buff *tesserae* just mentioned, serves to formalise the appearance of the panel, so adding depth to the central portrait.

That this portrait represents Medusa is indicated by the matted hair clearly manifesting itself as 'hissing' snakes; the M-shaped fillet beneath the chin; the well-documented, glaring eyes and the characteristic rounded face without neck or shoulders. As suits its importance as the central device, it is worked in finer *tesserae* than are observed elsewhere (frequently less than 7.5mm). The array of snakes is surprisingly realistic for this form of stylised representation. The 'hair' is clearly depicted by black *tesserae* on a brown ground. The face is brought to life with careful highlighting of the cheeks, forehead, and lower lip by the use of cream on brown. At the very centre, Medusa's eyes are picked out by two black *tesserae*.

Mosaics with figural work are not common in the north of England; indeed, with Yorkshire we are dealing with the most northerly part of the province to produce important mosaic remains of any description. For this reason alone the panel would be interesting. However, it further testifies to the presence of a fairly accomplished craftsman who, to judge from other northern examples, would not have been easy to come by. Mistakes are apparent, as noted above. And to these can be added the awkward drawing of the urn-lotus motifs. But these are not errors of sufficient naivety or extent to suggest the work of an apprentice. Instead, they are better described as errors produced during the normal course of tessellation by a single mosaicist who, throughout the pavement, shows a greater facility with the use of colour and contrast than in the consistent organisation of space.

Dating and interpretation of the Structure J mosaics
Plough damage and the previous excavation of the site ensured that the amount of recoverable dating evidence was minimal. In most places the foundations of Structure J, Rooms 2 and 5, were no more than one course high, and were frequently robbed out. Moreover, by far the greatest number of finds in this area belonged to contexts 1000 and 1001, representing backfill material. No significant sealed deposits were encountered. The oven (1017, 1023) projecting into Room 2 (the geometric mosaic) produced pottery of the late 2nd to the late 4th centuries. The backfill material itself included two 4th-century coins, one of *c.* AD 330-340 (Chapter 4). Sherds of Dales ware pottery were found in a pit (912) in Room 3, and in a pit (1002) just beyond the walls of the apse.

However, none of this either confirms or contradicts the 3rd or 4th-century date suggested by both the coin evidence recorded by Procter and the general stylistic affinities of the mosaic. Procter records only nine coins, yet of these, four, and possibly six, are of the 4th century (including issues of Constantius and one of Valentinian: Procter 1855, 279). This supports a 4th-century date, probably of the early to mid-4th century; even those issues belonging to an earlier period suggest nothing earlier than the late 2nd, and more likely the 3rd century.

The stylistic details of the pavements in Rooms 2 and 5 do support this view. Apsidal mosaics in Britain are likely to be of the late 3rd or 4th century, rather than earlier. Good examples are known from at least fifteen sites, of which at least ten can be dated to this later period. The most convincing examples of concentric banded decoration, enclosing a single portrait head as at Dalton Parlours, are certainly of this period: the Bignor Gladiators mosaic in West Sussex (Lysons 1817, pl. XVI), or the mosaic from Fordington High Street, Dorchester, Dorset, for example (*RCHM* 1970, front).

As a subject for figural work in mosaic, Medusa appears throughout the Roman period in Britain. There are examples in an early pavement at Fishbourne in West Sussex (Cunliffe 1971a, pl. LXXXIV) and in 2nd-century pavements from Dyer Street, Cirencester, Gloucestershire

(Buckman and Newmarch 1850, pls II-III); whilst the late 3rd and 4th centuries see Medusa featured at Bignor twice (Lysons 1817, pls XXIV, XXVI and XXVII), Brading, Isle of Wight (Morgan 1886, 234-5), Bramdean, Hampshire (*VCH* 1900, 308, fig. 18) and, notably, Toft Green, York (*RCHM* 1962, pl. 24 and front). However, none of these individual portraits is either sufficiently well recorded or stylistically close enough to the present example to permit meaningful comparisons. There is no precedent for the Dalton Parlours 'M' fillet; its position is more traditionally taken by encircling snakes which contribute further to the rounded appearance of the face, as seen at Cirencester (Cookson 1984, pl. 10b). The Dalton Parlours mosaic, in fact, presents an original mixture of traditional gaze and facial composure; it contrasts with an Italian example, now displayed in the Terme Museum, Rome, which gives a good indication of the alternative, frantic expression. It certainly has not proceeded down the road to the comic stylisation visible at Bignor and Brading, or in the continental examples from Germany at Cologne, Lungengasse (Parlasca 1959, pl. 83, no. 2) and Trier, Weberbachstrasse (Parlasca 1959, pl. 49, no. 1).

It is in the actual depiction of the face therefore, that one must look for similarities with other mosaics. In this respect, two pavements in the north of England are worthy of special mention. First is the mosaic from Toft Green, York which, in addition to a central Medusa panel, features busts of each of the 'four seasons' in its angles. Characteristics of these busts include long noses each defined by a single line of dark *tesserae*; rounded, almost fat faces, highlighted by the same technique, and occasional single lines of cream-coloured *tesserae* to pick out the cheeks, brow and bridge of the nose. The lentoid eyes of the York busts do, admittedly, provide a clear contrast with those of Medusa; although the latter must be considered with regard to the particular expression which they were intended to depict. The second pavement is the Rudston Charioteer mosaic, North Humberside (Stead 1980, pl. VIII; Neal 1981, no. 69). Much of the work is of a higher quality than that seen in the Dalton Parlours mosaic. However, again one encounters a long nose and wide eyebrows, an austere form of draughtsmanship, and a subtle use of colour as the tones darken from the left to the right of the face.

These similarities, although not definitive, do point to a style of portraiture evident in other mosaics as well as that from Dalton Parlours. The Rudston mosaic has been tentatively dated to the second quarter of the 4th century (Smith 1980, 137). As has been suggested elsewhere (Cookson 1984, 95-6), this pictorial style and technique in the north of England can be assigned to a period after the early 4th-century growth of figural design in the south-west.

The non-figural motifs in the Structure J mosaics can be divided into those from the apsidal panel and those from the geometric arrangement to the south. The former include the ivy-scroll and gadrooned bowl, as well as the two urn-lotus motifs. The latter comprise scale-pattern and intersecting lines.

The ivy-scroll is of a type not uncommon in Britain. Comparable – if not closely related – examples are seen in a 2nd-century pavement from Winterton, Humberside (Neal 1981, no. 81); in the mosaic from Dorchester; in the Bignor mosaics; and in mosaics from the Gallic sites of Diekirch in Belgium (Stern 1960, pl. XXVII) and Auriebat in France (Balmelle 1980, pl. XLV). Yet these span the 2nd to 4th centuries. Consequently, they are of limited value for dating purposes.

The unusual urn-lotus is more promising. It has affinities with those comprising the border of the Rudston Aquatic mosaic (Neal 1981, no. 67), a work which has been attributed to the third quarter of the 4th century (Smith 1980, 137). Revised dating has suggested some mosaics – notably the Venus mosaic – to be of the 3rd rather than the 4th century (Johnson 1982, 29), but this has yet to be fully substantiated (Cookson 1984, 85). Clearly, there are differences in the setting and drawing techniques in these two examples, which render them dissimilar. Yet for this idiosyncratic motif the affinity is close. The Rudston examples are more crudely executed, and are exaggerated when compared with those found on either side of Medusa. But in this they are only exhibiting a quality more graphically illustrated by other, late and relatively accurately dated mosaics from Winterton (Smith 1976, 258). For the apsidal panel itself, therefore, this again indicates a date prior to the mid-4th century, probably of *c*. AD 320-350.

The geometric arrangement to the south is now lost. But from Procter's illustration it is plain that the motifs there did not reproduce any to be found in the apsidal panel. It is possible that the two rectangular panels are drawn to a different scale from the remainder of the pavement, but this must remain conjectural. What seems certain however, is that the geometric mosaic and the Medusa mosaic were laid at different times, with the geometric probably the later of the two. The evidence for this is provided by the panels of scale pattern and simple intersecting lines which make up the arrangement. The former is found in the Brantingham Tyche mosaic in Humberside (Neal 1981, no. 12), dated to *c*. AD 330-50 (Liversidge *et al.* 1973, 89). More particularly, it forms a significant part of the mosaic of room II from that site (Cookson 1984, 94, pl. 99b), which is likely to be of the same period. Here, a central panel of stylised *peltae* is enclosed by a single band of superposed triangles, in turn followed by a wide panel of scale pattern. Unlike the scales of the Dalton Parlours mosaic their tips are shaded; the bases of the scales also appear to be narrower. Nevertheless, the mosaics cannot have been too distant from one another in time, especially when their geographical proximity is taken into consideration. Indeed, if a cruder example of this type of scale pattern is required, the Fortuna mosaic from Winterton (Neal 1981, no. 84) should be mentioned. Two panels of scale pattern border the central roundel of a pavement which, in this instance, is loosely set in large *tesserae* (Stead 1976, pl. XXIIIb and is dated to *c*. AD 350 (Smith 1976, 258). If this evidence is considered with the evidence from Brantingham it seems likely that the Dalton Parlours pavement must also be of the mid-4th century, possibly later.

The remaining decoration of the geometric panel has few notable parallels. The simple nature of this form means that such parallels, if discovered, might not be particularly helpful. Such evidence as there is, however, does not conflict with a later, mid-4th-century dating of the scale-pattern panels; indeed, two pavements which display stylised scale and linear decoration, from Taron and Lalonquette, both in Aquitaine, France, are dated to the later 4th and early 5th centuries (Balmelle 1980, nos 108 and 120).

Significance of the mosaics

If, as seems likely, the mosaics of Rooms 2 and 5 in Structure J were laid at different times, this should not detract from their importance as decoration. Nor does it preclude the possibility that they possessed complementary functions. The two panels are of differing quality, but they nevertheless combined to provide one of the largest areas of tessellation in the region. The Medusa panel alone is likely to have required more than 50 man days of labour. The quality of the geometric panel may have left a little to be desired. Rudston, Brantingham, Horkstow and Winterton (all in Humberside) each boasts more mosaic remains than does Dalton Parlours. Yet the impression is that Dalton Parlours was a villa where, during the 4th century at least, such sophisticated decorations were to be expected.

The Medusa panel will have remained a distinctive, prestige product – even if not conceived of as a particular status symbol by its owners. The skillful use of colour and vivid representation of figural subject matter distinguishes the mosaic as one of importance not only within the site; its position within the most important part of the most notable building on site must be significant. Whether or not a wall separated the two mosaics remains unclear. Procter reported this to be the case, but little evidence to support the statement was encountered during the recent excavations. If the building comprised one large room with an apse and figural mosaic at one end, then one must surmise a structure serving a public or ceremonial use. (It does not appear to have had a regular means of heating.) If partitioned, the 'Medusa Room' would appear to be more of a cult room, probably never seen by more than one or two of the villa's leading inhabitants.

As a cult symbol, the Gorgon has a long history, extending back at least as far as archaic Greece, and possibly into the pre-Dorian era. Medusa, as the mortal Gorgon, is central to a series of myths based on the relationship of human endeavour and the underworld – most notably in the Perseus-Gorgon story. As far as Roman culture is concerned, the crucial point of transition occurs when the active underworld force is reduced to a symbolic image, thus taking on, in pre-Roman times, distinct but circumscribed apotropaic powers. As such, the head of Medusa is subdued by Minerva, whose aegis she then adorns. She is also frequently associated with Mars, and more generally with virility, in the form of a phallus (Dunbabin 1978, pl. LXV), as a counterbalance to the 'evil eye'.

There are few suggestions as to how the Medusa mask was interpreted on the present site (for Medusa generally see Croon 1955, 9-16). There are no associated cult burials to attest the protection of the dead (see Henig 1984, 185 and 196), nor were any noteworthy cult objects discovered in the vicinity of Structure J. However, the mask is deliberately faced to the north, and is therefore possibly associated with the belief that the 'invidus' originated behind the north wind (Henig 1984, 196). Certainly, the position of the mask, if coincidental, is inappropriate for any conventional use of the room: Dunbabin (1978, 163) believes that there is usually an apotropaic quality attendant on any Medusa image which retains its central and isolated position within a Roman floor. In this respect, the stylised urn-lotus may be significant, as art history recognises a long association of this floral form with the phallus. In other respects the mosaic may be related to the seasons or to military life. If the room was in use for the summer months only, one should recall the frequent association of Medusa with seasonal themes, as at Bignor, Cirencester and York. As the site is so close to York, and to other military centres, it is possible that the martial associations of Medusa are also relevant. Such functional and iconographical allusions will not however, bring us much closer to providing a specific interpretation of the mosaic. What remains to be emphasised is the vivid but unpretentious charm of the Gorgon, as a symbolically restrained embellishment to a developing settlement complex.

18 Painted Plaster

Painted wall and ceiling plaster was recovered from various locations within the villa (see Fig. 100). As would be expected on a heavily ploughed site, the most significant concentrations were found in the hypocaust basements, in the sunken-floored buildings and (on the north side) in the upper filling layers of ditches. The best preserved group of plaster came from Structure B: this is discussed in detail below. The plaster from other contexts was too fragmented to permit meaningful analysis of decorative schemes. A few decorative elements from Ditch 014 are illustrated below; otherwise, quantification of and notes on the remaining plaster appear in the Archive Report.

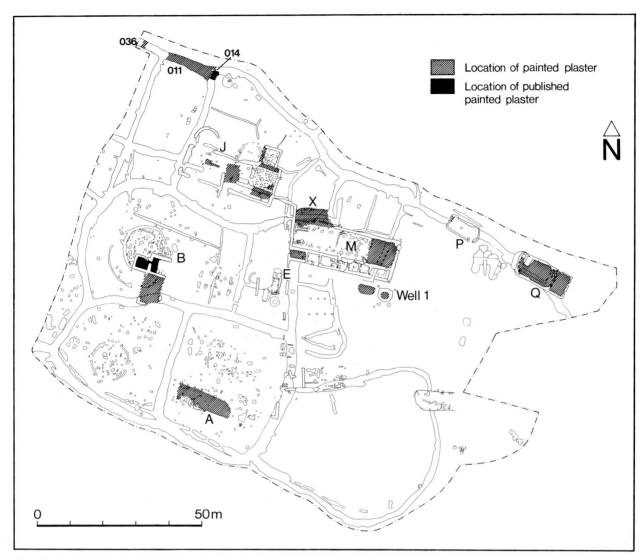

Fig. 100. The site distribution of painted plaster.

Painted Plaster from Structure B (Fig. 101; Pl. XXX) by Roger Ling

Most of the numerous fragments of painted plaster from the basements of Rooms 2 and 3 (layers 204-7 and 210-19) have been incorporated by Dr Norman Davey in three panels showing hypothetical decorative schemes. The panels have been described briefly elsewhere (Davey and Ling 1982, 102-6, no. 12).

Piece 1
The largest piece (Fig. 101, No. 1) carries a pattern of contiguous octagons containing roundels on a white ground. Both octagons and roundels are formed by broad bands of colours graded so as to give the effect of convex mouldings with highlights along the spines and shadows at the edges. Separate painted lines, with spots attached to the angles, accompany these frames, one on either side; stylised rosette and palmette ornaments are set at the centres of each medallion and of each of the square interspaces between the octagons. The main frames (those

forming the octagons) are in three grades of greyish-yellow, and those of the roundels are in grades of green, purple or orange; all have white highlights. The accompanying lines are greyish-yellow for the roundels and for some of the octagons, and purple for the remaining octagons. The rosette and palmette motifs are all red.

There can be little doubt that the reconstruction of the pattern is in all broad essentials correct. Although the fragments incorporated in it are very small, and no extensive joining areas could be found, there are sufficient pieces to indicate the width of the octagon and roundel frames (respectively 40mm and 55mm), the distance between these frames and the accompanying lines (10-14mm), the angles of the octagons and of the interstitial squares (respectively, of course, $45°$ and $90°$), and the curvature and thus the diameter of the roundels (externally about 305mm). That the roundels should fit inside the octagons is a reasonable inference, supported by parallels elsewhere (see below). What remains less certain is the size of the octagons. There seem to be no secure conjunctions of fragments which give the lengths of the sides; the best that can be found is a pair of joining pieces

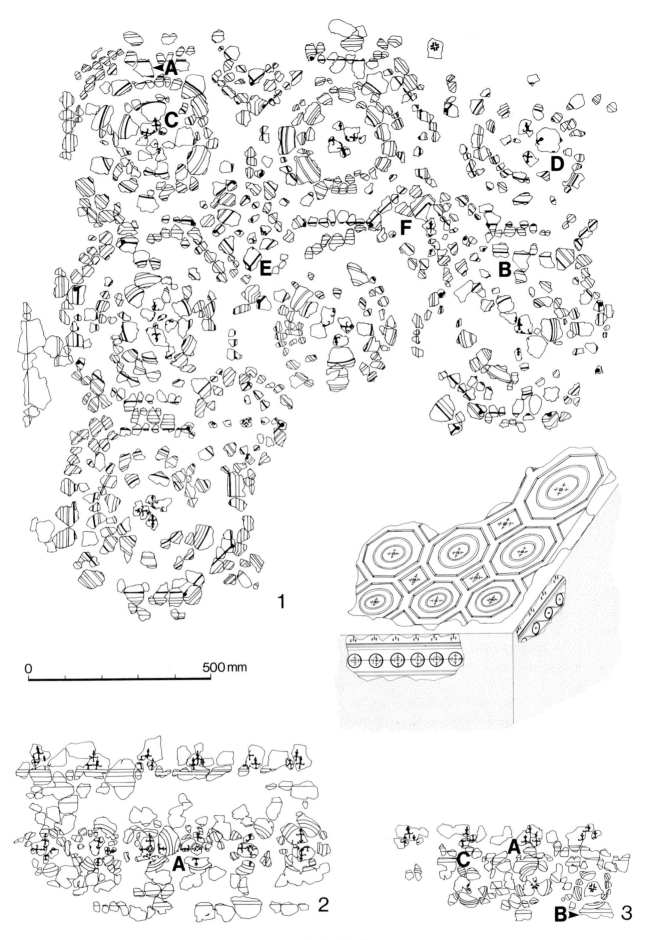

Fig. 101. Reconstructed areas of painted plaster from Structure B. Scale 1:10

0   500 mm

1

2

3

Pl. XXX. Reconstructed areas of painted plaster from Structure B. (Photos: English Heritage)

from a corner of one of the interstitial squares, indicating a minimum length of 100mm (Fig. 101, No. 1, F). Two small fragments, however, seem to bridge the gap between the inner borderline of an octagon and the outer one of a medallion (Fig. 101, No. 1, A and B). From these it is possible to estimate the minimum distance between these elements as about 35mm, which, when added to the known factors (the diameter of the roundel and the distance between the inner borders and the main frames), makes the inner measurement of the octagon approximately 425mm (rather less than in the restoration). This in turn enables us to calculate the length of each side as about 165mm.

If the restoration of the basic pattern is acceptable, the arrangement of the colours remains uncertain. Assuming that the fragments do indeed derive from a single decoration (which is by no means proven), the three different colours of the roundels must have been arranged in some kind of alternation. The writer knows of no repeating pattern with colour alternation of this type in Roman painting; but this may due to the defective nature of our evidence rather than to any real lack of parallels. Alternation of motifs, as opposed to colours, is a regular feature of repeating patterns in interior decoration, whether in painting, in stucco relief, or in mosaic; a favourite arrangement in such cases is in diagonal series (see e.g. *Antike Denkmäler* III, 1912-13, pls 16 and 18; Weege 1913, 181, fig. 26; Becatti 1961, pls LXII-LXIII; Ling 1977, 24-32, 45-7, figs 10-11, pls XV-XVI). A diagonal system may have underlain the colour scheme at Dalton Parlours. How the two different colours of the borderlines within the octagons were arranged in relation to the three different colours of the roundels is an open question. Neither of the two fragments which show the inner borderline of an octagon together with the outer one of a roundel (Fig. 101, No. 1, A and B) reaches far enough to indicate the colour of the roundel frame.

The rosette and palmette ornaments are certainly correctly restored within the roundels, because two fragments show parts of the palmettes combined with curving borderlines (Fig. 101, No. 1, C and D). The evidence for the presence of the same ornaments within the interstitial squares is more exiguous: a single piece with the tip of a palmette inside the corner of a square (Fig. 101, No. 1, E). That a single decorative motif should be repeated in roundels and squares alike seems reasonable enough. The precise form of the motif can be reconstructed without difficulty from numerous fragments, not all of which have been incorporated in Dr Davey's panel. It is a unique type: the rosette consisting of four V-shaped elements set together point inwards, and the palmettes, one of which sprouts from the fork of each 'V', of thin stalks terminating at each end in a knob, with two curling offshoots on either side, the outer pair smaller than the inner. More striking than the form of the motif, however, is the manner of its execution. Each palmette and each 'V' was applied not with a brush but with a stamp, a labour-saving procedure for which the only possible parallel among the surviving examples of Roman

painting known to the writer comes from another Yorkshire site, the fort at Malton (Davey and Ling 1982, 145, no. 28). The same stamped 'V's and palmettes were put together in different ways and with different colours on other fragments from the same deposit (see below).

The reconstructed scheme unquestionably belongs to a ceiling rather than a wall decoration. The reverse faces of the plaster fragments carry imprints of the reeds commonly used as a form of keying for plasterwork on wooden vaults and ceilings (Vitruvius, *The Ten Books of Architecture* VII, 3.2; Barbet and Allag 1972, 939-46). The pattern, too, points to derivation from a ceiling: schemes of contiguous octagons are at present, with one possible exception, never attested on Roman walls.

The earliest known examples of the pattern in the Roman world are two vaults in Italy, datable to the third quarter of the 1st century AD; both are executed in stucco relief. At Pompeii a vault in the Stabian Baths, decorated shortly before AD 79 (Mielsch 1975, 68, 144, K54 c1, pl. 53, 2), carries rows of octagons containing reliefs of Bacchic figures and armour, while the square interspaces are occupied by swastikas (a device repeated a few decades later in a vault from the headquarters building at Aquincum in Budapest (Kaba 1955, 255-72, figs 3, 4, 6 and 8, cf. 289-92)). At Rome there is an example above a stairway in the *nymphaeum* complex of Nero's *Domus Transitoria* in Rome (shortly before AD 64: Carettoni 1949, 54, fig. 5; Bastet 1971, 157-60, figs 7-9). Here the pattern is aligned differently from that of the Dalton Parlours ceiling, the interstitial squares being set parallel with, rather than diagonal to, the axes of the surface; but an important precedent for later decorations is provided by the insertion of roundels within some of the octagons. These roundels and the remaining octagons contained figure-reliefs, now broken away, while the squares were decorated with rosettes.

The painted versions of the pattern are all from the provinces and all probably later than the stuccoes in Rome and Pompeii. In every case the octagons contained roundels, and in almost every case both the roundels and the interstitial squares were decorated with rosettes. At Sabratha in Libya the octagonal framework was carried out in broad brownish-red bands on a white ground, while the roundels and the squares had coloured backgrounds, respectively pale ?blue and black; the petals of the rosettes alternated between purple and yellow (the roundels) and purple and blue (the squares) (Aurigemma 1962, 113, pl. 124, 3). At Marzoll, near Bad Reichenhall in Bavaria, all the fields were outlined with red lines and the rosettes had alternate green and red petals; Christlein (1963, 43-4, pl. I, 2) assigns them to both ceiling and walls. At Pierre-Buffière, near Limoges in France, the pattern was executed in white on a red ground (Delage 1953, 16, no. 23, fig. 14). Of two examples in Alsace-Lorraine, one from Strasbourg (Petry and Kern 1974, 70-72, fig. 7) was slightly anomalous in that the octagons (if correctly restored) had sides of irregular length and could perhaps be better described as squares with bevelled corners; moreover not only these pseudo-octagons but also the squares in the interspaces contained roundels. The Strasbourg frames were painted in brown, green and black on a white ground, but the interiors of the roundels were coloured, those within the octagons being divided into alternate purple and yellow quadrants, and those inside the squares being blue. For the octagonal pattern from Metz (mentioned by Eristov 1979, 20) no detailed information is available. Also in France, a recently reconstructed ceiling decoration from Rue de l'Abbé d'Épée in Paris (Eristov 1979, 15-21 and 29, figs 1-6 and 13) had octagons framed by green lines and roundels by red, all on a white ground; the rosettes in the roundels were green and yellow, and those in the squares red. Finally the palace at Aquincum, Budapest, has yielded at least two octagonal coffer-schemes from the 3rd century AD (Póczy 1958, 121-5, figs 29-31, 33, 35 and 37).

Apart from this last example, which includes imitation ovolo and astragal mouldings in the coffer-frames, all these painted decorations rely upon two-dimensional effects: they were predominantly linear in style and exploited contrasts between bright colours, chiefly against a white background. The Dalton Parlours ceiling, however, introduces an element of illusionism by the use of diluted colours with shading and highlights to suggest that the frames are in relief. A similar device is found in another British ceiling painting, that from the villa at Gadebridge, Hertfordshire (Davey and Ling 1982, 117-19, no. 19, fig. 24, pl. XLVI). In both cases it is clear that the painter was trying to convey the impression of a decoration in stone or stucco relief. The rhythmic, coffer-style pattern is in itself more appropriate to these media than to the freer, coloristic medium of painting; and it is possible that octagonal systems were first evolved on stone and stucco ceilings, and only subsequently borrowed by painters. There is no direct evidence to support this theory, but hexagonal if not octagonal coffering is found in stuccowork in Roman Italy, as well as in the stone arch at Glanum (Saint-Rémy-de-Provence, France), as early as the 1st century BC; it may perhaps be traced back to wooden or stone prototypes in Hellenistic times (Ling 1972, 31-3, 39 and 51-2, figs 3-4, pls XIIb and XIII; Barbet 1985a, 51, 77 and 81; cf. Rolland 1977, 31-2, pls 13, 63, 65-70 and 72-6; Delbrück 1912, 142, fig. 73; Lauter 1972, 157-8, fig. 10). The only known octagonal decorations earlier than those already cited are those of the painted vaults in a Late Hellenistic necropolis at Alexandria (Adriani 1952, 58, 61, 68, 82-4 and 111, figs 39 and 46; Adriani 1966, 191-4 and 196, figs 375-6 and 385-6). As this is at least a century, if not two, earlier than the first known examples in Roman Italy, it is best not to invoke it in the discussion; but, since it belongs to a decorative context in which painters clearly display their indebtedness to structural materials and forms (Barbet 1985a, 20-23), it suggests that there may already have been an interplay of ideas between relief and painting in the ceiling decorations of Hellenistic Egypt.

One other Romano-British ceiling painting employs the Dalton Parlours pattern of octagons containing roundels: that of the *caldarium* in the baths at Wroxeter,

Shropshire (Davey and Ling 1982, 200-201, fig. 55, pl. C). This decoration, which dates to the second half of the 2nd century or to the 3rd century, lacks an illusion of depth but is rendered in a monochrome technique which once again suggests a debt to stone or stucco relief.

Piece 2

The second piece restored by Dr Davey (Fig. 101, No. 2; Pl. XXX) shows a frieze of roundels on a ground half red and half green; the frieze is framed by bands of various colours, and along one side, on a white ground, are sets of grey-yellow palmettes arranged in threes, pyramid-style, above a purple stripe. The overall scheme is conjectural, for there appear to be no secure joins across the various elements; so we must look at the motifs individually.

The pyramidal groups of palmettes, which are produced with the stamps already described, could well belong to the ceiling; their grey-yellow colour, though setting them apart from the red of the ornaments in the ceiling roundels, matches the predominant colour of the frames in the ceiling, and the white ground is also, of course, consonant with derivation from the same source. Given the pyramidal structure of the groups, it is attractive to place them in the triangular fields which would result from a row of octagons at the edge of the ceiling. The purple stripe would form the hypotenuse of the triangle. In Davey's reconstruction of the ceiling, two of these triangular fields are given an isolated rosette of four 'V's; but there seems to be no overriding reason for placing such a motif in this position, and the inappropriateness of its shape is an argument against it: a more plausible position would be the much smaller triangle at the corner of the ceiling. Some of the fragments with three-palmette groups, on the other hand, show a yellow band beyond the purple stripe, and a similar yellow band appears adjacent to the frame of an octagon on fragments which Davey has placed at one edge of his reconstruction; so it is possible that a yellow band ran continuously along the edge of the ceiling, at least on one side.

The roundels are safely reconstructed from the evidence of several fragments. They have an external diameter of 130mm and are framed by contiguous bands of yellow (outside) and purple (inside), each about 10mm wide; within them we find replicas of the rosette and palmette ornaments already observed in the ceiling roundels. Here, however, the ornaments fit tightly within the smaller radius of the framing circles, and they are executed in white against a two-coloured background: a pair of palmettes masks the division of the field into two halves, one of which is red and the other green. The dichotomy of red and green continues outside the roundels. One crucial fragment (Fig. 101, No.2, A) shows the colour division, laid out with the aid of an impressed guide-line, running across the gap (about 4mm) between two roundels. Other fragments reveal that the roundels were not juxtaposed in the perpendicular direction (i.e. on the one-colour side). It is a possible inference from this evidence that there was, as suggested by Davey, a single row of roundels sitting astride the centre line of a two-colour horizontal frieze. But the joins with the white, yellow and purple stripes restored along the edges of this frieze look far from convincing; we can therefore countenance other schemes, such as a repeating series of red and green bands with roundels at every second or third colour division. More important, if Davey is right in attributing the roundels to a wall decoration, the brush marks on the background militate against derivation from a frieze. Assuming that they obey the normal rule of verticality on wall surfaces, the colour divisions must have been vertical rather than horizontal; in other words, the roundels came not side by side, as in a frieze, but one above the other. They may therefore, to cite just one possibility, have decorated the frames of, or the intervals between, large coloured fields of the type which usually form the dominant element in Roman wall decorations. A parallel for chains of roundels of roughly this size used as borders can be cited at Bordeaux, admittedly from a ceiling rather than a wall, and with a white rather than a coloured background (Barbet 1985b, 97, fig. 10.9 and 10.10).

Piece 3

The third restored piece (Fig. 101, No. 3; Pl. XXX) shows a frieze with a kind of cable or 'running dog' pattern. A series of small roundels framed by contiguous rings of lime green (outside) and black (inside) is set against a green background and linked by S-shaped ribbons of red running from the top of one roundel to the bottom of the next. Within each roundel is a white rosette formed by four 'V' stamps.

As restored, the frieze is flanked by a series of pyramidal triple-palmette motifs of the type and colouring described above, but once again there are no secure conjunctions between the fragments used to reconstruct the roundels and the fragments with palmettes. It is possible, therefore, to assign the palmette motifs, like those of Piece 2, to the ceiling. Here the coloured band beyond the purple stripe is red and not yellow, but this may be because the fragments involved come from a different part of the ceiling (compare the purple band along one edge of Davey's restoration) or even from a different ceiling altogether, perhaps that of a neighbouring room.

For the roundels a wall-top frieze is a possible position (Davey and Ling 1982, 106, fig. 17), but the 'grain' of the surface on two crucial fragments which show the beginning of S-ribbons (Fig. 101, No. 3, A and B) suggests that these ran vertically. The role of the roundels may thus have been similar to that postulated for those of Piece 2: the ornamentation of a vertical fascia in the main zone of the wall. Moreover, rather than a 'running dog', we could

postulate other possible restorations, such as the familiar type of continuous scroll in which circles or spirals spring alternately from one side and the other of an undulating stem. A couple of fragments suggest possible fluctuations in the width of the roundel frames, and one may even indicate a leaf-shoot on the black ring (Fig. 101, No. 3, C); both features would accord with the normal form of a stylised vegetal scroll (e.g. Barbet et al. 1977, 175-84 and 191-6, figs 2-10 and 16-18). Such scrolls are normally horizontal, but vertical instances occasionally occur (Barbet et al. 1977, 193, fig. 16C; for parallels in stone, see Toynbee and Ward-Perkins 1950, 20-21, 34-5 and 39-40, pls XVII-XVIII, XXIV, 2 and XXV, 1). Another possibility is a double scroll with stems interweaving in such a way as to create medallions, like the famous peopled scrolls on the pilasters in the Severan basilica at Lepcis Magna in Libya (Toynbee and Ward-Perkins 1950, 38, pls XXIV, 2 and XXV, 2). Though most examples of this interweaving type are in stone or stucco (Toynbee and Ward-Perkins 1950), it is possible to find analogous motifs in painting, for example among the elements from the site at Bordeaux already mentioned (Barbet 1985b, 97, fig. 10.11).

The evidence is insufficient to allow a final judgement on these different possibilities, and it is safest to leave the precise nature of the motif in doubt. On either side the frieze seems to have been bounded by a 10mm wide white stripe. Different fragments show different colours – red and purple – for the band or field beyond this, so we must conclude either that the scroll or cable had red on one side and purple on the other, or that different stretches of scroll were flanked by different colours.

Some of the other fragments of plaster from Structure B have been incorporated by Dr Davey in a restoration of framing elements from a wall decoration (Davey and Ling 1982, 106); they show the same bright colouring of red, green, purple and white found in the two frieze restorations (Pieces 2 and 3). More interesting are pieces with stamped ornaments in colours and combinations different from those already mentioned: they include pale green palmettes on a black ground and a reticulate pattern formed by yellow 'V's set back-to-back, again on a black ground, with a red band or field adjacent. None of these offers sufficient clues to determine its role in the decoration or decorations.

The material discussed seems to belong to the last structural phase of the building, when Room 3 was added to the pre-existing Rooms 1 and 2. The plaster fragments from Room 2 reveal evidence of an earlier decoration underlying the final one: its well-burnished surface and predominant use of yellow would seem to suggest a date no later than the early 3rd century.

Pl. XXXI. Wallplaster filling ditch intersection (Ditches 012 and 014) north of Structure J, facing east. (Photo: S. Wager)

Some Painted Plaster from Ditch 014 (Figs 102-104) by Stuart Wrathmell

Many plaster fragments were recovered from the partially excavated intersection of Ditches 014 and 012 (Pl. XXXI). They may have been derived from the nearest known Roman building, Structure J, but even so must have been transported a distance of more than 15m to reach their final positions. The deposit was only partially excavated, and it has proved impossible to reconstruct the overall scheme of decoration; but the fragments illustrated here (Figs 102-104) indicate elements of two designs. The fragments (or groups of joining fragments) Nos 1-5 (Figs 102-103) are all derived from a white-ground design featuring curving fronds and cornucopiae. The fronds, best seen in No. 1, are painted half green, half pale blue, and often follow compass-drawn guide grooves. They can be seen in Nos 2 and 5 to issue from cornucopiae, which are outlined in purple; in some instances the purple has been painted over yellow. On the evidence of Nos 3 and 4, some of the cornucopiae issue from the mouths of others, and No. 5 displays more intricate vegetal details, including a yellow ?stamen. All these fragments are oriented in the drawings to allow the ground painting to run vertically.

The other published fragments (Fig. 104, No. 6) are derived from an architectural scheme. They represent a column capital, with white volutes on a purple background, and part of an associated ?pediment.

Identification of the Painted Plaster Pigments
by G.C. McKenna (Report first submitted in 1981)

Two methods were used to identify the pigments used for the paintings at Dalton Parlours. First, energy dispersive X-ray fluorescence analysis was employed as a preliminary method to identify the major elemental constituents (with the exception of low atomic number elements). Secondly, X-ray diffraction was used to discover the crystalline structures of samples of the pigment. With these it was possible to identify the compounds present in the pigments. The results of this study, which was carried out as part of an archaeological sciences course at the University of Bradford, are given below:

Colour	Pigment
Dark red:	Almost pure haematite (Fe_2O_3), with small amounts of quartz and possibly goethite ($Fe_2O_3.H_2O$)
Orange-red:	A very impure form of haematite (containing large amounts of quartz), possibly the type known as 'reddle'
Yellow:	Mainly quartz coloured by goethite

157

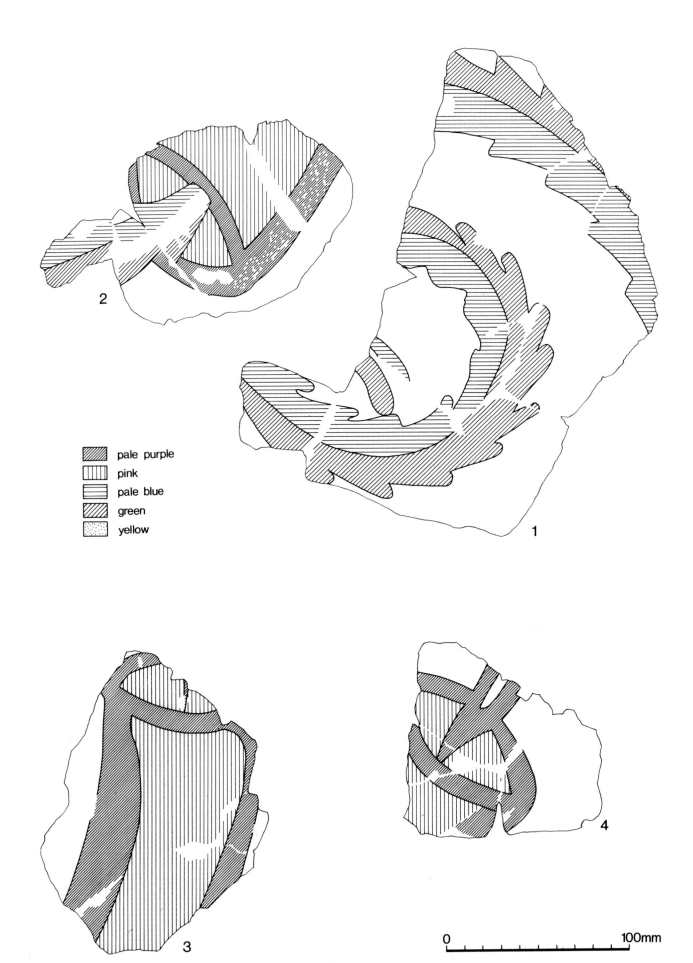

pale purple
pink
pale blue
green
yellow

Fig. 102. Plaster fragments from Ditch 014 (Nos 1-4). Scale 1:2

158

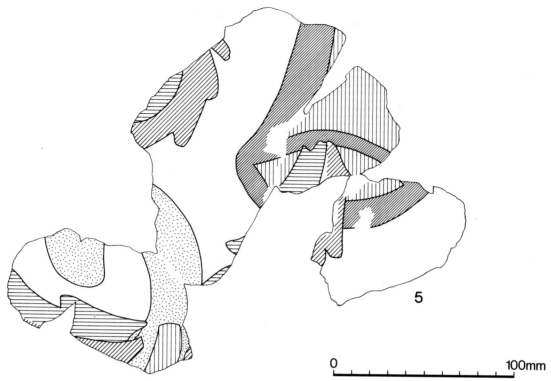

Fig. 103. Plaster fragments from Ditch 014 (No. 5). For key see Fig. 102. Scale 1:2

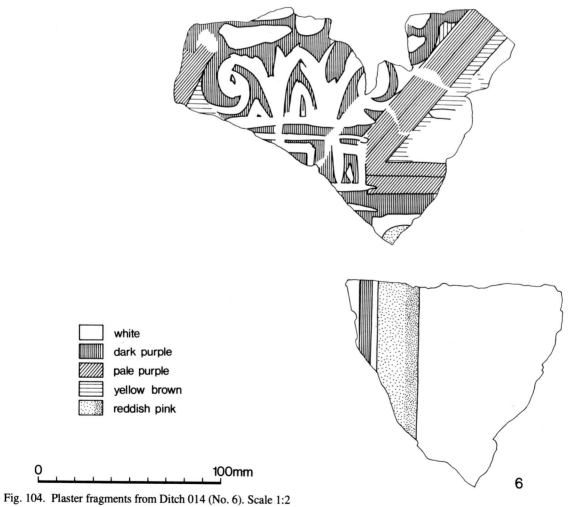

	white
	dark purple
	pale purple
	yellow brown
	reddish pink

Fig. 104. Plaster fragments from Ditch 014 (No. 6). Scale 1:2

Green: (from ditch) A mixture of the minerals celadonite and glauconite known as 'terre verte' (iron, magnesium, potassium and aluminium hydrosilicates)

Blue: A man-made pigment 'Egyptian Blue' (calcium copper silicate)

Green: (from Structure B) A man-made glass coloured with haematite

Purple: Unidentified but did contain iron

Brown: A brown ochre (quartz and clays coloured by iron)

Black: Carbon-based 'lamp black' (man-made)

White: 'Lime white' (made by calcining marble or shells)

Most of the pigments identified were of the common, easily obtained type. The more expensive ones (as indicated by the ancient authors) such as cinnabar, malachite, azurite and orpiment were not present. The major surprise of the study was the discovery of two previously unmentioned pigments. The unidentified purple, which appeared in a number of shades, the darkest being lightened by the addition of white in varying amounts, seems to be iron-based. The green from the friezes in Structure B seems to have been a man-made glass crushed into fairly large fragments, so as to preserve the colour, in a method similar to that commonly observed for Egyptian Blue.

19 Architectural Stonework (Figs 105-106) by T.F.C. Blagg

Catalogue

1* Column shaft with moulding; gritstone. Ht 330mm, the top and bottom are uneven, probably broken. Mouldings: a fillet and a torus (total ht 116mm). The shaft is oval in section, max. diam. 170mm

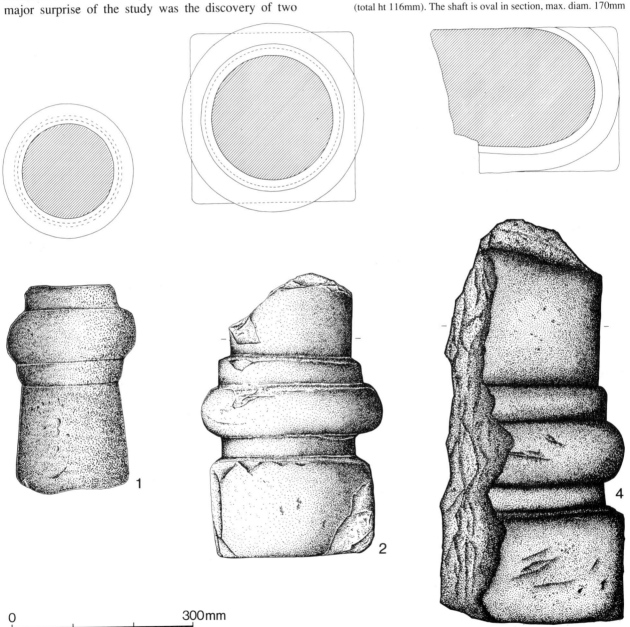

0   300mm

Fig. 105. Architectural stonework (Nos 1, 2 and 4). Scale 1:6

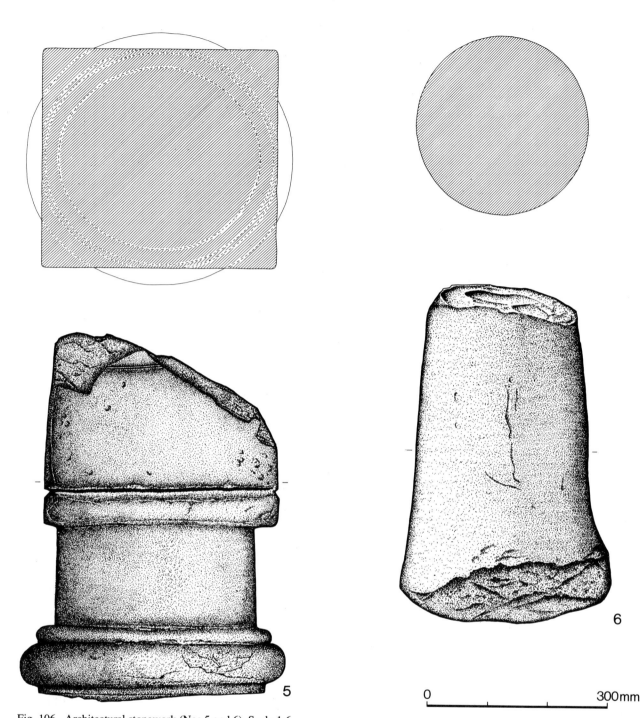

Fig. 106. Architectural stonework (Nos 5 and 6). Scale 1:6

by the mouldings, tapering to 198mm at the end. *5500M (Well 1); SF 1796*

2* Column shaft with moulding and plinth; gritstone. Ht 460mm, the shaft broken. Plinth 260 x 280 x 160mm high. Mouldings: a fillet and a torus (total ht 133mm), separated from the plinth by a square-cut scotia. The shaft is slightly oval in section, diam. 200-208mm. *5500J (Well 1); SF 1332*

3 Engaged column shaft with moulding; gritstone. Ht 610mm, in two joining pieces, the shaft broken. The mouldings are similar to No. 2, but very abraded (total ht 135mm), and are carved round half the circumference of the shaft, as is the block of the plinth. The shaft is 200mm diam., the rear part is very roughly dressed, and is likely to have been built into a wall. Reused as hypocaust *pila. 214 (Structure B); SF 656*

4* Engaged column shaft with moulding; gritstone. Ht 670mm, shaft broken. Similar to No. 3, except that the mouldings are taller (159mm), and the shaft tapers from diam. of 175mm above the mouldings to 192mm at the break. Reused as hypocaust *pila. 214 (Structure B); SF 655*

5* Pedestal; gritstone. Ht 600mm, broken at the top. The upper part is rectangular in section, with a slightly undercut bead moulding round the lower edge. Most of the upper part has been broken away, leaving only one side preserved for its full length (380mm) and short lengths of the two adjacent sides. The lower part is oval in section, with a shaft 165mm high and 289-326mm across the shortest and longest diams, and it has a fillet and torus mouldings at the bottom. The faces of the rectangular part are cut smooth, the mouldings dressed more roughly. *5500J (Well 1); SF 1333*

6* Column ?shaft; gritstone. Ht 550mm. It is tapered to an elongated bell-shaped profile, 248mm diam. at the top, 360mm at the bottom. A shallow recess 140mm square has been cut in the top. The dressed surface has the pitting characteristic of tooling with a punch. *1815 (Structure R); SF 1218*

7 Column shaft; gritstone. Ht 340mm, broken at one end, possibly both. Oval section, 201-209mm one end, 212-230mm the other. Reused in oven flue. *1606 (Structure P); SF 1795*

8 Column shaft; gritstone. Ht 295mm, broken one end, and in two joining pieces. Diam. 194-203mm. *5500K (Well 1); SF 1356*

9 Column shaft fragment; gritstone. Ht 160mm, broken both ends. Diam. 198-210mm. *5500K (Well 1); SF 1355*

Discussion

The pieces are all quite roughly executed. Except for the rectangular sides of the upper part of No. 5, which were dressed smooth, the carving was all done with a punch, leaving slightly pitted surfaces and ill-defined junctions between the mouldings. None of the columns is truly circular in section. The fillet and torus mouldings are very simple. It is quite possible that the same mouldings were used on both capitals and bases. The tapering shaft and smaller diameter of No. 1 indicate that it was more probably a capital, and the plinths on Nos 2, 3 and 4 suggest that they were bases. Numbers 3 and 4 are from engaged half-columns projecting from a wall, either at the ends of a colonnade running between two walls, or framing an entrance. They are not a pair, however, since the mouldings of No. 4 are appreciably taller. The diameters of the column shafts, about 200mm, indicate that the columns are not likely to have been much taller

Pl. XXXII. Structure B: column fragment reused as hypocaust *pila* in Room 2. (Photo: S. Wager)

than 1.75m when complete, more probably shorter, and standing on a low wall. The tapering shaft of No. 6 is of greater diameter, and the degree of taper is stronger than is usual; there is no indication that it was intended to have mouldings (never cut), but it may have served as the base of a crude column.

Number 5, described above as a pedestal, is very unusual in form, and its function may not have been simply architectural. The remainder, though poorly executed, suggest nevertheless that the building from which they came was intended to be impressive, in having a facade or features of classical appearance which are relatively uncommon in the Roman architecture of the area. There is no indication, however, that this primary use was in one of the structures excavated at Dalton Parlours. It is possible that they had been salvaged from an as yet undiscovered structure, or from another site for reuse as *pilae* (Pl. XXXII).

20 Other Structural Stonework (Fig. 107) by Stuart Wrathmell

A full list of the other architectural and structural stonework from the site appears in the Archive Report. Only one of these pieces merits illustration and discussion here.

27* ?Threshold stone; gritstone. A slab now broken into three pieces. At one corner is part of a rectangular socket with worn sides, originally at least 40mm deep; elsewhere, several grooves have been worn into the surface. The grooves all run in approximately the same direction, though some are on slightly divergent alignments, and some overlie or impinge upon each other. Laterally they are flattish-based, and are between 30-40mm wide. Longitudinally the depth of wear decreases gradually towards the ends of the grooves. Max. l. of stone *c.* 880mm; max. w. *c.* 530mm; th. *c.* 210mm. *1814 (Structure R); SF 1341-2*

The longitudinal profiles of the grooves suggest they resulted from wear caused by the iron tyres of cartwheels. The curvature suggests wheels of perhaps 1.2m in diameter or more. Some grooves terminate a short distance from the socket; this suggests that the latter held a block which acted to stop the wheels. The number, proximity and alignments of the grooves, and the evidence of the socket would be consistent with the threshold of a doorway where carts were unloaded. The stone was recovered from the fill of a sunken-floored building identified as a crop-processing facility (see Chapter 3).

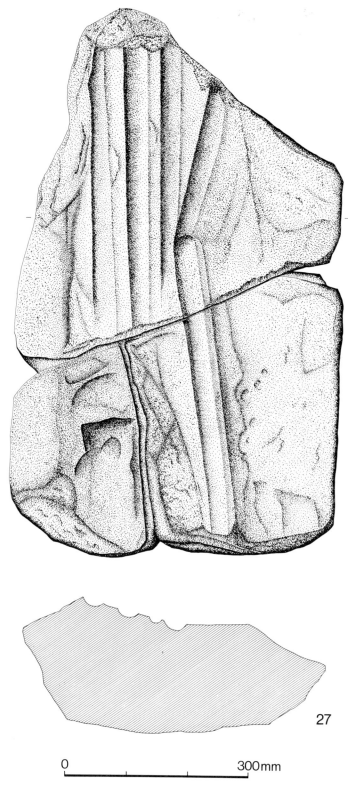

Fig. 107. ?Threshold stone (No. 27). Scale 1:6

0   300mm

27

21 Stone Roofing Slabs (Fig. 108)

by J.C. Clarke

The Archive Report describes pieces of at least 23 roofing slabs, of which four are illustrated here:

1* Micaceous siltstone; diamond-shaped slab with one peg hole. L. 400mm; w. 310mm; th. 20mm. *5500K (Well 1); SF 1944*

2* Micaceous siltstone; diamond-shaped slab with a peg hole off-set from the apex. L. 435mm; w. 320mm; th. 25mm. *5500K (Well 1); SF 2001*

3* Micaceous siltstone; fragment of slab broken through the peg hole. L. 426mm; w. 310mm; th. 24mm. *5500J (Well 1); SF 1994*

4* Micaceous siltstone; fragment of ?diamond-shaped slab with iron nail *in situ*. L. 310mm; w. 180mm; th. 25mm. *1213/1 (Structure M); SF 1997*

Discussion

The fragmentary nature of the 23 roof slabs makes it difficult to assess their shape, but it is likely that most were diamond shaped (Pl. XXV), like the example recovered from Brough-on-Humber (Wacher 1969, fig. 45, no. 11). Of particular interest is the one with its iron nail still *in situ* (No. 4), and those with iron staining (Nos 9 and 10; see Archive Report). The large proportion (70%) recovered from Structure M, Well 1 and adjacent areas suggests that

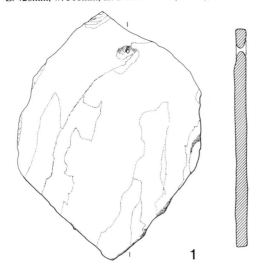

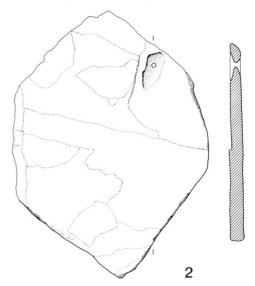

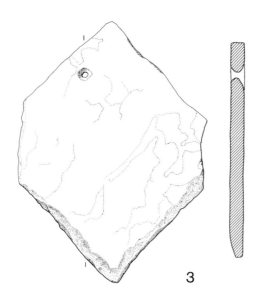

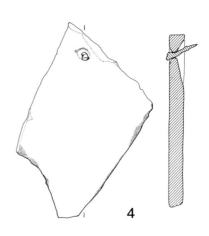

0   300mm

Fig. 108. Stone roofing slabs (Nos 1-4). Scale 1:6

they were used to roof Structure M and possibly also the well-head building.

Acknowledgements
The help of Dr G. Hornung of the Department of Earth Sciences, Leeds University in identifying the stone types is gratefully acknowledged.

22 Roman Brick and Tile (Figs 109-12)
by Ian M. Betts

The amount of tile recovered is only a small fraction of the total quantity of ceramic building material which must have originally been present. The surviving tile, which weighs over 250kg, includes *tegulae* and *imbrices*, box-flue tile and various sizes of brick. The majority is highly fragmentary, but several more or less complete tiles were recovered.

Fabric type

Using a low powered binocular microscope (x20) three fabric types were recognised:

> Fabric 1: Fine fabric
> Fabric 2: Sandy fabric
> Fabric 3: Red clay pellet fabric

By far the majority of tiles lay in the first two fabric groups. These were distinguished by differences in the amount and size of quartz grains present. The red clay pellet fabric is represented by only three fragments of roofing tile.

In order to test the validity of the groupings 38 bricks and tiles were analysed in greater detail: twenty by thin section analysis; fifteen by neutron activation analysis and a further three by both techniques. The results largely confirmed the initial fabric groupings, although the grain size of the red clay pellet tiles proved to be similar to certain tiles in Fabric 1.

The only change occurred in the fine fabric group where two separate sources of supply were recognised: one from York, the other from an as yet unknown kiln site. The only visual difference between the two is that the tiles from York tend to be slightly harder and deeper red, although this is not true in every case.

Because of the difficulty of distinguishing, without scientific analysis, tiles from York from fine fabric tiles originating elsewhere, the term 'Fabric 1' has been retained to cover tiles from both sources. Where analysis has been carried out the origin of the tile has been specified; the results are summarised below (see Table 7). Relatively few bricks were analysed as the majority of tile found is either box-flue and voussoir or roof tile.

Table 7. Fabric of tiles analysed.

Fabric	*Tegula*	*Imbrex*	Brick	Flue	?Form	Total
Fabric 1 (York)	4	1	2	2	–	9
Fabric 1 (Unknown)	1	2	–	7	–	10
Fabric 2	4	3	1	3	1	12
Fabric 3	1	2	–	–	–	3
(Uncertain)	1	2	–	1	–	4

Fabric 1: Fine fabric tiles
Source: York

Quartz grain size: predominantly <0.015 to 0.09mm, with occasional larger grains up to 0.45mm.

Thin section petrology: frequent quartz with common quartzite, muscovite mica and rounded clay inclusions; occasional chert, plagioclase feldspar, iron oxide, limestone, sandstone and small unidentified heavy minerals. Clino-pyroxene and mica-schist was found in one tile.

Fabric 1: Fine fabric tiles
Source: unknown

Quartz grain size: predominantly <0.015 to 0.09mm, with occasional grains up to 0.52mm.

Thin section petrology: frequent quartz and muscovite mica with common clay inclusions, quartzite and iron oxide; occasional chert, heavy minerals, limestone, sandstone and vein quartz. Siltstone and a small metamorphic rock fragment were noted in one tile.

Fabric 2: Sandy fabric tiles
Source: unknown

Quartz grain size: predominantly <0.015 to 0.12mm, with occasional grains up to 0.72mm.

Thin section petrology: frequent quartz, muscovite and clay inclusions; moderate amounts of iron oxide, plagioclase feldspar, quartzite and sandstone in most tiles; occasional chert, heavy minerals, limestone and vein quartz. Biotite and clino-amphibole and siltstone inclusions are present but are very rare.

Fabric 3: Red clay inclusion fabric
Source: unknown

Quartz grain size: predominantly <0.015 to 0.09mm, with occasional larger grains (rarer than in Fabrics 1 and 2) up to 1.14mm.

Thin section petrology: frequent rounded red clay inclusions mainly up to 3mm with frequent quartz and muscovite mica; occasional iron oxide, quartzite and sandstone. Certain tiles also contain small amounts of biotite, chert, plagioclase feldspar, vein quartz, siltstone and heavy minerals.

Forms of tile

Tegulae

Tegulae and *imbrices* are primarily used for roofing. At Dalton Parlours three main sizes of *tegulae* are represented:

Group	Context	Length	Breadth	Thickness	Comments
A	2007	430	326	21-31	–
B	1304 (Str. M)	380	303-23	20-23	Tapered
B	001	394	310	24-26	–
C	1304 (Str. M)	358	–	18-20	–
C	1213/3 (Str. M)	*c.* 350	–	20-21	Two tiles

All measurements are in mm

The only complete *tegula* in size group A is in Fabric 1 and has a sandal imprint in the middle of the top surface. This contrasts with the *tegulae* in the other two groups which are all in Fabric 2, and are thus presumably from the same source. Size group B comprises two complete *tegulae*. One tile is slightly tapered, whilst the other must have been made in a separate mould as it has parallel sides. The other *tegulae* in Fabric 2 are significantly shorter in length and form size group C. Unfortunately, none has surviving breadth measurements.

Only two areas of Roman tile production are known in Yorkshire: Grimescar, near Huddersfield, and York. The *tegulae* in size groups A and C differ from the examples manufactured at Grimescar and York (Betts 1985, 169). However, some unstamped *tegulae* from York are of the same size as the *tegulae* in size group B, and may be of similar date.

Nail holes are present in a number of *tegulae*: one is in a *tegula* in Fabric 1 (of York origin), and one in Fabric 3; the remainder are all in Fabric 2. Most nail holes are circular, 9-10mm in diameter, and are situated 21-8mm from the top edge. One tile has a square nail hole (Structure M, context 8104) which measures 10 by 10mm. Nail holes normally seem to have been positioned near the centre of the tile, roughly mid-way between the flanges, and were cut prior to the tile being fired. The only exception is a *tegula* with a 10mm diameter hole bored into the tile after firing (Structure M, context 1213/3). This nail hole is unusual in being situated in the top right-hand side of the *tegula*, 63mm from the top edge and only 85mm from the right-hand edge.

Not every *tegula* was attached to the roof by nails. The complete *tegulae* from Dalton Parlours have no nail holes whatsoever. In Britain as a whole only about one in five *tegulae* have nail holes (Brodribb 1987, 11). It seems possible that only the lowest few tile courses above the eaves were secured by means of nails.

The shape of the flanges on the *tegulae* varies widely, but two main types are apparent: flanges with square-shaped profiles (mainly in Fabric 1) and those with more rounded profiles (predominantly in Fabric 2). A shallow groove is often present along the bottom inside edge of the flange. Two *tegulae* are more unusual in having twin grooves (Structure M, context 1213 and Structure P, context 1603).

The lower cutaway occurs in three varieties (Fig. 109). Type A occurs predominantly on tiles in Fabric 1, whilst types B and C are mainly restricted to *tegulae* in Fabric 2.

A distinctive feature of certain *tegulae* is the curved shape of a number of examples. One *tegula* (Well 1, context 5500E) is so bent that it could not possibly have been used on a roof. This may be a waster brought in for use as rubble hardcore. Another possibility is that the curved tiles once formed part of a tile tomb. Similar, equally curved *tegulae* were used to form tile tombs at Roman cemeteries in the York area (Brodribb 1987, 22).

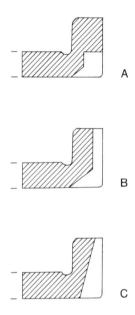

Fig. 109. Varieties of *tegula* cutaway.

Imbrices

The majority of *imbrices* are highly fragmentary and give little indication of their original size. One fragment has an incomplete length measurement of 305mm, but no indication of breadth (Structure M, context 4900A).

A unique feature is the presence of small, curved *imbrex*-shaped tiles all of which were found associated with Structure M (Fig. 110, Nos 1-3). They range in length from 150-55mm and are 16-21mm thick. One tile (Structure M, context 4900A) has a complete breadth of 138-45mm. The length of these small curved tiles is less than half that of all the surviving complete tegulae. They are also much smaller than any other *imbrex* tile found in Britain, the smallest of which is from Icklingham in Suffolk, and measures 360mm (Brodribb 1987, 26). This suggests that these small curved tiles may not be *imbrices* but served some other function. One possibility is that they may be ridge tiles although they would still be significantly smaller than similar tiles elsewhere.

Brick

Roman bricks were generally produced in more or less standard sizes corresponding to a whole or part of the Roman foot (1 Roman foot = 295.7mm). The complete bricks with surviving size measurements are listed below:

Fabric	Context	Length	Breadth	Thickness	Comments
?2	1300 (Str. M)	186	184	30-33	–
2	8004 (Str. M)	192-3	190-91	34	–
2	8104 (Str. M)	214-17	215	33-44	?Voussoir
2	5500 (Well 1)	215	–	36-39	–
2	511 (Str. E)	302	140	34-40	–

All measurements are in mm

The square-shaped bricks are all *bessalis* tiles. These are bricks approximately eight Roman inches square (198mm). In Britain as a whole they vary in size from 170-235mm (Brodribb 1987, 34). At Dalton Parlours the *bessales* seem to have been made in moulds of two sizes, one of which produced bricks 186-93mm square, the other bricks 214-17mm square. One *bessalis* has a slight taper as it ranges in thickness from 33-44mm. It is possible that this may be a *cuneatus* (solid voussoir). These are wedge-shaped bricks which were normally used to form arches.

The other complete brick is over one Roman foot long by almost half a Roman foot wide (Fig. 111, No. 8). Only one other brick near this size has been found in Roman Britain. This is a solitary brick from Slack in West Yorkshire which measures 290 by 150 by 65mm (Brodribb 1987, 57).

Box-flue tile

Box-flue tiles are keyed on two faces whilst the other two faces are left plain. At Dalton Parlours keying was normally carried out by means of a comb. A variety of different combs were used with between four and eight teeth. One flue tile, however, is unusual in having keying

Fabric	Context	Length	Breadth	Thickness	Comments
2	8104 (Str. M)	–	124	19-21	Plain side
1	8104 (Str. M)	317	–	20-21	Combed side
1	001	–	229	21-22	Combed side
1	5500 (Well 1)	–	c. 230	23	Plain side
1	5500 (Well 1)	–	122	20-24	Plain side

All measurements are in mm

applied by either the tip of a finger or the end of a blunt stick (Structure V, context 8201/3B, Fabric 2).

Vent holes were cut into the plain sides prior to firing. These are normally square or rectangular, but one tile has the remains of an irregularly cut circular vent hole 20-24mm in diameter (Well 1, context 5500, Fabric 1).

Very few box-flue tiles have surviving size measurements. The more complete tiles are listed above.

'Springer' and Voussoir tiles

From Structure Q came a complete example of a rare form of voussoir called by Brodribb a 'springer' (Context 1703, Fig. 110, No. 4). Only eight other sites in Roman Britain have so far produced such tiles (Brodribb 1987, 82-3). They seem to have been placed at the base of an arch linking voussoir tiles above with box-flue tile below (see reconstruction on Fig. 110). The Dalton Parlours example is in a slightly sandy fabric which could be a variant of either Fabrics 1 or 2.

The 'springer' is keyed by a four-tooth comb on its smallest face, whilst rectangular vent holes are cut into the two adjacent sides. The tile, which has a thickness of 15-18mm measures as follows:

	Height (mm)	Breadth (mm)
Keyed side	198	185
Plain side	215-19	185
Plain sides and vents	198 to 215-19	128-32

All measurements are in mm

Structures F, M and R produced fragments of probable voussoir tiles. They are similar in appearance to the 'springer' tile, but are shorter in height. Such tiles were used in conjunction with 'springers' in vaulted roofs (Fig. 110). Certain tiles are in Fabric 2, whilst others are slightly sandy and like the 'springer' could be variants of either Fabrics 1 or 2.

No complete tiles survive, but three fragments give an indication of size:

Context	Height	Breadth	Thickness
636, Str. F; Plain side and vent	c. 129-47	c. 125	13
1300, Str. M; Plain side and vent	129-?	133	14
5500, Well 1; Plain side	134	–	16-18

All measurements are in mm

The two plain sides of the voussoirs have vent holes, whilst the other two sides are combed. The vent holes are normally square or rectangular and vary in size from 22-36mm. One voussoir (Structure R, context 1803), however, has a circular vent hole 25mm in diameter.

Tesserae

The majority of *tesserae* are of stone, with smaller amounts of ceramic *tesserae* in Fabric 2.

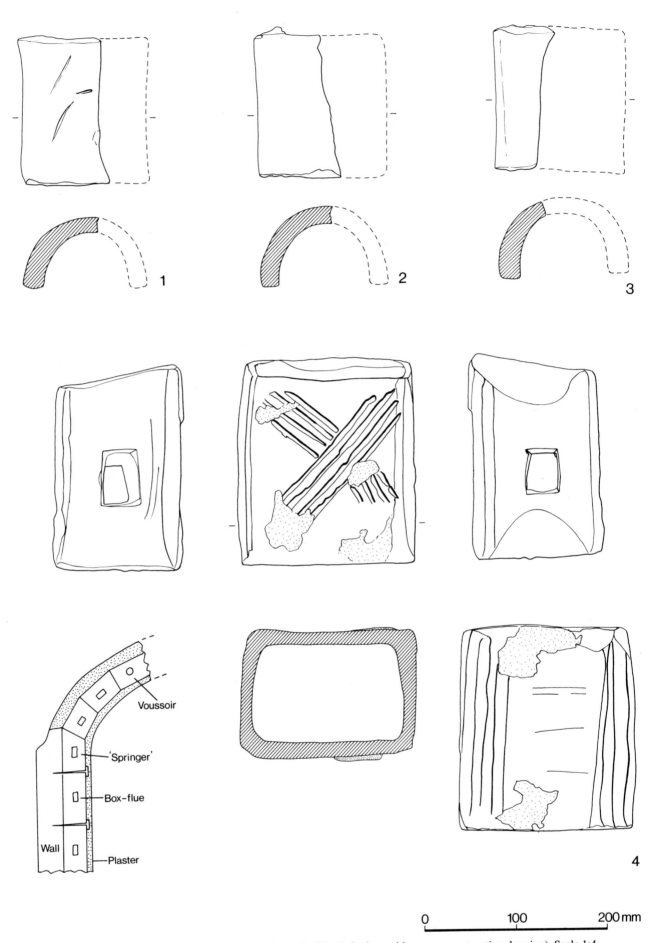

Fig. 110. Small *imbrex*-shaped tiles (Nos 1-3) and springer tile (No. 4; for its position see reconstruction drawing). Scale 1:4

Voussoir

'Springer'

Box-flue

Wall

Plaster

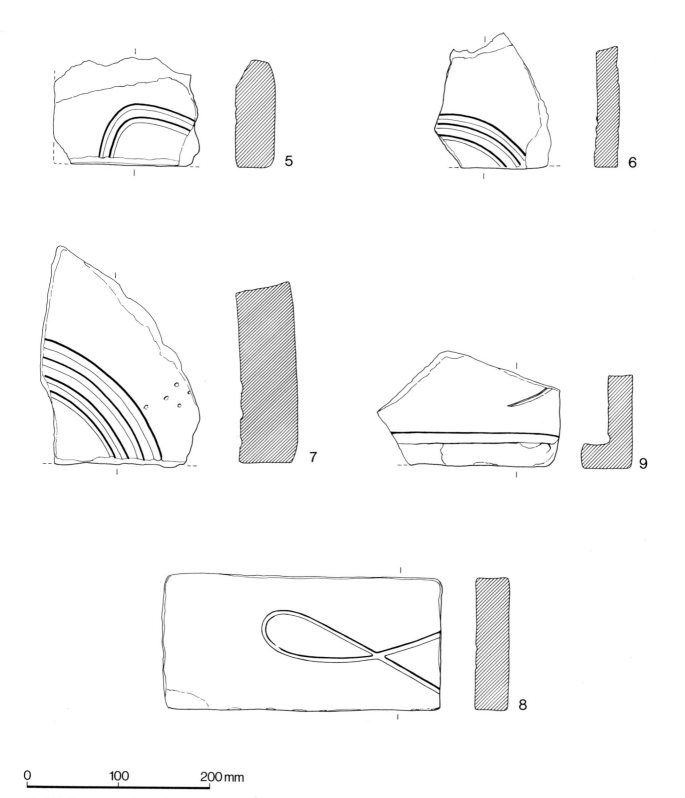

Fig. 111. Signature marks on tiles and brick (Nos 5-9). Scale 1:4

Markings

Tile stamps

Elgee and Elgee (1933, 140) record the presence of box-flue tiles with Sixth Legion stamp dies. Unfortunately, the whereabouts of these tiles is not known and none was found during the current excavations. At York the only box-flue tiles with Sixth Legion stamps are stamped with die types 26 and 48 (Betts 1985, 222).

Signature marks

These are marks on the top surface of roof tiles and bricks usually made with the tip of the fingers, or, less commonly, a stick or other blunt instrument. They are believed to represent the personal mark of the tiler who made them, although not every tile has such a mark.

The best signature marks are illustrated in Figure 111 (Nos 5-9). Most are of the semi-circular variety, which is by far the most common type in Britain as a whole (Brodribb 1987, 101). The single crossed loop variety (Fig. 111, No. 8) which occurs on unusual rectangular-shaped bricks from Structure E, is also known from York, London and Beauport Park in East Sussex.

Several *imbrices* have shallow grooves running along their length; they may be either signature marks or some kind of decoration. One *imbrex* has three grooves along what is probably the crest of the tile (Structure M, context 1213, Fabric 2), whilst another has a single wavy line running along one side parallel to the bottom edge (Structure M, context 4900A, ?Fabric 2).

Inscribed Tile (Fig. 112)

by R.S.O. Tomlin

Fragment of a buff tile at least 40mm thick, neatly inscribed in 'rustic capitals' before firing: [...]SCA.[...]. The fourth letter began with a diagonal stroke, suggesting M or N; it was not E or T. There is no knowing whether they belong to one word or two, but the space before and after 'S' is greater than that between the succeeding letters, suggesting perhaps a personal name: [...u]s Ca[ndidus].

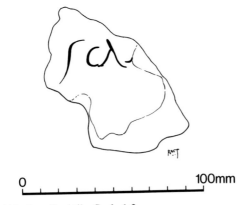

0   100mm

Fig. 112. Inscribed tile. Scale 1:2

Paw, hoof and other imprints

Procter noted in the last century that the tiles from Dalton Parlours were frequently marked with the impressions of dogs' feet (Procter 1855, 277). The current excavations produced five *tegulae* and bricks in Fabrics 1 and 2 with clear paw and hoof imprints. Four tiles, all in Fabric 1, have sandal imprints, one of which is above a signature mark (Structure M, context 8104).

One *tegula* has the top surface covered by small pits indicating that it was left out in the rain to dry prior to firing (Structure V, context 8201/2). The tile is in a fine sandy fabric (probably not Fabric 2) which is similar to certain Sixth Legion stamped tiles from York. Rain prints on Roman tile are relatively rare, indicating that the normal practice was to lay out tiles to dry under some sort of cover.

Roof mortar impressions

Several fragments of roof mortar were recovered; these give an indication of the position of the tiles on the roof. One fragment (Structure M, context 1213/3) shows that two adjacent *tegulae* were only 3-5mm apart, whilst the distance from the top of the flanges to the base of the overlying *imbrex* dipped from 30-35mm to around 10mm.

Conclusions

The evidence of analysis indicates that the villa obtained ceramic building material from four separate sources of supply. One of these was York, but the other three sources are unknown. Clearly there must be other production sites in Yorkshire which have not yet been identified. The tileries producing Fabrics 2 and 3 not only supplied Dalton Parlours but also sent a small quantity of their products to Castleford (Betts forthcoming).

The presence of brick and roof tile from York, some of which was apparently stamped by the Sixth Legion, suggests a possible military connection. In the Rhineland the spread of legionary stamped tiles around the fortress of Vetera at Xanten has been interpreted as a partial guide to the position of the *territorium legionis* on which were located farms supplying the needs of the military (Peacock 1982, 144). A *territorium* comprises land assigned to the garrison legion in holdings renewable every five years.

At Vindonissa in Switzerland many legionary stamped tiles were found on estates around the legionary fortress; Staehelin (1948) suggests that such tiles were obtained by private landowners in exchange for supplies of corn and other agricultural commodities. The estate at Dalton Parlours may well have supplied agricultural produce to the legionary garrison at York, perhaps in exchange for tiles. About 4km south-east of the villa the road system splits the land into strips. It has been suggested by Addyman (1984, 14) that this could have been part of a *territorium legionis*. This *territorium* may have extended to include the Dalton Parlours estate. It is possible that the estate was actually established by a retired army veteran.

Part Three
Environmental Evidence (excluding Well 1)

edited by David Berg

23 The Human Remains
by Keith Manchester, Helen Bush

The human remains from the excavations at Dalton Parlours were analysed between 1977-78 by Keith Manchester. Four additional infants (Nos 12-15) were identified during post-excavational analysis and were examined in 1987 by Helen Bush. Skeleton No. 1 was a post-Roman burial and is described, along with associated artefacts, in Appendix 2.

The remains are not from a planned and ordained cemetery but are isolated discrete burials. It is, therefore, valueless to consider these isolates as a single skeletal biological unit. No valid remarks or conclusions drawn from the examination of discontinuous morphological traits, or osteometry, can be made. It is perhaps noteworthy, however, that of the fourteen individuals examined from Roman contexts, ten are infants or neonates.

Summary data for each skeleton and their site locations are shown in Table 8 and Figure 113. Adult

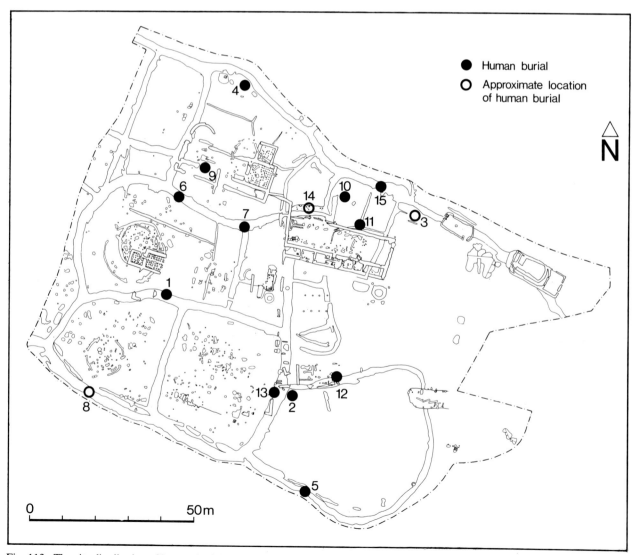

Fig. 113. The site distribution of human burials.

171

skeletal measurements are presented in Tables 9-10; and infant long bone measurements are given in Table 11. Dentition data are summarised in Table 12.

1   See Appendix 2.

2   Disturbed skeleton oriented SW-NE in shallow grave (602) cut into bedrock. Fragmented and poorly preserved. Probably female 1.51m tall and about 25 years of age at death. The individual shows slight dental calculus formation and upper left third molar absence. There is no other abnormality noted in this individual. *SF 285*

3   Well-preserved partial remains of disturbed infant skeleton lying in shallow pit (6101). Estimated age <15 months at death. Sex indeterminate. No abnormalities were noted in this individual. *SF 435*

4   Partial and fragmentary remains of poorly preserved skeleton lying in shallow pit (4300). Probably female of estimated height 1.68m and about 35 years of age at death. Evidence of mesial dental caries on upper right and left first molar and marked calculus formation. No other abnormality was noted. *SF 457*

5   Partial remains of well-preserved infant skeleton lying in ditch section (023/5). The individual of indeterminate sex was less than 12 months old at death. No dentition. *SF 542*

6   Partial and fragmented remains of infant skeleton lying in ditch section (016/1). Sex indeterminate. The age at death as estimated by neural arch union was under one year. The cranial skeleton is represented by the incus only. The complete upper and lower deciduous dentition was lost *post mortem.* No pathological features were apparent. *SF 576*

7   Partial remains of infant skeleton lying in ditch section (016/2-017/1). Sex of individual indeterminate. Age at death possibly less than one year. No dentition. *SF 601*

8   Fragmented remains of skeleton found on surface of Ditch 002. The collection consists of seven fragments. The individual was possibly male and in the age group 20-25 years at death. There is moderate dental hypoplasia and moderate shovel-shaped incisor teeth. The stature is not known. *SF 692*

9   Well-preserved remains of infant skeleton lying in small pit (1007). From the absence of epiphysial union and from the erupting upper central incisor it is estimated that the age at death was about 8-10 months. There is malposition within the mandible due to rotation of the lower right second incisor and canine. It was not possible to indicate the sex of the child. No other pathological feature has been noted. *SF 750*

10   Well-preserved adult skeleton, oriented NE-SW in shallow grave (5005) cut into bedrock (Pl. XXXIII). The individual was an adult male of 25-30 years at death. His height was 1.74m and he was of fairly muscular build. The feet are missing and, *in situ*, the lower third of both tibiae had been broken. The loss of feet and broken tibiae are presumed to be the result of plough damage. The individual was dolicocephalic, eurymeric and platycnemic. There is evidence of dental caries, abscess and slight periodontal disease with moderate calculus formation.

A small area of periostitis is present on the upper third of the medial surface of the right tibia. A surface irregularity of the medial facet of the left patella may indicate resolution of chondromalacia patella. There is evidence in the right wrist and hand of early arthritic change. On radiological grounds this possibly represents rheumatoid arthritis. It is fairly localised and may be early or quiescent. Apart from pain in the wrist and hand and possibly some effusion of the wrist joint there may not have been any symptoms. An ossification of the left femoral adductor magnus tendon at its insertion may be the result of a forced abduction of the left thigh.

The man was buried prone in a grave large enough to accommodate him fully extended. He was however in a position of opisthotonos, the neck in extreme extension and the vertebral column markedly extended. The legs were flexed slightly at the hip joints and the knees were flexed about 50-60°. The right upper and forearm were flexed with the right hand lying in front of the left shoulder. The left upper and forearm were positioned so that the left hand remained

Table 8. Human bone: summary of all skeletal remains.

Burial	SF	Age	Sex	Stature
1	235	*c.* 25 yrs	F	1.62m
2	602	*c.* 25 yrs	?F	1.51m
3	6101	<15 mths	I	–
4	4300	*c.* 35 yrs	?F	1.68m
5	542	<12 mths	I	–
6	576	<12 mths	I	–
7	601	?<12 mths	I	–
8	692	20-25 yrs	?M	–
9	750	8-10 mths	I	–
10	798	25-30 yrs	M	1.74m
11	839	6-9 mths	I	–
12	675	<6 mths	I	–
13	710	?0-3 mths	I	–
14	1848	birth ± 2 mths	I	–
15	1921	<9 mths	I	–

F = female, M = male, I = indeterminate, ? = probable

Table 9. Adult skull measurements.

Skeleton No. 10	
L	197.4
B	147.9
B'	104.5
B''	123.0
H'	132.5
LB	101.4
S1	114.0
S2	125.8
S3	100.0
S'1	133.0
S'2	137.0
S'3	124.0
Biast B	119.0
G'H	–
GL	–
G2	–
G'1	–
O'	–
O2	–
FL	35.4
FB	30.0
MH	50.5 (L)
NB	–
NH'	–
SO	–
NB4	–
DC	–
W1	–
ZZ	45.8
RB	40.1 (L)
H'	–
M_2H	32.5
CYL	25.0 (L)
CrH	73.0 (L) 71.0 (R)

All measurements in mm and as defined by Brothwell (1981)

172

Plate XXXIII. Skeleton No. 10 (5005), facing south-west. (Photo: S. Wager)

Table 11. Infant long bone measurements.

Skeleton	No. 3	No. 5	No. 6	No. 9	No. 11	No. 12	No. 14
Femur							
Diaphysis	73.0	–	74.0	73.6	78.7	(78.0)	78.8(L) 79.9(R)
Tibia							
Diaphysis	56.0	–	–	58.4	66.0	68.4	69.8(L) 70.3(R)
Humerus							
Diaphysis	56.0	68.0	62.0	65.7	68.0	67.3	–
Radius							
Diaphysis	48.0	–	48.0	52.0	53.3	56.3	55.2(L)
Ulna							
Diaphysis	55.0(L) 57.0(R)	–	56.0	59.5	62.2	–	–
Fibula							
Diaphysis	–	–	–	–	62.2	–	66.7

Measurements in brackets are estimated

Table 12. Dental formulae.

Skeleton	

2

```
                              NP
8 7 6 5 4 3 2 1 | 1 \\ 4 5 6 7 8
8 7 6 5 4 3 \ 1 |   \\\ 4 5 6 7 8
```

3

```
e d c b a | a b c d e
e d c b a | a \ \ d e
                O V
```

4

```
        C                   C
\ \ 6 5 4 3 2 1 | 1 2 3 4 5 6 7 \
8 7 6 5 4 3 2 1 | 1 2 3 4 5 6 7 8
```

10

```
        C
\ 7 6 5 4 3 2 1 | 1 2 3 4 5 6 X 8
8 7 6 5 4 3 2 \ | 1 2 3 4 5 6 7 8
C                       C A
```

Key to dental formulae:

X = ante mortem loss
\ = post mortem loss
NP = not developed
C = caries
A = abscess
E = pulp exposure
V = unerupted
O = erupting

Table 10. Selected adult long bone measurements.

Skeleton	No. 2	No. 10 (L)	No. 10 (R)
Femur			
FeL[1]	389.0	462.0	463.0
FeL[2]	385.0	459.0	460.0
FeLe	–	449.0	450.0
FeD[1]	20.9	33.0	33.0
FeD[2]	28.7	34.7	33.6
Tibia			
TiL[1]	–	394.0	–
TiL[2]	–	393.0	–
TiL[3]	–	374.6	370.8
TiD[1]	–	45.7	45.1
TiD[2]	–	26.6	26.1
Humerus			
HuL	(288.0)	343.0	338.0
HuD[1]	–	26.1	25.9
HuD[2]	–	20.4	19.0
Radius			
RaL[1]	(223.0)	251.0	249.0
Ulna			
UlL[1]	–	277.0	278.0
Fibula			
FiL[1]	–	–	380.0

All measurements in mm and as defined by Brothwell (1981)
Measurements in brackets are estimated

beneath the right side of the pelvis, i.e. over the right iliac fossa in life. *SF 798*

11 Partial remains of infant skeleton lying in fill of gully (5600/4). Age at death was 6-9 months. Estimation of the sex of the infant was impossible. No pathological features were noted. Cause of death unknown. *SF 839*

12 Infant skeleton lying in 'presumed' grave, pit 605. Generally well preserved although there is some damage to the ends of the long bones. No teeth have survived.

The absence of teeth makes ageing problematic. Measurements of the long bones indicate that the child died between birth and the first six months of post-natal life (Table 11). However, on the basis of size, comparison with skeleton No. 14 suggests that the two infants were of similar age at death, that is, that they died at birth or in the first few months of post-natal life.

No pathology or developmental abnormalities were noted. *SF 1675*

13 Infant fragments from ?post-hole 628. The remains of this individual are in very poor condition. The left side of the mandible is present, but there are no teeth, mandibular or maxillary.

The poor preservation of the long bones makes measurement impossible. Non-fusion of the mandible indicates an age of less than one year at death. Although there has been *post mortem* damage to both temporal bones, the right tympanic ring appears fused. Given the condition of the material, it is not possible to assign a more precise age-at-death to this infant than birth, or within a few months of the event. *SF 1710*

14 Infant skeleton from layer of destruction debris (1213). This burial is well preserved, with most of the skeletal elements represented. The mandible is complete, although unfused at its mid-point; only the left maxilla is present. The teeth which survive are only partially mineralised, and this, together with their immature morphology, makes them difficult to classify.

The unfused state of the mandible indicates an age of less than one year at death. This figure is refined by long bone measurements (Johnson 1962) which all indicate that the infant died between birth and six months of post-natal life (Table 11).

Comparison of the teeth with the dental development and eruption chart of Ubelaker (1978, 112-13) indicates that this baby died at birth (± 2 months). On the dental evidence it was suggested that the infant may, in fact, have been premature (Craig, pers. comm.), and this is supported by the early stage of development of the canine, which calcifies initially at five months *in utero* and is represented in this burial by an incisal tip 2.7mm long (lingual surface). However, the tympanic ring is fused, an event which can occur just prior to birth (Williams and Warwick 1980, 330), or up to two months of neonatal life, and the petromastoid and squamous portions of the temporal bone are united, their fusion normally occurring in the first year of post-natal life. The balance of the evidence therefore indicates a full-term infant.

There is no evidence of pathology or developmental abnormalities in this infant. *SF 1848*

15 Infant fragments from ditch fill 030/3. This burial consists of a well-preserved but very incomplete skeleton.

Little can be said of this infant, other than that the developmental stage of the teeth indicates that age-at-death was comparable to the other infants described above. *SF 1921*

Acknowledgements

Helen Bush would like to thank Dr. Geoff Craig, Department of Oral Pathology, University of Sheffield, for his assistance with dental identification.

24 The Mammal Bones

by David Berg

Introduction

The faunal material examined from Dalton Parlours was restricted to those contexts that could be confidently phased to either the pre-Roman native settlement (Iron Age) or the main period of villa occupation (Roman). This resulted in a small assemblage of 4432 bone fragments of which 741 (16.7%) could not be identified to species or element type.

A majority of the identified material derives from the major domesticated food animals, cattle, sheep/goat and pig. Minor species represented include dog, horse, red deer, hare and badger. Vertebrae and ribs were identified to species where practicable or classed as large, medium or small mammal but have been excluded from all frequency calculations of identified mammal bone unless stated otherwise.

The overall condition of the bone was good although fragmentary. Of the identified fraction 7.6% was freshly broken. There was a clear relationship between bone condition and some context types, most evident in the identified bone that was calcined and brittle (9.5%) which derived almost exclusively from the ditches and destruction levels, and from identified burnt material (32.1%) largely restricted to pits and hearths. Occupation layers and pits produced a majority of the identified bone showing evidence of carnivore damage (5.3%), although the eroded and fragmentary condition of much of the material from other feature types has probably caused the loss of this form of taphonomic evidence.

An additional 8421 fragments of mammal bone from Well 1 (context 5500) were examined at the University of Sheffield and are dealt with separately below (Chapter 31).

Methodology

In order to maintain compatibility all quantifications and element groupings follow the system employed by Cotton (1982) in the analysis of Well 1 mammal bone (Berg this volume). Fragment counts were based on a system of diagnostic zones (cf. Watson 1979). Long bones were counted if they were complete or included all or part of the proximal or distal epiphysis or unfused diaphysis. Additionally, complete barrels (diaphyses without articulations), fragments greater than 50% of the complete bone and unfused epiphyses were counted. Small shaft fragments were excluded. Elements that are prone to fracturing into numerous small pieces resulting in over-representation were treated as follows:

i   mandibles were counted if they included all or more than half of the tooth row, with or without extant teeth

ii scapulae fragments were only counted if they included all or part of the glenoid cavity

iii pelves were restricted to those fragments including all or part of the acetabulum

iv skull fragments had to include the occiput or, because of the low numbers of this zone, the orbit. Small fragments such as those from the frontal and temporal region were excluded.

All figures are absolute totals: no attempt has been made to correct the bias created by those elements that are more numerous than others within individual skeletons, nor those that differ in frequency between species. The small numbers of such bones, for example phalanges and pig metapodials, did not warrant recalculation. This information should avoid any possibility of misinterpretation.

The minimum number of individual animals present (MNI) was calculated on the basis of the most frequent non-reproducible body element for each species (after Chaplin 1971). The state of epiphysial fusion was taken into consideration in the quantification of the MNI but no attempt was made to pair elements because of the inherent problems and possible biases this can introduce (O'Connor 1984, 7). The total MNI was calculated on the basis of combining context information. This may have resulted in the inflation of some figures as context independence cannot be demonstrated and therefore totals for phases and features should be interpreted with this in mind.

All bone measurements follow the conventions given by von den Driesch (1976). The metrical analysis of dog skulls conforms to the recommendations of Harcourt (1974). Dentition was recorded using the methods of several authors: cattle – Halstead (1985); sheep/goat – Payne (1973); and pig – Maltby (1987). The toothwear of all species was also recorded using Grant's (1975; 1982) system. The full dental and metrical archive is available from West Yorkshire Archaeology Service. The anatomical distinctions described by Boessneck (1969) were employed to identify goat from sheep bones.

The Iron Age assemblage

Of the 1810 fragments phased to the pre-Roman settlement period, 608 (33.5%) were unidentifiable. The major stock species identified, in order of fragment frequency, were sheep/goat (71.2%), cattle (23.9%) and pig (4.9%) (Table 13). The high proportion of dog (30.5% of the identified mammal bone) in this phase was due to one complete and two incomplete articulated burials. The relative frequency based on the minimum number of individuals present, sheep/goat (55.7%), cattle (36.1%),

Table 13. Total mammal bone fragments – Iron Age.

	n 1 %		n 2 %		n 3 %	
Cattle	166	9.17	166	16.42	166	23.88
Sheep	495	27.35	495	48.96	495	71.22
Pig	34	1.88	34	3.36	34	4.89
Total					**695**	**100.00**
Dog	308	17.02	308	30.46		
Horse	8	0.44	8	0.79		
Total			**1011**	**100.00**		
Large vert/ribs	56	3.09				
Small vert/ribs	133	7.35				
Bird	2	0.11				
Unident.	391	21.60				
Unident. long bone	217	11.99				
Total	**1810**	**100.00**				

column 1 = total fragments
column 2 = total identified mammal
column 3 = total major species

Table 14. Minimum number of individuals – Iron Age.

	n 2 %		n 3 %	
Cattle	22	28.21	22	36.07
Sheep	34	43.59	34	55.74
Pig	5	6.41	5	8.20
Total			**61**	**100.00**
Dog	11	14.10		
Horse	6	7.69		
Red Deer	–			
Hare	–			
Small mammal	–			
Total	**78**	**100.00**		

and pig (8.2%), supported the dominance of sheep/goat in the assemblage (Table 14).

Animal bone was recovered from 32 phased contexts, although the thirteen ditch and eight pit contexts provided over 82% of the identified material. Tables 15 and 16 provide species frequencies by fragment count and MNI respectively for the major feature types in this phase.

Ditches

A majority of the fragments from ditch contexts came from the ditch sections north of Enclosures I and II; the remainder from the boundary ditch north of Structure M. The general condition of the bone was poor with a high percentage of surface erosion, pitting and evidence of root etching. This was particularly noticeable on material from the northern ditch.

The ditch contexts produced 70.5% of the total cattle fragments from this phase and 100% of the large mammal ribs and vertebrae. Cattle and sheep/goat each formed approximately 42% of the 266 identified fragments with pig and dog approximately 6%.

The distribution of element types for the major stock species is given in Table 17. For all species loose teeth proved to be the most dominant element (30.6% of total cattle, sheep/goat and pig fragments), as might be expected from such a fragmentary deposit. Cattle were mostly represented by head fragments (skull, mandible and loose teeth), scapula, pelvis and feet. The main meat-bearing long bones were poorly represented and those surviving were biased to the most robust parts of the skeleton e.g. distal humerus and proximal radius.

The sheep/goat assemblage was of a different character, again head fragments dominated but limb bones were better represented whilst very few bones of the feet were found. There was a noticeable absence of late fusing long bone epiphyses, i.e. distal radius and proximal humerus and tibia. Of the 42 surviving long bone and metapodial fragments, 23 (54.7%) were barrels, i.e. complete diaphyses, 11 of which retained clear evidence of carnivore damage.

Pits

Eight pits produced 703 fragments of which 571 were identified to species. Pits 3405, 3454 and 7105 contained

Table 15. Iron Age mammal bone fragments by feature type.

	Ditch		Pit		Slot		Hearth		Post-hole		Gully	
	n	%	n	%	n	%	n	%	n	%	n	%
Cattle	117	34.41	3	0.43	–		4	0.69	28	23.14	14	26.42
Sheep	114	33.53	269	38.26	5	50.00	63	10.81	25	20.66	19	35.85
Pig	17	5.00	12	1.71	–		4	0.69	–		1	1.89
Subtotal	248	72.94	284	40.40	5	50.00	71	12.18	53	43.80	34	64.15
Dog	15	4.41	286	40.68	–		1	0.17	–		6	11.32
Horse	3	0.88	1	0.14	4	40.00	–		–		–	
Red Deer	–		–		–		–		–		–	
Hare	–		–		–		–		–		–	
Small mammal	–		–		–		–		–		–	
Subtotal	266	78.24	571	81.22	9	90.00	72	12.35	53	43.80	40	75.47
Cow/horse	56	16.47	–		–		–		–		–	
Pig/deer	–		–		–		–					
Sheep/dog	12	3.53	79	11.24	–		–		37	30.58	5	9.43
Bird	–		2	0.28	–		–		–		–	
Unident.	2	0.59	36	5.12	1	10.00	350	60.03	–		2	3.77
Unident. long bone	4	1.18	15	2.13	–		161	27.62	31	25.62	6	11.32
Total	340	100.00	703	100.00	10	100.00	583	100.00	121	100.00	53	100.00

Table 16. Iron Age MNI by feature type.

	Ditch		Pit		Slot		Hearth		Post-hole		Gully	
	n	%	n	%	n	%	n	%	n	%	n	%
Cattle	14	42.42	2	8.00	–		1	20.00	2	50.00	3	37.50
Sheep	11	33.33	16	64.00	1	50.00	2	40.00	2	50.00	2	25.00
Pig	2	6.06	1	4.00	–		1	20.00	–		1	12.50
Subtotal	27	81.82	19	76.00	1	50.00	4	80.00	4	100.00	6	75.00
Dog	3	9.09	5	20.00	–		1	20.00	–		2	25.00
Horse	3	9.09	1	4.00	1	50.00	–		–		–	
Red Deer	–		–		–		–		–		–	
Hare	–		–		–		–		–		–	
Small mammal	–		–		–		–		–		–	
Total	33	100.00	25	100.00	2	100.00	5	100.00	4	100.00	8	100.00

a majority of the bone, with pits 2562, 3456 and 3801 containing only 42 fragments between them. The main feature of the larger pit groups were the dog burials, accounting for pits containing 92.8% of all the dog fragments in this phase. The relative proportions of species by fragment count were dog (50.0%), sheep/goat (47.1%) and pig (2.1%). Cattle were represented by only three fragments. MNI frequencies reduced the dominance of dog (20.0%) and increased that of sheep/goat (64.0%).

The overall condition of the bone was good and generally less fragmentary than the ditch assemblage; 82.3% of sheep/goat long bones and metapodials were complete. Loose teeth contributed only 1.7% of the total identified material.

Excluding dog fragments the assemblage was almost entirely sheep/goat, dominated by bones of the limb extremities. Two hundred phalanges, carpals and tarsals made up over 74% of the sheep/goat assemblage. However, even excluding these elements from percentage calculations, the body-part proportions remained heavily biased with metapodials 54.4%, scapula, pelvis and long bones 27.9%, and mandible 2.9%.

Pit 3405

Situated towards the centre of Enclosure IV, this shallow pit contained 112 fragments from the partially articulated skeleton of a dog, and four fragments from a second individual (Pl. XXXIV). A minimum number of twelve

Pl. XXXIV. Animal burial (3405) north of Structure B, facing east. (Photo: S. Wager)

Table 17. Selected element frequencies from major Iron Age features.

	Iron Age		Pits		Ditches	
	n	%	n	%	n	%
CATTLE						
skull	10	6.02	–		7	5.98
mandible	13	7.83	–		12	10.26
loose teeth	30	18.07	1	33.33	25	21.37
scapula	11	6.63	–		10	8.55
humerus	5	3.01	–		3	2.56
radius	8	4.82	–		7	5.98
ulna	3	1.81	–		3	2.56
pelvis	14	8.43	–		13	11.11
femur	6	3.61	–		4	3.42
tibia	7	4.22	–		6	5.13
metapodials	17	10.24	1	33.33	12	10.26
foot bones	42	25.30	1	33.33	15	12.82
Total	**166**	**100.00**	**3**	**100.00**	**117**	**100.00**
SHEEP						
skull	16	3.24	5	1.87	7	6.14
mandible	12	2.43	2	0.75	8	7.02
loose teeth	76	15.38	4	1.49	45	39.47
scapula	8	1.62	1	0.37	4	3.51
humerus	8	1.62	–		3	2.63
radius	25	5.06	2	0.75	7	6.14
ulna	6	1.21	3	1.12	2	1.75
pelvis	9	1.82	2	0.75	7	6.14
femur	18	3.64	6	2.24	7	6.14
tibia	23	4.66	6	2.24	14	12.28
metapodials	54	10.93	37	13.81	9	7.89
foot bones	239	48.38	200	74.63	1	0.88
Total	**494**	**100.00**	**268**	**100.00**	**114**	**100.00**
PIG						
skull	4	11.76	–		3	17.65
mandible	3	8.82	1	8.33	2	11.76
loose teeth	9	26.47	–		6	35.29
scapula	–		–		–	
humerus	2	5.88	–		2	11.76
radius	1	2.94	–		1	5.88
ulna	3	8.82	1	8.33	2	11.76
pelvis	2	5.88	2	16.67	–	
femur	2	5.88	1	8.33	1	5.88
tibia	1	2.94	1	8.33	–	
metapodials	1	2.94	–		–	
foot bones	6	17.65	6	50.00	–	
Total	**34**	**100.00**	**12**	**100.00**	**17**	**100.00**

sheep/goat were identified represented by a total of 313 fragments, including 63 vertebrae and ribs. Twelve fragments were identified as pig.

The articulated dog lay on its left side, the rear of the animal had been disturbed. The sides of the pit had been deliberately lined with sheep/goat and pig elements, a majority of which were metapodials and phalanges. At least one sheep/goat articulated lower limb (tibia, tarsals, metatarsal and phalanges) had been placed in the pit. Part of a sheep/goat articulated spinal column was also present.

The deliberate and careful burial of dogs has been noted on Iron Age sites (Griffith 1977); they are often recorded as 'special' deposits with inferred ritual significance (cf. Grant 1984)

Pit 3454
Also situated near the centre of Enclosure IV, this pit contained 130 fragments of which 121 were from the articulated skeleton of a dog. Other species were sheep/goat (8) and horse (1). The dog lay on its right side, the skull had collapsed from damage prior to excavation and the lower limbs were absent.

Pit 7105
Situated about 10m further west in the same enclosure, this pit contained 44 disarticulated dog bones. Only fragments of the skull, scapula and forelimbs were present.

Hearths
Three hearth contexts were examined although the bulk of the material originated from context 2514 near the centre of Enclosure I. The overall stock species frequency was sheep/goat (88.7%), cattle and pig (each 5.6%). A minimum number of one cow, one pig and two sheep were identified. The total percentage of loose teeth was 15.2%. Context 2514 contained 544 fragments of which 90.6% were either burnt or 'ivoried' and highly fragmented (average size <20mm). This accounted for the high percentage of unidentified fragments (89.2%) in this context. With the exception of one pig tooth all the material represented sheep/goat and consisted almost exclusively of phalanges, carpals, tarsals, metapodials and radius and tibia fragments.

The Roman assemblage

Contexts phased to the main villa occupation provided 2622 fragments of animal bone, of which 1409 (53.7%) were identifiable to species and 988 (37.7%) to vertebrae and ribs. In order of fragment frequency the proportions of major stock animals totalled sheep/goat (56.5%), cattle (25.8%), pig (17.7%) (Table 18). Other species present (by fragments) included dog (30), horse (26), red deer (9) and hare (1).

The sheep/goat majority was reduced in the MNI proportions (44.2%) with cattle 31.4% and pig 24.4% (Table 19).

Table 18. Total mammal bone fragments – Roman.

	n 1	%	n 2	%	n 3	%
Cattle	346	13.20	346	24.56	346	25.82
Sheep	757	28.87	757	53.73	757	56.49
Pig	237	9.04	237	16.82	237	17.69
Total					**1340**	**100.00**
Dog	30	1.14	30	2.13		
Horse	26	0.99	26	1.85		
Red Deer	9	0.34	9	0.64		
Hare	1	0.04	1	0.07		
Small mammal	3	0.11	3	0.21		
Total			**1409**	**100.00**		
Large vert/ribs	256	9.76				
Medium vert/ribs	112	4.27				
Small vert/ribs	620	23.65				
Bird	92	3.51				
Unident.	58	2.21				
Unident. long bone	75	2.86				
Total	**2622**	**100.00**				

column 1 = total fragments
column 2 = total identified mammal
column 3 = total major species

Table 19. Minimum number of individuals – Roman.

	n 2	%	n 3	%
Cattle	27	26.73	27	31.40
Sheep	38	37.62	38	44.19
Pig	21	20.79	21	24.42
Total			**86**	**100.00**
Dog	4	3.96		
Horse	6	5.94		
Red Deer	3	2.97		
Hare	1	0.99		
Small mammal	1	0.99		
Total	**101**	**100.00**		

In total 36 contexts were analysed (Tables 20 and 21), with most of the material deriving from occupation layers in Structures P and M, structure fills from Y and X, and destruction levels from Structure M. A majority of cattle fragments (72.2%) and large mammal ribs and vertebrae (55.0%) appeared in the destruction levels and structure fills, particularly Structure M. Destruction levels also contained over 66% of dog fragments. Sheep/goat and pig bones were most dominant in occupation layers and appeared most frequently in the sunken-floored Structure P. Cattle, sheep and pig element frequencies calculated for the major feature types are presented in Table 22.

Occupation layers

Relative frequencies of the major stock species for the occupation layers were sheep/goat (64.6%), pig (28.6%) and cattle (6.8%) by fragment. By MNI the proportion of cattle (16%) increased slightly at the expense of sheep/goat (56%) with pig remaining at 28%. Loose teeth formed 14.7% of the total identified fragments.

The dominance of sheep/goat in this feature type is in part explained by context 1613. The main filling layer in the north-east corner of Structure P, this context contained exclusively sheep/goat and pig remains (70.9% and 29.1%). Loose teeth formed a majority of the sheep/goat elements (17.2%) but long bones were all equally well represented. The context contained a minimum of nine sheep/goat and two pig. Despite the number of loose teeth the assemblage contained a high proportion of complete long bones, 77.2% of sheep and 50.8% of pig. A striking feature was the age of the animals at death. Of the 180 sheep/goat fragments some 164 (91.0%) were either foetal/newborn or a matter of weeks old, based on size, texture and fusion.

Regardless of the obvious age bias in this context the proportions of sheep/goat element types did not prove to be significantly different from the material in the remaining occupation layers at 1% level of chi-squared. Excluding context 1613 the relative frequency of the major stock species in this feature type was sheep 51.3%, pig 26.1% and cattle 22.5%.

Structure fills

Fills from Structure Y (context 1222) and Structure X (context 4903) provided only 158 fragments of the major domesticates plus two fragments of horse and one of dog. Cattle outnumbered sheep/goat in this feature type in fragment counts and MNI. The percentage of loose teeth was 14.5%.

The cattle assemblage consisted mainly of skull, jaw and loose teeth (36.8%). Proximal radius and distal tibia were well represented among the 31.6% radius, ulna and tibia fragments. The number of foot bones, however, was low. The cattle assemblage was clearly subject to differential preservation, being biased towards the more robust elements of the skeleton.

The 56 sheep/goat fragments were less fragmentary than the cattle assemblage. Over 50% of the sample was composed of humerus, radius, ulna, femur and tibia. The percentage of loose teeth was 5.4% and no skull fragments were identified.

The 26 fragments identified as pig comprised 38.5% loose teeth and 30.8% mandible. No evidence of scapula, humerus, femur or tibia remained.

Destruction levels

Four destruction levels from Structures M (contexts 1212 and 1213), Q (context 1701), and R (context 1813) provided 429 identified fragments. Cattle fragments (44.7%) were more frequent than sheep/goat (37.5%) and pig (17.7%). The MNI also reflected these proportions at 45.5%, 31.8% and 22.7% respectively. Minor species included twenty fragments of dog, nineteen fragments of horse and one of red deer.

Table 20. Roman mammal bone fragments by feature type.

	Layer		Fill		Pit		Ditch		Oven	
	n	%	n	%	n	%	n	%	n	%
Cattle	25	3.3	76	19.8	56	19.4	5	29.4	4	1.5
Sheep	237	40.0	56	14.6	83	28.7	4	23.5	70	25.7
Pig	105	13.7	26	6.8	9	3.1	1	5.9	8	2.9
Subtotal	**367**	**48.0**	**158**	**41.3**	**148**	**51.2**	**10**	**58.8**	**82**	**30.1**
Dog	9	1.2	1	0.3	–		–		–	
Horse	2	0.3	2	0.5	3	1.0	–		–	
Red Deer	3	0.4	–		5	1.7	–		–	
Hare	1	0.1	–		–		–		–	
Small mammal	–		1	0.3	–		–		2	0.7
Subtotal	**382**	**50.0**	**162**	**42.3**	**156**	**54.0**	**10**	**58.8**	**84**	**30.9**
Cow/horse	26	3.4	61	15.9	70	24.2	1	5.9	16	5.9
Pig/deer	56	7.3	–		–		–		–	
Sheep/dog	298	39.0	38	9.9	44	15.2	6	35.3	138	50.7
Bird	1	0.1	42	11.0	19	6.6	–		28	10.3
Unident.	2	0.3	18	4.7	–		–		6	2.2
Unident. long bone	–		62	16.2	–		–		–	
Total	**765**	**100.0**	**383**	**100.0**	**289**	**100.0**	**17**	**100.0**	**272**	**100.0**

	Destruction level		Post-hole		Slot		Gully		Well	
	n	%	n	%	n	%	n	%	n	%
Cattle	174	29.0	–		3	33.3	–		3	33.3
Sheep	146	24.4	152	62.3	4	44.4	–		5	55.6
Pig	69	11.5	–		1	11.1	18	51.4	–	
Subtotal	**389**	**64.9**	**152**	**62.3**	**8**	**88.9**	**18**	**51.4**	**8**	**88.9**
Dog	20	3.3	–		–		–		–	
Horse	19	3.2	–		–		–		–	
Red Deer	1	0.2	–		–		–		–	
Hare	–		–		–		–		–	
Small mammal	–		–		–		–		–	
Subtotal	**429**	**71.6**	**152**	**62.3**	**8**	**88.9**	**18**	**51.4**	**8**	**88.9**
Cow/horse	80	13.4	1	0.4	–		–		1	11.1
Pig/deer	38	6.3	–		1	11.1	17	48.6	–	
Sheep/dog	26	4.3	70	28.7	–		–		–	
Bird	2	0.3	–		–		–		–	
Unident.	22	3.7	10	4.1	–		–		–	
Unident. long bone	2	0.3	11	4.5	–		–		–	
Total	**599**	**100.0**	**244**	**100.0**	**9**	**100.0**	**35**	**100.0**	**9**	**100.0**

Skull, mandible and loose teeth formed the major elements in the cattle, sheep/goat and pig assemblages with loose teeth forming 20.2% of all identified material. Long bones were well represented in cattle and sheep/goat but again the cattle fraction was biased towards distal humerus, tibia and radius fragments.

Pits

Five pits produced animal bone, the majority originating from the fill of Structure V (context 8201) situated south of Structure M. The bone was highly fragmentary, with 27.7% loose teeth. A minimum number of five cattle, four sheep/goat and one pig were calculated from the pit

179

Table 21. Roman MNI by feature type.

	Layer		Fill		Pit		Ditch		Oven	
	n	%	n	%	n	%	n	%	n	%
Cattle	4	13.8	5	31.3	5	38.5	1	25.0	1	20.0
Sheep	14	48.3	4	25.0	4	30.8	2	50.0	3	60.0
Pig	7	24.1	4	25.0	1	7.7	1	25.0	1	20.0
Subtotal	**25**	**86.2**	**13**	**81.3**	**10**	**76.9**	**4**	**100.0**	**5**	**100.0**
Dog	1	3.4	1	6.3	–		–		–	
Horse	1	3.4	1	6.3	2	15.4	–		–	
Red Deer	1	3.4	–		1	7.7	–		–	
Hare	1	3.4	–		–		–		–	
Small mammal	–		1	6.3	–		–		–	
Total	**29**	**100.0**	**1**	**100.0**	**3**	**100.0**	**4**	**100.0**	**5**	**100.00**

	Destruction level		Post-hole		Slot		Gully		Well	
	n	%	n	%	n	%	n	%	n	%
Cattle	10	37.0	–		1	33.3	–		–	
Sheep	7	25.9	2	100.0	1	33.3	–		1	100.0
Pig	5	18.5	–		1	33.3	1	100.0	–	
Subtotal	**22**	**81.5**	**2**	**100.0**	**3**	**100.0**	**1**	**100.0**	**1**	**100.0**
Dog	2	7.4	–		–		–		–	
Horse	2	7.4	–		–		–		–	
Red Deer	1	3.7	–		–		–		–	
Hare	–		–		–		–		–	
Small mammal	–		–		–		–		–	
Total	**27**	**100.0**	**2**	**100.0**	**3**	**100.0**	**1**	**100.0**	**1**	**100.0**

groups, although sheep/goat formed the majority of identified fragments. The cattle assemblage consisted of 41.1% skull, mandible and loose teeth fragments and 30.4% phalanges and metapodials. The sheep/goat fraction had similar anatomical proportions. Pig was represented by only nine fragments, seven of which were from the head, and two foot bones. Three horse fragments included a fused proximal femur, proximal metacarpal and a mandibular molar. Red deer was represented by five fragments of antler, none of which possessed any signs of butchery or working.

Major species

Data for the major species is presented in the following tables: dentition – Tables 23-4; epiphysial fusion – Table 25; and metrical – Table 26.

Cattle

The Dalton Parlours animal bone comprised a calculated minimum number of 22 Iron Age and 27 Roman cattle. The ageing data from Iron Age contexts was limited with

only five mandibles surviving with tooth rows that could be assigned to relative age classes. Two mandibles had a first molar unworn, i.e. 1-8 months, and three possessed molars in heavy wear representing senile animals (Halstead 1985). Of the bones with fusion evidence, only 12.2% were unfused (all of which fuse prior to 3 years, based on the figures of Silver (1969)).

Despite the better retrieval of Roman material the number of cattle mandibles was still small with just nine suitable for ageing on the basis of tooth eruption and wear. With the exception of one mandible with the deciduous p4 unworn (0-1 month), all were from mature beasts with four classed as senile (M$_3$ beyond Grant's (1975) stage j). Grant (1984) has stated that the Iron Age cattle jaws at Danebury, Hampshire with mandible wear stages of between 38-51 represent fully mature animals possibly of an age of 4 years plus. Eight of the nine Dalton Parlours mandibles were within the range of mws 39-53. The fusion data similarly showed a majority of cattle reaching maturity.

The determination of cattle sex ratios was hampered by the small sample size and the fragmentary nature of the

Table 22. Selected element frequencies from major Roman features.

	Roman		Layer		1613		Fill		Pit		Destruction	
	n	%	n	%	n	%	n	%	n	%	n	%
CATTLE												
skull	29	8.4	–		–		12	15.8	5	8.9	12	6.9
mandible	36	10.4	5	20.0	–		6	7.9	4	7.1	21	12.1
loose teeth	56	16.2	4	16.0	–		10	13.2	14	25.0	26	15.0
scapula	18	5.2	2	8.0	–		2	2.6	5	8.9	8	4.6
humerus	30	8.7	2	8.0	–		6	7.9	1	1.8	20	11.6
radius	24	6.9	–		–		10	13.2	3	5.4	11	6.4
ulna	16	4.6	1	4.0	–		5	6.6	2	3.6	8	4.6
pelvis	27	7.8	3	12.0	–		5	6.6	1	1.8	16	9.2
femur	15	4.3	3	12.0	–		1	1.3	1	1.8	8	4.6
tibia	28	8.1	1	4.0	–		9	11.8	3	5.4	14	8.1
metapodials	24	6.9	2	8.0	–		3	3.9	4	7.1	11	6.4
foot bones	43	12.4	2	8.0	–		7	9.2	13	23.2	18	10.4
Total	**346**	**100.0**	**25**	**100.0**	**0**		**76**	**100.0**	**56**	**100.0**	**173**	**100.0**
SHEEP												
skull	106	14.1	14	5.9	11	6.1	–		3	3.6	9	6.2
mandible	60	8.0	17	7.2	12	6.7	7	12.5	5	6.0	21	14.5
loose teeth	110	14.6	32	13.5	31	17.2	3	5.4	24	28.9	32	22.1
scapula	31	4.1	13	5.5	10	5.6	4	7.1	1	1.2	5	3.4
humerus	47	6.2	19	8.0	16	8.9	5	8.9	4	4.8	10	6.9
radius	61	8.1	26	11.0	14	7.8	7	12.5	9	10.8	9	6.2
ulna	19	2.5	8	3.4	8	4.4	1	1.8	2	2.4	2	1.4
pelvis	29	3.8	14	5.9	10	5.6	3	5.4	3	3.6	3	2.1
femur	51	6.8	23	9.7	16	8.9	7	12.5	1	1.2	11	7.6
tibia	61	8.1	20	8.4	14	7.8	8	14.3	8	9.6	15	10.3
metapodials	79	10.5	29	12.2	20	11.1	8	14.3	9	10.8	18	12.4
foot bones	100	13.3	22	9.3	18	10.0	3	5.4	14	16.9	10	6.9
Total	**754**	**100.0**	**237**	**100.0**	**180**	**100.0**	**56**	**100.0**	**83**	**100.0**	**145**	**100.0**
PIG												
skull	35	14.9	18	17.5	16	21.6	2	7.7	3	33.3	9	13.0
mandible	32	13.6	8	7.8	5	6.8	8	30.8	1	11.1	11	15.9
loose teeth	53	22.6	18	17.5	13	17.6	10	38.5	3	33.3	20	29.0
scapula	14	6.0	5	4.9	3	4.1	–		–		7	10.1
humerus	13	5.5	3	2.9	2	2.7	–		–		8	11.6
radius	12	5.1	6	5.8	3	4.1	2	7.7	–		1	1.4
ulna	6	2.6	2	1.9	1	1.4	1	3.8	–		1	1.4
pelvis	7	3.0	4	3.9	3	4.1	1	3.8	–		1	1.4
femur	12	5.1	9	8.7	4	5.4	–		–		3	4.3
tibia	11	4.7	6	5.8	3	4.1	–		–		3	4.3
metapodials	11	4.7	7	6.8	5	6.8	1	3.8	1	11.1	1	1.4
foot bones	29	12.3	17	16.5	16	21.6	1	3.8	1	11.1	4	5.8
Total	**235**	**100.0**	**103**	**100.0**	**74**	**100.0**	**26**	**100.0**	**9**	**100.0**	**69**	**100.0**

material limiting any statistically valid metrical analyses. Horn cores were conspicuous by their almost complete absence in all phases.

Calculations made for the estimated withers heights of the Dalton Parlours cattle were based on the maximum length of the metapodials (Fock 1966). The Iron Age material produced figures of 1.06m and 1.08m for the metacarpal and 1.11m for the metatarsal. Bones from the Roman phase resulted in withers heights of 1.07m and 1.14m (cow) and 1.19m (bull) based on the metacarpals.

These figures are comparable to published data from other sites of these periods (cf. Wilson et al. 1978; Maltby 1979) but are larger than the mean of 1.03m estimated for cattle from the 1st-century Roman fort at nearby Castleford (Taylor 1985).

Evidence for butchery was restricted to the more robust parts of the anatomy and it is probable that much information has been lost due to the differential survival of material. Data were limited in the Iron Age bone to several fragments of tibia bearing defleshing cut marks on the distal shaft. The Roman evidence for butchery consisted almost entirely of scapulae and mandibles. One scapula had been chopped through the glenoid cavity and several fragments displayed knife cuts around the neck. Mandibles appear to have been heavily butchered which may account for the low numbers of ageable specimens. The most frequent evidence was chopping through the mandibular condyle and cut marks on the ramus. Knife marks were also found on the alveolar ridge anterior to the premolars. One fragment of maxilla had knife marks on

Table 23. Iron Age and Roman dentition.

CATTLE

Phase 1	Phase 2	Stage	Grant*	Age
	1	A	p4 unworn	0-1 mth
2		B	p4 in wear, M1 unworn	1-8 mths
	1	F	M3 posterior cusp in wear, M3 wear < g	young adult
	1	G	M3 wear at stage g	adult
	2	H	M3 wear at stage h or j	old adult
3	4	I	M3 wear > stage j	senile

SHEEP/GOAT

Phase 1	Phase 2	Stage	Grant*	Age
	7	A	d4 unworn	0-2 mths
1	4	B	d4 in wear, M1 unworn	2-6 mths
1	7	C	M1 in wear, M2 unworn	6-12 mths
2	6	D	M2 in wear, M3 unworn	12-24 mths
	5	E	M3 in wear, posterior cusp unworn	24-36 mths
1	2	F	M3 posterior cusp in wear, M3 wear < g	36-48 mths
3	3	G	M3 stage g, M2 stage g	48-72 mths
1	2	H	M3 stage g, M2 > g	72-96 mths
	2	I	M3 > stage g	96+ mths

PIG

Phase 1	Phase 2	Stage	Maltby	Age
	1	3	M1 in wear, M2 not in wear	9-14 mths
	1	4	M2 in wear, P4 not in wear	15-18 mths
2	9	5	P4 in wear, M3 not in wear	19-26 mths
	2	6	M3 in early wear (Grant stage b)	27-36 mths
1	1	7	M1 heavily worn (Grant stage j-n), M3 in moderate wear (Grant stage c)	>36 mths

Phase 1 = Iron Age, 2 = Roman
Cattle stages after Halstead (1985)
Sheep stages after Payne (1973)
Pig stages after Maltby (1987) with additions
* after tooth wear stages of Grant (1975; 1982)

the buccal surface above the tooth row. This evidence would suggest that cattle heads were not treated as waste at the primary slaughter and butchery stage but were fully utilised for their meat potential with the extraction of the tongue and possibly cheek meat.

Cattle husbandry

From the available evidence a majority of the cattle at Dalton Parlours were allowed to reach maturity and some individuals survived to a considerable age. There is no indication that the cattle slaughtered *on site* were being raised specifically for meat; a commodity that would have been exploited only when a beast had reached the end of its useful working life as a traction animal and milk supplier.

The dominance of older cattle is typical of Iron Age and Roman assemblages, although in the latter period the heaviest concentrations have appeared on military and urban sites, in contrast with villas and rural settlements which have produced a better representation of younger mortalities (Maltby 1981). The limited range of ages at Dalton Parlours could be an effect of differential preservation or the spatial variability of deposits. The possibility also exists that live cattle were being exported to other sites as tribute or as a marketable commodity once they had reached a suitable age for slaughter. Evidence for the marketing and redistribution of cattle has been put forward by Maltby (1984) for bone assemblages from urban consumer sites, but indicators of such activities on producer sites are difficult to detect. The absence or reduction in numbers of animals of specific ages may point to their removal from site.

Sheep/goat

Ovicaprid bones formed the majority of identified material in all phases, possibly representing some 34 Iron Age and 38 Roman individuals. No bones of goat could be confidently identified in the assemblage. Anatomical and metrical distinctions were examined on all suitable material using the methods of Boessneck (1969) and indices after Maltby (1979, 41). Their absence is 'typical of most Iron Age sites in Britain' (Maltby 1985, 101) and the species is poorly represented even in large bone assemblages of the Roman period.

Nine Iron Age mandibles were assigned age classes using the methodology of Payne (1973). Two individuals were less than 12 months at death and five were over 36 months. In each epiphysial fusion age class a majority of the epiphyses were fused, the total unfused being 19%.

The ageing data for the Roman period were more substantial with 39 ageable mandibles. Structure P contained ten of the eleven mandibles aged at less than 6 months at death (stages A-B). Seven mandibles with the d_4 erupting or erupted but unworn (0-2 months) were found in context 1613 whilst three of the four mandibles with M_1 unworn (2-6 months) were from context 1603. The epiphysial fusion evidence from Structure P, context 1613, comprised 116 fragments of which 100% were unfused. Among this total were 21 proximal metapodials and distal first phalanges, articulations that normally ossify prior to birth (Silver 1969).

With context 1613 excluded from the data in this phase the remaining mandibles spread between Grant's wear stages 8-52 with too few mandibles to indicate any marked peaks of slaughter. Payne's stage distribution in contrast shows a peak between stages C and E (6-36 months) accounting for 64% of aged mandibles.

Analysis of sheep pelves after Boessneck (1969) produced the following sex distribution: Iron Age – one female and one probable female; Roman – six females and one possible male. Metapodial indices after O'Connor (1982) resulted in the measurement of sixteen metacarpals and ten metatarsals from the Iron Age deposits all of which were female. From the Roman material seven metacarpals and five metatarsals were all females with the exception of one male (index 38.8).

The maximum distal width of the tibia is one of the elements most frequently measured due to its robust nature and therefore better survival in archaeological deposits. The Dalton Parlours mean of 22.5mm fits with Iron Age data and 23.2mm with Roman data from published sites of these periods as compiled by Maltby (1981, 190)

Withers heights for sheep were estimated from the metapodials using the formulae of Teichert (1975) producing a mean of 57.5cm on the metacarpals and

Table 24. Mandible wear stages after Grant (1975).

MANDIBLE WEAR STAGES

	Sheep					Cattle					Pig			
mws	IA	%	RM	%	mws	IA	%	RM	%	mws	IA	%	RM	%
2	–		7	17.9	2	1	20.0	1	11.1	2	–		–	
3	–		2	23.1	3	–		–		3	–		–	
5	1	11.1	2	28.2	5	1	40.0	–		5	–		–	
8	–		2	33.3	8	–		–		8	–		–	
10	1	22.2	1	35.9	10	–		–		10	–		1	7.7
11	–		1	38.5	11	–		–		11	–		–	
12	–		2	43.4	12	–		–		12	–		–	
15	–		1	46.1	15	–		–		15	–		–	
18	–		–		18	–		–		18	–		1	15.4
19	1	33.3	–		19	–		–		19	–		–	
20	1	44.4	1	48.7	20	–		–		20	–		1	23.1
22	–		–		22	–		–		22	1	50.0	1	30.8
23	–		1	51.3	23	–		–		23	–		1	38.5
24	–		3	59.0	24	–		–		24	–		2	53.8
26	–		–		26	–		–		26	1	100.0	1	61.5
27	–		–		27	–		–		27	–		2	76.9
28	–		2	64.1	28	–		–		28	–		1	84.6
29	–		2	69.2	29	–		–		29	–		–	
31	–		–		31	–		–		31	–		2	100.0
32	–		3	76.9	32	–		–		32	–		–	
34	1	55.5	–		34	–		–		34	–		–	
35	–		2	82.1	35	–		–		35	–		–	
36	2	77.7	–		36	–		–		36	–		–	
39	–		2	87.2	39	–		1	22.2	39	–		–	
40	1	88.8	1	89.7	40	–		–		40	–		–	
41	–		–		41	–		1	33.3	41	–		–	
42	1	100.0	2	94.9	42	–		–		42	–		–	
44	–		1	97.4	44	–		–		44	–		–	
46	–		–		46	2	80.0	2	55.5	46	–		–	
48	–		–		48	1	100.0	2	77.7	48	–		–	
51	–		–		51	–		1	88.8	51	–		–	
52	–		1	100.0	52	–		–		52	–		–	
53	–		–		53	–		1	100.0	53	–		–	
Total	**9**		**39**			**5**		**9**			**2**		**13**	

mws = mandible wear stage
% = cumulative percent

58.2cm on the metatarsals for the Iron Age bone. Shoulder heights calculated for the Roman sheep were slightly smaller than these figures with means of 55.6cm and 57.9cm respectively. Allowing for a degree of regional and environmental variation in the stature of sheep, the Iron Age and Roman heights fit well with published figures from sites of these periods, for example Ashville, Oxfordshire (Wilson *et al.* 1978) and Exeter (Maltby 1979). The Roman figures are however of a smaller mean size than those at the nearby sites of Castleford (Taylor 1985) and Garton Slack, Humberside (Noddle 1980).

Evidence of Iron Age butchery was largely restricted to bones of the feet. Metapodials, particularly the material from pit 3405, consistently displayed fine knife cuts on the proximal shafts. One astragalus had similar knife marks on the lateral aspect.

Identical cuts were found on Roman sheep metapodials and on one calcaneum. These marks would indicate dismemberment of the feet around the proximal articulation of the metapodials performed with a knife.

Several long bones from Roman contexts, including humerus, radius and tibia, bore knife cuts on the distal shaft comparable to filleting marks as described by Binford (1981). Knife marks on the pubis and ilium of a pelvis would also suggest this activity. From the later Roman contexts disjointing marks were found on the proximal condyle of a femur and on the lateral aspect of a second cervical vertebra.

Sheep husbandry

The evidence indicates a majority of animals reached maturity during the Iron Age occupation and certainly beyond the prime age of sheep raised purely for meat. The low numbers hamper any firm conclusions of the husbandry regime but older animals suggest wool would have been an important secondary product and artefactual evidence supports the presence of textile production.

The Roman mortality profile includes a high proportion of neonatal and first year deaths, as has been found on many Iron Age and Roman sites (Grant 1984;

Table 25. Epiphysial fusion data.

Element	Age (mths)	Iron Age			Roman		
		F	NF	% NF	F	NF	% NF
CATTLE							
Sd Hd Rp Pp	7-18	21	2	8.7	41	1	2.4
Mcd Td Mtd	24-36	12	4	25.0	16	2	11.1
Fp C	36-42	2	0	0.0	0	0	0.0
Hp Rd Up Fd Tp	42-48	8	0	0.0	18	11	37.9
SHEEP							
Sd Hd Rp	6-10	8	0	0.0	19	39	67.2
Pp Mcd Td Mtd	13-28	50	11	18.0	61	61	50.0
Rd Up Fp C	30-36	12	3	20.0	18	35	66.0
Hp Fd Tp	36-42	11	5	31.3	29	74	71.8

Roman phase excluding context 1613

Element	Age (mths)	Iron Age			Roman		
		F	NF	% NF	F	NF	% NF
SHEEP							
Sd Hd Rp	6-10				19	14	42.4
Pp Mcd Td Mtd	13-28				61	34	35.8
Rd Up Fp C	30-36				18	16	47.1
Hp Fd Tp	36-42				29	29	50.0
PIG							
Sd Hd Rp	12	0	1	100.0	8	10	55.6
Mcd Td Pp C Mtd	24-30	1	3	75.0	8	20	71.4
Hp Rd Up Fp Fd Tp	36-42	0	6	100.0	2	27	93.1

Element key:
S = scapula, H = humerus, R = radius, U = ulna, Mc = metacarpal,
P = phalanx1, F = femur, T = tibia, C = calcaneum, Mt = metatarsal
p = proximal, d = distal
Ages after Silver (1969)

Maltby 1981; Noddle 1984). An unknown proportion of these deaths could have resulted from natural mortality reflecting the level of husbandry efficiency. Their presence may indicate that ewes were brought onto or near to the site for lambing.

Whatever the nature of their deaths, the carcasses of these young animals were certainly exploited. Grant (1975) found that neonatal mortalities tended to be disposed of in wells, whereas at Dalton Parlours all the evidence for young deaths occurred in the lower levels of the sunken-floored Structure P, and from butchery evidence even the youngest lambs had their fleeces removed prior to disposal.

Half of the mandibles examined fall within Payne's (1973) stages C-E, approximately 6 months to 3 years. A similar cluster of deaths between these stages has been interpreted by Halstead (1985, 222) as conforming to Payne's meat model, i.e. weaned animals raised and slaughtered specifically for meat. This regime is unlikely from the evidence at Dalton Parlours for several reasons. Grant (1984, 508) suggests that sheep raised and slaughtered for meat will fall within mandible wear stages 17-27 with a peak at 19-21. As can be seen the Dalton Parlours mandibles do not cluster in this area. The number of newborn and very young lambs, if culled, is incongruous with the objectives of a regime raising sheep for prime meat.

A different interpretation is suggested when the dentition data are viewed with the fusion and sexing evidence; a high proportion of juvenile mortality and a

dominance of females fits the pattern of a milking regime (O'Connor 1982) in which selected unweaned lambs are slaughtered to reduce competition for milk. In addition, a regular cull of animals of all ages can be expected in order to remove from the flock those individuals surplus to requirements, especially young males not required for breeding stock, sick or injured individuals, and barren ewes. The presence of quite old sheep, perhaps beyond breeding age, would have provided wool which, as in the Iron Age phases, was being worked on site.

Pig

Relative age classes were recorded using the mandible stages of Maltby (1987) with estimated ages based on pooled data from Bull and Payne (1982). Pig was poorly represented in Iron Age deposits with a mere 34 fragments from which a minimum of five individuals were identified. Three mandibles were aged of which two were at stage 5, estimated age group 19-26 months, and one at stage 7, over 36 months. Of the eleven fragments with fusion evidence 91% were unfused.

Fourteen mandibles were aged from the Roman deposits. Thirteen were older than 15 months with only one specimen over 36 months (Table 23). The majority were assigned to age stage 5, 19-26 months. The epiphysial fusion evidence supplemented the dentition data. A majority of the bone in each fusion age class was unfused including 55.6% of bones fusing at or before 12 months. The problems of directly comparing age profiles from dentition and epiphysial fusion are well recognised and the latter needs to be used with caution (Bull and Payne 1982). The data from Dalton Parlours may however suggest a bias against the survival or retrieval of the mandibles of young pigs.

The morphology of the canine teeth identified one sow and one boar, both of which derived from Iron Age deposits. No material from the Roman phases could be sexed.

A limited amount of butchery evidence survived. Fine knife marks were noticed on the ilium of a pelvis from Iron Age pit 3405, and dismembering cuts on the distal humerus and distal femur from the Roman assemblage. This phase also produced evidence of butchery using a heavy instrument rather than a knife. One radius and one tibia had been chopped in the middle of the shaft, and a mandible had been chopped immediately posterior of the M3.

Pigs are prime meat animals offering no useful secondary products whilst alive. They are therefore raised purely for slaughter and their renowned fecundity results in very limited variability in husbandry policy. With the exception of breeding animals, pigs are slaughtered when they reach prime meat condition and this is usually prior to full dental or skeletal maturity. Absolute ages for slaughter are dependent on rates of maturity, quality of feeding, breed, level of husbandry and consumer preferences (such as the Roman desire for suckling pig). Based on modern ageing data the Dalton Parlours pigs seem to have been slaughtered in their second and third

Table 26. Metrical data.

CATTLE

Meas.	Phase	n	Min.	Max.	Mean	Range	SD	CV
Astragalus								
GLl	IA	1	–	–	60.5	–	–	–
GLl	RM	5	56.9	64.9	61.0	8.0	2.85	4.67
GLm	IA	1	–	–	54.9	–	–	–
GLm	RM	5	53.5	58.1	55.6	4.6	1.95	3.50
Dl	IA	1	–	–	33.5	–	–	–
Dl	RM	5	31.3	35.6	33.7	4.3	1.49	4.41
Humerus								
Dd	IA	1	–	–	61.3	–	–	–
Dd	RM	2	71.4	76.2	73.8	4.8	–	–
Bd	IA	1	–	–	73.6	–	–	–
Bd	RM	3	78.5	95.6	84.9	17.1	7.61	8.97
HT	IA	1	–	–	37.2	–	–	–
HT	RM	3	42.3	45.9	43.8	3.6	1.51	3.43
BT	IA	1	–	–	64.5	–	–	–
BT	RM	3	69.0	82.9	76.1	13.9	5.68	7.46
Metacarpal								
Bp	IA	2	50.2	51.2	50.7	1.0	–	–
Bp	RM	3	51.0	60.5	55.2	9.5	3.94	7.13
Dp	IA	2	29.9	31.2	30.6	1.3	–	–
Dp	RM	2	32.6	34.2	33.4	1.6	–	–
BD	IA	2	44.8	47.2	46.0	2.4	–	–
BD	RM	4	49.0	57.6	52.8	8.6	3.83	7.25
Dd	IA	2	22.9	23.6	23.2	0.7	–	–
Dd	RM	4	25.0	27.4	26.3	2.4	0.88	3.33
Bd	IA	2	50.9	51.7	51.3	0.8	–	–
Bd	RM	4	54.2	62.7	58.1	8.5	3.89	6.69
DFD	IA	2	27.1	28.4	27.8	1.3	–	–
DFD	RM	4	27.4	32.9	30.3	5.5	2.1	6.97
GL	IA	2	178.0	180.0	179.0	2.0	–	–
GL	RM	3	179.8	190.4	184.2	10.6	4.51	2.45
Metatarsal								
Bp	IA	1	–	–	41.4	–	–	–
Bp	RM	2	46.5	55.7	51.1	9.2	–	–
Dp	IA	1	–	–	39.7	–	–	–
Dp	RM	2	45.4	50.3	47.9	4.9	2.45	5.12
BD	IA	1	–	–	42.6	–	–	–
Dd	IA	1	–	–	25.1	–	–	–
Bd	IA	1	–	–	47.4	–	–	–
DFD	IA	1	–	–	27.8	–	–	–
GL	IA	1	–	–	208.0	–	–	–
Radius								
Bp	IA	3	70.1	76.3	73.0	6.2	2.45	5.12
Bp	RM	5	80.1	86.2	82.7	6.1	2.33	2.81
Bd	IA	1	–	–	60.4	–	–	–
Bd	RM	5	71.1	74.9	72.9	3.8	1.34	1.84
GL	IA	1	–	–	249.0	–	–	–
GL	RM	2	297.2	299.1	298.2	1.9	–	–
Scapula								
GLP	RM	2	58.9	74.2	66.6	15.3	–	–
LG	RM	2	51.3	61.7	56.5	10.4	–	–
Tibia								
Bd	IA	2	48.7	57.9	53.3	9.2	–	–
Bd	RM	10	52.3	65.8	58.7	13.5	3.8	6.56
Dd	IA	2	38.6	43.9	41.3	5.3	–	–
Dd	RM	10	39.5	54.3	44.9	14.8	4.63	10.30
GL	IA	1	–	–	323.0	–	–	–

SHEEP/GOAT

Meas.	Phase	n	Min.	Max.	Mean	Range	SD	CV
Astragalus								
GLl	IA	1	–	–	24.1	–	–	–
GLl	RM	3	25.0	27.8	26.1	2.8	1.24	4.74
GLl	6100	2	35.5	35.7	35.6	0.2	–	–
GLm	IA	1	–	–	23.5	–	–	–
GLm	RM	3	24.2	26.7	25.2	2.5	1.1	4.36
GLm	6100	2	33.5	33.8	33.7	0.3	–	–
Dl	IA	1	–	–	13.8	–	–	–
Dl	RM	3	13.7	19.9	17.7	6.2	2.88	16.19
Dl	6100	2	20.2	20.5	20.4	0.3	–	–
Calcaneum								
GL	IA	1	–	–	43.6	–	–	–
GL	RM	3	49.5	58.6	53.4	9.1	3.82	7.14
GL	6100	1	–	–	68.6	–	–	–
a	IA	1	–	–	8.2	–	–	–
a	RM	3	11.0	11.7	11.4	0.7	0.31	2.70
a	6100	1	–	–	17.5	–	–	–
b	IA	1	–	–	18.7	–	–	–
b	RM	3	20.5	21.8	21.3	1.3	0.57	2.68
b	6100	1	–	–	27.8	–	–	–
Humerus								
Dd	IA	1	–	–	22.2	–	–	–
Dd	RM	7	21.3	23.9	22.6	2.6	0.72	3.19
Dd	6100	1	–	–	32.3	–	–	–
Bd	IA	1	–	–	25.4	–	–	–
Bd	RM	8	24.8	29.9	26.9	5.1	1.43	5.30
Bd	6100	1	–	–	40.1	–	–	–
HT	IA	1	–	–	15.9	–	–	–
HT	RM	8	13.0	17.2	15.7	4.2	1.27	8.08
HT	6100	1	–	–	25.2	–	–	–
BT	IA	1	–	–	24.2	–	–	–
BT	RM	8	23.2	27.3	25.6	4.1	1.18	4.62
BT	6100	1	–	–	38.7	–	–	–
GL	IA	1	–	–	126.3	–	–	–
GL	RM	2	131.0	132.0	131.5	1.0	–	–
GL	6100	1	–	–	166.2	–	–	–
Metacarpal								
Bp	IA	17	17.8	20.6	19.6	2.8	0.81	4.14
Bp	RM	9	17.5	21.9	20.0	4.4	1.25	6.27
Dp	IA	17	13.1	16.1	14.4	3.0	0.73	5.05
Dp	RM	9	12.9	15.7	14.4	2.8	0.80	5.52
BD	IA	16	20.3	22.3	21.2	2.0	0.54	2.55
BD	RM	7	21.4	23.4	22.3	2.0	0.84	3.75
Dd	IA	16	10.1	12.3	11.5	2.2	0.52	4.49
Dd	RM	7	10.3	12.4	11.6	2.1	0.70	6.02
Bd	IA	16	20.0	23.5	21.8	3.5	0.97	4.46
Bd	RM	7	21.1	22.9	22.2	1.8	0.7	6.02
DFD	IA	16	12.9	15.6	14.3	2.7	0.74	5.16
DFD	RM	7	13.4	15.6	14.4	2.2	0.83	5.78
B	IA	18	10.3	12.2	11.4	1.9	0.53	4.67
B	RM	8	11.1	12.2	11.8	1.1	0.38	3.22
BC	IA	16	8.8	11.1	10.3	2.3	0.61	5.91
BC	RM	6	9.9	10.7	10.5	0.8	0.29	2.79
GL	IA	13	113.0	129.3	118.9	16.3	5.79	4.86
GL	RM	8	112.6	124.0	116.1	11.4	4.43	3.82

Table 26. Metrical data. (cont.)

SHEEP/GOAT

Meas.	Phase	n	Min.	Max.	Mean	Range	SD	CV
Metatarsal								
Bp	IA	12	16.3	18.8	17.9	2.5	0.75	4.22
Bp	RM	10	16.6	19.3	18.3	2.7	0.82	4.47
Bp	6100	2	27.5	28.5	28.0	1.0	–	–
Dp	IA	11	16.4	18.4	17.3	2.0	0.64	3.68
Dp	RM	10	16.5	19.3	17.6	2.8	0.86	4.86
Dp	6100	2	26.9	27.4	27.2	0.5	–	–
BD	IA	10	18.7	21.0	19.9	2.3	0.76	3.82
BD	RM	5	20.0	22.2	21.2	2.2	0.91	4.31
BD	6100	2	32.7	33.5	33.1	0.8	–	–
Dd	IA	10	10.7	13.1	11.6	2.4	0.68	5.84
Dd	RM	5	10.3	12.6	11.6	2.3	0.94	8.09
Dd	6100	2	17.6	17.7	17.7	0.1	–	–
Bd	IA	10	19.7	22.0	21.0	2.3	0.75	3.59
Bd	RM	5	19.9	22.5	21.3	2.6	1.10	5.17
Bd	6100	2	33.3	33.4	33.4	0.1	–	–
DFD	IA	10	13.2	15.0	14.36	1.8	0.64	4.46
DFD	RM	5	12.9	15.8	14.6	2.9	1.07	7.33
DFD	6100	2	21.7	21.8	21.8	0.1	–	–
GL	IA	10	123.1	39.4	128.3	15.9	4.47	3.49
GL	RM	5	122.9	136.3	128.6	13.4	6.24	4.85
GL	6100	2	144.8	144.8	144.8	–	–	–
Radius								
Bp	IA	3	26.1	28.2	27.1	2.1	0.86	3.16
Bp	RM	2	24.6	30.4	27.5	5.8	–	–
Bd	IA	3	23.3	25.5	24.7	2.2	1.04	4.19
Bd	RM	4	25.1	28.2	26.5	3.1	1.12	4.23
GL	IA	3	129.7	154.2	139.9	24.5	10.39	7.42
GL	RM	2	131.7	141.0	136.4	9.3	–	–
Scapula								
GLP	IA	6	25.9	33.1	28.7	7.2	2.21	7.68
GLP	RM	4	26.1	30.2	27.9	4.1	1.63	5.83
GLP	6100	1	–	–	43.9	–	–	–
LG	IA	6	20.1	25.8	22.3	5.7	1.72	7.68
LG	RM	4	19.8	23.9	21.4	4.1	1.51	7.06
LG	6100	1	–	–	33.8	–	–	–
SLC	IA	6	15.3	23.1	17.5	7.8	2.61	14.86
SLC	RM	4	16.2	19.1	16.9	2.9	1.24	7.33
SLC	6100	1	–	–	28.0	–	–	–
DLS	IA	1	–	–	28.5	–	–	–
DLS	6100	1	–	–	31.0	–	–	–
Tibia								
Bd	IA	5	21.5	23.5	22.5	2.0	0.87	3.88
Bd	RM	8	20.3	25.3	23.2	5.0	1.46	6.26
Bd	6100	2	36.1	37.5	36.8	1.4	–	–
Dd	IA	5	17.4	19.3	18.0	1.9	0.71	3.93
Dd	RM	8	16.6	19.8	18.4	3.2	0.96	5.18
Dd	6100	2	28.8	29.0	28.9	0.2	–	–
GL	IA	2	187.6	190.0	188.8	2.4	–	–
GL	RM	4	189.0	206.0	198.4	17.0	7.51	3.79
GL	6100	2	230.0	231.0	230.5	1.0	–	–

PIG

Meas.	Phase	n	Min.	Max.	Mean	Range	SD	CV
Tibia								
Bd	RM	1	–	–	30.8	–	–	–
Dd	RM	1	–	–	25.4	–	–	–

DOG

Meas.	Phase	n	Min.	Max.	Mean	Range	SD	CV
Femur								
GL	IA	4	184.1	193.8	188.6	9.7	4.1	2.17
Humerus								
GL	IA	4	172.5	177.0	174.5	4.5	1.74	0.99
Radius								
GL	IA	3	167.1	175.4	170.2	8.3	3.72	2.19
Skull								
I	IA	1	–	–	175.0	–	–	–
II	IA	1	–	–	104.6	–	–	–
III	IA	1	–	–	88.2	–	–	–
IV	IA	1	–	–	99.6	–	–	–
IX	IA	1	–	–	89.6	–	–	–
X	IA	1	–	–	59.4	–	–	–
XI	IA	1	–	–	68.6	–	–	–
XII	IA	1	–	–	36.7	–	–	–
XV	IA	2	73.0	73.7	73.4	0.7	–	–
INDEX 1		1	–	–	56.9	–	–	–
INDEX 2		1	–	–	50.4	–	–	–
INDEX 3		1	–	–	41.6	–	–	–
Tibia								
GL	IA	5	156.2	197.0	185.2	40.8	14.9	8.04
GL	RM	2	189.2	189.7	189.5	0.5	–	–

SD = Standard deviation
CV = Coefficient of variation
All 'phase' 6100 = context 6100
Calcaneum measurements a/b after Boessneck (1969)
Dog skull measurements after Harcourt (1974)
All measurements in centimetres

years from dentition, with the long bone fusion indicating the culling of younger pigs prior to their reaching a prime meat weight.

Dog

Of the eleven Iron Age and four Roman individuals identified only one complete and one fragmented mandible were found. Both were from mature dogs with the third molar fully erupted and all four cusps of the M_1 in wear. The individual in pit 3405 had reached a considerable age. The lower canines had been reduced by abrasion on the mesial and posterior aspects to narrow columns through occlusion with the upper canine and third incisor. The lingual surfaces of the upper incisors were also heavily worn and the lower incisors had been reduced to short stumps.

All long bones examined were fused with the exception of one proximal humerus in pit 3405 and one distal radius in pit 2539. These bones normally fuse at 15 months and 11-12 months respectively (Silver 1969). There was no dentition evidence for the Roman periods. All surviving long bones were fused and covered the fusion ages 11-18 months.

The estimated shoulder heights calculated from all available long bones produced the following results:

pit 3405	n=9	range 54.4-56.8	mean 56.1
pit 3454	n=7	range 57.4-59.5	mean 58.3
pit 3411	n=1	(tibia)	46.5
Str. M, 1212	n=1	(tibia)	56.3

(all figures in centimetres after Harcourt's (1974) formulae)

The estimated size of the individual in pit 3405 falls in the upper range of sizes for Iron Age dogs as described by Harcourt. The dog in pit 3454 is a large specimen, the humerus, radius and femur being of greater length than Harcourt records for this period; although its height is smaller than the dog found in the later Iron Age phases at Ashville, Oxfordshire, with an estimated shoulder height of 60.5cm (Wilson *et al.* 1978, 125).

Only one skull, from pit 3405, was in a suitable condition for metrical analysis. The specimen had a cephalic index of 56.9, a snout index of 50.4 and a snout width index of 41.6, matching well the type of animal Harcourt describes as 'plain "dog"' (Harcourt 1974, 160), i.e. typical of the period prior to the breed and size variations associated with the Roman.

There was no evidence that any of the dogs at Dalton Parlours had been skinned, dismembered or in any way utilised for meat.

Horse
The majority of horse remains from all phases were loose teeth. All were in wear and no deciduous or incisor teeth were retrieved. The fusion evidence consisted of one fused proximal radius (15-18 months) dated to the Iron Age. A proximal humerus in the process of fusing from Structure X (context 4903) and one unfused proximal femur epiphysis from Structure V (pit 8201) were the sum total of Roman evidence. Both these epiphyses fuse at 36-42 months (Silver 1969).

The data did not allow any reconstruction of the size or sex of horses at Dalton Parlours. They were no doubt working animals and would seem to have reached maturity. Although there is plentiful evidence that horse flesh was eaten during the Iron Age and Roman periods, there is no evidence of butchery amongst this small assemblage.

Deer
The Iron Age deposits produced no identifiable deer remains. Three red deer fragments were found in Structure M (context 1216), comprising a metatarsal and humerus diaphysis, and a radius fragment. Pit 8201 contained five small fragments of red deer antler. None of the antler pieces had any evidence of butchery or working.

Hare
This species was represented by one fused proximal ulna found in Structure M, context 1216.

Unphased contexts
Of the unphased bone material the following contexts are worthy of mention:

Context 6100 was a small isolated pit situated south-west of Structure P. It contained no finds that would indicate a phase and was not stratigraphically related to any other datable feature. The pit held 112 bone fragments including 87 vertebrae and ribs from a partially complete, though not articulated, male sheep. The burial was minus head and cervical vertebrae, left humerus and both metacarpals. The left femur was fragmented.

This specimen is notable for its size, which questions contemporaneity with the Iron Age or Roman phases. The maximum length of the metatarsals of 144.8mm equals the upper limit of the Roman Castleford material (Taylor 1985) and is smaller than the 148.0mm recorded at Garton Slack (Noddle 1980), but is over 5mm larger than any Iron Age or Roman metatarsals at Dalton Parlours. The withers height estimated from the long bones is 65.3cm (metatarsal), 69.3cm (tibia) and 70.7cm (femur). An animal of comparable size was found in the Middle Saxon levels of Hamwih (Southampton) where the maximum range of shoulder heights was recorded as 70.9cm (Bourdillon and Coy 1980, 109).

The long bones were notable for their thickness more than their overall length. For example, the measurement of the distal breadth of the tibia is 36.8mm; larger than data recorded in any of the published material quoted above. Excluding the greatest length, the breadth and depth measurements of the proximal and distal metatarsal exceed data recorded from medieval deposits in this region (Ryder 1971; Ryder *et al.* 1974) including the maximum recorded from a sample of 50 metatarsals at Walmgate, York, some of which were dated to the early 18th century (O'Connor 1984, 40).

Although the condition of the bone (i.e. colour, surface texture and density) is comparable with bone from the Roman phase and would suggest an 'archaeological' context, this cannot be demonstrated and given the size of the individual the possibility of recent intrusion must be considered.

Context 2733 was located in the area of Roundhouse 6 adjoining the west wall of Structure B. There was no evidence that could firmly assign the feature to an occupation phase. One hundred and twenty-one fragments of a mature badger were identified. There was no indication that the animal had been butchered or skinned. Although the presence of badger is not unusual on sites of these periods the possibility of intrusion cannot be ruled out.

Discussion
The analysis of any bone assemblage should attempt to establish the degree to which the material studied is representative of a site's economic activities. This question is a basic prerequisite to all interpretations and can have the most profound effects on the most tentative inferences.

The animal remains from Dalton Parlours in each phase fall short of Noddle's interpretation of Casteel (1977), requiring at least 1400 fragments or a minimum number of 200 individuals for any interpretation of statistical significance (1984, 105). Similarly King, discussing the relationship between bone numbers and minimum number of individuals, concludes that small sites producing up to 500 fragments have an average of twenty or less bone fragments per individual cow and that such a ratio 'is too low to allow meaningful use to be made of the data' (King 1978, 210).

Whilst on the basis of fragment numbers Dalton Parlours is not a site in King's 'low yield' class, the ratios of bone numbers to individuals are small:

	Cattle	Sheep	Pig
Iron Age	7.5	14.5	6.8
Roman	12.8	20.0	11.2

In both phases sheep have the higher ratio and pig the smallest – confirming King's findings that the number of bones per pig is less than for other species due to reasons of differential erosion and possibly butchery practices (King 1978, 227).

The low ratios in the assemblage under study may be due to several factors. Firstly, few contexts examined contained primary deposits of animal bone and therefore various taphonomic forces have played a role in the assemblage formation (see below). Secondly, ratios of bones per individual are subject to a wide degree of variability, being dependent on the methodology employed for the quantification of fragments and MNI. The Dalton Parlours MNI were calculated by amalgamating context data. As stated above such aggregation may have inflated the MNI figures for each phase (Casteel 1977; Grayson 1973; 1979).

Of relevance to the Dalton Parlours material is that the MNI calculations are purely an index of the number of animals represented in the *assemblage* being studied and as such can have little or no relation to the population dynamics of a live herd or to a representative death assemblage when applied to samples accumulated over long periods of time.

Several factors have contributed to the formation of the Dalton Parlours bone assemblage, each of which has added to the erosion of a firm relationship between the bone originally deposited on site and the assemblage judged suitable for final analysis. Their significance should be assessed against this background.

Retrieval bias

The early phases of the site had suffered from destruction and rebuilding during later occupation, restricting the Iron Age contexts available for excavation. Historical disturbance, 19th-century excavation and recent plough damage have all contributed to the exclusion of a considerable amount of animal bone because it derived from contexts which could not be confidently assigned to an occupation phase. Additionally, some features such as the ditches were selectively excavated and this may be expected to have affected the proportions of larger mammals in the assemblage which tend to be deposited on the periphery of an occupation area (Wilson 1985). None of the bone examined resulted from sieved deposits.

Differential preservation

The assemblage is biased towards the more robust parts of the skeleton, that is, the denser elements such as distal humerus, distal tibia and astragalus. This is particularly noticeable amongst the cattle bones. The evidence of epiphysial fusion and bone texture in some contexts suggests the presence of more neonatal and very young animals than is indicated by the surviving mandibles; this has exaggerated or possibly accounts for the skewed dentition mortality profiles.

On the basis of the presence of dogs on site and the frequency of carnivore-damaged bone it can be expected that considerable material has been lost due to the activities of these animals (see Stallibrass 1986). The degree of carnivore damage is also likely to have been underestimated due to the eroded condition of the bone from some features.

Spatial variation and disposal strategies

Differences between feature types were examined using the chi square test. Only the larger features were used in order to avoid distorted results due to low cell frequencies. The relative frequency of cattle, sheep and pig fragments was tested as well as the distribution of element types for cattle and sheep.

The Iron Age features, pits, ditches, and hearths, proved to be significantly different. This is not surprising in view of the diverse nature of these deposits. The pits contained almost exclusively non-random assemblages comprising dog burials with a very high proportion of selected sheep elements. Ditches contained the remains of primary and secondary butchery waste and had been subjected to a variety of taphonomic agents. In contrast, the major hearth material reflects food preparation and cooking and is composed of a high frequency of burnt and unidentifiable bone.

The Roman features, layers, destruction levels, structure fills, and pits also proved significantly different, with the exception of the structure fills and destruction levels in Structure M for which there was no significant difference in species frequency or element distribution. Both these features contained a heterogeneous assemblage of bone suggesting secondary deposition.

By fragment count and MNI cattle were most frequent in the Iron Age ditches and Roman demolition levels and structure fills. Sheep occurred most frequently in Iron Age pits and Roman demolition levels and layers, particularly in Structure P which, despite the dominance of very young individuals, was not significantly different from the remaining layer assemblages in element distribution. These two feature types also contained a majority of the Roman pig bone. Dog remains were almost entirely restricted to Iron Age pits and horse bones to ditches and Roman demolition levels.

The total absence of complete horn cores and the sparse number of fragments surviving may suggest differential disposal rather than preservation bias, in that these elements were removed for horn working. Bone was certainly utilised on site as a raw material, as evidenced by the finds of bone working waste. This industrial demand for suitable bone will have resulted in the selected removal of some elements.

Animal husbandry

It is clear that during the Iron Age and Roman occupation of Dalton Parlours the maximum use was gained from each animal. In addition to meat, secondary products would have been of prime importance and cattle and sheep were fully exploited for their provision of traction power, milk, wool and no doubt manure. Pigs were kept in low numbers during the Iron Age but may have become more important during the villa occupation in supplying meat.

The relative proportions of the major stock species for the two phases were assumed to be similar and this hypothesis was tested using the chi square statistic. The difference between the Iron Age and Roman assemblages proved significant for both fragment counts and MNI.

The element frequencies for cattle and sheep were also examined; pig was excluded because of low frequencies. Again there was a significant difference between Iron Age and Roman assemblages.

The quantification of the major species showed sheep to be the dominant species in the assemblages examined. Pig bones increased in the later phase at the expense of sheep, whilst cattle increased their percentage by fragment numbers but were represented by proportionately fewer individuals.

	Iron Age				Roman			
	n	%	mni	%	n	%	mni	%
Cattle	166	23.9	22	36.1	346	25.8	27	31.4
Sheep	495	71.2	34	55.7	757	56.5	38	44.2
Pig	34	4.9	5	8.2	237	17.7	21	24.4

The species proportions, when compared to King's (1978) survey, fit the pattern of Iron Age and Romano-British native settlements rather than that of a Roman villa site, and it would appear that the subsistence regimes of the Iron age occupation of Dalton Parlours continued into the Roman period.

The trend in later Roman Britain towards an increase in cattle is not reflected in this small assemblage, despite the fact that King's findings show the movement away from sheep was more noticeable on 'romanised' rather than native sites.

Dalton Parlours at its peak was a substantial and affluent villa complex and so several factors may account for the faunal assemblage, assuming it is representative of the economy, being more akin to a 'native' rather than 'romanised' settlement. The husbandry of domesticated animals is to a degree governed by environmental constraints and the dominance of sheep at Dalton Parlours reflects the surrounding environment which may have

been considered less suitable for raising cattle in large numbers.

The low proportion of cattle may also be explained by the movement of live animals off the settlement. It is difficult to establish if stock were being raised specifically for the commercial market, but it is feasible that Dalton Parlours became a producer site particularly if, as Addyman (1984) has suggested, it fell within the *territorium legionis* of York. Additional local military sites that may have provided a market for livestock include Tadcaster and Newton Kyme, both in North Yorkshire.

25 The Carbonised Plant Remains from Selected Roman Deposits

by Josephine Murray

Introduction

During the excavation numerous samples were extracted for environmental analysis. These analyses were not carried out at the time and the samples remained in cold storage until the current investigation was initiated. Thirteen samples were chosen from within five structures (Structures F, P, R, X and Y). Although the site had suffered plough damage and there was the problem of contamination, the samples from Structures X and Y had remained sealed by the make-up for the second phase flooring of Structure M.

The aim of the investigation was to determine if carbonised plant remains were extant; their presence in these deposits would then facilitate a cursory examination of the Roman economy and environment at Dalton Parlours. More specifically it was hoped that the botanical remains would give some indication of the use of these structures.

Methods of analysis

The samples were processed by flotation and wet sieving. Cohesive samples were disaggregated by immersion for 24 hours in a 10% solution of sodium hexametaphosphate. Bulk processing of samples from 1-7kg (see Table 27 for record of individual weights of samples) was carried out using a flotation machine. The material from this was retrieved in 2mm, 1mm and 350 micron mesh sieves. These sizes of mesh were chosen as the larger size meshes (2mm and 1mm) would collect the majority of charred remains present whilst the smaller mesh would catch smaller particles such as chaff and some weed seeds. The residue was retained in the flotation machine by a 500 micron mesh. Both the float and the residue were air dried at *c*. 20° C. The residue was then dry sieved using 4mm, 2mm, 1mm and 500 micron sieves.

Table 27. Frequency of cultivated plants.

Structure Sample no.		X 4905 441	X 4905 442	F 613 386	F 636 391	F 607 411	P 1603 351	R 1809B 338
Mass of earth floated (kg)		7.0	2.0	2.0	2.0	7.0	0.5	2.0
Triticum								
T. spelta:	glume bases	1301	346	–	–	–	–	1
	grains	54	11	–	–	–	–	–
T. spelta/aestivum:	grains	59	25	–	–	–	–	–
T. aestivum:	rachis internodes	82	12	–	–	–	–	–
	grains	12	1	–	–	–	–	–
T. indet.:	rachis internodes	15	–	–	–	–	–	–
	grains	68	–	1	–	2	–	1
Hordeum								
Hordeum:	6 row rachis internodes	8	7	–	–	–	–	–
	indet. rachis internodes	14	–	–	–	–	–	–
	hulled assymetric grains	2	–	–	–	–	–	–
	naked assymetric grains	4	1	–	1	–	–	–
	hulled symmetric grains	23	8	–	–	–	–	–
	naked symmetric grains	15	–	–	1	–	–	–
	hulled grains	–	–	–	–	–	–	1
	naked grains	–	–	–	–	–	–	–
	indet. grains	35	3	1	–	–	1	–
Avena								
Avena/Bromus:	grains	12	25	–	–	–	–	–
Avena indet.:	grains	14	3	–	–	–	–	–
Cereal grains:	indet.	48	60	–	–	–	–	–
Total cultivated seeds		346	137	2	2	2	1	2
Number cultivated seeds/kg		49.4	68.5	1	1	0.3	2	1
Ratio wheat : barley		2.4	3.0	1	–	–	–	1
Ratio wheat glume bases : grain		6.7	9.4	–	–	–	–	1
Ratio barley grain : internode		3.6	1.7	–	–	–	–	–
Ratio B. secalinus : cultivated seed		0.8	0.4	1	–	–	2	–
Ratio weed seed : cultivated seed		2.2	1.5	2	1	4	2	9.5

Identifications

Nine out of the thirteen float samples yielded carbonised remains of cultivated and wild plants (Tables 27 and 28 provide a synopsis of this). The samples were examined under a Vickers stereo-microscope and a Russian MC6 stereo-microscope. In the initial scanning x10 was used, but for identification magnifications up to x70 were employed. The identification of cereal grains was based on morphology. The barley grains include both twisted and straight types. Six row barley (*Hordeum vulgare*), which has both types, is therefore shown to be present while the presence of two row barley (*H. distichon*), which has only straight grains, cannot be demonstrated. The quantities of either type compared to the indeterminate grains were not sufficient to allow calculation of a ratio of straight to twisted grains to determine if one sort predominates. The better preserved grains also bear characteristics that are indicative of hulled and naked barley.

Identifications of glume bases and rachis internodes were based on criteria used by G. Jones (pers. comm.). The presence of spelt wheat (*Triticum spelta*) was confirmed by the glume bases, and bread wheat (*T. aestivum/compactum*) by rachis internodes. Six row barley was confirmed by rachis internodes, and oat (*Avena* spp.) has been identified. It is apparent from the two oat grains, complete with lemmas and part of the floret base, that they are wild as they display the oval articulation scar characteristic of the wild species (*Avena fatua*). Although wild oats are a common arable weed, the presence of cultivated species cannot be ruled out. The wild species were identified using reference material held at West Yorkshire Archaeology Service and Sheffield University. Initial identifications were checked and corrected where necessary by Dr G. Jones.

Table 28. Frequency of non-cultivated plants.

Structure Species sample no.	X 4905 441	X 4905 442	Y 1226 443	F 613 386	F 636 391	F 607 411	P 1603 351	P 1606 354	R 1809B 338	Ecol. pref.
Mass of earth floated (kg)	7.0	2.0	3.0	2.0	2.0	7.0	0.5	0.5	2.0	
CARYOPHYLLACEAE										
Stellaria media (chickweed)	–	–	–	–	–	1	–	–	–	A
Stellaria spp.	3	1	–	–	–	–	–	–	–	
CHENOPODIACEAE										
Atriplex sp. (orache)	17	4	–	–	–	–	–	–	–	A(M)
Chenopodium cf. *album* (fat hen)	31	12	–	–	–	–	–	1	–	A
Chenopodium spp.	–	3	–	–	–	–	–	–	–	
COMPOSITAE										
Matricaria inodorum (scentless mayweed)	3	1	–	–	–	–	–	–	–	A
Compositae spp.	7	–	–	–	–	–	–	–	–	
CYPERACEAE										
Carex sp. (sedge)	105	51	5	1	–	–	–	–	–	M
Isolepis setacea (bristle scirpus)	1	–	–	–	–	–	–	–	–	Ma
Scirpus sylvaticus (wood club moss)	–	2	–	–	–	–	–	–	–	M
Scirpus sp. (club moss)	6	–	–	–	–	1	–	–	–	M
GRAMINEAE										
Agrostis sp. (bent grass)	36	6	3	–	–	2	–	–	2	
Bromus secalinus/mollis – floret bases	36	11	–	–	–	–	–	–	–	D/A
(rye brome/lop grass) – grains	289	58	1	2	–	–	2	–	–	D/A
Poa sp. (meadow grass)	31	12	1	1	2	1	–	–	–	
Sieglingia decumbens (heath grass)	58	23	19	–	–	–	–	–	–	Gb
JUNCACEAE										
Juncus articulatus (jointed rush)	–	1	–	–	–	–	–	–	–	Ma
LEGUMINOSE										
Leguminose indet.	15	15	2	–	–	–	–	–	–	
PLANTAGINACEAE										
Plantago media (hoary plantain)	1	1	–	–	–	3	–	–	14	A
P. lanceolata (ribwort)	2	–	–	–	–	–	–	–	–	A
POLYGONACEAE										
Polygonum cf. *aviculare* agg. (knotgrass)	62	3	4	–	–	–	–	–	2	A
Polygonum amphibium (amphibious bistort)	6	–	–	–	–	–	–	–	–	M
Polygonum sp.	53	1	3	–	–	–	–	–	–	
Rumex sp. (dock, sorrel)	25	5	–	–	–	–	–	–	1	A
PAPAVERACEAE										
Papaver dubium (long headed poppy)	2	–	–	–	–	–	–	–	–	A
PAPILIONACEAE										
Medicago lupulina (black medick)	–	1	–	–	–	–	–	–	–	D/G
POTAMOGETONACEAE										
Potamogeton sp. (pondweed)	9	2	–	–	–	–	–	–	–	M
URTICEAE										
Urtica dioica (stinging nettle)	4	–	–	–	–	–	–	–	–	A
Total charred seeds	766	202	38	4	2	8	2	1	19	

Ecological Preference:
A – weed of arable land and disturbed places
D – plant of disturbed places on field margins and waysides
G – plant of grassland
M – plant of marshy or very damp soil
a – acid soils
b – basic soils

Results

Table 27 indicates the presence and frequency of the cultivated plant remains. Each of the figures given is the actual frequency of that plant remain, be it a grain or a glume base. Table 28 provides the frequency of occurrence of non-cultivated species. In addition to this, information regarding the ecological preference of each species is also given, albeit in broad ecological groups.

All the samples are Roman in age. Structures X and Y both represent sunken-floored structures and provide the only securely sealed Roman deposits outside Well 1. The remaining deposits had all suffered some degree of plough damage.

It is evident that samples 441 and 442 are the richest in terms of charred plant remains, for both cultigens and non-cultigens. The implications of this with regard to the aims of the study are discussed below. The remaining samples all have some carbonised plant remains present and the significance of these is considered below.

The plant remains

The recognition of economic plants in a sample of charred seeds is normally based on the relative quantities with which seeds of the various species occur and a knowledge of their suitability for food (Jones 1978). Of the material recovered cereal grains and chaff, notably spelt, form the largest single component of the samples, in particular samples 441 and 442. However it is also noted that 50% of the samples have the non-cereal *Bromus secalinus/mollis* present; the significance of this will be discussed below.

Triticum (wheat)

The wheat remains include the grains themselves, fragments of rachis internodes, glume bases and spikelets. These can be divided into spelt wheat (*T. spelta*) and bread wheat (*T. aestivum/compactum*). Only those grains which showed little or no visible signs of distortion and maintained the embryo end were assigned to species. The majority of wheat grains were similar to *T. spelta* and the remainder resembled *T. aestivum/compactum*. There is a group *T. spelta/aestivum* where it was difficult to distinguish between the two. This may be the result of the interfertility of the two species when grown together and which produce grains of indeterminate characteristics (Reynolds 1981).

Although spelt wheat is slightly less productive than ordinary wheat, and possesses the disadvantage of brittle ears from which the true grain cannot be extracted without special mills (Percival 1921), it has many advantages that allow it to compete successfully with other forms of *Triticum*. Spelt will grow on a range of soil types, from the heavier soils associated with bread wheat, to lighter and drier soils (Jones 1981, 106). Its main characteristic and advantage to early farmers is its hardiness to cold, wind, diseases and pests (Jones 1981, 106). In addition to this,

the viability of the grain is retained longest when it is enclosed in the glumes (Percival 1921) and thus it can be stored for some time before use. Spelt was the most important wheat species in Britain during the Roman period. Emmer had been the principal wheat crop during the earlier prehistoric periods, but was gradually replaced by spelt wheat during the 1st millennium BC (Helbaek 1952; Jones 1981).

Hordeum (barley)

The barley remains include the grain, fragments of palea and lemma adherent to the grain and the internodes. As it was not possible to distinguish between six and two row barley it will now be referred to as one unit.

The wild species

The non-cereal species represented at Dalton Parlours are from a range of ecotypes indicative of cultivated ground, waste ground and wet/damp ground. The predominant species are mostly weeds of cultivated land; however, species of damp ground are also present. It might be expected that the seed impurities accidentally gathered in with the grain harvest would be entirely of the habitual weeds of cultivated land (Jones 1978). It is not unusual, however, for plants normally associated with other habitats to occur in small quantities in arable fields, normally as intrusive species or persisting from the vegetation existing before the area was cultivated (Jones 1978). This may account for the presence of seeds of damp ground; if so, it would imply exploitation of land several kilometres from the site in a north and west direction, if not as far as the River Wharfe then to the spring line at 200m, or to what is now Waver Spring Pond.

The most common damp ground species is that of sedge (*Carex* spp.). There were several species of sedge present but none was identified further. Seeds of orache (*Atriplex* spp.) were found throughout and this species is also commonly associated with moist and wet habitats on cultivated ground and/or waste places. The presence of pondweed (*Potamogeton* sp.) and amphibious bistort (*Polygonum amphibium*) is very interesting as both species require either flowing or standing water, neither of which is present in the immediate environs of the site.

The presence of two species that prefer acid soils is also of interest here, these being bristle scirpus (*Isolepis setacea* and jointed rush (*Juncus articulatus*). The former prefers damp places, sometimes among taller herbage in marshy meadows, and the latter wet ground, especially on acid soils preferring meadows or moors which are mown or grazed. As this type of habitat does not appear to be readily accessible to Dalton Parlours it is suggested that these elements were intrusive or that localised soil variation had created suitable pH for the growth of these plants.

The presence of heath grass (*Sieglingia decumbens*) is of interest as it is not found as a weed of arable crops today, although it was in prehistory (Hillman 1981). This perennial is found in acid grasslands and locally on damp base rich soils, such as would be expected in this area at wetter parts of the year. Heath grass has also been used as an indicator of ard cultivation (Hillman 1981). The ard disturbs the soil little, allowing the perpetuation of this weed and its presence at this site may be indicative of ard cultivation.

The high frequency of chess/soft brome (*Bromus secalinus/mollis*) has already been mentioned above. In samples 441 and 442 it is the most plentiful non-cereal, accounting for 37.7% and 28.7% of those samples respectively. It is also present in smaller quantities in the other samples (see Table 28). It has been suggested that this plant was cultivated in antiquity on the basis of its repeated occurrences in archaeological assemblages (Hubbard 1975). It does have some recent history of collection: in the early 20th century its seeds were gathered by Danish farmers when the rye crop failed (Jones 1981), and it has been proposed that it may have been used in a similar way by Roman farmers (Jones 1978). In this instance it seems unlikely that the species was deliberately cultivated as it predominates in what is essentially a waste deposit. However, the mutual exploitation of plants that are now considered to be weeds with 'cereal crops' should not be underestimated for prehistoric deposits where they may have been seen as an economic asset.

Discussion

Samples of carbonised plant remains are not random in composition and thus do not directly represent the prevailing economy. They are biased by numerous factors, notably the type and usage of each plant, and the circumstances under which the sample was carbonised (Dennell 1976). Before discussing the relationship of these data to the economy and environment it is essential to examine, as far as possible, the nature and origin of the plant remains. Although plant remains are present throughout, samples 441 and 442 (Structure X) exhibit the greatest diversity of species and components and will be dealt with first.

In both these samples the ratio of wheat glume bases to wheat grains is high (9.4:1 for sample 442, and 6.7:1 for sample 441; see Table 27 for these and other ratios). In the original plant the ratio would be 1 grain to 1 glume base. This suggests therefore that the deposit represents the residue of the crop cleaning process which was subsequently burnt for fuel. This is supported by the high number of weed seeds present, for example twice as many weed seeds than grain in samples 441 and 442. However, given that this deposit was not in a situation that suggested *in situ* burning, it may be the result of the mixing of several deposits. Both 441 and 442 come from the same context – 4905 – which is a discrete unit; although the exact spatial relationship of the two samples is unknown, the range and frequency of occurrence of species throughout is similar, suggesting some homogeneity.

Examination of the ratio of barley grain to rachis internode reinforces the idea that this context was a fuel residue, where the source of fuel or the material coming into contact with the fire varied. In the original plant the ratio of grain to rachis internode would have been 3:1. In sample 442 it is 1.7:1, indicating more chaff than grain. In 441 the ratio is 3.6:1; this might suggest a cleaned or semi-cleaned crop as there is a higher grain to rachis internode ratio than expected. However for a free-threshing cereal, like barley, it is unlikely that chaff will be found with the grain as it is removed with the straw in the early stages of crop-processing. The situation is different for glume wheats which have the chaff removed when the grain is needed (Hillman 1981). Therefore to find barley chaff and wheat chaff together in the same deposit is unusual and suggests again that the samples represent the residues from crop cleaning that were used as fuel. The deposit has either been mixed at source (in the hearth or oven), or is a result of the cleaning of these structures and the use of one dump for the waste (context 4905). Alternatively the barley may represent a residual field crop whose elements became processed together, resulting in a ratio of barley grain to rachis internode that is similar to the original plant.

The charred plant remains from the samples from other structures do not contribute any more to the understanding of the Roman economy and environment at Dalton Parlours. The ranges of wild and cultivated species present are similar to those found in samples 441 and 442.

The material associated with the carbonised seeds in sample 338 (Structure R) is interesting: it is made up predominantly of large charcoal fragments, perhaps representing fuel of some sort. The seeds found with this charcoal come from cultivated land and disturbed ground and could easily have come from anywhere within and around the site. This does not, however, provide any insight into the function of this structure.

Sample 411 (Structure F) has traces of metallurgy waste products indicative of high temperatures. However further analysis of these products is necessary before any interpretation can be attempted. The charred plant remains from the other samples in this structure (386 and 391) provide no conclusive evidence for function: cereal grains and weeds of arable land are present in both but the frequency of these is too small to allow interpretation. It is suggested that these carbonised remains represent the fortuitous inclusion of cultivated plants as part of the fuel.

The presence of the damp ground species is unexpected for a site that is situated on sloping ground on Magnesian Limestone. However these species are inclusions, predominantly, of samples indicative of crop-processing residues and thus it is suggested that land was being exploited beyond the immediate environs of the site, towards the north and west where surface water exists. Those species indicative of very wet conditions (pondweed and amphibious bistort) are represented by a few seeds, and those of damp acid environs by one seed each. These can therefore only be used to indicate the existence of these types of habitats and not their exploitation. Species such as sedge are more profuse and contribute as much as 25% of some samples (441 and 442). This would suggest the exploitation of an area of marsh ground. Spelt is known for its ability to thrive in a range of conditions and it is unlikely that sowing in fairly moist conditions would be detrimental to productivity.

Acknowledgements

I am indebted to Glynis Jones for help in identifying the plant remains and without whom this report would not have been possible. Also to Mark Beech for assisting in the sorting of the residues and to Pinilla who provided invaluable help.

Part Four
The Assemblage from Well 1

(environmental reports edited by David Berg)

26 Well 1 and its Layers (Figs 114-15)

by Stuart Wrathmell

Introduction

This was one of two wells discovered in the excavations. The other (Well 2, context 4017), at the south-east corner of Structure E, was not excavated below a depth of *c.* 1.5m. Well 1 was, in contrast, fully emptied: it yielded up numerous artefacts, including some of wood and leather, as well as important environmental evidence. On a site which had been almost completely destratified by ploughing, any closed group of finds would be valuable. The well assemblage has added significance because of the quantity and range of the objects. For this reason, data concerning both the contexts and the finds are published together in this fourth part of the report.

Context description

The main portion of the well was in the form of a simple, rock-cut shaft about 2.2m in diameter. The topmost 1.5m had, like the top of Well 2, been cut as a wider 'basin' (Pl. XXXV). This was because the more fragmented surface bedrock would otherwise have eroded into the shaft; the basin was formed to allow a masonry lining to be inserted. Part of this lining survived in Well 2. The basin of Well 1 contained no trace of a lining, but division G, redeposited natural limestone, was probably the material which had backed the revetment. When the stone lining had been

robbed out, its place had been taken partly by division F, a brown soil which overlay G, partly by the now unconfined shaft fill.

The shaft proper was 16m deep. It was excavated as six separate units (H-N), based on changes in the composition of the filling layers. These changes were not invariably clear-cut, and do not necessarily represent discrete events in the process of filling. For these reasons, the catalogue entries for the finds include the recorded depth below datum, as well as the context code. It will be observed that there are some marginal discrepancies in the attribution of codes to depths: these reflect inconsistencies in the site records.

As excavation proceeded, the following divisions were identified:

Divisions H and J

These extended to a depth of about 11.30m below the datum. The material was a continuation of division E: limestone and gritstone building rubble in brown soil. The proportion of stone to soil gradually increased with depth. Below 10.50m there were large fragments of architectural and other worked stone, and very little soil.

Pl. XXXV. Well 1 (5500), facing north-west.
(Photo: S. Wager)

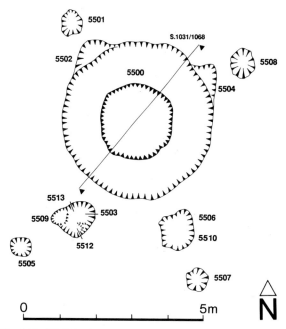

Fig. 114. Well 1: plan.

195

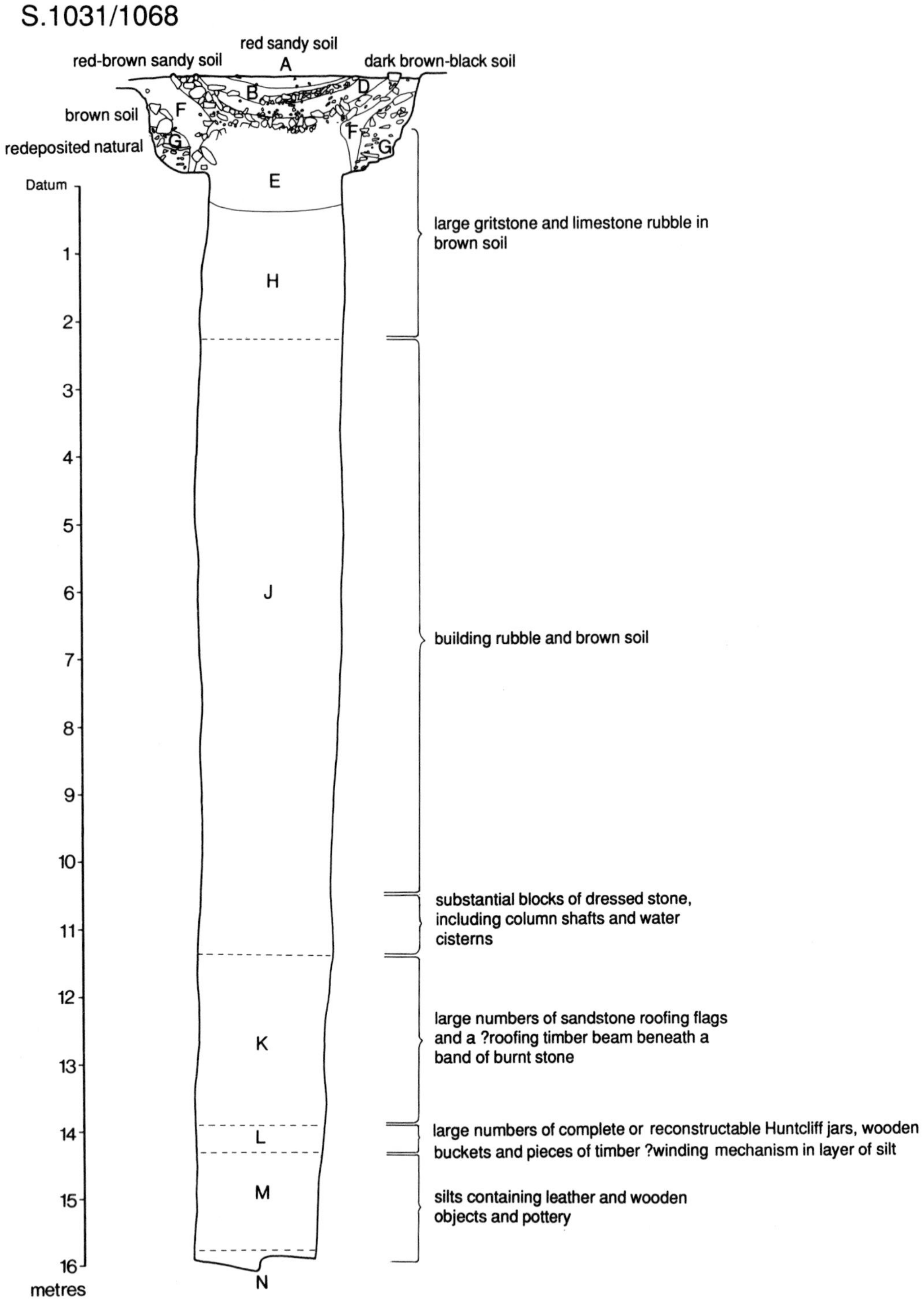

Fig. 115. Well 1: section, showing the depths and composition of the main recording divisions.

Division K

From a depth of about 11.50m below datum there was waterlogging, and consequently preserved timber. A band of burnt stone overlay a deposit of numerous sandstone roofing flags. Below these were deposits of small stone and organic matter.

Division L

The uppermost silt layer began at about 13.90m below datum. It contained many complete or near-complete pottery vessels, and the remains of several iron-bound wooden buckets.

Division M

The lower silt layer was sealed by a lens of sandy material 14.50m below datum. Besides organic material, there were a few large undressed blocks of stone and clay roofing tile (both *tegulae* and *imbrices*).

Division N

The bottom 0.25m of the fill was a very compacted silt layer.

Four pairs of post-holes set around the surface of the well may have supported a wooden superstructure. Equally, a stone well-house could have been robbed out entirely. These possibilities are considered further in the discussion.

Finds from the well

The main elements of the well assemblage have been grouped together here to facilitate comparison and discussion. Some classes of find, for example the leather artefacts, survived nowhere else. In other cases (notably ironwork and pottery) the character of the well groups was very different from that of the collections from the rest of the site: a large proportion of the iron, wooden and pottery objects from the well was related specifically to the drawing of water. The associated environmental evidence is, again, of particular significance for the history of the well, and for documenting the processes of its abandonment.

Some other classes of artefact, for example coins and architectural stonework, were also represented in the well, but are not treated separately here. Where relevant, these objects have been noted in the discussion which concludes this part of the report; they are listed in Appendix 3, pp. 287-9.

27 Ironwork from Well 1 (Figs 116-21)

by Ian R. Scott

The bulk of the ironwork from the well consists of fittings from buckets; these have been classified by function – handles, mounts and hoops – and are catalogued and discussed below. A few of the fittings have been attributed to specific wooden buckets; such attributions are noted in the catalogue entries of both this and the wood report (Chapter 28). Except in the case of Bucket 1 (Fig. 122), the matching of iron fittings and wooden buckets is, however, very tentative, because of the large number of similar vessels represented.

Buckets and fittings

A few complete Roman buckets, and some sets of fittings are known: for example, buckets from Newstead, Scotland (Curle 1911, 310, pl. LXIX) and Silchester, Hampshire (Reading Museum), and sets of fittings – complete or otherwise – from Gadebridge Park villa, Hertfordshire (Manning 1974, 187, fig. 79), Woodcuts, Wiltshire (Pitt-Rivers 1887, 85, pl. XXVII), Northchurch, Hertfordshire, (Neal 1977, 21-2, fig. XIII), and from Kastell Niederberg (*ORL* B, Nr. 2a Kastell Niederberg,

Taf. VII, no. 27) and Heilbronn-Böckingen (Schönberger 1967, 142, Abb. 7, no. 9) in Germany.

Bucket handles (Figs 116-17)

The Woodcuts, Gadebridge Park, and Northchurch buckets all have handles with a loop at the top to take a hook or rope, and to prevent the bucket from slipping and spilling its contents; an elementary precaution on a bucket intended for drawing water from a well. There is a bucket handle from Kastell Okarben in Germany (Schönberger and Simon 1980, 48, Taf. 7, no. B12) with the same feature. The handle of the Niederberg bucket has a hole punched through it, from side to side, and a ring fixed through the hole, to serve the same purpose. This bucket is small, being less than 200mm in diameter.

Surprisingly, loops or rings are absent from the bucket handles in the Dalton Parlours well group, but in a number of cases the handles have grips. There are complete handles, or pieces of handles, for fourteen buckets; of these five have U-sectioned grips, and three definitely have no grips. Of the other six, five have no surviving grips, but may originally have had them; one of these (No. 25) may have had a flattened grip not unlike that on a second handle from Okarben (Schönberger and Simon 1980, 48, Taf. 7, no. B13). The one other handle from Dalton Parlours (No. 34) has a split, or cut, at the top of the handle. The plain handles without grips are readily paralleled: the bucket from Newstead, cited earlier, has a plain semi-circular handle, and there are similar handles without grips from Heilbronn-Böckingen, from Okarben (Schönberger and Simon 1980, 48, Taf. 7, no. B14), and from Straubing, Germany (Walke 1965, 163, Taf. 135, nos 15-16). U-sectioned handles are equally common on Roman sites; the handle of the Silchester bucket, mentioned above, is of this type. For both handles without grips, and those with U-sectioned grips, see the examples catalogued by Manning (1985, 102-3).

21* Bucket handle fragment and mount. Handle of rectangular cross-section tapering from U-sectioned grip towards hooked end; mount with pointed end and one nail hole (see Nos 36-42). L.: handle 220mm, mount 118mm. *5500M (14.8m); SF 1583*

22* Bucket handle. Rectangular cross-section with U-sectioned grip; hook at one end lost. L. 267mm. *5500L (14.1m); SF 1412*

23* Bucket handle. Rectangular cross-section with U-sectioned grip; both hooks lost. L. 317mm. *5500M (14.5m); SF 1579*

24* Bucket handle. Fragment of rectangular cross-section with U-sectioned grip. L. 165mm. *5500M (14.5-15.5m); SF 1735*

25* Bucket handle. Two pieces; rectangular cross-section with hooked ends; no grip, but cross-section flattening out towards centre of arc. L. 195mm and 170mm. *5500M (15.9m); SF 1657*

26* Bucket handle fragment. Rectangular cross-section. L. 173mm. *5500M (15m); SF 1567*

27* Bucket handle. Rectangular cross-section; attributed to Bucket 2 (see p. 206 and Fig. 123). Original l. c. 366mm. *5500K (13.9m); SF 1401a*

28* Bucket handle. Fragment of stout handle; square cross-section; hooked at one end. L. 215mm. *5500M (14.5m); SF 1578*

29* Bucket handle. Square cross-section; attributed to Bucket 1 (see p. 206 and Fig. 122). L. 321mm. *5500K (13.9m); SF 1401b*

30* Bucket handle. Square cross-section without distinct grip; complete. L. 313mm. *5500L (14.1m); SF 1411*

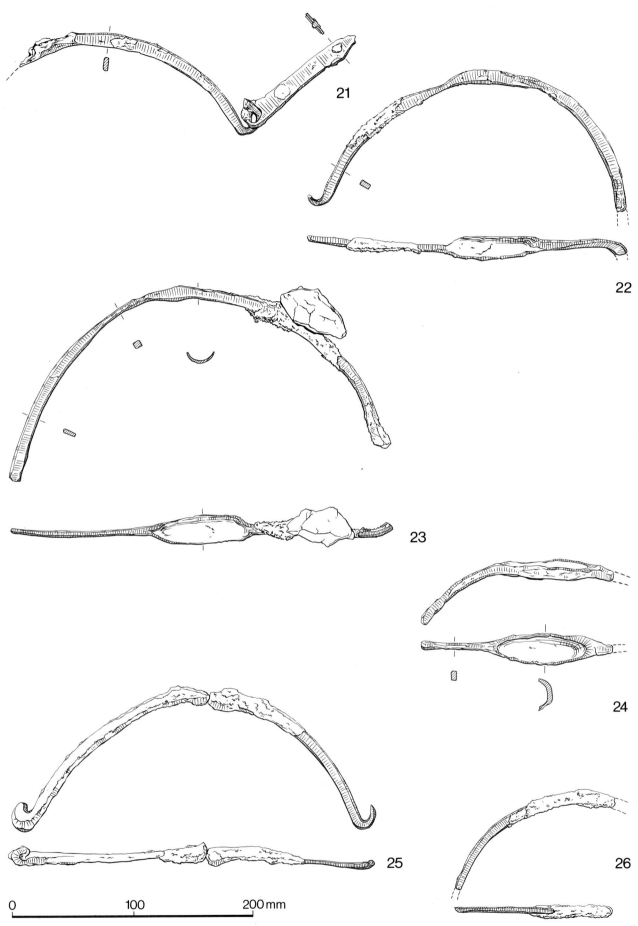

0   100   200 mm

Fig. 116. Iron bucket handles from Well 1 (Nos 21-6). Scale 1:3

198

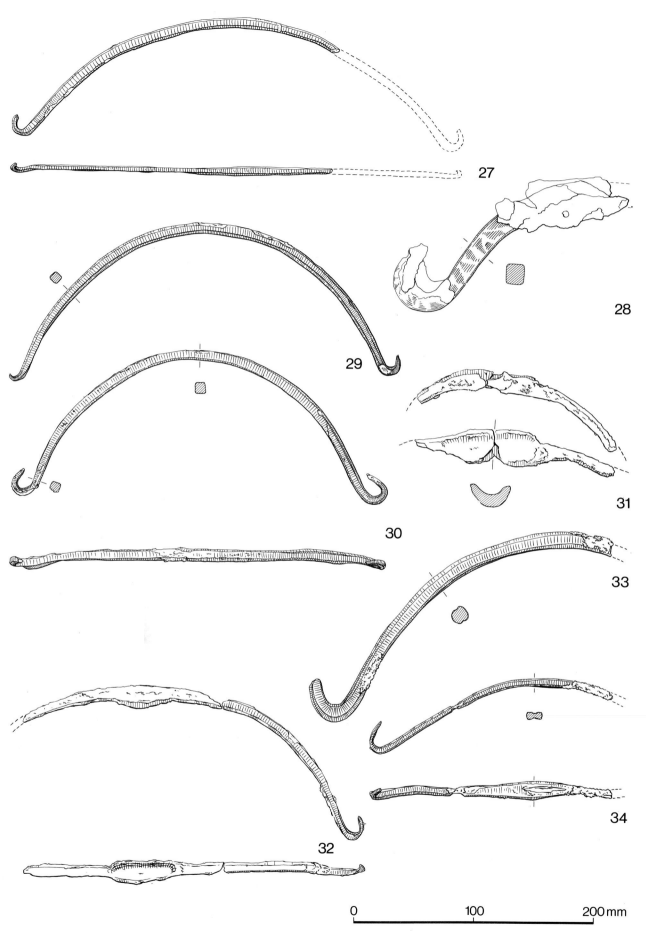

Fig. 117. Iron bucket handles from Well 1 (Nos 27-34). Scale 1:3

0   100   200 mm

31* Bucket handle. Fragment of circular cross-section with U-sectioned grip. L. 175mm. *5500M (15.6m); SF 1595*

32* Bucket handle. Two fragments; circular cross-section, one ending in a hook. L. 155mm (hooked piece) and 166mm. *5500L (14.4m); SF 1414*

33* Bucket handle. Fragment of large handle; sub-rectangular cross-section; hooked at one end. L. 285mm. *5500M (14.6m); SF 1575*

34* Bucket handle. Sub-rectangular cross-section with grip marked by thickening of the handle and a split at its centre; one hook missing. L. 210mm. *5500L (14.4m); SF 1420*

Handle mounts (Fig. 118)

The bucket handle mounts from Dalton Parlours, with a few exceptions, fall into four main categories:

Type 1

Long mounts, which extend the full length of the side of the bucket. They are secured between the bucket sides and the binding hoops, and their bottom ends are rolled over to form a hook, which is caught under the edge of the lowest hoop, or under the bottom of the bucket. Sometimes they are also nailed. There are good examples on the Gadebridge Park villa and Newstead buckets (both cited above), and from Pfünz, Germany (*ORL B*, Nr. 73 Kastell Pfünz, Taf. XVII, no.7), and Verulamium (Manning 1984, 95, fig. 41, no. 75). The hooked end is very clear on the latter examples. There are incomplete examples from Heddernheim, Germany (Fischer 1973, 127, Abb. 39, no. 12) and again from Verulamium (Manning 1972, 178, fig. 66, no. 54). The form is represented in this group by one example (No. 35).

Type 2

Short mounts with pointed ends. Some examples of this type have an elongated point that was bent inwards to fasten into the side of the bucket to help secure the mount (Manning 1985, 102). None of the Dalton Parlours examples can be said certainly to fall into this category, although several have points that may have been broken off through use in this way (Nos 36-38). Another has a point that was not bent (No. 39), and a further example, which is still attached to its stave, clearly was not fixed by its point (No. 41; see Fig. 125). Some examples have only one nail hole near the point, others have a second nail hole at about their mid-point. It is probable that the mounts were fitted under the upper bucket hoop. The loops for the handles, on the Dalton Parlours examples, were formed by punching a hole through the thickened top of the mount. In other examples a thin extension of the mount is rolled over and welded to form the loop. See the mount from Kingsholm, Gloucestershire (Hurst 1985, 38, fig. 15, no. 20), and the examples of both variants from Stockstadt, Germany (*ORL B* Nr. 33 Kastell Stockstadt, Taf. IX, nos 83 and 87, and Taf. X, no. 53). See also the brief discussion by Manning (1985, 102).

Type 3

Short mounts similar in appearance to those with pointed ends but instead rounded at the bottom and fixed by a single nail. The upper end was not nailed to the bucket, but secured between the bucket wall and the top hoop. There

are examples attached to the handle in the Heilbronn-Böckingen hoard cited above.

Related to both Types 2 and 3 is No. 53 which has a more elaborately shaped terminal.

Type 4

Small mounts formed from a bar of circular cross-section, whose ends have been flattened, laid side by side, and welded together. The bottom end is rolled over into a slight hook. Since there are no nail holes, attachment to the bucket would have been by means of the hooked end, which caught under the lower edge of the upper bucket hoop, while the mount itself was sandwiched between the hoop and the bucket side. The evidence of Bucket 1 (p. 206 and Fig. 122) suggests that these mounts may have been used in association with hoops of shallower depth, thicker in cross-section. Certainly, the fact that this form of mount is shorter than the other three types would tend to confirm this view. I am not aware of any parallels for this form of mount.

Long mount (Type 1)

35* Mount. Long, tapering with no obvious nail holes; broken off at bottom end. L. 170mm. *5500M (14.8m); SF 1580a*

Mounts with pointed ends (Type 2)

In addition to those mounts of this type listed below, see also No. 21, a broken handle and mount.

36* Mount. One certain nail hole near point; a very uncertain one, which does not show on an X-ray, near suspension loop; point at lower end is broken. L. 114mm. *5500M (14.5-15.5m); SF 1736*

37* Mount. Squared-off top; one nail hole near point, which is broken off. L. 113mm. *5500M (14.5-15.5m); SF 1582a*

38* Mount. Similar to above, but with enlarged loop for handle; only one nail hole near the point, which is broken. L. 120mm. *5500M (15.5-16.2m); SF 1629*

39* Mount. Similar to above, but larger; point is intact, but not bent. The point may not have been intended for use in that way, because there are two nail holes, one of which is near the point; the other is in the middle of its length. L. 154mm. *5500M (15.5m); SF 1656*

40* Mount. Similar to No. 38, but broken off above the point; no nail holes in the extant portion. Probably of Type 2, but could be Type 3 (see below). L. 95mm. *5500M (14.7m); SF 1488*

41 See Fig. 125: mount with pointed end and squared-off top; still attached to a stave by a nail. This example was never fixed by its point which does not appear to have been elongated; attributed to Bucket 4 (p. 209 and Fig. 125). L. 95mm. *5500L (14.4m); SF 1434di*

42* Mount. Lower end is broken. L. 118mm. *5500M (14.5-15.5m); SF 1590*

Mounts with rounded lower end (Type 3)

43* Mount. Lower end round, with square nail hole; oval hole for handle at the top end; both ends slightly squared off. L. 98mm. *5500M (15.8m); SF 1667*

Mounts of Types 1, 2 or 3

44* Mount. Broken; one nail hole. L. 73mm. *5500M (15.5m); SF 1658*

45* Mount. Broken; no extant nail holes. L. 56mm. *5500L (14.1m); SF 1410*

Short mounts with hooked ends (Type 4)

46* Mount. Bottom end is rolled over into a slight hook; no nail holes. L. 60mm. *5500L (14-14.5m); SF 2018*

47* Mount. As above. L. 52mm. *5500M (15.5-16m); SF 1608*

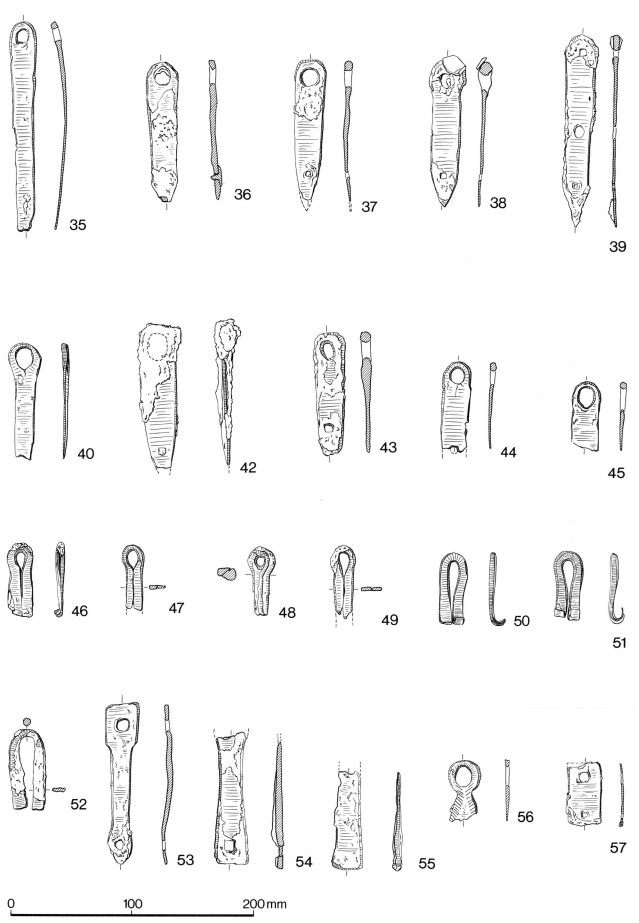

Fig. 118. Iron bucket mounts from Well 1 (Nos 35-40 and 42-57). Scale 1:3

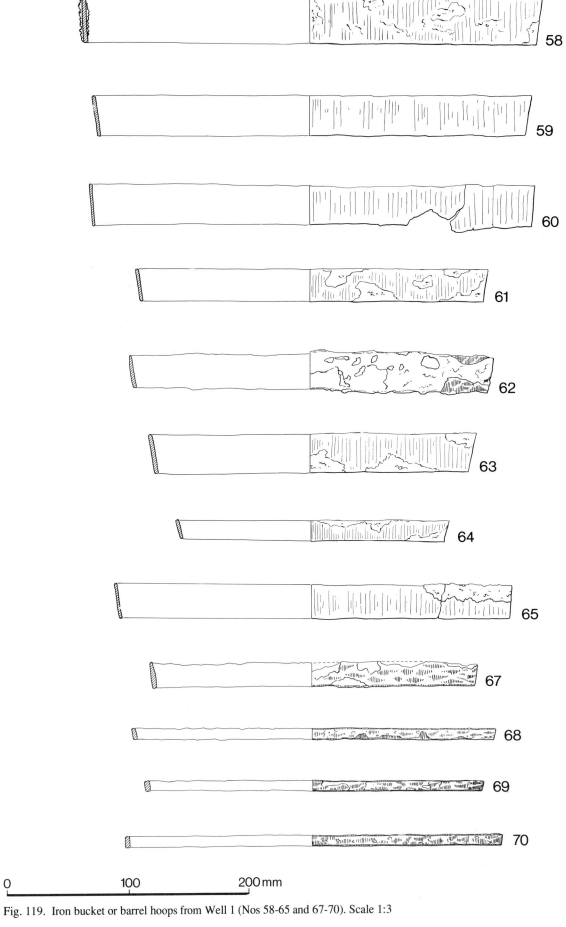

58

59

60

61

62

63

64

65

67

68

69

70

0   100   200 mm

Fig. 119. Iron bucket or barrel hoops from Well 1 (Nos 58-65 and 67-70). Scale 1:3

48* Mount. As above. Found with No. 49. L. 55mm. *5500L (14-14.5m); SF 1513a*

49* Mount. As above. Found with No. 48. L. 59mm. *5500L (14-14.5m); SF 1513b*

50- Pair of mounts. As above; attributed to Bucket 1 (see p. 206 and
51* Fig. 122). L. 58mm and 56mm. *5500K (13.9m); SF 1401c-d*

52* ?Mount. Unwelded, with partly formed hook end; ?unfinished. L. 67mm. *5500L (14.4m); SF 1417*

Miscellaneous other handle mounts

53* Mount. Leaf-shaped lower terminal with nail hole; top is rectangular with hole for the handle. L. 131mm. *5500L (14.3m); SF 1457d*

54* ?Mount. Keyhole shaped, but lacking suspension loop; one nail hole at bottom end. L. 105mm. *5500M (14.8m); SF 1498c*

55* ?Mount. As above, but with no evidence of a nail hole; chased decoration, or impression of leaf on its surface; lacks a loop. L. 79mm. *5500L (14.4m); SF 1422*

56* Mount. Incomplete, but with well-made loop. Exact form unclear, but both loop and broken plate are decorated with hatched lines chased into the metal. This is comparable in form to two objects in the Carlingwark hoard in Scotland (Piggott 1955, 32-3, nos C11-12). Furthermore, one of these (C11) has similar decoration to our object; it was riveted to another decorated plate with three arms. There is a similar object from Verulamium (Manning 1984, 95, fig. 41, no. 77). It was possibly attached to a metal vessel rather than a wooden bucket. L. 48mm. *5500 (sieving); SF 1753*

57* Mount. Short; rectangular with square nail hole, and a hole to take bucket handle. L. 55mm. *5500M (15.5m); SF 1619a*

Bucket or barrel hoops (Fig. 119)

58* Bucket, or barrel hoop. W. 40mm; diam. *c.* 385mm. *5500M (14.8m); SF 1658a*

59* Bucket, or barrel hoop. In two pieces. W. *c.* 33mm; diam. *c.* 365mm. *5500M (14.9m); SF 1585a-b*

60* Bucket, or barrel hoop. Four fragments. W. 32mm; diam. *c.* 365mm. *5500M (14.8m); SF 1580b-e*

61* Bucket hoop. Attributed to Bucket 5 (see p. 211 and Figs 127-8). W. 27mm; diam. *c.* 290mm. *5500M (15.5m); SF 1632c*

62* Bucket hoop. In two pieces; attributed to Bucket 5 (see p. 211 and Figs 127-8). W. 30mm; diam. *c.* 295mm. *5500M (15.5m); SF 1632a-b*

63* Bucket hoop. W. 32mm; diam. *c.* 272mm. *5500M (14.8m); SF 1501c*

64* Bucket hoop. Attributed to Bucket 4 (see p. 209 and Figs 125-6). W. 17mm; diam. *c.* 230mm. *5500L (14.4m); SF 1434*

65* Bucket hoop. Two pieces. W. 28mm; diam. *c.* 330mm. *5500M (14.8m); SF 1580f-g*

66 Bucket hoop fragment. W. *c.* 28mm. *5500M (14.5-15.5m); SF 1568a*

67* Bucket hoop. Three fragments. W. *c.* 19mm; diam. *c.* 270mm. *5500M (14.5-15.5m); SFs 1574a-b; 1568b*

68* Bucket hoop fragment. Narrower than all other hoops except those of Bucket 1; attributed to Bucket 2 (see p. 206 and Fig. 123). W. 10mm; diam. *c.* 300mm. *5500L (14m); SF 1394*

69- Pair of bucket hoops. Attributed to Bucket 1 (see p. 206 and Fig.
70* 122). The narrower thicker hoops are probably used with Type 4 mounts. W. 10mm; diam. 280mm and 310mm. *5500K (13.9m); SF 1401*

71 Bucket hoop fragment. W. *c.* 27mm. *5500M (14.5-15.5m); SF 1582b*

72 Bucket hoop fragment. W. *c.* 35mm. *5500M (15.6m); SF 1599*

73 Bucket hoop fragment. W. *c.* 20mm. *5500M (14.5-15.5m); SF 1732*

Other finds from the Well (Figs 120-21)

74* Sledgehammer, or block anvil of octagonal cross-section. The object tapers, and has an eye, or punching hole running through it from side to side. Both ends show considerable signs of battering, but it is especially marked at the narrower lower end. There are three unusual features that would suggest that the object is not an anvil. Firstly, the punching hole does not run down from the face. Secondly, both ends are heavily battered; wider end would have been the anvil face, while narrower end would have been set into the anvil block. Thirdly, stem lacks the step often found on anvils. See Manning (1985, 1-3, fig. 1) for a discussion of anvils and references. It is more probable that the object is a large sledgehammer head. See the large head from Pompeii (Gaitzsch 1980, 348, Taf. 14, no. 66 and 15, no. 66) L. *c.* 160mm. *5500 (depth not recorded); SF 2020*

75* Heavy mason's pick. Rectangular cross-section, tapering to a point at either end. Manning type 1, with paired spike-blades (Manning 1985, 30, fig. 6). The object curves less than one might have expected in longitudinal section. L. 350mm. *5500M (15.7m); SF 1669*

76* Spade sheath. Straight mouth and deeply grooved arms. Conforms to Manning type 2A (Manning 1970, 21-4; 1985, 44-7). L. 190mm. *5500M (16.1m); SF 1626*

77* ?Small reaping hook. Socket with broken blade. See in particular the examples from London and from Cranborne Chase, Dorset (Manning 1985, 53-8, especially nos F49 and F52). L. 45mm. *5500L (14- 14.5m); SF 1512*

78* ?Prong. Square cross-section, with flattened end opposite point. Possibly from a hay rake, but comparison with surviving examples shows that the identification is uncertain, for these all have a thin tang, not a flattened end. See the discussion and the examples listed by Rees (1979, 484 and 737-40, figs 225-6). L. 83mm. *5500L (14-14.5m); SF 1431*

79* Ox-goad, with end of rod *in situ*. Found with No. 80. For parallels see the examples from Verulamium (Manning 1972, 170, fig. 62, no. 21; 1984, 87, fig. 38, nos 17-18), from Vindolanda, Northumbria (Jackson 1985, 138, fig. 49, no. 41), and from Heddernheim (Fischer 1973, 134, fig. 45, no. 10). See discussion and examples listed by Rees (1979, 7-9, 294-302, fig. 73). L. 27mm. *5500M (14-15.5m); SF 1680*

80 Ox-goad, or spiral ferrule, with wood in socket. Found with No. 79. L. 20mm. *5500M (14-15.5m); SF 1680a*

81* ?Spatula with twisted stem. L. 90mm. *5500L (14-14.5m); SF 1514*

82* Knife. Curved blade with upturned tip, tanged. Manning type 23 (Manning 1985, 116, fig. 29, no. 23). L. 192mm. *5500K (12.9m); SF 1385*

83* Knife. Uncertain form, blade incomplete; handle or tang, decorated with twisting, and now covered in an ?organic material. The twisted decoration suggests a handle rather than a tang. Twisted handles are quite common. See the examples from Fishbourne, West Sussex (Cunliffe 1971b, 134, fig. 60, no. 43), and from Silchester, Hampshire (Manning 1985, 119, no. Q87). L. 84mm. *5500L (14-14.5m); SF 1429*

84* ?Knife blade. No surviving tang; blade form is uncertain. L. 95mm. *5500J (4.4m); SF 1281*

85* Tethering ring, or ?door knocker. Consisting of plate shaped like a fleur-de-lys with rolled over loop at the end to which is attached a large ring, of circular cross-section; there are nail holes in the plate. No exact parallel is known to the writer, therefore the identification is uncertain. The only object comparable in shape and size, though not in function, is the drop-hinge plate from the Brampton (Cumberland) hoard (Manning 1966, 29-30, no. 38). L. of plate 267mm; diam. of ring 135mm. *5500M (15.9m); SF 1603*

86* L-shaped lift key. Damaged bit; otherwise well preserved with decorative nicks around ring and upper part of stem. Attached to a decorated bronze strip crudely rolled into a ring. This is better made than is usually the case with iron lift keys, although this may be a reflection of its state of preservation. There is a neatly made L-shaped lift key from Straubing, Germany (Walke 1965, 158, Taf.

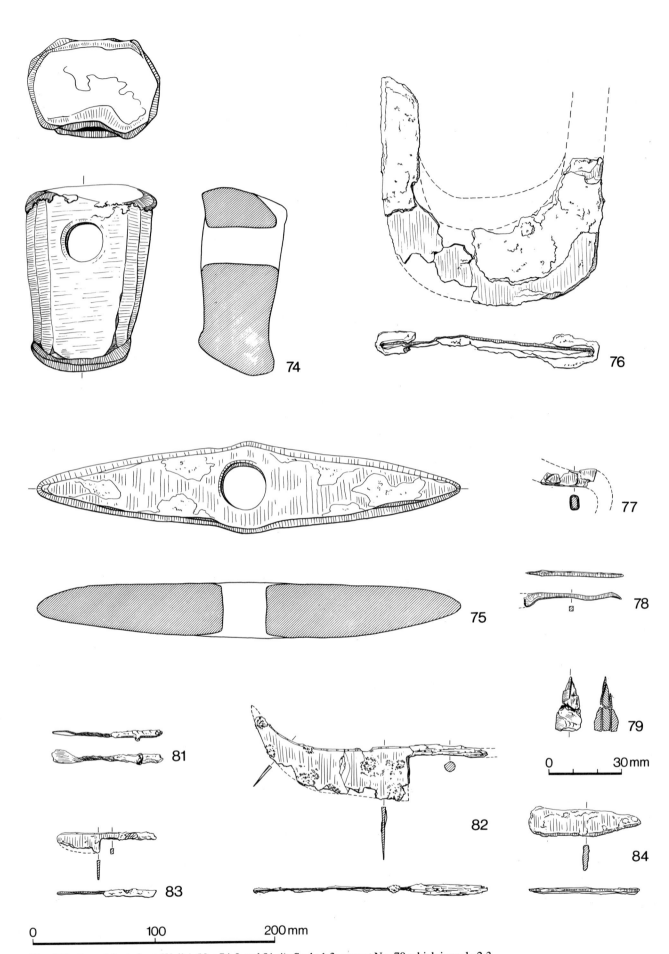

Fig. 120. Iron objects from Well 1 (Nos 74-9 and 81-4). Scale 1:3, except No. 79 which is scale 2:3

204

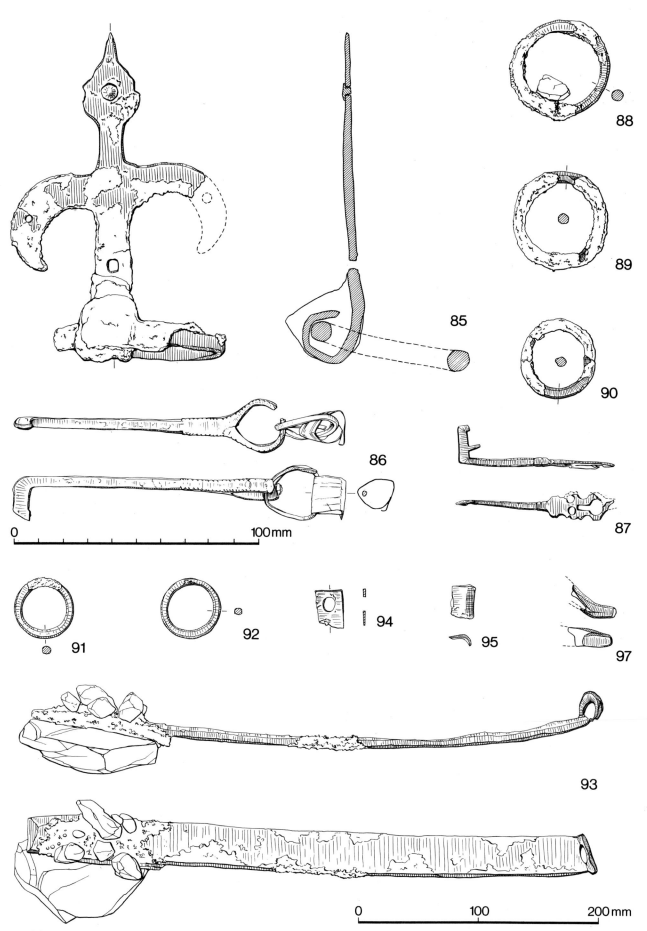

Fig. 121. Iron objects from Well 1 (Nos 85-95 and 97). Scale 1:3, except No. 86 which is scale 2:3

122, no. 9; see also Manning 1985, 90-92, fig. 25, nos 2-3). L. 108mm. *5500L (14.2m); SF 1405*

87* L-shaped lift key. Bit with two teeth, and damaged ornate handle with holes cut through it. Unusually elaborate handle for a lift key, with no parallel known to the writer. L. 135mm. *5500M (14.7m); SF 1576*

88* Ring of circular cross-section. Diam. 85mm. *5500M (14.5m); SF 1462*

89* Ring of circular cross-section. Diam. 80mm. *5500M (15.5m); SF 1664*

90* Ring of circular cross-section. Diam. 65mm. *5500L (14.1m); SF 1418*

91* Ring of circular cross-section. Diam. 50mm. *5500M (14.9-15.5m); SF 1596*

92* Ring of sub-rectangular cross-section. Diam. 48mm. *5500 (sieving); SF 1729*

93* Strip of rectangular cross-section, with one end bent and pierced; possibly binding. L. 470mm. *5500M (14.4m); SF 1465*

94* Binding fragment. Consisting of a broken rectangular sheet pierced by a large nail hole. Found with No. 95. L. 32mm. *5500M (14-15.5m); SF 1684a*

95* Binding fragment. Consisting of a strip bent along one edge. Found with No. 94. L. 28mm. *5500M (14-15.5m); SF 1684b*

96 Bar. Small rolled over loop at one end. L. 135mm. *5500M (14.3m); SF 1464*

97* Bar. Broken fragment that has been bent and welded. L. 43mm. *5500M (14-15m); SF 1619*

28 Wooden Finds (Figs 122-41)

By Carole A. Morris with species identifications by Allan Hall

A large collection of wooden coopered buckets with iron fittings was found in the waterlogged silts and organic layers of the well. A few of the buckets are complete (or nearly complete), while others survive only as one or two fragments, but they represent the largest associated group of Roman wooden buckets yet to be found in Britain. The waterlogged levels in the well also preserved other wooden objects including lathe-turned cups and a plate, pegs, stakes, beams and offcuts, a tally stick, a possible writing tablet fragment and a series of objects (Nos 48-57) which were originally termed 'yokes' and are now interpreted as part of the lifting mechanism connected with the buckets.

Fragments of at least 97 (and possibly over 100) vertical bucket staves were found at depths ranging between 13.9-15.8m below the well datum point. The staves appear to be from at least sixteen different buckets (Nos 1-16) which are represented by complete staves, and the additional incomplete fragments (Nos 17-28) could belong to these sixteen or to further vessels. Also found between these levels were fragments of probably sixteen different circular vessel bases (Nos 29-44) and additional fragments (Nos 45-7) could well belong to any of these. These sixteen bases are in addition to the five bases

already associated with Buckets 1 to 5, thus suggesting that there could have been as many as 21 vessels in the well. The material is very fragmentary, however, and since some fragments of Nos 29-44 could be from the same vessel base, it is possible that the final number is nearer the sixteen suggested by the staves.

The surviving iron bucket fittings also suggest that the number of vessels in the well was less than 21. There appear to be fragments of at least fourteen individual bucket handles. This number of buckets would also have had at least 28 iron hoops and 28 handle mounts, but there is nowhere near this number surviving, showing the incomplete nature of the archaeological remains. It seems reasonable to suggest, therefore, that the stave evidence is probably closer to the actual number at sixteen vessels.

An attempt is made here to group staves or base fragments together by comparing and contrasting their timber form (radially split or tangentially split/sawn), species, dimensions, and worked features such as basal grooves and edge chamfers. This method is very critical and detailed and should have resulted in pieces being placed with others most likely to be from the same vessel. The staves, bases and iron fittings were, however, found mainly in unrelated groups and jumbled heaps; they could not be grouped exhaustively or accurately. For future research, therefore, information recorded about the wooden objects includes description, timber form, species (where known), dimensions and worked features.

This report contains, at various places, suggestions as to which iron hoops or handles might have belonged to a group of staves/bases. These identifications must be viewed as very tentative indeed because of the lack of corroborative evidence.

The complete buckets (Figs 122-8)

1* Stave-built bucket. Thirteen staves and circular base. Vessel reconstructed. Staves wider at top, bucket therefore tapered from top to bottom; rounded squared top and bottom edges; croze groove 25mm above bottom edge for base to fit into. Iron stains on external surface of staves show the positions of two iron hoops (Fig. 119, Nos 69-70) which must have been shrunk onto the staves as there are no rivet holes through either the iron bands or the staves; complete iron handle (Fig. 117, No. 29) with square cross-section and simple hooked ends fastened through holes in two iron mounts (Fig. 118, Nos 50-51); these are sandwiched between the upper ends of two opposite staves and the upper iron band, and their lower ends terminate in hooks which loop under the iron band (see also p. 203). H. (not including handle) 270mm; diam. (top) 290mm; diam. (bottom) 265mm; w. (widest stave top) 91mm; w. (widest stave bottom) 51mm; th. 14mm. *Abies alba* (silver fir). *5500K (13.9m); SF 1401b*

2* Stave-built bucket. Many fragments of eleven or twelve staves, and at least twelve fragments of circular one-piece base. All pieces appear to have been made from radially split timber. Staves are wider at the top, vessel therefore tapered from top to bottom; staves have squared upper edges and a sloping chamfer cut across their lower edges; shallow U-shaped croze groove 2-3mm deep, 2-3mm wide; most staves are curved in cross-section thus displaying the cooper's technique of shaping staves by hollowing on the inside and backing on the outside; some of these staves have tool marks on their internal surfaces where they have been hollowed with a round shave. Base is plano-convex in cross-section with very smoothly shaved edges sloping to point. Several iron fittings were found at a similar depth to this group of wooden staves and base fragments and could be part of the same vessel. These are a handle for a vessel

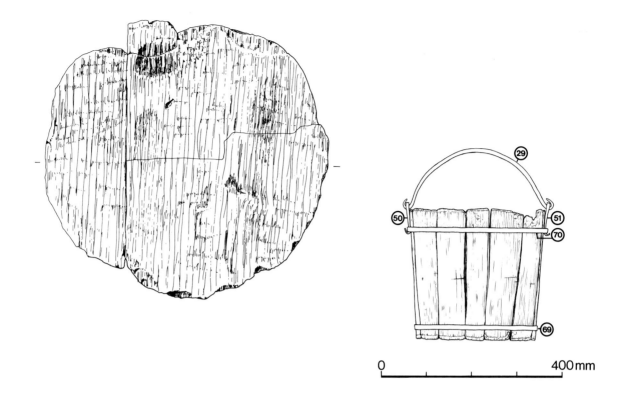

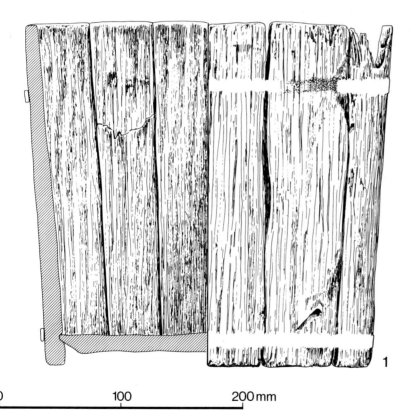

Fig. 122. Wooden bucket (No. 1). Scale 1:3

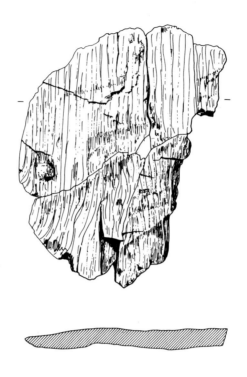

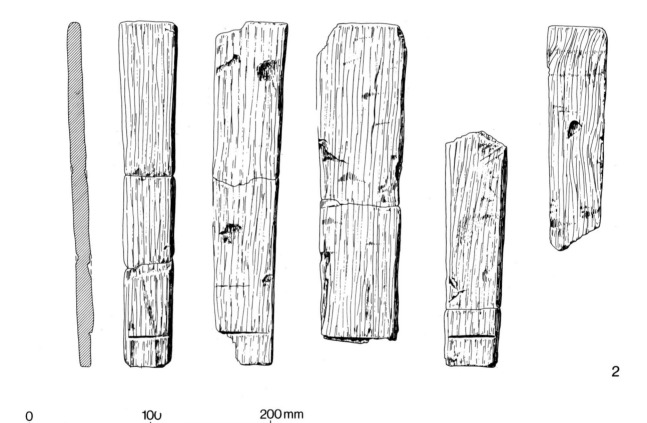

0   100   200 mm

Fig. 123. Wooden bucket (No. 2). Scale 1:3

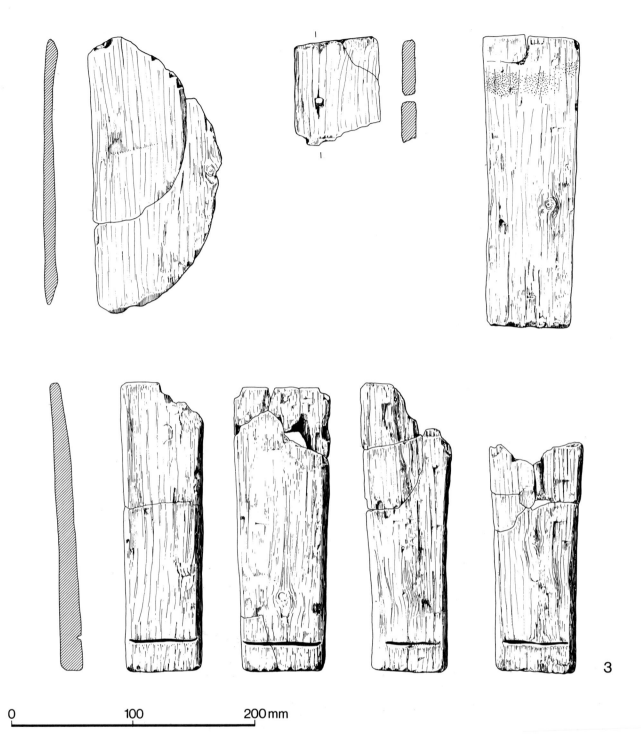

Fig. 124. Wooden bucket (No. 3). Scale 1:3

up to *c*. 340mm wide (Fig. 117, No. 27), and a hoop between 270-340mm diam. (Fig. 119, No. 68). H. 277mm; w. (widest stave top) 74mm; w. (widest stave bottom) 68mm; th. 11-15mm; th. (base) 14mm. *Acer pseudoplatanus* (European sycamore). *5500K (13.9m); SF 1402*

3* Stave-built bucket. Fragments of six staves (SFs 1423b, c, e, and f, 1425 and 1434a) and one half of a two-piece circular base (SF 1423a). All pieces are tangentially sawn/split timber. Staves are wider at the top, bucket therefore tapered from top to bottom; top and bottom edges are squared; deep V-sectioned croze groove 24-6mm above bottom edge; most staves show marked hollowing on the inside which has left top of stave much thinner than bottom. Semi-circular base with edges chamfered on one side only; very worn. H. 235mm; w. (widest stave top) 80mm; w. (widest stave bottom) 65mm; th. 8-20mm; diam. (base) 250-60mm. Base:

Quercus sp., oak; staves: *Alnus* sp. (alder); one *Quercus* sp. (oak). *5500L (14.3-14.4m); SFs 1423a-c, e-f, 1425 and 1434a*

4* Stave-built bucket. Thirteen staves and one-piece circular base. All made from tangentially sawn/split timber. All staves are wider at top, therefore vessel would have tapered from top to bottom; staves have rounded squared rim edges; V-sectioned croze groove 2mm wide, 18-19mm above bottom edge. One stave (SF 1434k) narrows from top width of 31mm to only 7mm at the bottom; this stave was one used by the cooper to make the bucket's staves fit accurately in the diameter required. Iron stains on the external surface of all staves show the original position of two iron hoops, probably 26mm and 17-18mm wide; one of these survives (Fig. 119, No. 64, 230mm diameter, 17mm wide). One stave (SF 1434dii) has iron handle mount 96mm long (No. 41, in two fragments) with squared upper end perforated by circular hole 9mm diameter for the end of

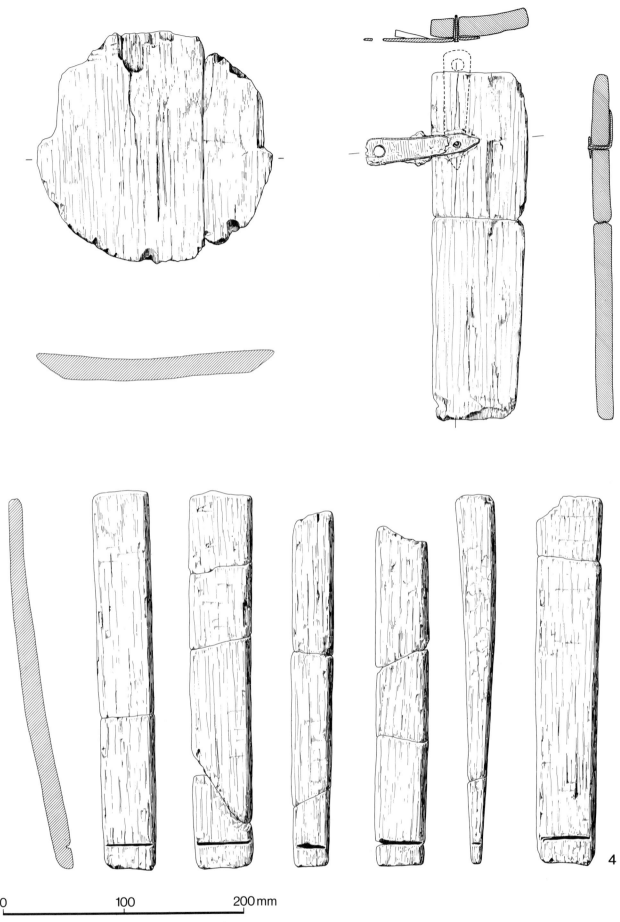

0   100   200 mm

Fig. 125. Wooden bucket (No. 4, part). Scale 1:3

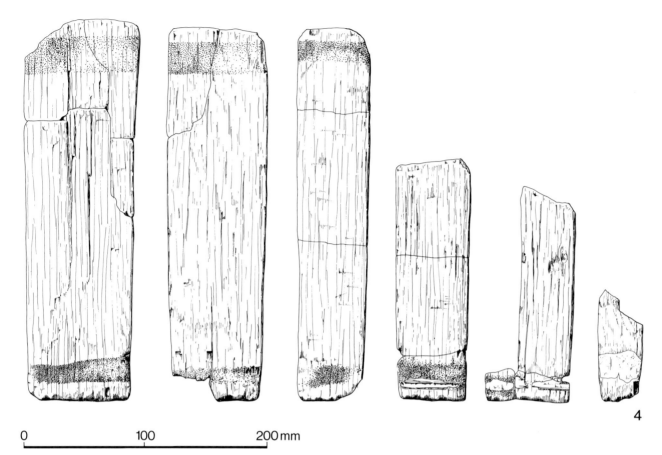

0   100   200mm

Fig. 126. Wooden bucket (No. 4, part). Scale 1:3

the bucket handle, and pointed lower end where it is fixed to the stave by an iron nail; the mount has slipped through 90° from its original position. H. 305mm; w. (widest stave top) 82mm; w. (widest stave bottom) 70mm; th. 14mm; diam. (base) 190-200mm; th. (base) 18mm. All *Quercus* sp. (oak). *5500L (14.4m); SF 1434b-p*

5*   Stave-built bucket. The twelve staves are all wider at top, therefore vessel would have tapered from top to bottom; rim edges squared; deep U-shaped croze groove; staves are hollowed on inside at top and are therefore much thicker at bottom. One stave has a rounded depression in its upper edge and a rivet hole below this suggesting that it originally had a handle mount with the handle rubbing the depression. All staves have iron stains on external surface showing position of two wide iron bands; these iron bands both survive (Fig. 119, Nos 61-62) and are 27mm and 30mm wide, and 290mm and 295mm in diameter respectively; latter is penannular, and the broken fragments still adhere to the widest stave. The one-piece base found with these staves is only 209mm diameter, and cannot be part of this bucket; a complete base of appropriate diameter, found at a similar depth, is No. 40 (see below); it could well be the base for this bucket. H. 277mm; w. (widest stave top) 115mm; w. (widest stave bottom) 92mm; th. 14-20mm; diam. (base) 209 x 205mm; th. (base) 15mm. Base: *Fraxinus* sp. (ash); Staves: *Abies alba* (silver fir). *5500M (15.5m); SF 1632*

Bucket staves and bases (Figs 129-34)

6*   Stave-built bucket. Ten staves, all fragmentary, but some surviving complete. All tangentially split/sawn timber. Staves are slightly wider at the top, indicating vessel probably tapered slightly from top to bottom; croze groove 26mm above bottom edge. One stave has iron rivet 95mm below top edge, probably from handle mount (as No. 4). H. 290mm; w. (widest stave) 82mm; th. 10-15mm. *Quercus* sp. (oak). *5500L (14.3-14.4m); SFs 1482b-f and 1484*

7*   Bucket stave in two fragments. Probably made from radially split timber. Tapers from top to bottom; shallow, U-shaped croze groove

15mm from bottom edge. H. 238mm; w. (top) 57mm; w. (bottom) 38mm; th. 14mm. *Quercus* sp. (oak). *5500M (14.6m); SF 1509*

8*   Two bucket staves. Probably from same vessel. Tangentially split/sawn timber. Staves taper from top to bottom; squared top and bottom edges; squared croze groove; H. 232mm; w. (top) 41mm; th. 9mm: h. 239mm; w. (top) 58mm; th. 11mm. Both *Quercus* sp. (oak). *5500L (14.3m); SF 1457a-b*

9*   Two bucket staves. Probably from same vessel. Both radially split timber. SF 1423g tapers from top to bottom; has squared rim edge and is broken across croze groove. Staining on external surface shows that upper iron hoop was 20mm below rim edge and 25mm wide. L. 260mm; w. (top) 80mm; w. (bottom) 68mm; th. 11mm (SF 1423g). *Quercus* sp. (oak). *5500L (14.1-14.3m); SFs 1423g and 1450*

10* Four bucket staves. Probably from same vessel. Radially split timber. Staves taper from top to bottom; squared top edges; three staves have each two croze grooves cut 20mm and 35mm above bottom edge, suggesting that either the bucket base needed to be reseated and a fresh groove was cut, or that the cooper made a mistake when he cut one groove and had to cut another at the time the bucket was first assembled. This is not uncommon in vessel staves although the only comparable ones are from medieval levels, for example at Dublin, Perth and Exeter (Morris 1984, fig. 103, C176iii and C185iii and fig. 117, C341). H. 248mm; w. (widest top) 61mm; w. (widest bottom) 45mm; th. 9-11mm (SF 1498b). *Pinus* sp. (pine). *5500M (14.9m); SFs 1498b and 1572a-c*

11* Bucket stave. Very narrow; tapers from top to bottom; top edge rounded squared; V-sectioned croze groove 13mm above bottom edge. H. 225mm; w. (top) 22mm; w. (bottom) 13mm; th. 7mm. *Pinus* sp. (pine). *5500M (14.6m); SF 1500a*

12* Bucket stave, complete. Possibly two other fragments from same vessel, although this is not definite; croze grooves 18-22mm above bottom edge. H. 230mm; w. (top) 24mm; th. 10-13mm. *Fraxinus* sp. (ash). *5500M (15m); SFs 1572d and f*

13* Bucket stave. Wider at top than bottom; top edge slopes slightly to one side; shallow, V-sectioned croze groove. Iron stains on

211

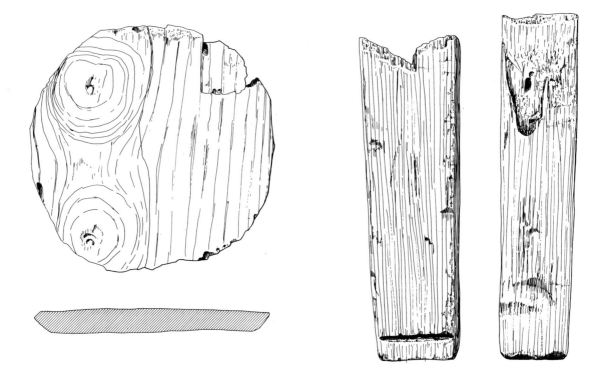

5

0   100   200 mm

Fig. 127. Wooden bucket (No. 5, part). Scale 1:3

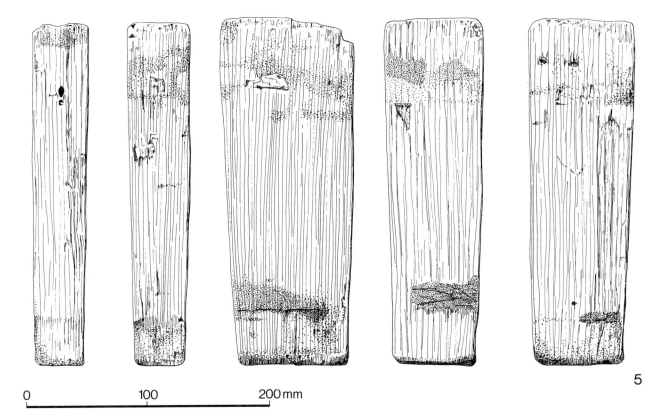

5

0   100   200 mm

Fig. 128. Wooden bucket (No. 5, part). Scale 1:3

external surface near top and bottom show positions of original iron bands *c.* 30mm wide. H. 237mm; w. (top) 46mm; w. (bottom) 35mm; th. 10mm. *Quercus* sp. (oak). *5500M (14.8m); SF 1480*

14* Bucket stave. Tangentially sawn/split timber. Tapers from top to bottom; croze groove above bottom edge. H. 269mm; w. (top) 80mm; th. 14mm. *Quercus* sp. (oak). *5500L (14.4m); SF 1482a*

15* Fragments of two bucket staves, one complete. Probably from same vessel. Tangentially sawn/split timber. More or less parallel-sided; squared top edge; croze groove above bottom edge. H. 169mm; w. (top) 64mm; th. 13mm (SF 1483a). *Quercus* sp. (oak); *Fraxinus* sp. (ash). *5500L (14.4m); SFs 1483a and g*

16* Fragments of three staves, one complete. Probably from same vessel. Tangentially split/sawn timber. More or less parallel-sided; deep squared U-shaped croze groove (SF 1483b); H. 149mm; w. 70mm; th. 18mm (SF 1483b). *Alnus* sp. (alder). *5500L (14.4m); SF 1483b-d*

17* Fragment of lower end of bucket stave (not from Nos 3 or 9). Croze groove 5mm wide, 23mm above bottom edge. L. 112mm; w. 65mm; th. 13mm. *Alnus* sp. (alder). *5500L (14.3m); SF 1423d*

18* Fragment of upper end of bucket stave. Tangentially split/sawn timber. Parallel-sided. L. 73mm; w. 80mm; th. 10mm. *Alnus* sp. (alder). *5500L (14.3m); SF 1457c*

19 Fragment of lower end of bucket stave. Broken above croze groove. L. 38mm; w. 38mm; th. 16mm. *Quercus* sp. (oak). *5500L (14.5m); SF 1518a*

20 Fragment of lower end of bucket stave (not from same vessel as No. 19). Broken above croze groove. L. 42mm; w. 35mm; th. 16mm. *Quercus.* sp. (oak). *5500L (14.5m); SF 1518b*

21 Fragment of lower end of very thick bucket stave (not from same vessels as Nos 19 or 20). Radially split timber. Faceting marks on surfaces from ?axe. L. 115mm; w. 40mm; th. 30mm. *Acer* sp. (maple). *5500L (14.5m); SF 1518c*

22 Bucket stave fragment. Top and bottom edges missing. L. 84mm; w. 40mm; th. 10mm. Unknown species. *5500L (14.5m); SF 1503a*

23 Bucket stave fragment. Top and bottom edge missing. L. 115mm; w. 28mm; th. 9mm. Unknown species. *5500M (14.6m); SF 1499b*

24 Three bucket stave fragments. One has trace of croze groove; one has possible top edge. Th. 10mm. *Quercus* sp. (oak). *5500M (14.7m); SF 1635a-c*

25 Two bucket stave fragments. Tangentially sawn/split timber. No top or bottom edge survives; wider at one end (probably top). L. 140mm; w. 51mm; th. 16mm. Unknown species. *5500M (14.9m); SF 1498a*

26 Fragment of upper end of bucket stave. Tapers towards bottom. L. 99mm; w. 49mm; th. 10mm. Unknown species. *5500M (14.9m); SF 1526a*

27 Fragment of upper end of bucket stave. Rounded squared top edge; broken at side and across middle. L. 92mm; w. 29mm; th. 9mm. *Pinus* sp. (pine). *5500M (15.5m); SF 1654b*

28* Fragment of lower end of large bucket stave. Tangentially sawn/split timber. Basal groove was either cut with a croze or sawn. L. 101mm; w. 92mm; th. 23mm. *Fraxinus* sp. (ash). *5500M (15.6m); SF 1600a*

29* Cant stave of circular piece-built bucket base. Tangentially split/sawn timber. Curved edges chamfered on one side only. Diam. (recon.) *c.* 220mm; th. 12mm. *Quercus* sp. (oak). *5500L (14.3m); SF 1451*

30* Eleven conjoining fragments of circular one-piece bucket base. Tangentially sawn timber. Curved edges chamfered on one side only; edges now very fragmentary. Diam. (recon.) *c.* 220mm; th. 18mm. *Quercus* sp. (oak); 13 growth rings per 20mm. *5500L (14.4m); SF 1435*

31* Semi-circular cant stave of circular two-piece bucket base. Curved edges are irregularly chamfered on both sides; straight edge is cut smooth and flat; Diam. 225mm; th. 10mm. *Abies alba* (silver fir). *5500M (15.8m); SF 1615b*

32* Semi-circular cant stave of circular two-piece bucket base. Curved edge has steep chamfer on one side and very slight small chamfer on the other; latter side is probably underside of bucket since it has many blade cuts in its surface which do not carry over onto the small chamfer and which were probably made when base was *in situ* (with bucket turned upside down). Diam. 227mm; th. 24mm. *Quercus* sp. (oak). *5500M (15.8m); SF 1663*

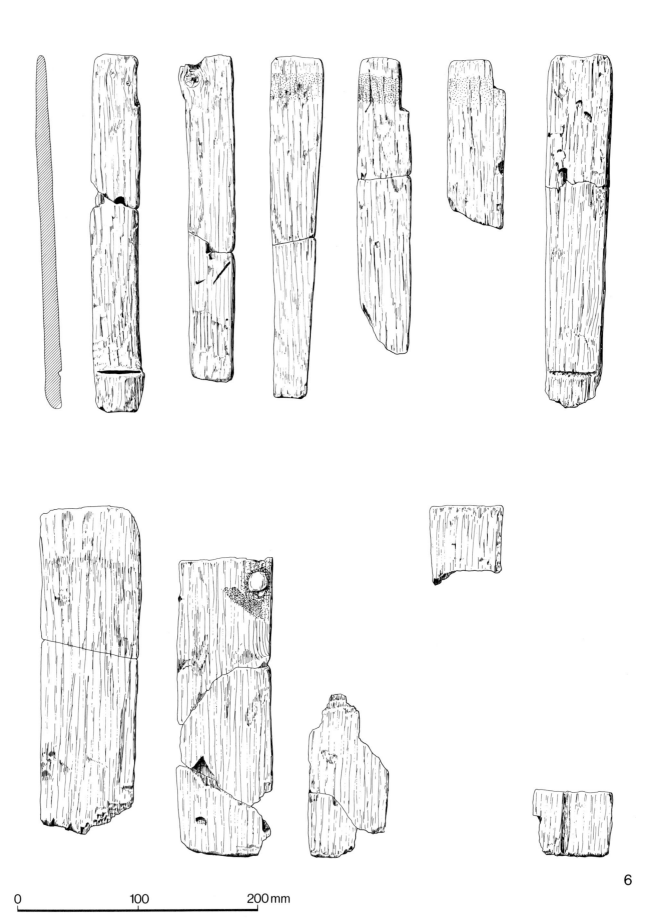

0   100   200 mm

6

Fig. 129. Wooden bucket (No. 6). Scale 1:3

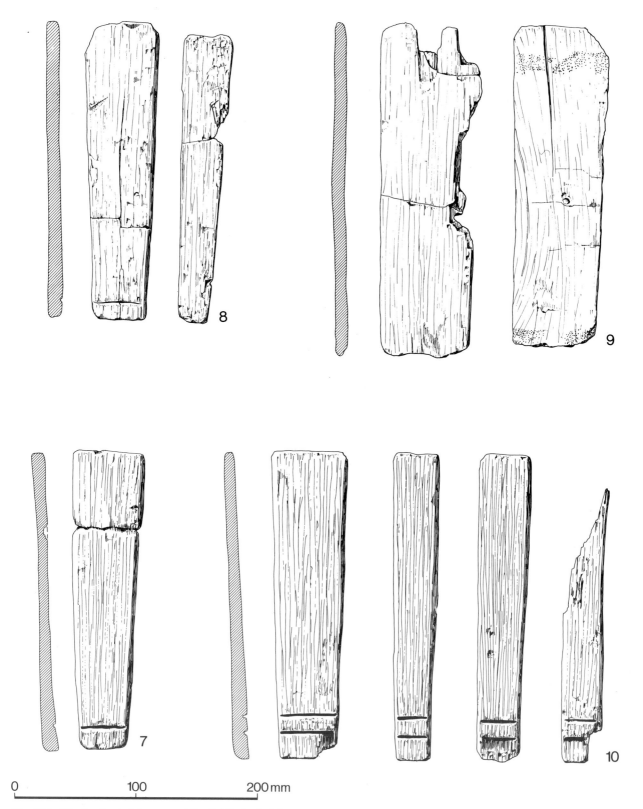

0   100   200 mm

Fig. 130. Wooden bucket fragments (Nos 7-10). Scale 1:3

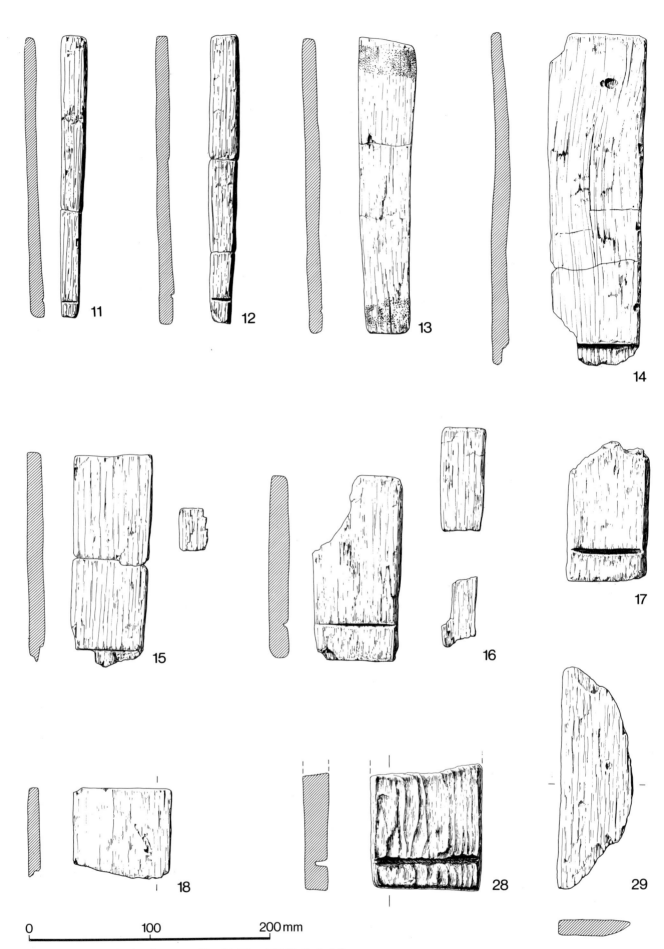

0   100   200 mm

Fig. 131. Wooden bucket fragments (Nos 11-18 and 28-9). Scale 1:3

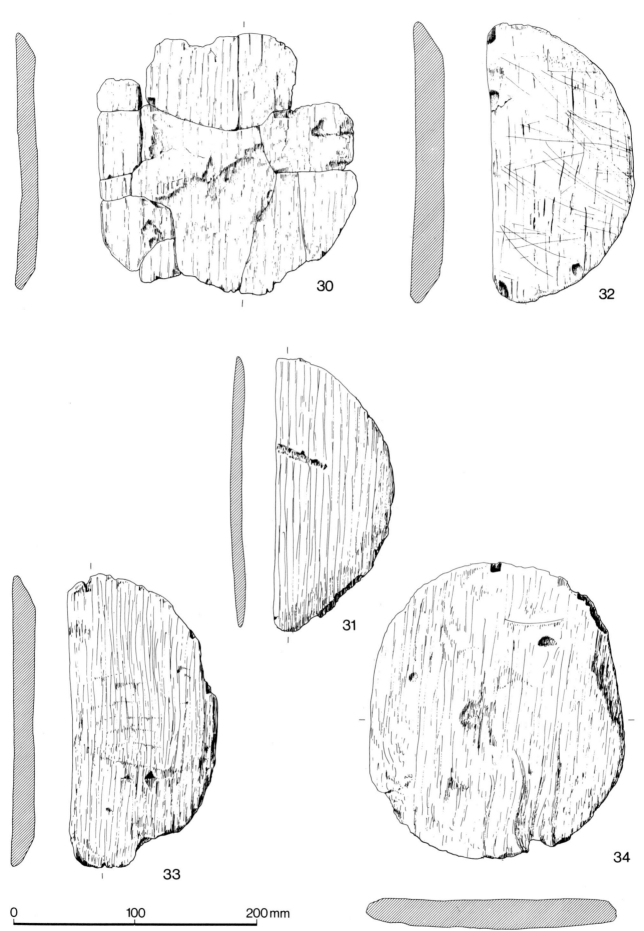

0   100   200 mm

Fig. 132. Wooden bucket bases (Nos 30-34). Scale 1:3

33* Semi-circular fragment of, probably, originally one-piece circular bucket base. Edges have wide chamfer on one side only. Diam. 240mm; th. 17mm. *Quercus* sp. (oak). *5500M (15.8m); SF 1615a*

34* One-piece circular bucket base. Curved edges have wide chamfer on one side only; edges damaged in places. Diam. 243mm; th. 25mm. *Quercus* sp. (oak). *5500M (15.8m); SF 1666*

35* Three fragments of staves from a circular piece-built bucket base. One fragment is probably a 'middle' stave with two flat edges and curved ends; the others are fragments of middles or cants. Curved edges chamfered on one side only. Diam. 242mm; th. 15mm. *Quercus* sp. (oak). *5500M (14.6m); SF 1470b*

36* Fragment of cant stave of circular piece-built bucket base. Curved edges chamfered on both sides. Diam. (recon.) 248mm; th. 10mm. *Quercus* sp. (oak). *5500M (15.8m); SF 1622b*

37* Semi-circular cant of circular two-piece bucket base. Tangentially split/sawn timber. Edges are chamfered on both sides, but are now very broken; chamfering was probably made with a drawknife. Diam. 250mm; th. 19mm. *Quercus* sp. (oak). *5500L (14.4m); SF 1419*

38* Complete two-piece circular bucket base. Very heavy and thick timber. Curved edges have wide chamfer (30mm) on one side only. Diam. 255mm; th. 23-5mm. *Fraxinus* sp. (ash). *5500M (14.9m); SF 1520*

39* Three fragments of, probably, one-piece circular bucket base. Tangentially sawn/split timber. Curved edges chamfered on one side only. Diam. 250-60mm; th. 16mm. *Quercus* sp. (oak). *5500M (14.8m); SF 1489a*

40* Three fragments of one-piece circular bucket base (not three separate staves, as appears). Tangentially sawn/split timber. Curved edges chamfered on both sides; tool marks on both flat surfaces in the form of parallel 'chatter' lines were probably made when surfaces were smoothed perhaps with a drawknife or shave. Diam. 260mm; th. 15mm. *Quercus* sp. (oak). *5500M (15.8m); SF 1614*

41* Six conjoining fragments of one-piece circular bucket base. Tangentially sawn/split timber. Curved edges chamfered on one side only. Diam. 260mm; th. 20mm. *Fraxinus* sp. (ash); 5 growth rings per 20mm. *5500L (14.5m); SF 1439*

42 Fragments of circular one-piece bucket base. Curved edges chamfered on one side only. Diam. 270mm; th. 20mm. *Quercus* sp. (oak). *5500L (14.4m); SF 1436*

43* Fragment of one-piece circular bucket base. Not cant stave. Wide chamfer on one side of curved edge. Diam. (recon.) 306mm; th. 25mm. *Quercus* sp. (oak). *5500M (14.6m); SF 1470a*

44 Four fragments of piece-built circular bucket base. Curved edges have deep chamfer on one side only. Diam. (recon.) 308mm; th. 12mm. *Alnus* sp. (alder). *5500L (14.5m); SF 1438*

45 Two small fragments of circular bucket base. Only a small section of curved edge survives but this is chamfered on one side only. Largest fragment: l. 95mm; w. 47mm; th. 17mm. *Quercus* sp. (oak). *5500M (15.6m); SF 1600c*

46 Four fragments of circular bucket base. Curved edges chamfered on one side only; flat surface shows tool marks in the form of chatter lines, possibly from drawknife or shave? Diam. (recon.) *c.* 240mm; th. 11mm. *Quercus* sp. (oak). *5500M; SF 1573*

47 Fragment of circular bucket base. Tangentially split/sawn timber. Wide chamfer on one side of curved edge. L. 132mm; w. 52mm; th. 13mm. *Quercus* sp. (oak). *5500M (14.8m); SF 1489b*

All the buckets from Well 1 are open-topped, straight-sided, stave-built vessels which taper from top to bottom. They have separate circular bases fitted in grooves at the bottom of the staves. Some bases are a single piece of timber, whilst others are piece-built with separate cants or arc-like pieces and sometimes middles between two of these. Although some of these grooves are V-sectioned, and others U-shaped and squared in section,

most were made by a cooper's croze, a tool with a serrated blade set in a wooden frame which can cut a continuous groove around an assembled bucket. Some staves show signs of hollowing and backing, i.e. rounded on the outside and inside using a drawknife and round shave.

The species of wood used to make the buckets include oak, ash, alder, maple and fir. Oak is usually the species preferred by coopers for buckets and cask staves, and this was used almost exclusively throughout the medieval period for buckets (Morris 1984, fig. 10, no. 5). This does not appear to be the case in Roman Britain, where many of the surviving wooden bucket staves are coniferous, and nearly always silver fir (*Abies alba*). As well as many of the Dalton Parlours group, there are others from York (Williams 1978, 47-9, fig. 26), Vindolanda, Northumbria (Birley 1977, 24) and Silchester, Hampshire (Boon 1974b, 86), and a larch stave from Segontium (Caernarvon), Gwynedd (Boon 1975, 53). Whereas the oak, ash and maple staves were most probably locally produced, silver fir and larch are not native species. Silver fir's natural habitat is among the mountains of central and southern Europe where it has a wide and irregular distribution and grows at altitudes of up to 6000 feet (Williams 1978, 48-9). It was not introduced into Britain until *c.* AD 1603. The Roman silver fir buckets must therefore have come to Britain in one of three ways: either they were manufactured on the continent and imported to Britain as complete vessels; or they were manufactured from silver fir timber brought to Britain as raw material; or they were manufactured from other artefacts of silver fir imported to Britain as complete objects. Since there is certain evidence that the Romans used silver fir for stave-built casks, for example those found reused as well-linings at Silchester (Reid 1901, 253), it is possible that many of the smaller Roman silver fir buckets found in Britain (including those from Dalton Parlours) were made by reusing wood from redundant casks.

It is very interesting to note that many of these Roman staves were tangentially sawn or split, as opposed to being cleft radially along the principal planes of weakness which follow the medullary rays. Most Anglo-Saxon, medieval and post-medieval staves were cleft radially using wedges, as were many objects which needed to be made from flat boards or planks. Roman woodworkers were well acquainted with large two-man pit and frame-saws (e.g. Goodman 1964, figs 122-4), tools which were ideal for sawing large planks and staves, but which may not have been used again in post-Roman Britain until the 15th century.

None of the Dalton Parlours buckets appear to have had two opposing staves higher than the rest with perforations cut through the wood for the hooked ends of the handle. This method of fastening handles was very popular in Anglo-Saxon and medieval Britain (Morris 1984, 140, figs 100-102) where an iron mount often acted as a hole reinforcement. It does not appear to have been a common technique of Roman coopers in Britain if one looks at surviving wooden and iron bucket components. All the Dalton Parlours buckets have curved iron handles

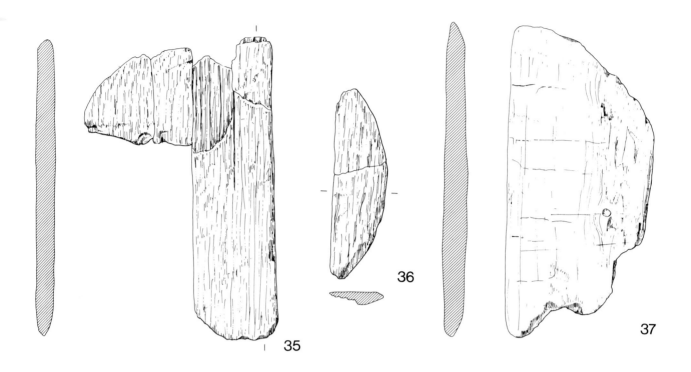

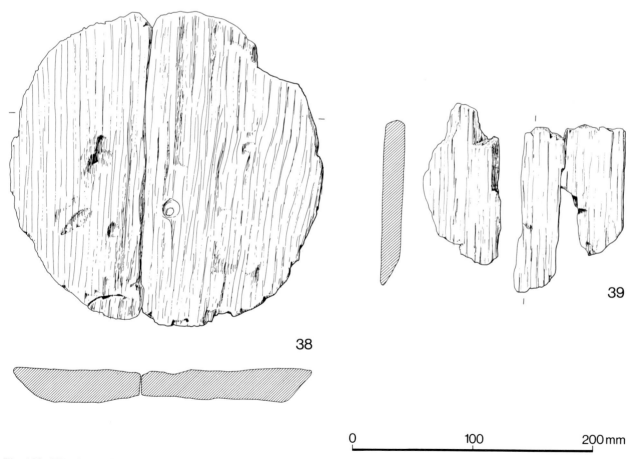

Fig. 133. Wooden bucket bases (Nos 35-9). Scale 1:3

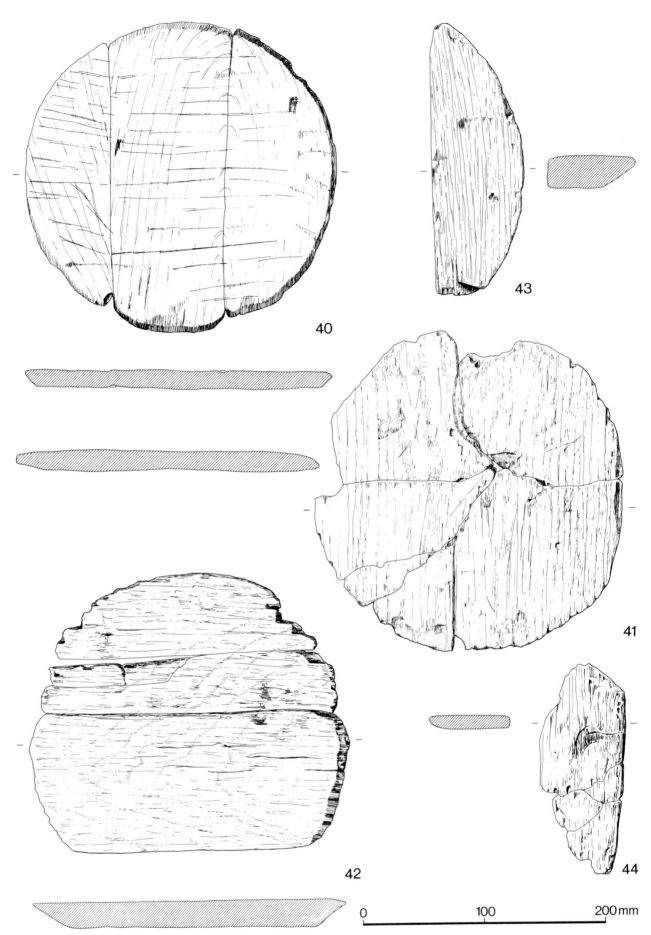

Fig. 134. Wooden bucket bases (Nos 40-44). Scale 1:3

0   100   200 mm

with hooked ends fastened through holes in iron mounts which project above the upper edge of two opposed staves. These iron mounts are of four types (see p. 200), three of which appear to have been nailed to the bucket staves. Mounts of the fourth type have their bottom ends rolled over into a small hook (a feature found on some of the other types) but have no nail holes. This lack of nail holes on the handle mounts, along with a general lack of nail holes on the iron bucket hoops, is very useful for indicating some methods of bucket construction used by the coopers who made them. These include assembling the wooden staves and base in a temporary (probably wooden) hoop, then heating the forged circular iron hoops and fitting them in place on the bucket whilst still hot. When the hoops cooled, they would 'shrink' tightly onto the staves and hold them all in place. If the iron handle mounts had been placed with their hooks under the hoops whilst they were also still hot, they would presumably have been tightly clamped into place and capable of supporting the bucket when the handle was lifted.

The water level in Well 1 would originally have been over 40 feet below the ground surface and the buckets used to lift water must therefore have been let down on a strong rope. None of the fourteen iron bucket handles from the well, however, had provision for securely attaching a rope which would not slip down the handle and either spill the contents or prevent the bucket filling properly when it reached the water. The handles are either plain rods or have a hand grip (U-shaped or flattened). Genuine well buckets of any period have either a looped constriction in the handle at the top of the arch, like the Roman well buckets from the Saalburg, Germany (Jacobi 1927, fig. 32), Woodcuts, Wiltshire (Pitt-Rivers 1887, pl. XXVIII), Gadebridge Park, Hertfordshire (Neal 1974, fig. 79) and Northchurch, Hertfordshire (Neal 1977, figs 23 and 25a), or a swivel mechanism fixed through a hole at the top of the arch as in the medieval well buckets from Brightlingsea, Essex (Erith 1972, fig. 6, no. 1), Tong, Shropshire (Wharton 1978, fig. 9) and York (Morris forthcoming b). It is reasonable to suggest, therefore, that none of the Dalton Parlours buckets represented by surviving iron handles was originally manufactured as a well bucket. They could have been ordinary household or farm buckets designed to be carried around by hand but which ended their life in the farmyard well.

The wooden and iron bucket components were found at various depths in the waterlogged well layers, suggesting that they were used and lost over a period of time by people who did not go to the lengths of obtaining vessels with suitable handles. This policy may go some way to explaining why so many of the vessels were lost!

Objects directly connected with the buckets (Figs 135-6)

48* Two fragments of curved object. Manufactured from length of roundwood timber and adjoining outcurving branch. Roundwood timber shaped to rectangular cross-sectioned bar, and above junction of main stem and branch the roundwood has been cut away leaving bar to taper into side branch. L. 850mm; w. (branch) 45mm; th. (branch) 40mm. *Prunus* sp., or Pomoideae (e.g. apple, pear, rowan, hawthorn, etc.) *5500L (14.3m); SF 2041a-b*

49* Similar curved object. Manufactured from length of roundwood timber and adjoining outcurving branch. Roundwood timber was shaped to rectangular cross-sectioned bar (57 x 37mm), and above junction of main stem and branch the roundwood has been cut away leaving bar to taper into side branch; latter has circular/oval cross-section (37 x 32mm). Found at same level as Bucket 2. L. 400mm; w. 57mm; th. 37mm. *Alnus* sp. (alder). *5500K (13.9m); SF 1402c*

50* Similar curved object. Manufactured from length of roundwood timber and adjoining outcurving branch. Roundwood timber was shaped to rectangular cross-sectioned bar (45 x 33mm), and above junction of main stem and branch the roundwood has been cut away leaving bar to taper into side branch; latter has roughly squared cross-section (36 x 28mm). L. 200mm; w. 45mm; th. 33mm. *Prunus* sp. (cherry or blackthorn). *5500L (14.5m); SF 1437a*

51* Two fragments of similar curved object. Manufactured from length of roundwood timber and adjoining outcurving branch. Roundwood timber was shaped (but not squared) with bladed tool to form bar 54mm wide; the roundwood above junction of main stem and branch has been cut away leaving bar to taper into side branch; latter is roughly squared roundwood branch (31 x 23mm) with faceted end, and is perforated by small hole 7mm diam. containing peg (6mm diam.). L. 324mm; w. 54mm; th. 36mm. *Corylus* sp. (hazel). *5500L (14.5m); SF 1437b*

52* Similar curved object. Manufactured from length of roundwood timber and adjoining outcurving branch. Roundwood timber was faceted to roughly hexagonal cross-sectioned bar which was cut away above junction of main stem and branch; bar tapers into side branch which has a carefully squared cross-section (22 x 21mm) and faceted end. L. 194mm; w. 35mm; th. 29mm. Pomoideae (e.g. apple, pear, rowan or hawthorn). *5500L (14.5m); SF 1437g*

53* Three fragments of similar object. Manufactured from length of roundwood timber and adjoining outcurving branch. Roundwood timber was faceted and cut to smooth-sided rectangular cross-sectioned bar (42 x 30mm); this was cut away above junction of roundwood and branch leaving bar to taper into side branch; latter is very worn but was originally faceted to roughly circular cross-section; the end was split down into half-section roundwood over *c.* 115mm. L. 430mm; w. 53mm; th. 35mm. *Corylus* sp. (hazel). *5500; SFs 2009a and d*

54* Similar curved object. Manufactured from originally roundwood timber and adjoining outcurving side branch. At junction of main stem and branch the timber has been shaped to roughly rectangular cross-section and it slopes away in both directions from central 'apex'; main stem has been split below junction into half-section timber, and branch has been converted similarly; both ends have semi-circular cross-sections and taper away from squared middle section; one end is slightly longer than the other; ends are faceted. L. 590mm; w. 48mm; th. 38mm. *Quercus* sp. (oak). *5500L (14.5m); SF 1437f*

55* Fragment of similar object. Manufactured from roundwood timber and adjoining outcurving branch. Surviving piece comes from junction of the two where cross-section is rectangular and surfaces are roughly faceted. L. 96mm; w. 55mm; th. 33mm. *Corylus* sp. (hazel). *5500L (14.5m); SF 1437d*

56* Three fragments of straight bar. Manufactured from radially split or quarter-section timber. Roughly rectangular cross-section; ends slightly tapered and roughly squared. L. 331mm; w. 28mm; th. 25mm. *Fraxinus* sp. (ash). *5500L (14.5m); SF 1437h*

57* Three fragments of straight bar. Manufactured from radially split or quarter-section timber. Roughly rectangular cross-section; ends squared. L. 365mm; w. 30mm; th. 29mm. *Fraxinus* sp. (ash). *5500L (14.5m); SF 1437e*

Although one (No. 54) and possibly two (No. 55) of these curved objects are approximately symmetrical with two similar sloping ends, it seems very unlikely that they are yokes in the sense of a wooden frame carried across the neck to carry a couple of buckets. There is neither a

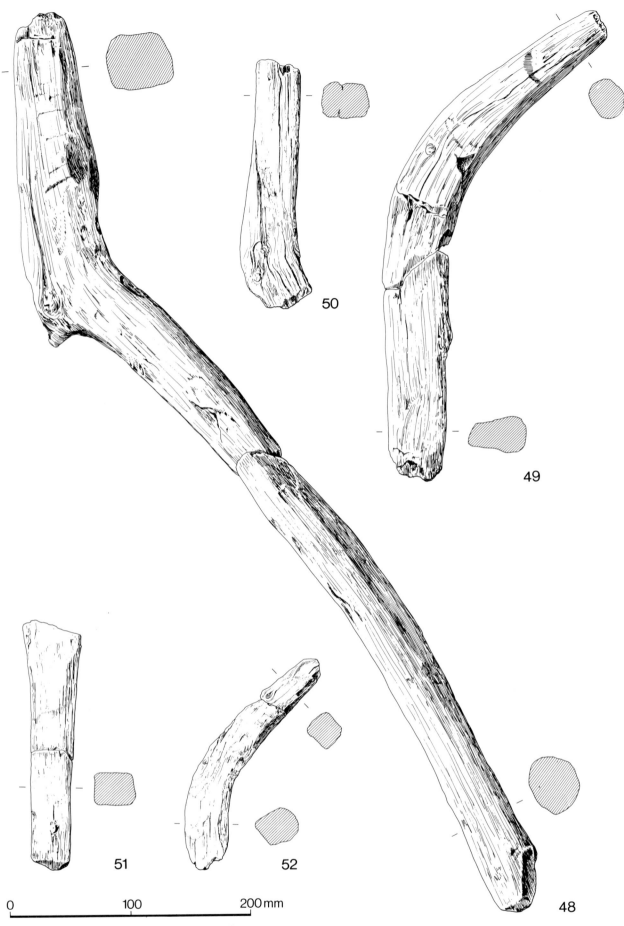

50

49

51

52

48

0   100   200 mm

Fig. 135. Wooden objects (Nos 48-52). Scale 1:3

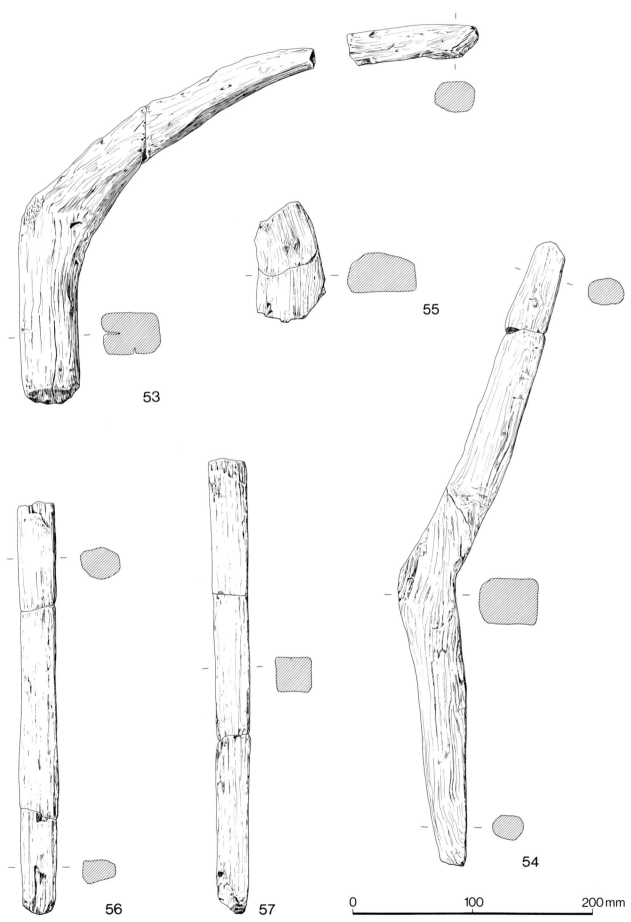

53

55

54

56

57

0   100   200 mm

Fig. 136. Wooden objects (Nos 53-7). Scale 1:3

neck hole nor any provision for attaching ropes to the ends.

The most important fact to note, and this is common to all the curved objects, is that they were cut from timber at the junction of a main stem and a side branch. This form of timber is usually specially selected when the proposed use of an object requires the strength provided by this naturally curved shape. Most of the thicker ends cut from the main stem are squared, shaped or faceted in some way, whereas some of the thinner branch wood ends are rounded or have little squaring off. Some branch ends are quite worn, suggesting they have been handled.

As yet there are no parallels for this type of object either from Roman or later collections of wooden artefacts. We can make only tentative suggestions, therefore, as to what they were used for. Since they were found in the well, in layers which also contained the wooden buckets and sometimes in direct association with a vessel (e.g. No. 49 was found with Bucket 2), it seems reasonable to suggest they were used at the same time. Numbers 50-52, 54 and 55 were all found together at the same depth and suggest that a number of these objects might have been in use all at the same time. They could either be part of a winding mechanism at the top of the well shaft which hauled the buckets to the surface, or part of a braking mechanism which might have secured a winding mechanism and prevented the bucket being plummeted back down the well before being emptied.

Lathe-turned vessels (Fig. 137)

58* Three conjoining base/wall fragments of lathe-turned vessel. Probably from a drinking cup. Spindle-turned (i.e. wood grain runs parallel to axis of lathe mandrel); almost vertical-sided vessel with slight outcurving rim; very worn pointed rim edge; base is thicker than walls; H. 50mm; th. (base) 10mm; th. (wall) 6mm. Pomoideae (e.g. apple, pear, rowan or hawthorn). *5500M (14.6m); SF 1471*

59* Two small rim/wall fragments of lathe-turned vessel. Rounded rim. Th. 7-8mm. *Betula* sp. (birch). *5500M (15.6m); SF 1600b*

60* Twelve base/wall fragments of lathe-turned vessel. Probably a drinking cup or bowl. Spindle-turned; deep, rounded walls; slightly convex base with rounded edges; turning lines prominent on internal surface, and internal bottom has raised disc of wood with a rough central knob as a remnant of the turning process (see below). Diam. *c*. 180mm; diam. (base) 80mm; th. (base) 15mm; th. (wall) 8mm. Pomoideae (e.g. apple, pear, rowan or hawthorn). *5500M (14.8-15.8m); SFs 1630, 1610 and 1497*

The presence of fragments of small, turned wooden vessels in the well is very predictable since people would have dipped such vessels into a hauled up bucket of water for a drink. They might have been accidentally lost, or thrown in the well when broken.

61* Nine fragments of circular ?platter. Probably lathe-turned using face-turning technique (i.e. wood grain is perpendicular to main axis of lathe mandrel); very flat profile with lower surface curving upwards slightly at edges into flat rim 31mm wide; upper surface has shallow circular hollow *c*. 165mm diam. forming the 'interior' of the vessel. Diam. (recon.) 228mm; th. (edge) 14mm; th. (middle) 11mm. *Quercus* sp. (oak). *5500M (14.8m); SF 1519*

Miscellaneous wooden fragments and objects (Figs 137-41)

62* Possible fragment of a sneck, i.e. a fastening mechanism for door, chest, box, etc., which uses double-ended catch pivoting on central nail or peg. Tangentially split timber. Small block which originally had two rectangular bars projecting from opposite ends (one now missing); surviving bar has rounded square end; rectangular cross-section; middle block is partially perforated by a nail hole and a circular stain around hole suggests it could have had a wide domed or flat head. L. 88mm; w. 40mm; th. 15mm. *Fraxinus* sp. (ash). *5500; SF 2009c*

63* Peg. Made from radially split section of timber. Short shaft with circular cross-section 18mm diam.; large faceted square head with vertical sides above which is a four-sided pyramid tapering to small square top. L. 74mm; head 27 x 26mm. *Quercus* sp. (oak). *5500L (14.5m); SF 1517*

64 Dowel-like peg. Made from full-stem roundwood. Faceted sides; no head; now oval cross-sectioned shaft. L. 69mm; w. 25 x 19mm. Unknown species. *5500L (14.5m); SF 1503b*

65* Peg or small stake. Made from quarter-section timber. Sides faceted with axe or knife cuts; rounded point; no head; roughly circular/oval cross-section. L. 103mm; w. 44 x 30mm. *Quercus* sp. (oak). *5500M (15.9m); SF 1859*

66* Peg. No head; cross-section is circular at 'head' end narrowing to rectangular at other end. L. 105mm; tapering from *c*. 25 x 25mm to 20 x 10mm. *Quercus* sp. (oak). *5500K (12.5m); SF 2032a*

67* Peg. Circular head; shaft cut down to narrow rectangular cross-section. L. 120mm; tapering from 36 x 31mm to 25 x 10mm. ?*Alnus* sp. (alder). *5500M (14.7m); SF 2038a*

68* Peg. L. 180mm; tapering from 34 x 26mm to 28 x 14mm. *Fraxinus* sp. (ash). *5500M (14.7m); SF 2038b*

69 Peg. *Sambucus nigra* (elder). *5500M (15.8m); SF 2042a*

70* Stake or peg. Squared head which is sub-rectangular in cross-section and asymmetrically positioned at one side of the shaft which tapers to blunt end. L 215mm; head 67 x 45mm. *Alnus* sp. (alder). *5500K (12.9m); SF 2027b*

71* Fragment of tally stick. Made from small full-stem roundwood branch which was debarked before notching. Traces of twelve V-sectioned notches cut on one side only; notches probably cut from two directions with a knife. L. 65mm; diam. 11mm. Unknown species. *5500L (14.5m); SF 1421*

Tally sticks such as this were marked with notches either to indicate sums of money owed, or to serve as a duplicated account, tag or label. Tallies of many different kinds have been used in all periods all over the world, but it seems that only the English Exchequer formalised their use as an official accounting procedure and many exchequer tallies dating from the 12th century to 1826 still survive in the Public Records Office (Jenkinson 1911). This Roman tally is unlikely to have been an official 'document' and is probably a fragment of a local trader's tally.

72* Very small fragment of thin, probably sawn, board of the type usually used for making stylus writing tablets. No diagnostic features or edges, but in character the fragment is exactly like the more complete boards from Castleford (Morris forthcoming a) and other Roman sites. This type of writing tablet was usually hollowed on one side to take a thin layer of wax on which a message could be written. *Abies alba* (silver fir). *5500L (14.5m); SF 1518e*

73* Small stake. Made from quarter-section timber. No head; roughly rectangular cross-section; tapers to pointed end which is now broken; fully perforated at upper end by circular augered hole 30mm diam. at one side and 27mm diam. on the other; hole filled by circular cross-sectioned peg made from split section timber (not

224

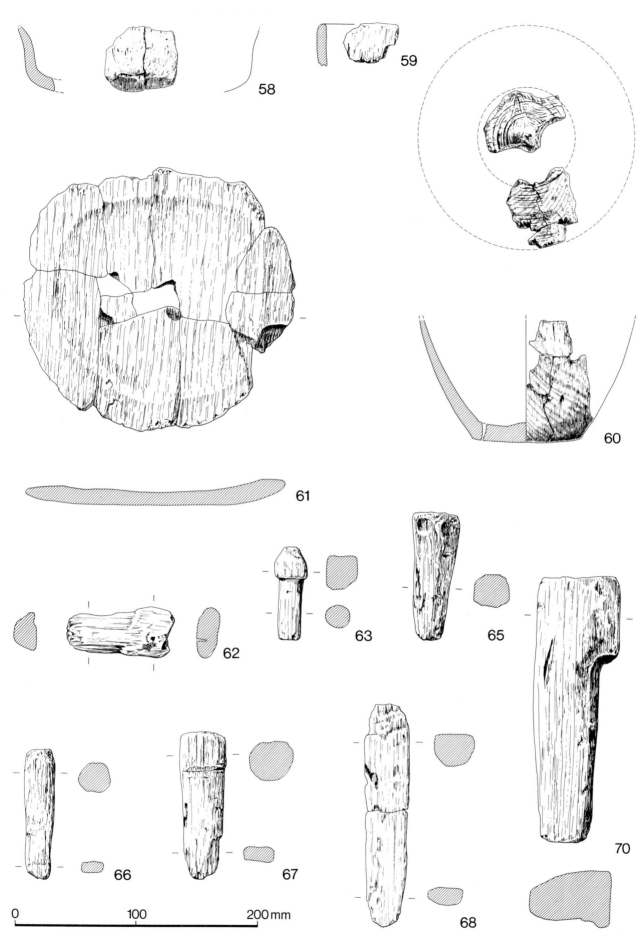

Fig. 137. Wooden objects (Nos 58-63, 65-8 and 70). Scale 1:3

58

59

60

61

62

63

65

66

67

68

70

0   100   200 mm

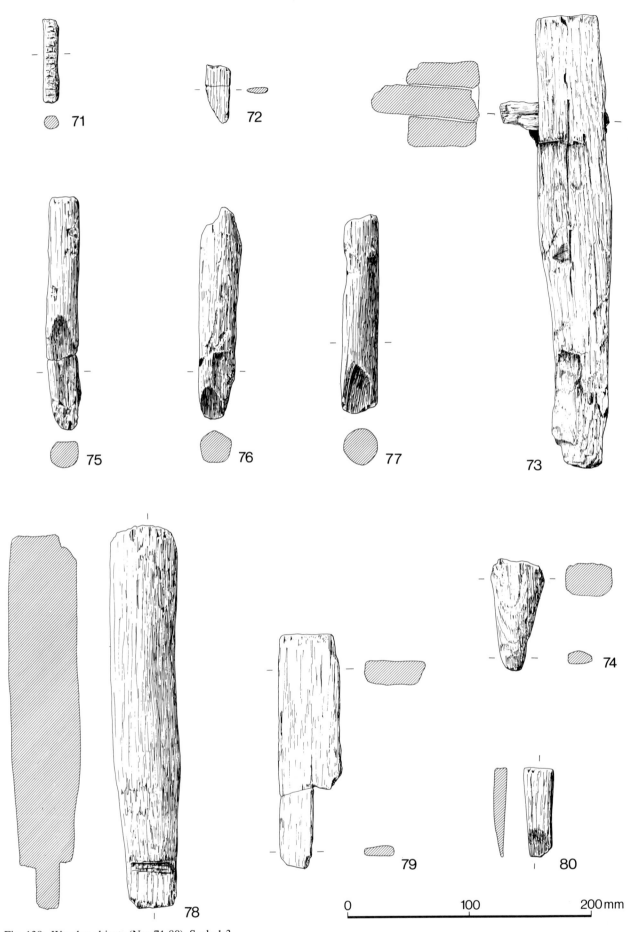

Fig. 138. Wooden objects (Nos 71-80). Scale 1:3

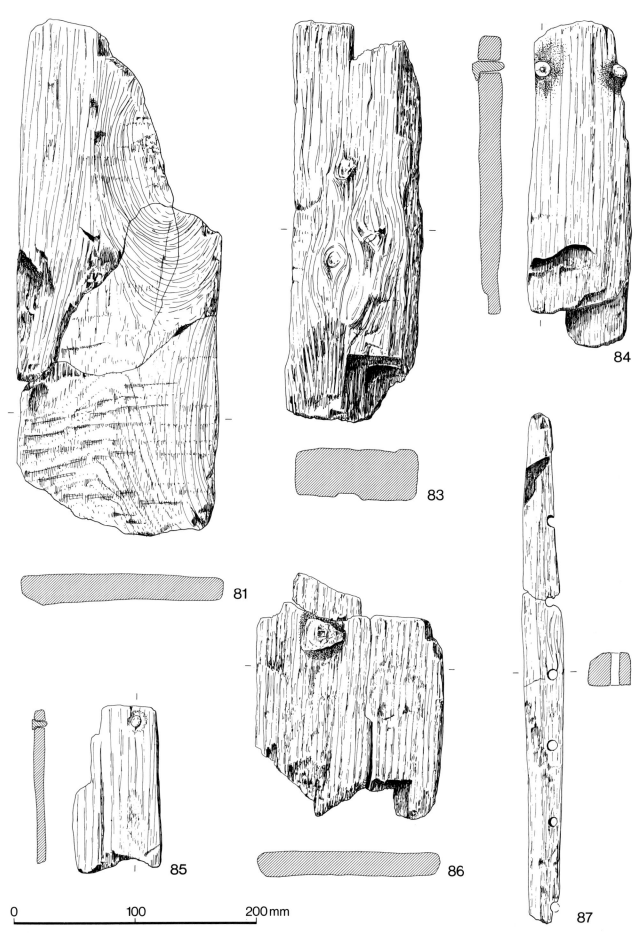

0   100   200 mm

Fig. 139. Wooden objects (Nos 81 and 83-7). Scale 1:3

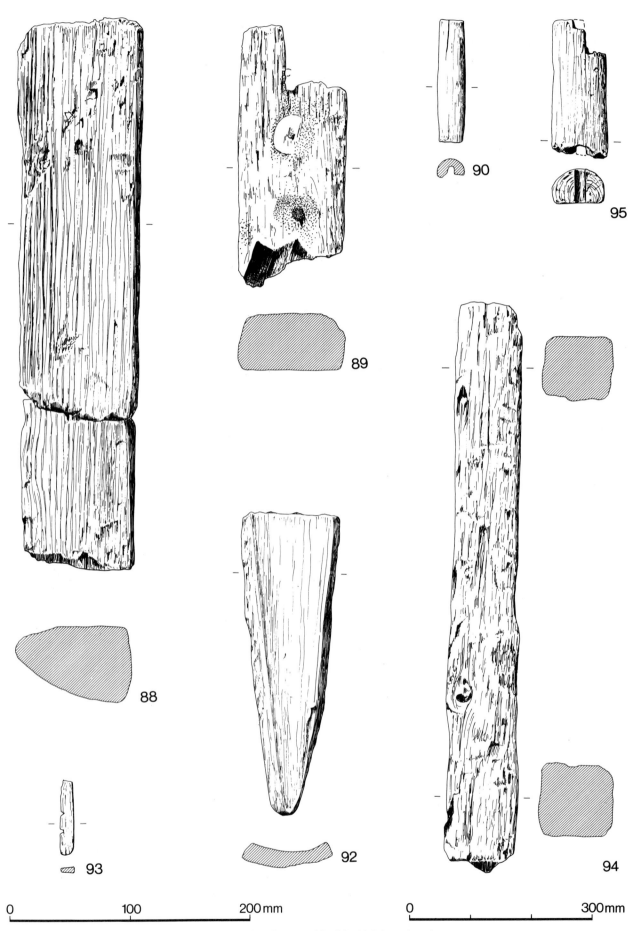

Fig. 140. Wooden objects (Nos 88-90 and 92-5). Scale 1:3, except No. 94 which is scale 1:6

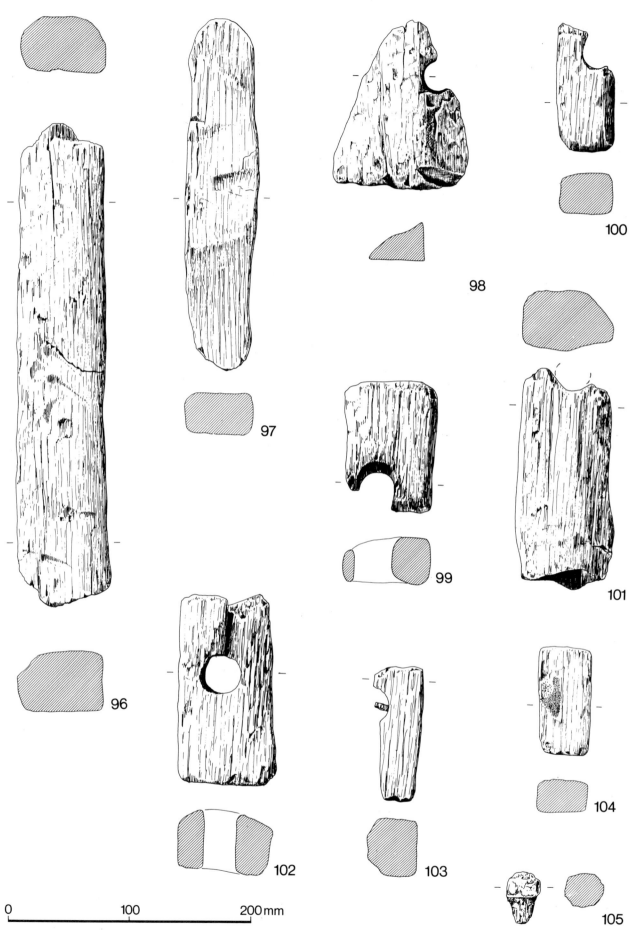

96

97

98

99

100

101

102

103

104

105

0   100   200 mm

Fig. 141. Wooden objects (Nos 96-105). Scale 1:3

roundwood); peg held in place by small oak wedge, and there are traces of black substance adhering to the stake at this end also. L. 365mm; w. 70mm; th. 53mm. *Quercus* sp. (oak). *5500K (14m); SF 2010*

74* Stake fragment. Broken shaft; rounded point remains. L. 89mm; 39 x 25mm tapering to 20 x 10mm. *Quercus* sp. (oak). *5500K (12.8m); SF 2043b*

75* Small stake. Sub-circular cross-section; no head; other end has facet cut and rounded point. L. 188mm; diam. *c.* 22mm. *Corylus* sp. (hazel). *5500K (13.8m); SF 2029a*

76* Stake. Upper end broken; sub-circular cross-section; blunt faceted point. L. 170mm; diam. *c.* 26mm. Pomoideae (e.g. apple, pear, rowan or hawthorn). *5500K (13.8m); SF 2029b*

77* Stake. Circular cross-section; facet-cut, blunt pointed end. L. 160mm; diam. *c.* 28mm. *Corylus* sp. (hazel). *5500K (13.8m); SF 2029c*

78* Stake or pole. Made from full-stem roundwood debarked before working. Heavy; oval cross-sectioned shaft; one end broken; the other end tapers and has been shaped with long faceted axe cuts; at the very end is a rectangular cross-sectioned tenon 39 x 19mm. L. 310mm; w. 60 x 50mm. *Quercus* sp. 9oak). *5500M (14.6m); SF 1499a*

79* Two fragments of ?wedge. Radially split section. Rectangular cross-section; tapers markedly in profile. L. 186mm; w. 51mm; th. 18mm. *Fraxinus* sp. (ash). *5500M (14.6m); SF 1499c*

80* Wedge. Radially split timber. Rectangular cross-section; tapers in profile; thinner end has wide facet cut across entire width. L. 72mm; w. 24mm; th. 10mm. *Quercus* sp. (oak). *5500M (15.5m); SF 1654a*

Radially split oak wedges such as this were themselves used for splitting long lengths of timber into planks.

81* Narrow plank. Rectangular cross-section; tangentially split/sawn; broken at both ends. L. 415mm; w. 168mm; th. 18-25mm. *Quercus* sp. (oak). *5500K (12.4m); SF 2030*

82 Plank. *Quercus* sp. (oak). *5500K (11.8m); SF 2031*

83* Plank. Rectangular cross-section. L. 320mm; w. 101mm; th. *c.* 40mm. *Quercus* sp. (oak). *5500K (12.7m); SF 2033*

84* Plank fragment with nails. L. 260mm; w. 85mm; th. 18mm. *Quercus* sp. (oak). *5500M (15.5m); SF 1652a*

85* Plank fragment with nail. L. 134mm; w. 72mm; th. 9mm. Unknown species. *5500M (15.5m); SF 1652b*

86* Five fragments of plank. Made from tangentially split/sawn board. One end and surviving fragments of straight sides appear to be rounded squared; traces of two iron nails through the plank, which are probably clench nails with square heads fixed through triangular iron plates; one is very corroded. Such nails are often used in boat construction, but it is impossible to say whether or not this plank once formed part of a boat. W. 160mm; th. 20mm. *Fraxinus* sp. (ash); 2 growth rings over 15mm showing that this plank was made from relatively fast-grown timber. *5500M (16.1m); SF 1624*

87* Beam. Made from half-section roundwood timber. D-shaped cross-section, shaped on all sides; one side is flat, others are faceted with long axe cuts; both ends broken, and beam is also broken by a split along the grain; traces of six augered holes 8mm diam. spaced roughly evenly down the long axis. Fragments of a similar beam with multiple holes were also found in the well at Rothwell Haigh (Morris in prep.) suggesting, perhaps, that such timbers are associated with the use of wells or with their superstructures. L. 420mm; w. 31mm; th. 28mm. *Quercus* sp. (oak). *5500M (15.8m); SF 1622a*

88* Two fragments of beam. Made from split quarter-section timber. Roughly triangular cross-section with rounded apex. SF 1501: l.

450mm; w. 92mm; th. 63mm. *Fraxinus* sp. (ash). *5500M; SFs 1501 and 1572g*

89* Beam. Rectangular cross-section; broken at both ends; row of three nails down long axis. L. 210mm; w. 89mm; th. 45mm. Unknown species. *5500M (15.6m); SF 2028*

90* Fragment of handle. Probably lathe-turned. Originally circular cross-section with circular hole (?tang hole) augered down entire length. L. 98mm; w. 22mm; th. 19mm. *Betula* sp. (birch). *5500M (15.9m); SF 1966*

91 Traces of wooden handle on iron whittle tang of knife. See Chapter 27, No. 82.

92* Fragment of vessel wall. Possibly reused as scoop. Original vessel was probably cylindrical and hollowed from length of full-stem roundwood timber; this technique of making a vessel also involves inserting a separate base into a basal groove in a similar way to that used for a stave-built vessel; surviving fragment is triangular, and if it was used as a scoop, the narrow apex would have served as a handle; it is curved in cross-section. L. 246mm; w. 85mm; th. 15mm. *Fraxinus* sp. (ash). *5500; SF 2011b*

93* Fragment of thin, flat object. Pattern of growth rings shows that it was probably made from tangentially sawn lath or a strip made like a veneer by shaving a length from roundwood. Broken at one end and along one side; originally rounded at other end; traces of two possible nail holes along broken edge. L. 60mm; w. 11mm; th. 5mm. Unknown species. *5500M (15.9m); SF 1858*

94* Beam. Squared roundwood. Possibly part of well structure or lifting gear? L. 920mm; w. 120mm; th. 112mm. *Quercus* sp. (oak). *5500K (12.1m); SF 2039*

95* Fragment of beam. D-shaped cross-section; perforated by at least two small square holes. L. 110mm; w. 44mm; th. 27mm. *Fraxinus* sp. (ash). *5500M (15.8m); SF 2035a-b*

96* Beam. Rectangular/D-shaped cross-section; rounded; broken at both ends. L. 390mm; w. 70mm; th. 49mm. *Quercus* sp. (oak). *5500L (14.2m); SF 2036a*

97* Beam. Rectangular cross-section; rounded ends; possible traces of tool marks. L. 283mm; w. 57mm; th. 33mm. *Quercus* sp. (oak). *5500K (12.5m); SF 2032b*

98* Triangular block or offcut. One possible sawn surface; perforated by augered hole 25mm diam., now broken. L. 135mm; w. 111mm; th. 60mm. *Quercus* sp. (oak). *5500M; SF 2011a*

99* Small block. Rectangular cross-section; perforated by augered hole with a countersunk chamfer. L. 105mm; w. 71mm; th. 39mm. *Quercus* sp. (oak). *5500K (13.7m); SF 2034*

100* Small block. Rectangular cross-section; broken ends; one perforated by augered hole. L. 104mm; w. 45mm; th. 33mm. *Quercus* sp. (oak). *5500K (12.9m); SF 2040b*

101* Block. Broken at both ends; probably perforated by circular augered hole. L. 179mm; w. 76mm; th. 49mm. *Quercus* sp. (oak). *5500K (12.8m); SF 2043a*

102* Block or offcut. Augered hole. L. 150mm; w. 79mm; th. 48mm. *Quercus* sp. (oak). *5500L (14.2m); SF 2036b*

103* Block. Rectangular cross-section; perforated by augered hole; iron nail fixed into one side, projects into the hole and probably originally into a peg or dowel in the hole. L. 110mm; w. 41mm; th. 46mm. *Quercus* sp. (oak). *5500L (14.2m); SF 2036c*

104* Block. Rectangular cross-section; straight cut ends. L. 87mm; w. 42mm; th. 27mm. *5500M (14.7m); SF 2038c*

105* Dome-headed iron rivet or nail with short shaft. Fragments of wood adhering to the shaft sides suggest it was hammered into the end grain of a piece of timber. L. 40mm; diam. 30mm. *5500M (15.9m); SF 1870*

Other fragments and offcuts are listed in the Archive Report.

A Note on the Timber Identifications

by Allan Hall

For objects in both the published report and Archive Report the full list of probabilities/possibilities is as follows.

Abies: probably *A. alba* Mill., the central European fir.
Acer: probably *A. campestre* L., the native field maple unless otherwise indicated.
Acer ?pseudoplatanus: possibly *A. pseudoplatanus* L., the central European sycamore.
Alnus: probably *A. glutinosa* (L.) Gaertner, the native alder.
Betula: probably one or both of *B. pendula* Roth or *B. pubescens* Ehrh., the two native tree birches or their hybrids.
Buxus: *Buxus sempervirens* L., the ?native/introduced box (see p. 146).
Corylus: probably *C. avellana* L., the native hazelnut.
Fraxinus: probably *F. excelsior* L., the native ash.
Pinus a species of pine, but uncertain whether native Scots pine, *P. sylvestris* L., or one of the several European spp.
Pomoideae: probably one or more of apple (*Malus sylvestris* Mill.), pear (*Pyrus communis* L.), rowan (*Sorbus aucuparia* L.) or another *Sorbus* sp., or a hawthorn (*Crataegus* sp.). Smaller pomoid Rosaceae like *Cotoneaster* can be ruled out.
Prunus: probably one of the native or ?introduced cherries (*Prunus cerasus* L./*P. avium* (L.) L.) or plums (*P. domestica*, *sensu lato*), or blackthorn (*P. spinosa* L.).
Quercus: one or more of the native oaks, *Quercus robur* L. and *Q. petraea* (Matt.) Liebl. (or their hybrid).
Salix: one or more of the many species of willow, *Salix* spp (fragments recorded in Archive Report only).
Sambucus: probably the native elderberry, *S. nigra* L.

29 The Leather Objects (Figs 142-3)

by Quita Mould

The leather was examined dry after conservation by freeze-drying. Where possible species identification was made by grain pattern using low-powered magnification. Hobnailing patterns on nailed bottom units are described using either the classification proposed by van Driel-Murray and Gechter (1983, 21, fig. 3) or by Rhodes (1980, 105-7), and hereafter referred to as van Driel-Murray type and Rhodes type respectively.

Additional abbreviations:

E/F   edge/flesh
G/F   grain/flesh
inc.   incomplete
s.   seat
SL   stitch length
st.   stitch (es)
tr.   tread
wst   waist

Catalogue

Leather one-piece shoes

1*   One-piece shoe. Backpart fragment with butted G/F back seam SL 5mm, oversewn using a single thong, and part of a thonged G/F seam SL 6mm around the heel on one side; remaining edges worn/torn away. Leather delaminated calf/cattle. L. 111mm inc.; back seam ht 36mm inc. *5500K (12.2-12.7m); SF 1369*

2*   One-piece shoe. Backpart with butted E/F thonged back seam SL 6mm and thonged E/F seams SL 8mm around the heel; remains of elongated upper loop present on right side; other edges worn/torn away; child's shoe. Leather calf/cattle. L. 97mm inc., back seam ht 40mm. *5500K (12.7m); SF 1384*

3*   One-piece shoe. Right backpart with butted E/F back seam SL 7mm; series of five fastening loops, upper and second loop joined with a decorative lobe; other edges worn/torn away. Leather calf/cattle. L. 155mm inc.; back seam ht 57mm. *5500M (14.9m); SF 1495*

4*   One-piece shoe. Left backpart with butted E/F back seam SL 5-8mm and thonged E/F seam SL 11mm around the heel; series of fastening loops; upper loop, with denticulated decoration of five lobes, is joined to second loop with decorative paired lobes; other edges worn/torn away. Leather calf/cattle. L. 101mm inc.; back seam ht 84mm. *5500M (15.5-16m); SF 1609a*

5   One-piece shoe. Five fragments, possibly from No. 4; largest fragment from right side with three fastening loops; other edges worn/torn away. Leather calf/cattle. L. 84mm inc.; w. 90mm inc. Also two loop fragments and two scrap fragments torn from the sole area. *5500M (15.5-16m); SF 1609b*

6*   One-piece shoe. Right side upper edge with fastening loop and remains of a further two torn away. A line of irregularly spaced G/F st. runs beneath torn loops along the top edge possibly from the attachment of an internal lining or a repair; other edges cut and worn/torn away. Leather calf. L. 188mm inc.; w. 39mm inc. *5500M (15.5-16m); SF 1609c*

7   One-piece shoe. Fragments, largest with remains of straight G/F seam SL 8mm and a thonged seam at right angles to it. Leather calf/cattle. L. 59mm inc.; w. 55mm inc. Also two waste and four scrap fragments likely to be broken from shoe fragments. *5500M (14.5-15.5m); SF 1743a*

8   One-piece shoe. Four fragments, two joining, with remains of fastening loops, one with line of G/F st. SL 7mm probably from a back seam. Leather calf/cattle. *5500 (sieving); SF 1820b*

9   One-piece shoes. Numerous small fragments from a minimum of two shoes, including ten fragments with G/F st. from back and heel seams; one fragment with decorative denticulation similar to No. 4, and fragment with elongated loop with decorative paired lobes at the base. Leather calf/cattle. *5500 (sieving); SF 1881*

10*   One-piece shoe. For child's left foot, toe missing, cut and torn away across the tread; butted E/F back seam SL 6mm and E/F seam SL 5mm to join back seam wings to heel seat; ends of elongated fastening loops present on each side; series of thonged G/F st. below second and third loop stub on right side, probably a repair. Leather calf/cattle. L. 132mm inc.; back seam ht 32mm; max. w. 113mm. *5500 (sieving); SF 2023*

Leather nailed shoes

11*   Nailed shoe. For right foot, comprising sole, middle, middle lamina, insole, heel stiffener and fragment of right side of upper.

Bottom unit: sole, middle and insole with gently pointed toe, medium tread and wide waist tapering to medium seat; sole has Rhodes type A/B nailing with widely spaced peripheral nailing and decorative nailing of four groups of three at the tread; sole survives only at the waist revealing the middle which has thonging running around the perimeter, inside the peripheral nailing, securing the upper; the insole, worn grain upward to the foot, has central thonging holding a middle lamina in position. Insole leather calf. Insole l. 213mm; w. tr. 73mm; w. wst 51mm; w. s. 37mm.

Upper: part of right side with short length of curving throat, other edges torn away above nailed and thonged lasting margin which lies between the insole and the middle; upper decorated by three sets of double impressed lines. Leather sheep/goat.

Small sub-triangular heel stiffener worn grain toward the foot with nailed and thonged lasting margin. Leather delaminated calf. *5500L (14.4m); SF 1415a*

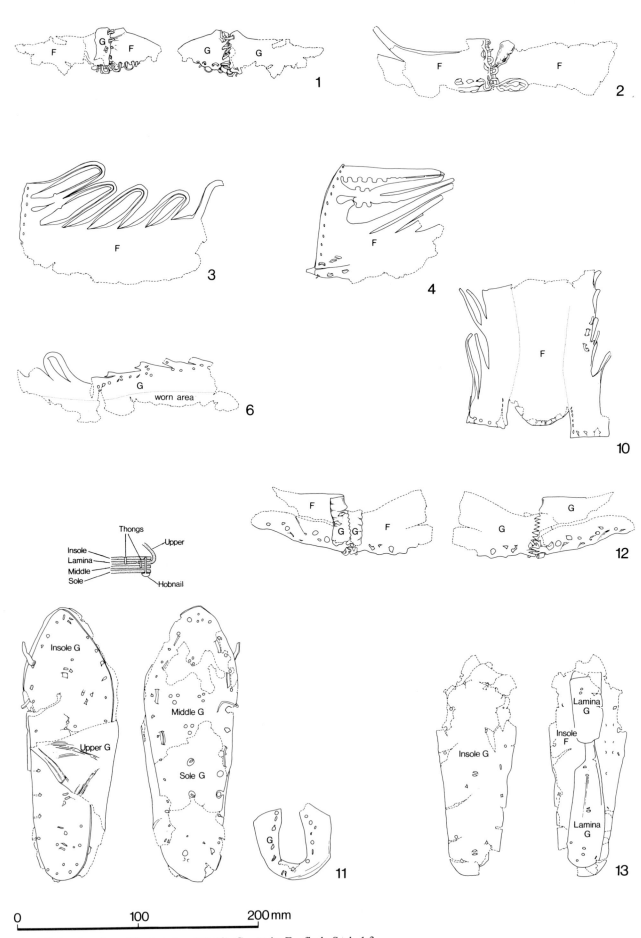

Fig. 142. Leather shoes (Nos 1-4, 6 and 10-13); G = grain, F = flesh. Scale 1:3

12* Nailed shoe. Upper backpart fragment with nailed lasting margin and line of small G/F holes with thread impressions from bracing along the edge which has been protected and is unworn; straight seam, probably back seam, has two edges folded back to form a closed seam and held on flesh side by whipped st.; seam is stitched with a thong, tightly pulled so that the individual st. interlock like teeth; right side top edge is knife-cut and folded, other edges torn away. Leather sheep/goat. L. 151mm inc.; back seam ht 52mm. *5500L (14.4m); SF 1415b*

13* Nailed shoe. Bottom unit comprising insole and two middle laminae; insole worn grain upward to foot with occasional nail holes around perimeter, suggesting Rhodes type B nailing; central thonging holds two middle laminae strips with cut edges on the flesh side; tunnel st. present at forepart on flesh side for attachment of the upper. Leather calf. L. 180mm inc.; w. tr. 67mm inc.; w. wst 53mm; w. s. 40mm. Also three waste and numerous small scrap fragments torn from a shoe and an iron hobnail. *5500L (14.4m); SF 1424*

14* Nailed shoe. For right foot, comprising sole, middle, middle packing, insole and heel stiffener.

Bottom unit: sole with oval toe, medium tread, wide waist and seat with van Driel-Murray type 1a nailing; insole worn grain upward to foot is centrally thonged to the middle which has a possible tunnel st. at right forepart visible; various fragments of middle packing lie beneath. Insole leather calf/cattle. Insole l. 198mm; w. tr. 60mm inc.; w. wst 46mm; w. s. 44mm.

Upper: low heel stiffener worn grain to foot with nailed lasting margin and st. hole with thread impression from bracing.

Also numerous small fragments of middle packing and insole. *5500M (15.2m); SF 1569*

15* Nailed shoe. Bottom unit for left foot comprising sole, middle lamina and insole; sole and insole have oval or gently rounded toe, medium tread, waist and seat; sole has van Driel-Murray type 1a nailing; the insole, worn grain upward to foot, is centrally thonged to the middle lamina. Leather calf/cattle. Insole l. 202mm; w. tr. 75mm; w. wst 53mm; w. s. 48mm. *5500M (14.8m); SF 1581*

Leather sandal

16* Sandal. For child's left foot comprising sole, middle, decorated insole, toe thong and one-piece quarters.

Bottom unit: the unnailed bottom unit has a broad, round toe with big toe scallop, tapering to a medium waist and narrow seat; sole, worn grain to the ground, middle and insole are joined by thonging around the perimeter *c.* 6-10mm from the edge; thonging did not penetrate full thickness of insole and sole and appears on grain surface of each as series of cracks and worn slits caused by wear; waist and seat area of middle only remains; insole, worn grain upward to foot has impressed linear decoration and a large double horizontal thong slit at the toe. Leather insole worn calf/cattle. Insole l. 136mm; w. toe 60mm; w. wst 38mm; w. s. 35mm.

Upper: toe thong with large semi-circular tab end passes through thong slit in insole and divides into two branches, each passing through a hole in the quarters latchet before returning back through the insole thong slit and tying together with a knot beneath the tab.

One-piece quarters cut away at the heel to form a sling back and extending at front edges into latchets with holes for the divided toe thong; held between insole and middle apparently by tunnel st. along the lasting margin (insole and middle have been stuck together in conservation so this cannot be verified at present). Leather worn ?sheep/goat. Quarters ht 55mm. *5500M (15.6m); SF 1665*

Leather shoe scrap fragments

17 Shoe scrap fragments. Including fragment with a cut and a denticulated edge. Leather calf/cattle. *5500M (14-15.3m); SF 1621*

18 Shoe scrap fragments. About twenty small fragments, two likely to come from loops and a short length of thong; also an iron hobnail. *5500; SF 2024*

Leather trimming

19 Trimming. With cut edges and torn ends. Leather delaminated ?sheep/goat. L. 103mm inc.; w. 13mm. *5500 (sieving); SF 1743b*

Discussion

Approximately 79 fragments of leather were found in Well 1 at Dalton Parlours. The leather comprises discarded shoes, including a complete sandal; however, the majority are small, worn fragments. There is no evidence for shoemaking, the single trimming found being of limited significance, nor were any non-shoe items recovered.

Three types of shoe were found: the one-piece shoe, the nailed shoe and the sandal. They can be paralleled by many examples from Britain and the continent, occurring primarily on sites with military associations. This may only reflect the fact that the bulk of Roman leather has so far been found at military sites and their *vici*. With the exception of the sandal (No. 16), dating of the shoes according to style is difficult because of their fragmentary nature and the absence of many of the shoe uppers; however, there is no reason to believe that the shoes do not belong to the period of the well's use and the early years of its abandonment in the second half of the 3rd century.

The problem of differential leather shrinkage during burial, after excavation and during conservation makes estimation of equivalent modern shoe sizes unreliable. Seen in the broadest terms, however, the Dalton Parlours shoes include both adult and children's footwear (after an allowance for a conservative 10% shrinkage has been made).

The majority of the shoe fragments from Dalton Parlours come from one-piece or moccasin type shoes of cattle hide, corresponding to the term *carbatina* frequently used in the archaeological literature. Two styles of one-piece shoe could be recognised: firstly, a plain shoe with simple fastening loops (e.g. Nos 2, 8 and 10); secondly, a more decorative shoe with multiple fastening loops with decorative lobes (e.g. Nos 3, 4 and 9). Both styles of one-piece shoe were joined with a straight, butted back seam and E/F seams joining the back seam wings to the heel seat, sewn with narrow thongs. The back seams were usually joined with an E/F seam; however, an example with an oversewn G/F seam (No. 1) occurred, as well as another where the thong was no longer preserved (No. 7). The additional G/F thonged stitching present below the fastening loops on two shoes (Nos 6 and 10) is likely to come from the attachment of sole repairs.

One-piece shoes are commonly found throughout the north-west provinces (see Rhodes 1980, 127-8). In Britain they occurred principally on sites of 1st and 2nd-century date (being virtually absent from the early to mid-3rd-century assemblage from St Magnus House, London, for example (MacConnoran 1986, 225-6, fig. 89). On the continent, however, this shoe type continues in popularity until the mid-3rd century after which time the evidence for all shoe types becomes insufficient for comment (van Driel-Murray 1986, 139-45). That the one-piece shoes from Dalton Parlours derive from deposits which

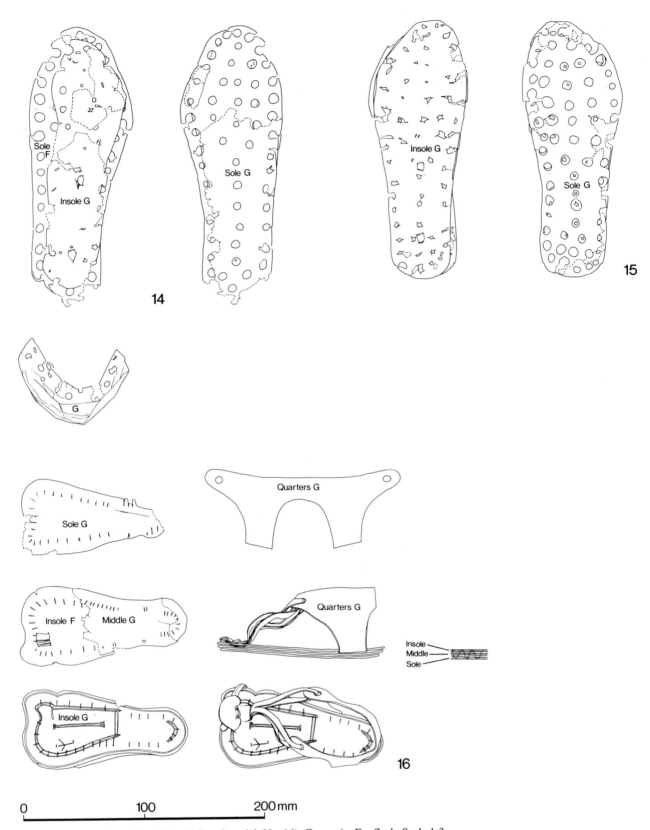

Fig. 143. Leather shoes (Nos 14 and 15) and sandal (No. 16); G = grain, F = flesh. Scale 1:3

accumulated during the use of the well in the second half of the 3rd century (Nos 3-7) and its deliberate infilling, probably closely following its abandonment shortly after *c*. AD 370 (Nos 1 and 2), is of some interest, echoing as it does the continental evidence.

Recently, one-piece shoes have also been recovered from a 4th-century well at Rothwell Colliery, West Yorkshire. They have a number of features in common with the Dalton Parlours material both in style, namely the multiple decorative lobes, and construction, thonged back seams and the use of thonging to attach sole repairs. The constructional similarities are shared with the later one-piece shoes found on the continent and must be seen as being characteristic of late 3rd and 4th-century footwear (van Driel-Murray 1986).

Four bottom units and a separate fragment of goatskin upper come from shoes of nailed construction, the most commonly found type of Roman footwear. Again they occurred in deposits dating to the use of the well during the third quarter of the 3rd century and its abandonment shortly after *c*. AD 370.

The pointed-toed shoe (No. 11) has remains of its goatskin upper and calfskin heel stiffener, the fragment of curved throat present suggests that the shoe had a closed upper originally. The upper and heel stiffener were secured to the middle by a nailed and thonged lasting margin. This construction is comparable with a bottom unit from Billingsgate Buildings, London (Rhodes 1980, no. 523, figs 59-60) which has peripheral thonging on the insole rather than the middle, but similarly has a decorative nailing pattern and a centrally thonged insole and middle lamina. The decorative nailing pattern of groups of three nails seen on the pointed-toed shoe (No. 11) can also be paralleled amongst the shoes from Rothwell Colliery (van Driel-Murray pers. comm.).

The other nailed bottom units also have insoles thonged to a middle or middle lamina. One insole (No. 13) has tunnel stitching on the flesh side, visible at the tread, by which the upper had been attached. The marks made on the insole by hobnails suggest it to have been a relatively lightly nailed shoe. The remaining two bottom units (Nos 14 and 15) have heavily nailed soles suggesting they came from outdoor, working shoes. No indication of the method of upper attachment was visible so that a one-piece moccasin type upper or, more likely, an upper with a nailed lasting margin may have been used. The separate goatskin upper fragment (No. 12) has a nailed lasting margin which had been held in place by bracing during construction when the individual components were nailed together on the last. The upper has a closed seam, a feature also noted on a nailed shoe of probable mid-4th-century date from Eastgate Street, Gloucester (Goudge 1983, fig. 102, no. 6).

A virtually complete child's sandal with divided toe thong and latcheted, one-piece quarters (No. 16) occurred in a deposit which accumulated during the use of the well during the third quarter of the 3rd century. It is of interest as rarely is the upper found so well preserved. The sandal has an unnailed bottom unit, the individual components

being held together by peripheral thonging only. The decoration on the insole is comparable with that on similar broad-toed sandals from Cologne in Germany (Fremersdorf 1926, 50, Abb. 8-9). Work done by van Driel-Murray on continental material and study of the shoes from London (Ross 1971, I, 25; MacConnoran 1986, 221-3) has shown that this broad-toed sandal type dates to the 3rd century, being found from *c*. AD 230 in London, *c*. AD 250 on the continent and disappearing from the archaeological record by the end of the 3rd century. The Dalton Parlours sandal fits well into this chronology.

Sandals occur much less frequently than the other two shoe types found at Dalton Parlours; they correspond to the term *solea* and, no doubt, were used predominantly for indoor wear in Britain.

30 Pottery from Well 1 (Figs 144-50)
by A.B. Sumpter

Introduction

The quantity of pottery recovered totals 5940 sherds, of which the bulk was stratified. The major concentration was towards the foot of the shaft where 90% of stratified sherds occurred in the lowest 3m of fill (13-16m below datum), though only 17% lay in the bottom 1.5m. The distribution by depth and class of ware is summarised in Table 29. Cross-matches between sherds of individual vessels from different depths are shown in Figure 144.

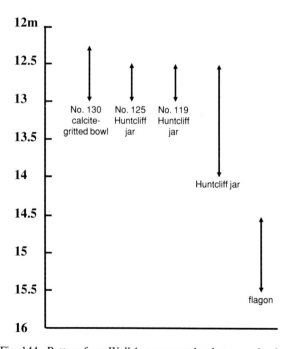

Fig. 144. Pottery from Well 1: cross-matches between sherds of the same vessels from different depths.

Table 29. Pottery from Well 1: sherd distribution by depth and class of ware.

Depth below datum (see Fig. 115)	TOTALS	Samian ware	Colour-coated ware	Flagons	Mortaria	Amphorae	Dales ware	Other gritted ware	Coarse gritted ware	Bowls in cream ware	Grey wares			Huntcliff jars
											Source uncertain	Throlam	Crambeck	
unstratified	256	1					2				46	46	49	112
A	4										3			1
B	4		2								2			
C	–													
D	5										4			1
E	41						3				30			8
F-G	–													
0.35-2.30m	78		3				3	1	3		46			22
2.30-12m	61		1			1		1			21		3	34
12-13m	144										7		4	133
13-14.5m	4360	6	29	3	7		7	11		2	269	179	1504	2343
14.5-15.5m	312	14	1	3	1	1	4				140	61	51	36
15.5-16m	675	7	8	4	3		4	4	2		209	406	18	10
TOTALS	5940	28	44	10	11	2	23	17	5	2	777	692	1629	2700

The assemblage displays no great variety, and there is an overwhelming prevalence of two vessel types: lug-handled jars in grey ware, and Huntcliff jars. The condition of the sherds is good, especially those from the lower levels, with little post-breakage abrasion or erosion. There are four complete vessels (Nos 90, 98 and 105-6), and 22 other vessels were reconstructed to 70% or more complete. The sieving procedure during excavation ensured a high rate of recovery, and the amount of reconstruction would have been greater had time and resources permitted.

The order of description is from the bottom of the shaft upwards; depths are measured from local datum (see Fig. 115). Sixty-five vessels have been illustrated; unillustrated sherds are recorded in the Archive Report.

Catalogue

All references to Gillam types are from Gillam 1970.

15.5-16m (Figs 145-6)

71* Bowl in hard, light grey ware with darker surfaces smoothed overall. cf. Gillam 223, dated AD 120-210. Three sherds, including one from 14.5-15.5m.

72* Jar in BB1; external carbon deposit. cf. Gillam 144, dated AD 160-280. Possibly the same vessel as in Structure F (context 600).

73* Mortarium with reeded rim in soft, coarse, orange fabric with cream slip; mixed trituration grit.

74* Flanged inturned jar in sandy, light grey ware with darker surfaces. A similar rim came from pit 8201. cf. Brough no. 741, suspected to be a Throlam bowl (Wacher 1969, 202, fig. 80); but at Castleford in a post-fort ditch, a rim of similar form and fabric with Throlam-style sloping line decoration was certainly a jar (Rush forthcoming). Three sherds, including two from 14.5-15.5m.

75* Large two-handled jar in sandy, medium grey ware with alternate smoothed bands; reconstructed to 90% complete, one handle missing; base very worn, most broken away probably before despatch. Light grey kiln marks from vessels of different sizes. Frilled collars occurred at both Throlam and Crambeck; and though the form is paralleled at neither, this is more likely to be a Throlam product.

76* Lugged jar in sandy, grey sandwich fabric; reconstructed to 95% complete, both lugs missing. Kiln marks from other vessels. cf. Throlam no. 72 (Sheppard and Corder 1934, 28, fig. 14).

77* Jar made without handles in light, medium grey ware; reconstructed to 80% complete. Kiln indentation on side. Base very worn, almost half broken away, first riveted then replaced by a large lead patch. The groups of burnished sloping lines are a typical Throlam decoration. cf. Throlam no. 95, shown with handle (Sheppard and Corder 1934, 30, fig. 15).

78* Globular jar in sandy, grey sandwich fabric with smoothed bands; reconstructed to 70% complete. Similar funnel necks occurred at Throlam, but no complete profile of this form. cf. Throlam nos 96 and 97 (Sheppard and Corder 1934, 30, fig. 15).

79* Globular jar in a grey sandwich fabric less sandy than No. 78, with smoothed bands; reconstructed to 60% complete. Including three sherds from 14.5-15.5m.

14.5-15.5m (Fig. 146)

80* Bowl in dark grey ware with thin, light grey cortex. cf. Gillam 225, dated AD 200-250 on the Northern Frontier.

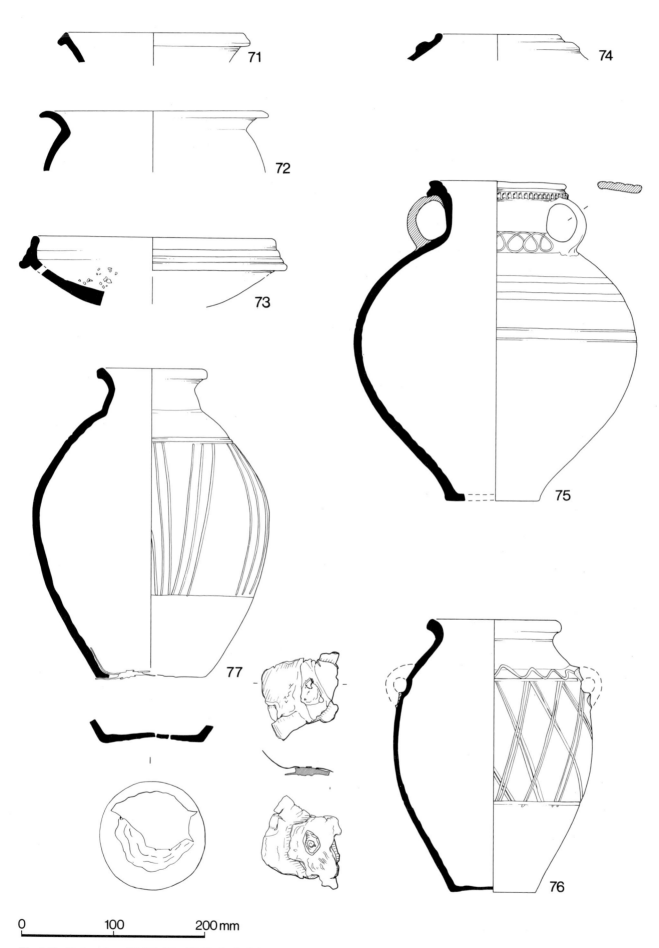

Fig. 145. Pottery from Well 1 (Nos 71-7). Scale 1:4

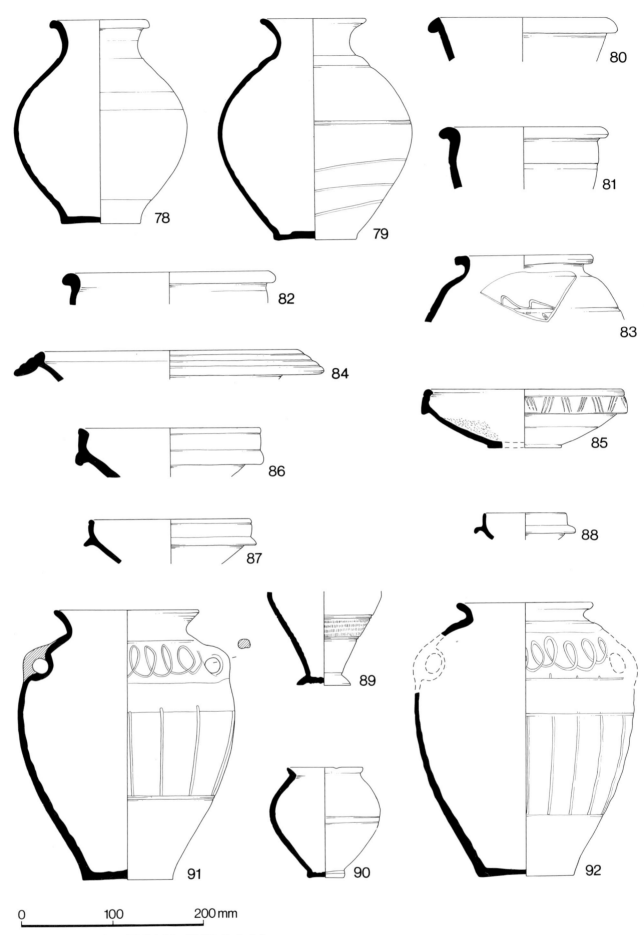

0   100   200 mm

Fig. 146. Pottery from Well 1 (Nos 78-92). Scale 1:4

13-14.5m (Figs 146-50)

81* Wide-mouthed bowl in sandy, medium grey ware with light grey core. Possibly a South Yorkshire product.

82* Wide-mouthed bowl in sandy, grey sandwich ware. Possibly a South Yorkshire product.

83* Jar in medium grey ware with smoothed bands. Rim warped; a second.

84* Mortarium with reeded flange in off-white fabric with eroded yellowish slip; mixed trituration grit. Discoloured by post-breakage burning.

85* Mortarium in fine cream fabric with red-brown paint decoration; reconstructed to 30% complete. Crambeck type 7 (Corder and Birley 1937, 401-3, fig. 3).

86* Segmental flanged bowl in very hard, over-fired, whitish-grey ware with dark grey smoothed surfaces. Chips on the rim and flange have been ground to remove sharp edges. Crambeck type 5a (Corder and Birley 1937, 401, fig. 3).

87* Segmental flanged bowl in fine cream fabric, undecorated. Discoloured by post-breakage burning. Crambeck type 5b (Corder and Birley 1937, 401, fig. 3).

88* Small delicate segmental flanged bowl in faintly pinkish-cream fabric with smooth, uniform orange colour-coat, slightly eroded; a passable imitation of samian form 38. For the form cf. Crambeck type 5b (Corder and Birley 1937, 401, fig. 3), where it occurred with orange-painted ornamentation rather than coating.

89* Beaker in cream fabric with dark brown colour-coat; zone of faint rouletting. Discoloured by burning.

90* Small jar in hard, pale grey ware with medium grey, very smooth surfaces. Complete but for minor rim and basal chips, a hole 11 x 7mm through the girth, and kiln spalling across 30% of the exterior; a second. Burnt on one side. cf. Crambeck type 11 (Corder and Birley 1937, 403, fig. 4).

Numbers 91-106 inclusive are lug-handled jars of Crambeck type 3 (Corder and Birley 1937, 399, fig. 2). Unless otherwise stated the fabric is hard, light to medium grey ware with darker surfaces, though varying in appearance within these limits; no two of the following sixteen vessels are in identical fabric. It is not uncommonly overfired to a hard, brittle, whitish-grey, contrasting markedly with the darker surfaces. The scheme of decoration was evidently well established: three smoothed zones, at the foot, above the girth and below the rim – the uppermost not always present – separate two reserved zones sometimes delineated by shallow horizontal grooves; lightly incised ornamentation in the lower reserved zone is by spaced vertical lines, and in the upper zone by a looped or wavy line level with the lugs. This upper line is sufficiently free-form to have autographical value, but close comparison within the groups could recognise no two vessels embellished by the same potter. The degree of surface finish differs, though bases are invariably turned. Light grey kiln marks from other vessels are common. Some of the jars have worn bases, chipped rims and lugs, and abrasions round the girth; others were relatively undamaged when deposited. Preservation conditions enabled some smoothed areas to retain a lustrous appearance, while a few sherds have been partly leached to a paler colour.

91* Lugged jar; reconstructed to 90% complete.

92* Lugged jar; reconstructed to 70% complete, lugs missing.

93* Lugged jar in whitish-grey ware with darker surfaces, overfired; reconstructed to 90% complete.

94* Lugged jar; reconstructed to 90% complete.

95* Lugged jar; reconstructed to 90% complete.

96* Lugged jar; reconstructed to 80% complete.

97* Lugged jar in whitish-grey ware with darker surfaces, overfired; reconstructed to 80% complete.

98* Lugged jar, complete and undamaged but for minor abrasions.

99* Lugged jar; reconstructed to 95% complete.

100* Lugged jar, with a 4mm hole through the girth repaired by a small lead plug; reconstructed to 95% complete.

101* Lugged jar in whitish-grey ware with darker surfaces, overfired; reconstructed to 90% complete.

102* Lugged jar with unusual upper zone decoration by hatching; reconstructed to 90% complete.

103* Lugged jar; reconstructed to 90% complete.

104* Lugged jar in whitish-grey ware with darker surfaces, overfired; reconstructed to 80% complete.

105* Lugged jar, complete but for minor rim chips, damaged lugs and a hole 35 x 30mm at the girth.

106* Lugged jar in whitish-grey ware with darker surfaces, overfired; complete but for badly chipped rim and a hole 65 x 35mm below the girth.

107* Jug in uniform, sandy, medium grey ware; spout missing. cf. Crambeck type 15 (Corder and Birley 1937, 405, pl. 87, no. 2: also Corder 1928, 40, pl. 8, nos 185-7).

108* Jug in sandy whitish-grey fabric, overfired; handle and most of spout missing. cf. Crambeck type 15, as above.

Numbers 109-129 inclusive are Huntcliff jars with hand-made bodies and wheel-finished rims: Gillam 163; a type considered to have been manufactured at more than one location. The fabric is coarse and can vary in colour even within the same vessel; usually dark grey or black, it may be lighter grey or brown. Surfaces are most often dark grey or black, the exterior not infrequently light brown or a lighter grey. Conspicuous rather than profuse inclusions mostly of calcite are in the order of 0.5-2.5mm. Decoration is scarce. Many of the jars have heavy carbonaceous deposits and sooting, especially on the shoulder and below the rim, and internal calcareous scaling from hard water.

109* Jar with internal rim groove; an exceptional fabric for this form: coarse, sandy, medium grey ware, externally lighter grey; roughly incised decoration.

110* Jar with marked rim groove; external carbon deposit; reconstructed to 85% complete.

111* Jar with rim groove; external carbon deposit; reconstructed to 65% complete.

112* Jar without rim groove; external carbon deposit, internal scaling; reconstructed to 80% complete.

113* Jar with marked rim groove; external carbon deposit, internal scaling; reconstructed to 90% complete.

114* Jar with marked rim groove; external carbon deposit; reconstructed to 50% complete.

115* Jar with rim groove; external carbon deposit, internal scaling; reconstructed to 40% complete. Including two sherds from 12.8-13m.

116* Jar with slight rim groove; external carbon deposit. Two diametrically opposite holes each 3.5mm diam. bored through the shoulder after firing; reconstructed to 30% complete.

117* Jar with rim groove; external carbon deposit, internal scaling.

118* Jar with marked rim groove; external carbon deposit.

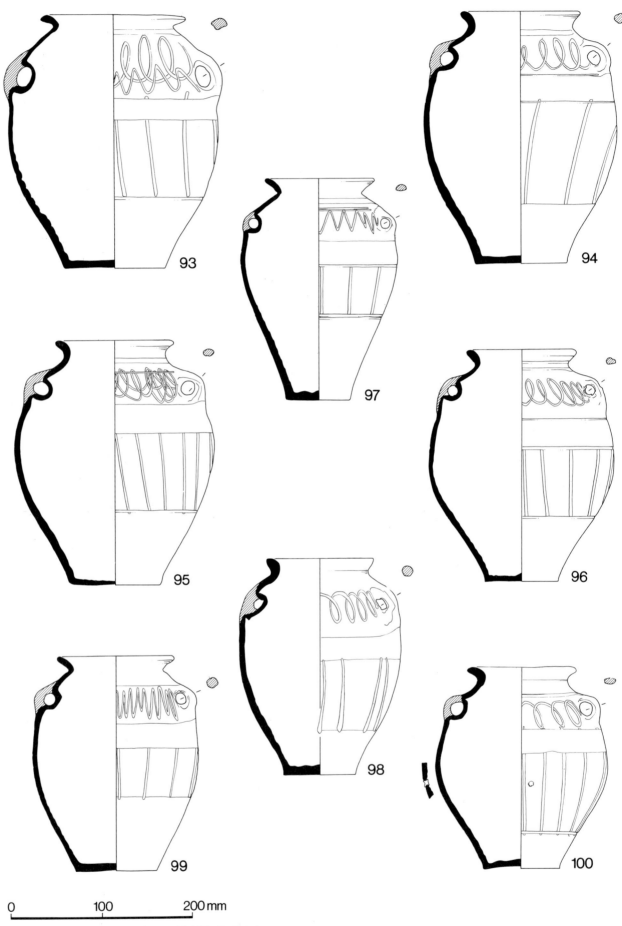

0   100   200 mm

Fig. 147. Pottery from Well 1 (Nos 93-100). Scale 1:4

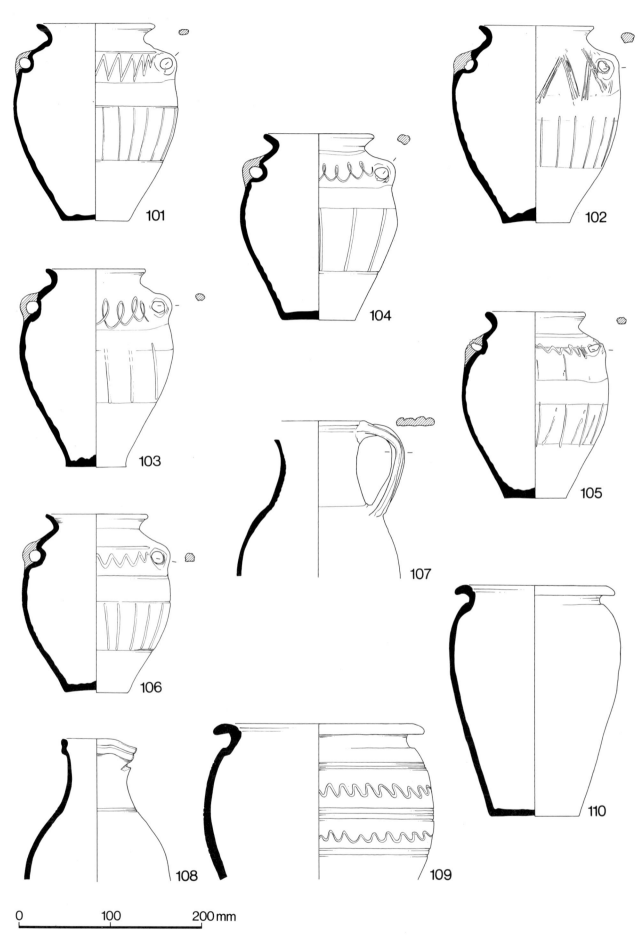

Fig. 148. Pottery from Well 1 (Nos 101-10). Scale 1:4

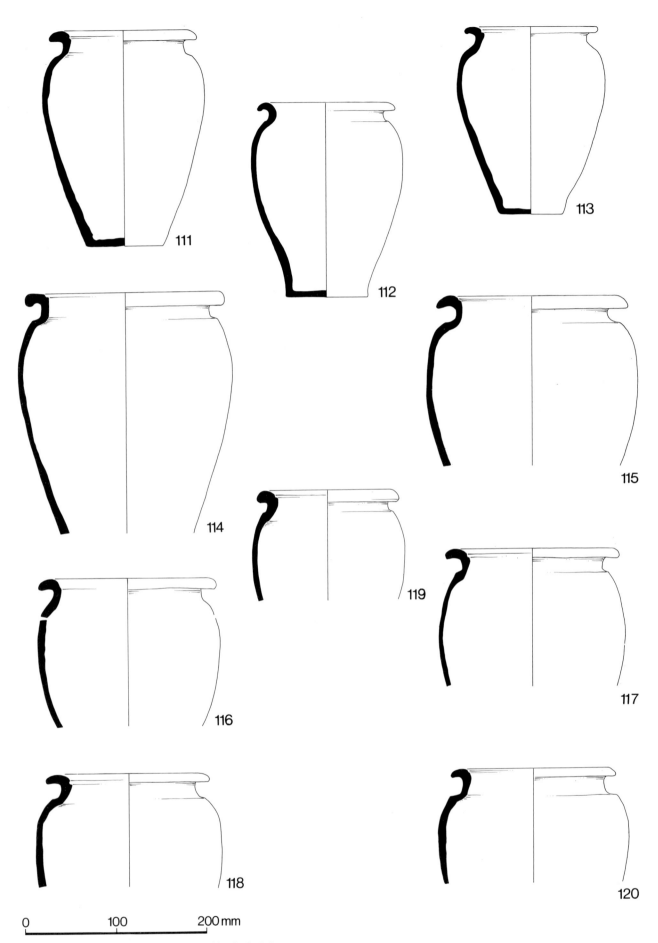

0   100   200 mm

Fig. 149. Pottery from Well 1 (Nos 111-20). Scale 1:4

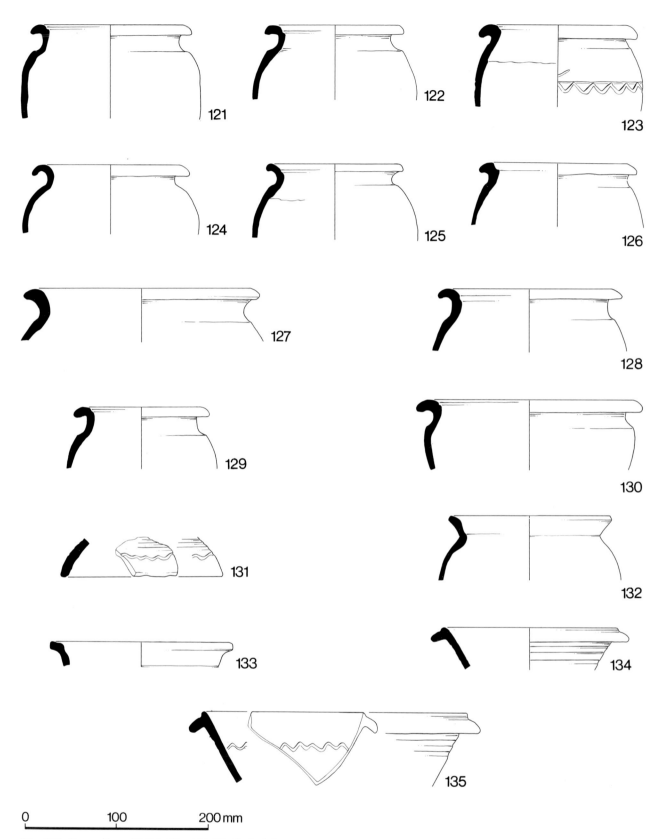

0   100   200 mm

Fig. 150. Pottery from Well 1 (Nos 121-35). Scale 1:4

119* Jar with rim groove; external carbon deposit, internal scaling; reconstructed to 40% complete. Including one sherd from 12-12.5m.

120* Jar with slight rim groove; external carbon deposit, internal scaling.

121* Jar with rim groove; external carbon deposit, internal scaling.

122* Jar with marked rim groove; external carbon deposit, internal scaling.

123* Jar with rim groove; external carbon deposit, internal scaling; roughly incised decoration.

124* Jar without rim groove; external carbon deposit, internal scaling.

125* Jar with slight rim groove; external carbon deposit. Including one sherd from 12-12.5m.

126* Jar with marked rim groove; external carbon deposit, internal scaling; roughly incised decoration.

127* Unusually large jar without rim groove; external carbon deposit.

128* Jar with rim groove; external carbon deposit, internal scaling.

129* Jar with slight rim groove.

130* Wide-mouthed bowl with hand-made body, and wheel-finished Huntcliff jar-type rim, with rim groove in calcite-gritted fabric with surfaces smoothed overall by a narrow tool. A single example in this fabric was found at Crambeck (Corder 1928, 39, pl. 6, no. 166). Two sherds including one from 12.2m.

131* Lid, hand-made in calcite-gritted fabric with roughly incised decoration; carbon deposit on the underside.

132* Jar with hand-made body and wheel-finished rim in dark grey fabric with profuse small shell grit; external carbon deposit.

133* Jar with wheel-finished rim in the same shell-gritted fabric as No. 132; external carbon deposit.

12-13m (Fig. 150)

134* Flanged bowl in light grey ware with medium grey surfaces. Discoloured by burning after breakage. cf. Crambeck type 1 (Corder and Birley 1937, 398-9, fig. 2).

135* Flanged bowl in light grey ware with dark grey surfaces smoothed overall, except for below the flange and an internal reserved zone bearing wavy line decoration. cf. Crambeck type 1b (Corder and Birley 1937, 399, fig. 2).

Discussion

The pottery might be expected to provide dating evidence for three phases of activity: the construction of the well, its use, and its infilling. For the initial phase, however, evidence was absent; the layers which had backed the retaining wall around the upper part of the well were devoid of pottery.

It remains to assess the extent to which the lower deposits had accumulated during the working life of the well. In the course of excavation this seemed unlikely to be large because of the penetration of sizeable stones to the full depth of the shaft. Furthermore, the concentration of 73% of stratified sherds between 1.5 and 3m from the base could have resulted mainly, if not wholly, from deliberate backfilling. In addition, there was no clear-cut grouping of early pottery such as samian ware at the foot of the shaft: the analysis summarised in Table 29 confirms that samian was broadly distributed throughout the lowest 3m.

On the other hand, it should be noted that the highest proportion of Throlam ware, over 400 sherds, lay in the lowest 0.5m of the fill. At this level there were only eighteen sherds identified as Crambeck grey ware and ten of Huntcliff jars, both types which peaked higher up in the

concentration at 1.5-3m from the foot. Since mainstream Throlam production is the earliest of the mass-produced coarse wares present in quantity, this argues that the lowest 0.5m represented deposition during use, albeit disturbed by the subsequent descent of heavy material. Between 0.5 and 1.5m from the bottom Throlam ware still outnumbered Crambeck grey ware and Huntcliff jars, though less overwhelmingly, implying that at least part of this level too had first accumulated while the well was in use. The number of Throlam jars suggests that the well was in being by the second half of the 3rd century; but there is insufficient evidence either to confirm or disprove an earlier starting date.

The inferred life of the well is protracted beyond AD 340 by the large number of Huntcliff jars clearly associated with its function. Quantification was attempted by dividing the weight of an average vessel into the gross sherd weight; but as the quotient was less than the total of different rims, it was concluded that not all the jars were complete when jettisoned. Later forms are few: two Crambeck type 7 painted mortaria (Gillam 289) including No. 85, and two Crambeck type 5b cream bowls (Gillam 207), unpainted, including No. 87 – both types dated to AD 370-400 on the Northern Frontier. All four vessels were in the major concentration between 1.5 and 3m from the bottom and therefore probably entered in backfilling. The well probably continued in use up to the abandonment of the villa, at some point during the late 4th century. From the vessel types noted above the final infilling post-dated AD 370.

Despite the number of iron-bound wooden buckets, handled jars also served for drawing water. This is shown by the scrap of cord still attached to a lug, and the frequency of girth abrasions consistent with damage from the sides of the shaft. The prevalence of chipped rims may also be symptomatic. The introduction of the Crambeck type 3 jar was a technological advance with countersunk lug handles substantially stronger than the luted appendages of its Throlam predecessor, as witnessed by scars where some of the latter had parted company. Experiment shows that the high-set position of the Crambeck type 3 handles is another crucial design feature, self-protecting and allowing suspension by one lug without significant loss of the liquid-carrying capacity.

The Huntcliff jars also provide functional evidence in the form of heavy carbonaceous deposits and internal scaling, which indicate the regular boiling of water on an open fire. Since kitchen wares are few, the hot water was probably for ablutions in the adjacent bath suite of Structure M.

Excluding those vessels accidentally lost in use, the likeliest explanation for the mass deposition of pottery is that Crambeck lugged jars and Huntcliff jars were stored in quantity close by, probably in the well-house, and were despatched together at an early stage in an organised backfilling operation.

Lug-handled and Huntcliff jars are characteristic finds from wells at other villas excavated in the region, for example Langton (Corder and Kirk 1932, 49-55) and

Rudston (Rigby 1980, 45, 73-89, 92-4). At Rudston the well lay next to a bath suite and the Huntcliff jars were sooted, suggesting that the interpretation of their use at Dalton Parlours might also apply there.

31 Mammal bones from Well 1 (Figs 151-4) by David Berg

The faunal remains from the Dalton Parlours well were analysed at the University of Sheffield as part of a postgraduate MA thesis (Cotton 1982). Edited sections of that report are reproduced below, particularly the analysis methodology and original quantifications. The assemblage and species descriptions, with additions, are also included. Only a summary of the comprehensive large mammal metrical data has been reproduced here; the complete archive is held at West Yorkshire Archaeology Service and is available on request. The overview is a reappraisal of Cotton's data in the light of further evidence from the well and the study of additional faunal remains from the Dalton Parlours site.

Provenance

Animal bone was analysed from the well divisions H to M and grouped into depth units below datum. A considerable variation in the colour, texture and hardness of bone fragments was noted during the analysis. This appeared to be related to changes in soil condition down the well and affected, to a certain extent, the level to which the bones could be identified (much of the unidentifiable fraction being heavily weathered and eroded specimens).

Division H (0.35-2.3m)
Total fragments 37.9%. Identified fragments 33.9%.
Bone 'bleached' white, surface texture powdery and bones have heavily weathered, pitted surface. Evidence of carnivore damage. Unfused specimens often in poor condition.

Division J (2.3-11.0m)
Total fragments 16.5%. Identified fragments 14.3%.
Bone in better condition than division H. Frequent hairline cracks on surface of bone.

Division K (11.9-13.9m)
Total fragments 37.6%. Identified fragments 42.8%.
Bone very well preserved. Surface stained dark reddish-brown and flaking off certain bones, particularly mandibles. Unfused bone very porous. Some heavily weathered specimens.

Division L (14.0-14.3m)
Total fragments 3.7%. Identified fragments 4.3%.
Bone frequently gnawed but well preserved with hard, smooth, grey surface.

Table 30. Well 1: bone fragment quantification.

	Fragments	%	%	%	MNI	%	%
Cattle	1321	15.7	27.4	48.4	29	19.7	32.2
Sheep	1047	12.4	21.7	38.4	41	27.9	45.6
Pig	360	4.3	7.5	13.2	20	13.6	22.2
Total A	**2728**	**32.4**	**56.5**	**100.0**	**90**	**61.2**	**100.0**
Horse	597	7.1	12.4		14	9.5	
Dog	1350	16.0	28.0		31	21.0	
Badger	101	1.2	2.1		6	4.0	
Hare	15	0.2	0.3		3	2.0	
Human	37	0.4	0.8		3	2.0	
Total B	**4828**	**57.3**	**100.0**		**147**	**100.0**	
Ribs	1564	18.6					
Vertebrae	449	5.3					
Scapulae	3	0.03					
Skull	533	6.3					
Total C	**2549**	**30.3**					
Shaft frags	396	4.7					
Unidentified	648	7.7					
Total D	**1044**	**12.4**					
Total bone	**8421**	**100.0**					

+ unstratified bone 15

A = Total major domestic species
B = Total identified to species
C = Total identified to element
D = Total unidentified

Division M (14.3-16.2m)
Total fragments 4.2%. Identified fragments 4.8%.
Bone well preserved with hard, smooth surface texture.

Soil samples from various levels within the well were analysed for pH value using the method described by Briggs (1977). The results should be viewed with caution as a period of some four years had elapsed between excavation and pH analysis.

The upper levels of the well fill (H and J) were somewhat alkaline which may explain the powdery surface texture of the bone from this area. The lower waterlogged levels containing considerable organic matter were slightly acidic (K) tending towards neutrality in the bottom levels (L and M). It is possible that the degree of acidity in level K is responsible for the poor condition of very young unfused bones.

All the soil and silt removed from divisions K, L and M was wet-sieved on site with the exception of samples taken for soil analysis. The retrieval of animal bone is therefore assumed to be near 100% and the sample is considered to be largely free from the types of bias noted by Payne (1972).

Methodology

The minimum number of individuals (MNI) was calculated in the following manner for each species in

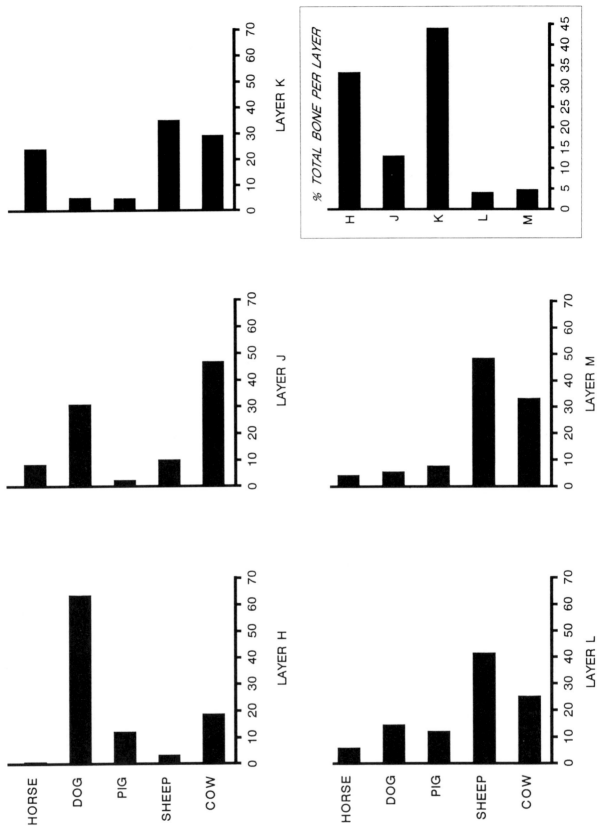

Fig. 151. Animal bone from Well 1: species fragment percentage frequency.

246

Table 31. Well 1: number of bone fragments for each unit and species – division H (from Cotton 1982).

	0.35-0.45		0.6-1.0		0.9-1.1		1.0-1.5		1.3-1.6		1.5-2.0		1.8-2.0		2.0-2.3		Total	
	F	%	F	%	F	%	F	%	F	%	F	%	F	%	F	%		
Sheep	1	50.0	0	0.0	0	0.0	10	1.8	13	1.6	24	3.2	4	0.9	7	1.6	59	1.8
Cattle	1	50.0	9	33.3	30	20.7	49	8.9	24	3.0	88	11.8	30	6.5	65	14.6	296	9.3
Pig	0	0.0	5	18.5	56	38.6	85	15.4	6	0.7	26	3.5	10	2.2	6	1.3	194	6.1
Horse	0	0.0	0	0.0	1	0.7	1	0.2	0	0.0	0	0.0	0	0.0	16	3.6	18	0.6
Dog	0	0.0	2	7.4	8	5.5	101	18.3	359	44.2	213	28.6	166	35.8	147	33.0	996	31.2
Badger	0	0.0	0	0.0	0	0.0	2	0.4	15	1.8	26	3.5	8	1.7	13	2.9	64	2.0
Hare	0	0.0	0	0.0	0	0.0	0	0.0	0	0.0	0	0.0	0	0.0	8	1.8	8	0.3
Human	0	0.0	0	0.0	0	0.0	0	0.0	0	0.0	0	0.0	0	0.0	0	0.0	0	0.0
Total identified	2	100.0	16	59.3	95	65.5	248	44.8	417	51.4	377	50.7	218	47.0	262	58.7	1635	51.2
Ribs	0	0.0	5	18.5	0	0.0	112	20.3	241	29.7	207	27.8	171	36.9	81	18.2	817	25.6
Vertebrae	0	0.0	0	0.0	0	0.0	54	9.8	24	3.0	35	4.7	25	5.4	21	4.7	159	5.0
Scapulae	0	0.0	0	0.0	0	0.0	3	0.5	0	0.0	0	0.0	0	0.0	0	0.0	3	0.1
Skull	0	0.0	3	11.1	12	8.3	23	4.2	38	4.7	10	1.3	0	0.0	22	4.9	108	3.4
Shaft	0	0.0	2	7.4	12	8.3	21	3.8	49	6.0	25	3.4	5	1.1	34	7.6	148	4.6
Unidentified	0	0.0	1	3.7	26	17.9	92	16.6	43	5.3	90	12.1	45	9.7	26	5.8	323	10.1
Total unidentified	0	0.0	11	40.7	50	34.5	305	55.2	395	48.6	367	49.3	246	53.0	184	41.3	1558	48.8
TOTAL	2		27		145		553		812		744		464		446		3193	

each depth unit and each division as a whole. Taking each bone element in turn, the fragments were separated into left and right and the greatest number taken as the MNI for that element. The origin of small fragments, measurements, epiphysial fusion and dentition data were considered during the analysis and only true paired elements were counted as pairs. Thus the MNI was the number of mutually exclusive bone fragments for a particular element. The MNI for each species was taken to be the greatest element MNI, again considering measurements and ageing data.

Matching pairs of elements were frequently identified in all the species except cattle. Paired bones often came from different depth units within divisions, but were never observed from different divisions. Consequently only the MNI for the well divisions are discussed, not for the different depth units as these are considered spurious.

Ageing data were recorded using the tooth eruption and wear stages of Grant (1975). Approximate ages of epiphysial fusion were based on the data of Silver (1969). Because of the difficulties in distinguishing the bones of sheep and goat any reference in the text to 'sheep' refers to 'sheep and/or goat' unless otherwise stated.

Sample description

The faunal sample from the well consisted of 8421 fragments of large mammal bone; 87.6% of the sample was identified to bone element level and 57.3% to species level (Tables 30-34). Unidentifiable fragments fell into two categories: those which could be identified to bone element but not species, e.g. scapulae, ribs, vertebrae and skull fragments, and those which were not identifiable to species or element type. The latter category was further

Table 32. Well 1: number of bone fragments for each unit and species – division J (from Cotton 1982).

	2.3-3.0		3.0-4.0		4.0-5.0		5.0-6.0		6.0-7.0		7.0-8.0		8.0-9.0		9.0-10.0		10.0-11.0		Total	
	F	%	F	%	F	%	F	%	F	%	F	%	F	%	F	%	F	%		
Sheep	7	2.6	4	2.1	2	3.6	2	2.0	10	7.0	2	7.4	27	7.0	7	3.3	2	28.6	63	4.5
Cattle	42	15.6	13	6.9	3	5.4	21	21.0	50	35.2	11	40.7	70	18.1	76	35.3	2	28.6	288	20.7
Pig	2	0.7	4	2.1	2	3.6	3	3.0	1	0.7	1	3.7	3	0.8	1	0.5	0	0.0	17	1.2
Horse	9	3.3	3	1.6	1	1.8	9	9.0	2	1.4	1	3.7	27	7.0	1	0.5	0	0.0	53	3.8
Dog	34	12.6	56	29.6	17	30.4	30	30.0	9	6.3	0	0.0	14	3.6	30	14.0	1	14.3	191	13.7
Badger	19	7.1	12	6.3	1	1.8	2	2.0	0	0.0	0	0.0	0	0.0	0	0.0	1	14.3	35	2.5
Hare	6	2.2	0	0.0	0	0.0	1	1.0	0	0.0	0	0.0	0	0.0	0	0.0	0	0.0	7	0.5
Human	1	0.4	3	1.6	0	0.0	4	4.0	5	3.5	4	14.8	20	5.2	0	0.0	0	0.0	37	2.7
Total identified	120	44.6	95	50.3	26	46.4	72	72.0	77	54.2	19	70.4	161	41.6	115	53.5	6	85.7	691	49.6
Ribs	85	31.6	54	28.6	26	46.4	5	5.0	16	11.3	3	11.1	19	4.9	14	6.5	0	0.0	222	15.9
Vertebrae	14	5.2	6	3.2	3	5.4	1	1.0	9	6.3	1	3.7	3	0.8	4	1.9	1	14.3	42	3.0
Scapulae	0	0.0	0	0.0	0	0.0	0	0.0	0	0.0	0	0.0	0	0.0	0	0.0	0	0.0	0	0.0
Skull	0	0.0	4	2.1	0	0.0	14	14.0	13	9.2	0	0.0	38	9.8	7	3.3	0	0.0	76	5.5
Shaft	8	3.0	0	0.0	0	0.0	1	1.0	21	14.8	4	14.8	72	18.6	50	23.3	0	0.0	156	11.2
Unidentified	42	15.6	30	15.9	1	1.8	7	7.0	6	4.2	0	0.0	94	24.3	25	11.6	0	0.0	205	14.7
Total unidentified	149	55.4	94	49.7	30	53.6	28	28.0	65	45.8	8	29.6	226	58.4	100	46.5	1	14.3	701	50.4
Total	269		189		56		100		142		27		387		215		7		1392	

Table 33. Well 1: number of bone fragments for each unit and species – division K (from Cotton 1982).

	11.9 F	11.9 %	12.0-12.7 F	12.0-12.7 %	12.5-13.0 F	12.5-13.0 %	13.0-13.9 F	13.0-13.9 %	Total F	Total %
Sheep	6	21.4	268	20.9	71	14.3	386	28.4	731	23.1
Cattle	11	39.3	268	20.9	85	17.1	246	18.1	610	19.2
Pig	0	0.0	38	3.0	8	1.6	61	4.5	107	3.4
Horse	1	3.6	188	14.6	176	35.3	139	10.2	504	15.9
Dog	0	0.0	17	1.3	45	9.0	49	3.6	111	3.5
Badger	0	0.0	0	0.0	0	0.0	2	0.1	2	0.1
Hare	0	0.0	0	0.0	0	0.0	0	0.0	0	0.0
Human	0	0.0	0	0.0	0	0.0	0	0.0	0	0.0
Total identified	18	64.3	779	60.7	385	77.3	883	65.0	2065	65.2
Ribs	0	0.0	196	15.3	77	15.5	138	10.2	411	13.0
Vertebrae	0	0.0	144	11.2	16	3.2	65	4.8	225	7.1
Scapulae	0	0.0	0	0.0	0	0.0	0	0.0	0	0.0
Skull	10	35.7	124	9.7	18	3.6	164	12.1	316	10.0
Shaft	0	0.0	0	0.0	0	0.0	48	3.5	48	1.5
Unidentified	0	0.0	41	3.2	2	0.4	61	4.5	104	3.3
Total unidentified	10	35.7	505	39.3	113	22.7	476	35.0	1104	34.8
Total	28		1284		498		1359		3169	

Table 34. Well 1: number of bone fragments for each unit and species – divisions L and M (from Cotton 1982).

	L 14.0-14.3 F	L 14.0-14.3 %	M 14.3-15.5 F	M 14.3-15.5 %	M 15.5-BTM F	M 15.5-BTM %	Total M F	Total M %
Sheep	82	26.3	76	35.0	36	26.1	112	31.5
Cattle	50	16.0	41	18.9	36	26.1	77	21.7
Pig	24	7.7	11	5.1	7	5.1	18	5.1
Horse	12	3.8	5	2.3	5	3.6	10	2.8
Dog	39	12.5	13	6.0	0	0.0	13	3.7
Badger	0	0.0	0	0.0	0	0.0	0	0.0
Hare	0	0.0	0	0.0	0	0.0	0	0.0
Human	0	0.0	0	0.0	0	0.0	0	0.0
Total identified	207	66.3	146	67.3	84	60.9	230	64.8
Ribs	52	16.7	39	18.0	23	16.7	62	17.5
Vertebrae	18	5.8	4	1.8	1	0.7	5	1.4
Scapulae	0	0.0	0	0.0	0	0.0	0	0.0
Skull	15	4.8	10	4.6	8	5.8	18	5.1
Shaft	13	4.2	14	6.5	17	12.3	31	8.7
Unidentified	7	2.2	4	1.8	5	3.6	9	2.5
Total unidentified	105	33.7	71	32.7	54	39.1	125	35.2
TOTAL	312		217		138		355	

Table 35. Well 1: major species frequencies.

Division		M	%	L	%	K	%	J	%	H	%	Total F	Total %
Cattle	F	77	33.5	50	24.2	610	29.6	288	47.1	296	18.9	1321	28.3
	MNI	4	23.5	4	28.6	11	20.8	4	25.0	6	17.1	29	21.5
Sheep	F	112	48.7	82	39.6	731	35.4	63	10.3	59	3.8	1047	22.4
	MNI	5	29.4	3	21.4	26	49.1	4	25.0	3	8.6	41	30.4
Pig	F	18	7.8	24	11.6	107	5.2	17	2.8	194	12.4	360	7.7
	MNI	2	11.8	3	21.4	7	13.2	2	12.5	6	17.1	20	14.8
Dog	F	13	5.7	39	18.8	111	5.4	191	31.2	996	63.7	1350	28.9
	MNI	4	23.5	2	14.3	3	5.7	4	25.0	18	51.4	31	23.0
Horse	F	10	4.3	12	5.8	504	24.4	53	8.7	18	1.2	597	12.8
	MNI	2	11.8	2	14.3	6	11.3	2	12.5	2	5.7	14	10.4
Total	F	230	100.0	207	100.0	2063	100.0	612	100.0	1563	100.0	4675	100.0
	MNI	17	100.0	14	100.0	53	100.0	16	100.0	35	100.0	135	100.0

subdivided in order to quantify the unidentifiable long bone shaft fragments. The difficult excavation conditions and the brittle nature of the bone contributed to the large number of very small, freshly broken fragments that were unidentifiable, particularly from divisions H and J.

The relative percentage frequency for each species throughout the well divisions is presented in Table 35 calculated from the number of identifiable fragments and the MNI. The relative distribution of species by fragments is also shown in Figure 151.

Sheep

Sheep formed 21.7% of the total identified fragments representing 41 individuals (27.9%). Table 36 shows a breakdown of the fragments into the principle anatomical elements and the MNI represented by each class.

The bones were frequently weathered and this precluded the measurements of the distal metacarpi condyles for sheep/goat discrimination as described by Payne (1969). In the few cases where these measurements were taken the results proved inconclusive. Metapodial indices of maximum proximal width to maximum length and maximum distal width to maximum length were calculated after Boessneck (1969). For the metacarpi these indices were consistently 0.16-0.17 and 0.18-0.19 respectively. In all but two metatarsi the indices were 0.13-0.15 and 0.15-0.16. The two exceptions had values of 0.18 which may suggest they are from goat.

From the analysis of cranial sutures three of the seventeen near-complete ovicaprine skulls were identified as goat; two of the sheep specimens were polycerate having four horns.

In divisions L and M most elements of the skeleton were evenly represented whilst in division K the assemblage was dominated by bones of the skull, carpals, tarsals, metapodials and phalanges. A similar pattern was produced by the bone in division J although far fewer fragments were present. The 59 fragments in the upper level H were heavily biased towards fragments of the head and foot elements.

Ageing data for the mandibles are presented in Table 37. Two mandibles from immature individuals derived from divisions L and M and the remaining 33 ageable specimens were all associated with division K. These jaws ranged from mandible wear stages 5-51 with no definite peaks at any age stage although the majority were dentally

Table 36. Well 1: sheep – principal anatomical elements in each level.

	H F	H M	J F	J M	K F	K M	L F	L M	M F	M M	Total F	Total M
Mandible	4	2	0	0	38	26	5	3	5	3	52	34
Maxilla	1	1	0	0	33	20	3	2	2	1	39	24
Tooth	5	2	9	2	40	3	6	2	6	2	66	11
Skull	5	2	9	2	131	18	10	3	10	3	165	28
Scapula	4	2	5	4	15	8	2	2	6	4	32	20
Humerus	0	0	4	2	15	8	2	1	5	4	26	15
Radius	1	1	2	1	16	10	5	3	6	4	30	19
Ulna	1	1	0	0	8	6	2	1	0	0	11	8
Carpal/tarsal	10	2	7	2	64	5	3	1	7	2	91	12
Metacarpal	5	2	3	3	38	18	4	2	8	4	58	29
Pelvis	0	0	3	1	13	10	4	2	5	4	25	17
Femur	1	1	2	1	21	13	7	3	5	3	36	21
Tibia	2	1	3	2	35	16	3	1	15	5	58	25
Astragalus	0	0	0	0	11	6	0	0	1	1	12	7
Calcaneum	1	1	0	0	13	6	0	0	2	2	16	9
N. cuboid	0	0	0	0	16	9	0	0	2	1	18	10
Metatarsal	4	3	3	2	60	23	5	2	10	5	82	35
Metapodial	0	0	0	0	4	2	0	0	0	0	4	2
Phalange 1	6	2	4	2	62	7	8	2	6	2	86	
Phalange 2	7	2	1	1	42	5	4	1	8	2	62	
Phalange 3	2	1	7	2	34	5	1	1	0	0	44	
Atlas	0	0	0	0	7	7	0	0	0	0	7	7
Axis	0	0	0	0	10	10	0	0	0	0	10	10
Vertebrae	0	0	1	1	5	2	8	2	3	1	17	6
Total frags/ greatest MNI	59	3	63	4	731	26	82	3	112	5	1047	41

F = fragments, M = minimum number of individuals (from Cotton 1982)

immature. Division K also produced the bulk of sheep bones with fusion evidence (Table 38).

Withers heights were estimated using the method of Teichert (1975) giving a means of 56.0cm on the metacarpals (min. 53.2, max. 59.5, n=11) and 56.8cm on the metatarsals (min. 53.7, max. 60.0, n=17). Selected long bone measurements are compared with data from other Roman assemblages in Table 39.

Butchery evidence was frequently noted. Two sheep skulls had been split along the frontal suture presumably for brain removal. Several skulls had cut marks across the occipital condyles as did atlases and axes indicative of head removal. Hyoid bones also displayed a high frequency of cut marks. All horn cores that had been severed from the skull included part of the frontal bone.

Cut marks on the scapula necks, pelves, distal humeri and astragali were similar to those described by Binford (1981) as resulting from dismemberment.

Overcrowding of teeth was frequent in the sheep mandibles, and one case of periodontal disease was noted. Two metatarsals were deformed and the diaphyses curved. Both were enlarged at the proximal end although this did not appear to be due to the regeneration of bone.

Table 37. Well 1: mandible wear stages after Grant (1975).

MANDIBLE WEAR STAGES

mws	Sheep M	%	Sheep L	%	Sheep K	%	Cattle M	%	Cattle K	%	Cattle H	%	Pig L	%	Pig K	%	Pig H	%
1	–		–		–		–		–		–		3	100.0	2	20.0		
2	–		–		–		–		1	8.3	–		–		–		1	100.0
3	–		–		–		–		1	8.3	–		–		–		–	
4	1	100.0	–		–		–		–		–		–		–		–	
5	–		–		3	9.1	–		3	25.0	–		–		–		–	
9	–		–		2	6.1	–		–		–		–		2	20.0	–	
10	–		–		1	3.0	–		–		–		–		–		–	
11	–		–		1	3.0	–		–		–		–		–		–	
12	–		–		2	6.1	–		–		–		–		–		–	
13	–		–		1	3.0	–		–		–		–		–		–	
14	–		–		1	3.0	–		–		–		–		–		–	
15	–		–		1	3.0	–		–		–		–		–		–	
16	–		1	100.0	4	12.1	–		–		–		–		–		–	
17	–		–		1	3.0	–		1	8.3	–		–		–		–	
20	–		–		–		–		–		–		–		1	10.0	–	
21	–		–		–		–		–		–		–		2	20.0	–	
22	–		–		1	3.0	–		–		–		–		1	10.0	–	
23	–		–		–		–		–		–		–		1	10.0	–	
25	–		–		2	6.1	–		–		–		–		1	10.0	–	
26	–		–		1	3.0	–		–		–		–		–		–	
29	–		–		1	3.0	–		–		–		–		–		–	
30	–		–		1	3.0	–		–		–		–		–		–	
31	–		–		1	3.0	–		–		–		–		–		–	
32	–		–		2	6.1	–		–		–		–		–		–	
34	–		–		2	6.1	–		–		–		–		–		–	
37	–		–		–		–		–		1	100.0	–		–		–	
38	–		–		–		–		1	8.3	–		–		–		–	
39	–		–		3	9.1	–		1	8.3	–		–		–		–	
40	–		–		1	3.0	–		–		–		–		–		–	
43	–		–		–		1	50.0	1	8.3	–		–		–		–	
44	–		–		–		–		1	8.3	–		–		–		–	
46	–		–		–		1	50.0	–		–		–		–		–	
48	–		–		–		–		2	16.7	–		–		–		–	
51	–		–		1	3.0	–		–		–		–		–		–	
Total	**1**		**1**		**33**		**2**		**12**		**1**		**3**		**10**		**1**	

mws = mandible wear stage
% = cumulative percent

Table 38. Well 1: epiphysial fusion data.

Element	Age (mths)	H F	H NF	H % NF	J F	J NF	J % NF	K F	K NF	K % NF	L F	L NF	L % NF	M F	M NF	M % NF
CATTLE																
Sd Hd Rp Pp	7-18	32	10	23.8	8	19	70.4	45	68	60.2	2	2	50.0	6	3	33.3
Mcd Td Mtd	24-36	4	6	60.0	2	9	81.8	15	26	63.4	0	2	100.0	9	1	10.0
Fp C	36-42	1	1	50.0	1	1	50.0	0	4	100.0	0	0	0.0	0	0	0.0
Hp Rd Up Fd Tp	42-48	10	23	69.7	2	11	84.6	7	14	66.7	4	2	33.3	5	5	50.0
SHEEP																
Sd Hd Rp	6-10	0	2	100.0	1	2	66.7	23	6	20.7	4	0	0.0	6	1	14.3
Pp Mcd Td Mtd	13-28	1	5	83.3	3	3	50.0	28	51	64.6	4	2	33.3	4	10	71.4
Rd Up Fp C	30-36	0	1	100.0	0	2	100.0	7	11	61.1	2	2	50.0	0	2	100.0
Hp Fd Tp	36-42	2	1	33.3	0	5	100.0	11	35	76.1	5	2	28.6	4	10	71.4
PIG																
Sd Hd Rp	12	0	27	100.0	2	2	50.0	1	4	80.0	1	4	80.0	1	0	0.0
Mcd Td Pp C Mtd	24	0	16	100.0	0	0	0.0	0	5	100.0	0	0	0.0	0	0	0.0
Hp Rd Up Fp Fd Tp	36-42	0	53	100.0	0	3	100.0	0	11	100.0	1	7	87.5	1	3	75.0
DOG																
Sd Pp	6-7	85	5	5.6	27	0	0.0	17	0	0.0	0	0	0.0	0	0	0.0
Hd Up Mcd Mtd	8-10	98	28	22.2	28	6	17.6	13	0	0.0	0	0	0.0	0	0	0.0
Rp Rd	11-12	16	7	30.4	4	5	55.6	4	0	0.0	0	0	0.0	0	0	0.0
Hp Td C	13-16	24	13	35.1	3	4	57.1	3	0	0.0	0	0	0.0	0	0	0.0
Fp Fd Tp	18	27	21	43.8	6	6	50.0	5	0	0.0	0	0	0.0	0	0	0.0

Element key:
S = scapula, H = humerus, R = radius, U = ulna, Mc = metacarpal, P = phalanx1, F = femur, T = tibia, C = calcaneum, Mt = metatarsal
p = proximal, d = distal
Ages after Silver (1969)

Table 39. Well 1: sheep metrical comparisons.

Metatarsal – maximum width distal fusion point	n	range (mm)
Dalton Parlours Well 1	18	19.4 - 23.8
Dalton Parlours villa	5	20.0 - 22.2
Exeter (Roman)	12	18.9 - 21.3
Braughing	12	15.1 - 23.5
Sheepen	8	18.8 - 21.7
Winterton	2	15.4 - 22.0

Tibia – distal width	n	range (mm)
Dalton Parlours Well 1	5	21.5 - 23.2
Dalton Parlours villa	8	20.3 - 25.3
Exeter (Roman)	66	21.3 - 29.2
Braughing	56	18.3 - 28.4
Sheepen	33	20.5 - 25.6
Winterton	21	19.8 - 27.7

Metacarpal – greatest length	n	range (mm)
Dalton Parlours Well 1	11	110.0 - 123.0
Dalton Parlours villa	8	112.6 - 124.0
Exeter (Roman)	3	112.0 - 117.0
Sheepen	12	111.0 - 122.5

Sources: Exeter – Maltby (1979); Sheepen – Luff (1982);
Dalton Parlours villa – Berg (this volume);
Winterton, Braughing – Fifield (1980)

Cattle

Cattle bones comprised 27.4% of the identifiable fragments and represented some 29 individuals (19.7%). Table 40 shows the principal anatomical elements present in the bovine sample according to fragments and MNI represented.

In divisions L and M cattle limb bones were well represented as were loose teeth although skull, mandible and bones of the feet were relatively few. Division K showed a similar element distribution to that of the ovicaprids with very few limb bones, the majority of fragments deriving from the skull and limb extremities. Loose teeth formed the majority in division J with mandible and skull fragments whilst in the upper division H a more even representation of all the major elements was apparent.

Cattle dentition data are presented in Table 37. Two mature mandibles were present in division M and one in division H with the remaining twelve ageable specimens deriving from division K. These few mandibles formed two distinct clusters at mandible wear stages 2-5 and 38-48. Four of the near-complete skulls from this division possessed intact maxillae with full adult and well-worn dentition. The epiphysial fusion data (Table 38) confirmed the presence of very young and fully mature specimens. The majority of bones, nevertheless, appeared to be from immature animals with at least one foetal or neonatal specimen present. Throughout the well young cattle were underrepresented in the mandible data.

Withers heights were calculated after the method of Fock (1966) on the metapodials. The results produced means of 111.7cm on the metacarpals (min. 105.3, max.

Table 40. Well 1: cattle – principal anatomical elements in each level.

	H		J		K		L		M		Total	
	F	M	F	M	F	M	F	M	F	M	F	M
Mandible	25	5	52	4	23	11	3	2	4	3	107	25
Maxilla	7	2	2	2	31	8	1	1	1	1	42	14
Tooth	25	4	64	4	34	6	6	2	12	2	141	18
Skull	35	4	22	3	83	11	0	0	3	2	143	20
Scapula	18	3	3	1	8	4	7	4	4	4	40	16
Humerus	21	6	9	3	21	7	4	2	5	2	60	20
Radius	13	5	5	2	6	3	6	2	5	2	35	14
Ulna	7	4	0	0	6	4	1	1	1	1	15	10
Carpal/tarsal	12	3	17	2	76	5	2	1	1	1	108	12
Metacarpal	6	3	11	4	28	11	4	2	3	3	62	23
Pelvis	19	5	13	3	10	5	2	1	3	1	47	15
Femur	14	6	9	4	13	6	2	1	8	3	46	20
Tibia	9	4	13	4	13	6	1	1	10	4	46	19
Astragalus	2	2	3	2	2	2	0	0	2	2	9	8
Calcaneum	2	2	3	2	5	3	0	0	2	1	12	8
N. cuboid	0	0	2	1	7	4	0	0	1	1	10	6
Metatarsal	7	3	13	4	36	10	2	1	5	2	63	10
Phalange 1	16	4	15	3	72	11	1	1	2	1	106	20
Phalange 2	16	3	13	3	60	8	1	1	1	1	91	16
Phalange 3	7	2	4	2	19	3	1	1	1	1	32	9
Atlas	3	1	0	0	4	4	0	0	0	0	7	5
Axis	0	0	1	1	3	3	0	0	0	0	4	4
Vertebrae	32	2	14	2	40	5	6	1	3	1	95	11
Total frags/ greatest MNI	**296**	**6**	**288**	**4**	**610**	**11**	**50**	**4**	**77**	**4**	**1321**	**29**

F = fragments, M = minimum number of individuals (from Cotton 1982)

Table 41. Well 1: cattle metrical comparisons.

Astragalus – greatest length lateral aspect	n	range (mm)
Dalton Parlours Well 1	8	55.4 - 68.9
Dalton Parlours villa	5	56.9 - 64.9
Exeter (Roman)	32	50.7 - 62.0
Braughing	36	54.7 - 69.8
Portchester	–	–
Winterton	23	53.5 - 72.7
Watercrook	16	55.5 - 68.6

Tibia – distal width	n	range (mm)
Dalton Parlours Well 1	1	59.9 -
Dalton Parlours villa	10	52.3 - 65.8
Exeter (Roman)	20	49.7 - 65.1
Braughing	31	49.4 - 65.6
Portchester	143	50.0 - 69.0
Winterton	23	52.3 - 69.2
Watercrook	8	45.6 - 65.1

Metatarsal – greatest length	n	range (mm)
Dalton Parlours Well 1	8	202.1 - 221.0
Dalton Parlours villa	–	–
Exeter (Roman)	15	190.0 - 219.0
Braughing	8	182.0 - 249.0
Portchester	108	183.0 - 240.0
Winterton	8	198.0 - 231.0
Watercrook	5	193.0 - 214.0

Sources: Exeter – Maltby (1979); Portchester – Grant (1975); Dalton Parlours villa – Berg (this volume); Watercrook, Winterton, Braughing – Fifield (1980)

118.7, n=7) and 114.8cm on the metatarsals (min. 110.1, max. 120.4, n=8). Selected long bone measurements are compared with data from other Roman assemblages in Table 41.

The bovine mandibles were often very fragmentary with the coronoid process and condyle frequently chopped, perhaps to facilitate the removal of the tongue. Skulls were also very fragmented except in division K where ten fairly complete skulls were recorded. All but one were missing the nasals, premaxillae and portions of the frontals. Only four had maxillae and palatine bones present. Two of the skulls had evidence of having been severed from the body above the occipital condyles and at least four of the individuals had the centre of the frontal bone pierced suggesting pole-axing was part of the slaughter process.

Other butchery evidence included dismembering cut marks on the necks of scapulae, defleshing marks on radii and distal humeri and cut marks on astragali and distal metapodials.

One mandible displayed a congenital abscess of the second permanent premolar.

Pig

The pig bones comprised only 7.5% of the identified fragments but represented some twenty individuals (13.6%).

Divisions M, L, and J contained very few pig fragments. Division K produced selected elements biased towards the head and feet whilst in division H all elements of the skeleton were equally well represented with no obvious peak in element distribution (Table 42).

Tooth eruption and wear analysis in Table 37 shows that over half of the fourteen ageable mandibles were at Grant stages 1, 2 and 9 with the remainder grouped between stages 20-25. Although the vast majority of pig

Table 42. Well 1: pig – principal anatomical elements in each level.

	H		J		K		L		M		Total	
	F	M	F	M	F	M	F	M	F	M	F	M
Mandible	13	5	0	0	10	7	5	3	2	1	30	16
Maxilla	10	3	0	0	8	5	0	0	1	1	19	9
Tooth	16	5	1	1	18	3	0	0	4	1	39	10
Skull	7	2	4	2	6	3	6	3	0	0	23	10
Scapula	9	6	0	0	2	2	2	2	0	0	13	10
Humerus	15	6	2	1	3	2	3	2	1	1	24	12
Radius	11	6	1	1	2	2	0	0	0	0	14	9
Ulna	9	4	0	0	3	3	3	3	1	1	16	11
Carpal/tarsal	5	2	1	1	3	1	0	0	0	0	9	4
Pelvis	12	3	0	0	3	2	1	1	0	0	16	6
Femur	16	6	1	1	0	0	1	1	4	2	22	10
Tibia	22	6	0	0	3	2	0	0	1	1	29	9
Astragalus	8	6	0	0	3	3	0	0	0	0	11	9
Calcaneum	6	3	1	1	2	2	1	1	0	0	10	7
Metapodial	25	2	5	1	6	2	1	1	0	0	37	6
Phalange 1	1	1	0	0	13	2	0	0	1	1	15	4
Phalange 2	5	1	0	0	3	2	1	1	1	1	10	5
Phalange 3	2	1	0	0	15	3	0	0	2	1	19	5
Atlas	2	1	1	1	0	0	0	0	0	0	3	2
Vertebrae	0	0	0	0	1	1	0	0	0	0	1	1
Total frags/ greatest MNI	**194**	**6**	**17**	**2**	**107**	**7**	**24**	**3**	**18**	**?**	**360**	**20**

F = fragments, M = minimum number of individuals (from Cotton 1982)

bones came from division H, the fragmented nature of the assemblage resulted in only one mandible surviving with a complete tooth row (mws 2). The fusion data (Table 38) shows only two specimens in the over three years age range. For division H 100% of the 96 fragments with fusion evidence were unfused, indicating the presence of far more immature pigs than the mandible data alone revealed.

Due to the immaturity of the pig bones, a large proportion of which appeared foetal or neonatal, metrical data were limited and analysis not considered applicable.

A high proportion of the bones were complete or freshly broken and evidence of butchery was limited to one scapula, two astragali and one calcaneum displaying cut marks.

Horse

Horse bones represented 12.4% of the identifiable fragments and fourteen individuals (9.5%). Table 43 presents the distribution of principle anatomical elements.

Most of the horse bones were complete or recently broken; however the varied representation of elements and the presence of heavily gnawed bone, particularly in divisions L, M and J, indicated that some of the material was the result of secondary deposition. Division K contained the majority of horse bones and represented primary deposition. Four near-complete horse skulls were present, three of which had straight or slightly dished profiles with the fourth being smaller and noticeably more

Table 44. Well 1: horse withers heights.

	Radius		Metacarpal		Tibia		Metatarsal	
	L	WH	L	WH	L	WH	L	WH
	346.0	13.9	228.0	13.4	353.0	13.8	258.0	13.3
	332.0	13.4	225.0	13.2	362.0	14.1	293.5	15.1
			187.0	11.0	325.0	12.7	274.0	14.1
			243.0	14.3			272.0	14.0
			226.0	13.3			271.0	14.0
			186.5	11.0			225.0	11.6
			227.0	13.3			254.0	13.1
			242.6	14.3			238.5	12.3
			232.5	13.7				
min.			186.5	11.0	325.0	12.7	225.0	11.6
max.			243.0	14.3	362.0	14.1	293.5	15.1
mean	339.0	13.7	222.0	13.1	346.7	13.5	260.6	13.4

L = maximum length (mm)
WH = withers height (hands)

convex. Division K also contained two complete sets of ribs and one complete spinal column. A second articulated spinal column was partially complete lacking the lower lumbar and coccygeal vertebrae and one cervical vertebra.

All of the horse bones were fused except for one metatarsal from division M. This came from an individual of perhaps less than 20 months. At least one foetal or neonatal individual was represented. Although several complete mandibles were recovered many had suffered the *post mortem* loss of the incisor teeth. Nevertheless, the dentition generally supported the fusion data indicating that a majority of the horses deposited in the well were mature (i.e. over 42 months). The smallest individual, possibly a pony, was aged at 10-15 years at death.

Withers heights were calculated using methods described by Luff (1982) from the radii, metacarpi, tibiae and metatarsi (Table 44). A range of sizes was represented from a small pony of 11 hands (metacarpal) to a quite large specimen of 15.1 hands (metatarsal). Luff (1982) records that most Romano-British horses were of small pony size (11-13 hands) but larger individuals (over 14 hands) occur on many villa sites e.g. Barton Court Farm, Oxfordshire, Gadebridge Park, Hertfordshire, and Lynch Farm, Cambridgeshire (Luff 1982, 136).

Evidence of butchery was noticed on one distal humerus and on several fragments of mandible chopped behind the third molar.

Cut marks were also noted on the lateral aspect of ribs and on vertebrae spines belonging to the articulated spinal column.

Dog

Dog bones comprised 28.0% of the total number of identifiable fragments. In division H, where dog bones were most prolific, this figure was over 60%. Thirty-one individuals were identified from the deposits (21.1%).

Anatomical representation is presented in Table 45. The few fragments of dog recovered from the lower divisions of the well (L and M) were almost wholly restricted to head fragments: skull, mandible and loose teeth. In division K a more even representation of

Table 43. Well 1: horse – principal anatomical elements in each level.

	H F	H M	J F	J M	K F	K M	L F	L M	M F	M M	Total F	Total M
Mandible	0	0	6	1	11	6	2	1	0	0	19	8
Maxilla	1	1	3	2	0	0	1	1	0	0	5	4
Tooth	2	1	22	2	25	3	1	1	1	1	51	8
Skull	2	2	4	2	23	6	0	0	0	0	29	10
Scapula	0	0	0	0	5	3	2	2	0	0	7	5
Humerus	0	0	1	1	11	6	0	0	0	0	12	7
Radius	0	0	0	0	6	4	0	0	0	0	6	4
Ulna	0	0	0	0	2	2	0	0	0	0	2	2
Carpal/tarsal	4	1	1	1	66	6	2	1	0	0	73	9
Metacarpal	3	1	5	2	21	5	1	1	0	0	30	9
Pelvis	0	0	0	0	7	4	1	1	0	0	8	5
Femur	0	0	1	1	8	4	1	1	0	0	10	6
Patella	0	0	0	0	5	3	0	0	0	0	5	3
Tibia	0	0	2	2	10	5	0	0	3	2	15	9
Fibula	0	0	0	0	6	3	0	0	0	0	6	3
Astragalus	0	0	0	0	5	4	0	0	0	0	5	4
Calcaneum	0	0	0	0	6	4	0	0	0	0	6	4
N. cuboid	0	0	0	0	4	2	0	0	0	0	4	2
Metatarsal	3	1	3	2	20	6	0	0	4	2	30	11
Phalange 1	0	0	1	1	19	6	0	0	0	0	20	7
Phalange 2	2	1	0	0	16	5	1	1	0	0	19	7
Phalange 3	1	1	1	1	15	4	0	0	0	0	17	6
Distal sesamoid	0	0	1	1	11	3	0	0	1	1	13	5
Atlas	0	0	0	0	7	6	0	0	1	1	8	7
Axis	0	0	0	0	5	5	0	0	0	0	5	5
Vertebrae	0	0	2	1	111	4	0	0	0	0	113	5
Rib	0	0	0	0	76	3	0	0	0	0	76	3
Sternum	0	0	0	0	1	1	0	0	0	0	1	1
Sacrum	0	0	0	0	2	2	0	0	0	0	2	2
Total frags/greatest MNI	18	2	53	2	504	6	12	2	10	2	597	14

F = fragments, M = minimum number of individuals (from Cotton 1982)

Table 45. Well 1: dog – principal anatomical elements in each level.

	H		J		K		L		M		Total	
	F	M	F	M	F	M	F	M	F	M	F	M
Mandible	38	18	6	4	3	2	2	1	2	2	51	27
Maxilla	14	9	3	3	1	1	3	2	0	0	21	15
Tooth	90	6	24	3	0	0	2	1	1	1	117	11
Skull	66	10	3	2	2	1	16	2	8	4	95	19
Scapula	51	13	3	2	1	1	1	1	1	1	57	18
Humerus	46	16	8	4	3	2	0	0	0	0	57	22
Radius	35	14	7	4	5	2	0	0	0	0	47	20
Ulna	33	14	3	2	2	2	0	0	0	0	38	18
Carpal/tarsal	18	4	5	2	1	1	0	0	0	0	24	7
Pelvis	53	14	4	2	2	2	0	0	0	0	59	18
Femur	35	11	8	3	1	1	0	0	0	0	44	15
Tibia	40	13	5	3	6	3	0	0	0	0	51	19
Fibula	5	3	1	1	5	3	0	0	0	0	11	7
Astragalus	7	5	4	4	2	2	0	0	0	0	13	11
Calcaneum	8	7	10	4	2	2	0	0	0	0	20	13
Metapodial	130	8	34	3	9	2	0	0	0	0	173	13
Phalange 1	46	3	10	2	11	2	0	0	0	0	67	7
Phalange 2	27	3	16	2	5	1	0	0	0	0	48	6
Phalange 3	11	2	3	1	2	1	1	1	1	1	18	6
Atlas	11	9	0	0	1	1	0	0	0	0	12	10
Axis	8	8	0	0	2	2	0	0	0	0	10	10
Vertebrae	205	6	31	2	44	2	14	1	0	0	294	11
Sternum	17	5	2	1	0	0	0	0	0	0	19	6
Os penis	2	2	1	1	1	1	0	0	0	0	4	4
Total frags/ greatest MNI	996	18	191	4	111	3	39	2	13	4	1350	31

F = fragments, M = minimum number of individuals (from Cotton 1982)

elements occurred including atlas and axis vertebrae and a notable lack of loose teeth. Divisions J and H broadly followed this pattern, although loose teeth became quite numerous, and the assemblage suggests the deposition of some complete dog carcasses in the upper levels of the well.

The Dalton Parlours dogs were aged on the basis of tooth eruption using the dates of Silver (1969). Of the twelve specimens in division H six were aged at less than 6 months as was one of the two mandibles from division M. The epiphysial fusion data (Table 38) supported the presence of young dogs but indicated that the majority reached skeletal maturity i.e. over 18 months.

Estimated shoulder heights (Table 46) were calculated from complete long bones using the methods described by Harcourt (1974). The dogs examined ranged in size from 36-64cm displaying the variability associated with the Romano-British period.

Butchery evidence was limited to one mandible in level M displaying cut marks. Several sections of

Table 46. Well 1: dog shoulder heights.

	Humerus		Radius		Femur		Tibia	
	L	SH	L	SH	L	SH	L	SH
	171.1	57.6	172.5	55.5	213.0	64.1	192.5	56.2
	170.1	57.3	156.0	50.2	160.5	48.3	195.5	57.1
	156.2	52.6	112.9	36.3	187.0	56.3	209.0	61.0
	179.0	60.3			205.5	61.9	177.0	51.7
	180.0	60.6			172.0	51.8	210.5	61.5
					171.5	51.6	211.0	61.6
					192.8	58.0	138.3	40.3
							138.0	40.3
min.	156.2	52.6	112.9	36.3	160.5	48.3	138.0	40.3
max.	180.0	60.6	172.5	55.5	213.0	64.1	211.0	61.6
mean	171.3	57.7	147.1	47.3	186.0	56.0	184.0	53.7

L = maximum length (mm)   SH = shoulder height (cm)

articulated vertebrae were found although no one complete spinal column.

Minor species
Additional species represented in the sample included badger (*Meles meles*: 101), hare (*Lepus capensis*: 15) and human (37) bone.

Badger (Meles meles)
The bones of at least six individuals were found in divisions H, J and K. The long bones were all complete, or freshly broken and unfused representing only immature individuals. Certain elements, particularly scapulae and pelves, were absent.

Hare (Lepus capensis)
Hare bones were present in divisions H and J and at least three individuals were partially represented. The long bones were heavily weathered and appeared unfused.

Human
Human bone was identified only in division J. A minimum of three individuals were represented. Three left fused distal tibia fragments indicate that the individuals were all over 21 years of age at death.

Overview
Recent work by the West Yorkshire Archaeology Service has expanded the environmental data from Dalton Parlours. Well 1 produced some 5297 small mammal and amphibian bones of which 3308 were identified to species in the West Yorkshire Archaeology Service laboratory (Tables 47 and 48). A further 2622 fragments of mammal bone have been identified and analysed from Roman deposits from the villa complex (Chapter 24) against which the well material can be viewed. Mandibles from the well were re-examined and recorded in a manner compatible with the ageing data from the villa assemblage for direct comparison (Table 49).

Of the many questions raised by the material from the well the two most fundamental must include the nature of the activities that resulted in the well being backfilled, and the period of time over which these actions took place. The extent to which the animal bone data can assist in answering these questions was one of the main objectives of the reappraisal. Examination of the faunal remains reveals a clear picture of several distinct activities: the disposal of primary butchery and kitchen waste, the secondary deposition of domestic rubbish and the primary dumping of complete or semi-complete animal carcasses. Also noticeable is a marked change in the frequency of bone fragments for each species and their relative presence ratio throughout the well divisions together with an obvious hiatus in bone deposition between 6-12m below datum. These observations are presented graphically in Figures 152 and 153.

The bottom divisions N, M and L represented silt levels. Only divisions M and L contained animal bone and

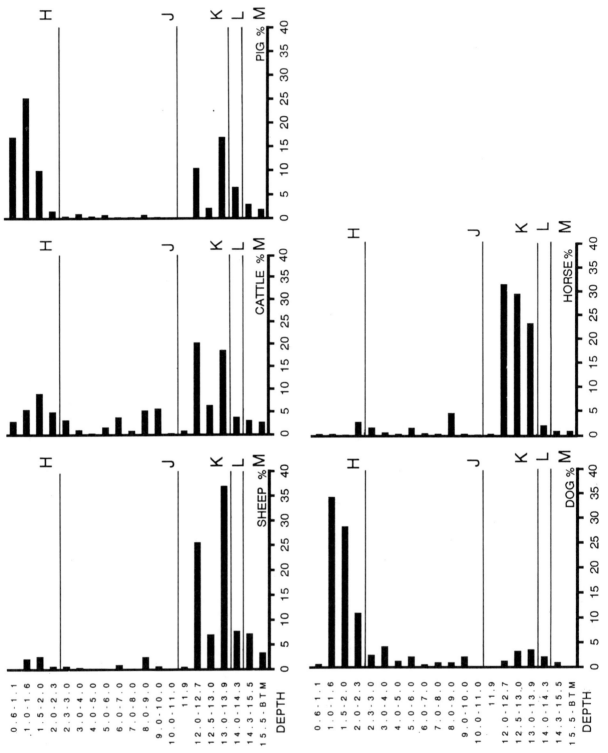

Fig. 152. Animal bone from Well 1: major species fragment percentage distribution.

254

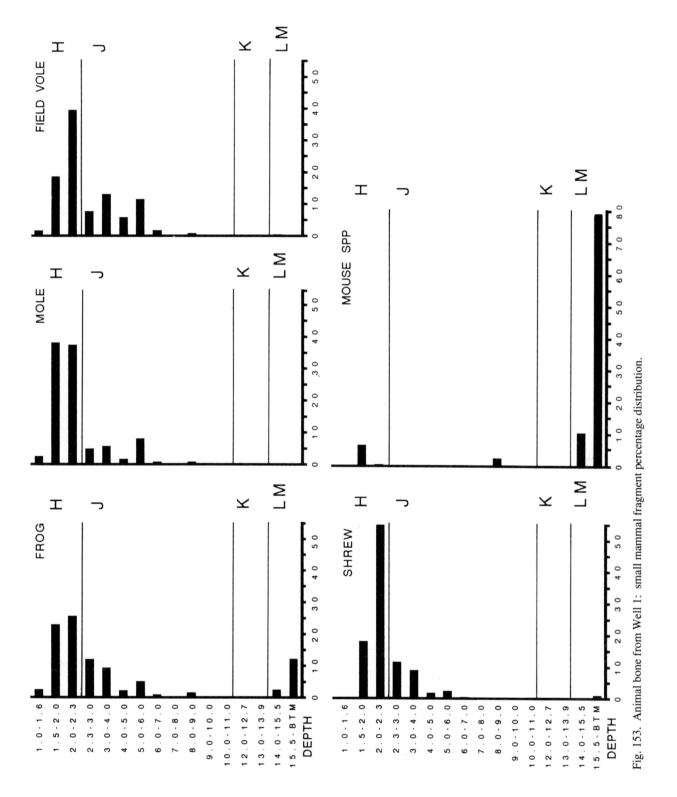

Fig. 153. Animal bone from Well 1: small mammal fragment percentage distribution.

Table 47. Well 1: small mammal bone identified fragments.

	Frog		Mole		Shrew		Bank vole		Field vole		Mouse spp.		Hedgehog		Rat	
	n	%	n	%	n	%	n	%	n	%	n	%	n	%	n	%
Depth H																
1.0–1.5	27	1.9	1	0.8	1	0.3	1	16.7	1	0.08	–		–		–	
1.3–1.6	10	0.7	2	1.6	–		–		1	0.08	–		–		–	
1.5–2.0	335	23.0	47	38.2	67	18.0	1	16.7	222	18.6	10	6.6	2	100.0	–	
2.0–2.2	375	25.7	46	37.4	205	55.1	1	16.7	472	39.5	1	0.7	–		–	
Total H	**747**	**51.2**	**96**	**78.0**	**273**	**73.4**	**3**	**50.0**	**696**	**58.3**	**11**	**7.3**	**2**	**100.0**		
Depth J																
2.3–3.0	177	12.1	6	4.9	43	11.6	–		93	7.8	–		–		–	
3.0–4.0	137	9.4	7	5.7	33	8.9	1	16.7	157	13.1	–		–		–	
4.0–5.0	34	2.3	2	1.6	7	1.9	–		69	5.8	–		–		–	
5.0–6.0	76	5.2	10	8.1	9	2.4	1	16.7	138	11.6	–		–		–	
6.0–7.0	15	1.0	1	0.8	2	0.5	–		20	1.7	–		–		–	
8.0–9.0	24	1.6	1	0.8	–		1	16.7	10	0.8	4	2.6	–		–	
9.0–10.0	21	1.4	–		–		–		–		–		–		–	
Total J	**484**	**33.2**	**27**	**22.0**	**94**	**25.3**	**3**	**50.0**	**487**	**40.8**	**4**	**2.6**				
Depth K																
12.0–12.7	5	0.3	–		–		–		3	0.3	–		–		–	
13.0–14.0	5	0.3	–		–		–		–		–		–		–	
Total K	**10**	**0.7**							**3**	**0.3**						
Depth L/M																
14.0–15.5	38	2.6	–		1	0.3	–		5	0.4	16	10.6	–		–	
15.5–Btm	180	12.3	–		4	1.1	–		3	0.3	120	79.5	–		1	100.0
Total L/M	**218**	**14.9**			**5**	**1.3**			**8**	**0.7**	**136**	**90.1**			**1**	**100.0**
Total	**1459**		**123**		**372**		**6**		**1194**		**151**		**2**		**1**	

as both were contemporary with the well's use there is no reason why they need to be treated separately. The majority of the fragments derived from sheep and cattle and represented domestic kitchen waste, some of which is likely to be intrusive from the division above. Small numbers of pig, dog and horse bones were also present. Minor species included frog (*Rana temporaria*), field vole (*Microtus agrestis*) and common shrew (*Sorex araneus*). The most abundant small mammal was mouse, over 80% of the total well population being retrieved from divisions L and M (Fig. 153). A majority were identified as wood mouse (*Apodemus sylvaticus*) with at least one specimen of house mouse (*Mus musculus*).

Division M also produced the partial skull of black rat (*Rattus rattus*). The occipital and parietal were absent having separated along the parieto-frontal suture. The upper incisors and left maxilla tooth row were complete with only the second molar extant on the right maxilla. Initial identification was made using comparative material at West Yorkshire Archaeology Service and with the aid of diagnostic features as described by Armitage *et al.* (1984). The specimen (ref. DP/SF 2049) was confirmed to be that of *Rattus rattus* by D. Whiteley of Sheffield City Museum Natural History Unit.

Black rat is now known to have been present in Britain during Roman times and, although still rare in archaeological deposits, specimens have been identified from securely dated contexts in Roman York and London (Armitage *et al.* 1984; Rackham 1979; O'Connor 1987). Its presence at Dalton Parlours with the other small mammals identified is compatible with an active farmyard environment.

The two metres of deposit that made up division K contained the majority of identified faunal material, although very few small mammal bones were recovered, reason why they need to be treated separately. The majority of the fragments derived from sheep and cattle and represented a period when the well was no longer used as a source of water. The domestic animal bone derived from kitchen, butchery and slaughter waste and from the dumping of partial, and possibly complete, carcasses. In total a minimum of 26 sheep/goat, 11 cattle, 7 pigs, 6 horses and 3 dogs were represented.

Sheep/goat dominated in this division by fragment numbers and MNI as was the case in the relative proportion of major species from the villa contexts (Table 50). The element distribution suggests the deposition of selected body-parts from the 26 individuals, in the main heads and limb extremities.

Age stages of the sheep mandibles from division K peaked at Payne's stage C and over 75% fell within stages C-E. Compared to the mandible mortality profile from the villa assemblage the percentage culled at stages D and E was very similar whilst the number of mandibles aged at

Table 48. Well 1: small mammal bone – minimum number of individuals.

	Frog		Mole		Shrew		Bank vole		Field vole		Mouse spp.	
	n	%	n	%	n	%	n	%	n	%	n	%
Depth H												
1.0–1.5	1	3.1	1	2.4	1	0.7	1	16.7	1	0.4	–	
1.3–1.6	1	3.1	1	2.4	–		–		1	0.4	–	
1.5–2.0	7	21.9	14	33.3	34	23.9	1	16.7	46	19.1	5	8.6
2.0–2.2	4	12.5	11	26.2	57	40.1	1	16.7	75	31.1	1	1.7
Total H	**13**	**40.6**	**27**	**64.3**	**92**	**64.8**	**3**	**50.0**	**123**	**51.0**	**6**	**10.3**
Depth J												
2.3–3.0	1	3.1	4	9.5	21	14.8	–		25	10.4	–	
3.0–4.0	2	6.3	3	7.1	17	12.0	1	16.7	34	14.1	–	
4.0–5.0	1	3.1	2	4.8	4	2.8	–		15	6.2	–	
5.0–6.0	1	3.1	4	9.5	4	2.8	1	16.7	32	13.3	–	
6.0–7.0	1	3.1	1	2.4	1	0.7	–		4	1.7	–	
8.0–9.0	2	6.3	1	2.4	–		1	16.7	1	0.4	4	6.9
9.0–10.0	1	3.1	–		–		–		–		–	
Total J	**9**	**28.1**	**15**	**35.7**	**47**	**33.1**	**3**	**50.0**	**111**	**46.1**	**4**	**6.9**
Depth K												
12.0–12.7	1	3.1	–		–		–		3	1.2	–	
13.0–14.0	1	3.1	–		–		–		–		–	
Total K	**2**	**6.3**							**3**	**1.2**		
Depth L/M												
14.0–Btm	8	25.0	–		3	2.1	–		4	1.7	48	2.8
Total	**32**		**42**		**142**		**6**		**241**		**58**	

Small mammal MNI based on mandibles

Table 49. Well 1: major species dentition.

CATTLE

Division HKLM	Stage	Grant*	Age
5	B	p4 in wear, M1 unworn	1-8 mths
1	C	M1 in wear, M2 unworn	8-18 mths
1 2	F	M3 posterior cusp in wear, M3 wear < g	young adult
1 1	G	M3 wear at stage g	adult
1	H	M3 wear at stage h or j	old adult
2 1	I	M3 wear > stage j	senile

SHEEP/GOAT

Division HKLM	Stage	Grant*	Age
3 1	B	d4 in wear, M1 unworn	2-6 mths
13 1	C	M1 in wear, M2 unworn	6-12 mths
5	D	M2 in wear, M3 unworn	12-24 mths
7	E	M3 in wear, posterior cusp unworn	24-36 mths
2	F	M3 posterior cusp in wear, M3 wear < g	36-48 mths
1	H	M3 stage g, M2 > g	72-96 mths
2	I	M3 > stage g	96+ mths

PIG

Division HKLM	Stage	Maltby	Age
2 1	1	d4 not in wear	0-8 wks
1 2 1	2	d4 in wear, M1 not in wear	2-8 mths
3	3	M1 in wear, M2 not in wear	9-14 mths
5	5	P4 in wear, M3 not in wear	19-26 mths

Cattle stages after Halstead (1985)
Sheep stages after Payne (1973)
Pig stages after Maltby (1987) with additions
* after tooth wear stages of Grant (1975; 1982)

Table 50. Major species relative frequencies – well division K and villa.

	Cattle %	Sheep %	Pig %
Well fragments	42.1	50.5	7.4
Villa fragments	25.8	56.5	17.7
Well MNI	25.0	59.1	15.9
Villa MNI	31.4	44.2	24.4

below stage C were far fewer in the well deposits (Fig. 154). This trend is supported by the epiphysial fusion data suggesting the selection of animals of a specific age group the remains of which were deposited in this layer of the well.

The surviving cattle mandibles showed a greater number of very young beasts (M1 unworn) deposited in the well than elsewhere. This was also demonstrated by the epiphysial fusion data with over 62% of the bones with fusion evidence unfused compared to 15.7% from the villa material. In part this variance can be attributed to differential survival of very young bone between the waterlogged well deposits and the villa contexts which produced very abraded and weathered bone.

In addition to the mandible evidence a minimum of ten cattle were represented by complete, or near-complete

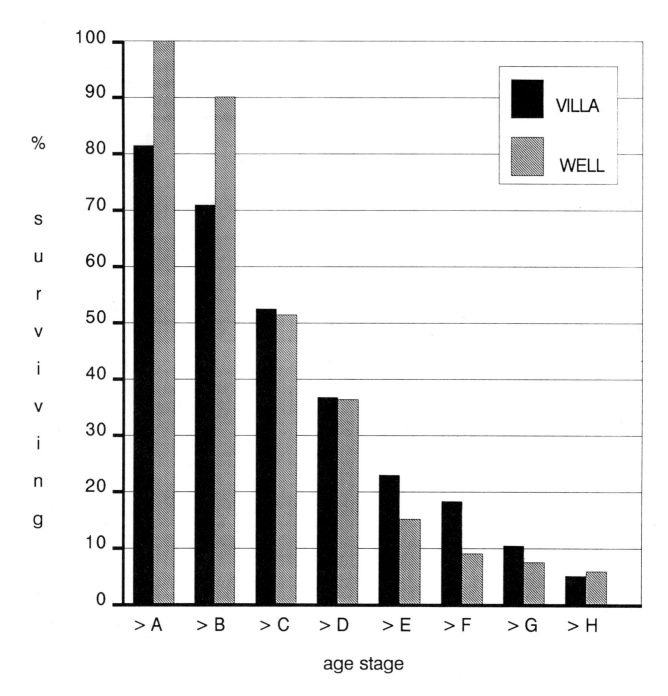

Fig. 154. Sheep mandible age stages (after Payne 1973).

skulls, all of which possessed complete and worn tooth rows. At least four of these cattle displayed evidence of being slaughtered by pole-axing.

The large number of horse bones in the lower half of division K (12-13.9m) derived from both primary and secondary deposition. It was clear from the evidence of carnivore gnawing that some bones had been fed to, or scavenged by dogs prior to arriving in the well. Primary deposits were present in the form of four complete and two partial horse skulls and at least two articulated spinal columns. The bone suggests that several articulated limbs may have been present in this layer but the nature of the deposit and the extreme difficulties of excavating at this depth precluded the excavation or even, in some instances, recognition of bones as articulated units. Numerous rib fragments bore marks compatible with skinning and knife

marks on one mandible posterior to the M3 may have been caused during the removal of the tongue.

The minimum number of six horse skulls is comparable to material found in other Roman well deposits such as the nine horse skulls found in pit 17 at Newstead, Scotland (Ross and Feachem 1976). The burials of complete or partial horse carcasses are also often described as 'votive' or 'ceremonial' deposits (Grant 1975; Luff 1982; Noddle 1973). In this respect the bones from division K fulfil one of Grant's two criteria for the designation of deposits as 'special', i.e. 'complete or near complete skulls and, in the case of horses, complete mandibles' (Grant 1984, 533). Three of the Dalton Parlours horse jaws were complete with joined left and right mandibles, a further two specimens were freshly broken during excavation. The density and condition of horse bones in this layer of the well may therefore be associated with Roman 'ceremonial' activities. Viewed with the remaining faunal and, in particular, botanical evidence from this division these activities may have been connected with the abandonment of the site.

The bulk of division J, between 5-11m, and the upper one metre of division K appears to have been a single activity in which building rubble and disturbed animal and human primary deposits were dumped into the well. There was very little animal bone (<35 fragments) between 10-11.9m where large masonry blocks and column bases had been deposited.

Only 14.3% of identified bone derived from division J although it was the largest by volume covering a depth of some 8.7m. A large proportion of the animal bone occurring within the main body of the fill resulted from secondary deposition. The presence of heavily eroded specimens with badly pitted surfaces, and the quantity of carnivore-damaged bone in the sample revealed that material had been derived from surface accumulations which had been discarded around the site some time prior to becoming incorporated into the well.

Several fragments of human bone were also found throughout this division representing at least three adult individuals. The presence of only partial skeletons again suggests the redeposition of disturbed primary deposits from areas around the site and within dumping distance of the well.

Among the animal bone were several matching bone fragments recovered from various levels within division J. This would point to the bulk of material from this layer being deposited in one single event over a relatively short period of time.

The results of this activity ended at between five and six metres below datum. Above this point the well appears to have remained as an open pit with fill accumulating over time. The open well clearly acted as a trap for small creatures such as (in order of MNI frequency): field vole (*Microtus agrestis*), common shrew (*Sorex araneus*), mole (*Talpa europaea*), frog (*Rana temporaria*), mouse spp. and bank vole (*Clethrionomys glareolus*). The bones of badger (*Meles meles*) and hare (*Lepus capensis*) were also present as were fragments of human bone although large mammal bones were relatively few, the majority being those of dog.

This assemblage continued up to about two metres below datum, after which in division H the quantity of large mammal bone increased. The general condition of the bone was poor, showing considerable surface erosion and evidence of carnivore damage. Much of the material was the result of secondary deposition although the disposal of complete carcasses was also evident. The major food animal was cattle with very few sheep/goat fragments recovered. Pig were equal in MNI to cattle but were represented in the main by complete foetal skeletons possibly representing the disposal of a litter and perhaps indicating the breeding of this animal on or near the site.

Division H produced large quantities of dog bones representing at least eighteen individuals, seven of which were immature and again may have derived from the deposition of one litter. A majority of the remaining individuals were sub-adult. Measurements of the cranial indices described a dolichocephalic breed, i.e. comparable to modern greyhound or collie breeds.

Various wild species from this division included field vole (*Microtus agrestis*), common shrew (*Sorex araneus*), mole (*Talpa europaea*), frog (*Rana temporaria*), bank vole (*Clethrionomys glareolus*), wood mouse (*Apodemus sylvaticus*), hedgehog (*Erinaceus europaeus*), hare (*Lepus capensis*) and badger (*Meles meles*).

The eroded nature of the division H assemblage has resulted in the loss of valuable information, e.g. ageing and metrical data. As it stands there was little evidence of prime butchery or kitchen waste in this level of the well. The picture presented is of a dump for secondary deposits and the complete carcasses of dead animals i.e. pigs and dogs; in this respect the abandoned well was probably a convenient distance away from any habitation area.

The animal bone from the Dalton Parlours well has indicated that the structure went through a range of uses and associated activities: the disposal of kitchen and butchery waste, the deliberate dumping of large quantities of animal bone (possibly associated with 'ceremonial' or 'votive' practices immediately preceding the site's abandonment) and in the upper levels, above the main fill of stone and masonry, an open pit employed to dump general site refuse and animal carcasses. Unfortunately the animal bone does not help to separate these actions temporally and therefore the time span between the well going out of use in division K and being used as an open dump in division H will have to be gauged from evidence other than faunal remains.

32 Botanical Remains (Pl. XXXVI)

by Margaret Bastow and Josephine Murray

Introduction

The lower part of Well 1, from 13.0-13.5m downwards, was cut into impervious shale, and below 11.5m the presence of free water and the creation of waterlogging conditions provided an ideal environment for the preservation of organic material. The major fill divisions were divided into seventeen different layers, and samples of soil were taken from all these for the recovery of botanical remains.

Methods

Macroscopic remains

A 1kg sample of soil was processed from each of the seventeen layers (large pieces of limestone, mortar, tile, pottery, bone and shell were first removed by hand). Nitric acid was added gradually to each sample, in order to avoid excess effervescence. Following dilution to 50% the

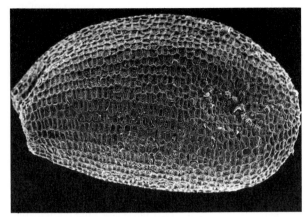

Capsella bursa-pastoris (sheperd's purse).

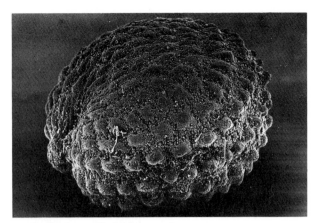

Stellaria media (chickweed).

Agrostemma githago (corn cockle).

Chara sp. (oogonium).

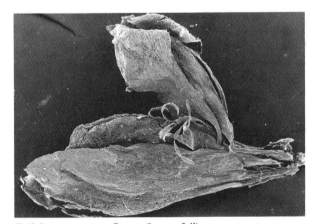

Trifolium campestre flower (hop trefoil).

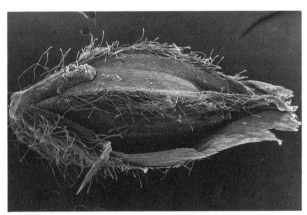

Poa pratensis (meadow grass).

Pl. XXXVI. Plant macrofossils from Well 1. (Photo: M. Bastow)

samples were left overnight, then washed through a 200 micron sieve to remove the fine sediment. The residue was examined under a low power light microscope and the botanical remains were removed for identification.

Pollen extraction

The samples contained a large proportion of mineral matter so the bromoform flotation method for extracting pollen was used, as described in Moore and Webb (1983). The material removed was stained with safranine and mounted on slides in glycerol jelly. These were examined under a light microscope at a magnification of x400.

Identification

Identification of seeds was aided by reference to seed atlases (e.g. Beijerinck 1947; Katz *et al.* 1965). Final identifications were always verified by comparison with type specimens. For other macroscopic remains, floras (Clapham *et al.* 1978; Harley and Lewis 1985; Keble-Martin 1965; Schauer 1982), plant drawings (Ross-Craig 1948-73) and various plant guides (Phillips 1981; Lousley and Kent 1981; Snorne 1979) were useful, but final identifications were again carried out using live plants and specimens from the herbarium collection in the Department of Pure and Applied Biology, University of Leeds. Similarly, mosses were identified by reference to moss floras (e.g. Dickson 1973; Watson 1968; 1978), herbarium specimens and a collection of type specimen slides.

Pollen grains were identified by reference to pollen atlases (e.g. Nilsson *et al.* 1977; Punt and Clarke 1981) and pollen analysis textbooks (Faegri and Iversen 1964; Moore and Webb 1983), plus modern type specimen slides (also from a collection at the University of Leeds). Confirmation of the identification of some specimens necessitated examination using a scanning electron microscope.

Quantification

Macroscopic remains: Identifications of the plant material recovered are given in Table 51. Each figure given represents one whole seed, nut or fruit. Fragments, parts of mosses and ferns, thorns, twigs and buds are all difficult to quantify, so an asterisk is inserted where these have been located. The main exceptions to note are *Rubus idaeus* (raspberry) whose numbers include thorns, *Calluna vulgaris* (heather) leaves, calices of *Prunella vulgaris* (self-heal), and some fruits of *Linum catharticum* (flax) and *Viola tricolor* (heartsease).

Pollen: For each sample, approximately 500 grains were counted. The frequency of occurrence of different species is represented as a percentage of the total pollen or %TP (Table 52). A note was also made of other material present (Table 53).

Results

Due to extreme alkalinity and dryness, the first twelve layers (0-12m below ground level) yielded neither macroscopic remains nor pollen. The lower five waterlogged layers, K1-M2 (12.1-16.0m), yielded macroscopic remains including seeds, fruits, perianths, leaves, stems, thorns, twigs, and fragments of charcoal and wood from 100 different species. There were also microscopic remains including pollen, fern spores, diatoms and whipworm eggs. Table 51 provides a synopsis of all the results for the samples from the well.

The pollen and macrofossil records generally show a similar range of plant taxa, although often there is no consistent correlation between their relative frequencies. Certain species, e.g. *Pinus* (pine), *Tilia* (lime) and *Poterium sanguisorba* (salad burnet), are only represented by pollen. Also, when a particular herb family contributes a high proportion of total pollen, as in the case of Umbelliferae in layer K1, it is difficult to attribute any particular environment to the level without further details of the species present. Individual species are visible in the macrofossil record. However, the two types of botanical evidence tend to reflect different processes by virtue of their differing modes of introduction into archaeological deposits, so considerable caution is necessary.

The plant macrofossil data in the following descriptions have been divided into ecological groupings. These are, of necessity, broadly defined and are somewhat arbitrary due to the overlap of certain habitat types. Plants may also change their habitats locally with variations in competition between species, as may be introduced by human agency or animal activity. The definitions are listed at the end of Table 51 and are based on Clapham *et al.* (1962; 1978) and Fitter (1987); also see Watson (1968; 1978), Dickson (1973) and Dalby (1980) for non-herb remains.

The following discussion considers the pollen remains only in a very general way after each description of the macroscopic remains. There is no information for the precise origin of any of the pollen samples other than the layer, some of which are up to a metre in depth.

Layer M2 (15.5-16.0m)

Layer M2 represented the basal deposit of the well; a rich, black organic material containing grit, artefacts and biological remains. Macroscopic remains representing 44 species were recovered. These were mainly seeds but included fruits of *Linum catharticum* (purging flax) and *Viola tricolor* (wild pansy), the leaves and perianths of *Calluna vulgaris* (heather) and flowers of *Trifolium campestre* (hop trefoil). This layer produced carbonised cereal grains but due to deterioration these could only be identified as *Hordeum* sp. (barley) and *Triticum* sp. (wheat). There was also a seed of *Linum usitatissimum* (cultivated flax).

The predominant ecotypes are species which belong to arable and waste places, for example, *Papaver rhoeas* (field poppy), *Polygonum aviculare* (knotgrass) and *Stellaria media* (chickweed). Six species of likely arable weed were identified. These include the annuals *Agrostemma githago* (corn cockle), *Capsella bursa-pastoris* (shepherd's purse) and *Urtica urens* (small

Table 51. The macroscopic remains from Well 1.

Depth (metres) Corresponding archaeological layer	12-12.7 K1	13-14 K2	14-14.3 L	14.5-15.5 M1	15.5-16 M2	Ecological preference
SPECIES						
Trees and shrubs						
Alnus glutinosa (alder)	–	–	1	–	1	W\M
Betula pubescens (birch)	–	–	–	1	1	W
Corylus avellana (hazel)	*	–	*	–	–	W\HG
Crataegus monogyna (hawthorn)	*	*	*	–	–	W\HG
Populus tremula (aspen)	*	*	*	–	*	W
Pinus sp. (pine) – only pollen						
Prunus spinosa (sloe)	–	*	–	–	–	W\WP\HG
Sambucus nigra (elder)	–	–	1	–	–	W\WP
Tilia sp. (lime) – only pollen						
Grasses						
Anthoxanthum odoratum (sweet vernal grass)	–	4	–	–	–	G
Bromus mollis (lop grass)	–	–	–	–	1	G\WP
Holcus lanatus (Yorkshire fog)	–	–	–	–	1	W\G\WP
Hordeum murinum (wall barley)	1	–	–	–	1	W
Phleum pratense (timothy grass)	–	2	–	–	–	G
Poa pratensis (meadow grass)	–	1	–	–	2	G
Poa trivialis (rough-stalked meadow grass)	–	1	–	–	–	G
Rushes and Sedges						
Carex sp. (sedge)	–	–	–	1	2	M
Eleocharis palustris v. vulgaris (spike rush)	–	–	–	1	–	M
Isolepis setacea (bristle scirpus)	–	–	–	–	2	M
Juncus effusus (soft rush)	4	7	–	2	–	W\M
Juncus subnodulosus (blunt-flowered rush)	–	4	–	–	–	M
Cultivated Plants						
Hordeum sp. (barley)	–	–	1	–	3	
Linum usitatissimum (cultivated flax)	–	–	–	1	1	
Triticum sp. (wheat)	–	1	–	–	1	
Pteridophytes						
Pteridium aquilinum (bracken)	*	*	*	*	*	W\H
Polypodium sp. (polypody) – only spores						W
Bryophytes						
Camptothecium lutescens	–	–	–	–	*	G
Dicranum scoparium	–	–	*	–	–	W\M
Eurhynchium praelongum	–	–	–	–	*	W\WE
Eurhynchium speciosum	*	*	*	*	*	G
Hylocomium splendens	–	–	–	*	*	H
Hypnum cupressiforme	–	–	*	*	*	H
Plagiomnium undulatum	–	*	–	–	–	W
Rhytidiadelphus squarrosus	–	*	–	–	–	G
Tortula ruralis	*	–	–	–	–	WP
Algae						
Chara sp. (oogonium)	–	–	*	–	–	WE
Herbs						
Aegopodium podagraria (gout weed)	1	–	–	–	–	WP
Aethusa cynapium (fool's parsley)	1	1	–	–	–	A\WP
Agrostemma githago (corn cockle)	1	1	1	–	2	A
Alchemilla conjuncta (lady's mantle)	–	–	–	–	1	G
Anagallis arvensis (scarlet pimpernel)	–	4	3	–	–	A\WP
Anthriscus caucalis (bur chevil)	1	–	–	-	–	WP\HG
Apium nodiflorum (fool's watercress)	–	1	–	–	–	M
Arctium lappa (great burdock)	–	4	–	–	–	WP(W)
Arenaria leptoclados (lesser thyme-leaved sandwort)	–	2	–	–	–	A\G\WP
Arenaria serpyllifolia (thyme-leaved sandwort)	2	23	5	2	1	A\G\WP
Artemesia absinthium (wormwood)	2	–	–	–	–	WP
Atropa belladonna (deadly nightshade)	–	–	1	–	–	W\H\WP

Table 51. The macroscopic remains from Well 1. (cont.)

Depth (metres) Corresponding archaeological layer	12-12.7 K1	13-14 K2	14-14.3 L	14.5-15.5 M1	15.5-16 M2	Ecological preference
Herbs (cont.)						
Calluna vulgaris (heather)	–	5	2	3	7	W\M\H
Capsella bursa-pastoris (shepherd's purse)	14	48	4	4	12	A\WP
Cardamine pratensis (cuckoo flower)	–	1	–	4	1	G\M
Cerastium arvense (field mouse-ear chickweed)	–	–	8	–	–	A\G\WP
Cerastium holosteoides (common mouse-ear chickweed)	–	–	8	–	–	A\G\WP
Chenopodium album (fat hen)	14	–	7	–	–	A\WP
Chenopodium bonus-henricus (good King Henry)	3	–	–	10	6	A\G\WP d\n
Chenopodium polyspermum (all seed)	9	–	4	–	3	A\WP
Cirsium arvense (creeping thistle)	1	–	1	–	1	A\WP
Conium maculatum (hemlock)	15	28	1	–	–	M\W(WP)
Daucus carota (wild carrot)	–	2	–	–	–	G\W
Euphrasia nemorosa (eyebright)	–	3	–	–	–	G\W
Galeopsis angustifolium (narrow-leaved hemp nettle)	–	1	–	–	–	A\H
Hyoscyamus niger (henbane)	–	–	1	–	–	WP
Lapsana communis (nipplewort)	1	7	8	–	–	W\WP\HG
Leontodon autumnalis (autumnal hawkbit)	1	–	–	–	–	G\M\WP
Leontodon hispidus (rough hawkbit)	–	2	–	–	–	G\M
Linum catharticum (purging flax)	5	20	37	5	12	G\H
Papaver dubium (long headed poppy)	–	3	1	4	–	A\WP
Papaver rhoeas (field poppy)	6	14	2	–	21	A\WP
Picris echioides (bristly ox-tongue)	–	–	–	1	–	WP\HG
Plantago lanceolata (ribwort plantain) – only pollen						G
Polygonum arenastrum (small-leaved knotgrass)	–	22	–	–	–	A\WP
Polygonum aviculare (knotgrass)	12	4	10	17	24	A\WP
Polygonum convolvulus (black bindweed)	–	–	–	–	1	A\WP
Polygonum hydropiper (water pepper)	–	8	–	–	–	M
Polygonum lapathifolium (pale persicaria)	–	–	–	1	–	A\M\WP
Potentilla erecta (common tormentil)	–	3	1	2	1	G\M\H
Potentilla palustris (marsh cinquefoil)	–	17	–	–	–	M\H
Poterium sanguisorba (salad burnet) – only pollen						G
Prunella vulgaris (self-heal)	7	21	8	3	5	G\W\WP
Ranunculus acris (meadow buttercup)	–	–	5	2	4	G\M
Ranunculus repens (creeping buttercup)	–	6	–	–	–	G\M
Rorripa microphylla (one-rowed watercress)	1	–	–	–	–	M
Rubus idaeus (raspberry)	–	3	2	–	–	W\H
Rubus saxatilis (stone bramble)	–	–	–	1	–	W
Rumex acetosa (sorrel)	–	18	4	–	3	G\W
Rumex acetosella (sheep's sorrel)	7	3	11	–	–	A\G\H\WP
Rumex crispus (curled dock)	12	3	3	5	–	A\G\WP
Senecio jacobaea (ragwort)	–	12	1	–	–	G\WP
Sherardia arvensis (field madder)	–	–	–	1	–	A\WP
Sisymbrium officinale (hedge mustard)	–	1	7	2	1	A\WP\HG
Sonchus asper (spiny milk thistle)	–	–	4	–	1	A\WP
Sonchus oleraceus (milk thistle)	5	–	–	–	1	A\WP
Stellaria graminea (lesser stitchwort)	–	8	7	6	14	G\W\H
Stellaria media (chickweed)	11	24	667	15	18	A\WP
Stellaria pallida (lesser chickweed)	–	7	–	–	–	A\WP
Torilis japonica (upright hedge-parsley)	6	33	18	–	–	HG\G
Trifolium campestre (hop trefoil)	–	–	–	–	2	G\WP
Urtica dioica (stinging nettle)	41	147	225	24	47	G\W\HG d\n
Urtica urens (small nettle)	6	16	32	17	8	A\WP
Viola tricolor (wild pansy)	–	2	–	–	1	A\G\WP

Ecological preference:

A – arable land	WP – waste places
G – grassland	WE – well
W – woodland	d\n – disturbed, nitrogen rich soils
M – marshy ground and damp places	1 = 1 fruit, seed or nut
H – heathland	* = other parts of plant recorded, e.g. twigs, buds, frags of mosses, nutshell,
HG – hedges	thorns, etc.

nettle). Grassland species and grasses are also frequent in this deposit. Species that flourish in nitrogen-rich environments or disturbed places, particularly *Urtica dioica* (stinging nettle), maintain consistently high values throughout. This particular species, however, is frequently found in large numbers on archaeological sites. Also present throughout the well samples are heathland species, such as *Calluna vulgaris* (heather), and they occur most frequently in this layer although it seems unlikely that heathland would have been located near to the villa in view of the calcareous nature of the surrounding soil.

The other plant groups present in all five samples are the ferns and the mosses, although their exact status on archaeological sites is often equally unclear. *Polypodium* and the shade loving moss *Eurhynchium praelongum* were possibly growing on the well walls. Other mosses, such as *Hylocomium splendens* and *Hypnum cupressiforme*, have been noted in Roman well deposits elsewhere, e.g. at Rothwell (Bartley in prep.), Skeldergate and the Bedern in York (Hall *et al.* 1980; Kenward *et al.* 1986). Both these mosses are common, but not exclusive to grassy heathland and may be associated with heather.

Only a few of the species present have a preference for specific types of soil (and they are not necessarily confined solely to these). The following list suggests a range of soil types within the locale of Dalton Parlours: limestone soils – *Linum catharticum* (purging flax) and *Daucus carota* (wild carrot); acid soils – *Calluna vulgaris* (heather); light soils – *Potentilla erecta* (common tormentil) and *Stellaria graminea* (lesser stitchwort); dry soils – *Hordeum murinum* (wall barley) and damp soils – *Isolepis setacea* (bristle scirpus).

The pollen profile for M2 also indicates high values for the grasses. Gramineae comprise 38% TP and cereals achieve their highest represented values in this layer. Tree and shrub pollen show only very low values and it seems unlikely that woody vegetation was growing very close to the well.

Layer M1 (14.5-15.5m)

Layer M1 was a black organic soil, similar to M2 but with fewer botanical remains. Thirty species are represented, mostly as seeds and fruits but perianths of *Rumex crispus* (curled dock) and the preserved remains of the moss *Hylocomium splendens* were also found. Arable and waste ground species still form the major component of this level. In absolute numbers the likely arable weed species account for almost half of this total but they are only represented by two species, *Urtica urens* (small nettle) and *Capsella bursa-pastoris* (shepherd's purse). This list of arable and disturbed land species is a fairly common one for such deposits on Roman and Iron Age sites (see for example Greig 1980). Some species, such as the thistles (*Sonchus* spp.), have a particularly efficient dispersal mechanism, which means they are more likely to dominate locally. The chickweeds (*Stellaria* spp.) and nettles (*Urtica* spp.) also produce large numbers of small light seeds which wells are ideally placed to catch.

An increase in woodland is indicated by both macroscopic remains and pollen. For the pollen this is mainly attributable to *Alnus*, an inhabitant of damp and riverine environments, and whilst there is an increase in marsh species in the macrofossil record, e.g. *Cardamine pratensis* (cuckoo flower), *Carex* sp. (sedge), *Eleocharis palustris v. vulgaris* (common spike rush) and *Juncus effusus* (soft rush), it is again important to recognise the different modes of entry of this material into a deposit.

Layer L (14.0-14.3m)

This deposit was the uppermost silt layer and it is apparent that a change took place here. Botanical remains representing 44 species were recovered, including 667 seeds of *Stellaria media* (chickweed) and 225 seeds of *Urtica dioica* (stinging nettle). In addition to seeds and fruits, twigs of *Populus tremula* (aspen) and thorns of *Crataegus monogyna* (hawthorn) and *Rubus* spp. were found, plus *Pteridium aquilinum* (bracken) frond fragments.

Arable and species from waste ground again dominate but this is overemphasised by the abundance of *Stellaria media* (chickweed) which on its own accounts for 60% of the total. *Urtica dioica* (stinging nettle) maintains the high profile for species characteristic of nitrogen-rich environments. This plant, however, also lives in other habitats such as hedgebanks, woods, grassy places, fens or near buildings, and it characterises waste ground colonisation lasting more than a single season (Kenward *et al.* 1986).

There are increased occurrences of various tree and shrub species: *Crataegus monogyna* (hawthorn), *Populus tremula* (aspen), *Corylus avellana* (hazel) and *Sambucus nigra* (elder), plus their associated herb species, *Torilis japonica* (upright hedge-parsley), *Rubus idaeus* (raspberry), *Atropa belladonna* (deadly nightshade), *Hyoscyamus niger* (henbane) and *Conium maculatum* (hemlock). This latter species, although usually attributed to marsh environments (Clapham *et al.* 1962), has been noted in waste places and at woodland edges (Kenward *et al.* 1986).

The preserved oogonium of *Chara* sp. (stonewort) found in this layer may represent algae growing in the well, perhaps with *Polypodium* and Filicales. Oogonia form under adverse conditions such as temporary drought and are often found in warm climate, freshwater deposits (Kelly 1968, cited in Evans 1978, 33).

Interestingly, the apparent increase in tree and shrub species does not show up in the pollen record, although associated herb species e.g. *Rubus* spp. continue to be represented. The profile is totally dominated by herb pollen, particularly that of grassland species and Umbelliferae, a family with many edible species, also appears.

Layer K2 (13.0-14.0m)

Although this layer contained much grit, building rubble, pottery fragments and animal bone, the waterlogged conditions prevailed.

Table 52. The pollen remains from Well 1.

Depth (metres) Corresponding archaeological layer	12-12.7 K1	13-14 K2	14-14.3 L	14.5-15.5 M1	15.5-16 M2
SPECIES					
Trees and Shrubs					
Alnus	–	–	2	14	6
Betula	–	–	–	3	3
Corylus	–	1	1	–	1
Pinus	–	–	–	1	1
Tilia	–	1	–	1	–
Total tree pollen	–	2%	3%	19%	11%
Grasses and cereal					
Cerealia	4	2	3	7	13
Cyperaceae	–	1	–	–	1
Gramineae	19	19	21	12	38
Total grass pollen	23%	22%	24%	19%	51%
Herbs					
Calluna	4	3	5	16	4
Caryophyllaceae	–	33	20	15	12
Chenopodium sp.	4	1	–	1	1
Compositae liguliflorae	20	7	20	14	11
Compositae tubuliflorae	16	1	2	–	–
Labiatae (*Prunella* type)	2	1	1	1	1
Plantago lanceolata	–	10	2	–	–
Polygonum (*aviculare* type)	–	–	1	1	–
Potentilla sp.	–	1	–	3	–
Poterium sanguisorba	–	3	4	1	1
Ranunculus sp.	4	4	5	5	6
Rosaceae	–	–	1	–	–
Rubus sp.	–	2	4	5	2
Rumex (*acetosella* type)	–	1	1	–	–
Succisa sp.	–	–	1	–	–
Umbelliferae	27	8	6	–	–
Viola sp.	–	1	–	–	–
Total herb pollen	77%	76%	73%	62%	38%

All figures = percentage of total pollen (% TP)

The macroscopic remains include thorns and twigs, and 53 species are represented. There is little change in the frequency of hedgerow or heathland species. A considerable increase of plants associated with arable and waste ground can be seen, for example, *Capsella bursa-pastoris* (shepherd's purse), *Polygonum arenastrum* (small-leaved knotgrass), *Prunella vulgaris* (self-heal) and *Urtica dioica* (stinging nettle); also, some purely arable weeds. *Rubus idaeus* (raspberry) and *Crataegus monogyna* (hawthorn) twigs and thorns indicate the continuation of bushes and shrubs from the previous layer. Species that tend to be found on marshy ground or in damp places show an increase, for example the rushes, *Conium maculatum* (hemlock) and *Polygonum hydropiper* (water pepper). The mosses occurring in this layer include the grassland species *Eurhynchium speciosum*, *Rhytidiadelphus squarrosus* and *Plagiomnium undulatum*.

The pollen count shows many grassland herbs and a further increase in Caryophyllaceae pollen (e.g. *Stellaria* spp.). Pollen of *Plantago lanceolata* (ribwort plantain) and Umbelliferous species is also present in significant amounts. These could all reflect plants that were growing around a farmyard. Tree and shrub species continue to be represented, but by almost negligible values, and cereal pollen persists at a low level.

Layer K1 (12.0-12.7m)

The uppermost of the waterlogged layers contained much building rubble, grit, pottery and metal fragments, animal bone and insect remains. The botanical remains include bracken fronds and stems, twigs and moss fragments. Of the species represented, arable and waste ground species remain the most frequent. Hedgerow species show some increase, and species associated with damp ground continue to be represented although this is largely due to *Conium maculatum* (hemlock) which, as stated above, will colonise waste ground.

The pollen profile for this layer shows no tree/shrub pollen at all. There are considerable increases in pollen of Compositae and Umbelliferae. The range of herb species

Table 53. Other microscopic remains from Well 1.

Archaeological layer	K1	K2	L	M1	M2
			No. of spores, etc.		
Diatoms	–	–	–	–	2
Filicales	–	13	15	14	12
Polypodium sp.	2	–	3	4	4
Trilete sp.	3	1	3	5	1
Whipworm eggs	2	13	4	3	1

represented shows a decrease although Gramineae continues to be important.

Deposition of plant remains

Before discussing the environmental and possible economic implications of the data, it is essential to examine briefly the mode of formation of the fills. Although the stratigraphy of such fills often appears simple, the mechanism of strata formation, and of the entry of biological material into them, may have been complex both in space and time (Hall *et al.* 1980, 122). The following discussion focuses on the macroscopic data. The situation is somewhat different for pollen which is dispersed by a variety of means, and is thus indicative of a larger catchment.

It is evident from the finds recovered that the waterlogged fills and their associated biota are Roman in date, so potentially they could serve as evidence for the environment and economy of that period. The finds do, however, span a considerable period of time: from the late 2nd to late 4th centuries AD. It is also not entirely clear how these are related to the stratigraphic development of the well. The nature of the sediments should have provided a more reliable picture, but no particle size analyses were carried out for these deposits. Nor were there detailed descriptions of the sediments *in situ* which might have determined whether they formed rapidly or otherwise. Nevertheless the field descriptions indicate that the waterlogged layers were not formed as a result of collapse from the well mouth: no collapse cone was noted.

No plant remains survived in the top 12m; the next 4m all contained biological remains and appear to have represented accumulation during and immediately after the use of the well. Stratigraphically, dumped material was present even at the lowest levels, and particularly from 12.0-14.3m, although it was more limited in extent. Hence, at least some of the botanical material could have entered the well this way. Layer M1 was, however, sealed by a sandy lens at *c.* 14.50m and in terms of botanical content layers M1 and M2 might not have been expected to produce such distinct remains as the previous

discussion has suggested. Layer L was a very narrow horizon, apparently little mixed with K2 above or M1 below. The extent to which K1 and K2 had been disturbed and had received material from above is difficult to assess. The ratio of structural debris to soil in the upper levels of divisions K and J was very high. Whilst they themselves preserved no plant remains, the possibility that material from these trickled down the shaft cannot be ruled out. This would have happened very quickly though, as the waterlogged material showed an excellent state of preservation. A band of waterlogging towards the top of K1 also suggested that movement of material into and within K was restricted.

Dumping is only one possible source for the plant material in the well and various interpretations are possible. Hypothetically at least, evidence for conditions in and around the well is likely to be limited. A well in use, with a protective rim, as postulated for this site, does not provide a favourable situation for the deposition of fruits and seeds, except as wind-dispersed propagules (note, for example, the species present in layer M1) through bird droppings, from species growing on the well wall, or via species growing at the well mouth after abandonment (Hall *et al.* 1980; Kenward *et al.* 1986). It should also be noted that an equal density in the distribution of plant remains is unlikely; there is a strong possibility that concentrations will occur. The samples discussed here represent only a small proportion of the total sediment available from layers which were sometimes up to a metre in depth. Sampling units can also be less relevant to actual levels than to convenience, or perhaps to some subjective cut-off point. In view of these comments, the following discussion can provide no more than a general picture of the environment around the well head.

Discussion

The range of plant taxa present is indicative of a mosaic of communities, essentially arable land, grassland, disturbed and waste places, heathland, hedges and woodland, and some damp places. The species found in the lowest two layers are suggestive of local cultivation. Most of the cultivated species, meagre as they are, were recovered from these; also the annual species *Urtica urens* (small nettle), *Polygonum aviculare* (knotgrass), *Stellaria media* (chickweed) and *Capsella bursa-pastoris* (shepherd's purse). These are characteristic of land repeatedly cleared or otherwise disturbed, as, for example, by regular cultivation or trampling (Kenward *et al.* 1986).

The presence of heathland and marshland species may indicate the exploitation of other habitats, although these could also have been brought on to site accidentally by animals. In addition, some marshland species may have grown in isolated niches around the site which developed through soil compaction caused by animal trampling. Plants like *Calluna vulgaris* (heather) and the rushes could, nevertheless, have been valuable commodities to the local population because of their variety of uses, e.g. in thatching, bedding, floor matting and for fuel. A picture of a wide range of exploitation, at least for the period when the well was in use, is also hinted at by the number of species that are specific to particular soil types.

Regarding the presence of ferns and mosses on archaeological sites, it is often unclear whether human activity is involved or whether they simply reflect local ecological conditions. They too have a variety of uses, e.g. for furnishings, bedding, packing, caulking and so on. On the other hand, mosses are never so abundant at Dalton Parlours that it must be concluded that they were consciously gathered (see Bartley in prep.).

The relative abundance of different plant taxa overall suggests that the area around the well-head was open and grassy with many weed species, indeed not unlike what would be expected for a working villa courtyard. The remains of tree and shrub species also point to the availability of other important resources nearby, and their increased occurrence in layers L and K adds weight to the hypothesis of more widespread abandonment.

The increase in species of disturbed and waste places in layers L and K2 could also reflect the abandonment of the site itself. The ruderals *Rumex* spp. (docks) and *Urtica dioica* (stinging nettle) indicate waste ground colonisation lasting more than a single season (Kenward *et al.* 1986). In addition, species such as *Aethusa cynapium* (fools parsley), *Polygonum aviculare* (knotgrass) and *Sonchus asper* (spiny milk thistle) will grow well in crumbling or rough masonry, as for example around the well-head (cf. Wilson 1981). However, some of these are also common agricultural weeds, e.g. *Rumex crispus* (curled dock), and it remains unclear whether they reflect wholesale abandonment or merely an area around the well itself.

Food plants were poorly or ambiguously represented throughout the well deposits. This does not deny their existence, in fact it illustrates the differential disposal and survival of plant remains on an individual site. Samples of carbonised material from the site (Murray, this volume) have provided considerable evidence for the use of a number crop plants at the villa, and have hinted that many were locally grown.

Plants that are of traditional medicinal value, such as *Hyoscyamus niger* (henbane), *Atropa belladonna* (deadly nightshade), *Conium maculatum* (hemlock) and *Linum catharticum* (purging flax), were present in the well. However, these may all have grown wild in the disturbed, arable or woodland environments nearby. As they predominated in the upper layers it is likely that the latter observation is applicable here.

Conclusion

The study of the botanical remains from the well has given a general picture of the environment in which the villa was situated. It is tentatively suggested, on the basis of the evidence presented here, that accumulation of material occurred throughout usage and abandonment of the well area, and perhaps the site as a whole. It is essential to recognise that the samples analysed here provide only a partial picture due to the processes involved in transportation of plant material from the places in which it grew; also the depositional and post-depositional effects, in particular, the nature of the deposit and the way in which it filled up. It is difficult to provide a definitive account of the environment around the villa, or of the economic potential, if any, of the plants recovered. There was, however, excellent preservation of botanical remains and together they have provided insight, at least, into the existence of different habitats around the villa. These included woodland, grassland, marshland, waste ground and, of course, arable fields.

33 The Insects from Well 1

by Tina Sudell

Introduction

During the excavation of Well 1 a number of samples were extracted for environmental analysis, of which sample 362 was examined for insect remains. The sample, from level M1, had been sealed by a sandy lens and had not been disturbed by the final purposeful backfilling of the shaft (see Bastow and Murray this volume). The bulk of the sample represented material deposited during the occupation of the villa.

Methods

Processing

A subsample of the 14.28kg bulk sample was found to contain sufficient insect remains to be numerically representative of the sample as a whole (see Kenward 1978). As a consequence only 3.68kg of sample 362 was processed.

The subsample was disaggregated in water and washed out over a 300 micron sieve after which the retained material was subjected to the process of paraffin flotation as described by Kenward *et al.* (1980). The resultant flot was thoroughly washed in detergent and hot water and then stored in alcohol prior to the subsequent sorting and identification stages.

Identification

The identifiable insect fragments were sorted in an alcohol-filled petri dish under low power light microscope and transferred onto dampened filter paper for identification. The classification of the remains into genus and species, where possible, was carried out under higher powered magnification, and in addition to the entomological reference collection housed at the University of Sheffield, a number of literary sources were utilised in final identifications (Balfour-Browne 1958; Freude *et al.* 1961-1981; Joy 1932; Tottenham 1954; Britton 1956; Duffy 1953; Lindroth 1974; 1986).

Table 54. Insect remains from Well 1.

INSECTA	Minimum No. Individuals	INSECTA	Minimum No. Individuals	INSECTA	Minimum No. Individuals
DERMAPTERA		STAPHYLINIDAE		PTINIDAE	
FORFICULIDAE		*Micropeplus staphilinoides* (Marsh.)	1	*Tipnus unicolor* (Pill. and Mitt.)	5
Forficula auricularia (L.)	10	*Megarthus depressus* (Payk.)	2	*Ptinus fur* (L.)	1
		Lesteva heeri (Fauv.)	7	*Ptinus* sp.	1
COLEOPTERA		*Lesteva* spp.	4	NITIDULIDAE	
CARABIDAE		*Omalium caesum* (Grav.)	1	*Brachypterous glaber* (Steph.)	1
Nebria salina	1	*O. rivulare* (Payk.)	2	*Meligethes* sp.	1
Trechus quadristriatus (Schr.)	1	*Omalium* sp.	2	*Epuraea* sp.	1
Bembidion lampros (Hbst.)	8	*Bledius* sp.	1	RHIZOPHAGIDAE	
B. properans (Steph.)	5	*Carpelimus rivularis* (Mots.)	6	*Monotoma* sp.	2
B. cf. *assimile* (Gyll.)	1	*Carpelimus* sp.	1	CRYPTOPHAGIDAE	
Bembidion sp.	2	*Platystethus arenarius* (Fourc.)	3	*Cryptophagus* sp.	1
Pterostichus gracilis (Dej.)	2	*P. cornutus* (Grav.)	15	*Atomaria* sp.	1
P. niger (Schall.)	2	*P. nitens* (Sahl.)	9	LATHRIDIIDAE	
Pterostichus sp.	1	*Platystethus* sp.	1	*Lathridius minutus* group	14
Calathus ambiguus (Payk.)	1	*Anotylus nitidulus* (Grav.)	12	*Lathridius* sp.	3
C. fuscipes (Goez.)	2	*A. rugosus* (Fab.)	5	*Corticaria* cf. *crenulata* (Gyll.)	1
C. melanocephalus (L.)	4	*A. sculpturatus* (Grav.)	8	*Corticaria/Corticarina* spp.	8
Ophonus sp.	2	*A. tetracarinatus* (Block)	7	CISIDAE	
Harpalus rufipes (Deg.)	2	*Anotylus* spp.	4	*Cis* sp.	1
Harpalus sp.	1	*Oxytelus* spp.	12	CHRYSOMELIDAE	
Dromius melanocephalus	1	*Stenus* spp.	3	*Oulema lichens* (Voet)	1
Amara eurynota (Panz.)	1	*Xantholinus* spp.	5	*Phyllodecta* sp.	1
A. familiaris (Duft.)	1	*Philonthus* cf. *longicornis* (Steph.)	2	*Phyllotreta aerea* (All.)	4
Amara spp.	2	*Philonthus* spp.	3	*P. consobrina* (Curt.)	4
DYTISIDAE		*Staphylinus olens* (Mull.)	1	*Phyllotreta* spp.	6
Hydroporus sp.	1	*Tachyporus chrysomelinus* (L.)	1	*Chaetocnema concinna* (Marsh.)	4
HYDROPHILIDAE		*T. nitidulus* (Fab.)	1	*C. arida* (Foud.) or *hortensis* (Fourc.)	1
Helophorus flavipes group	3	*Falagria* sp.	6	*Chaetocnema* sp.	1
H. aquaticus (Ill.)/*grandis*	1	*Aleocharinidae* indet.	1	*Psylliodes* sp.	1
H. obscurus (Muls.)	1	*Drusilla canaliculata* (Fab.)	1	APIONIDAE	
H. rufipes group	3	GEOTRUPIDAE		*Apion* sp.	4
Helophorus sp.	2	*Geotrupes* sp.	1	CURCULIONIDAE	
Cercyon analis (Payk.)	1	SCARABAEIDAE		*Polydrosus* sp.	1
C. quisquilius (L.) or *unipunctatus* (L.)	1	*Aphodius contaminatus* (Herb.)	2	*Ceutorhynchus* cf. *erysimi*	2
Cercyon spp.	3	*A. fimetarius* (L.)	1	*Ceutorhynchus* sp.	1
Megasternum obscurum (Marsh.)	4	*A.* cf. *foetens* (Fab.)	1	SCOLYTIDAE	
HISTERIDAE		*A. granarius* (L.)	9	*Leperisinus varius* (Fab.)	29
Plegadens dissectus (Erich.)	1	*A. rufus* (Moll)	2	DIPTERA	
Acritus homeopathicus (Woll.)	1	*A. sphacelatus* (Panz.)	3	*Dilophus* sp.	1
HYDRAENIDAE		*Aphodius* sp.	1	indet.	36
Ochthebius minimus (Fab.)	2	*Phyllopertha horticola* (L.)	2		
Hydraena riparia (Kug.)	1	SCIRTIDAE			
PTILIDAE		*Cyphon* cf. *padi* (L.)	2		
Pteridium cf. *pusillum* (Gyll.)	2	*Helodidae* indet.	4		
Pteridium sp.	1	BYRRHIDAE		**COLEOPTERA**	
HEIODIDAE		*Byrrhus* sp.	1	Total number of species	108
Catops sp.	2	ANOBIDAE		Total number of individuals	333
SILPHIDAE		*Anobium* sp.	5		
Silpha sp.	1				

Time did not allow for any further analysis of the Diptera which have, as a consequence, been counted as one group and not used in the interpretation.

Formation of the insect death assemblage

Prior to any consideration of the ecological requirements of the insect species and the possible range of habitats they indicate for the villa area, it is necessary to consider how the insects actually came to be in the well. It has been stated above that level M1 probably represented the period of Roman occupation at the site and theoretically, therefore, the species should be representative of conditions at and around the villa at that time. The analysis of a modern well has indicated that habitats in the vicinity contribute a discernible background component to the contained death assemblage (Hall *et al.* 1980), and the well at Dalton Parlours is no exception.

A well, even if protected by a revetment wall, would have acted as a pitfall trap especially to the locally active ground-dwelling Carabidae; and if the shaft was open to the air above, or acted as a receptacle for any insects collecting on the roof of the well building, it is likely to have accumulated a variable assortment of insects in flight, feasibly from a relatively wide catchment around the villa. Almost half of the Coleoptera recovered from the well can be associated with decaying organic material, with a number of the more synanthropic species closely associated with indoor habitats. This high proportion rules out the possibility of their accidental incorporation into the shaft, especially considering the presence of the revetment wall, and suggests that these insects were deliberately dumped into the shaft perhaps in floor sweepings. It is unlikely that this would occur whilst the well was still in use as a clean water source, which makes it feasible that at some point, prior to the final backfilling of the shaft, the well went into a period of disuse.

The entry of many insects into the well shaft would have been a random process, but at the same time affected by the selective filtering produced by the presence of a revetment wall and well building. It is highly probable that the recorded insects are not representative of all the types of environmental conditions at and around the villa and it may be that selective processes have caused some habitats to be overstated. However, keeping this in mind, it has been possible to arrive at a tentative interpretation concerning the environment and living conditions around the local area, and the results do appear to bear out those from the analysis of the seeds from the well.

Results: the species

The identified insect taxa were counted in terms of the minimum number of individuals, based on counts for the commonest element. All of the Diptera and Coleoptera, with the exception of *Geotrupes* sp. which was counted on the presence of diagnostic leg parts, were quantified on the numbers of heads, thoraces and elytra present. The total

for *Forficula auricularia* was calculated on the basis of the numbers of male and female *cerci*.

The state of preservation of the recovered insect remains was good although some of the larger Carabidae had been fragmented, probably as a result of mechanical damage during storage or processing. As a group the Coleoptera make up the bulk of the assemblage, with a minimum number of 108 species and 333 individuals. In addition, ten individuals of the earwig *Forficula auricularia* were extracted, together with 37 members of Diptera.

All the identified taxa and their minimum totals are listed in Table 54 according to the nomenclature and ordering procedure of Kloet and Hincks (1977).

Discussion: the environment and living conditions around the villa

The insect assemblage from the well at the villa represents a wide range of environmental conditions including tracts of grassland, cultivated and/or disturbed areas with their associated weeds, bodies of surface water and waterside vegetation, accumulations of organic detritus and the more artificial conditions associated with buildings. There is also some evidence for the presence of some tree cover albeit at some distance from the villa itself.

There is no evidence for the presence of any local breeding populations of Coleoptera either on the walls of the shaft or in the water itself. Ten individuals of water beetle of the *Helophorus* genus were recorded, together with one individual of *Hydraena riparia* and two of *Ochthebius minimus* and, although commonly known from still or sluggish fresh water, the low level in the shaft would have precluded the development of an autochthonous aquatic fauna. The water beetles are strong flyers and the water-filled well, if accessible, would have attracted such species, especially as there is little evidence for any further areas of standing water in the immediate vicinity (WYAS pers. comm.). The presence of a number of aquatic-marginal Staphylinidae does suggest that there were some source areas of surface water or damp conditions in the vicinity. Murray (this volume) has suggested that such conditions existed, and were possibly exploited, at some distance to the north and west of the site. If wetland vegetation were collected and transported to the site it would likely have contained some species of insect. *Platystethus cornutus*, a species known to burrow into mud on the banks of ponds and rivers (Hammond 1971), is particularly numerous with fifteen individuals recorded. *Bledius sp.* is fossorial in similar environments, and further evidence for marginally aquatic habitats comes from the presence of *Anotylus rugosus*, *Anotylus nitidulus* and *Platystethus nitens*; the latter of which is well represented despite being towards its northern limit of distribution in England (Hammond 1971). The ground beetle *Pterostichus gracilis* is associated with wet vegetated soil close to water and such localised conditions around the well-head cannot be ruled out.

It is the Carabid species which perhaps provide the best indication of ground condition around the well and in the immediate environs around the villa. The majority of the ground beetles suggest rather dry and open conditions with only a sparse cover of vegetation. *Nebria salina*, *Trechus quadrisriatus*, *Bembidion lampros* (the most numerous Carabid), and *B. properans* are all common to this habitat although the latter has a tendency towards less dry, clay-like soils (Lindroth 1986). Some species are eurytopic in character and known from a variety of ground conditions; *Amara familiaris* for example is recorded from meadows, fallow fields and waste ground amongst weeds, and *Calathus fuscipes* is to be found in dry meadows, grassland or cultivated soils (Lindroth 1986). Rather exposed and weedy conditions in the vicinity of the well are also suggested by some of the phytophagous species: *Brachypterous glaber* is indicative of its host *Urtica* spp., which thrive in nitrogen-rich environments, and *Chaetocnema concinna* is phytophagous on Polygonaceae and particularly the weed of cultivation *Polygonum aviculare*.

Many of the phytophagous plant feeders, although not restricted to a grassland habitat, are, in conjunction with the evidence from the dung beetles, suggestive of tracts of grazed grassland around the villa. The root feeder *Phyllopertha horticola* is a common grassland pest and would have found the light calcareous soils of the limestone region very favourable. Perhaps the best indication of pasture comes indirectly from the evidence for dung beetles, and particularly those associated with dung under field conditions. As a genus they are more influenced by the climatic and microclimatic conditions of their habitat than its source (Landin 1961). *Aphodius rufus* and *A. contaminatus* are restricted to dung but of various types. However, *A. foetens*, the only oligotopic member of the genus, does suggest the presence probably of cow dung in rather exposed sandy locations (Landin 1961). *Geotrupes* sp. is also confined to dung in field conditions.

Although the insects do not directly indicate cereals or other cultigens, there are a number of potential crop pests recorded which are suggestive at least. *Phyllotreta* spp., *Ceutorynchus erysimi*, *Meligethes* sp., and some species of *Helophorus* are known as pests on cultivated Cruciferae. *Psylliodes* sp. can reach pest distinction. The introduction of new cultigens in the Roman period increased the potential host plants for species previously more commonly associated with wild varieties.

Considering the proximity of some of the crop processing areas to the well, species directly associated with cereals and grain might have been expected. It may be that there was no infestation of the grain. This lack of obligate grain beetles is a factor common to many rural Roman sites in contrast to contemporary urban areas where granary pests often turn up in vast proportions (e.g. Kenward and Williams 1979). However, it is difficult to assess the significance of this apparent lack of grain beetles at Dalton Parlours as there was also a noticeable lack of grain extracted from the well. This might suggest

that it is the result of differential disposal especially as cultivated spelt, breadwheat and barley are in evidence from several other contexts at the site (see Chapter 25).

The evidence for wooded areas in the local environs is limited. *Pterostichus niger* favours shaded woody areas but can also be found in hedgerows (Lindroth 1986), and the one individual of *Cis* sp. would most likely derive from fungi in or around wood (Joy 1932). *Plegadens dissectus*, represented by only one possible individual, tends to inhabit rotten wood; and *Epuraea* sp., although sometimes taken on flowers, is known equally from under bark or at the sap of trees (Joy 1932). Pieces of wood and brushwood were recovered from the well in addition to the well buckets worked from ash and oak. It is interesting that, despite a general lack of true woodland species, the most common beetle recorded from the sample was the timber feeder *Leperisinus varius*. The 29 individuals make up 8% of the total number of Coleoptera. This species can live on a variety of host trees, and most particularly *Fraxinus excelsior*. Ash wood was recovered from the well in both 'natural' and worked form but was noticeably absent from the lists for the seeds and pollen (see Chapter 32). *Leperisinus varius* has been known to emerge in large numbers from logs imported to sites (Hall *et al.* 1983) and its presence may suggest that areas of mixed woodland with ash existed, perhaps on the more acidic higher land at some distance from the villa, and were exploited for their wood.

Five individuals of the *Anobium* genus were recorded. Normally associated with old timbers, or seasoned wooden artefacts or structures, such beetles would have found many suitable habitats around the villa, even as close to the shaft as the wooden well building.

Out of a total of 108 species and 333 individuals recovered, 45 species and 173 individuals are able to exploit some kind of rotting organic material. This large and variable group covers an array of habitats from dung and rather foul rotting matter through to the drier 'sweeter' compost as described by Kenward (1982). Many of these species, notably the Staphylinidae, are very eurytopic making ecological definition problematic.

The majority of the 'foul' compost species are associated with dung which may suggest that dung was allowed to accumulate in the yards or other domestic areas. *Aphodius fimetarius*, *A. sphacelatus*, and most numerous of the dung beetles, *A. granarius*, are often associated with piles of dung or rotting vegetation, and the indication of this type of habitat is further supported by the presence of many associated Staphylinid, Histerid, Hydrophilid and Ptilid species. *Pteridium pusillum* for example is recorded from decaying manure and dung carts (Freude *et al.* 1971); and dung, rotting vegetation and fungi are associated with *Megasternum obsurum* (Freude *et al.* 1971). There may have been some rotting carrion around the site as *Silpha* sp. and *Catops* sp. are in evidence. However, these two species only total three individuals between them and can also be found in other types of habitat, and so provide no conclusive evidence for such. Overall, there are nothing like the numbers and variety of species found at urban York to suggest particularly unsavoury living conditions around the site.

There are a number of species recorded which are associated more with drier compost conditions and similar habitats. The fungal feeder *Monotoma* sp. is commonly recorded from relatively dry compost together with *Atomaria* sp. and *Cryptophagus* spp. That stores of hay or similar dry plant materials might have been present in the vicinity is suggested by the relatively large numbers of *Forficula auricularia* (earwig) and the *Lathridius minutus* group. The latter are commonly recorded in Britain within primitive buildings and haystacks (Hinton 1945). The synanthropic species *Tipnus unicolor* and *Ptinus fur* can also be found associated with straw or hay waste, or alternatively in roofing thatch or old wood. Both species are characteristic of poorly heated buildings, and being flightless have a tendency to wander. This latter factor may explain their presence in the well deposits, although on the basis of the proportion of species present, associated with the stores of organic materials, it seems more likely that such species reached the well as a result of human activity.

Conclusion

The insect assemblage from the well represents a variety of ecological conditions and is suggestive of several different habitat types in the vicinity of the villa and in the area around it. The faunal assemblage is dominated essentially by a background component with 72 out of the 110 species represented by two individuals or less.

There were no autochthonous species in evidence from the well and the species present must have entered the well through a variety of means either accidentally or as a result of man's activities. On the basis of the species present, and having taken into consideration the probable mechanisms of entry of the insects into the well, a general picture of conditions around the site has been made.

The assemblage tends to suggest an open, dry environment around the villa with areas of short and/or weedy vegetation. There is little to suggest that conditions around the site were particularly unsavoury with the exception of some areas where dung may have been allowed to accumulate. The more synanthropic species are associated with rather dry materials either inside buildings or in outdoor situations.

There is some suggestion of areas of grazed grassland and cultivated fields around the villa, and areas of wetland and mixed woodland located outside the immediate area are also implied by a small proportion of the fauna.

Acknowledgements
I am very grateful to Paul Buckland who provided invaluable help during the processing and identification of the insects. Thanks are also due to Dave Berg and Tony Sumpter together with their colleagues at the West Yorkshire Archaeology Service for the information regarding the other aspects of the site.

34 Discussion of Well 1 and its Contents by Stuart Wrathmell

The lowest silt deposits in the well, occupying the bottom 1.5m of the shaft, were excavated as divisions M and N. They are interpreted as accumulations during the period of use, mainly on the basis of ceramic evidence: the succession of jar types in these and higher divisions conforms to chronological changes in the products of regional industries (Chapter 30, Table 29). The predominance of Throlam ware in these divisions indicates use of the well during the second half of the 3rd century. The Throlam jars, many reconstructed to a near-complete state, were presumably employed to draw water. So, too, was bucket No. 5 (p. 211), found at a depth of 15.5m below datum and presumably an accidental loss.

These divisions also produced a small number of artefacts which pre-date the mid-3rd century: some samian sherds and two coins (Nos 2 and 4, Chapter 4) of the 2nd and early 3rd centuries. Several of the one-piece shoes from these layers (e.g. Nos 3-6, Chapter 29) might be equally early losses, given the dating of comparable footwear on other sites; the presence of two other one-piece shoes at a higher level, in the abandonment-phase fill, suggests, however, that examples of this type need not all pre-date the 4th century.

It is impossible to say whether this relatively early material indicates use of Well 1 in the 2nd and early 3rd centuries. The sherds and coins could have become incorporated in the silt long after their breakage and loss; on the other hand, cleaning operations before the later 3rd century could easily have removed evidence of water-drawing at an earlier date. Though the villa would probably have been furnished with a well from the beginning (perhaps *c*. AD 200), the initial water source could have been the largely unexcavated Well 2.

Division L was a band of artefacts which had accumulated on the surface of the silt. The objects included four reconstructable wooden buckets (two from the base of division K) and fragments of several others. There were also numerous curved and angled lengths of roundwood (Chapter 28) which have been interpreted as part of the well-head winding mechanism, and large numbers of Crambeck lug-handled jars and Huntcliff jars. Two of the pottery vessels were intact, and many others could be reconstructed to a near-complete state, suggesting that they entered the shaft whole. These vessels have been interpreted as water containers, like the earlier and underlying Throlam jars. Several had been repaired with lead plugs or cramps, and one Crambeck jar retained a scrap of cord attached to the lug.

Such an accumulation of water containers and related artefacts cannot have resulted from accidental loss; rather, it suggests that, immediately upon the decision to abandon the well, the water-drawing equipment – which had probably been stored in the well-house – was thrown down the shaft. On the evidence of the pottery types present in and absent from the well, the date of abandonment was soon after *c.* AD 370; that is, probably at the same time as the entire settlement was abandoned.

The simultaneous deposition of large numbers of artefacts suggests a symbolic or ritual act which may have been related to the desertion of the villa as a whole; it was followed immediately by substantial dumping. The lower 2m of division K contained large quantities of animal bone: butchery and kitchen waste, as well as the partial skeletons of six horses and three dogs which may again, have some symbolic significance.

The upper part of K comprised an accumulation of stone roofing slabs below burnt stone and structural timber. This, the lowest element of the main filling of building debris, possibly represents the demolished well-house, levelled to facilitate the dumping of larger masonry in the shaft. The larger blocks, occupying much of division J, included at least one cistern (possibly two) from the water supply system; again, the deposition of items related to the drawing and distribution of water. The rest of the masonry seems to have been derived from the nearest building, the bath suite in Structure M: division J contained monolithic *pilae* and short columns reused as *pilae* (Chapter 19). Among the largest blocks was a threshold stone of estimated weight one tonne.

This main deposit contained little animal bone; what there was provided matching elements from various depths, confirming that it represents a single activity. It has previously been suggested that the dumping of building debris marks deliberate attempts to eliminate the structures systematically (Sumpter 1988, 192). The well would, however, have had very limited capacity for holding the Structure M hypocaust suite; indeed, most of the hypocaust structures survived into the 19th century (Procter 1855, 271-4). A much more acceptable explanation is that the operation was carried out in order to prevent others using the well; to make it more difficult for anyone to reoccupy the site. This would account for the effort expended in dumping very large blocks of masonry.

Whatever the intentions of the departing inhabitants there is some evidence of later, though undated, reoccupation. The main filling ended at (or subsided to) a depth of about 5m below datum; above this, the shaft seems to have remained open for some time, and to have been subject to gradual silting to a point in division H about 2m below datum. The rest of H contained a larger concentration of animal bone, representing food waste and indicating that the shaft was now used as a rubbish dump for a nearby settlement. This indication is supported by the deposition of foetal pigs and dogs.

Part Five
Dalton Parlours and its Context

35 The Cropmark Evidence (Fig. 155)

by R.E. Yarwood

Until 1986 relatively few cropmarks had been recorded in the immediate vicinity of Dalton Parlours, and none on the excavated area itself, despite reconnaissance for the previous fifteen years. Much of the detail shown in Figure 155 was recorded in the summer of 1986 and, surprisingly, in March-April 1989. The ditches shown in the excavated area are the principal ones recorded during excavation rather than cropmarks. Marks arising from features identifiable as more recent field boundaries have been omitted.

The inherent limitations of cropmark evidence are well known and, in this region, both geophysical survey and limited excavation have again shown how misleading or incomplete a picture is frequently gained from cropmarks (Yarwood and Marriott 1988). Interpretation of cropmark landscapes in the county is further hindered by the often fragmentary nature of the marks, by the paucity of surface remains, and by the relative lack of excavation evidence. Furthermore, a morphological study of numerous cropmark enclosures suggests that many have unique identifying characteristics and that any typology must be of the simplest and most general nature. Therefore any discussion of Figure 155 cannot go far beyond a cursory description of the cropmarks before entering the realms of speculation. There is little superimposition of features in the Dalton Parlours cropmarks and this again typifies the cropmark landscapes of this region.

Three elements recur in Figure 155: enclosures, linear ditches and ditched lanes or tracks. The last appear in part as a single broad cropmark rather than two parallel ditches, a feature which has been attributed to rutting during use. The central enclosure group, found to be of Iron Age date in the area excavated, is without parallel in the region. The majority of West Yorkshire enclosures occur singly and in only one other case, at Huddleston, North Yorkshire (SE 455 321), has such a number of enclosures been recorded in a nucleated group. There, however, the enclosures, both D-shaped and sub-rectangular, line both sides of a trackway for a distance of 430m. At Dalton Parlours, there is no obvious single routeway through the Iron Age settlement and nor was one found during excavation. It is now clear from the cropmarks recorded after excavation was completed that this settlement is about 375m in length, encompassing *c.*

3.4 hectares. Excavation results at first suggested a gap of up to 200 years between the apparent demise of the Iron Age settlement and the foundation of the villa (Sumpter 1988, 181): there were very few finds of the 1st and 2nd centuries AD. The possibility must now be entertained that Iron Age or native occupation continued on the western part of the central enclosure group up to and conceivably during the villa period, and that this accounts for the finds of early Roman date.

There is no sign in the air photographs of the 'Ancient Road' leading from the north-west side of the excavated area towards the west-north-west, as shown on sheet 189 of the 1850 1:10560 Ordnance Survey map. The central settlement area is clearly approached by three contemporary tracks leading from the north, west and east. The sinuous form of at least two of these (A and B, Fig. 155), compared with the straighter ditches which abut them, suggests that they were primary features in the surrounding cropmark landscape. It has been speculated that Dalton Lane is itself of Roman origin, but there is no proof of this; it certainly post-dates track B and its associated linear ditches. The land divisions marked by linear ditches abutting tracks A and B are seen as a secondary feature and could be of Iron Age or Roman date. Track C, possibly heading for the natural spring at Compton, could also be of either date.

Cropmark evidence from the region generally suggests that most, but not quite all, ditched trackways run for only short distances (less than 1km) in the immediate vicinity of settlement sites; they may therefore be the result of protecting arable areas from stock using the tracks. Such an interpretation implies the existence of 'fields' adjacent to the tracks. If, therefore, the land divisions around Dalton Parlours are of much later date (?Roman) than the tracks, then it may be speculated that they replaced earlier land divisions of a form which did not give rise to cropmarks. We do not know the extent to which hedges, fences or markers were used to demarcate fields, and such features could well have existed at the same time as the linear ditches as well as before them. The irregular size and shape of the areas defined by linear ditches in Figure 155 allow little further comment on the morphology of fields contemporary with either the Iron Age or the Roman settlement. Only to the south-east of the central settlement (and mostly just outside the area shown on Fig. 155) is there a small area. of linear ditches which may reflect a more regular arrangement of fields in a brickwork pattern.

The remaining cropmark features comprise a large sub-rectangular enclosure (D) which was not contemporary with track C, a small rectangular enclosure

Fig. 155. Cropmarks in the vicinity of Dalton Parlours (recorded by D.N. Riley, Cambridge University, RCHM(E) and WYAS).

274

(E) in direct association with track A, and a possible curvilinear enclosure (F) of unknown date.

Despite the obvious relevance of the surrounding cropmark landscape to the Dalton Parlours site, the limited description given here does not lead to the level of detailed interpretation which might be desired. Whilst further cropmark recording may usefully add to the picture, it is felt that substantial progress in our understanding of this landscape will be made only by using other techniques. For example, geophysical survey of selected areas to determine the limits of the trackways, and the judicious use of small area trial excavations are more likely to answer specific questions than is continued aerial survey. In conclusion, it cannot go unnoticed that the Iron Age settlement, of a character unique in the region, was also chosen as the site of one of the very few Roman villa establishments in the area. However, the problem of identifying the particular status or function of this Iron Age site, and its relationship, if any, to the villa cannot be resolved on the basis of current archaeological evidence alone.

36 Discussion (Figs 156-8)

by Stuart Wrathmell

A small collection of stone implements – arrowheads, scrapers and axes – bears witness to some kind of human activity in the vicinity of Dalton Parlours before the 1st millennium BC. On the basis of radiocarbon determinations, however, the excavated pre-Roman farmstead can be ascribed to the latter half of the 1st millennium BC; it may, of course, have begun earlier and/or continued later (Table 55). More precise dating is impossible because of the provenance of the samples: they were taken mainly from animal bones in the filling layers of the enclosure ditches. Some of the bones may have been residual in their excavated contexts, and there is no means of determining whether the ditches were kept free from silt over a long period, or were recut late in the life of the settlement. Two other samples came from human burials, but again there is no way of telling whether the burials took place before, during or after the domestic occupation. The duration of occupation is equally problematical, especially since as much as two-thirds of the settlement lay outside the area of excavation (see Chapter 35); this matter is considered below.

The Iron Age settlement

Unlike its Roman successor, the Iron Age settlement seems to have evolved and expanded gradually. It may have been established in an already cleared, enclosed and cultivated landscape, but the immediate area appears to have been open ground: the shape of the initial enclosures (II and, possibly, VI) indicates that they were not required to conform to pre-existing boundaries. Morphologically,

the rounded corners and, in some cases, rounded sides of both these and later enclosures are diagnostic of piecemeal encroachments into open space. Growth by subdivision – the creation of enclosures within a larger defined space – would almost certainly have produced sharper angles and straighter sides.

The enclosures were defined by ditches of variable profile, up to 3.3m wide and cut into bedrock to a maximum surviving depth of 1.6m. Apart from the possible entrance causeway between Enclosures I and III there was no visible means of access between the various units; timber bridges may have been used. Nor was there firm evidence of internal or external banks; on the contrary, some earth-cut features, such as the west entrance post-holes of Roundhouse 2, imply that contemporary banks did not exist. Nevertheless, it is possible that lengths of ditch became redundant as the settlement expanded, and were backfilled before some of the internal features were created.

Most of the enclosure boundaries were ditches, but some, in their primary phases, were represented by trenches which had accommodated palisades. The earliest additions to Enclosure II on both east and west sides were in part, at least, defined by palisade trenches. It is, indeed, conceivable that there was a pre-ditch settlement bounded solely by palisades, the evidence for which was largely obliterated by the ditches. Nevertheless, in terms of the surviving evidence there was no clear chronological distinction between palisades and ditches as boundary markers.

Figure 156, No. 1 shows the suggested arrangements in the early phases of the settlement: Enclosure II with the more central of the two roundhouses (No. 1); the palisade on each side; Roundhouse 3, with its entrance possibly aligned to a gap in the west palisade, and Roundhouse 5. In the second period (Fig. 156, No. 2) Enclosures I and III had been formed as fully ditched units; the now redundant stretches of Enclosure II ditch may or may not have been backfilled. The bend in the centre of the Enclosure I north side ditch implies not only the prior existence of Roundhouse 5, but also its continuation. Roundhouse 4 is assigned to this period because it was centrally located in Enclosure I. Enclosure VI may already have existed as an independent unit.

The next plan in the sequence (Fig. 156, No. 3) shows further expansion: the creation of Enclosure IV, the curving perimeter of which seems specifically designed to enclose a space around Roundhouse 6. The palisaded east side appears to have contained an entrance. At some stage Roundhouse 1 in Enclosure II was replaced by Roundhouse 2. The fourth plan (Fig. 156, No. 4) shows further development, including the expansion of Enclosure IV to the east in two stages, the first perhaps to accommodate the site of Roundhouse 7. The linking of Enclosures IV and VI may, in view of the ditch running westwards from the south-west corner of Enclosure I, have brought the settlement within a much larger enclosure. The final plan (Fig. 156, No. 5) shows the creation of Enclosure VII, apparently designed to

Table 55. Radiocarbon dates.

Sample	Context	Harwell reference	Radiocarbon Age bp±1 σ[1]	Min. and max. of calibrated age ranges[2]	Calibrated ages (incorporating +1 σ)	
					Calibrated age ranges with relative percentages under the probability distribution[3]	
Animal bone	**003/2** Fill of ditch on west side of Enclosure I	HAR 6716	2090 ±80	346-1 BC	347-321 BC 277-224 BC 208-87 BC 83-66 BC 64-37 BC 32-21 BC 12 BC- AD 1	10 1 61 8 11 4 5
Animal bone	**006/2** Fill of ditch on north side of Enclosure I	HAR 6727	2320 ±120	743-212 BC	755-691 BC 589-579 BC 542-528 BC 524-459 BC 450-350 BC 321-227 BC 224-208 BC	15 2 3 18 32 25 4
Animal bone	**020/1** Fill of ditch on west side of Enclosure II	HAR 6726	2950 ±100	1372-1012 BC	1368-1364 BC 1348-1344 BC 1320-1070 BC 1065-1050 BC 1035-1021 BC	1 1 88 5 4
Human bone	**602** Burial No. 2	HAR 6715	2140 ±70	355-94 BC	353-293 BC 231-218 BC 213-95 BC	31 7 62
Animal bone	**3455/2** Fill of gully of Roundhouse 6	HAR 6725	2320 ±90	480-235 BC	752-720 BC 716-695 BC 520-463 BC 448-351 BC 298-229 BC 220-211 BC	8 5 18 40 23 3
Human bone	**5005** Burial No. 10	HAR 6714	1780 ±80	AD 130-377	AD 131-263 AD 275-340	67 33

1. Uses half-life of 5570 years

2. Stuiver 1987, method A

3. Stuiver 1987, method B

accommodate an existing Roundhouse 8. It was followed by a number of smaller enclosures along the east side of IV and VII, and by the extension eastwards of the main north side ditch.

A total of eight roundhouses has been identified. Of these, three were unquestionably replacements for three others, so no more than five could have been used or occupied simultaneously. Some were visible through the survival of 'ring-grooves' – the trenches in which the walls were founded. Others were marked simply by pairs of elongated post-holes which flanked the entrance positions. Dalton Parlours is one of numerous settlements where entrance posts and adjacent sectors of walling seem to have been founded more deeply than the rest of the wall, with the result that (on ploughed sites especially) these are frequently the only indication of the house's full extent (see Guilbert 1981, 300-302).

Figure 157 shows the eight roundhouses identified principally by means of wall-trenches and post-holes;

these definitive elements are shown in black. Additional post-holes, marked in outline, have been selected as possibly associated structural elements, derived from the background scatter of cut features. They have been chosen on the basis of 'axial-line symmetry' (Guilbert 1982, 69-71) and, more generally, concentricity. To justify this procedure there is no need to invoke the concept of prehistoric builders taking trouble over the finer points of design, or having pride in the appearance of their houses (Guilbert 1982, 67). With pegs and a line it would, quite simply, have been quicker and easier to mark out a structure with perfectly concentric circular elements; irregularities would have introduced complications. Precise concentricity and symmetry would have produced a more stable structure; it would have allowed the correct number of timbers with appropriate diameters and lengths to be collected together prior to construction – the only rational way of erecting a timber building in a farming landscape.

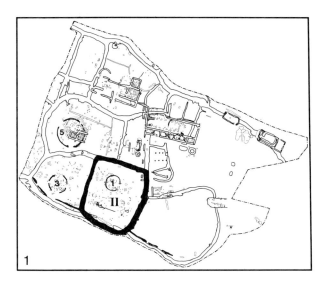

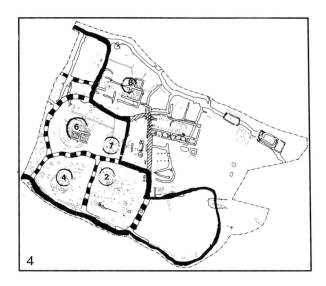

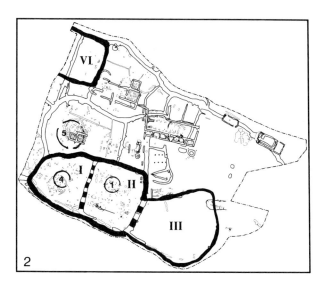

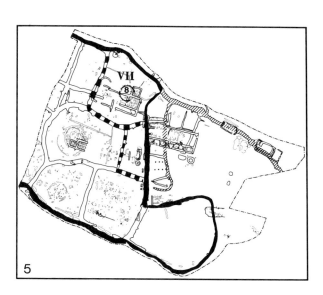

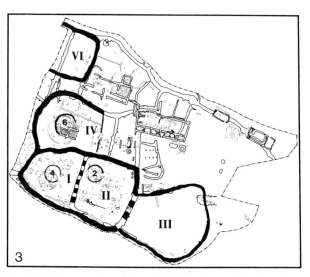

ditches and houses assigned to a phase
earlier ditches, possibly backfilled in a phase
ditches added to a phase

Fig. 156. Suggested evolution of the Iron Age enclosed settlement.

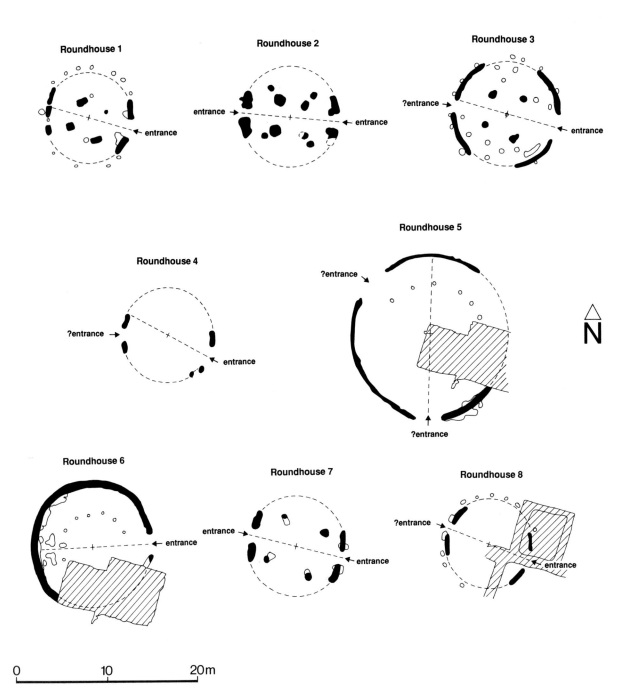

Fig. 157. Comparative plans of the roundhouses.

One of the roundhouses illustrated here, No. 5, stands out from the rest. It has a much larger diameter than the remainder, which are relatively uniform in their estimated sizes (17m diameter as against *c.* 9-11m). In fact, the proposed (incompletely recovered) internal post-ring of Roundhouse 5 was more closely comparable to the overall size of the others. It may also have had a south-facing entrance, whereas all the others seem to have had entrance alignments varying between east to west and south-east to north-west. On the other hand it should be noted that a gap in the north-west sector of the Roundhouse 5 wall-trench might indicate a doorway, and that the south-east sector had been obliterated by Structure B. Of the remaining roundhouses at least three (Nos 2, 7 and 8) seem to have had diametrically opposed entrances like those proposed

for roundhouse D3 at Whitton, South Glamorgan (Jarrett and Wrathmell 1981, fig. 35). Two others (Nos 3 and 4) had entrances less precisely opposed, in the manner of Pimperne, Dorset (Guilbert 1981, fig. 7C). The surviving extent of wall-trenches in Roundhouse 3 offers the prospect of two pairs of opposed entrances, one narrow, one wide, though this may be an accident of preservation, through a symmetrical variation in the depth of the trenches.

Three roundhouses (Nos 3, 5 and 6) provide (incomplete) evidence consistent with internal post-rings; for Roundhouses 3 and 6 it would be possible to construct more than one ring (all incomplete) on the same centre. Two others (Nos 2 and 7) with, possibly, two further roundhouses (Nos 1 and 3), seem to have contained four internal posts placed symmetrically; Roundhouse 2 may have had two different sets of four posts. The innermost set of Roundhouse 2 is reminiscent, in spacing and position, of the four-post setting in house I at Little Woodbury, Wiltshire (Guilbert 1981, fig. 7G). One roundhouse (No. 3) may have contained a central post, a feature recorded in roundhouses at Thorpe Thewles, Cleveland and a few other sites (Heslop 1987, 118).

Finally, there is evidence (again incomplete) of post-rings just within and just outside the external (or assumed external) walls; this comes from four roundhouses (Nos 1, 3, 6 and 8). As in any earthfast timber structure the lower parts of the external walls will have been most readily susceptible to rotting and consequent replacement. This could have taken place whilst the rest of the building remained standing – hence the concentric positioning.

None of the roundhouses contained evidence of hearths, which may be accounted for by the extent of plough damage. There were, however, four burnt hollows, identified as cooking-pits, in three of the enclosures. They were typically circular, about 1m in diameter and 0.30m deep (from the excavation surface), with near-vertical sides. Along with black ashy material, two of them produced Iron Age potsherds. The large parts of two jars from hearths 2558 (Chapter 13, No. 11) and 2600 (Chapter 13, No. 12) were externally sooted, and had presumably been used in these positions. There was no sign of enclosing structures.

Larger oval pits, also with steep sides and flat bases, were interpreted as storage pits: they were similar to those from Ledston, West Yorkshire, identified as grain-storage pits (Sumpter and Marriott in prep.). At Dalton Parlours, 15 of the 23 pits were located peripherally within the enclosures; the five which lay within the areas of the roundhouses may or may not have been contemporary with those houses. Dalton Parlours is situated in what is thought to have been an important grain-growing area of Brigantian territory (Ramm 1980, 31-2); several fragments of quernstone used as packing in post-holes provide firm if slight evidence of crop-processing on this site.

The paucity of finds datable to the 1st and 2nd centuries AD led initially to the suggestion that there was a gap in occupation between the abandonment of the Iron Age farmsteads and the erection of the Roman villa (Sumpter 1988, 181). Recently, new cropmark evidence (Chapter 35) has emphasised that the excavations covered only about one-third of the total area of settlement enclosures. In view of this, it would be unwise to rely upon negative evidence. The 1st and 2nd-century objects recovered were mainly portable ornaments (brooches, beads and bangles), precisely the kind of objects likely to be lost on the periphery of a settlement. Therefore it is more probable that the native farmsteads shrank in size or number, or were moved westwards, and that the villa was built by the side of an existing settlement. Some native homesteads may have continued in occupation until the abandonment of the villa, providing the agricultural and domestic labour force.

The Roman villa

The investigations failed to establish the condition of the excavated site just prior to the erection of the villa. Some at least of the ditches must have been filled up by then, otherwise it is difficult to account for the positioning of walls. The west wall of Structure J, for example, was seated in the fill of Ditch 012. Had that ditch been an obvious hollow at the time of construction, one might have expected the builders to have positioned the entire structure 2m further east to avoid subsidence, or at least to have consolidated the ditch fill; they did neither. Similarly, the south-west corner of Structure B and the west wall of M were founded in ditch fills (though the latter was a final-phase wall, not part of the original structure).

On the other hand, there are clear indications that the positions and orientations of the buildings were affected, if not by the ditches, at least by the boundaries which the ditches had once helped to define. The west walls of J and M not only overlay ditches, they followed the same alignments; so, too, did Structure F and its underlying ditch, on a markedly different orientation. It may be that some Iron Age boundaries, perhaps banks or hedges originally associated with the ditches, had survived either in use or at least as reusable features in the landscape, and that the villa builders retained some of the pre-existing enclosures. This would account for the way in which the wall separating the two villa compounds runs along the western edge of Ditch 022/026.

The siting of the sunken-floored buildings P and Q seems also to have been influenced by the location of Iron Age ditches. On a site where bedrock was generally close to the surface the creation of sunken floors might have entailed a considerable amount of quarrying. If, however, Ditch 033/034 was visible either as a depression, or as a zone supporting distinct vegetation, it would have indicated where such floors could most easily be located.

It is possible, too, that a number of the peripheral ditches were recut as boundary markers: those on the south and west sides (Ditches 021, 002 and 003) had distinct upper filling layers containing Roman material. In some areas it would, however, be difficult to distinguish between filled recuts and hollows which had been levelled with debris.

The numismatic and ceramic reports agree that occupation began c. AD 200 and probably ended soon after AD 370. All the Roman structures therefore fall within a period of two centuries at most, more probably 150 years. In these circumstances it would not be surprising to find some of the main buildings surviving from beginning to end, albeit with alterations reflecting changes in social status or economic organisation.

Structure J, which was clearly at some time the principal dwelling, may have fulfilled this role throughout the life of the villa. In plan form it can be assigned to the

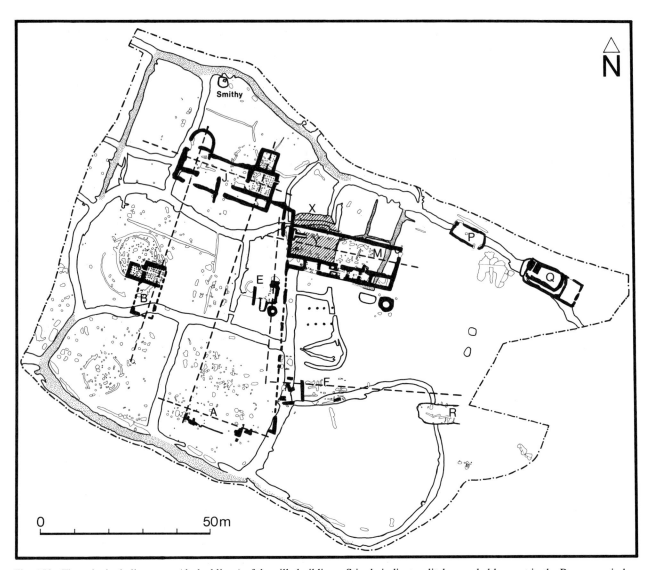

Fig. 158. The principal alignments (dashed lines) of the villa buildings. Stipple indicates ditches probably recut in the Roman period.

'winged-corridor' type of dwelling, more particularly to what Smith has called the 'debased form', found on the fringes of the Lowland Zone and represented in Yorkshire and Humberside at Langton and Rudston (Smith, D.J. 1978, 141-3).

The building was composed basically of three rooms: a central oblong and two flanking squares which had projecting 'wings'. The corridor, with central entrance, was on the opposite side to the wings; it presumably gave independent covered access to the three main parts of the dwelling. The eastern rooms were hypocausted; the apsidal and square units on the west were furnished with mosaics in the early and mid-4th century respectively. It is possible that the two wings and corridor were additions to the original structure: the extensive robbing would have removed any firm evidence of multi-phase development. The north-south wall on the west side of the corridor entrance makes little sense in terms of the known plan, and may therefore indicate structural alterations. It is also possible that the apsidal wing was installed at the same time as the Medusa mosaic, though the floor could equally have been added to an existing apse; the geometric mosaic

in the square room must, on the suggested dating, be an addition.

Though Structure J was too depleted to provide much evidence of function, it offers at least a basic plan for comparison with villa structures elsewhere, and an opportunity to identify recurrent patterns which reflect generally perceived requirements in domestic accommodation. The basic suite of central oblong and flanking square rooms seems to have been repeated in house II at Langton (Smith, D.J. 1978, 141); it may also underlie the plan of the west building at Beadlam, also in North Yorkshire (Stead 1971, fig. 4). At the level of the components, there are square rooms at Beadlam, Langton and Dalton Parlours which all measure about 6-7m square internally, and which have attached to them smaller square rooms, forming in each case a projecting wing, measuring between 3.5m square and 6m square internally. At Langton and Dalton Parlours both large and small rooms had hypocausts; the smaller, projecting room at Beadlam also had this facility. Such a specific repetition in plan form is surely indicative of a housing need common to the occupiers of all these buildings.

Unlike Rudston and Beadlam, the Dalton Parlours corridor house had no integral bath suite. Instead, it seems to have had a separate bath block, Structure B, about 24m to the south. There is, of course, no certainty that this bath house served Structure J, but a connection is indicated by their relative positions and alignments: the bath house seems to have been laid out in relation to the west wing of Structure J (Fig. 158).

Besides the winged-corridor dwelling, Dalton Parlours also contained an aisled building, Structure M, which included domestic accommodation. There is nothing to indicate in absolute terms its period of occupation. It was not, however, an original villa building, since its site had previously been taken up by the ancillary Structure Y. Furthermore its aisle posts had been renewed at least once, suggesting lengthy rather than short-lived occupation. Given that Structure J was certainly in use during the first half of the 4th century (on the evidence of the mosaics), it is a reasonable inference that the aisled building was contemporary with, rather than a predecessor of, or replacement for the winged-corridor dwelling. Building M seems, therefore, to fall into Morris' second category of aisled buildings: a subsidiary structure which has both domestic facilities 'of a comfortable standard' and agricultural functions (Morris 1979, 56).

The domestic facilities were marked by the row of small rooms in the *porticus* on the south side of the building. These included a hypocaust suite, and Procter (1855, 272) noted large amounts of painted wallplaster in them. He also recorded quantities of *tesserae* from the easternmost room (Room 7) as well as from the larger, square room to the north, in the eastern end of the main building. A comparison of the quern and wallplaster distributions in Structure M (Figs 80 and 100) is particularly instructive.

The rest of Structure M, the part which was aisled, was probably devoted to non-domestic uses. The T-shaped kiln and the oven flue are common features in aisled buildings (Hadman 1978, 192). The problems of relating them to the phases of Structure M have already been discussed (p. 58): they may pre-date the building; alternatively they may be associated with its initial phase, for which there is no evidence of a domestic function. It is possible, therefore, that the aisled building at Dalton Parlours was at first wholly given over to agricultural use, and only later acquired a domestic function. In its later phases it may be compared with the aisled building B at Winterton villa in Humberside: this had a group of small residential rooms at one end, partitioned off from a large open area containing furnaces and hearths (Stead 1976, 22-36).

The bath suite in the southern porticus of Structure M has been assigned to a final phase of the building. It is, however, possible that the structure already incorporated residential facilities before this addition. Some dual-purpose aisled buildings had separate bath houses (Morris 1979, 57); and the fragmentary Structure E, south-west of M, could be identified as a second free-standing bath block. Though only part of one

hypocausted room survived, there was an adjacent well (4017) and a feature (509) which might represent a plunge bath.

The rest of the excavated buildings were of agricultural, craft or other ancillary use. Amongst these, the most significant group comprised small, rectangular structures with sunken floors. They ranged in size from about 17 by 7m (Structure X), to about 12 by 4m (Structure Q); they were all located in the eastern half of the settlement, and had alignments varying between east to west and north-west to south-east. From their surviving fittings and associated debris, they all seem to have been concerned with crop-processing.

Their fittings were predominantly kilns and ovens, which ranged from T-shaped kiln flues and circular oven bases to unlined and rather irregular trenches with burnt sides. The simple trenches of Structure R are comparable to those contained in the aisled building B at Winterton, where several had unburnt, bowl-shaped access pits (Stead 1976, 32-3). The shorter, stone-lined flues at Dalton Parlours also find comparison at Langton, where one retained a number of stone slabs bridging the top of the flue; another had a stone-lined pit giving access to the stoke-hole (Corder and Kirk 1932, 56-7, figs 55-6).

Such fittings are generally identified as crop-processing facilities, whether for malting or for drying prior to milling (Morris 1979, 6-8). They were not confined to the sunken-floored buildings – the aisled Structure M, for example, produced both a T-shaped kiln flue and a Langton-type flue – but they are certainly characteristic of this type of building. They are often found in association with grinding stones (Morris 1979, 18), as in Structure P. Structure X, though without a kiln, contained four lower quernstones which were *in situ*, embedded in the floor; it also produced a mass of burnt crop-processing waste which may have been used to fuel the kilns in Structure M before being dumped. The use of husks and chaff to fuel grain-drying kilns has been common practice in the north in more recent times (Watts 1983, 16). The number of both beehive and flat quernstones from Roman structures is impressive (Fig. 80), and the presence of both forms suggests they were in simultaneous use, perhaps in order to achieve different products.

The plan forms of Structures P and Q are closely related, and in some phases identical; they are characterised by entrances in the centre of the east end wall, and in some phases by curved end walls. Structure R may have been similar. Comparable plans (though without sunken-floor areas) can be found in other Roman settlements of Yorkshire and Humberside. Building V at Hibaldstow, for example, had one curved end wall, and a central doorway in the opposite (east) end (Smith 1987, 191-2). Central, east end entrances also occurred in fully rectangular buildings at Ashton (Whitwell 1982, 379, fig. 14A) and Old Winteringham (Stead 1976, 6), in Humberside; both contained 'furnaces'.

Even more closely comparable are sunken-floored buildings from Welton Wold, Humberside. Several of these were identical in plan and arrangement to Structure Q, phase III; others contained evidence of milling, and the remains of circular domed ovens (Morris 1979, 13, 18; information from R.W. Mackay). The T-shaped kilns at Welton Wold were far better preserved than those at Dalton Parlours; the arrangement of flues and baffles shows that the drying floor, some distance above the sunken floor of the building, was at the same height as the ground outside. In view of this, and taking into account the usual positioning of flues against external walls, Mr R.W. Mackay has suggested, very plausibly, that grain would have been dumped on the drying floor from outside the building, perhaps offloaded directly from carts; the kiln would, of course, have been fuelled from inside the structure. The possible (reused) threshold stone from Structure R (Chapter 20, No. 27), which appears to have cartwheel grooves worn into its surface, would accord with this interpretation.

If kilns were isolated facilities, the simplest method of construction would involve cutting the flues into the ground, and also cutting a larger access pit at one end to fuel and fire the flue, and to regulate draught. If several kilns were to be erected near each other, or if fuelling a kiln was a major operation, a more economical method of construction might be to site all the facilities in a hollow, and then to build up the structures to ground level. This would account for the sunken floors.

Although the sunken-floored buildings at Dalton Parlours are most readily attributable to crop-processing, they may have had secondary or alternative domestic uses; the open hearth in the centre of Structure P might suggest this. Building V at Hibaldstow also had a central hearth, and the ovens were identified as secondary fittings; it was, therefore, interpreted as a domestic structure (Smith 1987, 191-2). At Welton Wold several sunken-floored buildings had no kiln, but contained large quantities of animal bone (information from R.W. Mackay). They, too, were identified as possible dwellings, for servants or slaves, although the animal bone could well have been produced by occupation elsewhere on the site, and then dumped in abandoned buildings. At Dalton Parlours it is equally possible, and perhaps more likely, that farm servants were housed in the native settlement to the west of the villa.

The sunken-floored buildings were, like the hypocausted structures, preserved because of their depth; even substantial masonry walls, like those of Structure B, had evidently been obliterated. Therefore our picture of the range of outbuildings associated with the villa is inevitably biased. Structures A and F remained in a very fragmentary condition; both contained furnace flues similar to those already described, but the latter also produced metallurgical waste. Structure Z, south of M, was a post-hole building perhaps with open sides, and Structure 4311, north of the principal house, marked the smithy. There were, no doubt, many other ephemeral, perhaps even substantial, ancillary buildings scattered about the settlement, but these have been lost to the plough.

The villa water supply is represented by two wells: 4017 (Well 2) at the south-east corner of Structure E, and 5500 (Well 1) at the south-east corner of Structure M. Since only one of these has been excavated – Well 2 has been preserved for a future occasion – it is impossible to establish beyond doubt whether these were successive or contemporary sources. The latter alternative is, however, favoured by the dating evidence from Well 1: the quantity of Throlam jars from the lowest layers suggests that it was in use during the later 3rd century; and the large numbers of Huntcliff jars indicate continued use until the abandonment of the villa, in the late 4th century.

Both wells were sited close to bath suites (if the interpretation of Structure E is correct); these buildings will obviously have required significant quantities of water. Well 1 was also probably associated with a series of cisterns and conduits found in the excavations of 1854 (Procter 1855, 272-3, pl. 7); unfortunately no trace of these remained to be discovered in the 1970s. Procter did not record the well; but about 4m north-east, just east of the Structure M bath suite, was a slab of concrete with raised edges, which he identified as either a cold plunge bath base or a cistern base (Fig. 2). A stone channel extended northwards from a point close to this feature, as far as a square cistern made of flagstones. A further stone channel was traced northwards from the square cistern for a distance of 40 yards (11m); it seems, therefore, to have continued beyond the northern limit of the excavated settlement. Though Procter suggested that the two channels both fed the square cistern, it seems more likely that they were part of a larger network which supplied buildings, yards and adjacent stock enclosures by means of pipes and aqueducts. The well produced a stone tank which had almost certainly formed a junction between wooden or lead piping and a stone channel similar to those located by Procter (Chapter 11, No. 42).

Conclusion

The functional interpretation, dating and relationships of the buildings, together with the character of associated artefacts, provide some basis for speculation about the occupants of Dalton Parlours villa. The evidence of both pottery and coins indicates that the villa was established at the beginning of the 3rd century. There is no sign that its erection was symptomatic of the gradual romanisation of native farmers, as found for example at Whitton, South Glamorgan (Jarrett and Wrathmell 1981, 250-53). Rather, it represents the plantation on this site of a high-status household with military associations. High status is attested by the proportion of silver to copper-alloy artefacts; it is also exemplified by the painted wallplaster (dated no later than the early 3rd century) which furnished at least one of the initial buildings (Structure B). Legionary connections are signified by items of military equipment among the copper-alloy objects, and also perhaps by the Medusa mosaic. More directly, the record of Sixth Legion stamped tiles from this site (Chapter 22) and the sourcing of excavated tiles to York indicates a close connection with Eburacum. These discoveries provide a measure of support for Dr Addyman's suggestion that the villa lay within the *territorium* of the legionary fortress (Addyman 1984, 14).

Other building materials besides tiles, as well as the craftsmen who built and furnished the domestic structures, were no doubt obtained from York or from those places which supplied York. Some of the hypocaust *pilae* of Structure B, for example, were reused parts of gritstone columns which were presumably made for (and perhaps first used in) imposing Roman buildings elsewhere in the region. The Millstone Grit was certainly exploited for York buildings (Addyman 1984, 15).

The villa seems to have expanded over time: reasons have been advanced for regarding the aisled dwelling as an addition to the residential facilities, rather than as a replacement for Structure J. The fully developed plan shows some replication of facilities – notably houses and bath suites – in the two separate courtyards. This may indicate joint proprietorship, of the kind proposed for other Yorkshire villas, like Beadlam (Smith, J.T. 1978, 164, 172). Alternatively, the development of Structure M may have been related to the installation of a subordinate family in the role of tenant or farm manager. There seems to be more emphasis on agricultural activities in the eastern enclosure; the western precinct may have been devoted to the domestic economy.

As indicated above, there is plentiful evidence of the importance of grain processing to the villa's economy.

The location and extent of its cultivated fields are, of course, unknown. The presence of damp-ground weeds among the plant remains suggests, however, that the fields extended several kilometres northwards to the spring line, or even to the River Wharfe beyond. The analysis of animal bones suggests that cattle meat was being produced for the market, and that sheep were kept for wool. The customers may well have been the inhabitants of York.

Given the extent of plough damage it is impossible to say whether the villa witnessed a period of decline before its abandonment, though the botanical evidence from the well shows an increase in waste, woodland-edge and grassy species in the later 4th-century silts (division L). The final act of desertion is encapsulated in the initial deliberate filling of the well: the ?ceremonial deposition of artefacts associated with drawing water; the dumping of large blocks of masonry and hypocaust *pilae* from the nearest building, in an apparent effort to ensure that the well could never be reinstated. The recovery of a lead sheet with a name stamped on it suggests an orderly desertion, with valuable materials being scrapped. There is some evidence of later activity at Dalton Parlours: the further, undated deposits of refuse in the well; the 5th to 7th-century burial. These may, however, signify no more than occasional use of a site which could have provided shelter for people and/or animals, and one which would have been an obvious source of building materials.

Appendices

Appendix 1

A Sub- or Post-Roman Pottery Vessel (Fig. 159) by Ailsa Mainman

Seven sherds from a single hand-made vessel were recovered from deposits within the recutting of an Iron Age ditch (002/1A). The sherds join to form part of a rim, below which is a horizontal zone of decoration.

The walls of the vessel are thick (varying from 10-12mm) and very dense. Inner and outer surfaces have been burnished though patches are now quite abraded; horizontal wiping marks are visible on the internal surface. The fabric is extremely coarse with frequent, large grains of quartz sand and possibly calcite or flint (2-3mm in size) being the most obvious inclusions. The larger grains protrude through the surfaces where the clay has shrunk around them during firing. There is also a lighter scatter of what appear to be small calcite grains visible in section.

The vessel is a fairly straight-sided form, as far as it can be reconstructed. The rim, which is slightly rolled, has a diameter of 150-60mm, suggesting a wide-mouthed form. The simply executed decoration consists of two rows of short incised slashes set at an angle to each other to form a herringbone pattern. These are contained within incised horizontal lines, two above and one below.

It is almost impossible to give a date to a vessel of this type. The decoration is well within the repertoire of the Anglian pottery tradition although the straight-sided form is a little unusual. The coarse nature of the fabric and the heavy, dense construction recall 4th-century pottery from York, however, and this might equally be a local sub-Roman vessel.

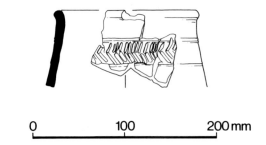

| 0 | 100 | 200 mm |

Fig. 159. Sub- or post-Roman pottery vessel. Scale 1:4

Appendix 2

A Post-Roman Burial (Pl. XXXVII)

An inhumation burial was discovered in the upper fill of Ditch 006, the northern ditch of Enclosure I (Fig. 113, No. 1). The grave (302), aligned north-west to south-east, had been cut through a band of rubble (306) which capped the earth filling. An associated annular brooch indicated a post-Roman date for the interment.

The Skeletal Remains
by Keith Manchester

The skeleton was orientated NW-SE and lying on left side with skull facing north. The individual was female of height 1.62m and about 25 years of age at death. There is evidence of mesial dental caries on the lower right first molar with slight calculus formation and slight dental

Table 56. Skeleton No. 1: long bone and skull measurements.

Long bone measurements		Skull measurements	
Femur			
FeL¹	429.0	L	180.3
FeL²	422.0	B	132.0
FeLe	406.4	B'	90.8
FeD¹	24.1	B''	113.0
FeD²	29.8	H'	130.0
		LB	106.5
Tibia		S1	109.0
TiL¹	346.0	S2	104.0
TiL²	346.0	S3	89.0
TiL³	329.4	S'1	125.0
TiD¹	33.0	S'2	116.0
TiD²	24.1	S'3	113.0
		Biast B	106.0
Humerus		G'H	61.0
HuL	326.0	GL	106.0
HuD¹	21.6	G2	41.0
HuD²	16.8	G'1	–
		O'	1.5
Radius		O2	29.0
RaL¹	236.0	FL	34.9
		FB	48.2
Ulna		MH	48.2
UlL¹	259.0	NB	23.2
		NH'	47.5
		SO	9.6
		NB4	10.4
		DC	23.1
		W1	–
		ZZ	43.4
		RB	32.6
		H'	27.9
		M₂H	25.4
		CYL	20.8
		CrH	56.1

All measurements in mm and as defined by Brothwell (1981)

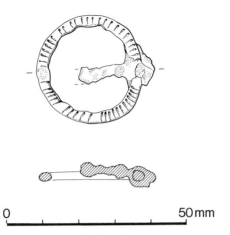

Fig. 160. Annular brooch. Scale 1:1

hypoplasia. There is bilateral upper and lower third absence and lower right double canine roots. The dental formula is (see Table 12 for key):

```
?NP  E                              V
    8 7 6 5 4 3 2 1 | 1 2 3 4 5 6 7 8
    8 7 6 5 \ 3 2 \ | 1 2 3 4 5 6 7 8
?NP  C                              ?NP
```

This individual shows a valgus deformity of mild degree of the distal phalanx on one great toe. No cause of death was determined. *SF 235*

Annular Brooch (Fig. 160)
by Tania M. Dickinson

Description
Circular ring. Cast; copper alloy; roughly D-sectioned, with a somewhat irregular profile. Traces of white metal near pin hinge may indicate an original white metal coating or a high tin composition. File marks on the inside edge indicate post-casting cleaning. The upper surface is decorated with transverse grooves, apparently applied after casting, and arranged in four irregularly spaced sections divided by three short plain areas and the pin hinge. The latter is obscured by the remnants of an iron pin, which originally extended across the brooch to rest on the surface of the opposite side. Greatest diam. 29.4mm; greatest w. of hoop 3.8mm; greatest th. 2.8mm. *SF 244*

Discussion
The brooch may be identified as an annular brooch of the type found in Anglo-Saxon cemeteries of the 5th to 7th centuries. These were broadly classified by E.T. Leeds (1945, 48) and the Dalton Parlours brooch clearly belongs to his stage f: brooches with half-round or oval section and, commonly, moulded or ribbed decoration. However, while considerable progress has now been made in reassessing the generally earlier and more southerly distributed brooches in his scheme, a-e (Ager 1985), there has been little advance in understanding Leeds' types f and g (brooches with narrow flat bands and punched/incised decoration). Yet these encompass the majority of annular brooches found in cemeteries north of the

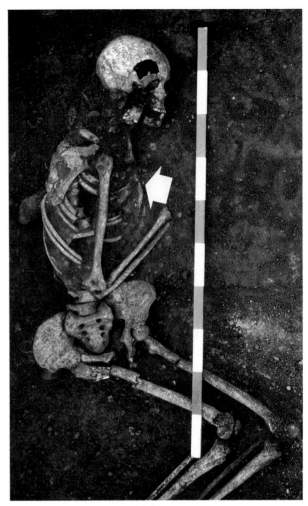

Pl. XXXVII. The post-Roman burial; position of brooch on left indicated by arrow. (Photo: WYAS)

'Stour-Severn' line, that is cemeteries of the 'Anglian' cultural area, where they are the most popular of all brooch forms, numbering at least 700 examples, and perhaps nearer 1000 (Hines 1984, 260-69). Without more exact classification of these or an exhaustive search through the literature, it is difficult to comment much further on the Dalton Parlours brooch.

Hines (1984, 262-3) gives a broad date range for the 'Anglian' annular brooches of the last quarter of the 5th century into the 7th century. This lower date is based on the occurrence of exceptionally small fine examples with bird-head terminals in Salin's Style II. But while the Dalton Parlours brooch is at the extreme lower end of the size range for annulars, it is not known whether this attribute alone is diagnostic of a late date.

The Dalton Parlours brooch is problematic in other respects. Although it does bear 'astragal' style ribbing, characteristic of many of Leeds' type f annular brooches, it is a poor version, and the initial impression is of a continuously ribbed band. Continuous ribbing would seem to be rare on annular brooches (but compare a pair from Upper Swell, Gloucestershire: Grinsell 1964, 13, fig. 1r) and is better evidenced on penannular brooches, notably of Fowler's type G (Dickinson 1982, especially 46-53). However, again, this feature alone cannot be used to imply a possible non-Anglo-Saxon context for the Dalton Parlours brooch: the current tenor of research is to deny British origins for annular brooches, and to stress rather their continental and Germanic beginnings (Ager 1985, especially 5-8; Hines 1984, 264-9; Hirst 1985, 56).

The final point of relevance is how the Dalton Parlours brooch was worn. The textile evidence (see below) suggests it was fastening the neck of a tunic at one shoulder, though sadly the disposition of the skeleton and absence of staining on the bones means we cannot know which one. Hines reports that annular brooches were usually worn either in pairs at the shoulders, or centrally with a pair of other brooches as shoulder fasteners, and he suggests that singletons may imply the loss, post-depositionally, of one of a pair (Hines 1984, 264). Whether this was possible at Dalton Parlours should be considered; if not, then the brooch was clearly not being used in the most common 'Anglian' mode.

All of which is relevant, but insufficient, to assessing the general date and cultural context of this brooch, given that its findspot lies at the very margin of the distribution of accompanied burials of 'Anglo-Saxon' type. It may indicate a burial, like other such burials in western Yorkshire and Bernicia, of later 6th or even 7th-century date (cf. Faull 1974; Miket 1980); it may have belonged to someone who regarded themselves as 'Anglian'; or it might even have been worn by a Briton, who had either acquired an 'Anglian' brooch, but none of the other attributes of 'Anglian' dress, or who had had an 'Anglian' style brooch manufactured locally, for whatever reasons of social emulation or integration. But none of these hypotheses can be confidently supported from the evidence currently available about the annular brooch alone.

Textile Fragments
by Elisabeth Crowfoot

At the pin attachment are remains of two textiles, the fibres of the threads almost completely replaced by metal oxides, but both originally obviously wool. Underneath, against the ring, is a clear area (a) *c.* 7 by 6mm, a layer of fabric with an appearance of tabby-weave, count 11-12 (Z spun)/9-10 (S spun) threads on 5mm, i.e. 22-24/18-20 threads per mm; this fabric is extremely solid, and the lie of the threads at the broken edges suggests that it is not a simple tabby, but a tablet-weave of a 2-hole technique, which has a tabby-weave appearance, as in an example in flax from Laceby, Lincolnshire (Crowfoot 1956). Lying above this (b) over an area 7 by 18mm, and in traces on the pieces of the pin, are remains of a coarser weave, Z-spun in both systems, almost certainly a twill, the most popular Anglo-Saxon garment weave; in one area threads lie 7-8 on 5mm in one system.

Weave (a) suggests part of the garment pinned by the brooch, probably a tablet braid decorating the neckline of the gown; the coarser (b) twill could be traces of the cloak, or a blanket laid over the burial.

Appendix 3

List of Finds by Context (excluding pottery vessels and tiles)

Context	Description	Finds
001	unstratified (u/s)	Coin Nos 10, 11, 14, 20, 22, 23, 26, 28, 29, 30, 36, 37, 40, 42, 43, 44, 54, 57, 60 and 63; Bronze Nos 4(s), 6(s), 9, 13, 18, 21, 23, 27, 32, 35, 49, 51, 58, 60, 61, 62, 65, 66, 71, 72, 73, 74, 77, 81, 83, 87, 90, 91, 93, 94, 95 and 133; Brooch Nos 2, 3 and 7; Lead Nos 2, 4, 5, 6, 10, 11, 15 and 16; Iron Nos 3, 5, 6, 8 and 15; Glass Nos 1, 12, 13, 19, 20, 21, 22a, 39 and 41; Quern Nos 3, 4, 8, 12, 14, 15, 16, 17, 18, 19, 20, 35, 37, 52, 57 and 73; Ceramic Obj. Nos 1, 7, 11, 12, 13 and 14; Jet No. 1; Stone Obj. Nos 1, 2, 3, 4, 5, 13, 14, 17, 18, 19 and 20; Bone Obj. Nos 20 and 28;
002/1B	Ditch fill	Bone Obj. No. 8
002/2A	Ditch fill	Glass No. 2
002/3	Ditch segment fill	Ceramic Obj. No. 15
002/4	Ditch segment fill	Bronze No. 88
002/9A	Ditch fill	Coin No. 7; Ceramic Obj. No. 2
004	Ditch fill	Glass No. 43
004/2	Ditch segment fill	Bone Obj. No. 6
005/2	Ditch segment fill	Ceramic Obj. No. 16; Stone Obj. Nos 6 and 21
006/1	Ditch segment fill	Bronze No. 92
006/6	Ditch segment fill	Bone Obj. No. 29
011	Ditch fill	Jet No. 2
011/1	Ditch segment fill	Bone Obj. No. 13
011/1A	Ditch fill	Iron No. 10
014/1A	Ditch fill	Coin No. 5; Glass Nos 3 and 22
016/1	Ditch segment fill	Bone Obj. No. 2
020/4	Ditch segment fill	Bronze No. 56; Glass No. 33
021/1	Ditch segment fill	Bone Obj. No. 4
021/2A	Ditch fill	Coin No. 73; Iron No. 14
030/2	Ditch segment fill	Brooch No. 4
031/2A	Ditch fill	Bronze No. 20
036/1	Ditch segment fill	Ceramic Obj. No. 3
039/1	Ditch segment fill	Bronze No. 43
100	u/s (Str. A)	Bronze No. 45; Quern No. 49; Bone Obj. No. 19
101	u/s (Str. A)	Glass Nos 8, 35, 37 and 38; Stone Obj. No. 22
102	Layer (Str. A)	Brooch No. 5
104	Wall (Str. A)	Bronze No. 42
200	u/s (Str. B)	Coin Nos 12, 39 and 41; Bronze Nos 52, 53 and 80; Ceramic Obj. No. 8

204	Layer (Str. B)	Coin No. 31
207	Layer (Str. B)	Bronze No. 59
212	Layer (Str. B)	Coin No. 1
214	Layer (Str. B)	Architectural Stone Nos 3 and 4
216	Layer (Str. B)	Coin No. 51; Bone Obj. No. 1
218	Layer (Str. B)	Stone Obj. No. 23
221	u/s (Str. B)	Iron No. 11
222	Layer (Str. B)	Coin No. 9
300	u/s (Str. B)	Coin No. 33; Bronze No. 41
302	Grave pit fill (Str. B)	Post-Roman Brooch
303	Layer (Str. B)	Coin No. 71; Glass No. 40; Jet No. 8
501	Flue fill (Str. E)	Iron No. 20
600	u/s (Str. F)	Coin Nos 16 and 17
603	Layer (Str. F)	Coin Nos 8 and 19
607	Flue fill (Str. F)	Bone Obj. No. 3
627	Post-hole fill	Quern Nos 10 and 29
802	Layer (Str. A)	Stone Obj. No. 24; Bone Obj. No. 15
900	u/s (Str. J)	Bronze No. 57; Brooch No. 1; Glass No. 36; Bone Obj. No. 24
901	Layer (Str. J)	Bronze No. 17
902	Layer (Str. J)	Glass No. 32
903	Layer (Str. J)	Coin No. 55; Bronze Nos 12, 50 and 69
918	Robber trench fill (Str. J)	Glass No. 31
1000	u/s (Str. J)	Bronze No. 24
1001	u/s (Str. J)	Coin No. 35; Stone Obj. No. 25; Bone Obj. Nos 10, 16 and 27
1003	Robber trench fill (Str. J)	Bronze No. 63; Bone Obj. No. 11
1023	Oven fill (Str. J)	Quern No. 40
1200	u/s (Str. M)	Coin Nos 18 and 25; Glass Nos 10 and 11; Quern No. 21; Jet No. 3
1201	u/s (Str. M)	Lead No. 3
1212	Layer (Str. M)	Bronze No. 75
1213	Layer (Str. M)	Bronze No. 31; Iron No. 12; Quern Nos 34 and 53; Stone Obj. No. 26
1213/1	Layer (Str. M)	Iron No. 13; Ceramic Obj. No. 17; Stone Obj. No. 27; Roofslab No. 4
1213/2	Layer (Str. M)	Lead No. 17; Iron No. 19; Glass Nos 4 and 7a
1213/3	Layer (Str. M)	Bronze No. 15; Lead No. 18; Iron No. 9; Glass Nos 5 and 6; Ceramic Obj. No. 4; Stone Obj. Nos 15, 28 and 29; Bone Obj. No. 7
1216/1	Layer (Str. M)	Quern Nos 42, 43 and 60
1216/2	Layer (Str. M)	Bronze No. 89; Iron No. 7
1220	Foundation trench fill (Str. Y)	Bronze No. 19

1221	Oven fill (Str. M)	Quern Nos 22 and 66
1222	Layer (Str. Y)	Quern No. 61
1222/1	Layer (Str. Y)	Bronze No. 2(s)
1300	u/s (Str. M)	Coin Nos 32, 38, 48, 50 and 83; Glass Nos 14, 15, 16, 24d and 24e; Bone Obj. No. 18
1302	Layer (Str. M)	Jet No. 9
1305	Layer (Str. M)	Glass No. 20b
1400	u/s (Str. M)	Coin No. 69; Iron No. 18; Glass No. 24c; Quern No. 59
1422	Layer (Str. M)	Bronze No. 28; Iron No. 4
1432-33	Post-hole fill	Quern No. 54
1463C	Post-hole fill (Str M)	Quern No. 32
1500	u/s (Str. O)	Jet No. 6
1600	u/s (Str. P)	Iron No. 2; Bone Obj. No. 17
1601	Layer (Str. P)	Lead No. 1
1602	Layer (Str. P)	Coin Nos 13 and 15; Quern Nos 1, 27, 46 and 62
1603	Layer (Str. P)	Quern Nos 48 and 71
1604	Layer (Str. P)	Bronze No. 11
1606	Flue fill (Str. P)	Quern No. 51; Architectural Stone No. 7
1611	Layer (Str. P)	Bronze No. 34
1612	Layer (Str. P)	Bone Obj. No. 9
1615	Wall (Str. P)	Quern No. 50
1616	Wall (Str. P)	Glass No. 42
1700	u/s (Str. Q)	Bronze No. 47
1701	Layer (Str. Q)	Coin No. 21; Bronze No. 68; Quern Nos 28, 47, 56 and 64; Stone Obj. No. 43
1702	Layer (Str. Q)	Brooch No. 6
1800	u/s (Str. R)	Coin No. 34; Glass No. 28
1801	Layer (Str. R)	Stone Obj. Nos 30 and 31
1803	Layer (Str. R)	Coin No. 61
1806	Post-hole fill (Str. R)	Stone Obj. No. 44
1809	Gully fill (Str. R)	Coin No. 45
1809A	Gully fill (Str. R)	Stone Obj. No. 45
1813	Layer (Str. R)	Coin No. 70; Brooch No. 8
1814	Layer (Str. R)	Architectural Stone No. 27
1815	Layer (Str. R)	Bronze No. 40; Glass No. 20a; Architectural Stone No. 6
1900	u/s (Str. S)	Quern No. 65
2010	Pit fill	Bronze No. 76
2518	Natural feature fill	Stone Obj. No. 32
2550/9	Trench fill	Jet No. 7
2558	Pit fill	Bronze No. 67
2601	Natural feature fill	Bronze No. 30
2604A	Pit fill	Wooden object
2747	Post-hole fill	Stone Obj. No. 7
2775	Pit fill	Bronze No. 64
2802	?Post-hole fill	Bronze No. 7

3211	Pit fill (Str. A)	Bronze Nos 33, 37, 38 and 39; Stone Obj. No. 8
3218A	Pit fill	Bronze No. 55
3222	Pit fill	Bronze No. 22
3312	Pit fill	Quern Nos 6 and 58
3413	Natural feature fill	Coin No. 27
3420/3	Natural feature fill	Coin No. 66
3436/ 3461	?Pit fill	Quern No. 72
3454	Pit fill	Bronze No. 79; Stone Obj. No. 16
3463	Pit fill	Bronze No. 44; Iron No. 16
3480	Post-hole fill	Glass No. 9
3491	?Post-hole fill	Coin No. 24
3493?	Post-hole fill	Coin No. 46
3505	Pit fill	Quern No. 5
3902	Post-hole fill	Iron No. 17
3916	Pit fill	Quern No. 31
3917	Post-hole fill	Quern Nos 30 and 33
3921	Pit fill	Bone Obj. No. 23
4017B	Well 2 fill	Bronze No. 54
4103	Pit fill	Quern No. 7
4200	Natural feature fill (Str. J)	Glass No. 29
4310	Gully fill	Bone Obj. No. 21
4900B	Oven fill (Str. M)	Coin No. 3
4903	Feature fill (Str. X)	Quern No. 36
4903/2	Feature fill (Str. X)	Bronze No. 70; Iron No. 1; Stone Obj. No. 46
4903/3	Feature fill (Str. X)	Bronze No. 86
4910	Pit fill (Str. X)	Quern No. 13
5008	Pit fill	Quern No. 24
5010	Feature fill (Str. X)	Quern No. 11
5020	Post-hole fill (Str. X)	Glass No. 30

(The main categories of artefact from Well 1 are to be found in Part 4 of this report. The rest as are follows:)

5500	Well 1	Coin Nos 2, 4, 6 and 47; Bronze Nos 1(s), 5(s), 8, 10, 14, 16 and 25; Lead Nos 7, 8, 9, 12, 13 and 14; Glass Nos 7, 18, 25 and 34; Quern Nos 9, 23, 25, 26, 41, 44, 45, 55 and 63; Ceramic Obj. Nos 5, 9, 18 and 19; Stone Obj. Nos 9, 10, 33, 39, 40, 41, 42, 47 and 48; Bone Obj. Nos 5, 25 and 26; Architectural Stone Nos 1, 2, 5, 8 and 9; Roofslab Nos 1, 2 and 3
5600/4	Gully fill	Bronze No. 48
5605	Ditch fill	Bronze Nos 29 and 84; Bone Obj. No. 14
5605/2A	Ditch fill	Bronze No. 26
6400	Layer	Glass No. 17
8000	u/s (Str. M)	Coin Nos 49, 80 and 82
8001	Layer (Str. M)	Coin No. 53
8004	Layer (Str. M)	Glass No. 24
8009	Layer (Str. M)	Glass No. 26
8010	Layer (Str. M)	Coin Nos 59 and 65; Glass Nos 24a, 24b, 24f and 27; Stone Obj. No. 11
8020	Layer (Str. M)	Glass No. 23
8023D	Layer (Str. M)	Stone Obj. No. 12
8023G	Layer (Str. M)	Ceramic Obj. No. 6
8102	Robber trench fill (Str. M)	Coin Nos 58 and 67
8104	Layer (Str. M)	Coin Nos 52, 56, 62, 64, 75, 76 and 77; Bronze No. 36
8200	u/s (Str. V)	Coin Nos 78, 79, 81, 84, 85, 86 and 87; Bronze No. 82; Jet No. 4
8201	Feature fill (Str. V)	Bronze No. 3(s)
8201/1	Feature fill (Str. V)	Jet No. 5
8201/2	Feature fill (Str. V)	Bronze No. 78; Bone Obj. No. 12
8201/4A	Feature fill (Str. V)	Coin Nos 68 and 72
8201/5	Feature fill (Str. V)	Stone Obj. No. 34
8201/6B	Feature fill (Str. V)	Coin No. 74
8202	Feature fill (Str. V)	Bronze No. 46
8300	u/s	Bronze No. 85; Stone Obj. No. 35
8301/1	Gully fill	Stone Obj. Nos 36, 37 and 38
8301/2	Gully fill	Ceramic Obj. No. 10; Bone Obj. No. 22

Bibliography

Addyman, P.V., 1984, 'York in its archaeological setting', in Addyman, P.V. and Black, V.E. (eds), *Archaeological Papers from York Presented to M.W. Barley*, 7-21

Addyman, P.V. and Priestley, J., 1977, 'Baile Hill, York', *Archaeol. J.* 134, 115-56

Adriani, A., 1952, 'Nécropoles de l'île de Pharos', *Annuaire du Musée Gréco-Romain (Alexandria)*, iii (1940-50), 47-128

Adriani, A., 1966, *Repertorio d'arte dell'Egitto greco-romano*, C.I-II

Ager, B.M., 1985, 'The smaller variants of the Anglo-Saxon quoit brooch', *Anglo-Saxon Stud. Archaeol. Hist.* 4, 1-58

Allason-Jones, L., 1983, 'Bronzes', in Miket, R., *The Roman Fort at South Shields. Excavation of the Defences 1977-1981*, 109-30

Allason-Jones, L., Bayley, J., Henig, M. and Snape, M., 1985, 'The objects of copper alloy and of other materials', in Bidwell, P.T., *The Roman Fort of Vindolanda at Chesterholm, Northumberland*, Hist. Buildings Monuments Comm. Archaeol. Rep. 1, 117-29

Allason-Jones, L. and Miket, R., 1984, *The Catalogue of Small Finds from South Shields Roman Fort*, Soc. Antiq. Newcastle-upon-Tyne Monogr. Ser. 2

Annable, F.K., 1960, *The Romano-British Pottery at Cantley Housing Estate, Doncaster: Kilns 1-8*, Doncaster Mus. Publ. 24

Armitage, P., West, B. and Steedman, K., 1984, 'New evidence of black rat in Roman London', *London Archaeol.* 4(14), 375-83

Aurigemma, S., 1962, *L'Italia in Africa. Le scoperte archeologiche (1911-1943). Tripolitania*, i. *I monumenti d'arte decorativa*, ii. *Le pitture d'età romana*

Balfour-Browne, F., 1958, *British Water Beetles* 3

Ball, F. and Ball, N., 1985, '"Rescue" excavation at Wall (Staffordshire) 1980-81, (Wall excavations report No. 13)', *Trans. South Staffordshire Archaeol. Hist. Soc.* 25 (1983-84), 1-30

Balmelle, C., 1980, *Receuil général des mosaiques de la Gaule: Province d'Aquitaine* IV.1, Gallia Supplément 10 (Paris)

Baratte, F., 1986, *Le trésor d'orfèvrerie Romain de Boscoreale* (Paris)

Barbet, A., 1985a, *La peinture murale romaine* (Paris)

Barbet, A., 1985b, 'Peinture murale romaine à Bordeaux', in Barbet, A. (ed.), *Peinture murale en Gaule*, Br. Archaeol. Rep. S240, 89-112

Barbet, A. and Allag, C., 1972, 'Techniques de préparation des parois dans la peinture murale romaine', *Mélanges de l'École Française de Rome, Antiquité* 84, 935-1069

Barbet, A., Davreu, Y., Le Bot, A. and Magnan, D., 1977, 'Peintures murales romaines d'Alésia, l'hypocauste no. 1', *Gallia* 35, 173-99

Bastet, F.L., 1971, 'Domus Transitoria I', *Bulletin van de Vereeniging tot Bevordering der Kennis van de Antieke Beschaving* 46, 144-72

Becatti, G., 1961, *Scavi di Ostia iv. Mosaici e Pavimenti Marmorei* (Rome)

Beck, H.C., 1928, 'Classification and nomenclature of beads and pendants', *Archaeologia* 77, 1-76

Beijerinck, W., 1947, *Zadenatlas der Nederlandsche Flora* (Wageningen)

Bestwick, J.D. and Cleland, J.H., 1974, 'Metal working in the North-West', in Jones, G.D.B. and Grealey, S. (eds), *Roman Manchester*, 143-58

Betts, I.M., 1985, 'A scientific investigation of the brick and tile industry of York to the mid-eighteenth century', unpubl. PhD Thesis, Univ. Bradford

Betts, I.M., forthcoming, 'Roman brick and tile', in Abramson, P., *Roman Castleford*, Yorkshire Archaeol.

Binford, L.R., 1981, *Bones: ancient men and modern myths*

Birley, R.E., 1977, *Vindolanda: A Roman Frontier Post on Hadrian's Wall*

BMC, 1950, Mattingley, H.B., *Coins of the Roman Empire in the British Museum* V

BMC, 1962, Carson, R.A.G., *Coins of the Roman Empire in the British Museum* VI

Boessneck, J., 1969, 'Osteological differences between sheep and goats', in Brothwell, D.R. and Higgs, E.S. (eds), *Science in Archaeology* (2nd ed.), 331-58

Boon, G.C., 1974a, 'Counterfeit coins in Roman Britain', in Casey, J. and Reece R. (eds), *Coins and the Archaeologist*, Br. Archaeol. Rep. 4, 95-171

Boon, G.C., 1974b, *Silchester: The Roman Town of Calleva*

Boon, G.C., 1975, 'Segontium fifty years on', *Archaeol. Cambrensis* 124, 52-67

Bourdillon, J. and Coy, J.P., 1980, 'The animal bones', in Holdsworth, P., *Excavations at Melbourne Street, Southampton, 1971-6*, Counc. Br. Archaeol. Res. Rep. 33, 79-121

Bramwell, D., Dalton, K., Drinkwater, J.F., Hassall, M., Lorimer, K.L. and Mackreth, D.F., 1983, 'Excavations at Poole's Cavern, Buxton: an interim report', *Derbyshire Archaeol. J.* 103, 47-74

Brewer, R., 1986, 'Other objects of bronze', in Zienkiewicz, J.D., *The Legionary Fortress Baths at Caerleon. Volume II. The Finds*, 172-89

Briggs, S.J., 1977, *Sources and Methods in Geography: Soils*

Britton, E.B., 1956, *Coleoptera: Scarabaeoidea*, Handbooks for the Identification of British Insects V.11

Brodribb, A.C.C., Hands, A.R. and Walker, D.R., 1971, *Excavations at Shakenoak Farm, Near Wilcote, Oxfordshire. Part II: Sites B and H* (privately published)

Brodribb, A.G.N., 1987, *Roman Brick and Tile*

Brothwell, D.R., 1981, *Digging Up Bones* (3rd ed.)

Brown, A.E. and Woodfield, C., 1983, 'Excavations at Towcester, Northamptonshire: The Alchester Road Suburb', *Northamptonshire Archaeol.* 18, 43-140

Buckland, P.C., 1988, 'The stones of York: building materials in Roman Yorkshire', in Price, J. and Wilson, P.R. (eds), *Recent Research in Roman Yorkshire*, Br. Archaeol. Rep. 193, 237-87

Buckland, P.C. and Dolby, M.J., 1980, *A Roman Pottery Kiln Site at Blaxton Quarry, Auckley*, Archaeol. Doncaster 4/1

Buckland, P.C. and Magilton, J.R., 1986, *The Archaeology of Doncaster 1: The Roman Civil Settlement*, Br. Archaeol. Rep. 148

Buckland, P.C., Magilton, J.R. and Dolby, M.J., 1980, 'The Roman pottery industries of South Yorkshire: a review', *Britannia* 11, 145-64

Buckley, D.G. and Major, H., 1983, 'Quernstones', in Crummy, N., *The Roman small finds from excavations in Colchester 1971-9*, Colchester Archaeol. Rep. 2, 73-6

Buckley, D.G. and Major, H., forthcoming, 'The quernstones', in Abramson, P., *Roman Castleford*, Yorkshire Archaeol.

Buckman, J. and Newmarch, C.H., 1850, *Illustrations of the remains of Roman art in Cirencester, the site of ancient Corinium*

Bull, G. and Payne, S., 1982, 'Tooth eruption and epiphysial fusion in pigs and wild boar', in Wilson, B., Grigson, C. and Payne, S. (eds), *Ageing and Sexing Animal Bones from Archaeological Sites*, Br. Archaeol. Rep. 109, 55-71

Carettoni, G., 1949, 'Contruzione sotto l'angolo sud-occidentale della Domus Flavia (triclinio e ninfeo occidentale)', *Notizie degli scavi di antichità*, 48-79

Casteel, R.W., 1977, 'A consideration of the behaviour of the minimum number of individuals index: a problem in faunal characterization', *Ossa* 3/4 (1976-77), 141-51

Caulfield, S., 1977, 'The beehive quern in Ireland', *J. R. Soc. Antiq. Ireland* 107, 104-38

Challis, A.J. and Harding, D.W., 1975, *Later Prehistory from the Trent to the Tyne*, Br. Archaeol. Rep. 20

Chaplin, R.E., 1971, *The Study of Animal Bones from Archaeological Sites*

Chapman, H., 1980, 'Wood', in Jones, D.M. and Rhodes, M., *Excavations at Billingsgate Buildings 'Triangle', Lower Thames Street, 1974*, London Middlesex Archaeol. Soc. Spec. Pap. 4

Charlesworth, D., 1959, 'Roman glass in northern Britain', *Archaeol. Aeliana* 37 (4th ser.), 33-58

Charlesworth, D., 1972, 'The glass', in Frere, S.S., *Verulamium Excavations: Volume I*, Rep. Res. Comm. Soc. Antiq. London 28, 196-215

Charlesworth, D., 1976, 'Glass vessels', in MacGregor, A., *Finds from a Roman Sewer System and an Adjacent Building in Church Street*, Archaeol. York 17/1, 15-18

Charlesworth, D., 1978, 'Glass vessels', in MacGregor, A., *Roman Finds from Skeldergate and Bishophill*, Archaeol. York 17/2, 54-7

Charlesworth, D., 1980, 'Glass', in Stead, I.M., *Rudston Roman Villa*, 124-5

Charlesworth, D., 1984, 'The glass', in Frere, S.S., *Verulamium Excavations: Volume III*, Oxford Univ. Comm. Archaeol. Monogr. 1, 145-73

Christlein, R., 1963, 'Ein römisches Gebäude in Marzoll, Ldkr. Berchtesgaden', *Bayerische Vorgeshichtsblätter* 28, 30-57

Clapham, A.R., Tutin, T.G. and Warburg, E.F., 1962, *Flora of the British Isles* (2nd ed.)

Clapham, A.R., Tutin, T.G. and Warburg, E.F., 1978, *Excursion Flora of the British Isles*

Clarke, G., 1979, *Pre-Roman and Roman Winchester Part II. The Roman Cemetery at Lankhills*, Winchester Stud. 3

Clarke, J.C., forthcoming, 'Stone finds', in Abramson, P., *Roman Castleford*, Yorkshire Archaeol.

Collingwood, R.G., 1931, 'Objects from Brough-under-Stainmore in the Craven Museum, Skipton', *Trans. Cumberland Westmorland Antiq. Archaeol. Soc.* 31 (new ser.), 81-6

Cookson, N.A., 1984, *Romano-British Mosaics*, Br. Archaeol. Rep. 135

Cool, H.E.M., 1983, 'A study of the Roman personal ornaments made of metal, excluding brooches, from southern Britain', unpubl. PhD Thesis, Univ. Wales

Cool, H.E.M. and Price, J., forthcoming, 'The glass from the burials', in Mould, Q., *The Romano-British Cemetery at Brougham, Cumbria*

Corder, P., 1928, *The Roman Pottery at Crambeck, Castle Howard*, Roman Malton Dist. Rep. 1

Corder, P., 1930, *The Defences of the Roman Fort at Malton*, Roman Malton Dist. Rep. 2

Corder, P., 1950, 'The pottery made at the kilns', in Hayes, R.H. and Whitley, E., *The Roman Pottery at Norton, East Yorkshire*, Roman Malton Dist. Rep. 7, 26-34

Corder, P., 1958, 'Parisian ware', *Yorkshire Archaeol. J.* 39 (1956-58), 48-52

Corder, P. and Birley, M.I., 1937, 'A pair of fourth-century Romano-British pottery kilns near Crambeck', *Antiq. J.* 17, 392-413

Corder, P. and Kirk, J.L., 1932, *A Roman Villa at Langton, near Malton, E. Yorkshire*, Roman Malton Dist. Rep. 4

Cotton, S.E., 1982, 'The animal bones from the well (F5500) at Dalton Parlours', unpubl. MA thesis, Univ. Sheffield

Crawford, O.G.S. and Röder, J., 1955, 'The quern-quarries of Mayen in the Eifel', *Antiquity* 29, 68-76

Cregeen, S.M., 1958, 'The Romano-British excavations at Cantley estate, Doncaster', *Yorkshire Archaeol. J.* 39 (1956-58), 364-88

Croon, J.C., 1955, 'The mask of the underworld demon – some remarks on the Perseus-Gorgon story', *J. Hellenic Stud.* 75, 9-16

Crowfoot, G.M., 1956, 'The textile and impressions', in Thompson, F.H., 'Anglo-Saxon sites in Lincolnshire: unpublished excavation material and recent discoveries', *Antiq. J.* 36, 188-9

Crummy, N., 1979, 'A chronology of Romano-British bone pins', *Britannia* 10, 157-63

Crummy, N., 1983, *The Roman small finds from excavations in Colchester 1971-9*, Colchester Archaeol. Rep. 2

Cunliffe, B.W., 1971a, *Excavations at Fishbourne, 1961-1969. Volume I: The Site*, Rep. Res. Comm. Soc. Antiq. London 26

Cunliffe, B.W., 1971b, *Excavations at Fishbourne, 1961-1969. Volume II: The Finds*, Rep. Res. Comm. Soc. Antiq. London 27

Curle, A.O., 1915, 'Account of excavations on Traprain Law in the parish of Prestonkirk, County of Haddington, in 1914', *Proc. Soc. Antiq. Scotland* 49 (1914-15), 139-202

Curle, J., 1911, *A Roman Frontier Post and its People*

Curnow, P.E., 1976, 'Coins', in Stead, I.M., *Excavations at Winterton Roman Villa*, Dep. Environ. Archaeol. Rep. 9, 234-44

Curwen, E.C., 1937, 'Querns', *Antiquity* 11, 133-51

Curwen, E.C., 1941, 'More about querns', *Antiquity* 15, 15-32

Dalby, M., 1980, 'Moss remains from the well', in Stead, I.M., *Rudston Roman Villa*, 168

Davey, N. and Ling, R.J., 1982, *Wall-Painting in Roman Britain*, Britannia Monogr. Ser. 3

Delage, F., 1953, 'Fouilles de la "Villa d'Antone" à Pierrebuffière (Haute-Vienne)', *Gallia* 10 (1952), 1-30

Delbrück, R., 1912, *Hellenistische Bauten in Latium* 2

Dennell, R.W., 1976, 'The economic importance of plant resources represented on archaeological sites', *J. Archaeol. Sci.* 3, 229-47

Dickinson, T.M., 1982, 'Fowler's type G penannular brooches reconsidered', *Medieval Archaeol.* 26, 41-68

Dickson, J.H., 1973, *Bryophytes of the Pleistocene*

Down, A., 1978, *Chichester Excavations* III

Down, A., 1979, *Chichester Excavations* IV

Duffy, E.A.J., 1953, *Coleoptera: Scolytidae and Platypodidae*, Handbooks for the Identification of British Insects 5.15

Dunbabin, K.M.D., 1978, *The Mosaics of Roman North Africa*

Elgee, F. and Elgee, H.W., 1933, *The Archaeology of Yorkshire*

Elsdon, S.M., 1982, *Parisian Ware*, VORDA Res. Ser. 4

Emeleus, C.H., 1974, 'Igneous rocks', in Rayner, D.H. and Hemingway, J.E. (eds), *The Geology and Mineral Resources of Yorkshire*, 265-9

Eristov, H., 1979, 'Les enduits peints d'époque gallo-romaine découverts rue de l'Abbé-de-L'Épée (5e)', *Cahiers de la Rotonde* 2, 13-29

Erith, F.H., 1972, 'The well at Bramford', *Colchester Archaeol. Group Annu. Bull.* 15, 1-11

Evans, J.G., 1978, *An Introduction to Environmental Archaeology*

Faegri, K. and Iversen, J., 1964, *Textbook of Pollen Analysis* (2nd ed.)

Faull, M.L., 1974, 'Roman and Anglian settlement patterns in Yorkshire', *Northern Hist.* 9, 1-25

Faull, M.L. and Moorhouse, S.A. (eds), 1981, *West Yorkshire: an Archaeological Survey to A.D. 1500* 4

Fifield, P.S., 1980, 'Faunal Studies and the Roman Economy in Britain', unpubl. M.Phil thesis, Univ. Sheffield

Fischer, V., 1973, *Grabungen im römischen Steinkastell von Heddernheim, 1957-1959*, Schriften des Frankfurter Museums für Vor- und Frühgeschichte, Band II (Frankfurt)

Fitter, A., 1987, *Collins New Generation Guide to the Wild Flowers of Britain and Northern Europe*

Fock, J., 1966, *Metrische Untersuchungen an Metapodien einiger Europäischer Rinderrassen*, Dissertation (Munich)

Fowler, E., 1960, 'The origins and development of the penannular brooch in Europe', *Proc. Prehist. Soc.* 26, 149-77

Fowler, P.J., 1983, *The Farming of Prehistoric Britain*

Fremersdorf, F., 1926, 'Ein Funde römischer Ledersachen in Köln', *Germania* 10, 44-56

Fremersdorf, F., 1959, *Römische Gläser mit Fadenauflage in Köln*, Die Denkmäler des römischen Köln 5 (Cologne)

Freude, H., Harde, K.W. and Lohse, G.A., 1961-1981, *Die Käfer Mitteleuropas*, Band 2-11 (Krefeld)

Gaitzsch, W., 1980, *Eiserne römische Werkzeuge*, Br. Archaeol. Rep. S78

Gaunt, G.D., 1970, 'A temporary section across the Escrick Moraine at Wheldrake, East Yorkshire', *J. Earth Sci.* 8, 163-9

Gaunt, G.D., 1981, 'Quaternary history of the southern part of the Vale of York', in Neale, J.W. and Flenley, J. (eds), *The Quaternary in Britain*, 82-97

Gillam, J.P., 1958, 'The coarse pottery', in Hildyard, E.J.W., '*Cataractonium*, fort and town', *Yorkshire Archaeol. J.* 39 (1956-58), 252-65

Gillam, J.P., 1970, *Types of Roman Coarse Pottery Vessels in Northern Britain* (3rd ed.)

Gilligan, A., 1920, 'The petrography of the Millstone Grit of Yorkshire', *Q. J. Geol. Soc. London* 75 (1919), 251-94

Gilyard-Beer, R., 1951, *The Romano-British Baths at Well*, Yorkshire Roman Antiq. Comm. Res. Rep. 1

Goodman, W.L., 1964, *The History of Woodworking Tools*

Goudge, C.E., 1983, 'Leather', in Heighway, C., *The East and North Gates of Gloucester*, Western Archaeol. Trust Excavation Monogr. 4, 173-8

Grant, A., 1975, 'The animal bones', in Cunliffe, B.W. (ed.), *Excavations at Portchester Castle. Volume 1: Roman*, Rep. Res. Comm. Soc. Antiq. London 32, 378-408; 437-450

Grant, A., 1982, 'The use of tooth wear as a guide to the age of domestic ungulates', in Wilson, B., Grigson, C. and Payne, S. (eds), *Ageing and Sexing Animal Bones from Archaeological Sites*, Br. Archaeol. Rep. 109, 91-108

Grant, A., 1984, 'Animal husbandry', in Cunliffe, B.W., *Danebury: an Iron Age hillfort in Hampshire. Vol. 2: The Finds*, Counc. Br. Archaeol. Res. Rep. 52, 496-548

Grayson, D.K., 1973, 'On the methodology of faunal analysis', *Am. Antiq.* 38, 432-9

Grayson, D.K., 1979, 'On the quantification of vertebrate archaeofaunas', in Schiffer, M.B. (ed.), *Advances in Archaeological Method and Theory* 2, 199-237

Green, C.S. and Gregory, T., 1985, 'Appendix 4: surface finds', in Hinchliffe, J. and Green, C.S., *Excavations at Brancaster 1974 and 1977*, East Anglian Archaeol. 23, 190-221

Greep, S.J., 1986, 'The objects of worked bone', in Zienkiewicz, J.D., *The Legionary Fortress Baths at Caerleon. Vol. II The Finds*, 197-212

Greep, S.J., forthcoming, 'Objects of bone, antler and ivory', in Blockley, K. and Day, M., *Excavations in the Marlowe Car Park and associated Areas*, Archaeol. Canterbury 5

Greig, J.R.A., 1980, 'Seeds from the well', in Stead, I.M., *Rudston Roman Villa*, 169-71

Griffith, N., 1977, 'The Animal Bone Remains from Knight's Enham, Andover, Hampshire', Ancient Monuments Lab. Rep. 2430

Grinsell, L.V., 1964, 'The Royce collection at Stow-on-the-Wold', *Trans. Bristol Gloucestershire Archaeol. Soc.* 83, 5-33

Guido, M., 1978, *The Glass Beads of the Prehistoric and Roman Periods in Britain and Ireland*, Rep. Res. Comm. Soc. Antiq. London 35

Guilbert, G., 1981, 'Double-ring roundhouses, probable and possible, in prehistoric Britain', *Proc. Prehist. Soc.* 47, 299-317

Guilbert, G., 1982, 'Post-ring symmetry in roundhouses at Moel y Gaer and some other sites in prehistoric Britain', in Drury, P.J. (ed.), *Structural Reconstruction*, Br. Archaeol. Rep. 110, 67-86

Hadman, J., 1978, 'Aisled buildings in Roman Britain', in Todd, M. (ed.), *Studies in the Romano-British Villa*, 187-95

Hall, A.R., Kenward, H.K. and Williams, D., 1980, *Environmental Evidence from Roman deposits in Skeldergate*, Archaeol. York 14/3

Hall, A.R., Kenward, H.K., Williams D. and Greig, J.R.A., 1983, *Environment and Living Conditions at Two Anglo-Scandinavian Sites*, Archaeol. York 14/4

Halstead, P., 1985, 'A study of mandibular teeth from Romano-British contexts', in Pryor, F., French, C., Crowther, D., Gurney, D., Simpson, G. and Taylor, M., *Archaeology and Environment in the Lower Welland Valley. Volume 1*, East Anglian Archaeol. 27, Fenland Project No. 1, 219-24

Hammond, P.M., 1971, 'Notes on British Staphylinidae 2. On the British species of *Platystethus* Mannerheim, with one species new to Britain', *Entomologists Monthly Magazine* 107, 93-111

Harbord, N.H. and Spratt, D.A., 1972, 'Petrological examination of Iron Age pottery from Cleveland', *Yorkshire Archaeol. J.* 43 (1971), 174-5

Harcourt, R.A., 1974, 'The dog in prehistoric and early historic Britain', *J. Archaeol. Sci.* 1, 151-75

Harden, D.B., 1958, 'Four Roman glasses from Hauxton Mill, Cambridge, 1870', in Liversidge, J., 'Roman discoveries from Hauxton', *Proc. Cambridge Antiq. Soc.* 51 (1957), 12-16

Harden, D.B., 1962, 'Glass in Roman York', in RCHM, *An Inventory of the Historical Monuments in the City of York, I: Eburacum, Roman York*, 136-41, R. Comm. Hist. Monuments (England)

Harden, D.B., 1968, 'The glass', in Brodribb, A.C.C., Hands, A.R. and Walker, D.R., *Excavations at Shakenoak Farm, near Wilcote, Oxfordshire. Part I: Sites A and D*, 74-81 (privately published)

Harden, D.B., 1974, 'Window-glass from the Romano-British bath-house at Garden Hill, Hartfield, Sussex', *Antiq. J.* 54, 280-81

Harden, D.B., 1979, 'Glass vessels', in Clarke, G., *Pre-Roman and Roman Winchester Part II. The Roman Cemetery at Lankhills*, Winchester Stud. 3, 209-20

Harden, D.B., Painter, K.S., Pinder-Wilson, R.H. and Tait, H., 1968, *Masterpieces of Glass*

Harley, J.L. and Lewis, D.H., 1985, *The Flora and Vegetation of Britain. Origin and Changes: The Facts and their Interpretation*

Hartley, B.R., 1966, 'The Roman fort at Ilkley: excavations of 1962', *Proc. Leeds Philos. Lit. Soc.* 12(2), 23-72

Hattatt, R., 1985, *Iron Age and Roman Brooches: a second selection of brooches from the author's collection*

Hawkes, C.F.C. and Hull, M.R., 1947, *Camulodunum*, Rep. Res. Comm. Soc. Antiq. London 14

Hayes, R.H., 1974, 'Querns: a survey of hand querns found in East Cleveland, the North Yorkshire Moors and the Vale of Pickering', *Ryedale Hist.* 7, 22-41

Hayes, R.H., Hemingway, J.E. and Spratt, D.A., 1980, 'The distribution and lithology of beehive querns in Northeast Yorkshire', *J. Archaeol. Sci.* 7, 297-324

Hayes, R.H. and Whitley, E., 1950, *The Roman Pottery at Norton, East Yorkshire*, Roman Malton Dist. Rep. 7, 41-2

Helbaek, H., 1952, 'Early crops in southern England',

Proc. Prehist. Soc. 18, 194-233

Henig, M., 1970, 'Zoomorphic supports of cast bronze from Roman sites in Britain', *Archaeol. J.* 127, 182-7

Henig, M., 1978, *A Corpus of Roman Engraved Gemstones from British Sites*, Br. Archaeol. Rep. 8 (2nd ed.)

Henig, M., 1984a, 'A bronze stamp found near Brough on Humber', *Yorkshire Archaeol. J.* 56, 167

Henig, M., 1984b, *Religion in Roman Britain*

Heslop, D.H., 1987, *The Excavation of an Iron Age Settlement at Thorpe Thewles, Cleveland, 1980-1982*, Counc. Br. Archaeol. Res. Rep. 65

Hicks, J.D. and Watson, J.A., 1975, 'The Romano-British kilns at Hasholme', *East Riding Archaeol.* 2, 49-70

Hillman, G.C., 1981, 'Reconstructing crop husbandry practices from the charred remains of crops', in Mercer, R.J. (ed.), *Farming Practice in British Prehistory*, 123-62

Hines, J., 1984, *The Scandinavian Character of Anglian England in the pre-Viking Period*, Br. Archaeol. Rep. 124

Hinton, H.E., 1945, *A Monograph of the Beetles Associated with Stored Products*, British Museum (Natural History), Dep. Entomology Monogr. 1

Hirst, S.M., 1985, *An Anglo-Saxon Inhumation Cemetery at Sewerby, East Yorkshire*, York Univ. Archaeol. Publ. 4

Hörter, F., Michels, F.X. and Röder, J., 1952, 'Die Geschichte der Basaltlava-Industrie von Mayen und Niedermendig', *Jahrbuch für Geschichte und Kultur des Mittelrheins und Seiner Nachbargebiete* 2-3 (1950-51), 1-32

Hubbard, R.N.L.B., 1975, 'Assessing the botanical component of human paleo-economies', *Bull. Inst. Archaeol.* 12, 197-205

Hull, M.R., 1933, 'The pottery from the Roman signal stations on the Yorkshire coast', *Archaeol. J.* 89 (1932), 220-53

Hull, M.R., 1958, *Roman Colchester*, Rep. Res. Comm. Soc. Antiq. London 20

Hurst, H., 1985, *Kingsholm*, Gloucester Archaeol. Rep. 1

Isings, C., 1957, *Roman Glass from Dated Finds* (Groningen)

Jackson, R., 1985, 'The objects of iron', in Bidwell, P.T., *The Roman Fort of Vindolanda, at Chesterholm, Northumberland*, Hist. Build. Monuments Comm. Archaeol. Rep. 1, 130-51

Jacobi, H., 1927, 'Bericht des Saalburgmuseums', *Saalburg Jahrbuch* 6 (1914-24) (Frankfurt)

Jarrett, M.G. and Wrathmell, S., 1981, *Whitton: An Iron Age and Roman Farmstead in South Glamorgan*

Jeffreys, T., 1775, *The County of York Survey'd ...*

Jenkins, F., 1952, 'Canterbury excavations June-December, 1947', *Archaeol. Cantiana* 65, 114-36

Jenkinson, H., 1911, 'Exchequer tallies', *Archaeologia* 62, 367-80

Johnson, F.E., 1962, 'Growth of the long bones of infants and young children at Indian Knoll', *Hum.*

Biol. 20, 249-54

Johnson, P., 1982, *Romano-British Mosaics*

Jones, M.K., 1978, 'The plant remains', in Parrington, M. (ed.), *The excavation of an Iron Age settlement, Bronze Age ring-ditches and Roman features at Ashville Trading Estate, Abingdon (Oxfordshire) 1974-76*, Oxfordshire Archaeol. Unit Rep. 1, Counc. Br. Archaeol. Res. Rep. 28, 93-110

Jones, M.K., 1981, 'The development of crop husbandry', in Jones M.K. and Dimbleby, G.W. (eds), *The Environment of Man: The Iron Age to Anglo-Saxon Periods*, Br. Archaeol. Rep. 87, 95-127

Jones, M.U., 1972, 'Aldborough, West Riding, 1964: excavations at the south gate and bastion and at extra-mural sites', *Yorkshire Archaeol. J.* 43 (1971), 39-78

Joy, N.H., 1932, *A Practical Handbook of British Beetles*

Kaba, M., 1955, 'Az Aquincumi parancsnoksági épület belsö dekorációja a laktanya utcában', *Budapest Régiségei* 16, 255-293

Katz, N.J., Katz, S. and Kipiana, M.G., 1965, *Atlas and Keys of Fruits and Seeds Occurring in Quaternary Deposits in the USSR* (Moscow)

Keble-Martin, W., 1965, *The Concise British Flora*

Keighley, J.J., 1981, 'The Iron Age', in Faull, M.L. and Moorhouse, S.A. (eds), *West Yorkshire: an Archaeological Survey to A.D. 1500* 1, 115-35

Kent, B.J.W. and Kitson Clark, M., 1934, 'A Roman settlement at Wetherby', *Yorkshire Archaeol. J.* 31 (1933), 170-84

Kenward, H.K., 1978, *The Analysis of Archaeological Insect Assemblages: A New Approach*, Archaeol. York 19/1

Kenward, H.K., 1982, 'Insect communities and death assemblages, past and present', in Hall, A.R. and Kenward, H.K. (eds), *Environmental archaeology in the urban context*, Counc. Br. Archaeol. Res. Rep. 43, 71-8

Kenward, H.K., Hall, A.R. and Jones, A.K.G., 1980, 'A tested set of techniques for the extraction of plant and animal macrofossils from waterlogged archaeological deposits', *Science and Archaeology* 22, 3-15

Kenward, H.K., Hall, A.R. and Jones, A.K.G., 1986, *Environmental Evidence from a Roman Well and Anglian Pits in the Legionary Fortress*, Archaeol. York 14/5

Kenward, H.K, and Williams, D., 1979, *Biological Evidence from the Roman Warehouses in Coney Street*, Archaeol. York 14/2

Kenyon, K., 1948, *Excavations at the Jewry Wall Site, Leicester*, Rep. Res. Comm. Soc. Antiq. London 15

Kilbride-Jones, H.E., 1938, 'Glass armlets in Britain', *Proc. Soc. Antiq. Scotland* 72 (1937-38), 366-95

King, A., 1978, 'A comparative survey of bone assemblages from Roman sites in Britain', *Inst. Archaeol. Bull.* 15, 207-32

Kloet, G.S. and Hincks, W.D., 1977, *A check list of British insects. Part 3. Coleoptera and Strepsiptera*,

Handbooks for the Identification of British Insects 9.3 (2nd ed.)

Landin, B.-O., 1961, 'Ecological studies on dung beetles (Col. Scarabaeidae)', *Opusc. Entomological Supplement* 19 (Lund.)

Lauter, H., 1972, 'Ptolemais in Libyen: ein Beitag zur baukunst Alexandrias', *Jahrbuch des Deutschen Archäologischen Instituts* 86 (1971-72), 149-78

Le Patourel, H.E.J. and Wood, P., 1973, 'Excavation at the Archbishop of York's manor house at Otley', *Yorkshire Archaeol. J.* 45, 115-41

Leeds, E.T., 1945, 'The distribution of the Angles and Saxons archaeologically considered', *Archaeologia* 91, 1-106

Lindroth, C.H., 1974, *Coleoptera, Carabidae*, Handbooks for the Identification of British Insects 4.2

Lindroth, C.H., 1986, *The Carabidae (Coleoptera) of Fennoscandia and Denmark*, Fauna Entomologica Scandonavica 15 (1) and (2) (Leiden)

Ling, R.J., 1972, 'Stucco decoration in pre-Augustan Italy', *Pap. Br. Sch. Rome* 40, 11-57

Ling, R.J., 1977, 'Stucco decorations at Baia', *Pap. Br. Sch. Rome* 45, 24-51

Liversidge, J., Smith, D.J. and Stead, I.M., 1973, 'Brantingham Roman villa: discoveries in 1962', *Britannia* 4, 84-106

Lloyd-Morgan, G., 1986, 'Small finds from the civil settlement, Doncaster', in Buckland, P.C. and Magilton, J.R., *The Archaeology of Doncaster 1. The Roman Civil Settlement*, Br. Archaeol. Rep. 148, 84-96

Loughlin, N., 1977, 'Dales ware: a contribution to the study of Roman coarse pottery', in Peacock, D.P.S. (ed.), *Pottery and Early Commerce: Characterization and Trade in Roman and Later Ceramics*, 85-146

Lousley, J.E. and Kent, D.H., 1981, *Docks and Knotweeds of the British Isles*, Botanical Soc. Br. Isles Workbook 3

Lowther, A.W.G., 1936, 'Roman "Votive Lanterns" and a fragment found in London', *Antiq. J.* 16, 204-5

LRBC, 1965, Carson, R.A.G., Hill, P.V. and Kent, J.P.C., *Late Roman Bronze Coinage* I and II

Luff, R.-M., 1982, *A Zooarchaeological Study of the Roman North-western Provinces*, Br. Archaeol. Rep. S137

Lysons, S., 1817, *Reliquiae Britannico-Romanae* III

McBirney, A.R., 1984, *Igneous Petrology*

MacConnoran, P., 1986, 'Leather', in Miller, L., Schofield, J. and Rhodes, M., *The Roman Quay at St Magnus House, London*, London Middlesex Archaeol. Soc. Spec. Pap. 8, 218-26

McIlwain, A., 1980, 'Quernstones', in Jones, D.M. and Rhodes, M., *Excavations at Billingsgate Buildings 'Triangle', Lower Thames Street, 1974*, London Middlesex Archaeol. Soc. Spec. Pap. 4

McWhirr, A.D., 1986, *Cirencester Excavations III: Houses in Roman Cirencester*

Maltby, J.M., 1979, *Faunal Studies on Urban Sites: the Animal Bones from Exeter 1971-1975*, Exeter Archaeol. Rep. 2

Maltby, J.M., 1981, 'Iron Age, Romano-British and Anglo-Saxon animal husbandry – a review of the faunal evidence', in Jones, M. and Dimbleby, G. (eds), *The Environment of Man: the Iron Age to the Anglo-Saxon Period*, Br. Archaeol. Rep. 87, 155-203

Maltby, J.M., 1984, 'Animal bones and the Romano-British economy', in Grigson, C. and Clutton-Brock, J. (eds), *Animals and Archaeology: 4. Husbandry in Europe*, Br. Archaeol. Rep. S227, 125-38

Maltby, J.M., 1985, 'The animal bones', in Fasham, P.J., *The Prehistoric Settlement at Winnall Down, Winchester and Excavations of MARC3 Site R17 in 1976 and 1977*, M3 Archaeol. Rescue Comm. Rep. 8, Hampshire Field Club Archaeol. Soc. Monogr. 2, 97-150

Maltby, J.M., 1987, 'The animal bones from excavations at Oswlebury, Hampshire: an Iron Age and early Romano-British settlement', unpubl. Ancient Monuments Lab. Rep. 6187

Manning, W.H., 1966, 'A hoard of Romano-British ironwork from Brampton, Cumberland', *Trans. Cumberland Westmorland Antiq. Archaeol. Soc.* 66, 1-36

Manning, W.H., 1970, 'Mattocks, hoes, spades and related tools in Roman Britain', in Gailey, A. and Fenton, A. (eds), *The Spade in Northern and Atlantic Europe*, 18-29

Manning, W.H., 1972, 'The iron objects', in Frere, S.S., *Verulamium Excavations: Volume I*, Rep. Res. Comm. Soc. Antiq. London 28, 163-95

Manning, W.H., 1974, 'Objects of iron', in Neal, D.S., *The Excavation of the Roman Villa in Gadebridge Park, Hemel Hempstead, 1963-8*, Rep. Res. Comm. Soc. Antiq. London 31, 157-87

Manning, W.H., 1984, 'The iron objects', in Frere, S.S., *Verulamium Excavations: Volume III*, Oxford Univ. Comm. Monogr. 1, 83-106

Manning, W.H., 1985, *Catalogue of the Romano-British Iron Tools, Fittings and Weapons in the British Museum*

Margary, I.D., 1957, *Roman Roads in Britain*

Marsden, P.R.V., 1966, *A Ship of the Roman Period, from Blackfriars in the City of London*

Marshall, F.H., 1911, *Catalogue of the Jewellery, Greek, Etruscan and Roman in the Departments of Antiquities, British Museum*

May, J., 1970, 'Dragonby: and interim report on excavations on an Iron Age and Romano-British site near Scunthorpe, Lincolnshire, 1964-69', *Antiq. J.* 50, 222-45

Mellor, W., 1934, 'Linton and Wetherby', *Yorkshire Archaeol. J.* 31, 331-2

Mielsch, H., 1975, *Römische Stuckreliefs*, Mitteilungen des Deutschen Archäologischen Instituts, römische Abteilung, Ergänzungsheft 21 (Heidelberg)

Miket, R., 1980, 'A restatement of evidence for Bernician Anglo-Saxon burials', in Rahtz, P., Dickinson, T.M. and Watts, L. (eds), *Anglo-Saxon*

Cemeteries 1979, Br. Archaeol. Rep. 82, 289-305

Milne, G., 1985, *The Port of Roman London*

Mitchelson, N., 1966, 'Roman Malton: the civilian settlement', *Yorkshire Archaeol. J.* 41, 209-61

Moore, C.N., 1974, 'A Roman bronze candlestick from Branston, Lincolnshire', *Britannia* 6 (1975), 210-12

Moore, P.D. and Webb, J.A., 1983, *An Illustrated Guide to Pollen Analysis*

Morgan, T., 1886, *Romano-British Mosaic Pavements*

Morris, C.A., 1984, 'Anglo-Saxon and medieval woodworking crafts – the manufacture and use of domestic and utilitarian wooden artifacts in the British Isles 400-1500 A.D.', unpubl. Ph.D thesis, Univ. Cambridge

Morris, C.A., forthcoming a, 'The wooden finds', in Abramson, P., *Roman Castleford*, Yorkshire Archaeol.

Morris, C.A., forthcoming b, *Anglo-Scandinavian and medieval wooden smallfinds from Coppergate, York*, Archaeol. York 17/13

Morris, P., 1979, *Agricultural Buildings in Roman Britain*, Br. Archaeol. Rep. 70

Mostyn-Lewis, J., 1966, 'Notes on kilns and sites', *Lincolnshire Hist. Archaeol.* 1(1), 46-7

Myres, J.N.L., Steer, K.A. and Chitty, A.M.H., 1962, 'The defences of *Isurium Brigantium* (Aldborough)', *Yorkshire Archaeol. J.* 40 (1959-62), 1-77

Nash-Williams, V.E., 1932, 'The Roman legionary fortress at Caerleon in Monmouthshire Report on the excavations carried out in the Prysg Field, 1927-9, Part II: the finds', *Archaeol. Cambrensis* 87, 48-104

Neal, D.S., 1974, *The Excavation of the Roman Villa in Gadebridge Park, Hemel Hempstead, 1963-8*, Rep. Res. Comm. Soc. Antiq. London 31

Neal, D.S., 1977, 'Northchurch, Boxmoor and Hemel Hempstead Station: the excavation of three Roman buildings in the Bulbourne Valley', *Hertfordshire Archaeol.* 4, 1-135

Neal. D.S., 1981, *Roman Mosaics in Britain*, Britannia Monogr. 1

Neal D.S. and Butcher, S.A., 1974, 'Miscellaneous objects of bronze', in Neal, D.S., *The Excavation of the Roman Villa in Gadebridge Park, Hemel Hempstead, 1963-8*, Rep. Res. Comm. Soc. Antiq. London 31, 128-50

Nilsson, S., Praglowski, J. and Nilsson, L., 1977, *Atlas of Airborne Pollen Grains and Spores in Northern Europe* (Stockholm)

Noddle, B.A., 1973, 'Animal bones from two wells at Tripontium', in Cameron, H. and Lucas, J., 'Tripontium: second interim report on excavations by the Rugby Archaeological Society at Cave's Inn, near Rugby, grid reference SP 57, 535795', *Trans. Birmingham Warwickshire Archaeol. Soc.* 85, 136-42

Noddle, B.A., 1980, 'Animal Bone Report', in Brewster, T.C.M., *The Excavation of Garton and Wetwang Slacks*, East Riding Res. Comm. Prehist.

Excavation Rep. 2, 771-99

Noddle, B.A., 1984, 'A comparison of the bones of cattle, sheep and pig from ten Iron Age and Romano-British sites', in Grigson C. and Clutton-Brock, J. (eds), *Animals and Archaeology: 4. Husbandry in Europe*, Br. Archaeol. Rep. S227, 105-23

O'Connor, T.P., 1982, *Animal Bones from Flaxengate, Lincoln c. 870-1500*, Archaeol. Lincoln 18/1

O'Connor, T.P., 1984, *Selected Groups of Bones from Skeldergate and Walmgate*, Archaeol. York 15/1

O'Connor, T.P., 1987, 'Why bother looking at archaeological wild mammal assemblages?', *Circaea* 4 (2), 107-14

Oldenstein, J., 1977, 'Zur Ausrüstung römischer Auxiliareinheiten', *Bericht der römische-germanischen Kommission* 57 (1976), 49-284 (Mainz am Rhein)

O.R.L. B, *Der Obergermanisch-rätische Limes des Römerreiches*, Abteilung B (Berlin)

Parlasca, K., 1959, *Die römischen Mosaiken in Deutschland*, Römisch-germanische Forschungen 23 (Berlin)

Payne, S., 1969, 'A metrical distinction between sheep and goat metacarpals', in Ucko, P.J. and Dimbleby, G.W. (eds), *The Domestication and Exploitation of Plants and Animals*, 295-305

Payne, S., 1972, 'Partial recovery and sample bias: the results of some sieving experiments', in Higgs, E.S. (ed.), *Papers in Economic Prehistory*, 49-64

Payne, S., 1973, 'Kill-off patterns in sheep and goats: the mandibles from Asvan Kale', *J. Anatolian Stud.* 23, 281-303

Peacock, D.P.S., 1968, 'A petrological study of certain Iron Age pottery from western England', *Proc. Prehist. Soc.* 34, 414-27

Peacock, D.P.S., 1969, 'A contribution to the study of Glastonbury ware from south-western Britain', *Antiq. J.* 49, 41-61

Peacock, D.P.S. (ed.), 1977, *Pottery and Early Commerce: Characterization and Trade in Roman and Later Ceramics*

Peacock, D.P.S., 1980, 'The Roman millstone trade: a petrological sketch', *World Archaeol.* 12, 43-53

Peacock, D.P.S., 1982, *Pottery in the Roman World*

Peacock, D.P.S., 1987, 'Iron Age and Roman quern production at Lodsworth, West Sussex', *Antiq. J.* 67(1), 61-85

Penny, L.F., 1974, 'Quaternary', in Rayner, D.H. and Hemingway, J.E. (eds), *The Geology and Mineral Resources of Yorkshire*, 245-64

Percival, J., 1921, *The Wheat Plant*

Petry, F. and Kern, E., 1974, 'Vestiges d'un important bâtiment romain à mosaique sous la chapelle Saint-laurent à la cathédrale de Strasbourg', *Cahiers alsaciens d'archéologie, d'art et d'histoire* 18, 63-74

Philips, J.T., 1950, 'A survey of the distribution of querns of the Hunsbury or allied types', in Kenyon, K.M., 'Excavations at Breedon-on-the-Hill, 1946',

Trans. Leicestershire Archaeol. Soc. 26, 75-82

Phillips, R., 1980, *Grasses, Ferns, Mosses and Lichens of Great Britain and Ireland*

Piggott, S., 1955, 'Three metal-work hoards of the Roman period from southern Scotland', *Proc. Soc. Antiq. Scotland* 87 (1952-53), 1-50

Pirie, E.J.E., 1971, 'A Constantian coin hoard from Womersley, W.R.', *Yorkshire Archaeol. J.* 42 (1967-70), 127-29

Pitt-Rivers, A.L.H.F., 1887, *Excavations in Cranborne Chase I: Excavations in the Romano-British Village on Woodcuts Common and Romano-British Antiquities in Rushmore Park*

Pitt-Rivers, A.L.H.F., 1892, *Excavations in Cranborne Chase* III

Póczy, K.Sz., 1958, 'Az Aquincum helytartói palota falfestészete', *Budapest Régiségei* 18, 103-48

Potter, T.W., 1979, *Romans in North-West England. Excavations at the Roman Forts of Ravenglass, Watercrook and Bowness on Solway*, Cumberland Westmorland Antiq. Archaeol. Soc. Res. Ser. 1

Price, J., 1980a, 'The Roman glass', in Lambrick, G., 'Excavations in Park Street, Towcester', *Northamptonshire Archaeol.* 15, 63-9

Price, J., 1980b, 'The glass', in Gracie, H.S. and Price, E.G., 'Frocester Court Roman villa', *Trans. Bristol Gloucestershire Archaeol. Soc.* 97 (1979), 37-46

Price, J., 1981, 'The glass', in Jarrett M.G. and Wrathmell, S., *Whitton: An Iron Age and Roman Farmstead in South Glamorgan*, 149-62

Price, J., 1983, 'The glass', in Webster G. and Smith, L., 'The excavation of a Romano-British rural establishment at Barnsley Park, Gloucestershire, 1961-1979', *Trans. Bristol Gloucestershire Archaeol. Soc.* 100 (1982), 174-85

Price, J., 1986, 'Roman glass from Wharram le Street Roman villa', in Rahtz P., Hayfield, C. and Bateman, J.,, *Two Roman villas at Wharram Le Street,* York Univ. Archaeol. Publ. 2, 12.18 and 26.12

Price, J., 1987, 'Glass from Felmongers, Harlow; a dated deposit of vessel glass found in an Antonine pit', *Annales du 10e Congrès de l'Association Internationale pour l'Histoire du Verre*, 185-206 (Amsterdam)

Price, J., 1988, 'Romano-British glass bangles from eastern Yorkshire', in Price, J. and Wilson P.R. (eds), *Recent Research in Roman Yorkshire*, 339-66

Price, J. and Cool, H.E.M., 1983, 'Glass from the excavations of 1974-76', in Brown, A.E. and Woodfield, C., 'Excavations at Towcester, Northamptonshire: the Alchester Road suburb', *Northamptonshire Archaeol.* 18, 115-24

Procter, W., 1855, 'An account of the excavation of the remains of a Roman villa near Collingham', *Proc. Yorkshire Philos. Soc.* 1 (1847-54), 270-81

Punt, W. and Clarke, G.C.S. (eds), 1981, *The North-west European Pollen Flora* III (Parts 1-28)

Purdy, J.G. and Manby, T.G., 1973, 'Excavations at the

Roman tilery at Grimescar, Huddersfield, 1964', *Yorkshire Archaeol. J.* 45, 96-107

Rackham, J., 1979, '*Rattus rattus*: the introduction of the black rat into Britain', *Antiquity* 53, 112-20

Ramm, H.G., 1980, 'Native settlements east of the Pennines', in Branigan, K. (ed.), *Rome and the Brigantes*, 28-32

Ravetz, A., 1964, 'The fourth-century inflation and Romano- British coin finds', *Numis. Chron.* 4 (7th ser.), 201-31

RCHM, 1962, *An Inventory of the Historical Monuments in the City of York, I: Eburacum, Roman York*, R. Comm. Hist. Monuments (England)

RCHM, 1970, *An Inventory of the Historical Monuments in the County of Dorset* II.3, R. Comm. Hist. Monuments (England)

Rees, S.E., 1979, *Agricultural Implements in Prehistoric and Roman Britain*, Br. Archaeol. Rep. 69

Reid, C., 1901, 'Notes on the plant-remains of Roman Silchester', *Archaeologia* 57(2), 252-6

Reynolds, P.J., 1981, 'Deadstock and livestock', in Mercer, R.J. (ed.), *Farming Practice in British Prehistory*, 97-122

Rhodes, M., 1980, 'Leather', in Jones, D.M. and Rhodes, M., *Excavations at Billingsgate Buildings 'Triangle', Lower Thames Street, London, 1974*, London Middlesex Archaeol. Soc. Spec. Pap. 4, 99-128

RIC, 1923-49, Mattingly, H.B. and Sydenham, E.A. (eds), *Roman Imperial Coinage* I-IV

RIC, 1966-73, Sutherland, C.H.V. and Carson, R.A.G. (eds), *Roman Imperial Coinage* VI-VII

Rigby, V., 1980, 'Coarse pottery', in Stead, I.M., *Rudston Roman Villa*, 45-94

Rigby, V. and Stead, I.M., 1976, 'Coarse pottery', in Stead, I.M., *Excavations at Winterton Roman Villa*, Dep. Environ. Archaeol. Rep. 9, 136-90

Rolland, H., 1977, *L'arc de Glanum (Saint-Rémy-de-Provence)*, Gallia Supplément 31

Ross, A. and Feachem, R., 1976, 'Ritual rubbish? The Newstead pits', in Megaw, J.V.S. (ed.), *To Illustrate the Monuments: Essays on Archaeology Presented to Stuart Piggott*, 230-37

Ross, L., 1971, 'Romano-British Shoes from London', unpubl. MA dissertation, Univ. London Inst. Archaeol.

Ross-Craig, S., 1948-1973, *Drawings of British Plants* 1-31

Runnacles, R.B., 1985, 'The Preparation and Analysis of the Ceramic Assemblages from Ledston and Dalton Parlours by Thin Section Petrology', unpubl. MA dissertation, Univ. Bradford

Rush, P., forthcoming, 'The pottery', in Abramson, P., *Roman Castleford*, Yorkshire Archaeol.

Ryder, M.L., 1971, 'The animal remains from Petergate, York 1957-58', *Yorkshire Archaeol. J.* 42 (1967-70), 418-28

Ryder, M.L., Hurst, J.G. and Le Patourel, H.E.J., 1974, 'Animal remains from Wharram Percy', *Yorkshire*

Archaeol. J. 46, 42-52

Schauer, T., 1982, *A Field Guide to the Wild Flowers of Britain and Europe*

Schönberger, H., 1967, 'Ein Eisendepot, römische Flossfesseln und andere Funde im Bereich des Kastells Heilbronn-Böckingen', *Fundberichte aus Schwaben*, Neue Folge 18/1, 131-51

Schönberger, H. and Simon, H.-G., 1980, *Kastell Okarben*, Limesforschungen, Band 19 (Berlin)

Scott, I.R., 1980, 'The iron objects', in Gracie, H.S. and Price, E.G., 'Frocester Court Roman villa', *Trans. Bristol Gloucestershire Archaeol. Soc.* 97 (1979), 31-7

Sheppard, T. and Corder, P., 1934, 'Roman kilns and pottery near Holme-on-Spalding Moor', *Trans. East Riding Antiq. Soc.* 27 (1931-33), 1-35

Silver, I.A., 1969, 'The ageing of domestic animals', in Brothwell D.R. and Higgs, E.S. (eds), *Science in Archaeology* (2nd ed.), 283-302

Smith, A.H., 1961, *Place Names of the West Riding of Yorkshire* V

Smith, D.J., 1976, 'The mosaics of Winterton', in Stead, I.M., *Excavations at Winterton Roman Villa*, Dep. Environ. Archaeol. Rep. 9, 251-72

Smith, D.J., 1978, 'Regional aspects of the winged corridor villa in Britain', in Todd, M. (ed.), *Studies in the Romano-British Villa*, 117-47

Smith, D.J., 1980, 'Mosaics', in Stead, I.M., *Rudston Roman Villa*, 131-8

Smith, J.T., 1978, 'Villas as a key to social structure,' in Todd, M. (ed.), *Studies in the Romano-British Villa*, 149-85

Smith, R.F., 1987, *Roadside Settlements in Lowland Roman Britain*, Br. Archaeol. Rep. 157

Snorne, K.R., 1979, *The Morphology of Pteridophytes*

Speight, H., 1902, *Lower Wharfedale*

Spratt, D.A. (ed.), 1982, *Prehistoric and Roman Archaeology of North East Yorkshire*, Br. Archaeol. Rep. 104

Spratt, D.A., 1987, 'The progress of the Yorkshire quern survey', *Counc. Br. Archaeol. Forum*, CBA Group 4, 21-2

Staehelin, F., 1948, *Die Schweiz in römischer Zeit* (Basel)

Stallibrass, S.M., 1986, 'Some Effects of Scavenging Canids on the Bones of Ungulate Species: Some Actualistic Research and a Romano-British Case Study', unpubl. Ph.D. thesis, Univ. Sheffield

Stead, I.M., 1972, 'Beadlam Roman villa: an interim report', *Yorkshire Archaeol. J.* 43 (1971), 178-86

Stead, I.M., 1976, *Excavations at Winterton Roman Villa*, Dep. Environ. Archaeol. Rep. 9

Stead, I.M., 1980, *Rudston Roman Villa*

Stern, H., 1960, *Receuil général des mosaiques de la Gaule: Province de Belgique* I.2 (Est), Gallia Supplément 10 (Paris)

Stevenson, R.B.K., 1956, 'Native bangles and Roman glass', *Proc. Soc. Antiq. Scotland* 88 (1954-56), 208-21

Stevenson, R.B.K., 1976, 'Romano-British glass bangles', *Glasgow Archaeol. J. 4*, 45-54

Stuiver, M., 1987, *Radiocarbon calibration program*, University of Washington, Quaternary Isotope Laboratory

Sumner, H., 1924, *Excavations at East Grimstead, Wiltshire*

Sumpter, A.B., 1988, 'Iron Age and Roman at Dalton Parlours', in Price, J. and Wilson, P.R. (eds), *Recent Research in Roman Yorkshire*, Br. Archaeol. Rep. 193, 171-96

Swain, H.P., 1987, 'The Iron Age pottery', in Heslop, D.H., *The Excavation of an Iron Age settlement at Thorpe Thewles, Cleveland, 1980-1982*, Counc. Br. Archaeol. Res. Rep. 65, 57-71

Swan, V.G., 1975, *Pottery in Roman Britain*

Sweatman, T.R. and Long, J.V.P., 1969, 'Quantative electron-probe microanalysis of rock-forming minerals', *J. Petrology* 10, 332-79

Taylor, F.J., 1985, 'Investigations into Meat Supply to the Roman Fort at Castleford, West Yorkshire, c. AD 75-85', unpubl. M.A. thesis, Univ. Sheffield

Teichert, M., 1975, 'Osteometrische Untersuchungen zur Berechnung der Widerrishöhe bei Schafen', in Clason, A.T. (ed.), *Archaeozoological Studies*, 51-69 (Amsterdam)

Toomey, J.P., 1976, *An Iron Age Enclosure at Oldfield Hall, Meltham*

Tottenham, C.E., 1954, *Coleoptera, Staphylinidae (a). Piestinae to Euaesthetinae*, Handbooks for the Identification of British Insects 4.8

Toynbee, J.M.C. and Ward-Perkins, J.B., 1950, 'Peopled scrolls: a Hellenistic motif in imperial art', *Pap. Br. Sch. Rome* 18, 1-43

Ubelaker, D.H., 1978, *Human Skeletal Remains: Excavation, Analysis, Interpretation* (Chicago)

van Driel-Murray, C., 1986, 'Shoes in perspective', *Studien in den Militargrenzen Roms III*, 13 Internationaler Limeskongress Aalen 1983, 139-45 (Stuttgart)

van Driel-Murray, C. and Gechter, M., 1983, 'Funde aus der fabrica der legio I Minervia am Bonner Berg', *Rheinsiche Ausgrabungen* 23, 10-25

VCH, 1900, *Victoria County History of Hampshire* I, 308

Viner, L., 1982a, 'Objects of copper alloy', in Wacher, J.S. and McWhirr, A.D., *Cirencester Excavations I: Early Roman Occupation at Cirencester*, 93-7

Viner, L., 1982b, 'Copper alloy objects', in McWhirr, A.D., Viner, L. and Wells, C., *Cirencester Excavations II: Romano-British Cemeteries at Cirencester*, B08-C04

Viner, L., 1986, 'Objects of shale and jet', in McWhirr, A.D., *Cirencester Excavations III: Houses in Roman Cirencester*, 116

von den Driesch, A., 1976, *A Guide to the Measurement of Animal Bones from Archaeological Sites*, Peabody Mus. Bull. 1 (Harvard)

Wacher, J.S, 1969, *Excavations at Brough-on-Humber 1958-1961*, Rep. Res. Comm. Soc. Antiq. London 25

Wahlstrom, E.E., 1947, *Igneous materials and rocks*

Wainwright, G.J., 1979, *Gussage All Saints*, Dep.

Environ. Archaeol. Rep. 10

Walke, N., 1965, *Das römische Donaukastell Straubing-Sorviodurum*, Limesforschungen, Band 3 (Berlin)

Ward-Perkins, J.B. and Claridge, A., 1979, *Pompeii AD 79*

Watson, E.V., 1968, *British Mosses and Liverworts* (2nd ed.)

Watson, E.V., 1978, *The Structure and Life of Bryophytes*

Watson, J.P.N., 1979, 'The estimation of the relative frequencies of mammalian species: Khirokitia 1972', *J. Archaeol. Sci.* 6, 127-37

Watts, M., 1983, *Corn Milling*

Webster, G., 1950, 'A Romano-British burial at Glaston, Rutlandshire, 1947', *Antiq. J.* 30, 72-3

Webster, J., 1981, 'The bronzes', in Jarrett, M.G. and Wrathmell, S., *Whitton: An Iron Age and Roman Farmstead in South Glamorgan*, 163-88

Weege, F., 1913, 'Das goldene Haus des Nero', *Jahrbuch des Kaiserlich Deutschen Archäologischen Instituts* 28, 127-244

Welfare, A.T., 1985, 'The milling-stones', in Bidwell, P.T., *The Roman Fort of Vindolanda at Chesterholm, Northumberland*, Hist. Buildings Monuments Comm. Archaeol. Rep. 1, 154-64

Wharton, A., 1978, *Excavation of the 14th century well at Tong Castle, Shropshire*, Tong Archaeol. Group Rep. 1

Wheeler, R.E.M., 1930, *London in Roman Times*, London Mus. Cat. 3

Wheeler, R.E.M., 1943, *Maiden Castle, Dorset*, Rep. Res. Comm. Soc. Antiq. London 12

Wheeler, R.E.M. and Wheeler, T.V., 1928, 'The Roman amphitheatre at Caerleon, Monmouthshire', *Archaeologia* 78, 111-218

White, K.D., 1970, *Roman Farming*

Whiting, W., Hawley, W. and May, T., 1931, *Report on the excavation of the Roman Cemetery at Ospringe, Kent*, Rep. Res. Comm. Soc. Antiq. London 8

Whitwell, J.B., 1982, *The Coritani*, Br. Archaeol. Rep. 99

Williams, D., 1978, 'Wood identification', in MacGregor, A., *Roman finds from Skeldergate and Bishophill*, Archaeol. York 17/2, 47-50

Williams, P.L. and Warwick, R., 1980, *Gray's Anatomy*

Wilson, B., 1985, 'Degraded bones, feature type and spatial patterning on an Iron Age occupation site in Oxfordshire, England', in Fieller, N.R.J., Gilbertson D.D. and Ralph, N.G.A. (eds), *Palaeobiological Investigations: Research Design, Methods and Data Analysis*, Br. Archaeol. Rep. S266, 81-95

Wilson, B., Hamilton, J., Bramwell, D. and Armitage, P., 1978, 'The animal bones', in Parrington, M. (ed.), *The excavation of an Iron Age settlement, Bronze Age ring-ditches and Roman features at Ashville Trading Estate, Abingdon (Oxfordshire) 1974-76*, Oxfordshire Archaeol. Unit Rep. 1, Counc. Br. Archaeol. Res. Rep. 28, 110-139

Wilson, D.G., 1981, 'The plant remains', in Jarrett M.G. and Wrathmell S., *Whitton: An Iron Age and Roman Farmstead in South Glamorgan*, 240-42

Wilson, M.G., 1968, 'Other objects of bronze, iron, silver, lead, bone and stone', in Cunliffe, B.W. (ed.), *Fifth Report on the Excavations of the Roman Fort at Richborough, Kent*, Rep. Res. Comm. Soc. Antiq. London 23, 93-114

Yarwood, R.E., 1981, 'The natural environment', in Faull, M.L. and Moorhouse, S.A. (eds), *West Yorkshire: an Archaeological Survey to A.D. 1500* 1, 34-45

Yarwood, R.E. and Marriott, J.J., 1988, *Methley Willow Grove, Rescue Excavation*, Interim Archive Rep., West Yorkshire Archaeology Service

Index

Ledston, West Yorkshire, grain storage pits, 279
Linch pins, iron, 97
Little Woodbury, Wiltshire, four-post structures, 279
    roundhouses, 279
Loomweights, tile, 122

Medusa mosaic, 2, 33, 35, 146-50, 280-82
Military equipment, copper alloy, 79, 86
    lorica segmentata, 81
    lorica squamata, 81, 86
Millstones, 105, 119-20, 282-3
Mortaria, 135-43, 145-6, 236-44
Mosaics, 146-50, 280-82
    see also Medusa mosaic, *Tesserae* (Brick and tile)

Nails, iron, 37, 40, 53-4, 62, 67, 164, 200, 209, 230
    lead, 95-7
Needles, bone, 128
    copper alloy, 80-81, 84
Newstead, Scotland, well deposits, 258

Old Winteringham, Humberside, winged villa, 33, 35, 281
Onyx, 2
Opus signinum, 34, 40-41, 52-3, 55-7
Ovens, 34-7, 47, 50-53, 58-60, 62, 69-74, 281-2
Ox-goads, iron, 203
Oyster shells, 2

Painted plaster, 33-4, 37, 40, 53, 55-6, 67, 70, 150-60, 281-2
Paint-pot, Dales ware, 145
Palette, slate, mixing, 126
Palisades, 7, 12-19, 275
    see also fences
Pick, masons', iron, 203
Pilae, 2, 35, 37-41, 55-8, 60-62, 161-2, 272, 283
Pimperne, Dorset, roundhouses, 278
Plant remains, *see* botanical remains
Plaque, copper alloy, 37
Plate, wooden, 206
Plugs, lead, 95-7
Pollen, 261-6
Pottery
    Iron Age, 17, 24, 34, 37, 47, 128-35, 279
    post-medieval, 34
    post-Roman, 285
    repairs, 95-7
    Roman, 24, 35, 37, 40-41, 45-7, 53-5, 60, 62, 67-8, 70, 75, 83, 135-46, 196-7, 238-45, 271, 279, 282
Fabrics
    Black Burnished ware, 135-9, 144, 236
    Cantley kiln products, 137
    Colour-coated ware, 40, 45, 239
    Crambeck ware, 40, 56, 68, 70, 236-44, 271
    Dales ware, 37, 62, 131, 133, 135-7, 143-6, 148
    Huntcliff wares, 40, 56, 68, 135-7, 141-6, 236-45, 271, 282
    Nene Valley colour-coated ware, 144

Oxfordshire colour-coated ware, 40, 137, 145
Parchment ware, 145
Parisian ware, 139-41, 144
Rhenish wares, 40, 144
Rustic ware, 143-4
Samian ware, 34, 130, 135, 143-5, 244, 271
Throlam ware, 135-7, 141, 144-5, 236, 244, 271, 282
West Yorkshire ware, 130, 135-7, 141-6
York red-painted ware, 145
see also amphorae, beakers, counters, dishes, flagons, jars, jugs, mortaria, paint-pots, spindlewhorls
Praefurnium, 33, 35
Precinct wall, 7-9

Quernstones, 45, 62, 67, 69, 105-20, 279, 281
    beehive, 43-5, 53, 62, 105-20, 126, 281
    lava, 105, 117-20
    Romano-British, flat, 105, 117-20
    saddle, 105-6

Radiocarbon dates, 16-17, 24, 275
Ritual deposits, 177, 272, 283
Rivets, iron, 211, 230
Roads, 'Ancient', 273
    Roman, 1, 170
Roofing slabs, stone, 164-5, 272
Rothwell, West Yorkshire, well deposits, 264
Roundhouse 1, 7-9, 16, 275, 278-9
Roundhouse 2, 7-9, 16, 24, 275, 278-9
Roundhouse 3, 12, 16-17, 275, 278-9
Roundhouse 4, 16-17, 275, 278
Roundhouse 5, 12, 19-24, 275, 278
Roundhouse 6, 24, 275, 278-9
Roundhouse 7, 19-24, 275, 278
Roundhouse 8, 26, 276-9
Rudston, Humberside, villa, 280-81

Sandal, leather, 233-5
    imprints on tiles, 166-70
Scoops, copper alloy, 80, 84
Scrapers, stone, 275
Seeds, 261-4, 266, 269-70
Shale, 123
Shoes, leather, 231-5, 271
Silver, coins, 75-6
    objects, 79, 83, 282
    see also bracelets, finger-rings, hairpins
Slags, 70, 133
Slate, mixing palette, 126
Sledgehammers, iron, 203
Smithy (Structure 4311), 282
Smithying, *see* ironworking
Sneck, wooden, 224
Spade sheath, iron, 203
Spatulae, iron, 203
Spindlewhorls, pottery, 120-22, 145
    stone, 123-6